Rethinking Popular Culture

Rethinking Popular Culture

Contemporary Perspectives in Cultural Studies

EDITED BY

Chandra Mukerji

AND

Michael Schudson

UNIVERSITY OF CALIFORNIA PRESS

Berkeley   Los Angeles   Oxford

University of California Press
Berkeley and Los Angeles, California
University of California Press, Ltd.
Oxford, England
© 1991 by
The Regents of the University of California

Library of Congress Cataloging-in-Publication Data
Rethinking popular culture: contemporary perspectives in cultural
studies / edited by Chandra Mukerji and Michael Schudson.
    p. cm.
  Includes bibliographical references and index.
  ISBN 0-520-06892-0 (alk. paper).—ISBN 0-520-06893-9 (pbk. :
alk. paper)
    1. Ethnology. 2. Popular culture. I. Mukerji, Chandra.
II. Schudson, Michael.
GN357.R48   1991
306.4—dc20   90-39009
                                                              CIP

9 8 7 6 5 4 3 2 1

CONTENTS

ACKNOWLEDGMENTS

This work is even more a collective project than most, not only because we have worked on it together but because its scope is so large, well beyond any domain where we could separately or jointly claim expertise. We have therefore relied on the kindness of both friends and strangers. The friends and colleagues include Todd Gitlin, Wendy Griswold, Robert Horwitz, Elizabeth Long, and Gaye Tuchman, who commented on earlier outlines of the project and later drafts of the introduction. The readers for the University of California Press, both friends and strangers, provided acute criticism. Sue Leibovitz Schudson provided editorial assistance, and Silvio Waisbord, research assistance. Our editor at the University of California Press, Naomi Schneider, offered gentle guidance and encouragement. Our students in courses on popular culture have road tested some of the essays represented here and some of the organizing ideas of the introduction. Our colleagues in both the Departments of Communication and Sociology at the University of California, San Diego, have long provided the intellectual atmosphere in which a rethinking of popular culture has been not only encouraged but enjoined.

ONE

Introduction
Rethinking Popular Culture

Chandra Mukerji and Michael Schudson

Popular culture studies have undergone a dramatic change during the last generation—from an academic backwater to a swift intellectual river where expansive currents from different disciplines meet. Anthropologists, historians, sociologists, and literary scholars have mounted impressive intellectual challenges to basic assumptions in their own fields, which had previously barred close attention to popular forms.

These intellectual developments, shaped by the general cultural upheaval of the 1960s, helped change the outlooks of conventional disciplines and helped define a number of hybrid fields, including communication and cultural studies, in the past twenty years. The rigid conceptual barrier between "high," or estimable, culture and popular, or representative, culture has broken down. Literary and art critics have come to recognize how much high culture and popular culture have in common as human social practices. The distanced and intentionally nonevaluative approach of the social sciences has come to influence thinking about culture in the humanities. Scholars have also come to see, as several of the articles in this volume make clear, how much the traditional division of high and popular culture has been a political division rather than a defensible intellectual or aesthetic distinction. They have begun to trace the mutual influence of high and popular culture. They have come to take popular culture more seriously as a terrain of political and social conflict and a weapon of political mobilization. In historical writing, in particular, attention to the beliefs and practices of ordinary people has very nearly displaced studies of political, diplomatic, and military elites. (The pendulum has not yet swung the other way, but several recent critical appraisals of "the eclipse of politics" in historical writing signal a change.)[1]

1

The redefinition of popular culture studies has made problematic earlier views of mass culture as degraded and elite culture as elevating. Instead, the new studies recognize the power of the ordinary, accept the commonplace as a legitimate object of inquiry, hammer away at the often arbitrary and ideological distinctions between popular, mass, and elite culture, and ask serious questions about the role of popular culture in political and social life.

We intend this volume to mark the emergence of this rethinking of popular culture by collecting some leading examples of both theoretical and empirical work, demonstrating to students and scholars in a range of disciplines the rich resources and significant problems for inquiry that have opened up. This is a limited selection of recent work; we do not pretend to have covered all the territory. We have tried to represent a range of key figures and key ideas, to include pieces that draw attention to a variety of popular culture forms, and to provide examples of different theoretical and disciplinary perspectives. We have also tried to choose, where possible, works of special clarity to make this book valuable in the classroom.

The new study of popular culture is institutionally as well as intellectually distinctive. Historically, colleges and universities have taken as part of their responsibility and as central to their identity the transmission of the greatest cultural achievements of human beings. In practice, of course, this mission has tended to be parochial, a parochialism in which many still take pride. But parochialism it is, or "educational fundamentalism," as Gerald Graff has called it.[2] Universities in the West have particularly emphasized the achievements of Western civilization; especially since the decline of classical studies, universities in a given country have emphasized the achievements of their own national elite culture.

Nowhere in the conventional university curriculum of fifty or a hundred years ago was there a place for the study of popular culture, but seeds of change had already been planted. In the eighteenth century, "culture" was a synonym for "civilization," the general process of becoming civilized or cultivated—an evolutionary process leading up, presumably, to eighteenth-century European culture as the pinnacle. The German philosopher Johann Gottfried von Herder attacked this view: "Men of all the quarters of the globe, who have perished over the ages, you have not lived solely to manure the earth with your ashes, so that at the end of time your posterity should be made happy by European culture. The very thought of a superior European culture is a blatant insult to the majesty of Nature."[3] Herder was the first to speak of "cultures" rather than "culture" in the singular. He began to use the term in a way that would become standard in anthropology and sociology a century later. Herder and others encouraged studies of "folk culture" in the early

nineteenth century, and under the influence of a new democratic romanticism, folkloric studies began in Europe. Still, substantial institutional recognition came only with the formal organization of the social
sciences in the late nineteenth century. If the popular arts of a primitive
tribe were still not included for study in a department of art or literature, they at least could be examined in anthropology. If they were not
to be studied as great human achievements, they could nonetheless be
examined as evidence of the kind of creatures human beings are.

At first, anthropological and other social scientific approaches to the
study of culture had little impact on central understandings of culture
in the humanities. Even within anthropology, the potential that existed
for reshaping the mission of the university itself was rarely exploited.
The anthropological focus on exotic and *traditional* cultures typically
blinded anthropology to the contemporary popular culture of the primitive groups they studied as these groups encountered "modernizing"
influences. Anthropologists did not see mass cultural forms such as Indian films or tourist art as worthy of scholarly attention. If they were
recognized at all, they were seen as symptoms of the breakdown of noble
traditions, impurities in the cultural soup rather than the soup itself. In
this way, even the relatively egalitarian discipline of anthropology carved
out its own academic niche while joining art and literary criticism in condemning modern popular culture. Even anthropology tended to praise
folk culture for its authenticity and decry mass culture for its commercial
origins and purposes, its ideological aims, or its aesthetic blandness.

The legitimation of contemporary popular culture as a subject for
study in universities and a subject of inquiry for serious scholars, although far from complete today, has grown enormously in a generation.
In both the social sciences and humanities, the study of popular culture
has been transformed and has, to some extent, transformed the definitions of the disciplines themselves. As evidence grows that "authentic"
folk traditions often have metropolitan or elite roots and that mass culture often is "authentically" incorporated into ordinary people's everyday lives, it has become hazardous to make an invidious distinction between popular culture and high culture or a rigid separation of authentic,
people-generated "folk" culture from unauthentic and degraded, commercially borne "mass" culture.

In this period of rethinking, "popular culture" is a difficult term to
define. We will sidestep a great many terminological disputes with the
inclusive claim that popular culture refers to the beliefs and practices,
and the objects through which they are organized, that are widely shared
among a population. This includes folk beliefs, practices and objects rooted
in local traditions, and mass beliefs, practices and objects generated in
political and commercial centers. It includes elite cultural forms that have

been popularized as well as popular forms that have been elevated to the museum tradition. In this way, we capture some of the subtleties of new cultural theories and can help convey the array of studies that have made traditional conceptions of popular culture untenable.

While studies of popular culture today are creating a truly interdisciplinary literature, scholars continue to speak to others of their own disciplinary backgrounds and come upon the scene of popular culture not entirely fresh but shaped by particular bents, traditions, and theories of their own fields. No single discipline has or will ever have a monopoly on the study of popular culture; no discipline represents the "best" approach. Each sees a different part of the elephant.

Moreover, each has used popular culture as a weapon in its own disciplinary wars. The process of legitimating popular culture studies in recent years has (in all the fields) been associated with major theoretical challenges to basic assumptions of the disciplines. Students of popular culture in each field have seen themselves as innovative, marginal, and as challenging traditional modes and objects of research, missionaries within their own disciplines who employ new subject matter and ideas imported from other disciplines to call into question the standards of their own.

For example, historians from the French *Annales* school (the name comes from the journal in which they have published) sought to move their discipline away from its traditional focus on the activities of elites and the political histories of nations based on documents written by the literate. Instead, they advocated studying the common people (who left few or no written records), using aggregate data (from birth, marriage, and death records or tax figures) or descriptions of collective, ritual life made by literate neighbors. This research agenda required historians to learn some social science. They learned statistics like sociologists or economists in order to analyze public records. They learned anthropology to better interpret the cultural lives of the nonliterate. Their new tools did not make a new generation of historians into social scientists, however. *Annales* historians wanted to understand a lost past, not unchanging cultural patterns or contemporary ones; they wanted to use data about the past to describe the passage of time and its human significance. Moreover, the methodological problems and principles of this type of research were meant to differ from those of statistical sociology or interpretive anthropology because historical records must be understood in their historical contexts before they can be used statistically *or* symbolically, and neither anthropologists nor sociologists have typically cultivated the appropriate skills for doing this. So although historians have been liberally borrowing theories and methods from social scientists, historical studies of popular culture remain surprisingly remote from those made by sociologists and anthropologists.

Similarly, Marxist historians devoted to understanding the role of culture in the political mobilization of disadvantaged groups have borrowed numerous sociological concepts and organized their research to answer theoretical questions posed in the social sciences, but they have also concentrated on unearthing new kinds of historical records in order to give voice to groups that have been absent from historical literature. Digging in the archives has become a self-conscious form of contemporary politics within the discipline of history, not a way to supply sociology with the answers to long-standing questions.

Students of popular culture, then, have simultaneously worked in the tradition of their disciplines and fought with their premises. The most successful of them have transformed their disciplines and made their style of research a new (and still somewhat threatening) model of good work. This is why we have organized the readings in this volume by discipline. Most of the works here are deeply interdisciplinary, if that is not an oxymoron (and we do not think it is). But most of them do emerge from specific disciplinary perspectives and can best be understood in light of related developments in their disciplines.

There is an irony in this. We think that unearthing the disciplinary underpinnings of popular culture studies is important now precisely because popular culture has become an interdisciplinary subject of research. Popular culture studies have embraced such a range of issues with such an array of methods that they have become bafflingly diffuse to many students. Many of the researchers exulting in the intellectual freedom of the field have had no interest in establishing clear boundaries around it. After all, they rebelled against the traditional territorial arrangement of disciplines and have in many cases been loath to draw a new set of territorial lines. The resulting freedom for researchers has had its costs for students. The field is not easily characterized by either its perimeter or its center. The boundaries are not clear, and there are multiple centers emerging from the parent disciplines. So students approaching the field have no coherent way to understand why analysts of popular culture care so much about, for example, the role of the working class, the meaning and development of literacy, the extent to which popular forms mirror reality or express dreams and wishes, or how reversals of meaning appear in popular culture objects or performances. By looking at how popular culture analysis has developed in history, anthropology, sociology, and literary studies, novices to the field can see more clearly how the intellectual traditions and politics of diverse fields have helped shape the issues within popular culture studies.

We confess here a preference, if not an elitism, of our own—not about what human phenomena merit study but about the theoretical sophistication of the approach to their study. Some may ask if baseball cards are as valuable for study as *The Scarlet Letter*. Is the baseball game as significant a cultural tradition in the United States as the novel? Or is the passion for statistics and for collecting among preadolescent males as much a part of American culture as a Puritan heritage and sense of sin? Or is the ritual of Little League or the World Series as vital to everyday life as the close study of a semisacred text in a high school classroom? And which students are to be judged more culturally literate—those who can identify Hester Prynne but not Babe Ruth or those who can identify Jackie Robinson but not Arthur Dimmesdale?

These are not our questions. What matters, it seems to us, is that a student of popular culture, as opposed to an enthusiastic fan of it or a hands-over-the-ears critic of it, should have good questions to ask. To date, the most sophisticated and fruitful questions have come from scholars using theoretical positions developed in anthropology, sociology, history, and literary studies. Because popular culture studies have developed in conjunction with major theoretical restructuring in these fields, researchers from them have generally been especially sensitive to theoretical issues.

The new theoretical approaches to the study of culture that we highlight no longer exclude topics like popular ceremonies or consumer goods from the range of possible research subjects. A historiography that can treat vital statistics as seriously as diplomatic correspondence necessarily accepts and calls for the expansion of appropriate subjects for study. Literary theory that focuses on relations between texts, their producers, and their audiences—and can conclude that a text is definable only by these relationships—necessarily reconsiders romance novels and science fiction and television soap operas and other denigrated literary forms as acceptable subjects for study.

This is not, of course, a matter of purely intellectual development detached from its social setting. Not only have the theoretical views in the different fields influenced one another, but all have been shaped by the changing politics of academic life since the 1960s. The antielitist tendencies of the intellectual movements that have promoted the study of popular culture are products of the radical questioning of higher education that marked the cultural revolution of the 1960s and since. In part, this led to a more receptive audience for Marxism in the academic world and therefore more sympathetic attention to the beliefs and practices of the working class and others lower in the social order. In part, it meant that less overtly political theories, and even theoretical views like structuralism, which could easily be politically conservative, were turned to the antielitist cause (which is not to say that, once established, these same movements have not created invidious distinctions of their own).

The disciplines we consider here all held elitist attitudes toward popular culture. There was a preciousness in anthropologists' tendency to deny the forces of change that were affecting the societies they studied. They wanted social groups to be ideal types, unaffected by changing conditions of ordinary life, but this stance was not necessarily helpful to the groups that they studied. Politically active anthropologists made this point well, helping to underscore anthropological elitism and to spark efforts to change the discipline. There was also an elitism among the sociologists who found religion or art (meaning conventionally understood "high" art) more fittingly academic than popular culture as a subject of study. There was an elitism among traditional historians connected in part to their reliance on written records to uncover the past but, more important, tied to a vision of history as a chronicle of "major" sociopolitical and cultural changes. With this conventional focus, one needed to uncover the actions, values, and motives only of elites, not of ordinary people.

But the new efforts of social historians to examine the everyday lives of slaves, women, children, and other groups, whom professional historians had almost entirely neglected, so richly changed the sense of the past in leading university history departments and so quickly were tied to demands of women and minorities for greater representation in the profession that the elitism of conventional historiography came to seem increasingly silly and stuffy. (In the end, opening up historical analysis to include the lives of ordinary people had practical benefits for the discipline: it gave history new subject matter and reason for continued scholarship. It has also given history departments a leading role in thinking about new curricula for new or nontraditional college students from ethnic minorities.)

Literary scholars, art and music historians, and cultural critics in general were the most committed of all academics to elitist concepts of culture. Indeed, defining taste and value was in many ways their raison d'être. Thus, they seemed the most stodgy of all when threatened by those who would study popular culture. And this may help explain why the changes in literary theory have been the most far-reaching of any we consider here. The traditional tools of literary scholarship seemed shockingly at odds with the antielitist tone of so much contemporary art and writing—the very subject of scholarship seemed to be escaping, or rejecting, its institutionalized study. The revolution in theories of interpretation could not help addressing new questions about the purpose of cultural criticism itself.

The result is a vastly restructured intellectual environment for the study of culture and society, one that not only allows room for the study of popular culture but requires it. We have tried to represent this new world of popular cultural studies here. In the pages that follow, we provide an overview of substantive issues in popular culture studies and an introduction to the specific works we have included in this anthology.

HISTORICAL STUDIES OF POPULAR CULTURE

Historians in general have given more sustained scholarly attention to popular culture than members of any other discipline, but their reasons for doing so have not been of a piece. Scholars specializing in the nineteenth and early twentieth centuries have most frequently looked to popular culture to try to understand the consequences of the industrial revolution, especially the role of culture in the development of the working class, the significance of the new commercial culture developing in the period, and the new uses of culture as a means of social control. In contrast, historians of the early modern period have more often engaged in a kind of archaeological exploration, turning to the unnoticed marks of cultural activity left by illiterate people. If a main task of the nineteenth-century historian is to preserve nineteenth-century popular culture from denigration and to explore its relationship to politics, the task of the early modernist is to save popular culture for history altogether. There is in this a strong egalitarian impulse, a reaction against a tradition of historiography that privileges literary evidence, but the resulting scholarship is often much less closely tied to contemporary political concerns than the work of the nineteenth-century historians who struggle with the web of politics, industrial capitalism, and culture.

Medievalists and early modernists look beyond the well-known characteristics of the elaborate court culture of their periods (reaching its height or depth, as the case may be, at Versailles) to the forgotten activities practiced by "the people" in other, less powerful social worlds.[4] In a kind of gesture of affirmative action, they turn to reading practices, carnival activities, songs, jokes, pictures, and dances to reinstate ordinary people in history, using new methods of research adapted from anthropology and sociology. Because popular practices could not be successfully understood by either extrapolating from the behavior of elites or reading elite accounts of them, methodology has been an abiding preoccupation of many of these scholars.

Some historians, for instance, began to use statistics. If there are few personal records (like diaries) of the thoughts and aspirations of individual peasants or poor urban dwellers, one can still get a sense of everyday life from various forms of aggregate data. Tax rolls can suggest general levels of wealth, prices and measures of household wealth taken for tax or other purposes can say something about consumption patterns, school enrollments or whether wills are signed or marked can speak to literacy rates, legal documents from the Inquisition can say something about the theological leanings of the population, and guild records can reveal the occupational structure of towns. These sources used in conjunction with the accounts of public events written down by the literate are providing historians with surprisingly detailed views of past ways of life. French historian Fernand Braudel argued that historians who use such materials could begin to "read" in Europe another kind of history running beneath the world of high-stakes politics and wealth, a history of slow changes transforming the lives of ordinary people in significant but undramatic fashion (the *"longue durée"*).[5]

Braudel is a central figure in the *Annales* school of historiography.[6] The *Annales* historians have sought to move their discipline away from elites and political history to studies of the common people and social history. They have advocated attention to bureaucratically gathered data and the use of statistics to analyze them, all in an effort to chart the *longue durée*. Because of the low literacy rates of the late middle ages and the early modern period, there was no other choice. It is perhaps no coincidence, then, that an early member of the *Annales* school, Lucien Febvre, turned to the question of literacy itself as a subject for research focusing on Europe from the twelfth to the sixteenth century. He and Henri-Jean Martin wrote a book on the subject that (true to form) depends crucially on statistical evidence about printing and literacy.[7] They tried to construct a model of literate culture and its changes after the introduction of print by examining the records of publishing houses. This effort was later supplemented by the work of Natalie Davis on patterns of literacy and reading among nonelites in early modern France (some of which is reprinted here), work on the cognitive effects of literacy developed by the anthropologist Jack Goody but taken up by historians, and the work done by Elizabeth Eisenstein on printing's crucial role in the Renaissance, Reformation, and the scientific revolution.[8]

One central problem for these researchers has been defining literacy. Natalie Davis discusses that issue carefully in her essay in this volume. She asks what people from different social ranks could read and what kinds of effects reading was likely to have had on them. She does not take the ability to read to be the same as having access to a literate culture. She does not even assume uniformity in the literate cultures people could find around them. She makes it clear that literate culture was something that spread beyond the bounds of the literate in the sixteenth century—the period covered in the article included here—because readers would read out loud to those who could not read themselves. She also notes that marginally literate people living in the highly literate culture of the cities could be affected more by literacy then the highly literate few in the countryside. Like Febvre and Martin, she is conservative in her assessment of literacy's effects, but because she pays more attention to reading than printing, she is much more precise in detailing patterns of literacy and the bounds of literate culture.

It is notable that Davis takes reading to be an active kind of behavior. Very often, she observes, readers "translated" as they read along from French to a local language or dialect and "edited" as they adapted small portions of long works for their particular purposes. And they had plenty of room to interpret as they chose—so much so, Davis observes, that the church began to include illustrations and notes in the Bible to guide readers toward the proper interpretation. All this demonstrates the theoretical point Davis makes in the beginning: A printed book is not so much a source of ideas as "a carrier of relationships." This is a point that has appeared, in an entirely different context and with extraordinary force, in contemporary literary theory, as we shall see.

What Davis does not do in this essay is indicate how people were thinking when they were reading. Carlo Ginzberg in *The Cheese and the Worms* suggests that not all readers extracted the same meaning from a text.[9] He seems to share Goody's idea that having literacy skills allows people to think in new ways, but that just being able to read and write does not automatically make people think in a "literate" fashion. People can be nonliterate members of a literate culture and show "literate" thought patterns, or readers coming out of a primarily oral culture can retain "oral" modes of thinking. Ginzberg studied a sixteenth-century miller who developed an idiosyncratic heretical theology based on his "readings" of a variety of religious and "historical" books. This man could "read," but he used the interpretive skills and liberties of someone in an oral culture. He gave just as much credence to books of myths as he did to theological and scientific texts; moreover, he saw them all as materials he could use for his own storytelling. With them, he developed an idiosyncratic creation myth that was so elaborate and about which he spoke so freely that the Catholic church thought he must be part of a heretical sect. Like the singer of tales or storyteller in an oral culture, Ginzberg's oral literate seemed to feel uninhibited in remaking texts to his own design.

Using this case as evidence, Ginzberg (much like Michel Foucault and Janice Radway in the selections here) argues that the meaning of a text comes from its mobilization in reading. He joins with those who contend that if we want to understand the effects of literacy, we need to know *how* people read as well as *what* they read.

It is hard to overestimate the importance of research on literacy for popular culture studies. Today it is common to use "reading" as a metaphor for the interpretation of any cultural object, a piece of art as much as a book, a social ritual as much as a pamphlet. It is also common to think of cultural objects as existing in and deriving from a "code" or "language." The whole field of communication grows out of a set of categories about how a "sender" "encodes" a "message" in a given "medium" that a "receiver" or "audience" then "decodes." That is a familiar model in communication of the central cultural or communicational act. So in communication studies, as elsewhere, when new light is shed on the uses and meaning of literacy in its most conventional sense—the reading and writing of texts in script or print—the whole field of cultural studies is illuminated.

The accessibility of "literacy" as a concept and "reading" as a metaphor creates some problems, too. Students of literacy patterns in Europe before the eighteenth century describe how low literacy rates have built barriers between us and the people we read about in the past. The lack of diaries and other firsthand accounts has certainly obscured our access to past voices, but the problem goes deeper. We read of the nonliterate past from the point of view of a deeply literate culture, using sensibilities nonliterates could not share. So part of the project for historians of popular culture from this period is the infinitely difficult one of finding ways to unearth the cultural assumptions of those times, which are unlike the ones we know today.

For this project, historians from the *Annales* school prescribed the use of anthropological theories and methods. After all, anthropologists developed their research tools for studying (primarily) nonliterate groups. Moreover, early modern and late medieval popular culture was often a performance culture, filled with rites and ceremonies, saints' days and other religious festivals, whose study appropriately fits into the intellectual domain of anthropology. (If "reading" is one master concept in the new study of popular culture, "performance" is another.) This original impulse was then expanded into more recent interest in material culture studies as a basis for historical thinking. The work of folklorists as well as anthropologists was applied to the problems of historiography.[10]

The most ambitious historians tried diligently to combine statistical and anthropological methods, sometimes with great success. Le Roy Ladurie's magisterial *Carnival in Romans* contains tax data and anthropological readings of popular rituals to excavate a political upheaval that reached its bloody apex in carnival.[11] He reconstructs the course of the events from the diaries of two wealthy men, trying to take into account and comment on their differing perspectives on the events, but he goes beyond this. He describes the major actors in the events in terms of social

characteristics he derived from tax rolls and residency patterns, and using anthropological methods, he dissects the symbolism in carnival that
aggravated the political tensions of the event.

To give a taste of the symbolic reading of political protest in this period and to suggest the influence of anthropology in history, we have
included here a celebrated study by historian Robert Darnton, "The Great
Cat Massacre." Darnton shows how the discontent of apprentices in a
sixteenth-century print shop (note the attention to printing again) led
them to express their hostility in violence. But they did not make their
master (the source of their oppression) or his wife (the source of many
of their frustrations) the object of their violence. They called on their
symbolic resources to transform their master's cat into a symbol of their
dissatisfaction and focused their violence on that animal. They were not
in any position to engage in overtly political acts to redress their griev-
ances—as many did in peasant rebellions—but they could lash out safely
through symbolic action. The result was still effective. The meaning of
their massacre was visible enough to their employers to constitute a threat.
Here cultural performance was a piece of cultural politics.

However much the carnival in Romans and the massacre of cats were
instances in which culture was mobilized for political protest, these were
not acts of political resistance of the sort to be found in the nineteenth
century. The low-level artisans in both cases used the symbols from the
common culture of their period to represent their subordination and to
vent their distress, but they did not resist the culture itself or protest
fundamentally the social hierarchy in which they lived. Darnton and
Ladurie do not tell us these stories to show the political power of culture,
but rather to give us access to the political intelligence expressed in these
acts. These symbolic protests were not the actions of dumb, rude peasants (if such a thing existed); these were the acts of shrewd readers of
political relations and cultural symbols.[12]

The archaeological work by historians of the early modern period has
given forgotten voices a place in historical accounts and has helped build
new images of and ideas about history. The work on peasant and artisanal culture was only a start. Its success helped legitimate research on
women and children. Family history and women's history have become
active areas of early modern studies as women and children have been
recognized as important populations historians had ignored in the past.
They, too, were found to be more interesting and lively than historians
had previously realized, and their lives were reconstructed to become
part of the record of popular forms.[13]

It is instructive to contrast the spirit in which historians have presented popular activities of peasants and families from the early modern
period to the tone of the research on the cultures of nineteenth-century

working-class groups and families. One can see immediately that historians of nineteenth-century popular culture look not so much for forgotten or lost cultural forms to give us something approaching an ethnographic record of earlier nonelites, but rather search out and describe the *political* meanings and uses of culture during industrialization (i.e., the way popular culture in the nineteenth century either helped outline an emerging system of social control by elites over nonelites, particularly workers and women, or articulated new bases for social integration and differentiation).

The focus on subordinate groups—slaves, laborers, immigrants, women—became central to historical research. History is now often written, as advocates began to say in the 1960s, "from the bottom up."[14] The landmark work published in 1963 by the independent British scholar E. P. Thompson, *The Making of the English Working Class,* was central in shaping scholarship on the working class.[15] This extraordinarily powerful, rich, and probing work argued that a working class in early industrial England became an organized and self-conscious entity not as an automatic and passive result of industrial change but as a willed force responding to economic transformation. Moreover, the English working class was not only working class but English, built on workers' sense of their political entitlement as citizens of England. Thompson stressed how much the political ambitions of these workers were shaped by their belief in a traditional moral order, their sense not of a new or revolutionary political vision but of their rights as "free-born Englishmen," in other words, their understanding of their cultural heritage. This understanding was passed down in songs and stories, in fraternal organizations, and in recalled history and myth. It crucially shaped the character of new working-class organizations and politics. Members of the working class saw a past on which to construct (and fight for) a future.

Thompson and other historians of the working class have become preoccupied with the relationship between culture and politics for the working class. They examine the imposition of work discipline (for example) that developed with the factory system and ask who was served by the growing cultural emphasis on punctuality and the abhorrence of drinking on the job. They also have asked questions about the political potential of working-class institutions: whether they have facilitated political mobilization or simply directed workers' attention away from political problems.[16] Historians of the working class often differ in their interests in working-class culture and its relationship to power. Some, like Thompson and Gareth Stedman Jones, are interested in the extent to which workers' culture led to the creation of a class consciousness that fed political action.[17] Others, like Kathy Peiss and Roy Rosenzweig, are more concerned with the preservation of cultural autonomy and maintenance of cultural traditions by workers in the nineteenth century.[18] They see a kind of class struggle written in the codes of cultural objects and practices cultivated by workers who did not bow to elite tastes. Not accidentally, Thompson and Stedman Jones look at England, where a strong working-class consciousness developed and a strong labor party emerged; Rosenzweig and Peiss examine the United States, where nine-teenth-century politics is more often characterized as "ethnocultural" than as strictly class based, with sectional, ethnic, and religious divisions often more sharply drawn than class antagonisms.[19]

The chapter from Rosenzweig's book reprinted in this volume illustrates patterns of working-class cultural recalcitrance and change visible in drinking habits. Rosenzweig describes drinking habits in working-class ethnic groups blatantly at odds with the perceived economic interests and hegemonic beliefs of the social elites. The drinking culture of workers who had traditionally drunk on the job, for example, threatened the efficiency of the factory and challenged employers' capacity to control their employees' work time as well as after-hours activities. Traditional drinking habits not only insulted the Protestant ethic by interfering with sober attention to work itself; they ran counter to American individualism because they stressed the fundamentally *social* nature of drinking. They also (in early stages) reduced the separation of the workplace and the home by supporting the growth of drinking establishments in working-class houses near factory sites. This drinking was not so much to resist elite control but to contest elite culture. Thus, it had political meanings even if it was not inspired by, or was not fated to inspire, political action.[20] (Although this selection emphasizes commonalities in the working class, other parts of Rosenzweig's work stress important variations. For instance, French-Canadian and Irish workers supported the saloons, but native Protestant workers and Swedish immigrants frequently supported efforts to control or close them. Religious differences were important, too: Protestant temperance groups rejected the saloon totally; Catholic temperance societies offered alternative recreational facilities that accepted the fellowship of the saloon—its spirit without its spirits.)[21]

As Rosenzweig hints, the issue of cultural resistance to elite control was important to women as well as to working-class men in the nineteenth and early twentieth centuries. Kathy Peiss and Dolores Hayden, among others, examine women's culture from this perspective.[22] They too want to understand the limits and effects of cultural domination by elites (elite men); and, in a parallel fashion, they illustrate how both women workers and elite women tried, in their different ways, to use their degrees of cultural freedom to articulate a gender culture that would serve their social and political interests. Sometimes the women drew on tradition (like the culture of the domestic economy), and other times they reappropriated hegemonic cultural forms to suit their purposes. Thus, elite women used the machines of industrialization to reorganize domestic life in collectives and other utopian housing schemes, trying to free themselves from the physical burden and social isolation of housework without becoming victims of the new division of labor by gender that accompanied industrialization. In a similar vein, working-class women, using their new independent wealth gained from factory work, bought clothing that copied reigning fashions but also used the bright colors and exaggerated designs associated with prostitutes. They reproduced the fashion consciousness of their gender role but reappropriated it to resist dominant tastes. These women responded to elite domination not by trying to change their political status but by demonstrating their ability to retain some control over their own actions.

The term "hegemony" has come into widespread use fairly recently in all the disciplines covered here (and Raymond Williams discusses it directly in his essay).[23] The term is now used—sometimes with great abandon—to describe any aspect of a culture, ideology, or set of practices through which elites impose their views and establish the legitimacy of their power and privilege over nonelites. In some uses, "hegemony" becomes a synonym for "domination." However, its original intent, in the works of the Italian communist political writer Antonio Gramsci, was to explain how dominant classes could rule *without* employing force.[24] The question to which "hegemony" is an answer is, "Why do dominated or oppressed groups accept their position in the social hierarchy?" Gramsci held that, in fact, oppressed groups accept the definition of the world of elites as common sense; their understanding of how the world works, then, leads them to collaborate in their own oppression. Gramsci's work, available in English translations and popularized in the academic community in Britain and the United States in the 1970s, helped lead Marxist historians and social scientists to a new interest in ideology and culture.

Historical studies of nineteenth-century popular culture, for all they hold in common, have *not* all focused on the issue of resistance to cultural hegemony. Many studies examine the social origins and cultural organization of hegemonic culture itself. Scholars like Rosalind Williams, represented here, as well as others like Gunther Barth and Alan Trachtenberg, have sought to understand why professional sports, commercial expositions, or department stores became shared objects of delight among people of different social positions.[25] They document the development of hegemonic cultural systems for a growing mass society. Other studies trace the emergence of work discipline in the new factories, moral indoctrination in the Sunday schools, uses of literacy to tame rather than liberate workers, and other new systems of social control of behavior "society" judges deviant.[26] Much of this work is less a tale of elite control than a saga of the breakdown of traditional class cultures that accompanied the rise of a more commercial, urban, mass-distributed culture. The new culture was an improvisation as much as an imposition, articulating a new set of relationships among members of diverse social classes.

Lawrence Levine's work (reprinted here) presents a striking picture of some changes in nineteenth-century definitions of popular and high culture.[27] Examining the reception of Shakespeare's plays in the United States, Levine shows that the dividing line between popular culture and high culture was shaped by complex cultural politics. He indicates that early in the century, these plays were treated as part of a distinctively "American" culture, integrating rather than differentiating diverse groups of Americans. Shakespeare was presented on makeshift stages in rural areas as well as in established urban theaters. Audiences were heterogeneous, more like the audience at an athletic event today than one attending contemporary theater. Only at the end of the century did Shakespeare become appropriated as high culture, deemed intellectually beyond the reach of the masses. This story is very much like the one Paul DiMaggio tells (in the sociology section of this book) about two "high culture" institutions established late in the nineteenth century: the Boston Symphony Orchestra and Boston Museum of Fine Arts. He shows that both were self-consciously and painstakingly created by elites to make visible their high status in an uncomfortably fluid and class-crossing culture. Both Levine and DiMaggio show that "high culture" emerged by the end of the century not so much from aesthetic decisions as from cultural politics—a restratification of culture through the establishment of a distinct set of elite cultural organizations and standards of taste.

Levine is less explicit than DiMaggio in describing the specific institutional and organizational ways in which this transformation took place, but he writes suggestively about the values embodied in Shakespeare that helped make his plays so congenial to nineteenth-century Americans. He sees some of the interest in Shakespeare stemming from the form of the plays, their oratorical style (like political speeches in the nineteenth century), and their melodrama. But he also points to their individualism and emphasis on morality. These were deep American values in the early nineteenth century, and Shakespeare's plays were a vehicle for celebrating and reinforcing them. The reappropriation of Shakespeare as literature rather than performed moral lesson left the value of individualism and moral reasoning to other forms of writing (like the sentimental novel that Ann Douglas describes).[28] Shakespeare became a carrier of American values for elites, part of a newly claimed territory (like museums and symphonies), but not before helping give body to an American culture that spoke to all about individual opportunity and responsibility.

Whereas Levine examines a part of popular culture that became exclusive culture, Rosalind Williams looks at the late nineteenth-century growth of a mass commercial culture, a culture of consumption and conspicuous display, that some elites originated and others almost instantly attacked. Williams's work may at first seem in the tradition of the *Annales* school in that it draws attention to a number of locales that are themselves relatively new to serious historical study—fairs and expositions (themselves a product, on the modern scale, of the rising industrial forces of the mid-nineteenth century), the department store and other modern arenas of shopping, movie theaters, and the nightlife made possible by electrical lighting.[29] But Williams does this work to consider more fundamental theoretical and political questions about the effects of mass culture on the general population. Indeed, she is writing something closer to intellectual history than to social history, but her work illustrates how precarious a distinction this can be. Consumer enjoyments once limited to elites were now spreading to a mass public. Was this good or bad for people? How did it affect the self-definition of elites? How did elite culture change in response? How was the aesthetic of mass consumption affected by the world economy that supported it?

As Williams shows, these questions are not only the recurrent questions of twentieth-century cultural critics when they address the subjects of advertising, popular amusements, or consumer culture in general; they were equally the questions of intellectuals present at the explosion of mass culture in the late nineteenth century. Williams resuscitates the nineteenth-century voices that first came to define mass culture as vulgar and unauthentically commercial, appealing to the lowest common denominator of taste. She argues that this kind of talk was part of an effort to redefine elite culture after its traditional forms had been put in the service of mass culture. Earlier in the century, taste leaders like Beau Brummel had abandoned the aesthetics of French court culture, turning to simplicity and perfection as markers of elite status. In this way, they had dissociated themselves from the models for mass culture design, dismissing them as "gaudy." Their efforts to set new tastes were later paralleled by the work of intellectuals who began to show concern about the depravity of fashion and conspicuous consumption now that the masses were driven by them.

Although Williams does not describe late nineteenth-century consumer culture as a precursor of the "postmodern," her description of it comes very close to what people in recent years have meant by that term. The fair, the department store, and the newspaper may have contributed to a modernist urban culture, but they also helped create a style Williams calls syncretistic, illogical, and flamboyant, a "chaotic-exotic" style. What her work demonstrates (and this may be a useful insight for understanding the "postmodern" today) is that "modern" forms of popular culture already had seeds of postmodernism in them because the institutional and technological sources of a vast consumer culture and cacophonous forms within it already existed in the nineteenth century.[30]

The study of popular culture in history has had a range of uses and benefits for historians as well as a diversity of analytic forms. The study of neglected groups, championed by early modernists but visible among other specialists, has corrected historical misconceptions and brought to the forefront of historical research areas (like social and cultural history) that have broadened the charge of historians. And the studies of cultural politics initiated mostly by specialists in nineteenth-century working-class or women's history have made it decisively clear that one should never again think that ordinary people have been unimportant to political history; they have been visibly engaged in the cultural realm in shaping and resisting the exercise of power.

ANTHROPOLOGICAL APPROACHES TO POPULAR CULTURE

Anthropology's catholic approach to the study of human societies has been essential to the revival (in many disciplines) of popular culture studies. Interest in understanding contemporary popular and mass cultural forms has hardly been universal in anthropology, and its tradition of cultural relativism has not until recently tempered a disciplinary disdain for modern mass culture. Documenting *traditional* cultural forms has remained the primary charge of most research. But two movements have encouraged anthropologists to apply their long-standing cultural relativism to the analysis of modern forms of popular culture. We label these, loosely, the structuralist and interpretivist wings in anthropology.

The former, inspired by the conceptual tools of linguistics and the work of French anthropologist Claude Lévi-Strauss, has affected anthropological research on a wide range of subjects from kinship structures to mythology. Lévi-Strauss and his followers work from the assumption that language is a fundamentally structured and structuring part of culture. Language systems give order to the experience of individuals as well as provide them with the means for generating complex cultural forms. On this basis, Lévi-Strauss has argued that even "simple" societies have complex cultures because all societies have relatively complex language systems. By extension, one could argue (and many have) that all cultural expressions have complex deep structures, and to the extent that all language systems have structural similarities, all cultural systems may be analyzed in comparable ways. Ironically, structuralism has *not* been used widely in anthropology to legitimate new attention to popular culture, but it has still had a great impact on popular culture studies, particularly in the French intellectual world where Lévi-Strauss works. There it has been picked up by literary and other cultural critics as a basis for reform of their critical enterprise.

The structuralists begin with the premise that the human mind universally orders the flux of experience into binary oppositions: male/female, sacred/profane, pure/impure, in/out, kin/other, and, most of all, nature/culture. People make sense of the world through these binary categories and make use of the sense data of the world—plants, animals, colors, human bodies, weather, geography—to arrive at cognitive order. Things that seem to bridge categories are "anomalous" and take on special powers of danger, magic, or heightened meaning. Religious systems and myths are cultural constructions that elaborate a society's cognitive categories. The cognitive categories hold social, moral, and intellectual significance.

Lévi-Strauss's essay on totemism, for instance, reconsidered an anthropological chestnut: How do we explain the origins, purposes, and meaning of totemic religions? Can any sense be made of the apparently arbitrary connections between social units (say, the "bear" clan and the "eagle" clan) and the totemic objects (an image of a bear and an image of an eagle) they worship? Lévi-Strauss gave a celebrated, aphoristic response to this old problem. Totems, he concluded, "are good to think with."[31] In other words, the object of analysis could not be the individual totemic animal but the *system* of totemic symbols as a whole, and the point of totemism could be seen as the differentiation of social groups around differentiable symbols. Through the readily distinguished symbols, the more abstractly experienced social groups could take on stronger form.

This structuralist explanation grants great importance to the cognitive experience of social groups. Religion is not about the spirit for Lévi-Strauss, but the mind. Similarly, for anthropologist Mary Douglas, consumer goods are not in the first instance about producing cheap goods for a mass market, but about providing a common culture for a population with few other meanings or presuppositions to hold it together. Consumer goods offer a readily recognizable and cognizable basis for social relations.[32] This is not simply a brand of functionalism. At any given moment in the history of society, neither religious symbols nor consumer goods are invented self-consciously to serve the intellectual or communicative functions they do; instead, communication and intellection become possible at all only within limits imposed by these symbolic or material categorizations of the world. As Lévi-Strauss wrote in his study of South American mythology, his work shows "not how men think in myths but how myths operate in men's minds without their being aware of the fact."[33]

These views have had enormous influence in the study of primitive myth, religion, and ritual. They have been applied to modern industrial societies, too. Will Wright applied a Lévi-Straussian framework to a study of Western movies. Judith Williamson did something similar for advertisements, E. A. Lawrence for rodeo, and Paul Bouissac for circuses.[34] Most notably, Roland Barthes developed structuralism as a tool for analyzing modern fashion, advertising, architecture, literature, and popular culture in general. In each case, structuralism has directed attention away from the anthropologists' omnibus definition of culture as a people's "way of life" and toward a view of culture as a people's shared mental categories and contents, the governing "rules" that order perception, thought, and action.

The second or interpretivist stream of anthropological theory has been much more strongly connected to popular culture studies within anthropology itself as well as in a number of the social sciences. It differs from structuralism in emphasizing structures or patterns of *feeling* or *sentiment* where structuralism typically emphasizes *cognitive organization*. It differs even more strikingly in stressing methodologically that the scholar should seek to understand human experience from the subject's point of view. Its products, then, are more often tapestries of native experience than, as in the structuralist case, recoding and categorizations of native beliefs or practices taken out of their local context.

The interpretivist tradition can be traced most of all to Clifford Geertz, an American anthropologist. Geertz's celebrity is today probably as pronounced in history, sociology, communication, and even literature departments as in anthropology (where he has come under attack for having been insufficiently self-conscious and reflexive a field-worker).[35] Geertz elaborates a notion of a "cultural system" that strictly distinguishes it from the social system (a term he borrows from the sociologist Talcott Parsons). Geertz takes the capacity for and reliance on the symbolic as the defining feature of the human species. Symbols, he says, exercise a cybernetic control over human behavior, expressing the social and the personality systems of a culture without being merely expressive. Like the structuralists, Geertz accords significance to symbols (and relationships within the symbol system). Unlike them, he does not adopt a formalist method of analysis that would divorce the symbolic from the social. Although in theory he separates "culture" (a system of symbols) from "society" (a system of social relations), in practice he seeks always to understand their mutuality.

This turns out to be both the strength and weakness of Geertz, as distinguished from the structuralists. Structuralist accounts of culture, it seems to us, often provide insights that seem absolutely right—side by side with observations that seem utterly arbitrary or demonstrably wrong.[36] The structuralist matrix offers a general method and approach that can be applied rather mechanically, but the results, even where they seem insightful, feel arbitrary or ungrounded. Suppose it is true, as Lévi-Strauss has argued, that the Oedipus myth is in some respect about the over-valuing versus the undervaluing of kin or that the "trickster" figure in American Indian mythology is important because it has an anomalous or mediating quality—so what? Just what does that explain? And what do the interpretive niceties have to do with the general role and meaning of culture in society?

Geertz's work never raises such a question. He is deeply concerned not only with the relations of symbols to one another but the relations of symbols to social order, the efficacy of culture, if you will. In the essay included here, Geertz's most celebrated piece of writing, he shows how the Balinese cockfight represents and heightens the importance of social solidarities and social divisions in Balinese society. He also shows how the cockfight represents and heightens important psychological tenden-cies in the Balinese personality, especially those surrounding the rela-tionship between the Balinese man and his "cock." Geertz treads familiar ground here in connecting a cultural object to its social and psychologi-cal moorings. But he then confronts a recurrent question in cultural analysis: If the culture just "expresses" the social order, why bother? If it "reinforces" the social order, to what end? Why does the social order need expression or reinforcement? Doesn't a reinforcement theory of culture suggest culture is redundant, a restatement without apparent issue of what already exists?

Geertz offers an intriguing answer: Culture is not only a reflection of a social setting or a psychological predisposition, but also a production of meaning. And that is its point: to offer the Balinese a text that rep-resents Balinese society to itself and so provides the opportunity and the occasion for the Balinese to think and rethink, feel and feel again what being Balinese means. Not all representations of a society to itself are the same. Each may feature or caricature the society in somewhat differ-ent ways—a point Geertz makes but does not himself explicitly empha-size. The cockfight does not precisely express what Balinese society is but what, in a kind of collective thought experiment, it might be if one important set of emotional tendencies were taken to a logical extreme. The cockfight is a safe way, culturally framed, to test what happens when certain tendencies in the social order go unchecked, just as, Geertz ar-gues, *King Lear* is a collective thought experiment about what happens when fathers and daughters do not show love and respect for one an-other. Geertz holds that an observer can read the cockfight as a text just as a critic can read *King Lear* as a text. The cockfight provides "sentimental education" for the Balinese. Not incidentally, Geertz's analysis of "high" art is just the same: Works of art, he writes—meaning all works of art, high, commercial, or popular—are important most of all because they "materialize a way of experiencing, bring a particular cast of mind into the world of objects, where men can look at it."[37]

Whatever the worth of this analysis for Bali—and critics in anthropology have complained that Geertz never really gives very much evidence of what the Balinese themselves imagine the cockfight to be about, nor does he offer even a ghost of an idea about how different segments of Balinese society might think of the cockfight differently (for instance, the view of women, excluded from cockfighting, versus the view of men, for whom cockfighting may be a central passion)—this view of the cockfight does articulate a general theory of culture. The influence of this essay—and other work of Geertz—on neighboring fields and on the study of popular culture generally has been twofold.

First, it has offered a democratization of the objects deemed appropriate for study. Geertz's influence has by no means been alone here, but it has been significant. The study of the cockfight especially, and not incidentally because of Geertz's intentionally provocative comparisons to Shakespeare and Dickens, has been seen to open up the range of things taken to be textual and accessible to interpretation. (In a review of four books on American boxing, Garry Wills sardonically comments that sportswriters now have become social historians, and so remarks, "Clifford Geertz has a lot to answer for.")[38]

Second, it has offered methodological guidance—at least a code phrase, "thick description." Unlike structuralists, interpretivists never make it very clear how you are to go about your work. How do you do thick describing? Geertz does not say how a thick description is to get one very far along the way toward explanation, but that seems to be its mission. Geertz rejects the notion that anthropology is a science like the natural sciences, but just what kind of a science he has in mind is not very clear. Is he restating the late nineteenth-century German distinction between hypothetico-deductive sciences and hermeneutic sciences, that is, between studies capable of arriving at empirical generalizations and laws open to disconfirmation, and studies primarily interpretive that can be judged only on the basis of internal consistency, thoroughness, and aesthetic criteria of elegance? Perhaps, but he seems to be wary of sequestering anthropology as "merely" interpretive. Although he is skeptical about scientific "explanation" in social studies, the idea of a thick description seems to be a claim that what social science can aspire to is not "mere" description but description at a certain high level of intensity and reliability, yielding a high concentration of insight into social relations that, say, a journalist popping into Bali for a few days or a week would not be able to provide.

Geertz's theoretical and methodological precepts offer no particular guidance about what one should be most interested to observe. It is not easy to predict, say, what Geertz himself will write on next. He has written on ideology, law, common sense, kingship, religion, and other topics, as well as versions of "cultural systems." What next? There is no telling.

In contrast, anthropologists we would label neo-Durkheimians, especially Victor Turner and his students, have concentrated attention on aspects of human activity that step self-consciously out of social life to negate and counterpoise daily existence with moments of high contrast in "antistructure," "hyperstructure," or what Elihu Katz and colleagues have called the "high holidays" of culture.[39] They have concentrated attention on ceremony, ritual, celebration, and spectacle. Victor Turner himself focused on "social dramas," "sustained public actions" in which social conflicts are dramatized, be it in a court of law, an assembly of elders, or some other ritual mode of redress. These dramas do not simply restate or mirror underlying social structure and social divisions. They are performances that belong to what Turner calls society's "subjunctive" mood. Ritual, carnival, festival, theater, and other cultural performances express "supposition, desire, hypothesis, possibility," rather than fact.[40] For anthropologists in the Turnerian as well as the Geertzian line, cultural forms can be read as a culture thinking out loud about itself. Barbara Babcock discusses Southwest Indian clown performances, for instance, as a kind of acted-out philosophizing, a metalanguage and commentary on social life that "disrupts and interrupts customary frames and expected logic and syntax and creates a reflexive and ironic dialogue, an open space of questioning."[41]

Geertz remarks that the virtue of Turner's work—the capacity of his concepts of ritual action to apply to a wide variety of social activities, from Mexican insurrections to Icelandic sagas to Caribbean carnivals to tribal rites of passage—is also its defect, for it makes "vividly disparate matters look drably homogeneous." All rituals, in the Turnerian formula, have an initial phase that separates the rite from daily life, a second "liminal" or "betwixt and between" phase that suspends normal psychological and social roles and rules, and a final phase of reintegration into everyday life. These social processes have formal similarities (and even emotional similarities), but, Geertz cautions, they "say . . . rather different things, and thus have rather different implications for social life."[42] It might be added that the Turnerian or neo-Durkheimian tradition is typically invoked not only to analyze but to celebrate performative genres. The anthropologists here, like the folklorists and historians elsewhere, are not only pointing out the performative elements in social life but (unlike Erving Goffman, for example) are "commending them" to our attention.

This is an inevitable potential in academic studies of popular culture. There is a chip on the shoulder of anyone in the academic world who dares take popular culture seriously because he or she does so always in the face of a tradition of high culture and is invariably reckoned by many colleagues alternately shallow or subversive.

Subversive, indeed, is the selection here by Marshall Sahlins, part of a chapter from his difficult and brilliant *Culture and Practical Reason*. It is an intriguing statement not because it argues for the priority of culture over economic or material forces as an explanation of human action—that, after all, is a kind of anthropological commonplace, in some quarters taken as the very rationale for anthropology as a discipline. But Sahlins has himself been a leading practitioner of economic anthropology, an exponent of a materialist orientation to anthropological studies, drawing the discipline's attention to economic and ecological underpinnings and causes of the arrangements of kinship and social organization anthropologists so regularly studied. *Culture and Practical Reason* turns this around. In Sahlins's own summary of his book, he writes, "This book amounts to an anthropological critique of the idea that human cultures are formulated out of practical activity and, behind that, utilitarian interest."[43] He thus attacks both economics as a discipline and Marxist thought, which incorporates economistic assumptions. Sahlins's task began with a question about Marx's analysis of society: Why is it so difficult to apply Marx to tribal societies? And his conclusion is the ironic one that Marx was a bourgeois ideologue, a creature of his class and times and presuppositions, someone who imbibed the spirit and preconscious cultural assumptions of a world that gave priority to motives of self-interest. Marx's theories provide an acutely perceptive description of the bourgeois world but unconsciously incorporate bourgeois presuppositions into the analysis.

So Sahlins, reanalyzing anthropological studies of Tallensi farmers, concludes, "Tallensi farmers are not related as father and son by the way they enter into production; they enter thus into production because they are related as father and son," thereby siding with a traditional British social anthropologist (Meyer Fortes) against his Marxist reviser (Peter Worsley).[44] Social and cultural relations organize practical activity rather than the other way around. And so, too, when he turns to some instances of American popular culture in the selection printed here, his stress is on the ways in which "culture" sets the bounds within which, even in this most bourgeois and utilitarian of societies, utilitarian and economically self-interested motives are defined. Sahlins's work is implicitly critical not only of the imperial tendencies of neoclassical economics to define as universal human motives what is the historically constituted motivational structure of the Western bourgeoisie, but equally of the Marxist spirit that instructs a significant amount of the new study of popular culture.

Indeed, in *Culture and Practical Reason,* "culture" comes to have a kind of priority and autonomy that sounds suspiciously Lévi-Straussian; the French structuralists have clearly influenced Sahlins in this work. In works published since, Sahlins has been seeking some way of articulating the relationship between culture and history, structure and action, the constraining presuppositions of social life and social thought, and the permeability of these presuppositions to the erosions of time and the upheavals of historical change.[45]

The final anthropological selection is also influenced by structuralism. In "Jokes," Mary Douglas makes a persuasive effort to combine a little Freud, a little structuralism, and a little old-fashioned sociological understanding of social groups and their conflicts. It is the kind of piece that has, we could say, the conventional virtue of anthropology, making us see something more than we did about ourselves by showing us how the X or Y or Z tribe does it. But it goes beyond this. Indeed, we include it in part because it is such a nice companion to the Robert Darnton essay on the cat massacre. Both are about jokes; both claim that jokes are commentary on social structure.

Douglas is reacting against conventional British social anthropology, which has treated "ritual joking" as a form of tension release for social relations that are structurally full of conflict—as, for instance, the relationship between a mother-in-law and a daughter-in-law in certain cultures. This tends to reduce the joke to a shout, an emotional outburst that appears at a particularly sore point in the social structure. Douglas, in contrast, sees the joke as providing cognitive as well as expressive satisfaction to those who tell it and hear it. Indeed, she suggests that a joke makes social sense—as commentary on social structure—because it provides cognitive satisfaction. Like Freud, she believes "the pleasure of the joke lies in a kind of economy," and she defines the joke as "a play upon form."

The joke, Douglas argues, as a play upon form, is necessarily subversive. But it is also what people have always popularly taken it to be: frivolous. It is not always acceptable to tell a joke, of course; some subjects or occasions are too sacred or too precarious for the challenge of a joke. So Douglas shifts her attention not only to what makes a joke but to what permits its telling. For her, the relationship of social and symbolic is very close. A joke is not a mirror of social structure; it is an experience called forth by social structure. As she puts it, "the experience of a joke form in the social structure calls imperatively for an explicit joke to express it." She closes her essay with a sympathetic commentary on Victor Turner's argument that ritual joking in Africa, far from being a mere ejaculation of social structural conflict, is a serious form of philosophy, that even though these jokes are not treated in their societies as "philosophy," they nonetheless are reflective commentaries on the relation of thought to experience. They may comment not only on social organization but also on the conditions of human knowledge.

Does this go too far? Does this give a seriousness to the joke that it cannot sustain? It is, from a different angle, the same kind of irreverent leveling we find in Geertz's comparison of Balinese cockfights and Shakespeare's tragedies. Here again, popular culture is held up as serious self-reflection. (All this is screwed up one more notch in Geertz's most recent essays on anthropologists as writers and in the essays by James Clifford and George Marcus and colleagues that, in a sense, hold up serious self-reflection in anthropology as popular culture.)[46] Here popular culture is taken to be a society thinking out loud about itself. The democratization, the leveling of cultural forms, and the societies that have produced them are brazen challenges anthropologists have flung at conventional Western thinking about culture. Once the cultic elements of structuralist thinking have been laid aside, once the hypnotic elegance of Clifford Geertz's writing has been bracketed, a defiant message remains.

PRODUCING CULTURE: THE SOCIOLOGICAL PERSPECTIVE

In the early twentieth century, when American sociology was primarily a native discipline, linked to Protestant social reform and to a strong emphasis on "social problems," popular culture entered unobtrusively into sociological studies. In sociology, more than in any other discipline, it was taken for granted that popular culture could be a legitimate subject of study. Early figures in and around American sociology manifested strong and unembarrassed interest in popular culture. Robert Park, an ex-journalist and a student of Georg Simmel, studied the newspaper; John Dewey, an influence on sociology, social psychology, and education, also wrote about the press. Thorstein Veblen, an economist and social critic, wrote about the "leisure class" and took an interest in everything from the wealthy classes' passion for sports to the livery of their servants.[47]

When sociology emerged as a discipline at the University of Chicago, students were encouraged to examine the everyday life of the ordinary and not so ordinary citizen. William I. Thomas and Florian Znaniecki in *The Polish Peasant in Europe and America* (1918–1920), a defining work for the Chicago school, used life histories, diaries, and letters of Polish immigrants to investigate social life and social organization in all of its variety. They looked at family, schools, the immigrant press, prostitution, the dance hall, and the nostalgia of the immigrants for a homeland left behind.[48] Out of a separate tradition of Christian social reform, Robert and Helen Lynd published *Middletown* in 1929 and so helped cement community studies as a central element in American sociology, and one deeply concerned with the whole range of human social activity. The Lynds approached "middle American" Muncie, Indiana, like anthropologists examining an exotic tribe. They were as attentive to dating patterns and the role of movies in the socialization of the young as they were to occupational stratification and other topics one might assume to be of greater sociological dignity.[49]

Despite this parentage, sociology developed its own ambivalence toward the study of popular culture. The Lynds saw mass culture as an integral—but unsettling—part of a whole way of life. The Payne Fund studies of mass entertainment in the 1930s saw the movies as a social problem, a cause of juvenile delinquency. When European social thought came to America in the 1930s and after, the sociological attitude toward popular culture darkened. Mass culture was seen increasingly as a central feature of the decay of civilization in a capitalist society. By the 1950s, the most influential work on popular culture in sociology was the work of or work influenced by the Frankfurt school (see the next section on literary criticism)—and, within a short time, its critics. David Manning White and Bernard Rosenberg's standard anthology, *Mass Culture* (1957), is centrally oriented to the "mass culture" debate, as it came to be known.[50] That debate weighed the dangers and prospects of mass-produced cultural forms for the political enlightenment and cultural enrichment of the citizens.

The debate (outlined in an early French version in Rosalind Williams's essay) persists today. It is regularly renewed by critics of new media (television, video games, and MTV in recent years), advertising, and consumer culture generally. Its contours were comprehensively restated and reconsidered by Herbert Gans in 1974.[51] Gans comes out a sharp critic of the critics of mass culture. He finds their arguments inconsistent, their evidence of the pernicious consequences of mass culture thin or nonexistent, and their tenor of argument less related to the political radicalism many critics profess than to the particular "taste culture" of upper-middle-class intellectuals they share. He sees the case against mass culture as more often parochial than political.

While the mass culture debate moved sociology away from empirical studies of cultural phenomena, attention to culture survived in sociology, notably in *The Lonely Crowd* (1950), by David Riesman, Nathan Glazer, and Reuel Denney, followed up by Riesman in other essays.[52] The complexity of sociological attitudes to popular culture is discussed in some of Riesman's work, where he defends mass culture from its highbrow critics (recommending, for instance, that a new supermarket might be a better arena for community leisure than a new park and arguing that it is by no means clear that books are more liberating than radio and television). But he is equally prepared to defend high culture minorities from "inverse snobbery and class romanticism."[53]

The mass culture debate continues in a variety of polemics that, in our view, too often only recycle the old (and still very readable) essays on the subject by Edward Shils, Dwight MacDonald, Hannah Arendt, C. Wright Mills, and others and rarely achieve the complex confrontation with the valuation of popular culture forms one finds in Riesman.[54] But recent sociological concern with popular culture has moved sharply from heated debate over the aesthetic and moral worth of popular culture to an acceptance that popular culture is legitimate to study as a symbolic object and, even more, as a manufactured thing produced in and by social organizations. As in literary studies, this newer sociological work has eschewed attention to the valuation of popular culture as good or bad, high or low. Much recent work on popular culture in the United States comes from the "production-of-culture" school, which uses analytical systems from the sociology of occupations and of organizations to see how social resources are mobilized by artists, filmmakers, and the like to make culture production possible. There has also been renewed interest among sociologists (including a large number in Europe) in the stratifying functions of cultural systems, the way social groups are identified by their cultural tastes or their abilities to create cultural institutions suited to members of their social strata. Both approaches provide new perspectives for analyzing cultural objects or systems without finding any reason to sharply distinguish elite culture from popular culture.

The production-of-culture route begins from the assumption that the production of cultural objects, be they "art" *or* "mass culture," involves social cooperation and group problem solving that can be approached with conventional tools of sociological analysis. Social commonalities across aesthetic categories make the study of popular culture no more and no less important than the study of fine art. In the hands of some production-of-culture writers, this assimilates the study of art to the sociology of organizations and markets; in the hands of others, it assimilates the study of art to the sociology of occupations.[55] In either case, the artist is dethroned as a genius whose creativity can only be appreciated rather than analyzed and replaced with a worker whose habits can be systematically investigated. Similarly, the cultural stratification school, if we may call it that (represented here by Pierre Bourdieu), begins from the assumption that cultural differences and social attention to cultural difference are important sociologically because they are linked to fundamental patterns of social stratification. Social stratification is buttressed by differences in the cultural attributes of people from different strata. Because understanding cultural stratification requires attention to the range of cultural forms, popular culture has a central (but not dominating) role.

Some American sociologists who study popular culture invoke the heritage of European social theory rather than of early American sociology. Emile Durkheim and Max Weber, they observe, both studied the sociology of popular religion. Durkheim is an important intellectual forebear of structuralism; Weber encouraged sociology to focus on how people make meanings in their world, and he is thereby a legitimating presence for any sociological study that centers on symbols and signification. (Geertz, in an oft-quoted line, cites Weber as having taught us that human beings are creatures who live suspended in webs of meaning they themselves have spun.)[56] But neither Weber nor Durkheim directly influenced new sociological work on popular culture. Weber offers warrant, but not precedent or example, for attention to popular cultural forms, the study of religion itself excepted.[57] The sociological studies of culture that most often acknowledge an American heritage grow out of symbolic interactionism. Here, in a direct line that goes back to Robert Park and George Herbert Mead at the University of Chicago (and can be traced back further to American pragmatism generally in John Dewey and William James and others), a distinctive emphasis on how people make meaning and make society through the experience of everyday social interaction emerged. This approach is tailor-made for the quietly leveling or more openly pedestal-blasting tendencies in popular culture studies.

The production-of-culture approach notes that, in spite of the Western emphasis on the role of creative *individuals,* social *groups* produce art, music, literature, television news, and so forth. What pop music and particle physics have in common is that both are symbolic structures produced by human beings who work in and are shaped by social organizations. This apparently unexceptional observation contrasts sharply with assumptions common in both lay and professional writing on culture. The organizational perspective denies that there is a close relationship between the intentions of an individual, even a powerful individual, in a corporate culture-producing organization, and the kind of product that gets created. The product is more the unplanned consequence of a large number of small choices than the intended result of a small number of critical decisions. Choices are shaped in large part by the internal needs of an organization and not the long-range goals of its executives or owners.

In this way, the production-of-culture approach to popular culture has in many instances been a self-conscious reaction against mass culture studies. Paul DiMaggio argues that left-wing critics of mass culture implicitly assume a "monopoly" situation: that there is a single producer of culture (the ruling class) and that the public will necessarily absorb whatever it offers. Right-wing critics, in contrast, implicitly assume a situation of "perfect competition" where there is a multitude of culture producers that create a practically unlimited assortment of cultural objects so that the public can choose whatever it desires. In DiMaggio's view, the central features of mass culture do not fit either right-wing or left-wing models because the key characteristics of mass culture vary by industry, not by society. Some mass culture industries are monopolistic—like the television industry (before cable) or school textbook publishing in the United States. But other mass culture industries—trade books, records, movies, magazines—create objects for specialized audiences; their situation more closely resembles one of free competition. The degree of diversity and innovation in the cultural goods available to the public depends, then, primarily on the market structures and organizational environments of specific industries, not on the preferences of either the masses or their masters.[58]

This approach also denies any simply stated relationships between cultural products and underlying social structure or cultural values. On the one hand, it is precisely the point of organizational studies to demonstrate that cultural products are more or less determined by social structure—the social structure of the producing organizations. On the other hand, the attention to the producing organization has grown out of dissatisfaction with studies that suggested a connection between culture and broad, underlying social and economic structures based on the axiomatic belief that culture mirrors the social order. In this regard, sociology squares off against anthropology or, at least, against reading very much from studies of simple societies for the understanding of complex societies. Perhaps there is a snug "fit" between culture and social organization in the societies anthropologists typically study, but it does not follow that in highly complex, differentiated, plural societies today we will find so neat a correspondence.

The sociological approach here breaks sharply from the anthropological tradition in a second way: It moves away from the study of meaning altogether to the study of culture as a manufactured product. Using a perspective honed earlier in his career in the sociology of occupations, Howard Becker, for example, examines material, social, and symbolic resources for the creation of meaningful cultural objects. He is not interested so much in what the final objects mean. He wants to understand what is *social* about them. He focuses on the wide array of cooperative links between "creators" and "support personnel" necessary for the production of cultural objects. Most work in both the sociology of art and cultural criticism looks for some "creator" or "artist" who is responsible for the final object. Becker, in contrast, opens his *Art Worlds* discussing the relationship of Anthony Trollope to his valet as essential to the production of the books we attribute to Trollope, and he goes on to reproduce a long list of the "credits" of a recent commercial film to illustrate the collectiveness of artistic production in another medium. The conventions of Western individualism and resulting aesthetic theory have made the support personnel behind culture production invisible servants. Those who develop film in laboratories, make paints, or print books are central to the production of culture, but rarely cited for their contribution. Studying these links, Becker contends, generates a fundamentally *social* vision of the creative process and its creations. Interestingly, Becker takes for granted that a sociology of art and popular culture need not be organized around understanding how some culture becomes "respected" and other kinds are critically lambasted. Critics, dealers, and museum personnel are, like everyone else in Becker's art worlds, simply doing their jobs. Their special power in the world of art and the relationship of aesthetic stratification of culture to social hierarchy are not things Becker singles out for central attention. Less to his credit, he does not emphasize how such hierarchical considerations (both social and aesthetic) enter into the production process. But others working in the production-of-culture school do.[59]

If production-of-culture studies are linked on one side to symbolic interactionism and the sociology of occupations, they are connected on the other side to the sociology of organizations. Take, for example, Paul Hirsch's essay on fads and fashions. Hirsch, like Becker, is not interested in interpreting culture (i.e., providing accounts of what cultural objects "mean"). There is no obeisance here to Weber and *Verstehen,* Geertz and thick description, or other heroes of the interpretive persuasion. Hirsch wants to know about the characteristics of industries that produce cultural products (typically nonmaterial goods that serve for their consumers an aesthetic or expressive rather than utilitarian function). The main problem for the industries he has in mind—trade books, movies, and records—is the uncertainty of popular demand for the products. The main economic feature that structures the way these industries operate is their cheap technology: It costs very little to produce a book, record, or low-budget film. The result is overproduction and differential promotion of cultural items: These industries produce far more cultural objects than they need or expect to make money for them. They count on the "gatekeeper" institutions of media critics and radio stations and so forth to identify to the public the best or most attractive cultural objects. They then put more marketing muscle behind those products so identified than the other objects they have produced (with the hopeful writers and artists wondering vainly why their books, records, or movies are not being promoted). Hierarchical ratings of cultural products are central to Hirsch's approach, but not as a means for distinguishing good from bad culture. They are central to the way participants in culture industries organize the production and distribution process.

Hirsch's essay has the virtues and defects of the general approach of production-of-culture studies. The virtue is that it really tells us something about how popular culture gets created. There are no vague references here to a relationship between something called "culture" and something called "society" that it somehow reflects. Instead, Hirsch describes a concrete set of organizations and individuals and entrepreneurial motives and organizational routines that concretely produces items of culture, some of which become popular and influential, most of which do not. This locates culture in concrete social and economic institutions.

As for defects, there are three. First, as practitioners of this viewpoint themselves recognize, the organizational approach is much better at explaining the normal mechanisms for creating "normal" culture than it is at explaining what happens when culture changes. It is not that the latter is impossible. Todd Gitlin makes an impressive effort in his study of prime-time television at explaining why "Hill Street Blues," a decidedly unusual and norm-breaking TV program, managed to get on the air and stay there in the 1980s. In the excerpt from his book on television included here, he also tries to get a grasp of typical routines by examining an exception. In this case, the exception very much proves the rule. Indeed, what Gitlin finds is that what began as an exception—a break from network television blandness, an effort to make a strong political statement—wound up bowdlerized, just another object on the cultural assembly line. Hegemony worked its wonders even though the "authors" had hoped to make a critical statement. Gitlin's is a particularly vivid description of this process.

Second, there is a tendency in production-of-culture work to assume that sociological factors are more determining than, in fact, they are. The danger is that organizational studies may come to assume that organizations are more limited by the need to respond to constraints in their environments than is actually true. Organizations (or rather, key decision makers within them) have some freedom to act within broad environmental constraints. Moreover, there are frequently alternative decisions that could lead to an equally acceptable outcome. Perhaps still more important, organizations may help create the environments they must then respond to—this is especially so in industries that are government regulated or oligopolistic. Finally, organizations respond not to their "real" environments but to their perception of the environment.[60] Even in the most pragmatic organizations, culture—in the form of traditions, ideologies, and presuppositions—enters into the formulation of problems. The "bottom line" is no less a "cultural" product than other humanly constructed lines (national borders, time zone demarcations, or newspaper deadlines).

Third, there is a tendency in production-of-culture studies to assume that they study the production of "culture." They do not. They study the production of cultural objects, and these objects become a part of and contribute to culture. But they are not culture as such. Production-of-culture studies examine *parole,* not *langue;* performance, not competence; or speech, not language, to borrow distinctions from linguistics. The whole production process and certainly the gatekeeping process Hirsch and Gitlin describe so nicely are not only socioeconomic but are also cultural processes, created and existing against a network of background assumptions, symbolic taken-for-granteds. And *that* is culture.[61] (Gitlin understands this. His work is as rooted in cultural criticism as in organizational sociology; if he is less systematic than some of the others who look at culture-producing organizations, he is more theoretically encompassing.)

The distinctive contribution of the sociological tradition is not limited to a focus on the organizations, structures, and processes that produce cultural objects. Sociologists, particularly those influenced by a Marxist tradition (which means nearly all European sociologists whether they are Marxists or not), have drawn attention to the connections between culture and social class. They have, more than anthropologists or literary scholars, centered work on the sociocultural dimensions of social differentiation and social stratification. In the Marxist-influenced tradition, this means primarily an emphasis on the relations between culture and class; in the American tradition, it is just as likely to examine the relations between culture and other social forms of differentiated power, notably ethnicity and gender.

A particular form of this kind of work examines especially the subjective experience of class or other relations of hierarchy and subordination. At one level, this becomes a study of expressive style in nations, classes, and subcultures of various sorts. Culture can be viewed as an expression of instrumental desires, as in Dick Hebdige's work on subculture.[62] Or it can be viewed as metonymically related to other matters of social difference and social cohesion, a shadow of social relations.

Bourdieu's essay gives a good sense of a highly developed articulation of the sociological vision of culture as an expression and instrument of social class divisions. (Bourdieu's work is most fully elaborated in *Distinction.*)[63] It is explicitly concerned with the "production" of culture, but it sets this interest in tandem with a concern about the consumption of culture. Ultimately, Bourdieu's interest in examining both the "supply" of a cultural entity (sports, in this essay) and the "demand" for it becomes a task of mapping the distribution of a given cultural object or cultural taste among the different subgroups (especially classes, but Bourdieu also attends in this essay to the distribution of sports activity across age groups) of a population. In this work, Bourdieu shows that modern sports have emerged under specific historical conditions and in specific class locations. He argues that, despite the presence of popular sport, the dominant sports tradition is a schooled one, associated with elite educational institutions where "the propensity towards activity for no purpose" is cherished and promoted in both the taste for art and the taste for sports. The popularization of sport offers no essential problem for this view; in fact, popularization goes hand in hand with the elaboration of a cultural division between professionals and the lay public reduced to the role of consumers. Here, indeed, Bourdieu suggests, is the area where sport produces "its most decisive political effects," condemning the greater public to "an imaginary participation which is only an illusory compensation for the dispossession they suffer to the advantage of the experts."

In this argument, Bourdieu connects leisure activities to the stratification systems traditionally tied in sociology exclusively to the work process. He argues that class, not status, is reproduced in sport. This is a major claim to be made for the role of culture in social life, and Bourdieu brings much evidence to bear on it. Unfortunately, his theoretical net does not capture all the richness of the empirical, historical knowledge he brings to the analysis. By dint of the focus on the hierarchical structuring of culture, Bourdieu's model is awkward to use for studying the kinds of cultural processes rendered so well by researchers in the production-of-culture school. The attribution of popular tastes and activities to class, for example, tends to obscure the complex ways people make sense of and use their tastes. Still, Bourdieu integrates the constellation of culture into a broader analysis of society as a whole, which the production-of-culture approach rarely even attempts. Not surprisingly, the elegant power of his model is a major factor leading new generations of students to the study of popular culture in sociology.

Paul DiMaggio's essay, certainly influenced by Bourdieu, nicely combines both the class-related vision of European sociology and the organization-related perspective of the production-of-culture school. DiMaggio examines the development of "elite culture" in late nineteenth-century Boston. The reason we include a work specifically concerned with "high" culture in a volume devoted to popular culture quickly becomes clear in this essay: Creating the Boston Symphony Orchestra and the Boston

Museum of Fine Arts was not a matter of finding an organizational basis for an already defined realm of "high culture" but a task of *inventing* a category of high culture *through* the creation of organizations that would mobilize elites around it. DiMaggio argues that the distinction between high culture and popular culture in the United States emerged in the late nineteenth century as urban elites created organizations that isolated a separate sphere of "high culture" and differentiated it from "popular culture." In Boston, a new organizational form—the nonprofit corporation governed by a self-perpetuating board of trustees—emerged to secure a separate sphere for high culture and its elite patrons. What DiMaggio documents is how a "status group"—the Boston "Brahmins"—sought to define an exclusive and prestigious culture that they could control. At the same time, as a dominant social class, the Brahmins sought to impose on the general public a respect for and deference to the culture they were claiming as exclusively their own.

DiMaggio's emphasis on the organizational basis of culture is a crucial contribution of the sociological perspective. However, it should not obscure the importance of the differentiation of high from popular culture on a symbolic as well as organizational basis. We just briefly note here an essay by William Weber on how a pantheon of musical "masters" developed in mid-nineteenth-century Europe. Because no Greek and Roman music had survived, European music could not draw on a classical tradition, as did literature, architecture, painting, and sculpture. With the rise of a mass public for music in the early nineteenth century, thanks in part to the growth of the printing industry and the availability of sheet music, elite professional orchestras began to establish a "classical" repertoire. In the 1820s, the works played by the Philharmonic Society of London were primarily works by living composers; by the 1850s, less than a third were by living composers; the Société des Concerts in Paris devoted only 11 percent of its repertoire to living composers by the 1860s. Weber's view, like DiMaggio's, is ultimately sociological and skeptical; it gives no quarter to those who would insist that the classical repertoire is "better" than more popular musical forms but argues that the creation of a classical repertoire is itself a social phenomenon dominated by struggles for power and standing among class and status groups.[64]

Clearly, then, a central lesson of the new studies of popular culture is that a radical distinction between high culture and popular culture cannot be maintained. Aspects of popular culture become high culture over time (Charles Dickens, folk art, early manufactured furniture, jazz). Aspects of high culture become popular culture (Pachelbel's "Canon in D," Handel's *Messiah*). Common people have sophisticated and refined craft knowledge and artistic capabilities; elites have their own folk beliefs (including the persistent belief in the nineteenth-century romanticist view of the individual genius as cultural creator). The borderline of elite and popular culture is patrolled, and the fences maintained, for identifiably social and political, rather than purely aesthetic, purposes. Now, in contrast to the "mass culture" debates in sociology in the 1950s, sociologists are a bit more inclined to sit on the sidelines and observe the very debates they once engaged in (and sometimes still do) as part of a social process by which valuation is attached to the particular tastes of particular social groups.

These considerations link up with new studies in literature and the arts on "canonization." Literary scholars are increasingly reflective about the extent to which their own activity is not abstractly critical but concretely political—that what counts as a piece of "literature" depends very much on what individuals and institutions connected with the dominant gender and dominant social classes declare literature to be. What counts as a masterpiece is a social and political process, not an exercise of pure reason.[65]

The legitimation of popular culture should not be taken—though it sometimes is—as an uncritical welcome to all that popular culture contains. The study of popular culture is too often its celebration. Although this celebration helps legitimate the aesthetic and political expressions of common people, the democratic aspiration of popular culture studies is sometimes undiscriminating. We can happily celebrate discoveries in popular culture of sociability, fellowship, and creative resistance to exclusionary cultural forms; but that should scarcely blind us to popular traditions of racism, sexism, and nativism that are just as deeply rooted. This is popular culture, too.

This raises a key issue, usually ignored in popular culture studies, about the relation of the popular to the public. There is, in the concept of "the public sphere," public spaces where people come together on equal terms and work out problems together through rational and critical discussion, a normative dimension and a political program that are not part of the general concept of the popular. A modern sense of the public is itself a historically specific notion, as the German philosopher and social theorist Jürgen Habermas makes plain in the short article we include in this volume. The work from which this paper is drawn was originally written in 1962 but translated into English only in 1989. Its influence on academic thought in the Anglo-American context, then, has yet to be fully felt. However, the emphasis on a "public sphere" that Habermas more than anyone else has insisted upon has drawn the attention of various scholars in several disciplines to the institutions that define and constitute a public realm in modern societies, especially the news media, private associations, and leisure activities in which political discussion is free to take place (as in the coffeehouses of the eighteenth century). As politics descended in the eighteenth century and after from the halls of aristocratic power restricted to the few to parties that recruit from the masses, newspapers that seek a broad readership, and streets where groups of people from different classes and backgrounds congregate to express their views, the study of democratic politics necessarily became a consideration of various institutions of popular culture.

This, clearly, adds a different kind of normative dimension to the analysis of popular culture. With a sense of the "public sphere" in mind, aspects of popular culture may be worth examining not simply because they are popular but because they may contribute to, or impede, rational and critical participation in the political world. The concept of the "public sphere" as a normative standard is a vital addition to the study of popular culture.

LITERARY AND OTHER FORMS OF CRITICISM

Perhaps the most dramatic rethinking of popular culture has been initiated by literary critics, many of whom have left behind altogether traditional allegiances to high culture as the privileged subject matter of serious criticism. They have led a series of critical revolutions with a proliferating set of theoretical schools (structuralism, semiology, poststructuralism, deconstruction, discourse theory) and a startling opacity of terminology that intimidates outsiders and makes not a few insiders shake their heads. But within this brave new world of literary theory are new tools of critical analysis and new outlooks on the nature of culture, broadly understood, that reach far beyond the confines of literature departments.

To begin a few steps back: Attention to popular culture in literary or, broadly, cultural criticism can be traced to both right-wing and left-wing dissatisfaction with the cultural inclinations of the general population. On the right, anxiety about democratic and egalitarian movements and about increasing working-class participation in politics was accompanied by disapproval of the mass culture that the general population seemed to take such pleasure in. Whether it was novels in the eighteenth century that attracted women readers, mass circulation newspapers in the late nineteenth century that attracted the working class, nickelodeons at the turn of the century that drew an audience of immigrants in the United States, or comic books in the 1940s and 1950s that attracted the young, guardians of elite culture saw in these works serious threats to the maintenance of high culture as the central standard for education and socialization. New mass cultural forms seemed debased in a variety of ways: they appealed to the senses and not to reason; they represented and thereby encouraged violence and sexual activity; they were easily acces-

sible to the uneducated or ill-educated and demanded little of their audiences.

If all this could be said from the side of elitists intent on defending
high culture, much the same critique could come from left-wing critics
intent on locating authentic and liberatory cultural elements in oppressed social groups. The Left as well as the Right deplored the influence of mass-produced commercial culture. Where the Right blamed the
low level of mass culture on the tastes of the masses, the Left blamed it
on elite efforts to domesticate a potentially unruly population. On the
Right, this brand of criticism did not develop in any systematic way, but
on the Left, it became a sophisticated set of critical perspectives in the
hands of the Frankfurt school. The Frankfurt school refers to the work
of scholars associated with or influenced by the Frankfurt Institute of
Social Research (Institut für Sozialforschung), founded in 1923 as an
independent research institute designed to pursue Marxist studies while
reexamining the philosophical underpinnings of Marxism itself from the
ground up. When Hitler came to power in 1933, the prospects of a Marxist
research institute, most of whose leading figures were Jewish, were obviously dim, and the institute moved to Geneva. Before long, many of
the key figures in the institute emigrated to the United States. The term
"Frankfurt school" did not arise until after the group left Frankfurt,
indeed, not until the institute returned to Frankfurt in 1950.[66]

Not surprisingly, much of the work of this group of scholars tried to
understand the success of Nazism, in part by considering the psychological and political effects of mass culture and its role in shaping popular
political consciousness. They perceived mass culture as aesthetically and
politically debilitating, reducing the capacities of audiences to think critically and functioning as an ideological tool to manipulate the political
sentiments of the mass public. They developed a new kind of Marxist
perspective, one still devoted to understanding how the power of the
capitalist class was sustained under industrial capitalism, but now grappling with the role of mass media in creating something unanticipated
by Marxist theory: conservatism and—a new term—"authoritarianism"
among workers.

As on the Right, so on the Left there was hostility to new cultural
forms and new technologies that reached the masses. One of the key
Frankfurt school critics, Theodor Adorno, criticized both popular music
(including jazz) and the radio technology that distributed it. He found
that the "commodity form" of capitalist culture, standardizing culture
and reducing it to a lowest common denominator, led toward a music
that emphasized recognition of the familiar rather than more active and
intelligent appreciation. Popular music encouraged passivity. As for radio itself, it isolated individuals and kept people apart from the sense of

community that a live performance can create; it encouraged "atomized listening."[67]

With the revival of Marxism in the American student movement and its European counterparts during the 1960s, critical theory, as the work of the Frankfurt school came to be known, gained a new constituency and was given new direction. Walter Benjamin's famous essay "The Work of Art in the Age of Mechanical Reproduction" became a touchstone for new critical discourse.[68] Benjamin was an uneasy ally of the Frankfurt school, connected with Frankfurt school scholars but always at arm's length from them. Benjamin was deeply influenced by Jewish theology and mysticism, on the one hand, and a cruder brand of materialism, on the other. Under the influence of Bertolt Brecht, he was optimistic about the revolutionary potential of popular art and new technologies in a way that other Frankfurt scholars were not. This is readily apparent in "The Work of Art," where he suggests that the mass production of imagery makes image makers seek constituencies rather than personal presence through their work. Thus, mass production necessarily and fundamentally politicizes communication. It removes the "other" (the author) from immediate view by audiences, and it can be used only where large numbers can be enticed into becoming an audience.

What made Benjamin's analysis so appealing to critical analysts in the 1960s is in part simply that his work is allusive, aphoristic, more poetic than analytic, and therefore interpretable in a wide variety of ways. In his emphasis on mass production, Benjamin's ideas seemed compatible with then-popular ideas espoused by Marshall McLuhan, claiming the medium as the message.[69] But unlike McLuhan and the earlier critical theorists, Benjamin did not believe that mass media necessarily had a particular character (good or bad, hot or cold). As a partisan of some still photography and an enthusiast of film, he believed these media could be used for aesthetically important purposes and could have politically progressive effects. In this way, Benjamin's work no doubt helped assuage the guilt of rock music fans or film aficionados who wanted to be critical thinkers; more important, it stimulated new debate about how to structure a liberatory communication system and gave it a distinguished pedigree. In the latter project, he was followed by several illustrious thinkers with Frankfurt ties, including Herbert Marcuse and Jürgen Habermas.

Interest in creating new communicative possibilities was very closely tied to the interests of the student radicals of the period. If political conservatism was taught through the dominant media, then how could other political positions be articulated and realized? Another way to answer the question was to turn to labor history and see how culture and oppositional politics had functioned together in the past. Particularly in

England, students of labor history and literary critics both began to ask themselves about the role of culture in mobilizing the working class. E. P. Thompson's *Making of the English Working Class*, already discussed, had extraordinary significance in this regard.

Other scholars tried to articulate formally the theories of cultural control and resistance Thompson raised for discussion, like the late Raymond Williams in the essay we have included here. Williams, a literary critic and historian, had a vital role in reinvigorating critical studies in England (and the rest of the English-speaking world). In his studies of mass media, from drama to the press and television, he describes how the messages conveyed by the media have been constructed according to the politicoeconomic as well as technological environment in which they have been mobilized. He sees their forms as an expression simultaneously of the social position of their "authors" (which he understands primarily in terms of Marxist categories of class analysis) and the social relations developed around the media.

In this article, Williams outlines a program for a Marxist theory of culture. Here he offers a kind of primer of key terms for a reconstituted Marxist theory, one that would abandon superficial notions of a "base" "determining" a "superstructure." In attacking all three terms and sketching in a history of other critical revisions of them, he presents a lexicon of concepts he believes improve a Marxist approach to culture: hegemony; dominant, alternative, and oppositional cultures; dominant, residual, and emergent cultures. Williams tackles head-on the conventional Marxist metaphor that the "base" of economic structure determines the "superstructure" of politics, law, religion, and—of central interest here—culture. He finds, as others have, that culture is more variable in its meaning and significance than Marxist theory has usually allowed. More than that, he essentially denies that culture is properly understood as superstructure at all. He argues that this view wrongly gives the impression that culture is a set of symbols or set of objects when it is more properly understood as a set of practices. That is, base and superstructure coexist within the world of culture itself. Even more important, he holds, the notion of the base as a fixed technological and economic system misrepresents what Marxist scholars should be attending to: the specific activities of people in real social and economic relationships, a process of productive activity and not a machine of determined proportion. If base and superstructure are misunderstood, so too is "determine" in the old Marxist formula. For Williams, "determine" should not mean "totally predicts or prefigures" but "sets limits."

Williams does not sit easily in any disciplinary category. He, like the other key figures in establishing the "cultural studies" movement in Britain (Stuart Hall and Richard Hoggart), is equally identifiable as a literary scholar, communication scholar, and even sociologist.[70] In Britain, the field of communication has become a center for the kind of popular culture studies we discuss here. In the United States, this is also increasingly true, as students of communication are influenced by various literary theorists (notably Mikhail Bakhtin), British cultural studies (especially Stuart Hall and Raymond Williams), and bits of a "hegemony theory" from sociology.[71]

Cultural studies in Britain, as John Fiske has defined it, is "concerned with the generation and circulation of meanings in industrial societies."[72] Most of this work speaks on the Marxist assumption (although this is an assumption shared by sociologists generally) that culture—the meanings by which people live—derives from social structure. Culture is important (and this is in part Williams's point) because it acts back on social structure to hold it in place. But none of this happens in an easily apprehensible way. That is, the ideology inscribed in popular culture—notably in television, which has been an important subject for British cultural studies—may be "decoded" by actual audiences in a variety of ways. In Stuart Hall's terms, there may be a "preferred reading," but audiences may also arrive at alternative or even oppositional readings of the same text.[73] When empirical studies examine how actual audiences read actual texts, even this formulation seems too simple; and works in cultural studies emphasize the "multivocality" or "polysemy" of texts, indeed arguing, as Fiske does, that the more popular a text, the more likely it is to be "open," allowing "the various subcultures to generate meanings from it that meet the needs of their own subcultural identities."[74] Once cultural studies have shifted this far from a view of popular culture as a medium for the transmission of a simple, dominant ideology, it is not easy to retain clearly any sense of domination or hegemonic authority, although even Fiske in the formulation cited here tries to. The dialogue between text and audience, he argues, must be understood not as anarchic or pluralistic, but in terms of dominant power relations in society. The television text, for instance, he holds is not anarchic. One cannot read any meaning out of it: "The diverse subcultures in a society are defined only by their relations (possibly oppositional) to the centers of domination, so, too, the multiple meanings of a text that is popular in that society can be defined only by their relationships (possibly oppositional) to the dominant ideology as it is structured into that text."[75]

Marxist theory today is itself full of contradictory and competing views. Williams represents, as do British cultural studies in general, a minimally deterministic, process-oriented, and activity-oriented version of neo-Marxist thought. This has led to an increasing need for essays, like Williams's here, that try to spell out what a Marxist cultural theory sensitive to empirical complexity will look like.

As Williams became more precise in articulating theory, he correspondingly moved farther away from the kind of work that established his reputation: interpreting cultural works in their sociohistorical context. Theory or no theory, "reading" culture as an expression of hierarchical and historical social relations is no easy task. John Berger takes a stab at it in his brief but telling analysis of a famous 1913 photograph by Auguste Sander of three peasants in dress suits on their way to a dance. He suggests from the photographs that the suit is not the same object on the body of a laborer as it is on the body of a businessman. It is made for the latter, reinforcing class relations while seemingly providing an egalitarian link among men. This is a graphic example of "hegemony" at work. The peasants look so awkward and ungainly in their suits because *they are*. The suit as we know it developed, Berger writes, as "a professional ruling class costume." Yet the workers and peasants come to accept this clothing as their own, thereby consigning themselves to clumsy appearance in an intrinsically foreign garment. In a nutshell, this is the story of cultural hegemony everywhere: The working class "accepts" and takes for granted not only the dress but the art, the language, the values of the bourgeoisie. Similarly, cultural hegemony is at work when women accept the standards of taste and value set by men, the Third World accepts the standards of behavior and worth defined by colonial powers, blacks accept the norms of whites, homosexuals accept the values of heterosexuals, and so forth. In each case, what is so powerful is not that a foreign system is viciously imposed on subordinates (though this is sometimes exactly what happens), but that the force of domination has succeeded in "naturalizing" the values of the dominant class so that their superiority is taken by everyone as obvious, as common sense.

In his writings. Berger takes images (like these photographs) to have clear and recognizable politicoeconomic significance. He assumes that configurations of social power and social interests are the essential forces behind the look and meanings of pictures, not the personal motives or gifts of an author. It is interesting to compare Berger's actual practice of reading culture in this little essay to Williams's prescriptions in his theoretical work. In one respect, Berger's study of the suit beautifully illustrates what it means to see culture as a practice rather than a symbol or object. But in other respects, Berger falls short. For someone as careful as Berger ordinarily is to see the artifactualness of images, it is odd to find him here taking Sander's photograph as transparent. He talks about the three men in their suits as if we (the viewers of the photograph) had through the photo direct access to empirical reality. He never asks if the social act of photographing three men in their suits is not itself part of the process of making the men appear awkward. He sees Sander as a scientist, not as a man among men, a middle-class and urban man at that, whose attitude and style and social position must surely have had something to do with making his rural subjects ill at ease. Yet Berger here talks only of suits, not of photographs of suits. His greatest strength, ordinarily, showing the ways in which a photograph or painting has been constructed, is here abandoned.

There is another matter curiously overlooked in this essay. Berger never asks how the observer's sense of beauty, the observer's sense of what is gainly or ungainly, comes to be formed. Not only does he see the photographer Sander as directly registering with his camera empirical reality, but he also takes himself (and his readers) to be objective observers, scientists with no social position or social background themselves. Would peasants also see the three men as ungainly? Would peasants of 1913 have seen them as ungainly?

All these problems acknowledged, there remains something compelling in this little gem of "reading" culture. Berger, other British Marxists, and Frankfurt school critics have persuasively urged attention to the relations between texts or pictures, the social power they exercise, and the aesthetic systems that govern judgment. The power of an individual image to define reality may emanate in part from its compelling use of a powerful aesthetic, but that too emanates from a social reality it helps to reproduce.

This point of view provides a set of tools for critical analysis that helps forge ties between social history and cultural exegesis, but it does not provide critics with a very refined set of techniques for approaching the content of some cultural objects. After the social relations are identified in the objects, what can you say about their other aesthetic characteristics? The ties between aesthetic and social movements are not always easy to identify, nor is there always a clear correspondence between the social origins of a cultural object and the social content of its message or, even more, its style. The antipathy of the founders of the Frankfurt school to mass culture of the twentieth century made attempts to analyze contemporary culture using this critical perspective more difficult for Marxists, so scholars interested in doing more than condemning contemporary literature and art tended to look to other schools of thought for theoretical guidance.

What some have identified as the most original Anglo-American contribution to literary theory, "New Criticism," arose in the 1930s as a specifically antihistoricist, anticontextual reading of texts.[76] New Criticism asserted that knowing the author's intentions or, indeed, anything at all about the author and the world in which he or she wrote, was irrelevant to deciphering the meaning of texts. The message was in the text itself, and the good reader could discover it without reference to external clues.

New Criticism seemed to have little to offer students of popular culture. After all, its practitioners were concerned with developing the techniques for distinguishing good from bad literature and did not generally
deign to touch mass culture because it was by definition less closely tied
to a distinctive authorial style. But still, their approach to reading had its
counterpart in film studies—in the guise of "auteur theory." Critics
working within this tradition tried to explain individual films by reference to the corpus of the director. They redefined film as an expressive
more than commercial medium, and they redefined the hierarchy of
control within filmmaking units. Before the 1950s (at least in the United
States), films were often thought to belong to their producers. (Why not?
They were industrial products, and the producers controlled the money.)
In contrast, auteur theory attributed film content to the decisions of film
directors, who were treated as authors. They were the aesthetic arbiters
in film units, so they were easy to anoint as the God figures who "created" films. With the director as artist, film could become art.[77]

Auteur theory was successful in elevating film this way in part because
it was a French import, designed for analyzing works following the art
film tradition in Europe. It also worked because auteur theorists were
able to apply models of literary analysis that assumed that the meaning
of a work resided in the techniques of expression chosen by a single
author. Finally, it worked because it did not question the importance of
distinguishing art from mass culture. It taught viewers how to distinguish art films (with a signature) from commercial works (expressing
collective commercial values, not a personal vision). In this way, auteur
theory reinforced the critical hierarchy in literary studies, simply taking
some films and placing them alongside "real" literature. The study of
film did not open up the academy to popular culture; it simply allowed
a new medium, or certain exemplars of a new medium, to enter into an
academy whose principles of operation could remain largely intact.[78]

Serious study of forms of popular culture *as popular culture*, using
techniques of literary criticism, had to wait for the semiotics of Roland
Barthes. Barthes was among the early structuralists to use Saussurian
linguistics as a means for cultural analysis. He went one step beyond
most structuralists, however. He did not simply use linguistic techniques
for analyzing patterns of literary writing; he proposed to use them for
studying nonelite imagery (film, photography, clothing) and other popular forms (like food and boxing).

The logic of this move was simple. Indeed, as Robert Alter has argued, the premise of semiotics and structuralism that the world is a set
of signs to be deciphered and not a set of objects to be known, led inescapably to "a global expansion of the concept of *text*." "Structuralist man,"
writes the not very sympathetic Alter, "encounters nothing but texts

wherever he looks."[79] Like other followers of Saussure, Barthes took oral speech as the model language form. Even to study written texts, one had to "translate" from one medium to another. This might be particularly easy with writing because alphabetic writing systems attempted to reproduce speech, but writing was still a medium separate from speech. It was less flexible and interactive than the spoken word; equating it with speech was an imperfect equation. If applying linguistic techniques to the written word was useful, then why not also apply these techniques to other systems of signification? All systems of signification could be treated as imperfect attempts to communicate with the mental equipment of speakers.

But what could this mean practically for the study of cultural forms? For one thing, it meant paying attention to how differences between types of objects are conceived, how a weed is distinguished from a flower in a garden, how a fashionable dress is distinguished from any old garment, or how a boxing match is distinguished from a brawl. If culture is a web of signs, and if Saussure is to be heeded in his argument that the meaning of a sign is its difference from other signs rather than some absolute meaning, then the analysis of culture must focus on classificatory schemes and must take *difference* as a central concept.

Structuralism in general and Barthes's semiology in particular share with Marxist structuralism the inclination to treat communication as an expression of a *system* more than an expression of an author. The fundamental structuring system in Marxist theory is class difference in the political economy; in linguistic structuralism, it is elementary phonemic differences in spoken language. For the latter, culture is an elaborate system of signification. Cultural analysis at its best would attempt to differentiate the subsystems of signification and the means for translating from one to the next. It would not be concerned as much with the social world as with the signs used to represent human actions and make them meaningful. All these themes are evident in "Written Clothing," a selection from *The Fashion System,* probably Barthes's most ambitious effort (not necessarily his most successful) to apply formal semiotic analysis to an apparently nonlinguistic aspect of culture.

In this piece, Barthes argues that fashion is produced not by designing and then producing exquisite clothing, but rather by a coincidence of three language systems. One language is the language of clothing construction. Clothes are made from a limited "vocabulary" of fabrics, shapes, and colors and the techniques used to produce them. This vocabulary limits how clothes are technically put together, which in turn limits what they could possibly mean, but it does not define fashion.

Fashion is also partially defined by an image-making system, fashion photography, which differentially emphasizes some aspects of clothing rather than others. Using camera angles and lighting effects, fashion photographs select certain aspects of clothing, reducing once again the vocabulary of fashion statements.[80] (Barthes adds that dress patterns are part of a visual system of signification with more or less the same role as photographs. Here he is on shakier ground. Paper patterns for dresses do not identify what is fashion; they describe techniques for constructing clothes. They do not evaluate the salience of technique to fashion as fashion photographs do implicitly and fashion writing does explicitly.)

Writing about clothes is (to Barthes) the third and most important language of clothes. It tells readers how to interpret clothing styles, what techniques to pay attention to, and how they function as meaningful parts of some fashion. Aspects of a dress design (like the location of the waistline) may in some periods be crucial to fashion (empire dresses or 1920s flapper dresses) but in other periods may not be so important. Fashion writings articulate a hierarchy of salience of the features of clothing as well as evaluative comments on the choices made by a particular designer.

Barthes flies in the face of convention in this analysis. Fashion designers are usually thought of as "authors" who express a certain sensibility that is personally their own. They are thought to express this in the techniques and materials they use for their clothing. Their role is completely ignored by Barthes, who sees their manipulation of cloth as only the most rudimentary part of fashion. The complex cultural system that Barthes is accounting for exists as a collective process; Barthes does not give pride of place to an "author." It is a social system; in particular, it is a capitalist system that Barthes not so subtly criticizes. But his techniques are far from those used by Raymond Williams and John Berger. The signs he studies are not (to Barthes) outcomes of *behaviors* that can be studied (as they are for Williams and Berger); they are part of the language systems that structure the life-world of the people who use them. (Note in this selection that he explicitly distinguishes sociological from semiological analysis.)

Marxist structuralists and Saussurian structuralists agree that human agency is less autonomous than we imagine in our daily life (and in the tradition of individualism in Western culture). But although Williams and Berger see human culture as organized and animated primarily by politicoeconomic structures and interests, linguistic structuralists see human culture as a set of language systems. Whether they agree with the idea that the human mind is structured for language, and therefore the structuring of language has a biological base, or whether they see language as socially developed (interactive, interpersonally shaped) does not so much matter as the belief in the primacy of this cultural-linguistic structuration. The market or the mind, history or culture—the impersonality of the outcomes is similar.

For literary or art theory, this means a reversal of the Renaissance-rooted inclination to identify works as the manifestation of an individual sensibility. For theorists trying to understand artworks of any sort, it means that authors are to be set aside as objects of study, and new objects are to be given center stage. Cultural forms are impersonally developed. They must be accounted for with an analysis of the *systems* by which languages are mobilized. Human agency is minimized, as is human feeling, as Robert Alter observes.[81] With the exception of the British school of Marxists, who have been particularly interested in working-class resistance to structural systems of control, little room is left in structuralist theories for concerted action, expressive or political. This is one of the problems of structuralism that helped spur the development of poststructuralist theories.

If no one is the author, perhaps everyone is the author. Probably the central tenet of poststructuralist analyses is that texts are multivocal. Texts are seen as having a variety of potential meanings, none of which is the real meaning to be derived by some superior reader. The Frankfurt school, New Criticism, and structuralism all have taken it for granted that the purpose of criticism is to discover "the" meaning of a text. They generated totalizing systems or theories meant to explain reality (or texts) in an exhaustive way. Members of the different schools have held distinct opinions about what "the" reading should be and have seen these differences as more than inherent difficulties of interpretation. They have taken them as expressions of the weaknesses of others' theories.

Poststructuralists have generally been more interested in the variability of readings than in the perfectibility of the reading process. They claim not only that different interpretations are a necessary part of reading because different readers approach texts with different assumptions about writing and reading, but also that texts themselves are multivocal or riddled with contradictions. A feminist piece might use language that is deeply patriarchal, negating part of its message; a collectivist piece might advocate ideas about personal freedom essential to Western individualism. In less blatant ways as well, writers present their readers with mixed messages, leaving them to construct a coherent meaning from a less than coherent text through the act of reading. All texts, the poststructuralists effectively teach, are "intertextual"; and just as they subtly or openly, intentionally or unconsciously, allude to or incorporate other texts, so they make themselves inevitably open to multiple readings.

From this viewpoint, the critic loses his or her special expertise. The act of criticism is an act of reading, like any other one. On the one hand, this gives the critic greater power than the writer in assigning meaning to a text simply because the critic is a reader. But the critic is no longer privileged vis-à-vis the general public. This means that popular readings of popular culture are just as interesting a subject matter for poststructuralist analysis as readings by critics within elite culture. At the same time, poststructuralists tend to think that what kinds of objects audiences are "reading" make a difference because the relationships between object and reader differ across media.[82]

Jacques Derrida argues, for instance, that writing cannot be studied as a derivative translation of spoken language.[83] The world of writing has its own life, and its textuality is part of how it communicates. It is spatial and visual, not simply aural. So language use on paper has its own meanings, problems, and possibilities. One of its special features is that it allows repeated study and careful comparisons of different passages within a text. This enables analysts (like Derrida and his followers) to seek out the conceptual contradictions in writing, contradictions so severe that written work is its own criticism, or, as one school of poststructuralism says, writing "deconstructs" itself.

A number of poststructuralists have also asked questions about the psychological factors that pervade the reading process. Michel Foucault, Roland Barthes, and Christian Metz, among others, have drawn attention to the sensual nature of the reading process.[84] They have asked what makes reading a book or watching a film pleasurable. With the revival of Freudian thinking in France based on the work of Jacques Lacan, critics have asked more about how human needs are addressed through culture.[85] They have picked up threads of Freudian critical discourse that had (in an earlier form) been central to the Frankfurt school, but dropped out in most later Marxist cultural analysis (Louis Althusser being a notable exception).[86]

Sex and power, then, have been reestablished as motivating forces, affecting the ways in which culture can be made and used. Sex and power have been particularly important categories in feminist theory, a critical movement that has developed in interaction with other streams of poststructuralist thinking. Feminists have contended that language is by its nature political as well as sensual and reveals or establishes systems of power in its every use. The class system is clearly imprinted on the tradition of "great writers and writing" and so is the system of gender stratification. Genres typically used by women, types of narratives employed by women, and ways of using language comfortable for women are disrespected, and the types of literature advocated and used by men are hailed as superior. These patterns, among others, are evidence that it is inappropriate to talk about the structuring nature of language without paying attention to the way language helps structure social relations while it structures thought. Interpreters of feminist drama, for instance, argue that contemporary feminist theater may seem unsatisfying to viewers raised on classical theater because it offers no "act of recognition" as its climactic moment. Macbeth or Lear or Oedipus come face to face with their own identities in self-recognition, but feminist drama questions the very notion of self these plays take for granted. Where traditional heroism lay in "this process of recognition and unveiling," in feminist drama, the self is not seen as stable and true, if hidden, but as "shifting, alterable, admirably and problematically varied."[87]

Foucault raises many of these issues in his essay on the author. He has been an extremely controversial thinker whose influence has touched literary criticism, sociology (especially the study of deviance and social control), and intellectual and cultural history. The essay here is one of his most important pieces of poststructuralist thinking because it focuses so precisely on the nature of language and power and so clearly draws a line between structuralism and poststructuralism. Like many structuralists, he sees the author as a cultural invention, embedded in the system of Western individualism, masking the extent to which all writers draw their ideas and language from a common culture. But unlike structuralists, Foucault does not think we should ignore authorship altogether. On the contrary, he thinks the author should be studied as a vital instrument of power that has been used in literary criticism to restrict access to print and its power. Authors are "given" (through attribution) both bodies of writing and distinctive ways of using language. When they are said to have invented new writing styles, it seems sensible enough because they have indeed written their books. But to the extent that they use characters from their culture and use language they have heard in others' mouths, they are inappropriately isolated as the sole source of their work. They should be more precisely seen as recipients of territories of language that are not distributed to ordinary people and keepers of language skills that help keep them esoteric. Assigning authorship is not merely a tool for criticism, then, but a means for allocating power.

Once this is understood, it raises new questions about what constitutes authorship. Is all "Freudian" writing authored by Freud because he developed its language and the style still bears his name? What would happen if we began thinking of it this way? What would happen if we attributed authorship to the ordinary people whose voices writers mimic in their fiction or their ethnographies? Would we want to say a book was written by Brooklyn? And if we wanted to redistribute power in society, how might we redistribute authorship? Foucault opens the concept of authorship like Pandora's box and lets the possibilities fly out. To distribute the power of authorship and its attribution more widely, he argues for a common poststructuralist vision of decentralized meaning. He con-

tends that all readers should assert their own views of authorship, rec-
ognizing the act of reading for what it is: a political act shaping and using
the power of language.[88]

Foucault's analysis suggests that we have so long kept standard ideas
about authorship in large part because without them the cultural critic
could no longer identify great work by its great author. That would be
dangerous because it would upset the system of power in language, including the stratified relationship of elite to popular culture. Popular
culture is often "authorless," unless, like film, it is elevated by the identification of its "real" author (the director). It is precisely because Foucault's analysis of literary authorship unravels so revealingly the politics
of cultural stratification that it is so important to students of popular
culture.

Foucault calls into question what it means to be an author, but Janice
Radway pointedly raises the issue of what it means to be a reader. Her
essay is that of a feminist engaged in a form of reader response analysis.
Reader response theory developed before poststructuralism and without
the concern for the multivocal quality of texts themselves. But Radway
is very much aware of and concerned about the mixed messages conveyed in texts. She is also aware of the sensual/sexual power of reading
and the ways language embodies power relations.

Radway's essay concerns her ethnographic study (more fully reported
in her book, *Reading the Romance*) of a group of women readers of romance novels.[89] She was curious about romance novel reading because
of critics' disdain for these books as mass cultural garbage and the more
recent feminist criticism of the politics of their messages. Both these
"readings" of romances were clearly political and had to do with gender
politics, but what was their relationship to romance readers' readings?
She identifies the attraction of these books to their readers with psychological satisfactions—on the one hand, turning away from the demands
of their families to read something for themselves and, on the other
hand, providing a fantasy world in which to certify repetitiously the value
of their choice to live as wives and mothers rather than as career women.
In their favorite novels, strong and attractive women make the same
choice over and over again, significantly, just as they convince some virile
man of the value of love and tenderness. The woman gives up her autonomy, but she scores a victory for feminine culture, civilizing an otherwise unruly male. The books temporarily make the cultural world of
housewives dominant, and this (Radway asserts) is part of their pleasure
for these readers. Still, it is also the basis for the criticism of romances
by some feminists. Radway concludes that these texts are multivocal and
allow contradictory political readings. How can this be with such stereo-
typed, formula fiction?

Radway fully recognizes that these texts are highly commercial and formulaic. But the reading of them, she argues, although patterned, is not formulaic. It is both patterned *and* personal. The psychopolitical situation that these books address (women at home who are asked to spend so much of their lives tending to the needs of others) is standard enough as a social form to make the formula "work" for many readers, but the readings are still made by individual women and *tailored* by them to their needs and dreams as domestic women. It is in this sense that romance readers act individually but still constitute an "interpretive community." In an interpretive community, common literary analysis or interpretation depends on a consensus of experience and attitudes of a particular group of readers.

Radway's essay begins by commenting on André Kertesz's photographs of people reading.[90] Again, reading itself is found problematic, and Radway calls, much as Natalie Davis has in her work, for "specific studies of what people do with printed texts." Although other advocates of an audience- or reader-oriented criticism have raised the same questions, no one else has so determinedly left the classroom to find readers to examine. In a sense, Radway takes seriously the theoretical conviction that reading is a social process and so turns to sociological investigation to study literature. She takes recent literary criticism that would view reading and writing as activities to a logical end: the study of the activities themselves.

But she sets herself a particularly daunting task: How is a feminist to evaluate romance reading for women? If she can set aside the bias of high culture looking at popular culture, she has no desire to set aside her political values. So if, on the one hand, she recognizes that the multivocality of these texts, like any texts, gives readers power to use them to serve their own needs, she also comes to her project suspecting that the language of romances and their formulaic character offer a dominant message that urges women to accept as natural the oppressive gender relations to which they are accustomed.

Radway finds that the women she studies use the act of reading itself to carve out for themselves private time in the face of demanding husbands and children. Even if the books are "escape" literature, they are an actual escape from the oppressive demands of everyday life; even if they make room for "fantasy" rather than rebellion, the value of fantasy deserves some reconsideration (as the British feminist, Angela McRobbie, has made explicit in recent work).[91]

Still, from her reading of the texts, the lessons romance novels seem to preach are not attractive to Radway. But what about the readings the romance readers themselves offer? Are their readings as "good" as her own feminist reading of the books? It is not a question Radway resolves, remaining on the whole, it seems, a relativist on this matter. But in her book, she makes some critical observations of the romance readers: that they read addictively (she compares their habit to liquor and drugs); that they claim to value diversity but will not finish a romance that strays from a basic plot line; that they identify so closely with the heroine that they will not read romances where something unpleasant happens to her and certainly will not approve a romance with a sad ending; that they are very literal readers with little sense of the possibilities of irony in an author or psychological complexity or self-deception in a character; and that they read therapeutically, rereading old romances when they are depressed or under stress (psychoanalysis can be understood as suggesting that all narrative is therapeutic).[92]

Still, Radway champions the power of reading over the power of writing, and she has more contempt for those who disdain these readers than she has for the messages they derive from the books. Her work is self-consciously multivocal, providing a critical analysis of the society that has put many women into a position to like formula romances but leaving room for both a critical and an appreciative view of the romance novel readers themselves.

In a sense, Radway shows that the global expansion of "the text" has also been its global evaporation. If more and more objects are taken to be textual, that is, capable of being interpreted, more and more the interpretation of the texts denies their objectness. The text decomposes into the readers who read it and the interpretive communities, more generally, whose norms and values sustain it and make its interpretation possible in the first place. Oddly enough, rather than thereby reducing the authority of the interpreter, this view gives the act of interpretation a new importance. Now, it seems, interpretation is the very act whereby a text is sustained; the practice of literary criticism, as Stanley Fish has written, "is absolutely essential not only to the maintenance of, but to the very production of, the objects of its attention." Interpretive communities, not the text or even the reader, in Fish's view, "produce meanings" and do so prior to the act of reading itself.[93]

The implications of this position are probably most evident in the studies of canonization and canonicity that are now popular in literary studies. In one elegant example, Jane Tompkins has written of the social, economic, and political underpinnings of the rise of Nathaniel Hawthorne's writings to "masterpiece" status. She challenges the commonplace notion of a "classic" as a text that retains its value even though times change. She argues that a "classic" is in constant change: "Rather than being the repository of eternal truths, they embody the changing interests and beliefs of those people whose place in the cultural hierarchy empowers them to decide which works deserve the name of classic and which do not. For the idea of 'the classic' itself is no more universal or interest-free than the situation of those whose business it is to interpret literary works for the general public."[94] If, in Radway, we find a literary scholar who has taken to sociological studies of actual readers, quite in accord with new literary theory, in Tompkins and others, we find a literary scholar who has taken on literary scholarship as an object of sociohistorical scholarship. Interpretation becomes the object of study of the interpreters in a way that cannot help leaving the student of popular culture wondering if the elite culture/popular culture distinction, and all the elaborate barricades and buildings and temples erected to sustain it, has finally been revealed as a house of cards.

CONCLUSION

The readings collected here reflect the disciplinary origins of the new research in popular culture, resulting from the broad reassessments of the nature of culture within these fields. The traditional "great man" history and "genius" approaches to literary analysis and art history have lost their special charm. Western individualism and the achievement ethic as conceptual systems (although certainly not as general normative systems) have been systematically and self-consciously undermined or turned on their heads as a kind of intellectual (and sometimes, ironically, a heroic) exercise. Many scholars have had to suspend belief in fundamental normative prescriptions of Western culture, a difficult move in its requirements of careful theoretical reasoning but a rewarding one in opening up for study a vast range of human activities. This work is inevitably "reflexive," asking us to rethink not only popular culture but the category of popular culture, not only the category of popular culture but the cultural institutions and interpretive communities that have created and preserved that category—including, of course, the university. The whole educational apparatus of departments and disciplines, professional associations and prestigious chairs and prizes, curricula reform and the assembling of a reader on popular culture are all elements in the social elaboration of culture. There is no Archimedean point outside culture from which to observe it objectively and no protection within the university for those wishing to be ignorant of the popular cultural environment.

As definitions of what objects are important for cultural analysis have changed, popular culture has found legitimacy for the very reasons it was previously derided: the scale of its social impact and its attractiveness to unschooled audiences. This has made it central to any understanding of Western societies and thought. The irony of this situation is that popular culture, the fluffy stuff so often described by academics as vacuous

and insignificant (and alien to the Great Tradition that previously defined Western culture) has arrived in the present intellectual environment as a fascinating and revolutionary object for academic thought.
That is why, although the rethinking of popular culture we document
here may be embedded in analyses of jokes, romance novels, and the
treatment of pets, it is not just about these subjects. It is also a commentary on broad intellectual changes initiated by scholars who, in strug-
gling to "see" Western culture without being totally blinded by its assumptions, began to think about and reject the taboos that had kept
thinkers away from everyday culture. They bravely redefined the role
and value of popular amusements and, in so doing, allowed their thinking and ours to be transformed.

NOTES

1. Theodore S. Hamerow, *Reflections on History and Historians* (Madison: University of Wisconsin Press, 1987); Gertrude Himmelfarb, *The New History and the
Old* (Cambridge, Mass.: Harvard University Press, 1987).

2. Gerald Graff, "Conflicts Over the Curriculum Are Here to Stay: They
Should Be Made Educationally Productive," *Chronicle of Higher Education*, February 17, 1988, p. A48.

3. Cited in Raymond Williams, *Keywords* (New York: Oxford University Press,
1976), p. 79.

4. Interestingly, these "people" were resuscitated by nineteenth-century Ro-
mantics who saw them as carriers of an authentic European tradition of vital
interest to elites. Contemporary historians want to know about them less to celebrate their authenticity than to determine more accurately their historical importance to their own periods. For a discussion of the history of historical attention to popular culture, see Peter Burke, *Popular Culture in Early Modern Europe*
(New York: Harper & Row, 1978). Burke has also written useful reviews of the
study of popular culture in "Revolution in Popular Culture," in Mikulas Teich
and Roy Porter, eds., *Revolution in History* (Cambridge: Cambridge University
Press, 1986), pp. 206–225, and "Popular Culture Between History and Ethnology," *Ethnologia Europaea* 14 (1984), pp. 5–13. For a provocative discussion of
the origins of the whole metaphor of "high" and "low" to indicate rank, see
Barry Schwartz, *Vertical Classification* (Chicago: University of Chicago Press, 1981).

5. See Fernand Braudel, *On History* (Chicago: University of Chicago Press,
1980).

6. For a discussion of the influence of the *Annales* school, see S. Clark, "French
Historians and Early Modern Popular Culture," *Past and Present* 100 (1983), pp.
62–99; Lynn Hunt, "French History in the Last Twenty Years: The Rise and
Fall of the *Annales* Paradigm," *Journal of Contemporary History* 21 (1986), pp. 209–
224; Lynn Hunt, "Introduction: History, Culture, and Text," in Lynn Hunt, ed.,
The New Cultural History (Berkeley: University of California Press, 1989), pp. 1–
22.

7. Lucien Febvre and Henri-Jean Martin, *The Coming of the Book*, trans. David Gerard (London: NLB, 1958, 1976).

8. Natalie Davis, *Society and Culture in Early Modern France* (Stanford: Stanford University Press, 1975). The essay reprinted here is from pp. 189–226. See also the interview with Natalie Davis in MARHO, the Radical Historians Organization, *Visions of History* (New York: Pantheon, 1983), pp. 97–122. Jack Goody, *The Domestication of the Savage Mind* (Cambridge: Cambridge University Press, 1977). See also Michael Cole and Sylvia Scribner, *The Psychology of Literacy* (Cambridge, Mass.: Harvard University Press, 1981). Elizabeth Eisenstein, *The Printing Press as an Agent of Change* (Cambridge: Cambridge University Press, 1979).

9. Carlo Ginzburg, *The Cheese and the Worms* (New York: Penguin, 1980).

10. For contemporary discussions of material culture and how to look at it, see T. J. Schlereth, *Material Culture Studies in America* (Nashville: American Association of State and Local History, 1982); Chandra Mukerji, *From Graven Images: Patterns of Modern Materialism* (New York: Columbia University Press, 1983); Neil McKendrick, John Brewer, and J. H. Plumb, *The Birth of a Consumer Society: The Commercialization of Eighteenth-Century England* (Bloomington: Indiana University Press, 1982); Arjun Appadurai, ed., *The Social Life of Things* (Cambridge: Cambridge University Press, 1986). For works that take a folkloristic or anthropological approach to social history, centering on aspects of ritual and performance in social life, see Susan Davis, *Parades and Power: Street Theater in Nineteenth-Century Philadelphia* (Philadelphia: Temple University Press, 1986); Rhys Isaac, *The Transformation of Virginia: 1740–1790* (Chapel Hill: University of North Carolina Press, 1982).

11. Emmanuel Le Roy Ladurie, *Carnival in Romans* (New York: Braziller, 1980).

12. Darnton's "Great Cat Massacre" was criticized by French historian Roger Chartier in "Text, Symbols, and Frenchness," *Journal of Modern History* 57 (1986), pp. 682–695, and Darnton responded in "The Symbolic Element in History," *Journal of Modern History* 58 (1986), pp. 218–234.

13. This is now a vast area of research. A key work is Lawrence Stone, *The Family, Sex and Marriage in England 1500–1800* (New York: Harper & Row, 1977). The seminal work on children is P. Ariès, *Centuries of Childhood* (New York: Vintage, 1969). See also J. H. Plumb, "The New World of Children in 18th-Century England," in McKendrick, Brewer, and Plumb, *Birth of a Consumer Society*. Natalie Davis describes women's lives in *Society and Culture in Early Modern France* (Stanford: Stanford University Press, 1975). See also Jean-Louis Flandrir, *Families in Former Times* (Cambridge: Cambridge University Press, 1979); Merry Weisner, *Working Women in Renaissance Germany* (New Brunswick, N.J.: Rutgers University Press, 1986).

14. Peter Novick traces the phrase to the 1920s but dates its general usage to the influence of American historian Jesse Lemisch in the 1960s. See Peter Novick, *That Noble Dream* (Cambridge: Cambridge University Press, 1988), p. 442.

15. E. P. Thompson, *The Making of the English Working Class* (New York: Vintage, 1963). See Novick, *That Noble Dream*, pp. 440, 461, and 484, for observations on E. P. Thompson's influence on the rise of social history.

16. See E. P. Thompson, "Time, Work-Discipline, and Industrial Capitalism," *Past and Present*, no. 38 (1967), pp. 56–97.

17. Gareth Stedman Jones, *Languages of Class: Studies in English Working Class History* (Cambridge: Cambridge University Press, 1983).

18. Kathy Peiss, *Cheap Amusements: Working Women and Leisure in New York City, 1880 to 1920* (Philadelphia: Temple University Press, 1985); Roy Rosenzweig, *Eight Hours for What We Will* (Cambridge: Cambridge University Press, 1983).

19. Sean Wilentz criticizes the notion of American "exceptionalism" in studies of working-class culture, arguing that the American case is startlingly different from European working classes only if one rather rigidly identifies working-class consciousness with organized working-class socialism. See his "Against Exceptionalism: Class Consciousness and the American Labor Movement," *International Labor and Working Class History* 26 (Fall 1984), pp. 1–24.

20. Drinking has been the subject of a number of important studies of politics and popular culture, including Joseph Gusfield, *Symbolic Crusade* (Urbana: University of Illinois Press, 1963); Brian Harrison, *Drink and the Victorians* (Pittsburgh: University of Pittsburgh Press, 1971).

21. Rosenzweig, *Eight Hours for What We Will*, pp. 98, 100, 106.

22. Dolores Hayden, *The Grand Domestic Revolution* (Cambridge, Mass.: MIT Press, 1981).

23. For a valuable essay on the use of the term in historiography, see T. J. Jackson Lears, "The Concept of Cultural Hegemony: Problems and Possibilities," *American Historical Review* 85 (1985), pp. 567–593. In American studies of the media, the concept has been most notably employed in the work of Todd Gitlin. See his *The Whole World Is Watching: Mass Media in the Making and Unmaking of the New Left* (Berkeley: University of California Press, 1980).

24. Antonio Gramsci, *Selections from the Prison Notebooks* (New York: International Publishers, 1971).

25. Gunther Barth, *City People: The Rise of Modern City Culture in Nineteenth-Century America* (New York: Oxford University Press, 1980); Alan Trachtenberg, *The Incorporation of America* (New York: Oxford University Press, 1982).

26. On work discipline in the factories, see Thompson, *Making of the English Working Class*. On Sunday schools, see Tom Laqueur, *Religion and Respectability: Sunday Schools and Working Class Culture* (New Haven, Conn.: Yale University Press, 1976). On literacy as social control, see Harvey J. Graff. *The Literacy Myth: Literacy and Social Structure in the Nineteenth-Century City* (New York: Academic Press, 1979). On new forms of controlling deviance, see Michel Foucault, *Madness and Civilization* (New York: Pantheon, 1965); David Rothman, *The Discovery of the Asylum* (Boston: Little, Brown, 1971); Andrew Scull, ed., *Madhouses, Mad-Doctors and Madmen* (Philadelphia: University of Pennsylvania Press, 1981).

27. Levine's essay on Shakespeare, included here, is now part of a book, *Highbrow/Lowbrow* (Cambridge, Mass.: Harvard University Press, 1988), which includes a parallel study of opera.

28. Ann Douglas, *The Feminization of American Culture* (New York: Knopf, 1977).

29. In this, she crosses paths with the historian Neil Harris, "Museums, Merchandising, and Popular Taste: The Struggle for Influence," in I. M. G. Quimby,

ed., *Material Culture and the Study of American Life* (New York: Norton, 1978), pp. 140–174.

30. This may have been especially true for women. See Sharon Zukin, "The Post-Modern Landscape: Mapping Culture and Power," in Scott Lash and Jonathan Friedmann, eds., *Modernity and Identity* (London: Basil Blackwell, 1990).

31. Claude Lévi-Strauss, *Totemism* (Boston: Beacon Press, 1963).

32. Mary Douglas and Baron Isherwood, *The World of Goods* (New York: Basic Books, 1979).

33. Claude Lévi-Strauss, *The Raw and the Cooked* (New York: Harper & Row, 1969), p. 12.

34. Will Wright, *Sixguns and Society: A Structural Study of the Western* (Berkeley: University of California Press, 1975); Judith Williamson, *Decoding Advertisements* (London: Boyars, 1978); E. A. Lawrence, *Rodeo: An Anthropologist Looks at the Wild and the Tame* (Knoxville: University of Tennessee Press, 1982); Paul Bouissac, *Circus and Culture: A Semiotic Approach* (Bloomington: Indiana University Press, 1976).

35. For some criticism of Geertz, see Vincent Crapanzano, "Hermes' Dilemma: The Masking of Subversion in Ethnographic Description," in George Marcus and James Clifford, eds., *Writing Culture: The Poetics and Politics of Ethnography* (Berkeley: University of California Press, 1986), and Aletta Biersack, "Local Knowledge, Local History: Geertz and Beyond," in Lynn Hunt, ed., *The New Cultural History* (Berkeley: University of California Press, 1989), pp. 72–96.

36. This is well illustrated in a critique of Lévi-Strauss. See Michael Carroll, "Lévi-Strauss, Freud, and Trickster," *American Ethnologist* 8 (1981), pp. 301–313.

37. Clifford Geertz, "Art as a Cultural System," *MLN* 91 (1976), p. 1478.

38. Garry Wills, "Blood Sport," *New York Review of Books*, February 18, 1988, p. 5.

39. See Victor Turner, *The Ritual Process: Structure and Anti-Structure* (Chicago: Aldine, 1969), for a discussion of antistructure; John J. MacAloon, "Olympic Games and the Theory of Spectacle in Modern Societies," in John J. MacAloon, ed., *Rite, Drama, Festival, Spectacle: Rehearsals Toward a Theory of Cultural Performance* (Philadelphia: Institute for the Study of Human Issues, 1984), pp. 241–280, for a discussion of hyperstructure. See also Elihu Katz, "Media Events: The Sense of Occasion," *Studies in Visual Communication* 6 (1984), pp. 84–89.

40. Victor W. Turner, "Liminality and the Performative Genres," in MacAloon, *Rite, Drama, Festival, Spectacle*, pp. 19–41.

41. Barbara Babcock, "Arrange Me in Disorder: Fragments and Reflections on Ritual Clowning," in MacAloon, *Rite, Drama, Festival, Spectacle*, p. 107.

42. Clifford Geertz, *Local Knowledge* (New York: Basic Books, 1983), p. 28.

43. Marshall Sahlins, *Culture and Practical Reason* (Chicago: University of Chicago Press, 1976), p. vii.

44. Ibid., p. 9.

45. Marshall Sahlins, *Islands of History* (Chicago: University of Chicago Press, 1985).

46. Clifford Geertz, *Works and Lives* (Stanford: Stanford University Press, 1988); Clifford and Marcus, *Writing Culture*.

47. Robert Park, "The Natural History of the Newspaper," *American Journal of Sociology* 29 (November 1923), pp. 273–289; Robert Park, *The Immigrant Press and Its Control* (Westport, Conn.: Greenwood Press, 1970; Harper, 1922); John Dewey, *The Public and Its Problems* (New York: Henry Holt, 1927); Thorstein Veblen, *The Theory of the Leisure Class* (New York: New American Library, 1953; Macmillan, 1899).

48. William I. Thomas and Florian Znaniecki, *The Polish Peasant in Europe and America* (Boston: Richard G. Badger, 1918).

49. Robert and Helen Lynd, *Middletown* (New York: Harcourt, Brace, 1929).

50. David Manning White and Bernard Rosenberg, eds., *Mass Culture* (Glencoe, Il.: Free Press, 1957).

51. Herbert J. Gans, *Popular Culture and High Culture* (New York: Basic Books, 1974).

52. David Riesman, with Nathan Glazer and Reuel Denney, *The Lonely Crowd* (New Haven, Conn.: Yale University Press, 1950).

53. David Riesman. *Individualism Reconsidered* (New York: Free Press, 1954), pp. 264–265.

54. Several key essays in this debate appear in White and Rosenberg, *Mass Culture*, including Dwight MacDonald, "A Theory of Mass Culture," pp. 53–59; Irving Howe, "Notes on Mass Culture," pp. 496–503; Ernest Van Den Haag, "Of Happiness and of Despair We Have No Measure," pp. 504–536. Edward Shils's contributions are "Mass Society and Its Culture," *Daedalus* 89 (1960), pp. 288–314, and "Daydreams and Nightmares: Reflections on the Criticism of Mass Culture," *Sewanee Review* 65 (1957), pp. 587–608. A number of relevant essays, including one by Hannah Arendt, appear in Norman Jacobs, ed., *Culture for the Millions* (Princeton, N.J.: Van Nostrand, 1961). C. Wright Mills comments on popular culture in *The Power Elite* (Oxford: Oxford University Press, 1956). For a fine intellectual history of the mass culture debate, see Leon Bramson, *The Political Context of Sociology* (Princeton, N.J.: Princeton University Press, 1961).

55. "It might be reasonable to say that what I have done here is not the sociology of art at all, but rather the sociology of occupations applied to artistic work. I would not quarrel with that way of putting it." Howard Becker, *Art Worlds* (Berkeley: University of California Press, 1982), p. xi.

56. Clifford Geertz, *The Interpretation of Cultures* (New York: Basic Books, 1973), p. 5.

57. We have not included studies of religion in this volume. The reasons for this have (we think) disciplinary origins. Literary scholars rarely look at religious writing, except students of early American literature, who necessarily read much religious writing. Cultural critics like Barthes rarely dare or want to tackle religious practices; they may study the worship of Garbo's face, but not sacred worship. Anthropologists and sociologists have tended to see religion as the most powerful form of culture, organizing and regulating other areas of social life, and thus clearly different from the everyday rites and fashions of popular culture. Only historians of the early modern period have routinely studied religious festivals as part of popular life. The burgeoning of popular culture studies has attracted the attention of more sociologists, anthropologists, and historians of the modern period to religious beliefs and practices, but religion still remains a

small part of the field of popular culture studies. Our volume simply reflects the limits of the field.

58. Paul DiMaggio, "Market Structure, the Creative Process, and Popular Culture: Toward an Organizational Reinterpretation of Mass-Culture Theory," *Journal of Popular Culture* 3 (1977), pp. 436–452.

59. Becker, *Art Worlds*.

60. Howard Aldrich and Richard Pfeffer, "Environments of Organizations," *Annual Review of Sociology* 2 (1976), pp. 79–105.

61. For other production-of-culture studies, see Richard A. Peterson, "Revitalizing the Culture Concept," *Annual Review of Sociology* 5 (1979), pp. 137–166; Richard Peterson, ed., *The Production of Culture* (Beverly Hills: Sage, 1976).

62. Dick Hebdige, *Subculture: The Meaning of Style* (New York: Methuen, 1979).

63. Pierre Bourdieu, *Distinction: A Social Critique of the Judgment of Taste* (Cambridge, Mass.: Harvard University Press, 1984).

64. William Weber, "Mass Culture and the Reshaping of European Musical Taste, 1770–1870," *International Review of the Aesthetics and Sociology of Music* 8 (1977) pp. 18–19.

65. There is now a small but impressive literature that treats politics itself as a form of popular culture and sees political debate and discourse as an instance of wider cultural forces. See, for instance, Jean Baker, *Affairs of Party* (Ithaca, N.Y.: Cornell University Press, 1983), for a Victor Turner–inspired examination of mid-nineteenth-century American presidential elections as collective rituals and "social dramas." See also Michael McGerr, *The Decline of Popular Politics* (New York: Oxford University Press, 1986), for a provocative study of "styles" of political campaigning as forms of popular culture with a significant impact on how Americans learn to conceive of politics and how they learn to care, or not care, about it. See also a discussion of politics as an expressive form of ethnic and social group conflict in Jonathan Rieder, *Canarsie: The Jews and Italians of Brooklyn Against Liberalism* (Cambridge, Mass.: Harvard University Press, 1985).

66. Martin Jay, *The Dialectical Imagination: A History of the Frankfurt School and the Institute of Social Research 1923–1950* (Boston: Little, Brown, 1973).

67. Ibid.

68. Walter Benjamin, "The Work of Art in the Age of Mechanical Reproduction," in Walter Benjamin, *Illuminations* (New York: Schocken, 1968), pp. 219–253.

69. Marshall McLuhan, *Understanding Media: The Extensions of Man* (New York: McGraw-Hill, 1965).

70. Richard Hoggart was founder and first director of the Center for Contemporary Cultural Studies at the University of Birmingham in 1964. He is best known for his book *The Uses of Literacy* (London: Chatto and Windus, 1957). Stuart Hall succeeded Hoggart as director of the "Birmingham school" and is widely known for lucid reviews, evaluations, and explorations of cultural theory. See, for instance, his "Cultural Studies: Two Paradigms," *Media, Culture and Society* 2 (1980), pp. 57–72; "The Rediscovery of 'Ideology': The Return of the Repressed in Media Studies," in Michael Gurevitch, Tony Bennett, James Curran, and Janet Woollacott, eds., *Culture, Society and the Media* (London: Methuen, 1982), pp. 56–90; "Signification, Representation, Ideology: Althusser and the

Post-Structuralist Debates," *Critical Studies in Mass Communication* 2 (1985), pp. 91–114.

71. M. M. Bakhtin, *The Dialogic Imagination* (Austin: University of Texas Press, 1981).

72. John Fiske, "British Cultural Studies and Television," in Robert C. Allen, ed., *Channels of Discourse* (Chapel Hill: University of North Carolina Press, 1987), p. 254.

73. Stuart Hall, "Encoding and Decoding," in Stuart Hall et al., eds., *Culture, Media, Language* (London: Hutchinson, 1980).

74. John Fiske, "Television: Polysemy and Popularity," *Critical Studies in Mass Communication* 3 (1986), p. 392.

75. Ibid.

76. For a history that discusses New Criticism and its influence, see Gerald Graff, *Professing Literature: An Institutional History* (Chicago: University of Chicago Press, 1987). See also Terry Eagleton, *Literary Theory: An Introduction* (Minneapolis: University of Minnesota Press, 1983), pp. 46–53.

77. For the early period in American film, see Benjamin Hampton, *The History of the American Film Industry from Its Beginnings to 1931* (New York: Dover [1931], 1970). Dudley Andrews speaks of "auteur theory" as not a theory but a critical method. In contrast, see the rethinking of film and film history in the late 1950s and early 1960s in Arthur Knight, *The Liveliest Art* (New York: Mentor 1957); Ralph Stephenson and Jean R. Debrix, *The Cinema as Art* (Baltimore: Penguin, 1965). See also J. Dudley Andrew, *The Major Film Theories: An Introduction* (London: Oxford University Press, 1976), p. 4.

78. Knight, *The Liveliest Art;* Stephenson and Debrix, *Cinema as Art* (Harmondsworth: Penguin, 1966); Gerald Mast and Marshal Cohen, *Film Theory and Criticism: Introductory Readings* (New York: Oxford University Press, 1974); and Peter Wollen, *Signs and Meaning in the Cinema* (London: Secker and Warburg, 1969).

79. Robert Alter, "Mimesis and the Motive for Fiction," *TriQuarterly* 42 (1978), p. 233. For more sympathetic treatments of structuralism, see Edith Kurzweil, *The Age of Structuralism* (New York: Columbia University Press, 1980); Richard T. DeGeorge, *The Structuralists from Marx to Lévi-Strauss* (Garden City, N.Y.: Doubleday, 1972).

80. For a sociological analysis of fashion photography that compares its style, ideology, and work organization with other forms of photography, see Barbara Rosenblum, "Style as Social Process," *American Sociological Review* 43 (1978), pp. 422–438, and *Photographers at Work* (New York: Holmes & Meiers, 1978).

81. Alter, "Mimesis and the Motive for Fiction," pp. 228–249.

82. Eagleton, *Literary Theory;* Julia Kristeva, *Desire in Language* (New York: Columbia University Press, 1980); and Jacques Derrida, *Writing and Difference* (Chicago: University of Chicago Press, 1978).

83. Ibid.

84. Roland Barthes, *The Pleasures of the Text;* Michel Foucault, "What Is an Author?" *Partisan Review* 4 (1975), pp. 603–614; Christian Metz, *The Imaginary Signifiers* (Bloomington: Indiana University Press, 1982). See also Kristeva, *Desire in Language.*

85. See Sherry Turkle, *Psychoanalytic Politics* (New York: Basic Books, 1978).

86. Louis Althusser, "Ideology and Ideological State Apparatuses," in Louis Althusser, *Lenin and Philosophy and Other Essays* (New York: Monthly Review Press, 1971) pp. 127–186.

87. Helene Keyssar, *Feminist Theatre* (New York: Grove Press, 1985), p. xiv. See also Kristeva, *Desire in Language.*

88. Foucault's ideas look on the level of academic practice at a politics of language that goes well beyond the university. Julia Kristeva has described ways that world politics shapes language use. She contends the peace treaty in Yalta that divided Europe into East and West, starting the cold war, made her give up her homeland, marry a Frenchman, and write in French. She claims this denied her the authorship of her own texts because politicohistorical forces shaped what she could and could not write and in what language. She connects this dissolving of the "I" to a passion for language on one hand and, on the other, the female experience.

89. Janice Radway, *Reading the Romance: Women, Patriarchy, and Popular Literature* (Chapel Hill: University of North Carolina Press, 1984).

90. André Kertesz, *On Reading* (New York: Grossman, 1971).

91. Angela McRobbie, "Dance and Social Fantasy," in Angela McRobbie and Mica Nava, eds., *Gender and Generation* (London: Macmillan, 1984), pp. 130–161.

92. Eagleton, *Literary Theory.*

93. Stanley Fish, *Is There a Text in This Class?* (Cambridge, Mass.: Harvard University Press, 1980), pp. 368, 14.

94. Jane Tompkins, *Sensational Designs: The Cultural Work of American Fiction 1790–1860* (New York: Oxford University Press, 1985), p. 37. See also the essays in Robert von Hallberg, ed., *Canons* (Chicago: University of Chicago Press, 1984).

PART ONE

Popular Culture in Historical Studies

TWO

Printing and the People

Natalie Zemon Davis

Here are some voices from the sixteenth century. "The time has come
. . . for women to apply themselves to the sciences and disciplines." Thus
the ropemaker's daughter Louise Labé addresses her sex when her collected poems are printed in Lyon in 1556. "And if one of us gets to the
point where she can put her ideas in writing, then take pains with it and
don't be reluctant to accept the glory." Ten years later in Cambrai, a
Protestant linen-weaver explains to his judges about the book in his life:
"I was led to knowledge of the Gospel by . . . my neighbor, who had a
Bible printed at Lyon and who taught me the psalms by heart. . . . The
two of us used to go walking in the fields Sundays and feast days, conversing about the Scriptures and the abuse of priests." And listen to the
printers' journeymen of Paris and Lyon in 1572, in a brief they printed
to convince Parlement and public that they needed better treatment from
their employers: "Printing [is] an invention so admirable, . . . so honor-
able in its dignity, and profitable above all others to the French. Paris
and Lyon furnish the whole of Christendom with books in every language." And yet "the Publishers and master Printers . . . use every strat-
agem to oppress . . . the Journeymen, who do the biggest and best part
of the work of Printing." And finally, Pierre Tolet, doctor of medicine,
justifying in 1540 his translation of some Greek texts into French, printed
for the use of surgeons' journeymen: "If you want a servant to follow
your orders, you can't give them in an unknown tongue."[1]

These quotations suggest the several and complex ways in which
printing entered into popular life in the sixteenth century, setting up

Reprinted from a slightly longer version in *Society and Culture in Early Modern France*, by
Natalie Zemon Davis, with the permission of the publishers, Stanford University Press.
© 1975 by the Board of Trustees of the Leland Stanford Junior University.

new networks of communication, facilitating new options for the people, and also providing new means of controlling the people. Can this be true? Could printing have mattered that much to *the people* in a period when literacy was still so low?

We can best understand the connections between printing and the people if we do two things: first, if we supplement thematic analysis of texts with evidence about audiences that can provide context for the meaning and uses of books; second, if we consider a printed book not merely as a source for ideas and images, but as a carrier of relationships. The data to support such an approach are scattered in the pages of the original editions themselves; in studies of literacy and dialects, book ownership and book prices, authorship and publication policy; and in sources on the customs and associational life of peasants and artisans. The theory to assist such an approach can be found in part in the work of Jack Goody and his collaborators on the implications of literacy for traditional societies—especially in their discussion of the relations between those who live on the margins of literacy and those who live at its center. Additional theoretical support exists in the fertile essays of Elizabeth L. Eisenstein on the impact of printing on literate elites and on urban populations in early modern Europe—especially when she talks of "cross-cultural interchange" between previously "compartmentalized systems." Both Goody and Eisenstein have insisted to critics that they do not intend technological determinism, and I am even more ready than they to emphasize the way that social structure and values channel the uses of literacy and printing.[2]

This essay, then, will consider the context for using printed books in defined popular milieus in sixteenth-century France and the new relations that printing helped to establish among people and among hitherto isolated cultural traditions. Were there new groups who joined the ranks of known authors? What was the composition of "audiences"—those who actually read the books—and of "publics"—those to whom authors and publishers addressed their works?*

These relations are especially interesting to trace in the sixteenth century. In the cities, at any rate, the basic innovations occurred quite rapidly. By mid-century all the major centers of publication had been established in France: Paris, Lyon, Rouen, Toulouse, Poitiers, Bordeaux, Troyes. Some forty towns had presses by 1550; at least sixty had them by 1600. Moreover, economic control in the industry was not yet firmly in the hands of merchant-publishers and commercial booksellers, as it would be after the Religious Wars. Decisions about what was profitable

---

*This distinction is a necessary one, but is not made in everyday speech. I follow the terminology of T. J. Clark, *Image of the People. Gustave Courbet and the Second French Republic, 1848–1851* (New York, 1973), p. 12.

and/or beneficial to print were made also by "industrial capitalists" and artisans, that is, by publisher-printers like Jean I de Tournes in Lyon and the Marnef brothers in Poitiers; such decisions were even sometimes made by simple master printers publishing their own editions. This diversity may help explain the wide range in the *types* of books that appeared before mid-century. In these decades there proliferated most of the forms to be published in France up to 1700. The same is true of patterns in book ownership. For example, virtually no Parisian artisans other than printers in the generation that died around 1500 owned printed books; by 1560, the percentage of Parisian artisans and tradesmen possessing books in inventories after death had reached the level (not very high, to be sure) that Henri-Jean Martin has documented for mid-seventeenth-century Paris.[3]

This brings me to a last point about method. Rather than thinking diffusely about "the people," I am trying wherever possible to ask how printing affected more carefully defined milieus—namely, cohesive social groups some of whose members were literate. In the countryside this means the entire settled population of a village where anyone was literate. In the cities this means the small merchants and the craftsmen (masters and journeymen), and even semiskilled workers (such as urban gardeners and fishermen) having some connection with urban organizations such as confraternities or guilds. It means their wives, themselves ordinarily at work in the trades, and even women in the families of the wealthier merchants. It means domestic servants, male or female, who might be living in their households. It does not include the unskilled dayworkers, the *gagnedenier* and *manouvriers,* the *portefaix* and *crocheteurs,* the vagabonds and permanent beggars. This floating mass was just illiterate; and however resourceful their subculture, the only reader to whom they listened with any regularity was the town crier ordering them to show up for work cleaning sewage or else leave town under penalty of the whip.

Nor am I including the lower clergy or the backwoods noblemen and their wives, even though they might in the sixteenth century sometimes cluster on the borderline between literacy and illiteracy and as individuals play a role in village social life. They are distinguished from the peasants and the urban *menu peuple* not by the criterion of literacy but by their estate and their relations to spiritual and emotional power, to jurisdiction and to property.

[I]

Let us look first to the peasants. The penetration of printing into their lives was a function not just of their literacy but of several things: the cost and availability of books in a language that they knew; the existence of social occasions when books could be read aloud; the need or desire for information that they thought could be found in printed books more easily than elsewhere; and in some cases the desire to use the press to say something to someone else.

Rural literacy remained low throughout the sixteenth century. Of the women, virtually none knew their ABC's, not even the midwives. As for the men, a systematic study by Emmanuel Le Roy Ladurie of certain parts of the Languedoc from the 1570's through the 1590's found that three percent of the agricultural workers and only ten percent of the better-off peasants—the *laboureurs* and *fermiers*—could sign their full names.* In the regions north and southwest of Paris, where the speech was French, the rates may have been slightly higher, and rural schools have been noted in several places. But the pupils who spent a couple of years at such places learning to read and write and sing were drawn from special families (such as that of a barber-surgeon in the Forez, who sent his boys to a school and rewarded its rector with a chapel in 1557) or were intended for nonagricultural occupations (such as the serf's son in the Sologne who went to school "to learn science" because he was "weak of body and could not work the soil").[4]

Surely a lad ambitious to be a *fermier* in the mid-sixteenth century would need to keep accounts, yet not all economic pressures pushed the prosperous peasant to literacy. Charles Estienne's agricultural manual advised the landed proprietor that his tenant farmer need not have reading and writing (one can lie on paper, too) so long as he was experienced and wise in agricultural ways. A peasant in the Haut-Poitou in 1601, designated tax assessor of his village, tried to get out of it by pleading illiteracy. As for sales of land, marriage contracts, and wills, there were itinerant scribes and notaries aplenty who were happy to add to their income by performing these services for the peasants.[5]

The country boys who really learned their letters, then, were most likely those who left for the city to apprentice to crafts or to become priests, or the few lucky sons of *laboureurs* who, at a time when fellowships for the poor were being taken over by the rich, still made it to the University of Paris. One such, the son of a village smith from Brie, be-

---

*Estimates of ability to read based on studies of ability to sign one's name are, of course, approximate. One can learn to read without learning to write and vice versa. Nevertheless, the two skills were most often taught together in the sixteenth century. Statistics on ability to sign, then, give us the order of magnitude of the number of readers. For a discussion of techniques of measuring literacy in the early modern period, see R. S. Schofield, "The Measurement of Literacy in Pre-Industrial England," in J. R. Goody, ed., *Literacy in Traditional Societies* (Cambridge, Eng., 1968), pp. 311–25, and F. Furet and W. Sachs, "La croissance de l'alphabétisation en France, XVIIIe–XIXe siècle," *Annales. Economies, Sociétés, Civilisations* 29 (1974): 714–37.

came a proofreader in Lyon after his university years, and at his death in 1560 was in possession of a precious manuscript of the Theodosian Code.[6]

But when they came back to visit, such men did not leave books in their villages. "Our little Thomas talks so profoundly, almost no one can understand him" was the observation of Thomas Platter's relatives when he passed through his Swiss mountain home during his student years in the early sixteenth century. One can imagine similar remarks exchanged by peasants in France about a son who had studied books in a strange language or learned his craft in a different dialect. As the peasants' inventories after death were virtually without manuscripts in the fifteenth century, so they were almost without printed books in the sixteenth.[7] Why should this be so? Surely a *laboureur* who could afford many livres worth of linens and coffers in the 1520's could afford three sous for a *Calendrier des bergers*, two sous for the medical manual *Le Tresor des povres*, or even two and a half livres for a bound and illustrated Book of Hours, which might be a credit to his family for generations.[8]

Yet just because one can afford books does not mean that one can have ready access to them or need them or want them. A literate *laboureur* in some parts of France during the sixteenth century might never meet a bookseller: his nearest market town might have no presses if it were a small place, and peddlers' itineraries still reached relatively few parts of the countryside.[9] If he did come upon a bookseller, his wares might be in a language the peasant had difficulty reading, since so little printing was done in vernaculars other than French. Only five books printed in Breton during the sixteenth century could be found by an eighteenth-century student of that language, and the first work in Basque came out in 1545 and had very few imitators.[10] Provençal was favored by several editions, mostly of poetry, but the various regional dialects, from Picard to Poitevin, rarely appeared in print at all.[11]

In any case, how much were printed books really needed in the sixteenth-century village? A *Shepherds' Calendar* was a useful, though not always essential, supplement to oral tradition. (Indeed, sometimes as I read the different sixteenth-century editions of the *Calendrier des bergers*, I wonder to what extent contemporary compilers and publishers envisaged a peasant public for them. They appear a cross between a folklorist's recording and a pastoral, a shaped vision of the peasant world for country gentlemen and city people and a way for such readers to identify themselves with the simple wisdom of "the great shepherd of the mountain." The appearance in Paris in 1499 of a *Shepherdesses' Calendar*, a literary contrivance modeled after the earlier *Calendrier* and printed by the same atelier, tends to support this view.[12] The *Shepherds' Calendar* told which sign the moon was in and its phases, the dates of fixed and movable feast days, and the timing of solar and lunar eclipses. For the most important findings about the year in which the calendar was printed, pictorial devices were given to aid the barely literate. For full use of the various tables, genuine ability to read was required.*

Now except for the eclipses, peasants had their own equivalent devices to calculate these results, which they then recorded "in figures on little tablets of wood." These "hieroglyphic Almanacs" were still being made by peasants in the Languedoc in 1655: "On a morsel of wood no bigger than a playing card," said an observer in the Albigeois region, "they mark by a singular artifice all the months and days of the year, with the feast days and other notable things."[13] Why should they then feel the lack of a *Shepherds' Calendar*?

And yet there were a few ways that printing did enter rural life in the sixteenth century to offer some new options to the peasants. The important social institution for this was the *veillée*, an evening gathering within the village community held especially during the winter months from All Saints' Day to Ash Wednesday.[14] Here tools were mended by candlelight, thread was spun, the unmarried flirted, people sang, and some man or woman told stories—of Mélusine, that wondrous woman-serpent with her violent husband and sons; of the girl who escaped from incest to the king's palace in a she-donkey's hide; of Renard and other adventuresome animals.[15] Then, if one of the men were literate and owned books, he might read aloud.

In principle, printing increased significantly the range of books available for the *veillée*. In fact, given the limited channels of distribution in the sixteenth century and the virtuosity of the traditional storyteller, even a rural schoolteacher might have very few books. According to Noel du Fail, a young lawyer from a seigneurial family in upper Brittany who wrote in 1547 a story of a peasant village, the village books were "old": *Aesop's Fables* and *Le Roman de la Rose*. Now both of these had printed editions and urban readers in the late fifteenth and early sixteenth centuries. By the 1540's, however, the learned were enjoying Aesop in fresh Latin and Greek editions or in new French rhyme; and, though still appreciative of the thirteenth-century *Roman*, they were feeling ever more distant from its sense and style, even in the updated version given them

---

*The *Shepherds' Calendar* was not published annually. The dates for the new moon could be read off for 38 years; the eclipses were predicted for a century or more. For any year after the year of its printing, the dates of the days of the week, the exact time of the new moon, and the position of the moon in the zodiac had to be worked out from the tables.

In Noel du Fail's *Propos rustiques*, the village copy of the *Calendrier des bergers* is owned by old Maistre Huguet, former village schoolteacher, who reads aloud from it from time to time (p. 15).

by Clément Marot. In contrast, peasants would have had no reason to supplant the early editions that Marot and his publisher disdained as full of printing errors and *"trop ancien langaige."*[16]

Did such reading aloud change things much in the village? *Reading aloud?* We might better say "translating," since the reader was inevitably turning the French of his printed text into a dialect his listeners could understand. And we might well add "editing"—if not for *Aesop's Fables,* whose form and plots were already familiar to peasants, then for the 22,000 lines and philosophical discourses of the *Roman.* In a community hearing parts of the *Roman* for the first time, new relationships were perhaps set up with old chivalric and scholastic ways of ordering experience; some new metaphors were acquired and varied images of women and love added to the listeners' existing stock.[17] Who do you yearn to be, or to love? Mélusine or the Rose? A good question, but it hardly constitutes a connection with the distinctive features of "print culture."*

As early as the 1530's, however, some *veillées* were being treated to a book that was in the vanguard and more disruptive of traditional rural patterns than Aesop, the *Roman de la Rose,* or the *Calendrier:* the vernacular Bible. In Picardy a cobbler reads it to the villagers at the *veillées* until he is discovered by a nearby abbey. Here the literalness of the text was important. The Bible could not be "edited" or reduced to some formulaic magic. It had to be understood, and there were probably no pictures to help. In the Saintonge and elsewhere during the 1550's, Philibert Hamelin, his pack filled with Bibles and prayer books that he had printed at Geneva, comes to sit with peasants in the fields during their noonday break and talks of the Gospel and of a new kind of prayer. Some are delighted and learn; others are outraged and curse and beat him. He is sure that one day they will know better.[18]

---

*Noel du Fail was quite particular about the books that he placed in the village. When a pirated edition of his *Propos* came out in Paris in 1548 with other books added to his list, he suppressed them in his new edition at Lyon in 1549. In 1573, however, the Parisian publisher Jean II Ruelle added five titles that may have had some hearing in the countryside: a late-fifteenth-century poetic history of the reign of Charles VII; two medieval romances (including *Valentin et Orson,* which has thematic material relating to the old rural custom of the chase of the wildman or of the bear); an account by Symphorien Champier of the chivalric deeds of the good knight Bayard; and the Miracles of Our Lady. Some of these were part of the *Bibliothèque bleue* of the seventeenth century (du Fail, *Propos,* pp. iv-xii, 138, 187).

On a rainy evening in February 1554, the Norman gentleman Gilles de Gouberville read to his household, including the male and female servants, from *Amadis de Gaule* (A. Tollemer, *Un Sire de Gouberville, gentihomme campagnard au cotentin de 1553 à 1562,* with introduction by E. Le Roy Ladurie [reprint of the 1873 ed., Paris, 1972], p. 285). This chivalric tale had only recently been translated from the Spanish and printed in France.

I think these books would have been received by peasants in the same way as the *Roman de la Rose* and *Aesop's Fables.*

In the Orléanais a forest ranger buys a vernacular New Testament, a French Psalter, and the Geneva catechism from a bookseller at a fair and goes alone into the forest of Marchenoir to read them. Over in the mountains of the Dauphiné a peasant somehow teaches himself to read and write French and divides his time between plowing and the New Testament. The story goes that when reproached by the priests because he did not know the Scripture in Latin, he laboriously spelled it out until he could contradict them with Latin citations.[19]

Finally, evangelical peddlers begin to work the countryside systematically. A carter, a native of Poitiers, loads up in Geneva with Bibles, Psalters, and Calvinist literature published by Laurent de Normandie and looks for buyers in the Piedmont and the rural Dauphiné. Five craftsmen from scattered parts of France are arrested in 1559 in a village in the Lyonnais with literature from Geneva in their baskets. Even the Inquisitor wonders why they should want to sell such books to *"gens rustiques."*[20]

Still, even if the Bible did not become a permanent fixture in most rural households, merely to think of selling to them on a large scale was something new. Who first opened up the rural markets for the peddlers' books of the seventeeth century? Not a simple printer of rural background; he would remember the illiteracy of his village. Not an ordinary publisher of popular literature; he would worry about meager profits. But zealous Protestants could overlook all that, could face the possibilities of destroyed merchandise and even death for the sake of "consoling poor Christians and instructing them in the law of God."[21]

If printing and Protestantism opened new routes for selling books in the countryside, the press also facilitated the *writing* of a few new books for a peasant public. What happened, I think, was that the printing of "peasant lore," as in the *Shepherds' Calendar* and in books of common proverbs, brought it to the attention of learned men in a new way. These men were discovering the thoughts not of their local tenants or of the men and women from whom they bought grain at market, but of The Peasants. And, dedicated to the "illustration" of the national tongue and to the humanist ideal of practical service, they decided that they must correct rural lore and instruct The Peasants. Thus, Antoine Mizaud, doctor of medicine, mathematician, and professor at Paris, writes an *Astrologie des Rustiques* to tell countryfolk without the time to acquire perfect knowledge of the heavens how to predict the weather by sure terrestrial signs. (Mariners, military commanders, and physicians should find it useful, too.)[22] Thus, somewhat later, the royal surgeon Jacques Guillemeau writes a book on pregnancy and childbirth "not for the learned . . . but for young Surgeons, little versed in the art, dispersed here and there, far away from the cities."[23]

Some new kinds of almanacs appear on an annual basis now, authored by doctors of medicine and "mathematicians," containing bits of possibly novel *agricultural* information, such as when to plant fruits and market vegetables. ("Tested by M. Peron and Jean Lirondes, old gardeners at Nîmes," says one edition, which then tells about the *choux cabus,* artichokes, melons, and other plants that distinguished the seventeenth-century Languedoc garden from its modest fifteenth-century forebear.)[24] Though these almanacs were conceived for a diverse public, they probably were expected to reach some peasant readers—certainly more than were the justly celebrated agricultural manuals of Charles Estienne, Jean Liebault, and others. These latter treatises were intended for landowners, gentlemen farmers, and seigneurs, who would then teach their lessees, tenants, and hired servants what to do.

What can we conclude, then, about the consequences of printing for the sixteenth-century peasant community? Certainly they were limited. A few lines of communication were opened between professor and peasant—or rather between bodies of cultural materials, as in the case of some traditional lore that was standardized and disseminated by the press, perhaps with a little correction from above. Expectations were higher by 1600 that a printed book might come into the village and be read aloud at the *veillée,* even where the little spark of Protestantism had burned out in the countryside. But oral culture was still so dominant that it transformed everything it touched; and it still changed according to the rules of forgetting and remembering, watching and discussing. Some printed medieval romances may have come to the peasants from the cities, but they cannot have played the escapist role that Mandrou has claimed for them in the seventeenth century. Peasants in the Lyonnais, in the Ile-de-France, and in the Languedoc put on tithe strikes just the same; villages in Burgundy forced their lords to enfranchise about half of their servile population; peasants in Brittany, the Guyenne, Burgundy, and the Dauphiné organized themselves into emergency communes, communicated with each other, and rebelled under traditional slogans, ensigns, and captains with festive titles—all neither deflected nor aided by what was being said in print.[25] Indeed, those who wished to control the countryside and bring it to order by means other than sheer force—whether bishop, seigneur, or king—would have to send not books but messengers, whose seals would not be mocked and who would disclose verbally the power behind the papers that they read.

[II]

In the cities, the changes wrought or facilitated by printing in the life of the *menu peuple* had greater moment. The literacy rate had long been higher among urban artisans and tradesmen than among peasants, but the gap widened—at least for males—in the early sixteenth century. The old choirboy schools still performed their service for the sons of some artisans and petty traders, and more important, the numbers of vernacular schoolteachers and reckonmasters multiplied. For instance, in Lyon in the 1550's and 1560's, some 38 male teachers of reading, writing, and arithmetic can be identified (very roughly one for every 400 males under the age of twenty in the city), quite apart from the masters at the Latin Collège de la Trinité. They marry the daughters of taverners and the widows of millers; they live in houses with pouchmakers and dressmakers; they have goldsmiths, printers, barber-surgeons, coopers, and gold-thread-drawers among their friends.[26] In addition to these teachers, newly established municipal orphanages in some cities provided simple instruction for poor boys, and at times even orphan girls were taught their ABC's.[27]

This press for literacy was associated with technological, economic, and social developments. Printing itself created a populous cluster of crafts (including bookbinding and typecasting) where literacy rates were high. Of 115 printers' journeymen assembled in Lyon in 1580 to give power of attorney, two-thirds could sign their names fully; and the journeymen were already demanding that all apprentices know how to read and write, even those who would be but simple pressmen. In other crafts, such as painting and surgery, literacy was spurred by the desire for a higher, more "professional" status and the availability of vernacular books for training. Even the royal sergeants, a group among the *menu peuple* previously noted only for their skill with the rod, began to live up to a 1499 decree requiring them to read and write.[28]

Literacy was not, of course, distributed evenly among the *menu peuple*. An examination of the ability to sign of 885 males involved in notarial acts in Lyon in the 1560's and 1570's spreads the trades out as follows (masters and journeymen combined):

Very high: apothecaries, surgeons, printers.
High: painters, musicians, taverners, metalworkers (including gold trades).
Medium (about 50 percent): furriers and leatherworkers, artisans in textile and clothing trades.
Low to very low: artisans in construction trades, in provisioning, transport; urban gardeners; unskilled dayworkers.

In Narbonne, for about the same time, Le Roy Ladurie found that one-third of the artisans could sign their names; another third could write initials; and only one-third were totally foreign to letters. At Montpellier the percentage of craftsmen who could make only marks was down to 25 percent. This range among the artisans contrasts both with the almost complete literacy of well-off merchants of all kinds and with the low rate of literacy among urban women outside the families of lawyers, merchant-bankers, and publishers.[29]

City-dwellers were also more likely than countryfolk to be able to understand French. Towns were, of course, constantly replenished by people from rural areas with their local patois and even by people from foreign lands, and the urban speech itself was not independent of the big patterns of regional dialect. Nevertheless, French was increasingly the language of royal government (after 1539 all judicial acts were to be in French) and of other kinds of exchange; in an important southern center like Montpellier it could be heard in the streets already by 1490.[30] Thus the urban artisan had potentially a more direct access to the contents of the printed book—whose vernacular was French, as we have seen—than a peasant who could read handwritten accounts in Provençal but would have had to struggle over a printed *Calendrier*.

From simple literacy to actual reading is something of a step. Studies based only on inventories after death in sixteenth-century Paris and Amiens suggest that the step was not always taken. In the early years of the century, if an artisan or small shopkeeper in Paris owns a book at all, it is likely to be a manuscript Book of Hours. By 1520 printed books appear, displacing the manuscripts but existing along with the religious paintings, sculpture, and wall hangings that even quite modest families possess. Most artisans, however, had no books at their death. They represent only about ten percent of book owners in Paris and twelve percent of book owners in Amiens (or seventeen percent, if we include barbers and surgeons), that is, well below the proportion of the *gens mécaniques* in the urban population at large. And when they do have books, outside of printers' stock, there are not very many of them. Out of all the editions in the Amiens inventories, only 3.7 percent were in artisanal hands (six percent, if we include barbers and surgeons); and apart from the latter group, the median size of the library was one book![31]

In Amiens that one book was most likely to be a Book of Hours, or perhaps a French *Golden Legend* (the medieval book of saints' lives popular throughout the sixteenth century), or a vernacular Bible. Or else it might be a technical work, such as a pattern book for cabinetmaking or painting. In Paris in 1549, a tanner dies owning a *Golden Legend* and the *Mer des Histoires,* a thirteenth-century historical work still being printed in the 1530's and 1540's; a barber-surgeon leaves behind six French volumes on the art of surgery.[32] Clearly the literate were often without private libraries and, at least on their deathbed, do not appear to have taken much advantage of the varied fruits of the "admirable invention."

There were some economic reasons for this, even though printed books were cheaper by far than manuscripts had been. A twenty-four page sermon on poor relief cost as much as a loaf of coarse bread in the 1530's; an easy little arithmetic, half a loaf. A few years later, a full news account of the seizure of Rhodes could be almost as expensive as a pair of children's shoes; a book of Christmas carols, as much as a pound of candlewax. In the 1540's a French history could cost more than half a day's wages for a painter's journeyman or a printer's journeyman, and almost a whole day's wages for a journeyman in the building trades.[33] In the 1560's the cheapest "hand-size" New Testament in French was not much less. Understandably, some artisans complained that they could not afford to buy it, thus prompting a Protestant polemicist to ask them whether "they didn't have all the Instruments of their craft, however much poverty made it difficult to buy them" and how could they pass up a Book of such utility as the Bible?[34]

In fact, artisans found ways to have access to printed materials without collecting them privately. They bought a book, read it until they were finished, or until they were broke or needed cash, and then pawned it with an innkeeper or more likely sold it to a friend or to a *libraire*. Thus one Jean de Cazes, a native of Libourne, purchased a Lyon Bible in Bordeaux for two écus (an expensive edition), read it, and sold it to someone from the Saintonge before he was arrested for heresy in 1566 at the age of 27.[35] Books were relatively liquid assets and were less subject to depreciation than many other personal items. One kept to the end, if one could afford it, only those editions that were needed for constant reference or were wanted as permanent family property—thus the Hours, the Bibles, and the workbooks that show up in the inventories after death. Possibly, too, in the absence of public libraries, literate artisans and shopkeepers lent each other books from their small stores as did more substantial collectors (the poet François Béroald had three leaves of his account book devoted to loaned books);[36] and they may even have passed on books as gifts more often than we know. Theirs was a world in which "secrets"—the secrets of craft, the secrets of women—had never been private possessions but corporate ones, shared, told, passed on so they would not be forgotten. What happens when scarce printed books enter such a world? They flow through the literate segments of the *menu peuple* rather than remain hoarded on an artisan's shelf.

Books were also shared in reading groups which, as in the countryside, brought the literate and illiterate together. The traditional winter *veillée* was not the regular setting, however; for outside the building trades many craftsmen worked winter and summer, by candlelight if necessary, till eight or even ten o'clock at night.[37] Gatherings of family and friends for singing, games, cards, storytelling, and perhaps reading were more likely special occasions, like feast days. Certain books were designed to be read aloud or consulted in the shop, such as pattern books for textile design and the French translation of Biringuccio's *Pirotechnia,* an excellent manual on metallurgical processes.[38] So, too, the oft-printed little arithmetics that taught petty business operations "by the pen" in Arabic numerals and by counting stones (*jetons*) "for those who don't know how to read and write" were resources for apprentices and adults in an atelier even more than for an instructor in a little school. One *Brief Arithmetic* promised to teach a tradesman all he needed to know in fifteen days' time and added mnemonic verses to help him catch on.[39]

Reading aloud in one connection or another must have been especially common in the printing shop. I am thinking not merely of the discussion of copy among scholar-printers, authors, and editors, but of reading in snatches that could reach out to the journeymen and to the spouses and daughters helping to hang up the freshly printed sheets. Thus one Michel Blanc, a simple pressman in Lyon in the late 1530's, knew enough of Marot's poems, which were printed in his shop, for his son to remember later how he had been "brought up in his youth on Marot."[40] Possibly men may sometimes have taken books into the tavern for reading. As for the women, they surely did some of their reading aloud among their own sex; an example might be the Life of Saint Margaret, with prayers for the pregnant and the parturient.[41]

But the most innovative reading groups were the secret Protestant assemblies on feast days or late at night in private homes—innovative among other reasons because they brought together men and women who were not necessarily in the same family or craft or even neighborhood. Thus a 1559 assembly in Paris included a goldsmith's journeyman from the Gâtinais, a university student from Lyon, a shoemaker's journeyman, and several others, all from different parts of the city. An early conventicle in the town of Saintes, organized by two poor artisans in 1557, had access to one printed Bible, from which passages were written down for discussion. Encouraged by Deuteronomy 6: 7 to speak of God's law however small their learning, the artisans scheduled written exhortations every Sunday by the six members who could read and write. Like the heretical linen-weavers of Cambrai, with their printed Bible in the fields, these Protestants read, talked, sang, and prayed.[42]

In short, reading from printed books does not silence oral culture. It can give people something fresh to talk about. Learning from printed books does not suddenly replace learning by doing. It can provide people with new ways to relate their doings to authority, new and old.

Nor should printing be viewed merely as purveying to the *menu peuple* the science of university graduates, the doctrine of the religious, the literary production of the educated, and the orders of the powerful. Artisans, tradesmen, and women composed themselves a few of the books they read.* To be sure, some such persons had in the fourteenth and fifteenth centuries quietly authored manuscripts—of craft secrets, of mechanical inventions, of poems. But the authors had failed to become widely known and, with the exception of outstanding figures like the literary Christine de Pisan, their works were not reproduced later by the presses.

But now many individuals without the ordinary attributes expected of an author in the later Middle Ages get their books printed—and they have an audience. Their tone might range from the confident ("I've tested sundials for a long time") to the apologetic ("Excuse my unadorned language ... I am not Latin"), but they are sure that their skills, observations, or sentiments give them something distinctive to say.[43] Like the learned writer, they imagine varied publics for their work: their own kind and those on a higher level. Like the learned writer, they present themselves to the unknown buyers of their books in proud author portraits quite different from the humble donor picture characteristic of the medieval manuscript. Thus Milles de Norry, previously a modest reckonmaster in Lyon, gazes from his 1574 commercial arithmetic, fitted out with a ruff and a Greek device.[44]

This widening of the circle of authors had diverse causes besides printing, but it was given some permanence by the new form of publication. Now practicing apothecaries get into print, like Pierre Braillier of Lyon, who dared to attack *The Abuses of Ignorance of Physicians,* and Nicolas Houel of Paris, who encroached on the physicians' field by writing on the plague and who published a treatise on poor relief as well.[45] Now surgeons write on their art and even on medicine (and we must remember that they are still considered *gens mécaniques* in the sixteenth century, despite the gains of some of them in learning, status, and wealth). Ambrose Paré's first book appears in 1545, when he is a mere army surgeon and master at the Hôtel-Dieu in Paris; and at least nineteen other surgeons have vernacular texts printed from the 1540's through the 1580's.[46] Sailors publish accounts of their travels to the New World. Poems come out from a cartwright in the Guyenne, a wine merchant in Toulouse, and a trader in Béthune, the last including a "Hymn to Commerce."[47]

The most self-conscious artisan-author, however, was the potter Ber-

---

*Anonymous city lore and song, like peasant sayings, found their way into print, as did innumerable stories and poems in which artisans and servants were the actors (such as *Le caquet de bonnes Chambrieres, declarant aucunes finesses dont elles usent vers leurs maistres et maistresses,* printed at Lyon about 1549). The authorship of such material and its relation to actual popular life and sources are such complex problems that we cannot consider them here.

nard Palissy. To the readers of his important dialogues on chemistry and agriculture he says that some will think it impossible that "a poor artisan . . . destitute of Latin" could be right and ancient learned theorists wrong. But experience is worth more than theory. If you don't believe what my books say, get my address from the printer and I will give you a demonstration in my own study.[48] What we see here is not merely fresh communication between craftsman and scholar (much discussed by historians of science), and between practice and theory (the participants in Palissy's dialogues); we see also a new kind of relation between an author and his anonymous public.*

Another entrant into the ranks of authors was, of course, the self-educated scholar-printer. Elizabeth Eisenstein has rightly stressed the novelty of this figure, who combined intellectual, physical, and administrative forms of labor.[49] Indeed, it was not only men like Badius, the Estiennes, Gryphius, and the de Tournes who had such a creative role; lesser masters and even journeymen could shape the content of the books they printed. Sometimes their names are appended to prefaces; sometimes, as with the proofreader Nicolas Dumont, it is only by luck that we catch a glimpse of their work as authors. A native of Saumur, Dumont was so busy preparing and correcting copy in Paris in the years 1569 to 1584 "that he scarcely had time to breathe." Yet he sometimes got hold of a press and printed pamphlets; he translated various works from Latin to French; and, in particular, he composed little news stories about Henri III's doings in France and Poland, the seizure of Tunis from the Turks, and other current happenings. Whether he presented his stories as "letters" from unnamed gentlemen observers or as anonymous eyewitness

---

*This formal invitation from the author for direct response from readers is found in other printed books as well. It is the product of a situation in which the author expects that a large number of unknown readers will be seeing his work in the near future and will be able to locate him easily. (It goes well beyond the practice of the medieval author who, as John Benton has informed me, either urged his readers to write improvements on the manuscript or—more likely—anathemized readers and scribes who tampered with his text, but who did not invite correspondence.) Robert I Estienne asked readers of his *Dictionaire Francoislatin* to send him any words he might have omitted that they found in Latin authors and "good French authors," as well as to correct any faults they found in his definitions of hunting terms (Paris: Robert I Estienne, 1549, *"Au lecteur"* and p. 664). Both the physician Laurent Joubert and the bibliophile François de La Croix du Maine asked for information from their readers, as we will see below. Authors may also have received unsolicited letters: Ambrose Paré asked young surgeons using his *Oeuvres* (1575) to let him know graciously of any faults they might find rather than slander him. The reckonmaster Valentin Mennher did not especially want to hear from readers about the mistakes in his arithmetic texts: "Please just make corrections on the page rather than by useless words." The errors in a 1555 Lyon edition of his work were the printer's fault, not his (*Arithmetique Seconde par M. Valentin Mennher de Kempten* [Antwerp, Jean Loc, 1556], f. Z viii').

accounts, Dumont in many ways anticipated the reporter of the periodical press.[50]

Female writers also appeared in print in noticeable numbers—more than twenty had some reputation. Mostly they came from families of gentlemen or lawyers, were involved in humanist circles, and published poems or translations.[51] Their works still show signs of womanly modesty: they are dedicated to other women ("because women must not willingly appear in public alone, I choose you for my guide"); they address themselves to "female readers"; they defend themselves against the reproach that silence is the ornament of women.[52] A few of them transformed the image of the author even more: Louise Labé, the ropemaker's daughter, whose appeal to women to publish we heard at the opening of this essay (and contemporary evidence indicates that many well-born women did shyly keep their poems in manuscript);[53] Nicole Estienne, printer's daughter and physician's wife, whose verses on "The Miseries of the Married Woman" had two editions; and the midwife Louise Bourgeois. Once midwife to the poor of her Paris neighborhood, later midwife to the family of Henri IV, Bourgeois wrote on her art, believing herself the first woman to do so. Her wide practice, she claimed, would show up the mistakes of Physicians and Surgeons, even of Master Galen himself. She looks out with poise from her engraving at the reader, this skilled woman who corrected men, publicly and in print.[54]

Finally, groups among the *menu peuple* sometimes spoke to the public collectively through the press. The *compagnonnages* of the journeymen of Lyon and Paris, as we have seen, printed the brief that they presented to the Parlement of Paris in 1572. This document raised a dozen objections to a royal edict on printing and attacked the journeymen's employers as tyrannical and avaricious oppressors, who worked them to poverty and illness. Their employers answered, also in print, that the journeymen were debauched conspiratorial "monopolists," trying to reduce their masters to servitude and destroy the industry. A printed protest was used again in Lyon in 1588, when master printers and journeymen were on the same side against the merchant-publishers, who were ignoring them in favor of the cheaper labor of Geneva.[55] Here are precocious examples of artisans trying to influence literate public opinion in a labor dispute.

Groups also tried on occasion to influence public opinion in regard to political matters. Here I am thinking of the urban Abbeys of Misrule, festive societies of neighborhood or craft, which directed their charivaris and mockery not only against domestic scandals but against misgovernment by their betters. For a long time, the Abbeys had left their recreations unrecorded; but in the sixteenth century they began to print them. Thus readers outside Rouen could learn about the 1540 Mardi Gras parade at that city—with its float bearing a king, the pope, the emperor, and a fool playing catch with the globe—and could ponder its mocking verses about hypocrisy in the church, about how faith was turning to contempt *(foy* to *fy)* and nobility to injury *(noblesse* to *on blesse).* In the Lyon festivals of the 1570's through the 1590's, the Lord of Misprint tossed printed verses to the spectators and subsequently published the scenarios, with their complaints about the high cost of bread and paper, about the fluctuations in the value of currency, and especially about the folly of war in France.[56]

This body of pamphlet literature, small and ephemeral though it is, suggests two interesting things about the relation of printing to the development of political consciousness. First, though most early polemical literature disseminated outward and downward the political and religious views of persons at the center (whether at the center of royal government or at the center of strong resistance movements like the Huguenots and the Holy Catholic League), it occurred to some city people on the margins of power to use the press to respond. Second, the addition of printed pamphlets to traditional methods for spreading news (rumor, street song, private letters, town criers, fireworks displays, bell-ringing, and penitential processions) increased the *menu peuple*'s stock of detailed information about national events. In the 1540's, the Rouen festive society could count on spectators and readers knowing the facts of local political life, but references to national or European events were usually general and even allegorical. By the end of the century in Lyon, however, the Lord of Misprint could expect that his audience would also recognize joking references to recent sumptuary legislation and to controversial decisions of the Parlement of Paris.[57]

Readers may be thinking that these varied works authored by the *menu peuple* were such a tiny fraction of the total printed corpus of sixteenth-century France that no educated contemporary would have paid attention to them. In fact they were noticed, favorably and unfavorably. The visionary bibliographer François de La Croix du Maine, who built up a library of thousands of volumes and who sent out printed requests all over Europe for information about authors, was happy to include most of the people and books we have been considering here in his *Bibliotheque* of 1584.* He made no critical exclusions: Nicole Estienne and Nicolas

---

*Thus among sixteenth-century authors either writing in French or translating into French, La Croix listed 110 physicians, but also 25 surgeons (22 of whom had works in print) and nine apothecaries (eight with works in print). He included 40 female writers from the end of the fifteenth century to 1584 (at least sixteen had works in print, as far as he knew); Christine de Pisan, composing her *City of Ladies* around 1405, seems to have been aware of no other contemporary female authors.

In 1579 at Le Mans, La Croix had 350 copies printed of the initial statement of his

Dumont are set in their alphabetical places just as are Pierre de Ronsard and Joachim du Bellay in his "general catalogue" of all authors, "women as well as men, who had written in our maternal French."[58]

We also have a reaction from a humanist and poet deeply concerned about the character of French culture. As a member of the Pléiade, Jacques Peletier had devoted himself to the vernacular tongue and had also celebrated the printing press:

> Ah . . . one can print in one day
> What it would take thirty days to say
> And a hundred times longer to write by hand.

High quality in vernacular publication would be guaranteed, so he had argued hopefully, by right and clear Method—right method for ordering poetry, mathematics, medicine, music, even spelling. But what would happen now that all kinds of people were publishing books? In an ironic anonymous essay, he urged every village, every curate, every trader, every captain to write his piece; every parish, every vineyard must have its historian. *"Ecrivons tous, sçavans et non sçavans!"* And if we do badly? Well, never mind. Our books can be used by the ladies who sell toilet paper at the Paris bridges.[59]

How indeed could the learned control not only aesthetic quality but also true doctrine and science if just anyone could get books printed, and if these books were being made available by the press in the vernacular to large numbers of ill-educated city people? The central book in the religious debate was, of course, the vernacular Bible, and for several decades the doctors of theology (strongly backed by secular law) tried to defend their monopoly on its interpretation by denying the right of the uneducated to read it. The debate was sometimes face to face, between doctor of theology and craftsman: "Do you think it's up to you to read the Bible," asked the Inquisitor in a Lyon prison in 1552, "since you're just an artisan and without knowledge?" "God taught me by His Holy Spirit," said the craftsman. "It belongs to all Christians to know it in order to learn the way to salvation."[60]

The debate also took place in print. "God does not want to declare his secrets to a bunch of *menu peuple,*" said the great Jesuit Emond Auger. "Intoxicated by I know not what phrases from the Apostles, badly quoted and even worse understood, they start to abuse the Mass and make up questions." Understanding comes not from "a bare and vulgar knowl-

project, including his request for information about or from authors. He received six answers. He repeated the request in the 1584 edition of the *Bibliotheque*, this time remembering to suggest ways in which mail might reach him at Paris (*Premier volume de la Bibliotheque du sieur de la Croix-du-Maine* [Paris: Abel l'Angelier, 1584], *"Preface aux lecteurs"* and pp. 523, 529, 538–39).

edge of the words," but from the special vocation of those who have studied.[61] A young Protestant pastor answered: the pope and his doctors of theology forbid the Bible to everyone but themselves, because they know that once their lives and doctrine are examined by the Word of God, they will have to give their goods to the poor and start working with their hands. They permit a poor craftsman to read a book on love or folly, to dance or play cards, but they see him with a New Testament in his hands and he is a heretic. But our Lord has commanded us "Search the Scriptures." And the early Fathers exhorted the people—craftsmen, women, and everybody in general—to read it in their houses and often, and especially before going to sermons so they could understand them.[62] The pastor ends up reminding his readers that reading *alone* was not the path to true doctrine. The Protestant method for guaranteeing orthodoxy was in the last instance censorship and punishment; but in the first instance it was *the combination of reading with listening to a trained teacher.*

Ultimately, despite the triumphs of the Counter-Reformation in France, the doctors of theology had to abandon their position, in fact if not always in public. Force simply would not work. What had guaranteed the clerical monopoly two hundred years before had really been a limited technology and the Latin language. Already at the end of the fourteenth century, vernacular Bibles, Biblical digests, and picture books were being used by lay families here and there. Once the first presses were installed in France, the stream of French Bibles and Bible versions began without waiting for the Reformation. No legislation, no inquisition, no procedures of censorship could stop the new relations between reading, listening, and talking that had grown up among city people—relations which Catholic humanists as well as Protestants had been ready to encourage. After the 1570's, it became legal for a French Bible—a Catholic revision of the Genevan Scripture approved by the Theology Faculty of Louvain—to circulate in France. In cheap, small format, the New Testament had some success among Catholic laymen in the cities.[63]

What was needed to maintain Catholic orthodoxy was a mode of control more suited to printing than an archaic form of sacerdotal monopoly and more effective than censorship. In 1542, a Franciscan religious who was translating and commenting a Book of Hours for a circle of noblewomen pointed the way. Everyone is admitted to preaching, no matter how unlearned, said Brother Gilles; need seeing words be more dangerous than hearing them? The answer was to make the bare text safe by clothing it with orthodox exposition. The Jesuits were to go on and fix the meaning of a devotional text by an accompanying standardized religious picture or emblem. By 1561 in Lyon, the Jesuit Possevino paid for the printing of orthodox little booklets and distributed them free in the streets. By the late sixteenth century, the Catholic laity had a growing body of spiritual literature *in which the eye was guided by exposition and illustration.*[64]

A similar though less intense debate occurred over the dissemination of medical information to laymen. Vernacular *Regimens against the Plague* and collections of remedies for ill health and women's disorders were old genres; printing did no more than increase their numbers. In the 1530's, however, doctors of medicine began to publish translations of Greek medical texts and of Doctor Guy de Chauliac's fourteenth-century Latin treatise on surgery, as well as systematic examinations of medicine and surgery in French for the specific use of surgeons' journeymen, "who have begged us to do it," "whose ignorance must be dispelled," and "who are today more studious than many physicians." These books were used by the young surgeons who attended occasional lectures and dissections given by physicians at the Hôtel-Dieu at Lyon, special courses at the Faculty of Medicine at Montpellier, and the classes supported by the surgeons' confraternity of Saint-Côme at Paris; they were used also by older surgeons in the cities who wanted to improve their skill.[65] The next step was the publication by doctors of medicine of new regimens of health and medical advice on child-rearing in the vernacular, very often dedicated to women.[66]

The arguments used in defense of these editions, offered by Catholic humanists and Protestants alike, resemble those used in defense of vernacular Bibles and doctrinal literature. As printers pointed out that Saint Jerome had translated the Bible into a vernacular, so the physician Vallembert pointed out in his 1565 pediatric manual that Galen and Avicenna had written in their vernacular. An English medical popularizer spoke against his critics in the very terms that the early Protestant Antoine de Marcourt had used against the engrossing "merchants" of the Faculty of Theology: "Why grutch [grudge] they phisike to come forth in Englysche? Wolde they have no man to know but onley they? Or what make they themselves? Marchauntes of our lyves and deathes, that we shulde bye our healthe onely of them, and at theyr pryces?" A French work by the Protestant Laurent Joubert makes the comparison explicit: those doctors of medicine who say that it is wrong to teach people how to maintain their health are no better than doctors of theology who deprive them of spiritual food. To those who objected to instructing surgeons in French, Joubert's son answered that good operations could be performed in any language and that misunderstanding of a Latin text was as possible as misunderstanding of a French one ("should we burn all Latin books because of the danger that some clerk will misinterpret the law therein?"). And anyway, if we are willing to read books aloud to surgeons' journeymen, why not put them in French? "Must we put a lower value on the living voice than on the written paper?"[67]

Laurent Joubert's volumes are especially useful for a study of the new relations between groups of people and between cultural traditions facilitated by printing. For twenty-five years he had been trying to stamp out false opinions in medicine, and in 1578 he decided to compile a new kind of book—*Erreurs Populaires* about health and medicine from conception to grave that he would collect and correct. "Popular errors" came from several sources, he explained: from weaknesses in the soul and human reasoning; from ignorant oral traditions, especially those of midwives; and from people's having heard too much from physicians and having a crude understanding of it. It seems to me, however, that as the sense of the errors in peasant lore was sharpened for the learned by the printing of that lore (as we have seen above), so the printing of all kinds of vulgar regimens, traditional books of secrets, and remedies created for Joubert the concept of general errors and made them accessible to correction.

In any case, in Volume One he got through conception and infancy, demonstrating, for instance, that it was *not* true that male children were born at full moon and female children at new moon and that it *was* true that at certain times of night or monthly period one could be sure of conceiving a male. He then told his readers that he would wait to publish Volume Two until they had had a chance to send him more popular errors. They could just address him at the University of Montpellier, where he was Chancellor of the Faculty of Medicine. Dr. Joubert received 456 sayings and queries from readers within a year, which he duly published and, where possible, corrected or explained in Volume Two.[68]

Joubert's *Popular Errors* illustrates the central paradox in the impact of printing on the people. On the one hand, it can destroy traditional monopolies on knowledge and authorship and can sell and disseminate widely both information and works of imagination. It can even set up a new two-way relationship between author and anonymous audience. But printing can also make possible the establishment of new kinds of control on popular thought. To quote once more the physician and translator Pierre Tolet, "If you want a servant to follow your orders, you can't give them in an unknown tongue."[69] Joubert's goal and that of the other popularizers was not to eliminate the distinction between expert and inexpert or to weaken the profession of medicine. It was to raise the surgeons from their "routine illiterate practice" while defining their field to keep even the most skillful of them under the authority of the physicians. It was to raise the people to a better understanding of how to take care of themselves while convincing them more effectively to obey the doctor's orders.

On the whole, it seems to me that the first 125 years of printing in France, which brought little change in the countryside, strengthened rather than sapped the vitality of the culture of the *menu peuple* in the cities—that is, added both to their realism and to the richness of their dreams, both to their self-respect and to their ability to criticize themselves and others. This is because they were not passive recipients (neither passive beneficiaries nor passive victims) of a new type of communication. Rather they were active users and interpreters of the printed books they heard and read, and even helped give these books form. Richard Hoggart, in his remarkable study of working-class culture in present-day England *(The Uses of Literacy)* has found a salty, particularistic, resourceful layer of culture existing along with a "candy-floss," slack, uniform one. If this is possible in the twentieth century, with its powerful and highly competitive mass media and centralized political institutions, all the more readily could the sixteenth-century populace impose its uses on the books that came to it. Oral culture and popular social organization were strong enough to resist mere correction and standardization from above. Protestantism and certain features of humanism converged with printing to challenge traditional hierarchical values and to delay the establishment of rigid new ones. Economic control of publishing was not concentrated in the houses of great merchant-publishers, but was shared by a variety of producers. Monopolies in knowledge had broken down but had not been replaced by effective political and religious censorship and by the theory and laws of private property in ideas.

If in a different context printing may lead the people to flaccidity, escape, and the ephemeral, in the sixteenth century the printers' journeymen could claim with some reason that printing was "the eternal brush which gave a living portrait to the spirit."[70]

NOTES

1. *Euvres de Louize Labé Lionnoize. Revues et Corrigees par ladite Dame* (Lyon: Jean I de Tournes, 1556), Dedication. Trial of *meulquinier* Antoine Steppen, native of Cambrai, in C. L. Frossard, "La réforme dans le Cambrésis au XVIe siècle," *Bulletin de la société de l'histoire du protestantisme français* 3 (1854): 530. *Remonstrances, et Memoires, pour les Compagnons Imprimeurs, de Paris et Lyon: Opposans. Contre les Libraires, maistres Imprimeurs desdits lieux: Et adiointz* (n.p., n.d. [Lyon, 1572]), f. A i^r (hereafter cited as *Remonstrances*). *Le Chirurgie de Paulus Aegineta . . . Ung Opuscule de Galien des Tumeurs . . . Le tout traduict de Latin en Francoys par Maistre Pierre Tolet Medecin de l'Hospital de Lyon* (Lyon: Etienne Dolet, 1540), p. 6.

2. J. R. Goody, ed., *Literacy in Traditional Societies* (Cambridge, 1968). Elizabeth L. Eisenstein, "Some Conjectures About the Impact of Printing on Western Society and Thought: A Preliminary Report," *Journal of Modern History* 40 (1968): 1–56; *idem*, "The Advent of Printing and the Problem of the Renaissance," *Past and Present* 45 (Nov. 1969): 19–89; *idem* (with T. K. Rabb), "Debate. The Advent of Printing and the Problem of the Renaissance," *Past and Present* 52 (Aug. 1971): 134–44; *idem*, "L'avènement de l'imprimerie et la Réforme," Annales ESC 26

(1971): 1355–82. For a study of popular culture that uses a "relational" approach, see M. Agulhon, "Le problème de la culture populaire en France autour de 1848," Davis Center Seminar, Princeton University (May 1974). For a critique of some of the techniques used by social historians in the study of books and literary culture in the eighteenth century, see R. Darnton, "Reading, Writing and Publishing in Eighteenth-Century France: A Case Study in the Sociology of Literature," in Felix Gilbert and S. R. Graubard, eds., *Historical Studies Today* (New York, 1972), pp. 238–50.

3. A. H. Schutz, *Vernacular Books in Parisian Private Libraries of the Sixteenth Century, According to the Notarial Inventories* (University of North Carolina Studies in the Romance Languages and Literatures 25; Chapel Hill, 1955). E. Coyecque, *Recueil d'actes notariés relatifs à l'histoire de Paris et de ses environs au 16e siècle* ("Histoire générale de Paris"; Paris, 1924).

4. Bernard Guenee, *Tribunaux et gens de justice dans le bailliage de Senlis à la fin du moyen âge (vers 1380–vers 1550)* (Paris, 1963).

5. Charles Estienne, *L'agriculture et maison rustique* (Paris: Jacques du Puys, 1564), chap. 7, f. 9ʳ. Paul Raveau, *L'agriculture et les classes paysannes. La transformation de la propriété dans le haut Poitou au 16e siècle* (Paris, 1926), p. 259. René Choppin, *Traité de Privileges des Personnes Vivans aux Champs* [1st ed. in Latin, 1575] in *Oeuvres* (Paris, 1662–63), 3: 16. René Fédou, *Les hommes de loi lyonnais à la fin du moyen age* (Paris, 1964), pp. 158–60.

6. E. Campardon and A. Tuetey, eds., *Inventaire des registres des insinuations du Châtelet de Paris pendant les règnes de François 1ᵉʳ et de Henri II* (Paris, 1906), no. 735. Archives Départementales du Rhône, B, Insinuations, Testaments, 1560–61, ff. 9ʳ–10ᵛ; Henri and Julien Baudrier, *Bibliographie lyonnaise* (Lyon, 1895–1912), 9:306.

7. Thomas Platter (1499–1582), *Autobiographie*, trans. M. Helmer (*Cahiers des Annales* 22 [Paris, 1964]), p. 42. Thomas taught one of his young cousins his ABC's in one day and that lad left the village soon after for a scholarly career (p. 50). When Platter returned much later to found a school for a short period, it was with a special evangelical mission.

No books are mentioned in the reviews of household possessions and wills made by Bézard, *Vie rurale;* Guérin, *Vie rurale;* Gonon, *Vie quotidienne;* and Raveau, *Agriculture.* Note the remarkably infrequent mention of books in notarial acts in the rural Mâconnais even in the seventeenth through nineteenth centuries (Suzanne Tardieu, *La vie domestique dans le mâconnais rural préindustriel* [Paris, 1964], p. 358 and p. 358, n. 2).

8. Albert Labarre, *Le livre dans la vie amie noise du seizième siècle. L'enseignement des inventions après decès* (Paris, 1971).

9. Martin, *Livre, pouvoirs et société*, pp. 319–20. When the Sire de Gouberville acquired books for his little library at the manor of Mesnil-au-Val in Normandy, they were purchased in Paris and Bayeux (A. Tollemer, *Un Sire de Gouberville, gentilhomme campagnard au cotentin de 1553 à 1562* [Paris, 1972], pp. 204–9). In the 1570's and early 1580's, the bibliophile François de La Croix du Maine found it much harder to acquire books in Le Mans and vicinity than in Paris (*Premier volume de la Bibliotheque du Sieur de la Croix-du-Maine* [Paris, 1584], Preface, f. a viiʳ). A 1635 Paris edition of a book on surgery and health by H. Fierabras was

purchased in July 1669 "a la foire de beaucaire" (written in the copy at the medical library of the University of California at San Francisco). It seems unlikely that books were sold at the Beaucaire fairs a century earlier.

10. On the variety of speech and dialect in sixteenth-century France and the growing separation between written and spoken language, see F. Brunot et al., *Histoire de la langue française des origines à 1900* (Paris, 1905–53), 1: xiii–xiv, 304ff; 2: 174–75.

Grégoire de Rostrenin, *Dictionnaire françois-celtique ou françois-Breton* (Rennes, 1732), preface; a Breton-French-Latin dictionary (Tréguier: Jean Calvet, 1499); a book of the Passion and Resurrection, the Death of the Virgin, and the Life of Man in Breton verse (Paris: Yves Quillevere, 1530); the Four Ends of Man in Breton verse (Morlaix, 1570); and two saints' lives in Breton.

G. Brunet, *Poésies basques de Bernard Dechepare . . . d'après l'édition de Bordeaux, 1545* (Bordeaux, 1847). Julien Vinson, *Essai d'une bibliographie de la langue basque* (Paris, 1891–98), 1, nos. 1–5 (only two of these entries were published in France; the others were printed in Pamplona or Bilbao).

11. *Chansons nouvelles en lengaige provensal* (black-letter; n.p., n.d.). Augier Gaillard, *Las Obras* (Bordeaux, 1574); L. Bellaud de la Bellaudière, *Obros et rimos provenssalos* (Marseille: P. Mascaron, 1595). La Croix du Maine lists four persons with manuscripts in Provençal (Jean de Nostredame, Guillaume Boyer, Olivier de Lorgues, and Pierre de Bonifaccis), but I cannot find any evidence of their being printed in that language.

12. *Cy est le compost et Kalendrier des bergeres . . . nouvellement compose sans contredire a celluy des bergiers* (Paris: "in the Hotel de Beauregart in the rue Cloppin at the Ensign of le Roy Prestre lehan" [Guy Marchant and Jean Petit], n.d. [1499]). Signature in the copy at the University of Toronto Rare Book Library: "N. Chomat." The shepherdesses are named Sebille and Beatrix.

Bollème points out that the *Shepherds' Calendar* did not become part of the peddlers' literature, in a cheap edition, until the mid-seventeenth century (Genevieve Bollème, *Les almanachs populaires aux XVIIe et XVIIIe siècles. Essai d'histoire sociale* [Paris, 1969], p. 40). Yet she sees the intended public for the work as always the peasants ("L'auteur qui, symboliquement, ne sait pas écire donne au lecteur qui ne sait pas lire le moyen de se conduire mieux selon la sagesse naturelle. . . . Le Berger parle au berger, au laboureur, au paysan"—p. 16). I am suggesting, however, that the initial public for the work was not the peasants ("Who wants to have knowledge of the heavens . . . like the shepherds without letters [can here have it]. It is extracted and composed from their calendar and put into letters so that everyone can understand and know it like them. . . ." *Cy est le compost et kalendrier des bergiers nouvellement reffait* [Paris: Guy Marchant, 1493], f. h vii^v).

13. *Kalendrier des bergiers* (1493), f. h vii^v. Some of the verbal memory devices are recorded: ff. a v^r-a vi^r. Pierre Borel, *Tresor de Recherches et Antiquitez Gauloises et Françoises* (Paris, 1655), f. k iii^v.

14. Roger Vaultier, *Le folklore pendant la guerre de Cent Ans d'après les lettres de rémission du trésor des chartes* (Paris, 1965); Robert Mandrou, De la culture populaire aux 17e et 18e siècles. La bibliothèque bleue de Troyes (Paris, 1964).

15. Marc Soriano, Les contes de Perrault. Culture savante et traditions populaires (Paris, 1968).

16. Du Fail, *Propos*, pp. 15, 51. French editions of Aesop: Lyon, 1490 and 1499, prepared by the Augustinian Julien de Macho; new rhymed edition by Guillaume Corrozet, Paris 1542 and after. Greek and Latin editions: Elizabeth Armstrong, *Robert Estienne, Royal Printer* (Cambridge, 1954), p. 97; Germaine Warkentin, "Some Renaissance Schoolbooks in the Osborne Collection," *Renaissance and Reformation* 5, 3 (May 1969): 37. Urban ownership of Aesop: Labarre, *Livre*, p. 208; Schutz, *Vernacular Books*, pp. 72–73.

Editions of the *Roman de la Rose* in its "ancient language": fourteen between 1481 and 1528 in Paris and Lyon; three prose versions "moralised" by Jean de Molinet, 1500–1521; four editions between 1526 and 1538 in the translation attributed to Marot. No further editions until 1735! (Clearly the *Roman* did not become part of the peddlers' literature.) On these editions, on interest in the *Roman* among poets and on Marot as probable translator, see Antonio Viscardi, "Introduction," in *Le Roman de la Rose, dans la version attribuée à Clément Marot,* ed. S. F. Baridon (Milan, 1954), pp. 11–90. Urban ownership of the *Roman:* Labarre, *Livre*, p. 210; Schutz, *Vernacular Books*, p. 67; Doucet, *Bibliothèques*, p. 87, n. 39.

17. I am grateful to E. Howard Bloch, Joseph Duggan, and John Benton for suggestions on this subject. Though many medieval manuscripts remain of the *Roman de la Rose*—some 300— they are unlikely to have circulated among the peasants in this form. There is a short version of the *Roman* in manuscript, with much of the philosophical material omitted (E. Langlois, *Les manuscrits du roman de la Rose. Description et classement* [Lille, 1910], pp. 385–86). Here again there is no evidence that these excisions were made to prepare it for reading to peasants.

18. Jean Crespin, *Histoire des Martyrs persecutez et mis a mort pour la verite d'Evangile, depuis le temps des Apostres jusques a present (1619),* ed. D. Benoit (Toulouse, 1885–89) 2: 423–25; 1: 335.

19. On the carter Barthélemy Hector: *Livre des habitants de Genève,* ed. P.-F. Geisendorf (Geneva, 1957), p. 55; H.-L. Schlaepfer, "Laurent de Normandie," in *Aspects de la propagande religieuse* (Geneva, 1957), p. 198; Crespin, *Martyrs,* 2: 437–38. On the peddlers in the Lyonnais, ADR, B, Sénéchaussée, Sentences, 1556–1559, Sentence of July 1559. Two of them, the dressmaker Girard Bernard, native of Champagne, and the shoemaker Antoine Tallencon or Tallenton, native of Gascony, purchased books from Laurent de Normandie a few months before their arrest (Schlaepfer, "Laurent de Normandie," p. 200).

20. See, for instance, Marcel Cauvin, "Le protestantisme dans le Contentin," BSHPF 112 (1966): 367–68; 115 (1960): 80–81. Le Roy Ladurie, *Paysans*, 348–51. For a picture of Protestant congregations in the seventeenth century in which individual *laboureurs* play their part, see P. H. Chaix, "Les protestants en Bresse en 1621," *Cahiers d'histoire* 14 (1969): 252–54.

21. Crespin, *Martyrs,* 2: 438. The publisher of Protestant propaganda sometimes shared part of the risk with the peddler, contracting, for instance, that if the books were seized within a two-month period by the "enemies of the Gospel," the *libraire* would bear all the loss (Schlaepfer, "Laurent de Normandie," p. 199, n. 10; P. H. Chaix, "Les protestants en Bresse en 1621," *Cahiers d'histoire* 14 (1969) 25, p. 59).

22. [Antoine Mizaud], *Les Ephemerides perpetuelles de l'air: autrement l'Astrologie des Rustiques* (Paris: Jacques Kerver, 1554), dedication. Signatures in the Hough-

ton Library copy: "Claude Lorot, nimdunois [?], Claude Rinart son nepveu. Arte collude." On Mizaud's other works, see La Croix de Maine, *Bibliotheque*, pp. 17–18.

23. Jacques Guillemeau (1550–1613), *De la grossesse et accouchement des femmes* . . . *Par feu Jacques Guillemeau, Chirurgien ordinaire du Roy* (Paris, 1620; 1st ed. Paris, 1609), f. a iii^{r-v}.

24. Le Sieur L'Estoile, *Ephemerides ou Almanach iournalier pour l'an 1625* (Lyon, n.d. [1625]), pp. 75–78. On gardens in the Languedoc, see Le Roy Ladurie, *Paysans*, pp. 60–68.

25. N. Weiss, Vidimus des lettres patentes de François Ier, 1529," BSHPF 59 (1910), 501–4; Le Roy Ladurie, *Paysans*, 380–404; Bézard, *Vie rurale*, 289–90; V. Carrière, *Introduction aux études d'histoire ecclésiastique locale* (Paris, 1936), 3: 319–52. S. Gigon, *La révolte de la gabelle en Guyenne* (Paris, 1906); G. Procacci, *Classi sociali e monarchia assoluta nella Francia della prima metà del secolo XVI* (Turin, 1955), pp. 161–73, 213–30; Choppin, *Oeuvres* (1662–63), 3: 22 ("*la multitude des Rustiques de la Guyenne, qui alloient tumultueusement armée de villages en villages en l'an 1594*"). Jean Moreau, *Mémoires . . . sur les Guerres de la Ligue en Bretagne*, ed. H. Waquet (Archives historiques de Bretagne, 1; Quimper, 1906), pp. 11–14, 75–76. A. Le M. de La Borderie and B. Pocquet, *Histoire de Bretagne* (Rennes, 1906), 5: 173–81. Henri Drouot, *Mayenne et la Bourgogne, Etude sur la Ligue (1587–1596)* (Paris, 1937), 1: 39–55; 2: 291–92. Claude de Rubys, *Histoire veritable de la ville de Lyon* (Lyon, 1604), pp. 430–31; Daniel Hickey, "The Socio-Economic Context of the French Wars of Religion. A Case Study: Valentinois-Diois" (unpublished Ph.D. dissertation, Dept. of History, McGill University, 1973), chap. 4; L. S. Van Doren, "Revolt and Reaction in the City of Romans, Dauphiné, 1579–80," *Sixteenth Century Journal* 5 (1974): 72–77. See also Madeleine Foisil, *La révolte des Nu-Pieds et les révoltes normandes de 1639* (Paris, 1970), 178–83, on nicknames and organization of the Nu-Pieds.

26. Archives Départementales du Rhône, 15G22, ff. 130^{r}, 288^{r}. Examples of schoolteachers and reckonmasters: ADR, 3E6942, ff. 315^{r}–316^{v}; 3E4984, June 20, 1564; 3E8029, Sept. 7, 1564; 3E336, f. 44^{r}; 3E7184, ff. 238^{v}–239^{r}; 3E7170, Feb. 4, 1561/62; B, Insinuations, Donations, 25, f. 88^{r}; Archives municipales de Lyon, GG384, f. 43^{r}, GG435, no. 415.

27. Jean-Pierre Seguin, *L'information en France de Louis XII à Henri II* (Geneva, 1961), p. 52.

28. Archives Départementales du Rhône, 3E821, July 5, 1580; *Remonstrances . . . pour les Compagnons Imprimeurs* (cited in n. 1), f. A i^{v}. Guenée, *Tribunaux*, pp. 213–14.

29. The Lyon analysis is based on a study of hundreds of contracts in ADR, 3E, for the decades of the 1560's and 1570's. Le Roy Ladurie, *Paysans*, pp. 333, 347, 882.

30. Le Roy Ladurie, *Paysans*, p. 333. According to André Bourde, in a lecture given at the University of California at Berkeley in December 1972, it was only in the course of the seventeenth century that French made important gains among the patriciate of Marseille, while the people continued to speak Provençal.

31. See Coyecque, *Recueil*, nos. 85–116; 241–270; 584–609; 3749–3791. The Amiens figures are calculated by me from the data given in Labarre, *Livre*,

pp. 118–26 and 62–104. I have defined the "artisanal" group slightly differently from M. Labarre for purposes of this paper; that is, I have *excluded* from my count the unskilled workers included on pp. 124–26 and *added* some of the goldsmiths, butchers, etc. that Labarre has categorized with the *"classe marchande."*

32. Labarre, *Livre*, pp. 260–63. Coyecque, *Recueil*, nos. 3768, 3791. A one-book library in Lyon in 1563 in a room rented by a mason's helper from a miller's daughter: *"une bible en francois."* A five-book library in Lyon belonging to a merchant with a lot of paintings and furniture: *"Le livre des croniques, Les ordonnances des privileges des foyres de Lyon, Les troys miroirs du monde, La premiere partie de nouveau testament, Une Bible en francoys"* (ADR, 3E7179, ff. 467ʳ–468ʳ, 576ʳ–577ᵛ).

33. The relation of prices to wages and purchases is, of course, rough:

Book	Price, place, date
Jean de Vauzelles, *Police subsidaire . . . des povres*	5 deniers, Montpellier, 1535
Livre d'arismetique	1½ deniers wholesale, Paris, 1522
Jacques de Bourbon, *Prinse . . . de Rodes*	3 sous, Paris, 1547/48
La bible des Noelz	2 sous, Paris, 1547/48
Philippe de Commines, *Les croniques du roy Loys unze*	5 sous, Paris, 1547/48

Sources: L. Galle, "Les livres lyonnais," *Revue du Lyonnais* 23 (5th ser., 1897): 431; Doucet, *Bibliothèques,* pp. 92, 119, 118, 126.

In the 1520's in "normal" years at Lyon, a loaf of *pain farain* cost 5 deniers. In the 1530's and 1540's, a pair of children's shoes might cost 4 s. 6 d.; a pound of candlewax, 2 s. Painters' journeymen and printers' journeymen had wages roughly equivalent to 8 s. per day in the 1540's; journeymen and workers in the building trades, about 5–6 s. per day.

34. Schlaepfer, "Laurent de Normandie," p. 207: 4 s. per copy of the New Testament, 16°. Presumably this is a wholesale price. Bibles and New Testaments varied enormously in price depending on format, illustration, etc. An illustrated New Testament in an Amiens Library in 1564 was estimated at 5 livres (Labarre, *Livre*, p. 311).

Le moyen de parvenir a la congnoissance de Dieu et consequemment à salut (Lyon: Robert Granjon, 1562; 1st ed. 1557), ff. g viiᵛ–viiiʳ.

35. Coyecque, *Recueil*, no. 588. Medieval university students often used manuscripts as security for loans. Crespin, *Martyrs,* 2: 430.

36. Bibl. Nat., Mss., Collection Dupuy, 630, f. 171ʳ: *Memoire des livres que iay presté.* On book loans in the circle of the Sire de Gouberville, see Tollemer, *Gouberville,* p. 205.

37. Henri Hauser, *Ouvriers du temps passé* (5th ed.; Paris, 1927), pp. 82–85. Hauser points out how often regulations against night work were violated. Even when they existed, they prohibited work after 8, 9, or 10 P.M. In 1539, the Lyon printing ateliers ran till 10 P.M.; in 1572, they closed at 8 or 9 P.M.

38. For instance, *Patrons de diverses manieres Inventez tressubtilement Duysans a Brodeurs et Lingieres . . . A tous massons, menusiers et verriers . . .* (Lyon: Pierre de Saint Lucie, n.d.).

Vannoccio Biringuccio, *La Pyrotechnie ou Art du feu . . . traduite d'Italien en François par feu maistre Iacques Vincent* (Paris: Guillaume Iullian, 1572; 1st ed. 1556).

39. *Art et science de arismetique moult utille et profitable a toutes gens et facille a entendre par la plume et par le gect subtil pour ceulx qui ne scavent lyre ne escripre* (Paris: the widow Trepperel and Jehan Jehannot, n.d. [ca. 1520]). Under the title *L'Arithmetique et maniere de apprendre a Chiffrer et compter par la plume et par les gestz,* this work or slight variants thereof appeared many times throughout the century. A late version is *Arithmetique facile à Apprendre a Chiffrer et compter par la plume et par les gects* (Lyon: Benoît Rigaud, 1594). See David Eugene Smith, *Rara Arithmetica* (4th ed.; New York, 1970).

Guillaume de la Taissonnière, *Brieve Arithmetique fort facile a comprendre et necessaire à tous ceux qui font traffiq de marchandise . . . le te veux faire en quinze iours Sçavoir autant d'Arithmetique, qu'elle suffira pour tous iours Exercer ton art et practique* (Lyon: Benoît Rigaud, 1570; Pierre Rigaud, 1610).

40. Jean Visagier, *Epigrammatorum Libri IIII* (Lyon: printed by Jean Barbou for Michel Parmentier, 1537), p. 282 (poem to Cathelin Pellin and Michel Blanc, thanking them for work on the edition). Baudrier, *Bibliographie lyonnaise* 12: 468. Bernard de Girard du Haillan, *De l'Estat et succez des affaires de France* (Geneva: Antoine Blanc, 1596), last-page note from the printer: "nourrie en ieunesse, avec Dolet, Marot, etc."

41. *La vie de Ma Dame saincte Marguerite, vierge et martyr, Avec son Antienne et Oraison* (n.p., n.d. [ca. 1520]). Gargamelle refers to this custom in the first edition of *Gargantua.* She would rather hear a quotation from John 16 during her delivery than "la vie de saincte Marguerite ou quelque autre capharderie" (François Rabelais, *Oeuvres complètes,* ed. J. Boulenger and L. Scheler [Paris, 1955], p. 22, n. 4).

42. Crespin, *Martyrs,* 2: 670–71; Palissy, *Recepte veritable,* in *Oeuvres,* pp. 106–7.

43. Jean Bullant, *Recueil d'Horlogiographie, contenant la description, fabrication et usage des Horloges solaires* (Paris: Léon Cavellat for the widow Cavellat, 1598; 1st ed. 1561), f. Aa ii^{r-v}. (Bound with Bullant's *Geometrie et horlographie,* the Bancroft Library copy of the *Recueil* was purchased for 25 sous in 1606 by Charles Cocquerel.)

44. *Larithmetique de Milles Denorry gentilhomme chartrain, contenant la reduction tant de toutes especes de monnoyes . . . que des aulnes . . . poids et autres mesures d'un pais à l'autre: la forme de l'achat, vente et distribution de toute sorte de marchandise* (Paris: Gilles Gorbin, 1574), f. A i^v.AML, EE25, f. 13^v, GG87, piece 18. IAML, CC150, CC275. De Norry was almost certainly not of noble origin. For further information on de Norry and the commercial arithmetic, see N. Z. Davis, "Mathematicians in the Sixteenth-Century French Academies: Some Further Evidence," *Renaissance News* 11 (1958): pp. 3–10; and "Sixteenth-Century Arithmetics on the Business Life," *Journal of the History of Ideas* 21 (1960): 18–48.

The significance of the author portrait in the printed book was made known to me by Ruth Mortimer in a lecture given at the University of Toronto in November 1971, "A Portrait of the Author in Sixteenth-Century Italy," shortly to appear in expanded form as a book with the same title. The distinction between the manuscript and the printed book is not absolute: there are portraits stressing the author in the former (e.g., Christine de Pisan) and pictures stressing the dedicatee in the latter (e.g., La Croix du Maine's *Bibliotheque* has an engraving of Henri III, not of the author). Other examples of French portraits of authors of the new kind: the poet Louise Labé; the midwife Louise Bourgeois; the surgeon Ambrose Paré in his 1561 *Methode curative des playes* and after; and the mathematical practitioners Lucas Tremblay (*Prediction merveilleuse sur les deux ecclypses* [Lyon: Benoît Rigaud, 1588]), Valentin Mennher, and Bartelemy de Renterghem (the latter two lived respectively in Antwerp and Aix-la-Chapelle, but published commercial arithmetics and books on accounting in French at Antwerp).

45. *Declaration des Abus et Ignorance des Medecins . . . Compose par Pierre Braillier, Marchand Apotiquaire de Lyon . . .* (Lyon: Michel Jove, n.d. [Jan. 1557/58], copy at British Museum owned by the Parisian surgeon and book-collector François Rasse des Neux, 1567). Braillier was an apothecary of only moderate wealth in Lyon from the 1540's to the 1560's (Archives municipales de Lyon, CC41, f. 26^v, CC1174, f. 17^r). Nicholas Houel, *Advertissement, et declaration de l'institution de la Maison de la Charité Chrestienne establie es fauxbourgs Sainct Marcel . . . 1578* (Paris, 1580). On Houel, see La Croix du Maine, *Bibliotheque*, pp. 346–47 and *Dictionnaire des lettres françaises* (Paris, 1951), *Le seizième siècle*, p. 381. La Croix du Maine mentioned six other apothecaries who had composed works.

46. Paré's first work was *La methode de traicter les playes* (1545), published four years after he had been raised from journeyman to master at the Hôtel-Dieu of Paris. For Paré's presentation of himself, his training, and his intended public, see the "Au lecteur" in his *Oeuvres* (Paris, 1575 and after) and the "Apologie" accompanying the 1585 *Oeuvres*. Concerning the conflict about his status and authority, see Paré, *Des monstres et prodiges*, ed. J. Céard (Geneva, 1971), pp. xiv–xv.

Apart from Paré, La Croix du Maine lists 24 other surgeons, 23 of them with compositions, nineteen publishing works from the 1540's through the 1580's.

47. Jacques Cartier, "one of the most knowledgeable and experienced Pilots of his time" (La Croix du Maine, *Bibliotheque*, p. 180). Auger Gaillard, dit Le Charron; Jean Barril; Guillaume Poetou (*Dictionnaire des lettres françaises, 16e s.*, pp. 339, 84, 577 for details on their works).

48. *Discours admirables, de la nature des eaux et fonteines . . . des metaux, des sels et salines . . . Avec plusieurs autres excellens secrets des choses naturelles . . . Le tout dresse par dialogues . . . Par M. Bernard Palissy* (Paris: Martin Le Jeune, 1580), Dedication, Advertissement aux Lecteurs, and afternote (f. * 8^r).

49. Eisenstein, "Advent of Printing," p. 68.

50. La Croix du Maine, *Bibliotheque*, pp. 348–51. Dumont was the proofreader for La Croix's own book. Ph. Renouard, *Imprimeurs parisiens, libraires, fondeurs de caractères, et correcteurs d'imprimerie* (Paris, 1898), pp. 229–30. Of the pamphlets listed by La Croix, I have used *Extraict d'une lettre escritte par un Gentilhomme du Roy de Polonne, à Miezerich, le xxv Ianvier, 1574* (Newberry Library, no title page; La Croix says the printer was Denis du Pré). On the general characteristics of this literature, see Seguin, *L'information en France*, pp. 9–53.

51. List compiled from La Croix du Maine, *Bibliotheque;* Antoine du Verdier, *La Bibliotheque d'Antoine Du Verdier, seigneur de Vauprivas* (Lyon: Barthélemy Honorat, 1585); and *Dictionnaire des lettres françaises, 16e s.*

52. Dedications to women in works by Marie Dentière (*Epistre tres utile . . . composée par une femme chrestienne . . . envoyee a la Royne de Navarre,* 1538); Louise Labé (*Euvres;* cited in n. 1); and Louise Bourgeois ("Helisenne aux Lisantes," from *Les Oeuvres de Ma Dame Helisenne de Crenne* [Paris: Etienne Grouleau, 1551], and "Epistre aux dames," from *Les Oeuvres de Mes-Dames des Roches de Poetiers mere et Fille* [Paris: Abel L'Angelier, 1578]).

53. Of the 40 female writers listed by La Croix du Maine, 23 kept their work in manuscript.

54. La Croix du Maine, *Bibliotheque,* p. 358; *Dictionnaire des lettres françaises, 16e s.,* p. 315; *Les Misères de la Femme mariée . . . mis en forme de stances par Madame Liebault* (Paris: Pierre Menier, n.d.), reprinted by E. Fournier, *Variétés historiques et littéraires* (Paris, 1855), 3: 321–31. Nicole Estienne was the wife of the physician Jean Liébault.

Louise Bourgeois (1563–1636), *Observations diverses sur la sterilité, perte de fruict, foecondité, accouchements et maladies des Femmes et Enfants nouveaux naix . . . par L. Bourgeois dite Boursier, sage femme de Royne* (1st ed., Paris [Abraham Saugrain, 1609]; 2d ed., Rouen [widow of Thomas Daré, 1626]), Dedication to the Queen; author portrait at age 45, 1608; au lecteur. *Apologie de Loyse Bourgeois dite Bourcier sage femme de la Royne Mere du Roy et de feu Madame Contre le Rapport des Medecins* (Paris, 1627), p. 9.

55. *Remonstrances . . . pour les Compagnons Imprimeurs* (cited in n. 1). *Plaidoyez pour la Reformation de l'imprimerie* (n.p., n.d. [Paris, 1572]), Archives municipales de Lyon, BB120, f. 105ᵛ (printers submit to the Consulate a printed discourse of eight leaves with their complaints against the merchant publishers).

56. *Les Triomphes de l'Abbaye des Conards, sous le Resveur en Decimes Fagot Abbé des Conards, Contenant les criees et proclamations faites, depuis son advenement iusques à l'An present . . .* (Rouen: Nicholas Dugord, 1587). This edition includes scenarios and poems from 1540 *and* from the 1580's. But the 1540 material was presumably first printed shortly after that date, for the 1587 work includes a permission to print from the lieutenant of the baillif of Rouen dated January 18, 1541.

Dictons Satyriques louez en la Ville de Lyon par les Trois Supposts de l'Imprimerie, avec le pauvre Monde et le Medecin. Accompagnez du Capitaine des Imprimeurs, ensemble des Compagnons, marchans en armes (Lyon: Nicolas Guerin, 1574). *Recueil des plaisants devis recites par les supposts du Seigneur de la Coquille* (Lyon, 1857) reprints the *Plaisans devis* of February 21, 1580; May 2, 1581; February 19, 1584; Carnival, 1589; March 8, 1593; and March 6, 1594. On the initial printing of the *Plaisans devis,* see Baudrier, *Bibliographie lyonnaise,* 6: 19–21.

The development of a new kind of national consciousness in pamphlet literature in the course of the sixteenth century has been studied by Myriam Yardeni in *La conscience nationale en France pendant les guerres de religion (1559–1598)* (Louvain, 1971).

57. *Plaisans devis* of 1580 and of 1594.

58. *Premier volume de la Bibliotheque du Sieur de la Croix-du-Maine Qui est un*

catalogue general de toutes sortes d'Autheurs, qui ont escrit en François depuis cinq cents ans et plus, iusques à ce iourd'huy (Paris: Abel L'Angelier, 1584), p. 529. Signature in the Bancroft Library (Berkeley) copy: "Belin archdiacre de l'eglise du mans."

59. *Euvres poetiques de Iaques Peletier du Mans, Intitulez Louanges* (Paris: Robert Coulombel, 1581), f. 14ᵛ. "Le profit qu'avons des lettres et livres et de la gloire de nos rimeurs," in *Discours non plus melancoliques que divers, de choses mesmement qui appartiennent a notre France* (Poitiers: Enguilbert de Marnef, 1557), chap. 15. On the attribution of this work to Peletier, and for further bibliography on Peletier as well as discussion of the problems of popularization and right method, see N. Z. Davis, "Peletier and Beza Part Company," *Studies in the Renaissance* 11 (1964), especially pp. 196–201 and n. 39.

60. Crespin, *Martyrs,* 1: 527.

61. Emond Auger, *Continuation de l'Institution, Verite et Utilite du Sacrifice de la Messe* (Paris, 1566), pp. 53, 115. See also Eugénie Droz, "Bibles françaises après le Concile de Trente," *Journal of the Warburg and Courtauld Institutes* 18 (1965): 213.

62. Crespin, *Martyrs,* 1: 647.

63. E. Delaruelle et al., *L'Eglise au temps du grand schisme et de la crise conciliaire (1378–1449)* ("Histoire de l'Eglise depuis les origines jusqu'à nos jours," 14; Paris, 1964), 2: 712–21. Droz, "Bibles françaises," p. 222. *La Saincte Bible* (Lyon: Barthélemy Honorat, 1578), f. * 1ᵛ: *"Voyant, amy Lecteur, que la S. Bible en langue Francoise estoit de plusieurs requise, et qu'il ne s'en trouvoit plus de celles qui ont esté par le passé imprimees et mises en vente avec privilege du Roy: i'ay de l'advis et conseil de plusieurs scavans Docteurs et Predicateurs Catholiques, faict sortir en lumiere ceste-cy, sans gloses, additions ny distractions qui la puissent rendre suspecte. . . ."* This Bible, with illustrations used earlier in the Protestant editions at Lyon, is the one approved by the Faculty of Theology at Louvain; its publisher had been a Protestant until only a few years before. See also, Martin, *Livre, pouvoirs et société,* pp. 102–4.

64. *Paraphrase sur les Heures de nostre Dame, Selon l'usaige de Rome: traduictes de Latin en Francoys, par frere Gilles Cailleau* (Poitiers: Jean and Enguilbert de Marnef, 1542), f. A iiᵛ. See also the work of Benjamin Beausport in Droz, "Bibles françaises," pp. 218–20. Jean Guéraud, *La chronique lyonnaise de Jean Guéraud,* ed. J. Tricou (Lyon, 1929), p. 150.

65. On this process, see Brunot, *Histoire de la langue française,* 2: 36–55; Howard Stone, "The French Language in Renaissance Medicine," *Bibliothèque d'humanisme et renaissance* 15 (1953): 315–43; V.-L. Saulnier, "Lyon et la médecine aux temps de la Renaissance," *Revue lyonnaise de médecine* (1958): 73–83; C. A. Wickersheimer, *La médecine et les médecins en France à l'époque de la Renaissance* (Paris, 1906), pp. 128–78. Alison Klairmont of the University of California at Berkeley is considering these subjects anew in her doctoral dissertation on the medical profession in sixteenth-century France.

Le troisieme Livre de la therapeutique ou Methode curatoire de Claude Galien (Lyon: printed by Jean Barbou for Guillaume de Guelques, January 1539/40), translated by "Philiatros" (that is, the physician Jean Canappe), "Philiatros au Lecteur," f. 29ʳ⁻ᵛ. Signature in the Houghton Library copy, f. 127ʳ: "faict par moy . . . compaignon sirurgien."

La Chirurgie de Paulus Aegineta . . . Ung Opuscule de Galien des Tumeurs contre nature . . . Le tout traduict de Latin en Francoys par Maistre Pierre Tolet Medecin de l'Hospital (Lyon: Etienne Dolet, 1540), p. 3: *"la continuelle priere (pour leur necessité et usage) des compaignons chyrurgiens de la ville de Lyon."* Signature in the Houghton Library copy: "Jehan Derssert de Lyon."

Opuscules de divers autheurs medecins, Redigez ensemble pour le proufit et utilité des Chirurgiens (Lyon: Jean I de Tournes, 1552), translations by Canappe and Tolet.

De l'usage des parties du corps humain, Livres XVII. Escripts par Claude Galien et traduicts fidellement du grec en François (Lyon: Guillaume Rouillé, 1565), translated by Jacques Dalechamps. *"Et pource que la lecture de ce livre est non seulement utile mais aussi necessaire aus cheirurgiens . . ."* (f. 9ᵛ). Signature in the copy at the Université de Montréal: "Margueritte."

Chirurgie Francoise, Recueillie par M. Iaques Dalechamps, Docteur Medecin et Lecteur ordinaire de ceste profession à Lyon (Lyon: Guillaume Rouillé, 1570), f. † 7ᵛ: *"Le tout en nostre vulgaire Francoys, en faveur des compagnons et maistres Chirurgiens qui n'ont point este nourris aux lettres Greques et Latines."*

66. *Raison de vivre pour toutes fievres . . . Par maistre Jean Lyege medecin* (Paris: M. Vascosan, 1557), dedication from Lyege to Antoinette de Bourbon, Duchesse de Guise. *Commentaire de la conservation de santé et prolongation de vie, Faict en Latin par noble homme Hierosme de Monteux . . . medecin ordinaire du Roy . . . traduict de latin en François par maistre Claude Valgelas, docteur en Medecine* (Lyon: Jean I de Tournes, 1559), dedication from Valgelas to Louise Dansezune, dame de St. Chamond. *Cinq Livres De la maniere de nourrir et gouverner les enfans des leur naissance. Par M. Simon Vallembert, Medecin de Madame la Duchesse de Savoye . . .* (Poitiers: 1565), dedication from Vallembert to Catherine de Médicis.

67. Vallembert, *Cinq Livres,* Preface. *The regiment of life . . . with the boke of children, newly corrected and enlarged by T. Phayre* (London, 1550), preface by Thomas Phayer to *The Boke of children. Seconde Partie des Erreurs populaires et propos vulgaires, touchant la Medecine et le regime de santé, refutés ou expliqués par M. Laurent Ioubert* (Paris: Lucas Breyer, 1580), f. B. iiᵛ. *Annotations de M. Laurent Ioubert sur toutte la chirurgie de M. Gui de Chauliac* (Lyon: Etienne Michel, 1584), dedication from Isaac Joubert to Jean Bellièvre, January 1, 1580, pp. 4–18.

68. *Erreurs populaires au fait de la medecine et regime de santé corrigés par M. Laurent Joubert . . . la premiere partie* (Bordeaux: S. Millanges, 1578), Dedication, Book 2, chap. 4, pp. 380ff., *au lecteur. Seconde Partie des Erreurs populaires:* f. c iᵛ, *"Catalogue de plusieurs divers propos vulgaires et erreurs populaires colligez de plusieurs"* and given to Joubert by Barthélemy Cabrol (there follow 123 entries); pp. 159–87, *"Ramas de propos vulgaires et Erreurs populaires avec quelques problemes, anvoyes de plusieurs a M. Ioubert"* (there follow 333 entries).

69. *Chirurgie de Paulus Aegineta* (cited in n. 65), p. 6.

70. *Remonstrances . . . pour les Compagnons Imprimeurs* (cited in n. 1), f. C iiiʳ.

THREE

Workers Revolt

The Great Cat
Massacre of the
Rue Saint-Séverin

Robert Darnton

The funniest thing that ever happened in the printing shop of Jacques Vincent, according to a worker who witnessed it, was a riotous massacre of cats. The worker, Nicolas Contat, told the story in an account of his apprenticeship in the shop, rue Saint-Séverin, Paris, during the late 1730s.[1] Life as an apprentice was hard, he explained. There were two of them: Jerome, the somewhat fictionalized version of Contat himself, and Léveillé. They slept in a filthy, freezing room, rose before dawn, ran errands all day while dodging insults from the journeymen and abuse from the master, and received nothing but slops to eat. They found the food especially galling. Instead of dining at the master's table, they had to eat scraps from his plate in the kitchen. Worse still, the cook secretly sold the leftovers and gave the boys cat food—old, rotten bits of meat that they could not stomach and so passed on to the cats, who refused it.

This last injustice brought Contat to the theme of cats. They occupied a special place in his narrative and in the household of the rue Saint-Séverin. The master's wife adored them, especially *la grise* (the gray), her favorite. A passion for cats seemed to have swept through the printing trade, at least at the level of the masters, or *bourgeois* as the workers called them. One bourgeois kept twenty-five cats. He had their portraits painted and fed them on roast fowl. Meanwhile, the apprentices were trying to cope with a profusion of alley cats who also thrived in the printing district and made the boys' lives miserable. The cats howled all night on the roof over the apprentices' dingy bedroom, making it impossible to get a full night's sleep. As Jerome and Léveillé had to stagger out of bed at four or five in the morning to open the gate for the earliest arrivals among the journeymen, they began the day in a state of exhaustion while the bourgeois slept late. The master did not even work with the men, just as he did not eat with them. He let the foreman run the shop and rarely appeared in it, except to vent his violent temper, usually at the expense of the apprentices.

One night the boys resolved to right this inequitable state of affairs. Léveillé, who had an extraordinary talent for mimickry, crawled along the roof until he reached a section near the master's bedroom, and then he took to howling and meowing so horribly that the bourgeois and his wife did not sleep a wink. After several nights of this treatment, they decided they were being bewitched. But instead of calling the curé—the master was exceptionally devout and the mistress exceptionally attached to her confessor—they commanded the apprentices to get rid of the cats. The mistress gave the order, enjoining the boys above all to avoid frightening her *grise*.

Gleefully Jerome and Léveillé set to work, aided by the journeymen. Armed with broom handles, bars of the press, and other tools of their trade, they went after every cat they could find, beginning with *la grise*. Léveillé smashed its spine with an iron bar and Jerome finished it off. Then they stashed it in a gutter while the journeymen drove the other cats across the rooftops, bludgeoning every one within reach and trapping those who tried to escape in strategically placed sacks. They dumped sackloads of half-dead cats in the courtyard. Then the entire workshop gathered round and staged a mock trial, complete with guards, a confessor, and a public executioner. After pronouncing the animals guilty and administering last rites, they strung them up on an improvised gallows. Roused by gales of laughter, the mistress arrived. She let out a shriek as soon as she saw a bloody cat dangling from a noose. Then she realized it might be *la grise*. Certainly not, the men assured her: they had too much respect for the house to do such a thing. At this point the master appeared. He flew into a rage at the general stoppage of work, though his wife tried to explain that they were threatened by a more serious kind of insubordination. Then master and mistress withdrew, leaving the men delirious with "joy," "disorder," and "laughter."[2]

The laughter did not end there. Léveillé reenacted the entire scene in mime at least twenty times during subsequent days when the printers wanted to knock off for some hilarity. Burlesque reenactments of incidents in the life of the shop, known as *copies* in printers' slang, provided a major form of entertainment for the men. The idea was to humiliate someone in the shop by satirizing his peculiarities. A successful *copie* would make the butt of the joke fume with rage—*prendre la chèvre* (take the goat) in the shop slang—while his mates razzed him with "rough music." They would run their composing sticks across the tops of the type cases, beat their mallets against the chases, pound on cupboards, and bleat like goats. The bleating (*bais* in the slang) stood for the humiliation heaped on the victims, as in English when someone "gets your goat." Contat emphasized that Léveillé produced the funniest *copies* anyone had ever known and elicited the greatest choruses of rough music. The whole episode, cat massacre compounded by *copies*, stood out as the most hilarious experience in Jerome's entire career.

Yet it strikes the modern reader as unfunny, if not downright repulsive. Where is the humor in a group of grown men bleating like goats and banging with their tools while an adolescent reenacts the ritual slaughter of a defenseless animal? Our own inability to get the joke is an indication of the distance that separates us from the workers of preindustrial Europe. The perception of that distance may serve as the starting point of an investigation, for anthropologists have found that the best points of entry in an attempt to penetrate an alien culture can be those where it seems to be most opaque. When you realize that you are not getting something—a joke, a proverb, a ceremony—that is particularly meaningful to the natives, you can see where to grasp a foreign system of meaning in order to unravel it. By getting the joke of the great cat massacre, it may be possible to "get" a basic ingredient of artisanal culture under the Old Regime.

It should be explained at the outset that we cannot observe the killing of the cats at firsthand. We can study it only through Contat's narrative, written about twenty years after the event. There can be no doubt about the authenticity of Contat's quasi-fictional autobiography, as Giles Barber has demonstrated in his masterful edition of the text. It belongs to the line of autobiographical writing by printers that stretches from Thomas Platter to Thomas Gent, Benjamin Franklin, Nicolas Restif de la Bretonne, and Charles Manby Smith. Because printers, or at least compositors, had to be reasonably literate in order to do their work, they were among the few artisans who could give their own accounts of life in the working classes two, three, and four centuries ago. With all its misspellings and grammatical flaws, Contat's is perhaps the richest of these accounts. But it cannot be regarded as a mirror-image of what actually happened. It should be read as Contat's version of a happening, as his attempt to tell a story. Like all story telling, it sets the action in a frame of reference; it assumes a certain repertory of associations and responses on the part of its audience; and it provides meaningful shape to the raw stuff of experience. But since we are attempting to get at its meaning in the first place, we should not be put off by its fabricated character. On the contrary, by treating the narrative as fiction or meaningful fabrication, we can use it to develop an ethnological *explication de texte*.

The first explanation that probably would occur to most readers of Contat's story is that the cat massacre served as an oblique attack on the master and his wife. Contat set the event in the context of remarks about the disparity between the lot of workers and the bourgeois—a matter of the basic elements in life: work, food, and sleep. The injustice seemed especially flagrant in the case of the apprentices, who were treated like animals while the animals were promoted over their heads to the position the boys should have occupied, the place at the master's table. Although the apprentices seem most abused, the text makes it clear that the killing of the cats expressed a hatred for the bourgeois that had spread among all the workers: "The masters love cats; consequently [the workers] hate them." After masterminding the massacre, Léveillé became the hero of the shop, because "all the workers are in league against the masters. It is enough to speak badly of them [the masters] to be esteemed by the whole assembly of typographers."[3]

Historians have tended to treat the era of artisanal manufacturing as an idyllic period before the onset of industrialization. Some even portray the workshop as a kind of extended family in which master and journeymen labored at the same tasks, ate at the same table, and sometimes slept under the same roof.[4] Had anything happened to poison the atmosphere of the printing shops in Paris by 1740?

During the second half of the seventeenth century, the large printing houses, backed by the government, eliminated most of the smaller shops, and an oligarchy of masters seized control of the industry.[5] At the same time, the situation of the journeymen deteriorated. Although estimates vary and statistics cannot be trusted, it seems that their number remained stable: approximately 335 in 1666, 339 in 1701, and 340 in 1721. Meanwhile the number of masters declined by more than half, from eighty-three to thirty-six, the limit fixed by an edict of 1686. That meant fewer shops with larger work forces, as one can see from statistics on the density of presses: in 1644 Paris had seventy-five printing shops with a total of 180 presses; in 1701 it had fifty-one shops with 195 presses. This trend made it virtually impossible for journeymen to rise into the ranks of the masters. About the only way for a worker to get ahead in the craft was to marry a master's widow, for masterships had become hereditary privileges, passed on from husband to wife and from father to son.

The journeymen also felt threatened from below because the masters tended increasingly to hire *alloués*, or underqualified printers, who had not undergone the apprenticeship that made a journeyman eligible, in principle, to advance to a mastership. The *alloués* were merely a source of cheap labor, excluded from the upper ranks of the trade and fixed, in their inferior status, by an edict of 1723. Their degradation stood out in their name: they were *à louer* (for hire), not *compagnons* (journeymen) of the master. They personified the tendency of labor to become a commodity instead of a partnership. Thus Contat served his apprenticeship and wrote his memoirs when times were hard for journeymen printers, when the men in the shop in the rue Saint-Séverin stood in danger of being cut off from the top of the trade and swamped from the bottom.

How this general tendency became manifest in an actual workshop may be seen from the papers of the Société typographique de Neuchâtel (STN). To be sure, the STN was Swiss, and it did not begin business until seven years after Contat wrote his memoirs (1762). But printing practices were essentially the same way everywhere in the eighteenth century. The STN's archives conform in dozens of details to Contat's account of his experience. (They even mention the same shop foreman, Colas, who supervised Jerome for a while at the Imprimerie Royale and took charge of the STN's shop for a brief stint in 1779.) And they provide the only surviving record of the way masters hired, managed, and fired printers in the early modern era.

The STN's wage book shows that workers usually stayed in the shop for only a few months.[6] They left because they quarreled with the master, they got in fights, they wanted to pursue their fortune in shops further down the road, or they ran out of work. Compositors were hired by the job, *labeur* or *ouvrage* in printer's slang. When they finished a job, they frequently were fired, and a few pressmen had to be fired as well in order to maintain the balance between the two halves of the shop, the *casse* or composing sector and the *presse* or pressroom (two compositors usually set enough type to occupy a team of two pressmen). When the foreman took on new jobs, he hired new hands. The hiring and firing went on at such a fierce pace that the work force was rarely the same from one week to the next. Jerome's fellow workers in the rue Saint-Séverin seem to have been equally volatile. They, too, were hired for specific *labeurs,* and they sometimes walked off the job after quarrels with the bourgeois—a practice common enough to have its own entry in the glossary of their slang which Contat appended to his narrative: *emporter son Saint Jean* (to carry off your set of tools or quit). A man was known as an *ancien* if he remained in the shop for only a year. Other slang terms suggest the atmosphere in which the work took place: *une chèvre capitale* (a fit of rage), *se donner la gratte* (to get in a fight), *prendre la barbe* (to get drunk), *faire la déroute* (to go pub crawling), *promener sa chape* (to knock off work), *faire des loups* (to pile up debts).[7]

The violence, drunkenness, and absenteeism show up in the statistics of income and output one can compile from the STN's wage book. Printers worked in erratic spurts—twice as much in one week as in another, the weeks varying from four to six days and the days beginning anywhere from four in the morning until nearly noon. In order to keep the irregularity within bounds, the masters sought out men with two supreme traits: assiduousness and sobriety. If they also happened to be skilled, so much the better. A recruiting agent in Geneva recommended a compositor who was willing to set out for Neuchâtel in typical terms: "He is a good worker, capable of doing any job he gets, not at all a drunkard and assiduous at his labor."[8]

The STN relied on recruiters because it did not have an adequate labor pool in Neuchâtel and the streams of printers on the typographical *tours de France* sometimes ran dry. The recruiters and employers exchanged letters that reveal a common set of assumptions about eighteenth-century artisans: they were lazy, flighty, dissolute, and unreliable. They could not be trusted, so the recruiter should not loan them money for travel expenses and the employer could keep their belongings as a kind of security deposit in case they skipped off after collecting their pay. It followed that they could be discarded without compunction, whether or not they had worked diligently, had families to support, or fell sick. The STN ordered them in "assortments" just as it ordered paper and type. It complained that a recruiter in Lyon "sent us a couple in such a bad state that we were obliged to ship them off"[9] and lectured him about failing to inspect the goods: "Two of those whom you have sent to us have arrived all right, but so sick that they could infect all the rest; so we haven't been able to hire them. No one in town wanted to give them lodging. They have therefore left again and took the route for Besançon, in order to turn themselves in at the *hôpital.*"[10] A bookseller in Lyon advised them to fire most of their men during a slack period in their printing in order to flood the labor supply in eastern France and "give us more power over a wild and undisciplinable race, which we cannot control."[11] Journeymen and masters may have lived together as members of a happy family at some time somewhere in Europe, but not in the printing houses of eighteenth-century France and Switzerland.

Contat himself believed that such a state had once existed. He began his description of Jerome's apprenticeship by invoking a golden age when printing was first invented and printers lived as free and equal members of a "republic," governed by its own laws and traditions in a spirit of fraternal "union and friendship."[12] He claimed that the republic still survived in the form of the *chapelle* or workers' association in each shop. But the government had broken up general associations; the ranks had been thinned by *alloués;* the journeymen had been excluded from masterships; and the masters had withdrawn into a separate world of *haute cuisine* and *grasses matinées*. The master in the rue Saint-Séverin ate different food, kept different hours, and talked a different language. His wife and daughters dallied with worldly abbés. They kept pets. Clearly, the bourgeois belonged to a different subculture—one which meant above all that he did not work. In introducing his account of the cat massacre, Contat made explicit the contrast between the worlds of worker and master that ran throughout the narrative: "Workers, apprentices, everyone works. Only the masters and mistresses enjoy the sweetness of sleep. That makes Jerome and Léveillé resentful. They resolve not to be the only wretched ones. They want their master and mistress as associates (*associés*)."[13] That is, the boys wanted to restore a mythical past when masters and men worked in friendly association. They also may have had in mind the more recent extinction of the smaller printing shops. So they killed the cats.

But why cats? And why was the killing so funny? Those questions take us beyond the consideration of early modern labor relations and into the obscure subject of popular ceremonies and symbolism.

Folklorists have made historians familiar with the ceremonial cycles that marked off the calendar year for early modern man.[14] The most important of these was the cycle of carnival and Lent, a period of revelry followed by a period of abstinence. During carnival the common people suspended the normal rules of behavior and ceremoniously reversed the social order or turned it upside down in riotous procession. Carnival was a time for cutting up by youth groups, particularly apprentices, who organized themselves in "abbeys" ruled by a mock abbot or king and who staged charivaris or burlesque processions with rough music in order to humiliate cuckolds, husbands who had been beaten by their wives, brides who had married below their age group, or someone else who personified the infringement of traditional norms. Carnival was high season for hilarity, sexuality, and youth run riot—a time when young people tested social boundaries by limited outbursts of deviance, before being reassimilated in the world of order, submission, and Lentine seriousness. It came to an end on Shrove Tuesday or Mardi Gras, when a straw mannequin, King Carnival or Caramantran, was given a ritual trial and execution. Cats played an important part in some charivaris. In Burgundy, the crowd incorporated cat torture into its rough music. While mocking a cuckold or some other victim, the youths passed around a cat, tearing its fur to make it howl. *Faire le chat*, they called it. The Germans called charivaris *Katzenmusik*, a term that may have been derived from the howls of tortured cats.[15]

Cats also figured in the cycle of Saint John the Baptist, which took place on June 24, at the time of the summer solstice. Crowds made bonfires, jumped over them, danced around them, and threw into them objects with magical power, hoping to avoid disaster and obtain good fortune during the rest of the year. A favorite object was cats—cats tied up in bags, cats suspended from ropes, or cats burned at the stake. Parisians liked to incinerate cats by the sackful, while the Courimauds (*cour à miaud* or cat chasers) of Saint Chamond preferred to chase a flaming cat through the streets. In parts of Burgundy and Lorraine they danced around a kind of burning May pole with a cat tied to it. In the Metz region they burned a dozen cats at a time in a basket on top of a bonfire. The ceremony took place with great pomp in Metz itself, until it was abolished in 1765. The town dignitaries arrived in procession at the Place du Grand-Saulcy, lit the pyre, and a ring of riflemen from the garrison fired off volleys while the cats disappeared screaming in the flames. Although the practice varied from place to place, the ingredients were everywhere the same: a *feu de joie* (bonfire), cats, and an aura of hilarious witch-hunting.[16]

In addition to these general ceremonies, which involved entire communities, artisans celebrated ceremonies peculiar to their craft. Printers processed and feasted in honor of their patron, Saint John the Evangelist, both on his saint's day, December 27, and on the anniversary of his martyrdom, May 6, the festival of Saint Jean Porte Latine. By the eighteenth century, the masters had excluded the journeymen from the confraternity devoted to the saint, but the journeymen continued to hold ceremonies in their chapels.[17] On Saint Martin's day, November 11, they held a mock trial followed by a feast. Contat explained that the chapel was a tiny "republic," which governed itself according to its own code of conduct. When a worker violated the code, the foreman, who was the head of the chapel and not part of the management, entered a fine in a register: leaving a candle lit, five sous; brawling, three livres; insulting the good name of the chapel, three livres; and so on. On Saint Martin's, the foreman read out the fines and collected them. The workers sometimes appealed their cases before a burlesque tribunal composed of the chapel's "ancients," but in the end they had to pay up amidst more bleating, banging of tools, and riotous laughter. The fines went for food and drink in the chapel's favorite tavern, where the hell-raising continued until late in the night.[18]

Taxation and commensality characterized all the other ceremonies of the chapel. Special dues and feasts marked a man's entry into the shop (*bienvenue*), his exit (*conduite*), and even his marriage (*droit de chevet*). Above all, they punctuated a youth's progress from apprentice to journeyman. Contat described four of these rites, the most important being the first, called the taking of the apron, and the last, Jerome's initiation as a full-fledged *compagnon*.

The taking of the apron *(la prise de tablier)* occurred soon after Jerome joined the shop. He had to pay six livres (about three days' wages for an ordinary journeyman) into a kitty, which the journeymen supplemented by small payments of their own *(faire la reconnaissance)*. Then the chapel repaired to its favorite tavern, Le Panier Fleury in the rue de la Huchette. Emissaries were dispatched to procure provisions and returned loaded down with bread and meat, having lectured the shopkeepers of the neighborhood on which cuts were worthy of typographers and which could be left for cobblers. Silent and glass in hand, the journeymen gathered around Jerome in a special room on the second floor of the tavern. The subforeman approached, carrying the apron and followed by two "ancients," one from each of the "estates" of the shop, the *casse* and the *presse*. He handed the apron, newly made from close-woven linen, to the foreman, who took Jerome by the hand and led him to the center of the room, the subforeman and "ancients" falling in behind. The foreman made a short speech, placed the apron over Jerome's head and tied the strings behind him, as everyone drank to the health of the initiate. Jerome was then given a seat with the chapel dignitaries at the head of the table. The rest rushed for the best places they could find and fell on the food. They gobbled and guzzled and called out for more. After several Gargantuan rounds, they settled down to shop talk—and Contat lets us listen in:

> "Isn't it true," says one of them, "that printers know how to shovel it in? I am sure that if someone presented us with a roast mutton, as big as you like, we would leave nothing but the bones behind. . . ." They don't talk about theology nor philosophy and still less of politics. Each speaks of his job: one will talk to you about the *casse*, another the *presse*, this one of the tympan, another of the ink ball leathers. They all speak at the same time, whether they can be heard or not.

At last, early in the morning after hours of swilling and shouting, the workers separated—sotted but ceremonial to the end: "Bonsoir, Monsieur notre prote [foreman]"; Bonsoir, Messieurs les compositeurs"; "Bonsoir, Messieurs les imprimeurs"; "Bonsoir Jerome." The text explains that Jerome will be called by his first name until he is received as a journeyman.[19]

That moment came four years later, after two intermediary ceremonies (the *admission à l'ouvrage* and the *admission à la banque*) and a vast amount of hazing. Not only did the men torment Jerome, mocking his ignorance, sending him on wild goose chases, making him the butt of

practical jokes, and overwhelming him with nasty chores; they also refused to teach him anything. They did not want another journeyman in
their over-flooded labor pool, so Jerome had to pick up the tricks of the
trade by himself. The work, the food, the lodging, the lack of sleep, it
was enough to drive a boy mad, or at least out of the shop. In fact,
however, it was standard treatment and should not be taken too seriously. Contat recounted the catalogue of Jerome's troubles in a light-
hearted manner, which suggested a stock comic genre, the *misère des apprentis*.[20] The *misères* provided farcical accounts, in doggerel verse or
broadsides, of a stage in life that was familiar and funny to everyone in
the artisanate. It was a transitional stage, which marked the passage from
childhood to adulthood. A young man had to sweat his way through it
so that he would have paid his dues—the printers demanded actual payments, called *bienvenues* or *quatre heures*, in addition to razzing the apprentices—when he reached full membership in a vocational group. Until he arrived at that point, he lived in a fluid or liminal state, trying out
adult conventions by subjecting them to some hell-raising of his own.
His elders tolerated his pranks, called *copies* and *joberies* in the printing
trade, because they saw them as wild oats, which needed to be sown
before he could settle down. Once settled, he would have internalized
the conventions of his craft and acquired a new identity, which was often
symbolized by a change in his name.[21]

Jerome became a journeyman by passing through the final rite, *com-
pagnonnage*. It took the same form as the other ceremonies, a celebration
over food and drink after the candidate paid an initiation fee and the
journeymen chipped in with *reconnaissance*. But this time Contat gave a
summary of the foreman's speech:[22]

> The newcomer is indoctrinated. He is told never to betray his col-
> leagues and to maintain the wage rate. If a worker doesn't accept a price
> [for a job] and leaves the shop, no one in the house should do the job for
> a smaller price. Those are the laws among the workers. Faithfulness and
> probity are recommended to him. Any worker who betrays the others,
> when something forbidden, called *marron* [chestnut], is being printed, must
> be expelled ignominiously from the shop. The workers blacklist him by
> circular letters sent around all the shops of Paris and the provinces. . . .
> Aside from that, anything is permitted: excessive drinking is considered a
> good quality, gallantry and debauchery as youthful feats, indebtedness as
> a sign of wit, irreligion as sincerity. It's a free and republican territory in
> which everything is permitted. Live as you like but be an *honnête homme*, no
> hypocrisy.

Hypocrisy turned out in the rest of the narrative to be the main characteristic of the bourgeois, a superstitious religious bigot. He occupied a
separate world of pharasaical bourgeois morality. The workers defined

their "republic" against that world and against other journeymen's groups as well—the cobblers, who ate inferior cuts of meat, and the masons or carpenters who were always good for a brawl when the printers, divided into "estates" (the *casse* and the *presse*) toured country taverns on Sundays. In entering an "estate," Jerome assimilated an ethos. He identified himself with a craft; and as a full-fledged journeyman compositor, he received a new name. Having gone through a rite of passage in the full, anthropological sense of the term, he became a *Monsieur*.[23]

So much for ceremonies. What about cats? It should be said at the outset that there is an indefinable *je ne sais quoi* about cats, a mysterious something that has fascinated mankind since the time of the ancient Egyptians. One can sense a quasi-human intelligence behind a cat's eyes. One can mistake a cat's howl at night for a human scream, torn from some deep, visceral part of man's animal nature. Cats appealed to poets like Baudelaire and painters like Manet, who wanted to express the humanity in animals along with the animality of men—and especially of women.[24]

This ambiguous ontological position, a straddling of conceptual categories, gives certain animals—pigs, dogs, and cassowaries as well as cats—in certain cultures an occult power associated with the taboo. That is why Jews do not eat pigs, according to Mary Douglas, and why Englishmen can insult one another by saying "son-of-a-bitch" rather than "son-of-a-cow," according to Edmund Leach.[25] Certain animals are good for swearing, just as they are "good for thinking" in Lévi-Strauss's famous formula. I would add that others—cats in particular—are good for staging ceremonies. They have ritual value. You cannot make a charivari with a cow. You do it with cats: you decide to *faire le chat*, to make *Katzenmusik*.

The torture of animals, especially cats, was a popular amusement throughout early modern Europe. You have only to look at Hogarth's *Stages of Cruelty* to see its importance, and once you start looking you see people torturing animals everywhere. Cat killings provided a common theme in literature, from *Don Quixote* in early seventeenth-century Spain to *Germinal* in late nineteenth-century France.[26] Far from being a sadistic fantasy on the part of a few half-crazed authors, the literary versions of cruelty to animals expressed a deep current of popular culture, as Mikhail Bakhtin has shown in his study of Rabelais.[27] All sorts of ethnographic reports confirm that view. On the *dimanche des brandons* in Semur, for example, children used to attach cats to poles and roast them over bonfires. In the *jeu du chat* at the Fete-Dieu in Aix-en-Provence, they threw cats high in the air and smashed them on the ground. They used expressions like "patient as a cat whose claws are being pulled out" or "patient as a cat whose paws are being grilled." The English were just as cruel. During the Reformation in London, a Protestant crowd shaved a cat to look like a priest, dressed it in mock vestments, and hanged it on the gallows at Cheapside.[28] It would be possible to string out many other examples, but the point should be clear: there was nothing unusual about the ritual killing of cats. On the contrary, when Jerome and his fellow workers tried and hanged all the cats they could find in the rue Saint-Séverin, they drew on a common element in their culture. But what significance did that culture attribute to cats?

To get a grip on that question, one must rummage through collections of folktales, superstitions, proverbs, and popular medicine. The material is rich, varied, and vast but extremely hard to handle. Although much of it goes back to the Middle Ages, little can be dated. It was gathered for the most part by folklorists in the late nineteenth and early twentieth centuries, when sturdy strains of folklore still resisted the influence of the printed word. But the collections do not make it possible to claim that this or that practice existed in the printing houses of mid-eighteenth-century Paris. One can only assert that printers lived and breathed in an atmosphere of traditional customs and beliefs which permeated everything. It was not everywhere the same—France remained a patchwork of *pays* rather than a unified nation until late in the nineteenth century—but everywhere some common motifs could be found. The commonest were attached to cats. Early modern Frenchmen probably made more symbolic use of cats than of any other animal, and they used them in distinct ways, which can be grouped together for the purposes of discussion, despite the regional peculiarities.

First and foremost, cats suggested witchcraft. To cross one at night in virtually any corner of France was to risk running into the devil or one of his agents or a witch abroad on an evil errand. White cats could be as satanic as the black, in the daytime as well as at night. In a typical encounter, a peasant woman of Bigorre met a pretty white house cat who had strayed in the fields. She carried it back to the village in her apron, and just as they came to the house of a woman suspected of witchcraft, the cat jumped out, saying "Merci, Jeanne."[29] Witches transformed themselves into cats in order to cast spells on their victims. Sometimes, especially on Mardi Gras, they gathered for hideous sabbaths at night. They howled, fought, and copulated horribly under the direction of the devil himself in the form of a huge tomcat. To protect yourself from sorcery by cats there was one, classic remedy: maim it. Cut its tail, clip its ears, smash one of its legs, tear or burn its fur, and you would break its malevolent power. A maimed cat could not attend a sabbath or wander abroad to cast spells. Peasants frequently cudgeled cats who crossed their paths at night and discovered the next day that bruises had appeared on women believed to be witches—or so it was said in the lore of their village. Villagers also told stories of farmers who found strange cats in barns and broke their limbs to save the cattle. Invariably a broken limb would appear on a suspicious woman the following morning.

Cats possessed occult power independently of their association with witchcraft and deviltry. They could prevent the bread from rising if they entered bakeries in Anjou. They could spoil the catch if they crossed the path of fishermen in Brittany. If buried alive in Béarn, they could clear a field of weeds. They figured as staple ingredients in all kinds of folk medicine aside from witches' brews. To recover from a bad fall, you sucked the blood out of a freshly amputated tail of a tomcat. To cure yourself from pneumonia, you drank blood from a cat's ear in red wine. To get over colic, you mixed your wine with cat excrement. You could even make yourself invisible, at least in Brittany, by eating the brain of a newly killed cat, provided it was still hot.

There was a specific field for the exercise of cat power: the household and particularly the person of the master or mistress of the house. Folktales like "Puss 'n Boots" emphasized the identification of master and cat, and so did superstitions such as the practice of tying a black ribbon around the neck of a cat whose mistress had died. To kill a cat was to bring misfortune upon its owner or its house. If a cat left a house or stopped jumping on the sickbed of its master or mistress, the person was likely to die. But a cat lying on the bed of a dying man might be the devil, waiting to carry his soul off to hell. According to a sixteenth-century tale, a girl from Quintin sold her soul to the devil in exchange for some pretty clothes. When she died, the pallbearers could not lift her coffin; they opened the lid, and a black cat jumped out. Cats could harm a house. They often smothered babies. They understood gossip and would repeat it out of doors. But their power could be contained or turned to your advantage if you followed the right procedures, such as greasing their paws with butter or maiming them when they first arrived. To protect a new house, Frenchmen enclosed live cats within its walls—a very old rite, judging from cat skeletons that have been exhumed from the walls of medieval buildings.

Finally, the power of cats was concentrated on the most intimate aspect of domestic life: sex. *Le chat, la chatte, le minet* mean the same thing in French slang as "pussy" does in English, and they have served as obscenities for centuries.[30] French folklore attaches special importance to the cat as a sexual metaphor or metonym. As far back as the fifteenth century, the petting of cats was recommended for success in courting women. Proverbial wisdom identified women with cats: "He who takes good care of cats will have a pretty wife." If a man loved cats, he would love women; and vice versa: "As he loves his cat, he loves his wife," went another proverb. If he did not care for his wife, you could say of him, "He has other cats to whip." A woman who wanted to get a man should avoid treading on a cat's tail. She might postpone marriage for a year— or for seven years in Quimper and for as many years as the cat meowed in parts of the Loire Valley. Cats connoted fertility and female sexuality everywhere. Girls were commonly said to be "in love like a cat"; and if they became pregnant, they had "let the cat go to the cheese." Eating cats could bring on pregnancy in itself. Girls who consumed them in stews gave birth to kittens in several folktales. Cats could even make diseased apple trees bear fruit, if buried in the correct manner in upper Brittany.

It was an easy jump from the sexuality of women to the cuckolding of men. Caterwauling could come from a satanic orgy, but it might just as well be toms howling defiance at each other when their mates were in heat. They did not call as cats, however. They issued challenges in their masters' names, along with sexual taunts about their mistresses: "Reno! Francois!" "Où allez-vous?—Voir la femme à vous.—Voir la femme à moi! Rouah!" (Where are you going?—To see your wife.—To see my wife! Ha!) Then the toms would fly at each other like the cats of Kilkenny, and their sabbath would end in a massacre. The dialogue differed according to the imaginations of the listeners and the onomatopoetic power of their dialect, but it usually emphasized predatory sexuality.[31] "At night all cats are gray," went the proverb, and the gloss in an eighteenth-century proverb collection made the sexual hint explicit: "That is to say that all women are beautiful enough at night."[32] Enough for what? Seduction, rape, and murder echoed in the air when the cats howled at night in early modern France. Cat calls summoned up *Katzenmusik,* for charivaris often took the form of howling under a cuckold's window on the eve of Mardi Gras, the favorite time for cat sabbaths.

Witchcraft, orgy, cuckoldry, charivari, and massacre, the men of the Old Regime could hear a great deal in the wail of a cat. What the men of the rue Saint-Séverin actually heard is impossible to say. One can only assert that cats bore enormous symbolic weight in the folklore of France and that the lore was rich, ancient, and widespread enough to have penetrated the printing shop. In order to determine whether the printers actually drew on the ceremonial and symbolic themes available to them, it is necessary to take another look at Contat's text.

The text made the theme of sorcery explicit from the beginning. Jerome and Léveillé could not sleep because "some bedeviled cats make a sabbath all night long."[33] After Léveillé added his cat calls to the general caterwauling, "the whole neighborhood is alarmed. It is decided that the cats must be agents of someone casting a spell." The master and mistress considered summoning the curé to exorcise the place. In deciding instead to commission the cat hunt, they fell back on the classic remedy for witchcraft: maiming. The bourgeois—a superstitious, priest-ridden fool—took the whole business seriously. To the apprentices it was a joke. Léveillé in particular functioned as a joker, a mock "sorcerer" staging a fake "sabbath," according to the terms chosen by Contat. Not only did the apprentices exploit their master's superstition in order to run riot at his expense, but they also turned their rioting against their mistress. By bludgeoning her familiar, *la grise*, they in effect accused her of being the witch. The double joke would not be lost on anyone who could read the traditional language of gesture.

The theme of charivari provided an additional dimension to the fun. Although it never says so explicitly, the text indicates that the mistress was having an affair with her priest, a "lascivious youth," who had memorized obscene passages from the classics of pornography—Aretino and *L'Academie des dames*—and quoted them to her, while her husband droned on about his favorite subjects, money and religion. During a lavish dinner with the family, the priest defended the thesis "that it is a feat of wit to cuckold one's husband and that cuckolding is not a vice." Later, he and the wife spent the night together in a country house. They fit perfectly into the typical triangle of printing shops: a doddering old master, a middle-aged mistress, and her youthful lover.[34] The intrigue cast the master in the role of a stock comic figure: the cuckold. So the revelry of the workers took the form of a charivari. The apprentices managed it, operating within the liminal area where novitiates traditionally mocked their superiors, and the journeymen responded to their antics in the traditional way, with rough music. A riotous, festival atmosphere runs through the whole episode, which Contat described as a *fête:* "Léveillé and his comrade Jerome preside over the *fête*," he wrote, as if they were kings of a carnival and the cat bashing corresponded to the torturing of cats on Mardi Gras or the *fête* of Saint John the Baptist.

As in many Mardi Gras, the carnival ended in a mock trial and execution. The burlesque legalism came naturally to the printers because they staged their own mock trials every year at the *fête* of Saint Martin, when the chapel squared accounts with its boss and succeeded spectacularly in getting his goat. The chapel could not condemn him explicitly without moving into open insubordination and risking dismissal. (All the sources, including the papers of the STN, indicate that masters often fired workers for insolence and misbehavior. Indeed, Léveillé was later fired for a prank that attacked the bourgeois more openly.) So the workers tried the bourgeois in absentia, using a symbol that would let their meaning show through without being explicit enough to justify retaliation. They tried and hanged the cats. It would be going too far to hang *la grise* under the master's nose after being ordered to spare it; but they made the favorite pet of the house their first victim, and in doing so they knew they were attacking the house itself, in accordance with the traditions of cat lore. When the mistress accused them of killing *la grise*, they replied with mock deference that "nobody would be capable of such an outrage and that they have too much respect for that house." By executing the cats with such elaborate ceremony, they condemned the house and declared the bourgeois guilty—guilty of overworking and underfeeding his apprentices, guilty of living in luxury while his journeymen did all the work, guilty of withdrawing from the shop and swamping it with *alloués* instead of laboring and eating with the men, as masters were said to have done a generation or two earlier, or in the primitive "republic" that existed at the beginning of the printing industry. The guilt extended from the boss to the house to the whole system. Perhaps in trying, confessing, and hanging a collection of half-dead cats, the workers meant to ridicule the entire legal and social order.

They certainly felt debased and had accumulated enough resentment to explode in an orgy of killing. A half-century later, the artisans of Paris would run riot in a similar manner, combining indiscriminate slaughter with improvised popular tribunals.[35] It would be absurd to view the cat massacre as a dress rehearsal for the September Massacres of the French Revolution, but the earlier outburst of violence did suggest a popular rebellion, though it remained restricted to the level of symbolism.

Cats as symbols conjured up sex as well as violence, a combination perfectly suited for an attack on the mistress. The narrative identified her with *la grise*, her *chatte favorite*. In killing it, the boys struck at her: "It was a matter of consequence, a murder, which had to be hidden." The mistress reacted as if she had been assaulted: "They ravished from her a cat without an equal, a cat that she loved to madness." The text described her as lascivious and "impassioned for cats" as if she were a she-cat in heat during a wild cat's sabbath of howling, killing, and rape. An explicit reference to rape would violate the proprieties that were generally observed in eighteenth-century writing. Indeed, the symbolism would work only if it remained veiled—ambivalent enough to dupe the master and sharp enough to hit the mistress in the quick. But Contat used strong language. As soon as the mistress saw the cat execution she let out a scream. Then the scream was smothered in the realization that she had lost her *grise*. The workers assured her with feigned sincerity of their respect and the master arrived. " 'Ah! the scoundrels,' he says. 'Instead of working they are killing cats.' Madame to Monsieur: 'These wicked men can't kill the masters; they have killed my cat.' . . . It seems to her that all the blood of the workers would not be sufficient to redeem the insult."

It was metonymic insult, the eighteenth-century equivalent of the modern schoolboy's taunt: "Ah, your mother's girdle!" But it was stronger, and more obscene. By assaulting her pet, the workers ravished the mistress symbolically. At the same time, they delivered the supreme insult to their master. His wife was his most precious possession, just as her *chatte* was hers. In killing the cat, the men violated the most intimate treasure of the bourgeois household and escaped unharmed. That was the beauty of it. The symbolism disguised the insult well enough for them to get away with it. While the bourgeois fumed over the loss of work, his wife, less obtuse, virtually told him that the workers had attacked her sexually and would like to murder him. Then both left the scene in humiliation and defeat. "Monsieur and Madame retire, leaving the workers in liberty. The printers, who love disorder, are in a state of great joy. Here is an ample subject for their laughter, a beautiful *copie*, which will keep them amused for a long time."

This was Rabelaisian laughter. The text insists upon its importance: "The printers know how to laugh, it is their sole occupation." Mikhail Bakhtin has shown how the laughter of Rabelais expressed a strain of popular culture in which the riotously funny could turn a riot, a carnival culture of sexuality and sedition in which the revolutionary element might be contained within symbols and metaphors or might explode in a general uprising, as in 1789. The question remains, however, what precisely was so funny about the cat massacre? There is no better way to ruin a joke than to analyze it or to overload it with social comment. But this joke cries out for commentary—not because one can use it to prove that artisans hated their bosses (a truism that may apply to all periods of labor history, although it has not been appreciated adequately by eighteenth-century historians), but because it can help one to see how workers made their experience meaningful by playing with themes of their culture.

The only version of the cat massacre available to us was put into writing, long after the fact, by Nicolas Contat. He selected details, ordered events, and framed the story in such a way as to bring out what was meaningful for him. But he derived his notions of meaning from his culture just as naturally as he drew in air from the atmosphere around him. And he wrote down what he had helped to enact with his mates. The subjective character of the writing does not vitiate its collective frame of reference, even though the written account must be thin compared with the action it describes. The workers' mode of expression was a kind of popular theater. It involved pantomime, rough music, and a dramatic "theater of violence" improvised in the work place, in the street, and on the rooftops. It included a play within a play, because Léveillé reenacted the whole farce several times as *copies* in the shop. In fact, the original massacre involved the burlesquing of other ceremonies, such as trials and charivaris. So Contat wrote about a burlesque of a burlesque, and in reading it one should make allowances for the refraction of cultural forms across genres and over time.

Those allowances made, it seems clear that the workers found the massacre funny because it gave them a way to turn the tables on the bourgeois. By goading him with cat calls, they provoked him to authorize the massacre of cats, then they used the massacre to put him symbolically on trial for unjust management of the shop. They also used it as a witch hunt, which provided an excuse to kill his wife's familiar and to insinuate that she herself was the witch. Finally, they transformed it into a charivari, which served as a means to insult her sexually while mocking him as a cuckold. The bourgeois made an excellent butt of the joke. Not only did he become the victim of a procedure he himself had set in motion, he did not understand how badly he had been had. The men had subjected his wife to symbolic aggression of the most intimate kind, but he did not get it. He was too thick-headed, a classic cuckold. The printers ridiculed him in splendid Boccaccian style and got off scot-free.

The joke worked so well because the workers played so skillfully with a repertory of ceremonies and symbols. Cats suited their purposes perfectly. By smashing the spine of *la grise* they called the master's wife a witch and a slut, while at the same time making the master into a cuckold and a fool. It was metonymic insult, delivered by actions, not words, and it struck home because cats occupied a soft spot in the bourgeois way of life. Keeping pets was as alien to the workers as torturing animals was to the bourgeois. Trapped between incompatible sensitivities, the cats had the worst of both worlds.

The workers also punned with ceremonies. They made a roundup of cats into a witch hunt, a festival, a charivari, a mock trial, and a dirty joke. Then they redid the whole thing in pantomime. Whenever they got tired of working, they transformed the shop into a theater and produced *copies*—their kind of copy, not the authors'. Shop theater and ritual punning suited the traditions of their craft. Although printers made books, they did not use written words to convey their meaning. They used gestures, drawing on the culture of their craft to inscribe statements in the air.

Insubstantial as it may seem today, this joking was a risky business in the eighteenth century. The risk was part of the joke, as in many forms of humor, which toy with violence and tease repressed passions. The workers pushed their symbolic horseplay to the brink of reification, the point at which the killing of cats would turn into an open rebellion. They played on ambiguities, using symbols that would hide their full meaning while letting enough of it show through to make a fool of the bourgeois without giving him a pretext to fire them. They tweaked his nose and prevented him from protesting against it. To pull off such a feat required great dexterity. It showed that workers could manipulate symbols in their idiom as effectively as poets did in print.

The boundaries within which this jesting had to be contained suggest the limits to working-class militancy under the Old Regime. The printers identified with their craft rather than their class. Although they organized in chapels, staged strikes, and sometimes forced up wages, they remained subordinate to the bourgeois. The master hired and fired men as casually as he ordered paper, and he turned them out into the road when he sniffed insubordination. So until the onset of proletarianization in the late nineteenth century, they generally kept their protests on a symbolic level. A *copie*, like a carnival, helped to let off steam; but it also produced laughter, a vital ingredient in early artisanal culture and one that has been lost in labor history. By seeing the way a joke worked in the horseplay of a printing shop two centuries ago, we may be able to recapture that missing element—laughter, sheer laughter, the thigh-slapping, rib-cracking Rabelaisian kind, rather than the Voltairian smirk with which we are familiar.

APPENDIX: CONTAT'S ACCOUNT OF THE CAT MASSACRE

The following account comes from Nicolas Contat, *Anecdotes typographiques où l'on voit la description des coutumes, moeurs et usages singuliers des compagnons imprimeurs,* ed. Giles Barber (Oxford, 1980), pp. 51–53. After a day of exhausting work and disgusting food, the two apprentices retire to their bedroom, a damp and draughty leanto in a corner of the courtyard. The episode is recounted in the third person, from the viewpoint of Jerome:

He is so tired and needs rest so desperately that the shack looks like a palace to him. At last the persecution and misery he has suffered throughout the day have come to an end, and he can relax. But no, some bedeviled cats celebrate a witches' sabbath all night long, making so much noise that they rob him of the brief period of rest allotted to the apprentices before the journeymen arrive for work early the next morning and demand admission by constant ringing of an infernal bell. Then the boys have to get up and cross the courtyard, shivering under their nightshirts, in order to open the door. Those journeymen never let up. No matter what you do, you always made them lose their time and they always treat you as a lazy good-for-nothing. They call for Léveillé. Light the fire under the cauldron! Fetch water for the dunking-troughs! True, those jobs are supposed to be done by the beginner apprentices, who live at home, but they don't arrive until six or seven. Thus everyone is soon at work—apprentices, journeymen, everyone but the master and the mistress: they alone enjoy the sweetness of sleep. That makes Jerome and Léveillé jealous. They resolve that they will not be the only ones to suffer; they want their master and mistress as associates. But how to turn the trick?

Léveillé has an extraordinary talent for imitating the voices and the smallest gestures of everyone around him. He is a perfect actor; that's the real profession that he has picked up in the printing shop. He also can produce perfect imitations of the cries of dogs and cats. He decides to climb from roof to roof until he reaches a gutter next to the bedroom of the bourgeois and the bourgeoise. From there he can ambush them with a volley of meows. It's an easy job for him: he is the son of a roofer and can scramble across roofs like a cat.

Our sniper succeeds so well that the whole neighborhood is alarmed. The word spreads that there is witchcraft afoot and that the cats must be the agents of someone casting a spell. It is a case for the curé, who is an intimate of the household and the confessor of Madame. No one can sleep any more.

Léveillé stages a sabbath the next night and the night after that. If you didn't know him, you would be convinced he was a witch. Finally, the master and the mistress cannot stand it any longer. "We'd better tell the boys to get rid of those malevolent animals," they declare. Madame gives them the order, exhorting them to avoid frightening la grise. That is the name of her pet pussy.

This lady is impassioned for cats. Many master printers are also. One of them has twenty-five. He has had their portraits painted and feeds them on roast fowl.

The hunt is soon organized. The apprentices resolve to make a clean sweep of it, and they are joined by the journeymen. The masters love cats, so consequently they must hate them. This man arms himself with the bar of a press, that one with a stick from the drying-room, others with broom handles. They hang sacks at the windows of the attic and the storerooms to catch the cats who attempt to escape by leaping outdoors. The beaters are named, everything is organized. Léveillé and his comrade Jerome preside over the fête, each of them armed with an iron bar from the shop. The first thing they go for is la grise, Madame's pussy. Léveillé stuns it with a quick blow on the kidneys, and Jerome finishes it off. Then Léveillé stuffs the body in a gutter, for they don't want to get caught: it is a matter of consequence, a murder, which must be kept hidden. The men produce terror on the rooftops. Seized by panic, the cats throw themselves into the sacks. Some are killed on the spot. Others are condemned to be hanged for the amusement of the entire printing shop.

Printers know how to laugh; it is their sole occupation.

The execution is about to begin. They name a hangman, a troop of guards, even a confessor. Then they pronounce the sentence.

In the midst of it all, the mistress arrives. What is her surprise, when she sees the bloody execution! She lets out a scream; then her voice is cut, because she thinks she sees la grise, and she is certain that such a fate has been reserved for her favorite puss. The workers assure her that no one would be capable of such a crime: they have too much respect for the house.

The bourgeois arrives. "Ah! The scoundrels," he says. "Instead of working, they are killing cats." Madame to Monsieur: "These wicked men can't kill the masters, so they have killed my pussy. She can't be found. I have called la grise everywhere. They must have hanged her." It seems to her that all the workers' blood would not be sufficient to redeem the insult. The poor grise, a pussy without a peer!

Monsieur and Madame retire, leaving the workers in liberty. The printers delight in the disorder; they are beside themselves with joy.

What a splendid subject for their laughter, for a *belle copie!* They will amuse themselves with it for a long time. Léveillé will take the leading role and will stage the play at least twenty times. He will mime the master, the mistress, the whole house, heaping ridicule on them all. He will spare nothing in his satire. Among printers, those who excel in this entertainment are called *jobeurs:* they provide *joberie.*

Léveillé receives many rounds of applause.

It should be noted that all the workers are in league against the masters. It is enough to speak badly of them [the masters] to be esteemed by the whole assembly of typographers. Léveillé is one of those. In recognition of his merit, he will be pardoned for some previous satires against the workers.

NOTES

1. Nicolas Contat, *Anecdotes typographiques où l'on voit la description des coutumes, moeurs et usages singuliers des compagnons imprimeurs,* ed. Giles Barber (Oxford, 1980). The original manuscript is dated 1762. Barber provides a thorough description of its background and of Contat's career in his introduction. The account of the cat massacre occurs on pp. 48–56.

2. Contat, *Anecdotes typographiques,* p. 53.

3. Ibid., pp. 52 and 53.

4. See, for example, Albert Soboul, *La France à la veille de la Révolution* (Paris, 1966), p. 140; and Edward Shorter, "The History of Work in the West: An Overview" in *Work and Community in the West,* ed. Edward Shorter (New York, 1973).

5. The following discussion is derived from Henri-Jean Martin, *Livre, pou-*

voirs et société à Paris au XVIIᵉ siècle (1598–1701) (Geneva, 1969); and Paul Chauvet, *Les Ouvriers du livre en France, des origines à la Révolution de 1789* (Paris, 1959). The statistics come from investigations by the authorities of the Old Regime as reported by Martin (II, 699–700) and Chauvet (pp. 126 and 154).

6. For a more detailed discussion of this material, see Robert Darnton, "Work and Culture in an Eighteenth-Century Printing Shop," an Englehard lecture at the Library of Congress to be published by the Library of Congress.

7. Contat, *Anecdotes typographiques,* pp. 68–73.

8. Christ to STN, Jan. 8, 1773, papers of the Société typographique de Neuchâtel, Bibliothèque de la Ville de Neuchâtel, Switzerland, hereafter cited as STN.

9. STN to Joseph Duplain, July 2, 1777.

10. STN to Louis Vernange, June 26, 1777.

11. Joseph Duplain to STN, Dec. 10, 1778.

12. Contat, *Anecdotes typographiques,* pp. 30–31.

13. Ibid., p. 52.

14. For a recent overview of the vast literature on folklore and French history and bibliographic references, see Nicole Belmont, *Mythes et croyances dans l'ancienne France* (Paris, 1973). The following discussion is based primarily on the material collected in Eugène Rolland, *Faune populaire de la France* (Paris, 1881), IV; Paul Sébillot, *Le Folk-lore de France* (Paris, 1904–7), 4 vols., especially III, 72–155 and IV, 90–98; and to a lesser extent Arnold Van Gennep, *Manuel de folklore français contemporain* (Paris, 1937–58), 9 vols.

15. In Germany and Switzerland, *Katzenmusik* sometimes included mock trials and executions. The etymology of the term is not clear. See E. Hoffmann-Krayer and Hans Bächtold-Stäubli, *Handwörterbuch des deutschen Aberglaubens* (Berlin and Leipzig, 1931–32), IV, 1125–32; and Paul Grebe et al., *Duden Etymologie: Herkunftswörterbuch der deutschen Sprache* (Mannheim, 1963), p. 317.

16. Information on the cat burning in Saint Chamond comes from a letter kindly sent to me by Elinor Accampo of Colorado College. The Metz ceremony is described in A. Benoist, "Traditions et anciennes coutumes du pays messin," *Revue des traditions populaires,* XV (1900), 14.

17. Contat, *Anecdotes typographiques,* pp. 30 and 66–67; and Chauvet, *Les Ouvriers du livre,* pp. 7–12.

18. Contat, *Anecdotes typographiques,* pp. 65–67.

19. Ibid., pp. 37–41, quotation from pp. 39–40.

20. A good example of the genre, *La Misère des apprentis imprimeurs* (1710) is printed as an appendix to Contat, *Anecdotes typographiques,* pp. 101–10. For other examples, see A. C. Cailleau, *Les Misères de ce monde, ou complaintes facétieuses sur les apprentissages des différents arts et métiers de la ville et faubourgs de Paris* (Paris, 1783).

21. The classic study of this process is Arnold Van Gennep, *Les Rites de passage* (Paris, 1908). It has been extended by subsequent ethnographic research, notably that of Victor Turner: *The Forest of Symbols: Aspects of Ndembu Ritual* (Ithaca, N.Y., 1967) and *The Ritual Process* (Chicago, 1969). Jerome's experience fits the Van Gennep-Turner model very well, except in a few respects. He was not considered sacred and dangerous, although the chapel could fine journeymen

for drinking with him. He did not live outside adult society, although he left his home for a makeshift room at the edge of the master's household. And he was not exposed to secret *sacra*, although he had to acquire an esoteric lingo and to assimilate a craft ethos after a great deal of tribulation climaxed by a communal meal. Joseph Moxon, Thomas Gent, and Benjamin Franklin mention similar practices in England. In Germany the initiation rite was much more elaborate and had structural similarities to the rites of tribes in Africa, New Guinea, and North America. The apprentice wore a filthy headdress adorned with goat's horns and a fox's tail, indicating that he had reverted to an animal state. As a *Cornut* or *Mittelding*, part man, part beast, he underwent ritual tortures, including the filing of his fingertips. At the final ceremony, the head of the shop knocked off the hat and slapped him in the face. He then emerged newborn—sometimes newly named and even baptized—as a full-fledged journeyman. Such at least was the practice described in German typographical manuals, notably Christian Gottlob Täubel, *Praktisches Handbuch der Buchdruckerkunst für Anfänger* (Leipzig, 1791); Wilhelm Gottlieb Kircher, *Anweisung in der Buchdruckerkunst so viel davon das Drucken betrifft* (Brunswick, 1793); and Johann Christoph Hildebrand, *Handbuch für Buchdrucker-Lehrlinge* (Eisenach, 1835). The rite was related to an ancient popular play, the *Depositio Cornuti typographici*, which was printed by Jacob Redinger in his *Neu aufgesetztes Format Büchlein* (Frankfurt-am-Main, 1679).

22. Contat, *Anecdotes typographiques*, pp. 65–66.

23. The text does not give Jerome's last name, but it stresses the name change and the acquisition of the "Monsieur": "It is only after the end of the apprenticeship that one is called Monsieur; this quality belongs only to journeymen and not to apprentices" (p. 41). In the wage book of the STN, the journeymen always appear with their "Monsieur," even when they were called by nicknames, such as "Monsieur Bonnemain."

24. The black cat in Manet's *Olympia* represents a common motif, the animal "familiar" of a nude. On Baudelaire's cats, see Roman Jakobson and Claude Lévi-Strauss, *"Les Chats* de Charles Baudelaire," *L'Homme*, II (1962), 5–21; and Michel Riffaterre, "Describing Poetic Structures: Two Approaches to Baudelaire's *Les Chats,"* in *Structuralism,* ed. Jacques Ehrmann (New Haven, 1966).

25. Mary Douglas, *Purity and Danger: An Analysis of Concepts of Pollution and Taboo* (London, 1966); and E. R. Leach, "Anthropological Aspects of Language: Animal Categories and Verbal Abuse," in *New Directions in the Study of Language,* ed. E. H. Lenneberg, (Cambridge, Mass., 1964).

26. Cervantes and Zola adapted traditional cat lore to the themes of their novels. In *Don Quixote* (part II, chap. 46), a sack full of howling cats interrupts the hero's serenade to Altisidora. Taking them for devils, he tries to mow them down with his sword, only to be bested by one of them in single combat. In *Germinal* (part V, chap. 6), the symbolism works in the opposite way. A mob of workers pursues Maigrat, their class enemy, as if he were a cat trying to escape across the rooftops. Screaming "Get the cat! Get the cat!" they castrate his body "like a tomcat" after he falls from the roof. For an example of cat killing as a satire on French legalism, see Friar John's plan to massacre the Furry Lawcats in Rabelais' *Gargantua and Pantagruel,* book V, chap. 15.

27. Mikhail Bakhtin, *Rabelais and His World,* trans. Helene Iswolsky (Cam-

bridge, Mass., 1968). The most important literary version of cat lore to appear in Contat's time was *Les Chats* (Rotterdam, 1728) by François Augustin Paradis de Moncrif. Although it was a mock treatise aimed at a sophisticated audience, it drew on a vast array of popular superstitions and proverbs, many of which appeared in the collections of folklorists a century and a half later.

28. C. S. L. Davies, *Peace, Print and Protestantism* (St. Albans, Herts, 1977). The other references come from the sources cited in note 14. Among the many dictionaries of proverbs and slang, see André-Joseph Panckoucke, *Dictionnaire des proverbes françois et des façons de parler comiques, burlesques, et familières* (Paris, 1748); and Gaston Esnault, *Dictionnaire historique des argots français* (Paris, 1965).

29. Rolland, *Faune populaire*, p. 118. See note 14 for the other sources on which this account is based.

30. Emile Chautard, *La Vie étrange de l'argot* (Paris, 1931), pp. 367–68. The following expressions come from Panckoucke, *Dictionnaire des proverbes françois;* Esnault, *Dictionnaire historique des argots françois;* and *Dictionnaire de l'Académie française* (Paris, 1762), which contains a surprising amount of polite cat lore. The impolite lore was transmitted in large measure by children's games and rhymes, some of them dating from the sixteenth century: Claude Gaignebet, *Le Folklore obscène des enfants* (Paris, 1980), p. 260.

31. Sébillot, *Le Folk-lore de France*, III, 93–94.

32. Panckoucke, *Dictionnaire des proverbes françois*, p. 66.

33. This and the following quotations come from Contat's account of the cat massacre, *Anecdotes typographiques*, pp. 48–56.

34. According to Giles Barber (ibid., pp. 7 and 60), the actual Jacques Vincent for whom Contat worked began his own apprenticeship in 1690; so he probably was born about 1675. His wife was born in 1684. Thus when Contat entered the shop, the master was about 62, the mistress about 53, and the bawdy young priest in his twenties. That pattern was common enough in the printing industry, where old masters often left their businesses to younger wives, who in turn took up with still younger journeymen. It was a classic pattern for charivaris, which often mocked disparities in age among newlyweds as well as humiliating cuckolds.

35. Pierre Caron, *Les Massacres de septembre* (Paris, 1935).

FOUR

The Rise of the Saloon

Roy Rosenzweig

In 1829 Ichabod Washburn, the co-owner of a small Worcester machine shop who was later to become the city's leading manufacturer, sought help in building his new house, specifying, however, that there be no provision of rum for the workers. The carpenter was skeptical, since a house-raising "without the stimulus of spirits . . . had not before been done for many years." Most of Washburn's own workmen refused to take part in the experiment. "The work, however," Washburn later recalled, "proceeded noiselessly and successfully to its completion without rum." The local newspaper celebrated the novel achievement under the caption "Progress of the Temperance Reform." Washburn's workmen, however, had a less approving reaction: They watched and, "by their jeers, ridiculed the undertaking, and did their best to make it a failure." [1]

While his workmen laughed, the sober and pious Washburn prospered. At his death in 1868 he presided over a million-dollar manufacturing concern that produced more than half the wire in the United States. The years that marked Washburn's rise from master of a shop with fewer than 30 craftsmen to president of a corporation with more than 700 employees also saw the triumph of his ideas about sobriety and order in the workplace. By the time of Washburn's death a series of seven factory whistles precisely dictated the daily comings and goings of his wireworkers, and detailed, written "Regulations" governed their movements within the factory gates. "There shall be *no change* of workmen from one department to another without *special permission* from the

From Roy Rosenzweig, *Eight Hours for What We Will* (New York: Cambridge University Press, 1983), pp. 35–64 and 240–249. Reprinted with the permission of Cambridge University Press.

office: in which case *both Time-Keepers* will consult with the pay-roll Clerk regarding the keeping of the time," commanded a typical rule.[2]

The large factories of late nineteenth century Worcester would not tolerate the casual informality—the gambling, storytelling, singing, debating, and especially drinking—that had characterized its small workshops in the earlier years of the century or its farms in the previous century. Yet while the factory workers of the 1870s faced a more structured work regimen than the artisans of the 1820s, they also generally had more free time in which to pursue some of the socializing that had been removed from their workday. The drinking that manufacturers like Washburn repressed on the job now found a new temporal and physical locus in public, commercial leisure-time institutions known as saloons. Thus, it was in response to a complex set of social forces—tightened work discipline, shorter workdays, intensified regulation of public recreation, increased working-class incomes—that the saloon emerged as a center of working-class social life.[3] Although the saloon was a commercial enterprise, its ethnic working-class customers still decisively shaped its ritual and character. Somewhat paradoxically, they infused the saloon with a set of values that differed from those of the dominant industrial capitalist society that had given rise to the saloon in the first place.

DRINK AND WORK: THE EMERGENCE OF LEISURE TIME

As Washburn's house-raising experience indicates, workers in the eighteenth and early nineteenth centuries considered drinking an inextricable, and even mandatory, aspect of work. In the shoe shops of Lynn in the 1820s, a half pint of "white eye" was an expected part of the daily wage and the workers themselves financed further heavy drinking. In Rochester workshops of the same period "drinking was universal" and "was embedded in the pattern of irregular work and easy sociability."[4] This intermingling of work and socializing, of work and drink, marked manual as well as artisanal labor. Account books from the building of Worcester's town hall in the 1820s record payments for "labor and grog." Similarly, for the unskilled laborers—mostly Irish immigrants—who toiled from sunrise to sunset building the nation's canals and railroads, the four to six daily breaks for a "jigger" of whiskey provided the only relief from a brutal work regimen. In Worcester the contractors on the Blackstone Canal and the Boston and Worcester Railroad distributed whiskey to Irish immigrant laborers as part of their daily wage. "The rum barrel," writes Worcester Irish antiquarian Richard O'Flynn, "was always near the work—ready for distribution, by this means they kept the men hard at work all day."[5]

The pervasiveness of workplace drinking was hardly surprising in an era when it suffused all areas of life. "Americans between 1790 and 1830," a carefully documented recent study shows, "drank more alcoholic beverages than ever before or since." Even the church was not immune. Under the pulpit of Worcester's Old South Church was a large cupboard containing, "for the accommodation of the congregation, at noon time, a home manufactured beverage from the choicest products of the orchard."[6]

The antebellum temperance crusades, which began in the late 1820s, rapidly undermined the universality of these drinking habits, particularly among the native upper and middle classes. Between 1830 and 1850, according to one estimate, annual per capita consumption of absolute alcohol plummeted from 3.9 gallons to 1 gallon. Testifying before a Massachusetts legislative committee in 1867, Emory Washburn, a Worcester lawyer and a former governor, described the social impact of this new abstinence: "Before 1828 I do not know of any families that pretended to anything like hospitality who did not make a free use of liquor." But by 1867 Washburn noted of these same "respectable" circles that "it was as rare to see liquor offered in a man's house as it would be to see medicine offered."[7]

The early temperance movement appealed particularly to the middle- and upper-class men and women who dined with Emory Washburn. Industrialists and others tied to "the emerging industrial society" led Worcester's temperance movement in the 1830s, according to a recent historian of that movement. And by the 1840s "there was mounting evidence of the broadening appeal of prohibition among not only manufacturers and their allies, but also all respectable and propertied elements in the community." Although some working people—particularly those attracted to revivalist religion—did join the temperance crusades, larger numbers remained attached to their traditional drinking habits and customs. In the 1830s, at least, Worcester workers showed little interest in the city's temperance movement. Of twenty-six temperance activists engaged in manufacturing, at least two-thirds were employers of labor and only one was definitely an employee—and he was a foreman at Ichabod Washburn's new wire works.[8]

The prohibitory ordinances passed by local temperance forces were never fully effective, but new workplace bans on drinking had a more direct impact on popular customs. The Worcester Temperance Society reported in 1831 that twenty-six "mechanics shops" and six "manufactories," employing more than 200 workers in all had banned drinking during work hours and had stopped employing intemperate workmen. Beginning around 1830, then, rules against workplace and workday drinking spread at an uneven pace through innumerable trades and cities. By the late nineteenth century most employers tended to view workplace drinking as part of a bygone era. Oliver Ames, the head of Ames Plow Company, with factories in Worcester and Easton, Massachusetts, commented in 1867 that about thirty years earlier "the work would be frequently broken up by the intemperance of the men. Now we have no trouble of that kind." A New York carriage maker placed the change in his trade in the 1860s. "I can remember twenty or twenty-five years ago," he told a Senate committee in 1883, "when in our trade, even in our shop, there was a constant sending out for beer and spirits, and it was universally permitted." Now, he noted, bringing liquor into the shop "is a violation of rule which affords reason for discharge."[9]

Rules against alcohol consumption were the firmest in the most mechanized industries. Where traditional production methods or heavy manual labor prevailed, drinking was more likely to be tolerated. As late as 1898 the superintendent of Worcester's Sewer Department accepted his workers' consumption of "copious amounts of beer" during their noon break, because "the men had a right to drink when off duty if they chose to do so." Drinking, Dr. Samuel Hartwell told the Massachusetts Bureau of Statistics of Labor, was heaviest among those "who perform labor physically exhaustive, and those who are exposed to extremes of heat and cold." Moreover, when labor was short, even the strictest manufacturers tolerated drinking. "We have to put up with it [intemperance] when help is scarce," one textile manufacturer admitted in 1881. Even where employers successfully repressed on-the-job drinking, they could rarely confine it entirely to weekends and holidays. Excessive Sunday drinking often meant high Monday absenteeism or "blue Mondays."[10]

Despite the exceptions and evasions, numerous government reports demonstrate the growing repression of workplace drinking in the course of the nineteenth century. In 1881, for example, the Massachusetts Bureau of Statistics of Labor questioned workers and manufacturers about intemperance in the textile mills. Only one-sixth of the workers and one-quarter of the manufacturers reported substantial drinking. Sixteen years later a U.S. Department of Labor survey of 30,000 employers found that more than three-quarters considered an employee's drinking habits in hiring decisions.[11]

The gradual tightening of workplace discipline—as exemplified by the anti-drink regulations—was accompanied by a more favorable change for the working class: the gradual shortening of the workday. The precise connection between these two developments is difficult to specify, but they appear to have occurred in tandem. Agitation for the ten-hour day, for example, began in the mid-1820s at the same time that men like Washburn were challenging such basic forms of workplace sociability as drinking. Rochester carpenters—"unable," according to one historian, "to control their conditions of work or to mix work and leisure"—struck in 1834 and announced: "We will be faithful to our employers during the ten hours and no longer." Although such other motives as the desire to reduce pervasive unemployment influenced movements for the shorter workday, the growing articulation of a "right to leisure" played an important part. What workers wanted, the Knights of Labor explained, was "more of the leisure that rightfully belongs to them." The "division and specialization of labor" and the "intensity" of work dictated by "modern methods in industry" had reduced "the social opportunities of the masses," an American Federation of Labor pamphlet similarly argued; the only solution was "more leisure, more physical and mental repose, more and larger periods of relief, from the strain which the specialized industrial life imposes."[12]

As early as the 1840s the ten-hour movement had begun to have some impact, particularly in Massachusetts. In 1845, for example, workers at T. K. Earle's Machine Shop and Foundry in Worcester won a two-hour daily reduction to ten hours. Early the following year the Worcester Workingmen's Association invited "the employers of this village to meet us at our weekly meetings and show cause, if they have any, why *men* ought to work more than ten hours a day." And by the early 1850s the ten-hour day was "all but universal" among Worcester's skilled mechanics.[13]

Progress was, of course, uneven and varied enormously by industry. Massachusetts textile workers, for example, made some gains in the 1850s, but many continued to work eleven and a half to twelve hours until the 1874 law mandated ten hours for women and children. Even then, longer hours remained quite common. In 1879 a letter writer to the *Worcester Evening Star* wondered: "Why is Packachoag Mill, South Worcester, allowed to run 13 hours a day, or is the ten hour law of any use but to fill the Statute book?" In general, however, the political and economic struggles of the working class brought shorter workdays. In 1830 eleven hours per day or more was the standard at more than half the establishments surveyed in a U.S. Census Bureau study; by 1860 the figure had dropped to less than one-third. In Massachusetts, at least, ten hours was the "normal" workday in the 1870s and 1880s with 80 percent of 2,500 firms surveyed by the Bureau of Statistics of Labor in 1883 reporting the ten-hour day.[14]

Workers used their increased leisure time in a wide range of ways: gossiping with neighbors, lounging in pool halls, studying in night classes, visiting dance halls, mending worn clothing, organizing temperance societies, tending gardens, raising money for their churches, arguing over trade union strategy, and watching melodramas. But for many, drinking occupied an important portion of their growing, but still limited, leisure hours. Indeed, it is hardly surprising that a diversion like drinking, which

had once played such a central role during work time, would also have
a central place in leisure time. In a similar way, the songs that had once
modulated the work rhythms of black manual laborers did not disappear
with mechanization and urbanization; black music—in the form of the
blues—found a new home in leisure time rather than work time.[15] In
both cases, the diverse customs and traditions that once dominated the
workplace continued to shape newly emerging leisure-time institutions.
The saloon and similar working-class leisure institutions thus developed
in the context of tightening work discipline and decreasing work hours.
But just as the saloon owed its existence to the growing temporal separation of drinking and working, of socializing and working, it was also
predicated on the growing spatial separation of male sociability from the
home.

FROM *SHEBEEN* TO SALOON: THE EMERGENCE OF LEISURE SPACE

Formal drink places—taverns—existed in Worcester almost from its first
founding in the late seventeenth century. By the 1730s Worcester had
five well-regarded taverns with four of the proprietors holding town of-
fices. By the time of the temperance crusades of the 1820s, however, the
taverns had begun to lose their social respectability: None of the seventeen tavernkeepers in 1828 held an important town office. Their status
declined further with the rise of temperance sentiment among the "respectable" citizens of Worcester and the passage of various prohibitory
ordinances, beginning in 1835 and remaining in effect with only temporary breaks until 1875.[16]

These anti-drink measures had a limited impact on the drink trade.
The city's small police force, which consisted of just one watchman before 1851, could not effectively enforce the law. When Mayor Henry
Chapin attempted to suppress liquor traffic in 1850, pro-drink protest-
ers responded by bombing his office. Even the use of special police and
vigorous prosecutions "did not substantially suppress the sale of liquor,"
one Worcester mayor admitted. In the late 1850s, for example, with
Worcester under a strict anti-drink ordinance, a socially prominent Worcesterite met an acquaintance of his from New Orleans on the street in
Worcester. The New Orleans man suggested they go for a drink. The
Worcesterite replied: "You cannot get anything to drink here, the places
for the sale of liquor have all been closed up." But the New Orleans man
(who had been in the city only two days) corrected him: "Why, yes you
can; I have been to more than twenty places here in this city."[17]

At least a few of these illicit drink places—the Bay State House, for
example—even catered to the city's more "respectable" citizens. But most

working-class drinking went on in much less formal and elegant surroundings. As early as the 1830s the city's pioneer Irish laboring community had established a number of popular *shebeens* (unlicensed and
home- or kitchen-based liquor sellers) of the type so common in nineteenth century Ireland. In the 1840s and 1850s on the immigrant and
working-class East Side of the city, Worcester Irish historian Vincent E.
Powers notes, "temperance laws had little effect and illegal shebeens and
blind-pigs continued to operate. Irish freighters and railroad crews found
an eager market for the liquor they easily smuggled into the city."
Throughout Massachusetts those in contact with working-class neighborhoods observed the same close connection of drink selling and home
life in the face of official prohibition statues. A Boston Catholic priest
observed that "among the poorer classes . . . in almost every house (and
every tenement having a number of families in it) they have some liquor,
and they sell it to those in the house." [18]

Although there is only limited descriptive evidence, it is unlikely that
these kitchen barrooms were especially lavish or spacious since they shared
the physical limitations of most working-class dwellings of this period.
Even skilled workers in Worcester could not expect to house a family of
five in anything larger than a five-room apartment. Unskilled laborers—
often immigrants with larger families—lived in more crowded conditions. An investigator for the Bureau of Statistics of Labor in 1875 found
a Worcester Irish laborer and his family of eight living in a four-room
tenement, which provided only "two privies for about fifty people." [19] In
such a setting a shebeen was likely to be little more than a table and a
few chairs set up in the kitchen or bedroom of a tenement or three-
decker apartment.

Massachusetts's passage of a comprehensive liquor license law in 1875,
which finally allowed the legal operation of public drink places, did not
immediately remove drink selling from its location in the kitchens and
bedrooms of these working-class tenements. In the poorest sections of
the city drinking continued to take place in the "amateur grog shops"
and kitchen barrooms that had predominated during the prohibition
era of the previous three decades. When City Marshal James Drennan
raided the home of Bridget McCarthy in the Irish working-class district
known as the Island, he found seven men and women sitting in the kitchen
with a number of beer glasses on the table and two barrels of beer on
draft in the front room. Leaving the apartment was a young woman
carrying a pail of beer home to her family. On the same day Drennan
also visited the house of John Mehan on nearby Ward Street and found
four people sitting in the front room "with beer glasses frothing" and a
table set with beer. "A man with a pail of beer was talking to Mehan
outside the door [and] went off in a hurry as we entered," Drennan

reported. Some raids turned up rather elaborate equipment and provisions. In the cellar of John Mehan's Ward Street neighbor John Daily police officers found fifty gallons of ale in two barrels, two gallons of whiskey in two jugs and three bottles, twenty-four bottles of lager beer, and smaller quantities of rum and gin. A pipe connected the barrels of ale to the kitchen faucet.[20]

Many of these Irish kitchen saloonkeepers did not bother to take out licenses under the 1875 law, particularly since they could not afford the $200 required for a first-class license or the $100 for a second-class license (beer and light wine only), given their marginal profits. Moreover, fines imposed on the few violators actually prosecuted were usually small ($10 and costs) and often could be avoided by appeal to sympathetic judges and juries. Of 245 people prosecuted for liquor violations during the first four years of the license law only 35 faced any immediate fine or imprisonment; most cases were simply lost in the drawn-out appeal process. The nature of search and seizure laws and the location of sales in private dwellings further hindered the process of obtaining liquor law convictions. City Marshal W. Ansel Washburn complained: "It is not hard to detect the places where the article is kept and sold, even though it be in the privacy of the kitchen or bedroom. Yet, as the law now stands, an officer, in attempting to enforce the same, would become a trespasser."[21]

The centrality of women as both sellers and consumers of liquor in the kitchen grog shops further emphasizes their close connection to immigrant home and family life. Arrest records give ample evidence of the prominence of Irish women drink sellers in Worcester. Whenever temperance-minded Worcester mayors of the 1850s and 1860s decided to crack down on illegal liquor selling, the most immediate impact was that "half a dozen Irish women [would] . . . be sent to the house of correction."[22]

Whereas Worcester officials viewed these female liquor dealers as disreputable and criminal, the Irish community apparently looked at them quite differently. In Ireland the keeping of a shebeen was a "recognized resource of widows," and they had a "privileged" status in the liquor trade. In Worcester Irish immigrants continued to insist on the propriety of this form of communal charity, despite the failure of American laws to recognize it. Almost invariably, a woman arrested for illegal liquor selling would plead, as did Honora Lyon, that "she was compelled to sell a little beer and whiskey in order to make a living. She was sick, destitute and unable to provide for herself and child without having recourse to liquor selling." Even Irish temperance supporters might also affirm the communal impulses behind the shebeen. On the same day that he denounced liquor dealers, James H. Mellen, editor of the *Worces-*

ter Daily Times, complained of police raids on "hard working honest women and cripples," who were entitled to "sympathy."[23]

The practices, as well as the proprietorship, of the kitchen grog shops indicate their close connection to the home and the everyday patterns of Irish immigrant life. Often operating outside the established legal framework, these shops casually dispensed liquor at all hours to friends and neighbors, men and women alike, for both on- and off-premise consumption. Although more formal and more public drink places existed well before the 1870s, much drinking in that decade and even later remained rooted in the more informal and less visible kitchen grog shop. The saloon, as a spatially distinct public and commercialized leisure-time institution, had not yet entirely triumphed.

Gradually, however, the tighter regulations did have some impact, and Worcester saloons began to emerge from the back rooms and kitchens and take on a more standardized and regulated form. Initially, the Board of Aldermen did not discriminate very carefully in their selection of licensees, issuing an average of 235 licenses yearly over the first four years of licensing. In 1879, however, the Board of Aldermen decided to cut back sharply and so issued only 131 licenses.[24] Although the Board of Aldermen never articulated their motives in the license cutbacks, their targets—women, economically marginal operators, and saloons outside of downtown—reveal their goal of ending the kitchen grog shop and fostering the public working-class saloon.

Women—the group most commonly identified with the kitchen trade—were the most visible victims of the license shake-up. Forty-one women, who comprised 22 percent of all saloonkeepers in 1878, lost their licenses during the next two years. Only two women managed to hang on in the drink trade by obtaining fourth-class grocer's licenses. R. G. Dun and Company credit ratings of Worcester saloonkeepers make clear the marginal financial status of those—both men and women—who lost their licenses after 1878. A rating of "worthless" in 1878 or 1879 invariably presaged the loss of one's liquor license within the next year or two. The saloonkeepers themselves were well aware of this economic discrimination in the award of licenses. "One Who Knows How the Thing Works" wrote to the *Worcester Evening Star* to complain of "the injustice shown vs. *small dealers* in liquor."[25] In addition to gender and economic status, location figured importantly in the 1878–80 license cutbacks. In those two years the Board of Aldermen eliminated more than 85 percent of the saloons in areas more than a half mile from City Hall. The Irish working-class Island district lost fifteen of its existing seventeen licensed drink places.

The effect of the license cutbacks was to eliminate the least public and visible, the hardest-to-regulate, and the least capitalized drink places. In

so doing, the board, in effect, endorsed the creation of a more standardized and public institution—the late nineteenth century saloon—as a leisure place clearly separated from both work and home. This spatial segregation was given legal force in 1880 with the passage of a state law
prohibiting liquor licenses for premises with "any interior connection or
communication with any apartments occupied as a residence or for lodging purposes." The passage that same year of a "screen law," which prohibited obstructions of "a view of the interior" of the saloon as well as
side and back doors, further removed drinking from the private, informal world of the home-based kitchen barroom and set it in a public,
recreational institution.[26]

Naturally, the kitchen barrooms that seem to have been the predom-
inant Irish drinking places in the 1850s and 1860s (and remained prominent in the 1870s) did not simply disappear with the decrees of the
Board of Aldermen. "Certain it is," one local paper commented in 1879
of those who lost their licenses, "that some of them will continue to sell
in the defiance of the law." The police records confirm this prediction.
Almost 30 percent of those prosecuted for illegal liquor sales between
May 1880 and May 1881 had been legal licensees before the 1878–80
purges. Typically, those prosecuted kitchen barroom proprietors lived
in working-class neighborhoods and operated out of either their home
or a small grocery store. In 1878, for example, Alice Dignan ran a saloon
out of her home on 23 Nashua Street, near the Washburn and Moen
North Works, where her husband, Peter, was a laborer. Although she
lost her license in the 1879 shake-up, the Dignans appear to have retained their kitchen saloon for which they were prosecuted at least once
in 1880 and twice in 1882. When police raided the Dignans in 1880, they
found Alice serving four large glasses of beer in the kitchen and ample
supplies of lager beer, ale, whiskey, and gin hidden in the bedroom and
cellar.[27]

Although unlicensed and kitchen-based liquor selling continued well
into the twentieth century, public, legal, and formal saloons dominated
the drink trade in Worcester by the mid-1880s. According to the R. G.
Dun credit records, unlicensed dealers appear to have stayed in business
for only about a year and a half on the average after they lost their
licenses. In part, the demise of the kitchen sellers reflected surveillance
and prosecutions by an increasingly professional police force. Between
1869 and 1878 prosecutions for liquor violations averaged about thirty-
two per year, but in the next ten-year period they quadrupled. A single
liquor seizure could be enough to put a marginal dealer out of business.
In addition, unlicensed liquor dealers could not easily obtain credit.[28]
Finally, the kitchen barrooms simply could not compete with the better
appointed and more spacious legal saloons. Working-class patrons, not

just government regulators, ultimately preferred the public saloon over the kitchen grog shop.

The gradual emergence of the saloon as a leisure space clearly distinct from home thus gave workers a more comfortable and appealing place to spend their leisure time. But most working-class women did not share in this modest improvement in working-class life. For married women who did not engage in paid labor, recreation was an integral part of everyday life; in effect, they mixed work and play much in the manner of the early nineteenth century artisan. Thus, despite their home-centered responsibilities, women could have an important place in the kitchen barrooms as both proprietors and customers. However, when leisure was removed from the home or its immediate vicinity, it became predominantly a male privilege. While some women continued to patronize saloons, these public leisure spaces increasingly became male preserves. In this way, the male saloon became a mirror image of the male factory.

THE LIQUOR BUSINESS: THE EMERGENCE OF LEISURE SPENDING

The development of the saloon as a leisure institution temporally distinct from work and spatially distinct from home thus represented a contradictory series of gains and losses for Worcester workers: a decrease in control over work combined with an increase in free time; the demise of a traditional, home-centered, and sexually integrated gathering place along with the development of a more ample and comfortable public meeting spot. The economic context for the rise of the saloon had an equally mixed character: a growth in working-class incomes coupled with the extraction of a portion of those incomes by a commercial liquor business.

Although statistics on nineteenth century working-class incomes are unreliable and controversial, most historians agree that real wages rose in the second half of the century. Clarence Long, for example, argues that both daily and annual earnings increased about 50 percent between 1860 and 1890.[29] Discretionary expenditures for such items as amusement and alcohol probably increased with these growing—albeit still inadequate—real incomes.

Yet discretionary spending could not expand in a vacuum; it was also necessary that amusement and alcohol become purchasable commodities. In fact, both processes occurred together. In the late nineteenth century such commodities became both available and affordable to more and more working-class consumers. In comparing working-class family budgets from 1874 and 1901, historian John Modell finds more spending for virtually all nonessential items. For example, workers were more likely to rely on cash-bought and publicly consumed alcohol than on home-produced drink. In 1889 only 30 percent of the native-American families and 42 percent of the Irish-born families completing family budgets for the Bureau of Statistics of Labor listed any annual expenditures for alcoholic beverages. By 1901, however, these figures had jumped by about half.[30]

In this context, increased public consumption of alcohol might indicate the growing prosperity of the working class rather than its pathological degeneration, as it is sometimes depicted. According to an 1889 survey by the U.S. Department of Labor, the best paid workers were 50 percent more likely to purchase "indulgences" like alcohol and tobacco than those at the bottom of the income scale. "The workers who drank the most," historian Michael Marrus writes similarly of *Belle Epoque* France, "were not the most miserable, not those who were drowning their socioeconomic sorrows, but rather those with time and money to spend." What happened, Marrus argues, "was that as working conditions began to improve, and as wages slowly went up, workers naturally turned to drink during a transitional period because they were still adjusting to a more affluent state of affairs. What was new to them was the prospect of having any pleasure at all which was not furtively snatched from the grip of necessity." Indeed, beneath the persistent middle- and upper-class complaints about the "extravagance" and "thriftlessness" of working-class drinking habits lay a recognition and resentment of this nascent "prosperity." Speaking of skilled mechanics in 1883, the secretary of the New York Board of Health admitted that "they all do what I would like to do now, and what I do a good deal of myself—they smoke a great deal; they drink considerable, more or less, and I think their families are extravagant."[31]

Drinking and the saloon, then, offered recreational diversions well suited to growing, but still modest, working-class incomes. As a result, a liquor business developed, particularly from the middle to the late nineteenth century, to take advantage of this emerging market. In Worcester the growth of the drink trade, which was especially rapid in the 1870s and 1880s, can be charted in the careers of successful liquor dealers and saloonkeepers. In 1860s Worcester, liquor selling offered neither social respectability nor economic security. In 1863, for example, R. G. Dun and Company entered its first report on George F. Hewitt, who had started a liquor business in Worcester in 1860: He "is entirely unworthy of credit . . . no reliance can be placed on him in the matter of business." A few months later they cautioned creditors: "Public opinion . . . added to the liquor law is great inducement to repudiate." These warnings proved prescient, as Hewitt suffered both arrest and bankruptcy in the next twelve years. But Hewitt's remarkable success in the late 1870s and early

1880s suggests "boom" conditions in the Worcester drink business in that period. By 1882 the previously bankrupt and disreputable Hewitt had been a member of the Board of Aldermen, erected a block of stores and tenements, and was estimated to be worth $50,000.[32]

Even more dramatic was the success of John and Alexander Bowler, who entered the brewery business in Worcester in 1883. Within three years they had tripled their output and within six years their net worth had multiplied more than six times. The success of Hewitt and the Bowlers reflected the expansion of the Massachusetts liquor industry in these years. Between 1865 and 1885 the capitalization of the industry multiplied almost ten times, the number of employees three times, and the number of firms four times.[33]

Worcester saloonkeepers shared in this prosperity. In December 1885 the *Worcester Sunday Telegram* recalled that in the late 1870s Worcester "rumsellers had just emerged from the trials of the prohibition years" and "were as poor as the men they had sent to the almshouse." But "of late years their incomes have rapidly increased, and they have indulged in fast horses, elegant apparel, a self-contented swagger, and above all, have from year to year increased their political power." This new affluence was reflected in more lavish and more businesslike saloons. "The old homely and ungrateful beer saloons of the last generation have given way to comfortable and costly premises where liquor is now dispensed to the impatient consumer," the *Sunday Telegram* commented in 1886. As the *Telegram*'s language indicates, the saloon had become more of a commercial institution with drink as a commodity, the worker as a consumer, and the saloonkeeper as a businessman. Although Worcester's rum sellers were hardly considered "respectable" by the city's Yankee elite, they were becoming reasonably stable small-business men. To cite just one example of many recorded by Irish antiquarian Richard O'Flynn and the credit reporters from R. G. Dun: John McGrail was "not worth anything of any account" in 1875, but by 1884 he was doing "a good business" and was worth at least $2,000.[34]

But one should not exaggerate saloonkeeper affluence: Very few managed any substantial accumulations of wealth. "Doing a modest living," "doing well in a small way," or "gets a living" were the most often reported comments in the credit reports. Indeed, the insufficiently capitalist mentality of the saloonkeepers seems to have frustrated the more aggressive credit investigators. They implicitly chastise the saloonkeepers for living too extravagantly, for failing to "accumulate," and for not being very "progressive."[35] Apparently, many saloonkeepers were content to earn a modest working-class income from their businesses and had no larger aspirations.

Although saloonkeepers were not always aggressive entrepreneurs,

by the late nineteenth century in Worcester (and perhaps earlier elsewhere) they presided over a clearly commercial leisure-time institution.
Indeed, the very term "saloon" was a relatively new one, which suggested the spaciousness and luxury of a French salon or a large cabin on
a passenger ship. The word was used as early as 1841, but it seems to
have only come into common usage in Worcester after the Civil War and
particularly in the 1870s. Richard O'Flynn, writing in 1880, refused to
use the newer term: "I must be pardoned for the use of the word 'Rum
Shop.' I cannot conscientiously give any other name no matter how magnificent the surroundings."[36]

Despite O'Flynn's resistance, the saloon had triumphed. Its emergence was rooted in long-term changes: the separation of work and play,
the segregation of recreation from home life, and the commercialization
of this leisure time and space. Although the changes were broad and
general, their impact was class-specific. The emergence of the saloon
depended upon and reflected improvements in working-class living
standards: the achievement of growing amounts of leisure time free from
the constraints of the workplace, the development of alternative spaces
to spend that leisure time away from crowded homes and tenements,
and the possession of sufficient disposable income to purchase more than
the bare necessities of life. Yet the rise of the saloon equally grew out of
the subordination of the working class: its lack of freedom at the workplace, its very limited free time and disposable income, and its inferior
housing conditions. Thus, as Worcester's saloons formalized and grew
in the late nineteenth century, they remained decisively shaped by the
circumstances—both economic and cultural—of the city's large immigrant working class.

THE ETHNIC WORKING-CLASS SALOON:
PROPRIETORS AND PATRONS

In April 1885 three Irish-Catholic pastors startled local liquor dealers,
as well as members of their congregations, with a bold attack on the
drink trade. The Reverend John J. McCoy reportedly "denounced the
saloons as hells, and their owners as murderers." What made this rebuke
surprising was its source in the Irish-Catholic clergy, who ministered to
most of the city's saloonkeepers. Seventeen of the nineteen applicants
for liquor licenses in Sacred Heart parish belonged to that church, its
pastor, the Reverend Thomas Conaty, ruefully admitted. And two-thirds
of all Worcester liquor license applicants were Irish, whereas only one-
third of the city's population was of Irish origin, the Reverend Thomas
Griffin added.[37]

The 1880 U.S. Manuscript Census confirms these clerical estimates.

Although only one-sixth of Worcester's people were born in Ireland, about half of the 1880 saloonkeepers who could be traced into the census were Irish natives, and another 10 percent were the children of Irish immigrants. Even more overrepresented in the drink trade, however, were the Germans, who made up less than 1 percent of the city's population but more than 15 percent of its saloonkeepers. A nativist rhyme popular in Worcester after the Civil War captured the ethnic flavor of its drink trade: "The Irish and the Dutch; they don't amount to much, / For the Micks have their whiskey and the Germans guzzle the beer, / And all we Americans wish they had never come here."[38]

Although nativists blamed the drink trade entirely on immigrants, at least one-fifth of the saloonkeepers in 1880 were identifiable as "American." A few of the native-stock saloonkeepers kept relatively respectable restaurants, which also dispensed beer and liquor, but the others were part of a "sporting crowd," which spurned the Protestant values of their fellow "Americans." "A little flashy . . . likes to live well and make a show," the R. G. Dun credit investigator wrote of one. "Rather fond of horseflesh," he observed of another. In 1875 when native-born Worcester machinist A. V. Newton wrote *The Saloon Keeper's Companion* and subtitled it *Sporting Manual*, he probably had these saloonkeepers in mind.[39]

As Worcester's other ethnic communities—French Canadian, English, and Swedish—grew in the late nineteenth century, they also developed their own drink centers. As early as the 1860s the Christopher brothers established the first French-Canadian saloon in Worcester, and there were four or five French-Canadian saloons throughout the 1870s and 1880s. Despite occasional rumblings of temperance sentiment among their clergy, French-Canadian liquor dealers generally received respect within their community. The local French newspapers, for example, proudly reported the number of French Canadians who had received liquor licenses each year. Revocation of one of these licenses could provoke community protests. In 1891, for example, the *Worcester Telegram* reported that "many of the Frenchmen are considerably annoyed because [Adrien] Girardin has been refused a license. His place is just below St. Jean Baptiste Hall, and was quite a rallying place for some of the French people when anything was going on in the hall."[40]

The smaller community of English carpet weavers in South Worcester also appears to have supported three or four saloons. Worcester's Swedes . . . were much less indulgent of the liquor trade. Nevertheless, Swedish saloons began to develop by the late 1880s despite the vociferous opposition of Swedish fundamentalists. The Swedish newspaper *Skandinavia* reflected the more indulgent view of at least one segment of the Swedish community when it asked: "Would it perhaps not be preferable to have our young men spend their time in a Scandinavian saloon as opposed to

Irish, German, and American saloons, where they now spend their time?"[41]

Although Worcester saloons drew on ethnic communities and ethnically rooted drinking habits, they also operated in a specifically working-class context.[42] In 1891 a temperance-minded publication complained about the after-work pattern of the city's ethnically diverse work force: "Watch the 'dinner pail' brigade as it files down, at nightfall, from the shops north of Lincoln Square and see how many men and boys drop into the saloons along the north end of Main Street." Whatever the views of its founder and its management, a location near Washburn and Moen's North Works usually proved quite lucrative for the saloonkeeper. Patrick J. Welch's business picked up considerably when he moved his saloon to that area. Washburn and Moen's South Works provided an equally eager clientele. In May 1893 John Reynolds managed to obtain a license in the vicinity of that factory. On the first day of business wireworkers—presumably representing the different ethnic groups that toiled at the South Works—flooded into Reynolds's saloon on the first floor of a Millbury Street tenement and crowded around the bar three-deep.[43]

Drinking, of course, was not limited to the working class. But saloon-going was. Those in the middle and upper classes who did drink—and the numbers were probably considerably smaller than among the working class in the late nineteenth century—generally drank at home, private clubs, or expensive hotels. At the exclusive Worcester Club, members apparently formed a "yellow label club" through which they purchased liquor as a group. Similarly, the Worcester Daily Times noted that the "rich scions of nobility" who are "not seen at a public bar . . . have the good stuff at home."[44]

Working-class dominance of public drinking places produced a corresponding working-class predominance among those arrested for public drunkenness. The published Worcester police statistics do not break down drunkenness arrests by occupation, but they do report all arrests by occupation. From these figures it is possible at least to infer that unskilled laborers made up a disproportionate number of those arrested for excessive drinking. During years in which drunkenness arrests went up, arrests of laborers always increased at a much faster rate than those of other occupational groups.[45] The same pattern appears in other criminal and drunkenness statistics. In an 1881 Bureau of Statistics of Labor study of Massachusetts "criminals," laborers were three times as likely to be excessive drinkers as clerks and only one-third as likely to be total abstainers. Similarly, of those arrested for drunkenness in Worcester during June 1880, who could be located in that year's Worcester Directory, almost three-quarters held unskilled or semiskilled jobs.[46] In part, this occupational profile helps to explain the Irish dominance of those arrested for drunkenness. The Irish were particularly concentrated in jobs—

especially manual, outdoor labor, and transport—that allowed and encouraged heavy drinking. Although heavy drinking and saloongoing were not necessarily equivalent, it seems likely that many of those arrested for public drunkenness were also regular saloon patrons.

Not only did the saloons draw a largely working-class clientele, they also possessed a "working-class" management. While saloonkeepers were by definition small-business people, they should not be automatically assigned to a "middle-class" category. In the late nineteenth century, at least, Worcester saloonkeepers seem to have shown strong ties to, and identification with, their working-class customers. The social origins of the saloonkeepers provide one clue. Of forty-seven saloonkeepers in 1900 who were traced back ten years in the *Worcester Directory*, thirteen were already saloonkeepers and four were bartenders. But of the thirty-one not in the drink trade in 1890, more than two-thirds held blue-collar positions. Saloonkeepers in 1880 and 1918 shared these humble origins. For example, Michael Murphy, an overweight, clean-shaven, and unmarried Green Street saloonkeeper known to his patrons as "Father Murphy," began his work life as a laborer. He entered the saloon business in 1874, but left in 1882 to visit Ireland. When he returned to Worcester, he worked in a boot and shoe shop for a few years before returning to the liquor trade.[47]

The occupational world of the saloonkeeper, then, was not particularly distinct from that of the blue-collar worker. And, according to the R. G. Dun and Company records, their economic standing was often only marginally better. Most important, many saloonkeepers demonstrated and preserved their working-class ties by living in the same neighborhood as their saloon. In 1880 half of the city's saloonkeepers lived in the same building as their saloon or next door; 90 percent lived within a half mile. In addition, those saloonkeepers who shared their dwelling with other families almost invariably lived alongside blue-collar workers and their families. The native-American saloonkeepers offered the only partial exception to this rule. However, the working-class links of the saloonkeepers began to wane very gradually with growing affluence. By 1900, for example, less than one-eighth lived at the same address or next door, but three-quarters lived within a half mile of their saloon.[48] Whether or not the late nineteenth century Worcester saloonkeeper was a member of the working class, he was part of a working-class community.

THE WORKINGMAN'S CLUB

What explains the strong ties between the working class and the saloon? Most simply, it effectively met the needs of workers. "The saloon, in relation to the wage-earning classes in America," noted Walter Wyckoff, who had studied it firsthand, "is an organ of high development, adapting itself with singular perfectness to its functions in catering in a hundred ways to the social and political needs of men." Public toilets, food, warmth, clean water, meeting space, check-cashing services, newspapers—often otherwise unavailable to workers in the late nineteenth century city— could be found free of charge in the saloon. Often the saloon served as a communications center, a place where workers picked up their mail, heard the local political gossip, or learned of openings in their trade.[49]

Different types of saloons emphasized different features and functions. The "occupational saloon," which drew on customers from a particular trade or factory, for example, promoted its free lunch and its check-cashing services. Ethnic saloons, which attracted more of an evening business, provided a center for such immigrant communal celebrations as weddings and holidays as well as a meeting place for fraternal orders and gangs. The neighborhood saloon might attract a local multiethnic working-class crowd and provide a constituency for small-time politicians.[50] Not all saloons fit neatly into these categories. Some Worcester saloons could be simultaneously "neighborhood," "occupational," and "ethnic." For example, Michael Taylor, a former English carpet weaver, located his saloon on Cambridge Street in the midst of fellow countrymen who worked in the nearby carpet mills.

The utilitarian services of these different types of saloons only partially explain the saloon's attraction to its working-class patrons. More fundamentally, the saloon flourished because of its social and recreational appeal. Social reformers and early sociologists who entered the saloon to "ascertain the secret of its hold" upon the workingman invariably found—often to their surprise—that it was "man's social nature" and his "craving for companionship," rather than a desire for strong drink, that led him to the saloon. Almost three-quarters of 540 people arrested for drunkenness in Boston around 1907 told an inquiring Columbia University graduate student that their "special reason for drinking" was "social." Only 8 percent attributed it to a "taste for drink." Without the benefit of graduate training, a seventy-year-old Irish Fall River worker similarly explained the social and recreational nature of the saloon: "In England, where I was reared, the habit was for a man, when he drew his pay every Saturday night, to go in and enjoy himself. He was not a drunkard; neither do I consider the people of Fall River drunkards. . . . They go in and get their glass of beer as they do in the old country."[51]

The saloonkeeper presided over and fostered this atmosphere of good-hearted, informal socializing. "As a rule," observed the author of the locally published *Saloon Keeper's Companion*, "the saloonkeeper is a jolly,

easy going fellow, free with his money." Even Worcester temperance
advocate Richard O'Flynn, with his hatred for the "vendors of the deadly
cup," found the word "genial" the most appropriate to describe Worcester's rum sellers when he wrote profiles of them: Michael J. Leach was
"a genial, generous man"; William Molloy, "a genial, warm hearted man,
harmless in all save his calling"; and William H. Foley, "full of fun—
always ready with a pleasant anecdote or story." Similarly, when *Light,* a
Worcester society weekly, complained in 1890 of "loud and boisterous
laughter, obscene pleasantries and curses," it also hinted at the cheerful
sociability that prevailed in Worcester saloons.[52]

Upper- and middle-class hostility to the saloongoer's "boisterous
laughter" is hardly surprising since these men and women were probably the butts of barroom humor. *The Saloon Keeper's Companion* provided
Worcester bar owners with about fifty pages of jokes and stories with
which to amuse their customers. The jokes most often ridicule hypocrit-
ical temperance advocates, dishonest police and politicians, unsophisticated and easily fooled clergy and churchgoers, and stupid or pompous
judges.[53]

Singing, like joke- and storytelling, was an important part of the informal socializing that formed the core of saloon life. In other cities saloons offered more formal entertainment, but in Worcester the singing
was usually informal and participatory. The Massachusetts Bureau of
Statistics of Labor denounced the saloongoer's music as "the ribald song
of fellow drunkards." But George Ade, a Chicago columnist who regularly frequented the city's saloons in the 1890s, discerned a more complex pattern. He thought songs about "dear old Mother" were most popular, followed by songs about "the poor girl who was tempted and who
either fell or did not fall." Third most popular were songs about "the
organized workingmen and their nobility of character as compared with
millionaire employers."[54]

In Worcester saloons ethnic music probably accompanied the products of Tin Pan Alley. John C. Blos called his German saloon on Mechanic Street Orchestrion Hall, and his advertisements featured a picture of that elaborate musical device. Patrick Curran, the Irish proprietor
of a saloon known as the Little House Round the Corner, was "fond of
story and song," and "being a very good comic singer, he attracted many
of the gay spirits to his place." No doubt the patrons at the Little House
Round the Corner as well as Worcester's numerous other Irish bars drew
on the rich Irish-American musical heritage. In the late nineteenth century, according to historian Michael Gordon, Irish Americans favored
laments about "loved ones still in Ireland" and "specific rural scenes," as
well as "evocative nationalist verses like Collins's 'Defiant Still.' " All these
songs, Gordon points out, "were fundamentally political because they

spoke of events and sentiments inseparable from a historical context shaped by English and Anglo-Saxon rule."[55]

The singing and storytelling of Worcester barrooms was undoubtedly punctuated by conversations about sports. *The Saloon Keeper's Companion* considered sports rules and the results of major sporting contests as essential knowledge for barkeepers. Patrick Ryan decorated his Mechanic Street saloon "with pictures of pugilists, sprinters, and clogdancers." Sometimes a popular local fighter, like Jack Gray, William H. Foley, or Robert Mahagan, might retire from the ring to become a saloonkeeper, placing his "well-worn boxing gloves" on "the shelf behind the bar" as a reminder of more glorious days. Other saloonkeepers, like Michael Kelley, gained some fame for their intimacy with sporting heroes like John L. Sullivan, whose picture adorned the walls of many, if not most, 1890s saloons.[56]

Prizefighting was illegal in nineteenth century Massachusetts, and, indeed, the saloon often championed the shadier or, at least, less socially approved side of sports. Gambling, whether on cards, billiards, horse races, or sports matches, enlivened many Worcester saloons. In the 1870s those arrested for gambling violations also often found themselves in trouble for illegal liquor sales. Even cockfighting, ostensibly eradicated much earlier in the nineteenth century, enjoyed the patronage of Worcester saloonkeepers and their customers. In 1886, for example, Washington Square saloonkeeper Tim Delaney reportedly led Worcester "sports" to Cherry Valley for cockfights each Sunday morning. The same secluded spot also furnished a locale for illicit prizefights.[57]

For all its importance as a social center, the saloon was not the only recreational outlet for workers in Worcester and other industrial cities. "In this town, as in all others," one worker told the Bureau of Statistics of Labor in 1870, "there is a great difference in the habits and tastes of the working classes." Even the small group who answered a bureau questionnaire on recreation that year amply demonstrated this diversity. Their pursuits included dancing, walking, gardening, skating, ball and billiard playing, bowling, attending minstrel shows and concerts, listening to lectures, and visiting lodge and union halls and reading rooms. Yet, despite this variety of pursuits, probably only the church and the home rivaled the saloon as working-class social centers. Both, however, had important limitations. Even those workers who owned homes usually lacked the space or furniture to accommodate large numbers of visitors. The homes of the unskilled and the immigrant lacked space not only for socializing but often for the needs of everyday life. Tenements in Fall River, complained a local union official in 1883, "have two bedrooms and a kitchen . . . and if a friend comes in they have got to meet him there. . . . There is no comfort at all. If a man had a little room where he could go and read his paper and be comfortable, I think he would be more likely to stay at home instead of going abroad to seek other kinds of enjoyment." A Worcester reformer reached the same conclusion some years later: "A large number of people, men and boys particularly, cannot possibly find or make this reasonable social life in the lodging house or in such a home as falls to their lot."[58]

Lodging-house life provided a particularly strong incentive to seek, as a Cambridge printer put it in 1883, "amusement in public places, in the billiard room, and in the saloon." "In the boarding house," he explained, "there is nothing to entertain or to cheer him; seldom any pictures, or books, or female companionship of the proper kind; and in order to gratify his social faculties he frequently seeks pleasure in the forms in which it is met with in the saloon." In late nineteenth century Worcester the majority of immigrant Irishmen in their early twenties were boarders.[59] And the city's boardinghouse district was within easy walking distance of its largest concentration of saloons.

Single workingmen and -women who lived at home rather than at a boardinghouse faced a different, but related, problem: socializing under the watchful gaze of their parents. This was particularly difficult for Worcester's second-generation Irish males, who did not marry until age thirty-one on the average. Drinking and the saloon seem to have had a central place in their "bachelor" subculture, as it did in Ireland. It is not surprising, then, that relatively young, single males were overrepresented among those arrested for drunkenness.[60]

As a social and cultural force the church undoubtedly had a greater importance than the saloon, particularly for women and fundamentalist Protestants. Nevertheless, many noted its failure to compete effectively with the saloon for the worker's recreational time. "The church doors," complained Worcester reformer U. Waldo Cutler, "are closed except an hour or two on one evening a week, when the 'social meeting' is in progress, and even if these people were to force their way in, the churches would not know how to adapt themselves to their needs." Such complaints, of course, reflect more on the native Protestant churches than on their immigrant, and usually Catholic, counterparts. One manufacturer explained to the Bureau of Statistics of Labor in 1870 that only the Catholics in his community attended services regularly: "The Catholic Church is democratic; the Protestant Church is too aristocratic for the clothes they (the working people) are able to wear." Even the immigrant churches did not reach all their potential parishioners. Only 46 to 66 percent of New York Catholics attended church on Sundays in the 1860s. Moreover, even regular churchgoers saw the saloon as filling recreational needs that were ignored at the church. Some saloongoers, columnist George Ade writes with an exaggeration born of nostalgia, found the church "about as cheerful as a mausoleum while the place on the corner reeked with the kind of unrestrained gayety which has been in partnership with original sin since the beginning of history."[61]

For these reasons, the saloon remained the axis of the recreational world for large numbers of working-class men. One Saturday night in December 1883, several temperance advocates canvassed fifteen saloons between 6 and 10 P.M. and counted 1,832 patrons, "mostly young men." Thus, even if the city's other ninety-three legal drinking places were only half as popular as these, more than 7,500 Worcesterites would have stopped at the saloon that night—a significant percentage of the city's 30,000 males and easily a majority of its young working-class males.[62]

THE CULTURE OF THE SALOON

For many Worcester workers the saloon offered a variety of attractive activities from social services to informal socializing to singing and gambling. But did the late nineteenth century saloon hold any significance beyond its role as a social service and recreational center? Does the nature of the late nineteenth century saloon suggest anything about the central values and beliefs of Worcester workers? Such cultural analysis is inevitably difficult and speculative, particularly in the absence of the firsthand observations that are the stock-in-trade of the cultural anthropologist. Such problems are compounded here because of the diversity of types of saloons (ethnic, neighborhood, and occupational), the diversity of saloongoers (Irish, French Canadians, English, and Yankees; first- and second-generation immigrants; skilled and unskilled), and the changing nature of the saloon, which was undergoing a process of commercialization through which it distinguished itself from the kitchen groggeries that had preceded it. No single set of generalizations can do justice to the range of experiences, social styles, and cultural meanings embodied in the late nineteenth century saloon. Nevertheless, based on the limited available evidence, it does seem possible to argue that many Worcester saloons of the late nineteenth century reflected and reinforced a value system very much different from that which governed the dominant industrial, market, and social relations of that era.

Many observers trumpeted the saloon as "the rooster-crow of the spirit of democracy." It was, proclaimed the Reverend George L. McNutt, "the one democratic club in American life," the "great democratic social settlement." Of course, the saloon was much less open and democratic in fact than these commentators would have us believe. Most saloons at least informally barred members of the "wrong" sex, ethnic group, race, neighborhood, or occupation. Still, the commentators were partially right; the saloon was actually a "democracy" of sorts—an *internal* democracy where all who could safely enter received equal treatment and respect. An ethic of mutuality and reciprocity that differed from the market exchange mentality of the dominant society prevailed within the barroom.[63] Although collective and cooperative social relations were not the exclusive property of the immigrant working class, the saloon was one of the few late nineteenth century institutions that publicly and symbolically celebrated these alternative values.

Some understanding of the potential role of drink and the saloon in fostering this ethic of reciprocity and mutuality can be gained by looking at rural Ireland, the birthplace of many Worcester saloon patrons. "Drinking together," notes anthropologist Conrad Arensberg, "is the traditional reaffirmation of solidarity and equality among males" in Ireland. The most important drink custom for fostering such sentiments was "treating"—"a social law in Catholic Ireland enforced with all the vigour of a Coercion Act," according to one commentator. "If a man happens to be in an inn or public-house alone, and if any of his acquaintances come in, no matter how many, it is his duty to 'stand,' that is, to invite them to drink and pay for all they take. . . . It is a deadly insult to refuse to take a drink from a man, unless an elaborate explanation and apology be given and accepted."[64] Treating thus provided the nineteenth-century Irishman with a crucial means of declaring his solidarity and equality with his kin and neighbors.

These drink rituals were not an isolated sphere of Irish life; they were firmly embedded in a reciprocal life-style that governed at least some social relationships in the Irish countryside. Although the Irish rural economy was subject to external, exploitative, colonial rule, local social and economic relations were often based on a system of mutual rights and obligations rather than a rationalized market of monetary exchange. Helping a neighbor with a house-raising, for example, was often part of that local system of mutual obligation, which existed outside of the realm of direct cash exchange. The liberal provision of liquor at such an event offered a means of reciprocating, of symbolizing one's acceptance of the mutuality, friendliness, and communality on which it was based. A similar mentality lay behind the American work rituals of the eighteenth century and early nineteenth, such as the "chopping frolic," where it was "the practice to *treat* all who came to work." According to Robert Bales, when Irish farmers aided one another or the local gentry with harvesting, the only acceptable "payment" was the abundant provision of liquor, because "it had no utilitarian taint, but indicated good will and friendship, and because it was not in any exact sense 'payment in full,' but implied a continued state of mutual obligation."[65]

The precise connection between these reciprocal Irish drink customs and the rituals of Worcester saloons is difficult to demonstrate. Even less certain is how the prior background of other Worcester workers shaped their saloon behavior. What is striking, however, is the degree to which reciprocal modes—similar to those found in rural Ireland—seem to have operated within the new context of the ethnic working-class saloon. The most persuasive evidence of these modes is found in what the Massachusetts Bureau of Statistics of Labor called "the prevailing custom of treating." Observers as diverse as Upton Sinclair, Jack London, Thorstein Veblen, and the Anti-Saloon League cited the centrality of treating in the saloon of the late nineteenth and early twentieth centuries. "Here in noisy carousal," commented an 1871 observer, "the 'treat' goes round, the poor vanity of the free-hearted meets its reward, the mean man is scorned."[66]

These treating rituals embodied a resistance of sorts to the transformation of social relationships into "commodities"—a means of preserving reciprocal modes of social interaction within a capitalist world. Jack London, for example, explained his realization of the non-economic mutuality behind treating: "I had achieved a concept. Money no longer counted. It was comradeship that counted." This ethic was probably strongest in the least commercialized saloons and drink places. Patronage of the shebeen, for example, rested on larger notions of communal obligation for the well-being of widows. Similarly, when Worcester City Marshal Drennan caught John Mehan illegally serving liquor on a Sunday in 1880, Mehan simply explained that "he was *treating* some friends and a greenhorn (girl) named Leonard." Bridget McCarthy offered precisely the same explanation for the illegal liquor trade going on in her house.[67] In a sense, these may not have been alibis: The system of treating was based on an ethic of mutuality that was simply not reducible to the sort of market exchange that the police sought as proof of illegal liquor sales.

Of course, this was only partially true. The saloon was an increasingly commercial institution and alcohol was a commodity to be bought and sold. Veblen even explained treating as a working-class variant of "conspicuous consumption." Temperance reformers complained that saloonkeepers manipulated "hospitality" and the "social instinct" to their own economic advantage. In an editorial calling "treating" the "curse of this age in the U.S." a Worcester Catholic temperance newspaper described what it saw as the saloonkeeper's manipulation: "If two men not previously acquainted . . . come into his bar-room together . . . he introduces them and sets the ball rolling. Two or three rounds of drink are not enough for him. He is getting the money. So he produces the dice box and proposes 'to shake' for the drinks. He never lets up as long as his customers can stand on their feet and there is any money in sight."[68]

Although few saloonkeepers so baldly "traded" on the "social instinct," saloongoers did increasingly enact their reciprocal treating rituals within the commercialized confines of the saloon. Despite the contradiction, the prevalence and persistence of the custom points to a continuing predilection for reciprocal forms of social interaction. Itself a product of a commercializing society, the saloon became a refuge for values implicitly hostile to such a society.

As "a norm of equality and solidarity," treating rituals implied resistance to individualism as well as acquisitiveness. Indeed, the whole saloongoing experience affirmed communal over individualistic and privatistic values. After 1800, historian W. J. Rorabaugh notes, "drinking in groups . . . became a symbol of egalitarianism. All men were equal before the bottle." Inebriation further encouraged the breaking down of social barriers.[69] For some, to be sure, saloongoing was a solitary experience, but for most it was a group activity. It was a way of carousing with friends, neighbors, and fellow workers whom one could not (or should not) bring into the home. And because such socializing took place outside the home, it was more of a public occasion, and therefore open to a much wider group than the kinfolk that one might normally bring into the home. More than just the size of the gathering, the nature of the event—the drinking, singing, talking, card playing, billiard shooting—brought workers together for a collective public sharing of their recreation. As such, the saloon rejected the developing individualistic, privatistic, and family-centered values of the dominant society.

The saloon clashed with the values of industrial America not just in its communality and mutuality but also in the unwillingness of some patrons to endorse fully the work ethic of that society. Critics of drinking frequently lumped together the very rich and the very poor as unproductive classes "most exposed to the temptation of intemperate drinking." Employers, beginning in Ichabod Washburn's day, depicted drinking as a major threat to steady work habits. Thus, the Washburn and Moen Wire Manufacturing Company petitioned against saloons in the vicinity of their North Works because "the opportunities for slipping into a dram shop either on the way to work or from work, make it so much easier for the men to squander their wages which means a lessening of their efficiency for us."[70]

Not only did drinking and the squandering of wages lead to a loss of work efficiency; it also made it difficult for workers to move ahead in socially approved ways. Temperance advocates repeatedly pointed out that the money spent on drink might instead go toward "a modest working class home." The Worcester Five Cents Savings Bank, "the poor man's bank," claimed a one-third increase in local deposits during one no-license year. "It cannot be emphasized too strongly," Stephan Thernstrom writes in his study of nineteenth-century social mobility, "that the real estate holdings and savings accounts of Newburyport laborers depended on underconsumption. . . . A recreational luxury like drinking, for example, was out of the question."[71] Moreover, it was the sober and thrifty worker who might win the approval of his employer or learn new skills and advance occupationally. It was perhaps no accident that unskilled workers predominated among those arrested for drunkenness. Drinking and saloongoing could represent a rejection—albeit not an articulated rejection—of the dominant social mobility ideology of nineteenth-century America.

The rejection of the success ideal was far from total. Ironically, saloonkeeping was the most accessible means of upward social mobility for immigrants. More than three-quarters of Worcester's Irish immigrants who had become small proprietors by 1900 were engaged in some aspect of the liquor trade. Still, even these exemplars of immigrant success were not always models of acquisitive individualism, as the R. G. Dun and Company reports demonstrate. Arguably, then, the saloon culture partook of a larger suspicion of materialism and ambition that was common among many immigrant groups, particularly the Irish. As Timothy J. Meagher points out in his study of the Worcester Irish, even Catholic clergy like the Reverend John J. McCoy and the Reverend Thomas Conaty, "who enthusiastically celebrated American opportunity before assemblies of Catholic young men, frequently blasted 'wild ambition' and praised resignation to low status in their Sunday pulpits." Material success was often depicted as a threat to the maintenance of more important ethnic, religious, and spiritual values.[72]

Not only did the saloongoers implicitly question and sometimes explicitly reject the goals and values of industrial society, such as homeownership, thrift, social mobility, and punctuality; they also often found themselves in direct legal conflict with the police authorities. Most commonly, this happened through public drunkenness, by far the most common late nineteenth century "crime"—an offense that accounted for approximately 60 percent of all arrests in Worcester in these years. Moreover, patrons sometimes joined with saloonkeepers in such illegal pursuits as gambling, prizefighting, and cockfighting. Nineteenth century saloon patrons thus found themselves part of a culture that operated outside of, if not against, the formal legal system.

Finally, and in a rather complex way, saloon culture increasingly clashed with the dominant culture because it segregated leisure by gender in a society in which family-centered recreation was becoming the middle-class norm. Women temperance advocates, argues a recent historian, sought "to curb the self-assertive, boisterous masculinity of the saloon, to support and protect the family, and to return the husband—the immigrant workingman in particular—to the home." "The purpose of prohibition," agrees another historian, "was to protect the values sheltered by the American nuclear family."[73]

This analysis should not imply that working-class women did not drink. As suggested previously, women were present in—and often ran—the kitchen dives that predominated earlier in the nineteenth century. Even after the emergence of the saloon as a spatially distinct and usually male institution, many immigrant working-class women continued to drink. One grim indicator of this pattern comes from the statistics on alcohol-related deaths. Among the Irish, at least, male and female rates in the late nineteenth century are remarkably close.[74] Most commonly, female drinking seems to have taken place at home. A study of Boston's South End in the 1890s notes that although "women . . . are forbidden by police regulation to patronize the bar-rooms," the "liquor habit . . . is practically universal among both men and women."[75]

Some women—German and English immigrants, for example—did drink in saloons, but these few exceptions emphasize the character of the saloon as "essentially a male refuge" pervaded by an "aura of free-wheeling masculinity." As a historian of Denver saloons observes, "the obsession with virility, with potency, with body building, with sports that characterized turn-of-the-century America permeated the saloon." In this context, hard drinking was an expression of both "hospitality and manliness." Significantly, even where women entered the saloon, they seem to have been excluded from "treating," which according to one commentator served as a "ritual of masculine renewal."[76]

In its maleness and gender segregation, the saloon both challenged and affirmed the dominant culture. On the one hand, the saloon was a male institution in an era when the middle-class ideal was increasingly that of family-centered leisure. On the other hand, both the saloon and the bourgeois family mandated subservient roles for women. Thus, whereas saloongoers apparently departed from some of the basic values of industrial America, they nevertheless shared some of its deepest patriarchal assumptions.

In general, however, the saloon stood outside the dominant cultural values of the late nineteenth century, even if neither the saloon nor its patrons mounted an organized or disciplined challenge to those values. In Raymond Williams's terms, the culture of the saloon was "alternative," that of "someone who simply finds a different way to live and wishes to be left alone with it," rather than "oppositional," that of "someone who finds a different way to live and wants to change society in its light." Thus, Worcester saloongoers may have shared the "conservative and defensive culture" that John Bodnar finds among Slavic-American industrial workers. Such a culture, Bodnar argues, was a synthesis of earlier peasant values with the exigencies of survival in urban, industrial, capi-

talist America. Among the dimensions of this culture were limited occupational mobility, traditional family ties, retention of ethnic culture,
antimaterialism, and collectivism. Unlike British workers, who responded to industrialization with class combativity, Bodnar's Slavic
workers—and Worcester saloongoers—adopted a conservative, defensive posture as the best means of coping with the new economic order.[77]

The nineteenth-century ethnic working-class saloon, then, was a form
of both accommodation and resistance to the capitalist order that workers faced. Unlike a trade union or a socialist party, the saloon did not
openly confront or challenge the dominant society, though neither did
it embrace the values and practices of that society. Instead, it offered a
space in which immigrants could preserve an alternative, reciprocal value
system. This was only partially an act of historical preservation, for the
saloon was a new institution and, as such, was a creative response by
immigrants to the trials of late nineteenth century urban life. The creation of such new, urban working-class styles, note two urban anthropologists, "is a living continuation, an active development and constant reworking of . . . traditions." Workers, they conclude, not only "survive
and build the industrial economy, the cities, and transportation networks, but they also create distinctive cultures."[78] The nineteenth-century saloon was one of the central institutions of that distinctive culture.

NOTES

Abbreviations in these notes are: AAS, American Antiquarian Society,
Worcester, Mass.; HCC, College of the Holy Cross Archives, Worcester, Mass.;
Mass. BLS, Commonwealth of Massachusetts, Bureau of Statistics of Labor; *WDT,
Worcester Daily Times; WEG, Worcester Evening Gazette; WEP, Worcester Evening
Post; WES, Worcester Evening Star; WST, Worcester Sunday Telegram; WT, Worcester
Telegram.*

1. Rev. Henry T. Cheever, ed., *Autobiography and Memorials of Ichabod Washburn* (Boston, 1878), 56–7. (Reference courtesy of Gary Kornblith.)

2. Joshua Chasan, "Civilizing Worcester: The Creation of Industrial and
Cultural Order, Worcester, Massachusetts, 1848–1876" (Ph.D. thesis, Univ. of
Pittsburgh, 1974), 148–62; C. E. Goodrich, "Story of the Washburn and Moen
Manufacturing Company, 1831–1899" (typescript, 1935); "Regulations to be
Observed by all Persons in the Employ of the Washburn and Moen Manufactur-
ing Company" (Apr. 11, 1871); "Washburn and Moen M'F'G Co. 1869 Time
Table"; Goodrich, the regulations, and the timetable can be found in the Amer-
ican Steel and Wire MSS, Baker Library, Harvard University Graduate School
of Business Administration, but were made available to me through the gener-
osity of the Community Studies Program of Assumption College, Worcester.

3. The development of the saloon as a distinct leisure institution is only one
example of a very long-term and gradual process through which "leisure" emerged

as a separate sphere of life. For discussions of this general process in non-American contexts, see Michael Marrus, ed., *The Emergence of Leisure* (New York, 1974); E. P. Thompson, "Time, Work-Discipline, and Industrial Capitalism," *Past and Present*, no. 38 (Dec. 1967): 56–97; Keith Thomas, "Work and Leisure in Pre-industrial Society," *Past and Present*, no. 29 (Dec. 1964): 50–66; James Walvin, *Leisure and Society* (New York, 1978); Robert Malcolmson, *Popular Recreations in English Society, 1700–1850* (New York, 1973); Hugh Cunningham, *Leisure in the Industrial Revolution, 1750–1880* (New York, 1980).

4. Paul Faler, "Cultural Aspects of the Industrial Revolution: Lynn, Massachusetts Shoemakers and Industrial Morality, 1826–1860," *Labor History* 15 (Summer 1974): 379; Paul Johnson, *A Shopkeeper's Millennium: Society and Revivals in Rochester, New York, 1815–1837* (New York, 1978), 56–7. See also W. J. Rorabaugh, *The Alcoholic Republic* (New York, 1979), 14; Ian R. Tyrell, *Sobering Up: From Temperance to Prohibition in Antebellum America, 1800–1860* (Westport, Conn., 1979), 103; Herbert Gutman, "Work, Culture, and Society in Industrializing America, 1815–1919," *American Historical Review* 78 (June 1973): 557; Harry Gene Levine, "Industrialization and Worker Drinking" (paper presented at the National Academy of Science, National Research Council Conference, Washington, D.C., Mar. 8–10, 1982).

5. Margaret A. Erskine, *Heart of the Commonwealth: Worcester* (Woodland Hills, Calif., 1981), 53; George Potter, *To the Golden Door: The Story of the Irish in Ireland and America* (Boston, 1960), 320; Richard Stivers, *A Hair of the Dog: Irish Drinking and American Stereotype* (University Park, Pa., 1976), 140; Richard O'Flynn, "Rumsellers of Worcester," Folio 2, 553–83, Richard O'Flynn MSS, HCC. See also Vincent E. Powers, " 'Invisible Immigrants': The Pre-Famine Irish Community in Worcester, Massachusetts, From 1826 to 1860" (Ph.D. thesis, Clark Univ., 1976), 122–3.

6. Rorabaugh, *Alcoholic Republic*, ix; Paul Mange, *Our Inns From 1718 to 1918* (Worcester, n.d., but probably 1918), 16.

7. Rorabaugh. *Alcoholic Republic*, 232; Massachusetts General Court, *Reports on the Subject of a License Law by a Joint Special Committee of the Legislature* (Boston, 1867), Appendix (testimony), 15. Emory and Ichabod Washburn were not related. On the beginning of the temperance movement, see Tyrell, *Sobering Up;* John A. Krout, *The Origins of Prohibition* (New York, 1925). (I have not yet seen Robert Hampel's recently published *Temperance and Prohibition in Massachusetts, 1813–1852* [Ann Arbor, Mich., 1982].)

8. Tyrell, *Sobering Up*, 96–7, 98, 272. On workers and temperance elsewhere, see Bruce Laurie, *Working People of Philadelphia, 1800–1850* (Philadelphia, 1980), 40–2, 53–66, 119–24; Faler, "Cultural Aspects of the Industrial Revolution"; Jill Siegel Dodd, "The Working Classes and the Temperance Movement in Ante-Bellum Boston," *Labor History* 19 (Fall 1978): 510–31; Johnson, *Shopkeeper's Millennium*, 79–83, 113–15, 121–2, 130–5.

9. Tyrell, *Sobering Up*, 108; *Reports on the Subject of a License Law*, Appendix, 461; U.S. Congress, Senate, *Committee of the Senate Upon the Relations Between Labor and Capital, Hearings*, 4 vols. (Washington, D.C., 1885), 2: 1110; hereafter cited as *Relations Between Labor and Capital*.

10. *WEG*, Sept. 6, 1898; Mass. BLS, *Third Annual Report, 1872* (Boston, 1872),

386; hereafter cited as Mass. BLS, *Report, 1872;* Mass BLS, *Report, 1881,* 414; Hyman Feldman, *Prohibition: Its Economic and Industrial Aspects* (New York, 1930), 200–1. See also *Relations Between Labor and Capital,* 1: 746, 2: 1110; Tyrell, *Sobering Up,* 297–8; Mass. BLS, *Report, 1870,* 228; John Fitch, *The Steel Workers* (New York, 1910), 226–7.

11. Mass. BLS, *Report, 1881,* 455; U.S. Commissioner of Labor, *Twelfth Annual Report: Economic Aspects of the Liquor Problem* (Washington, D.C., 1898), 69–72.

12. Joseph G. Rayback, *A History of American Labor* (New York, 1966), 59–60; Johnson, *Shopkeeper's Millennium,* 42; Marion Cotter Cahill, *Shorter Hours: A Study of the Movement Since the Civil War* (New York, 1932), 40; George Gunton, "The Economic and Social Importance of the Eight-Hour Movement," as reprinted in Leon Stein and Philip Taft, eds. *Wages, Hours and Strikes: Labor Panaceas in the Twentieth Century* (New York, 1970), 12–13. For an excellent overview of the eight-hour movement, see David Montgomery, *Beyond Equality: Labor and the Radical Republicans* (New York, 1967), 230–60. (I have only been able briefly to examine David Roediger's important recent study of "The Movement for a Shorter Working Day in the U.S. Before 1866" [Ph.D. thesis, Northwestern Univ., 1980].)

13. U.S. Bureau of the Census, *Tenth Census, 1880,* 22 vols. (Washington, D.C., 1883–8), 20: 187; Charles E. Persons, "The Early History of Factory Legislation in Massachusetts," in S. M. Kingsbury, ed., *Labor Laws and Their Enforcement* (New York, 1911), 41; Norman Ware, *The Industrial Worker, 1840–1860* (Boston, 1924), 160. See also Thomas Dublin, *Women at Work* (New York, 1979), 108–31.

14. Montgomery, *Beyond Equality,* 236; *WES,* July 1, 1879; Jurgen Kuczynski, *A Short History of Labour Conditions in the United States of America, 1789–1946* (1943; rpt. New York, 1973), 45; Mass. BLS, *Report, 1883,* 239. At Washburn and Moen the official workday was 11¼ hours (9¼ on Saturday) in 1869, but 10 hours by 1870; see "Time Table" and "Regulations" cited in note 2. Nevertheless, based on an examination of the Time Books for the North Works (available in the American Steel and Wire MSS), at least some workers apparently worked much longer days in the 1870s, 1880s, and 1890s.

15. Lawrence Levine, *Black Culture and Black Consciousness* (New York, 1977), 202–17.

16. Tyrell, *Sobering Up,* 27. See also Mange, *Our Inns;* Alexander H. Bullock, "Discourse on Early Worcester Taverns" (paper, 1880, available at AAS); Charles A. Nutt, *History of Worcester and Its People,* 4 vols. (New York, 1919), 2: 596.

17. Charles C. Buell, "The Workers of Worcester: Social Mobility and Ethnicity in a New England City, 1850–1880" (Ph.D. thesis, New York Univ., 1974), 60; *Illustrated Sketch of the Police Service of the City of Worcester* (Worcester, 1888), 20; Franklin P. Rice, ed., *The Worcester of Eighteen Hundred and Ninety-Eight* (Worcester, 1899), 23; *Reports on the Subject of a License Law,* Appendix, 350, 8.

18. Herbert M. Sawyer, *History of the Department of Police Service of Worcester* (Worcester, 1900), 27–9; Powers, " 'Invisible Immigrants,' " 252, 422 (see also 315); *Reports on the Subject of a License Law,* Appendix, 17; see also 19–20, 23, 31, 87, 105, 107, 216. On the shebeen in Ireland, see K. H. Connell, *Irish Peasant Society* (Oxford, 1968), 1–50. Paul Johnson finds similarly that in early nine-

teenth century Rochester working-class drink places "were not great beer halls and saloons (they would arrive much later in the century) but houses and little businesses where workmen combined drinking with everyday social transactions"; *Shopkeeper's Millennium*, 58.

19. Mass. BLS, *Report, 1875*, 275.

20. *Annual Report of the City Marshal, Year Ending, November 30, 1876* (Worcester, 1877), 23; hereafter cited as *City Marshal, 1876; WEG*, Apr. 5, 1875; *WDT*, Dec. 4, 1888; Arrest Cards, James Drennan MSS, WHM.

21. *City Marshal, 1876*, 24; *WEG*, Apr. 22, 1879; *City Marshal, 1875*, 51.

22. *Reports on the Subject of a License Law*, Appendix, 12. "When drinking was done at home, women played an important part in liquor sales"; Perry R. Duis, "The Saloon and the Public City" (Ph.D. thesis, Univ. of Chicago, 1975), 205. About one-quarter of those arrested for illegal liquor sales in the spring and summer of 1870 were women; *WEG*, May–Aug. 1870.

23. Connell, *Irish Peasant Society*, 18: *WT*, Mar. 10, 1896; *WDT*, Jan. 15, 1883. See also *WEG*, Mar. 21, 1874. Such arguments were not confined to the Irish; see *L'Opinion Publique*, Mar. 3, 1893.

24. First- and second-class licenses—those permitting on-premise drinking—accounted for about three-quarters of the annual licenses. Grocers, whose fourth-class licenses entitled them to sell liquor only for off-premise consumption, received most of the other licenses; *WEG*, May 7, 1879, May 1, 1880.

25. *WES*, May 9, 1879 (emphasis added); see also May 17, 1879. The earlier credit ratings of thirteen saloonkeepers who lost their licenses in 1879 or 1880 contained the term "worthless" or an equivalent; Massachusetts volumes of R. G. Dun and Co. Collection, Baker Library, Harvard University Graduate School of Business Administration; hereafter cited as RGD.

26. *WEG*, Apr. 26, 1880; *Le Travailleur*, May 7, 1881. The effort to foster *public* drinking is a major theme of Duis, "Saloon and the Public City," 207–11, 327–9.

27. *WES*, May 9, 1879; Arrest List and Arrest Cards, James Drennan MSS. Even as late as 1882, more than one-quarter of those similarly prosecuted had lost their licenses in the cutbacks. Significantly, more than one-third (thirty-two of ninety-three) of those prosecuted were women, and of these, close to two-thirds were listed as "widows" in the *Worcester Directory*. The Dignans are sometimes listed as Degnan, Deignan, and Dignon in the *Worcester Directory* and the newspapers. The James Drennan MSS contain other accounts of raids, many of them on Irish liquor sellers. Groceries were also an important outlet for illegal sales.

28. Although it is difficult to compare precisely, turnover was substantially slower for a comparable group of licensed dealers, who were also checked in the R. G. Dun and Company records. Data on liquor violation arrests are from the annual *City Marshal Reports*. Joshua Chasan discusses the increasing professionalization of the Worcester police beginning in 1867 in "Civilizing Worcester," 75–6. For an example of the impact of a liquor seizure on one liquor seller, see entry on Patrick J. Welch, RGD, 104: 793.

29. Clarence Long, *Wages and Earnings in the United States, 1860–1890* (Princeton, N.J., 1960), 61–8.

30. John Modell, "Patterns of Consumption, Acculturation, and Family In-come Strategy in Late-Nineteenth-Century America," in Tamara K. Hareven and Maris A. Vinovskis, eds., *Family and Population in Nineteenth-Century America* (Princeton, N.J., 1978), 212–14.

31. Modell, "Patterns of Consumption," 217; of Irish families earning be-tween $200 and $299, 36.9% spent money on both alcohol and tobacco, and 52.6% of those earning more than $600 showed similar spending. Among native families, the figures were 19.9% and 35.5%, respectively; Michael R. Marrus, "Social Drinking in the *Belle Epoque*," *Journal of Social History* 7 (Winter 1974): 132; *Relations Between Labor and Capital*, 2: 671, see also 537, 1360. Friedrich Engels, *The Condition of the Working Class in England*, trans. and ed. W. O. Hen-derson and W. H. Chaloner (Stanford, Calif., 1968), 141–4, offers a classic state-ment of the pathology of drink among workers.

32. RGD, 99: 204; 100: 72, 104: 633, 911. See also *WDT*, June 6, 1885; *WT*, Apr. 30, 1889; *WST*, July 24, 1910.

33. RGD, 102: 21, 371; *WST*, July 4, 1886; Mass. BLS, *Report, 1889*, 377. For earlier failures in brewery business, see RGD, 104: 782, 783; Mange, *Our Inns*, 28.

34. *WST*, Dec. 13, 1885, July 4, 1886; RGD, 101: 33. See also O'Flynn, "Rum-sellers of Worcester."

35. See, for example, RGD, 97: 756–8, 808; 99: 469; 101: 285. On the use of these records for studying immigrant business people, see David Gerber, "Ethnics, Enterprise and Middle Class Formation: Using the Dun and Bradstreet Collection for Research in Ethnic History," *Immigration History Newsletter* 12 (May 1980): 1–7.

36. O'Flynn, "Rumsellers of Worcester." On the term "saloon," see Mitford M. Mathews, ed., *A Dictionary of Americanisms on Historical Principles* (Chicago, 1951), 1448; Jim Marshall, *Swinging Doors* (Seattle, 1949), 170. As late as the early 1870s, the term "grog shop" seems to have been more common than "sa-loon." See, for example, Mass. BLS, *Report, 1871*, 594.

37. *WST*, Apr. 26, 1885; *WDT*, Apr. 20, 1885.

38. U.S. Manuscript Census, Worcester, 1880; Powers, " 'Invisible Immi-grants,' " 430. If second-class licenses (beer and wine only) had been included, the Germans would have been even more overrepresented. Additional data on the ethnic composition of the saloon trade in the published censuses for 1880 and 1885 tend to be somewhat contradictory, because of the manner of presen-tation.

39. RGD, 104: 842; 99: 342; Addison V. Newton, *The Saloon Keeper's Compan-ion* (Worcester, 1875).

40. *WT*, Apr. 23, 1891. See also *WEG*, May 18, 1880; Petition in Favor of Innholder License for Napoleon Guertin, May 7, 1883, Board of Aldermen MSS, Worcester City Hall; *L'Opinion Publique*, Apr. 21, 1893. O'Flynn, "Rumsellers of Worcester," mentions the Christopher brothers. The number of French-Cana-dian saloonkeepers can be discerned from annual listings in the *Worcester Direc-tory* and the French-Canadian press. Between 1883 and 1885, the total number of licenses issued to French Canadians fluctuated between eight and thirteen, but these included pharmacies, groceries, and hotels. See *Le Courrier de Worcester*, May 4, 1883; *Le Travailleur*, May 2, 1884, May 15, 1885.

41. *Scandinavia*, May 25, 1888. There was also drinking at the English Social Club; *WEP*, May 3, 1897; *WT*, May 8, 11, 1897.

42. For more on ethnic drinking customs, see Madelon Powers, "Faces Along the Bar: The Saloon in Working-Class Life, 1890–1920" (paper, Social Research Group, School of Public Health, Univ. of California, Berkeley, July 1979), 39–40; John C. Koren, *Economic Aspects of the Liquor Problem* (Boston, 1899), 228; O'Flynn, "Rumsellers of Worcester"; Stivers, *Hair of the Dog;* Andrew Greeley, William McCready, and Gary Theisen, *Ethnic Drinking Subcultures* (New York, 1980); Robert F. Bales, "Attitudes toward Drinking in the Irish Culture," in D. J. Pittman and C. R. Snyder, eds., *Society, Culture, and Drinking Patterns* (New York, 1962), 157–87; Thomas J. Noel, "The City and the Saloon: Denver, 1858–1916" (Ph.D. thesis, Univ. of Colorado, 1978), 118–47; James R. Barrett, "Why Paddy Drank: The Social Importance of Whiskey in Pre-famine Ireland," *Journal of Popular Culture* 11 (Summer 1977): 155–66.

43. "Editorial," *Light* 4 (Nov. 7, 1891): 291; RGD, 104: 793; *WT*, May 2, 3, 1893. See also *WST*, Apr. 19, 1896; *WT*, June 25, 1898; *Skandinavia*, Jan. 12, 1893; Olive Higgins Prouty, *Pencil Shavings* (Cambridge, Mass., 1961), 43.

44. Group purchases evaded the law against liquor sales at private clubs. Unidentified clipping, Jan. 8, 1922, Clipping File, AAS; *WDT*, Apr. 29, 1886. See also *WDT*, May 17, 1885, May 3, 1886, Dec. 4, 6, 1888, Nov. 29, 1886.

45. For example, between 1886 and 1888, when drunkenness arrests rose 65% (because of the end of no-license), arrests of laborers swelled 81%. Arrests of wireworkers rose only 1% and of machinists 10%. Arrest statistics are from the annual *City Marshal Reports*.

46. Mass. BLS, *Report, 1881*, 477–531. See also Mass. BLS, *Report, 1895*, 1–416; lists of drunkenness arrests were drawn from the Central District Court Docket books, Central District Courthouse, Worcester.

47. The biography of Murphy is drawn from RGD, 99: 14; O'Flynn, "Rumsellers of Worcester"; U.S. Manuscript Census, Worcester, 1880; and *Worcester Directory*.

48. The distance from home to saloon was calculated as a straight line rather than as actual walking distance. Data on the occupations of neighbors of saloonkeepers come from U.S. Manuscript Census, Worcester, 1880.

49. Wyckoff, quoted in Koren, *Economic Aspects of the Liquor Problem*, 239. For a similar statement, see Royal L. Melendy, "The Saloon in Chicago," *American Journal of Sociology* 6 (Nov. 1900): 291. On the social functions of the saloon, see Jon M. Kingsdale, "The 'Poor Man's Club': Social Functions of the Urban Working-Class Saloon," *American Quarterly* 25 (Oct. 1975): 472–89; Duis, "Saloon and the Public City," 509–87; Melendy, "Saloon in Chicago," 289–306; George Ade, *The Old-Time Saloon* (New York, 1931); Raymond Calkins, *Substitutes for the Saloon* (Boston, 1901), 1–24; Koren, *Economic Aspects of the Liquor Problem*, 210–40; Ronald Morris Benson, "American Workers and Temperance Reform, 1866–1933" (Ph.D. thesis, Univ. of Notre Dame, 1974), 95–120; Powers, "Faces Along the Bar," 1–50; Noel, "The City and the Saloon."

50. Noel, "The City and the Saloon," 118–47, 197–225; Powers, "Faces Along the Bar," 27–48; Robert A. Woods, ed., *The City Wilderness* (Boston, 1899), 118. On free lunch in Worcester, see *WDT*, Mar. 8, 1886; *WEG*, July 5, 1910.

51. Melendy, "Saloon in Chicago," 290; Mass. BLS, *Report, 1871*, 540; Fitch,

Steel Workers, 226–7; Maurice Parmelee, *Inebriety in Boston* (New York, 1909), 38–9; *Relations Between Labor and Capital*, 3: 631. See also Mass. BLS, *Report, 1895*, 40–1, 46.

52. Newton, *Saloon Keeper's Companion*, iii; O'Flynn, "Rumsellers of Worcester"; "In Leisure Moments," *Light* 1 (June 7, 1890): 14. See also *WT*, May 2, 1893.

53. Newton, *Saloon Keeper's Companion*, 11–59.

54. Mass. BLS, *Report, 1870*, 540; Ade, *Old-Time Saloon*, 128–30. See also Marshall, *Swinging Doors*, 171–4.

55. *Worcester Directory, 1875* (Worcester, 1875), 441; O'Flynn, "Rumsellers of Worcester"; Michael Gordon, "Studies in Irish and Irish-American Thought and Behavior in Gilded Age New York City" (Ph.D. thesis, Univ. of Rochester, 1977), xxvii–viii. Massachusetts saloons were not legally permitted to offer commercial entertainment.

56. RGD, 97: 758; *WT*, Dec. 6, 1885; O'Flynn, "Rumsellers of Worcester"; *WST*, May 2, 1885, Dec. 6, 1885; Ade, *Old-Time Saloon*, 32; Marshall, *Swinging Doors*, 163. James Gilrein recalls that some Worcester saloons attracted specialized crowds of sports fans: boxing at Jerry Regan's, track at Sanderson's, and harness racing at the Lincoln House; interview, Worcester, Mar. 1, 1978.

57. *WST*, Jan. 3, 1886. See also *WT*, June 6, 1886; *WST*, Apr. 12, 1897.

58. Mass. BLS, *Report, 1870*, 334, 266–7; see also Mass. BLS, *Report, 1871*, 589, 612–13; *Relations Between Labor and Capital*, 2: 649; U. Waldo Cutler, "A Problem in Public Welfare," *Worcester Magazine* 12 (Sept. 1909): 303. On working-class housing, see Mass. BLS, *Report, 1875*. In 1895 housing in the working-class Fifth Ward averaged .96 persons per room, whereas in the more affluent Eighth Ward it was .57. Timothy J. Meagher, " 'The Lord Is Not Dead': Cultural and Social Change Among the Irish in Worcester, Massachusetts" (Ph.D. thesis, Brown Univ., 1982), 55.

59. *Relations Between Labor and Capital*, 1: 44; Meagher, " 'Lord Is Not Dead,' " 123. See also *Relations Between Labor and Capital*, 1: 409, 854; Mass. BLS, *Report, 1871*, 543.

60. Meagher, " 'Lord Is Not Dead,' " 115; Duis, "Saloon and the Public City," 361; Parmelee, *Inebriety in Boston*, 25. Mass. BLS, *Report, 1895*, 112–3, shows that younger males dominated among drunkenness arrests (63% were between 20 and 39). For a discussion of the "bachelor subculture" and the Irish, see Stivers, *Hair of the Dog*, 51–135.

61. Cutler, "Public Welfare," 303; Mass. BLS, *Report, 1870*, 306; Jay P. Dolan, "Immigrants in the City: New York's Irish and German Catholics," *Church History* 41 (Sept. 1972): 366; Ade, *Old-Time Saloon*, 99–100. According to one printer, the "thinking mechanic" abstained from church membership because of his "inability, if he has a family, to come up to the social requirements of church membership, in dress and in contributions to the various objects that the church carries along with it"; *Relations Between Labor and Capital*, 1: 50. See also Walter A. Wyckoff, *The Workers: An Experiment in Reality—The West* (New York, 1899), 196–7; Fitch, *Steel Workers*, 225; George L. McNutt, "Why Workingmen Drink," *Outlook* 69 (Sept. 14, 1901): 115–18; Mass. BLS, *Report, 1871*, 591, 594–5, 606, 618; Woods, *City Wilderness*, 228–9; Marshall, *Swinging Doors*, 13.

62. "To the Voters of Worcester," Dec. 7, 1883, Broadside Collection, WHM.

63. Melendy, "Saloon in Chicago," 294; McNutt, "Why Workingmen Drink," 115, 118. Even the national field secretary of the Church Temperance Society called the saloon the "most democratic institution in America"; Clipping and Minutes, Jan. 11, 1920, Scrapbook, Twentieth Century Club of Worcester, Worcester Public Library. On reciprocity, see David Harvey, *Social Justice and the City* (Baltimore, 1972), 206–7, 209, 282; Karl Polanyi, Conrad M. Arensberg, and Harry W. Pearson, eds., *Trade and Market in the Early Empires* (1957; rpt. Chicago, 1971).

64. Bales, "Attitudes toward Drinking in the Irish Culture," 172.

65. Joseph Walker, *Hopewell Village* (Philadelphia, 1966), 381 (emphasis added); Bales, "Attitudes toward Drinking in the Irish Culture," 175. On drink customs of Irish artisans, see John Dunlop, *Artificial and Compulsory Drinking Usages of The United Kingdom*, 7th ed. (London, 1844), 84. On the twentieth-century Irish rural economy, see Conrad Arensberg and Solon Kimball, *Family and Community in Ireland*, 2nd ed. (Cambridge, 1968). On similar American economic arrangements, see Mike Merrill, "Cash Is Good to Eat: Self-Sufficiency and Exchange in the Rural Economy of the United States," *Radical History Review* 4 (Winter 1977): 42–71.

66. Mass. BLS, *Report, 1895,* 41; Mass. BLS, *Report, 1871,* 540–1. See also Kingsdale, " 'Poor Man's Club,' " 480; Upton Sinclair, *The Jungle* (1905; rpt. New York, 1960), 84–5; Thorstein Veblen, *The Theory of the Leisure Class* (1899; rpt. New York, 1953), 72–3; Ernest R. Cherrington, ed., *Standard Encyclopedia of the Alcohol Problem*, 6 vols. (Westerville, Ohio, 1930), 6: 2668. A recent sociological study finds that treating is still "the most general of bar forms"; Sherri Cavan, *Liquor License: An Ethnography of Bar Behavior* (Chicago, 1966), 41.

67. Jack London, *John Barleycorn* (1913; rpt. Westport, Conn., 1968), 84 (also quoted in Powers, "Faces Along the Bar," 21); Arrest Cards, James Drennan MSS (emphasis added). See also *WDT,* July 6, 1883.

68. Veblen, *The Theory of the Leisure Class,* 72–3; *Catholic Messenger,* May 17, 1907; see also Feb. 15, 1907.

69. Stivers, *Hair of the Dog,* 86–7; Rorabaugh, *Alcoholic Republic,* 151; Cavan, *Liquor License,* 43.

70. Mass. BLS, *Report, 1871,* 543; *WT,* Apr. 16, 1895. Significantly, the Knights of Labor with its emphasis on the dignity of labor and its producerist ideology was the labor organization most hostile to drinking and the saloon; see David Brundage, "The Producing Classes and the Saloon: Denver in the 1880's" (paper presented at the Knights of Labor Centennial Symposium, Chicago, Ill., May 17–19, 1979); Benson, "American Workers and Temperance Reform," 150–86.

71. Committee of Five, "A Statement to Businessmen," Nov. 17, 1893, copy of broadside found in Worcester Room, Worcester Public Library; Stephan Thernstrom, *Poverty and Progress: Social Mobility in a Nineteenth-Century City* (1964; rpt. New York, 1972), 136–7. For claims about the connection between temperance and homeownership, see *Relations Between Labor and Capital,* 2:960, 1285.

72. Meagher, " 'Lord Is Not Dead,' " 201, 182. The degree to which American workers accepted or rejected "acquisitive individualism" remains a subject of debate. For contrasting positions, see, for example, David Montgomery, *Workers'*

Control in America: Studies in the History of Work, Technology, and Labor Struggles (Cambridge, 1979), 4, 153, and Melvyn Dubofsky, "Hold the Fort: The Dynamics of Twentieth-Century American Working-Class History," *Reviews in American History* 9 (June 1981): 250–1.

73. Kingsdale, " 'Poor Man's Club,' " 485–7; Norman H. Clark, *Deliver Us from Evil: An Interpretation of American Prohibition* (New York, 1976), 13.

74. Robin Room, "Cultural Contingencies of Alcoholism: Variations Between and Within Nineteenth-Century Urban Ethnic Groups in Alcohol-Related Death Rates," *Journal of Health and Social Behavior* 9 (Mar. 1968): 99–113. The Irish male death rate was two times that for women for deaths from alcoholism. However, the male rate of deaths from liver diseases (except jaundice) was only 80% that of the female rate.

75. *Reports on the Subject of a License Law*, 19, 20; Woods, *City Wilderness*, 155. Stivers notes that women in Ireland drank but not in pubs; *Hair of the Dog*, 177. Noel found both a social and a legal taboo on women drinking in saloons in Denver; "The City and the Saloon," 242–3, 246. Legal prohibitions on women in saloons seem to have emerged gradually. In the 1880s in Boston and Chicago there was only a social taboo; Duis, "Saloon and the Public City," 221. There seem to have been some public drink places primarily for upper-class women in New York City in the 1880s, but such habits were viewed as "exotic" from the perspective of Worcester; *WST*, July 7, 1889.

76. Marshall, *Swinging Doors*, 13; Powers, "Faces Along the Bar," 16; Noel, "The City and the Saloon," 250; Stivers, *Hair of the Dog*, 86. On women (probably English immigrants) in Fall River saloons, see Jonathan Baxter Harrison, *Certain Dangerous Tendencies in American Life* (Boston, 1880) as excerpted in Alan Trachtenberg, ed., *Democratic Vistas, 1860–1880* (New York, 1970), 171–4; *Relations Between Labor and Capital*, 1: 647. Cavan notes that the treating of men by women was still a taboo in the 1960s; *Liquor License*, 114, 122–3. In the Fall River example cited above, Harrison notes an asymmetrical form of treating—men treat women but not the reverse.

77. Raymond Williams, "Base and Superstructure in Marxist Cultural Theory," *New Left Review*, no. 82 (Dec. 1973): 11; John Bodnar, "Immigration and Modernization: The Case of Slavic Peasants in Industrial America," *Journal of Social History* 9 (Fall 1975): 44–71. See also John Bodnar, "Materialism and Morality: Salvic-American Immigrants and Education, 1890–1940," *Journal of Ethnic Studies* 3 (Winter 1976): 1–19.

78. Angela Keil and Charles Keil, "In Pursuit of Polka Happiness," *Cultural Correspondence*, No. 5 (Summer–Fall 1977): 8, 6.

FIVE

William Shakespeare and the American People

A Study in Cultural Transformation

Lawrence W. Levine

The humor of a people affords important insights into the nature of their culture. Thus Mark Twain's treatment of Shakespeare in his novel *Huckleberry Finn* helps us place the Elizabethan playwright in nineteenth-century American culture. Shortly after the two rogues, who pass themselves off as a duke and a king, invade the raft of Huck and Jim, they decide to raise funds by performing scenes from Shakespeare's *Romeo and Juliet* and *Richard III*. That the presentation of Shakespeare in small Mississippi River towns could be conceived of as potentially lucrative tells us much about the position of Shakespeare in the nineteenth century. The specific nature of Twain's humor tells us even more. Realizing that they would need material for encores, the "duke" starts to teach the "king" Hamlet's soliloquy, which he recites from memory:

> To be, or not to be; that is the bare bodkin
> That makes calamity of so long life;
> For who would fardels bear, till Birnam Wood do come to Dunsinane,
> But that the fear of something after death Murders the innocent sleep,
> Great nature's second course,
> And makes us rather sling arrows of outrageous fortune
> Than fly to others that we know not of.[1]

Twain's humor relies on his audience's familiarity with *Hamlet* and its ability to recognize the duke's improbable coupling of lines from a variety of Shakespeare's plays. Twain was employing one of the most popular forms of humor in nineteenth-century America. Everywhere in the

This article first appeared in *American Historical Review* 89, no. 1 (February 1984): 34–66. Reprinted by permission of the author and the *American Historical Review*.

nation burlesques and parodies of Shakespeare constituted a prominent form of entertainment.

Hamlet was a favorite target in numerous travesties imported from England or crafted at home. Audiences roared at the sight of Hamlet dressed in fur cap and collar, snowshoes and mittens; they listened with amused surprise to his profanity when ordered by his father's ghost to "swear" and to his commanding Ophelia, "Get thee to a brewery"; they heard him recite his lines in black dialect or Irish brogue and sing his most famous soliloquy, "To be, or not to be," to the tune of "Three Blind Mice." In the 1820s the British comedian Charles Mathews visited what he called the "Nigger's (or Negroe's) theatre" in New York, where he heard "a black tragedian in the character of Hamlet" recite "To be, or not to be? That is the question; whether it is nobler in *de* mind to suffer, or tak' up arms against a sea of trouble, and by *opossum* end 'em." "No sooner was the word *opossum* out of his mouth," Mathews reported, "than the audience burst forth, in one general cry, '*Opossum! opossum! opossum!*' "—prompting the actor to come forward and sing the popular dialect song "Opossum up a Gum Tree." On the nineteenth-century American stage, audiences often heard Hamlet's lines intricately combined with those of a popular song:

> Oh! 'tis consummation
> Devoutly to be wished
> To end your heart-ache by a sleep,
> When likely to be dish'd.
> Shuffle off your mortal coil,
> Do just so,
> Wheel about, and turn about,
> And jump Jim Crow.[2]

No Shakespearean play was immune to this sort of mutilation. *Richard III*, the most popular Shakespearean play in the nineteenth century, was lampooned frequently in such versions as *Bad Dicky*. In one New York production starring first-rank Shakespearean actors, a stuttering, lisping Othello danced while Desdemona played the banjo and Iago, complete with Irish brogue, ended their revelries with a fire hose. Parodies could also embody a serious message. In Kenneth Bangs's version of *The Taming of the Shrew*, for example, Kate ended up in control, observing that, although "Shakespeare or Bacon, or whoever wrote the play . . . studied deeply the shrews of his day . . . , the modern shrew isn't built that way," while a chastened Petruchio concluded, "Sweet Katharine, of your remarks I recognize the force: / Don't strive to tame a woman as you would a horse." Serious or slapstick, the punning was endless. In one parody of the famous dagger scene, Macbeth continues to put off his insistent wife by asking, "Or is that dagger but a false Daguerreotype?" Luckily, Desdemona had no brother, or Othello "might look both black and blue," a character in *Othello* remarked, while one in *The Merchant of Venice* observed of Shylock, "This crafty Jew is full of *Jeux d'esprit!*" Throughout the century, the number of parodies with such titles as *Julius Sneezer, Roamy-E Owe and Julie-Ate,* and *Desdemonum* was impressive.[3]

These full-fledged travesties reveal only part of the story. Nineteenth-century Shakespearean parody most frequently took the form of short skits, brief references, and satirical songs inserted into other modes of entertainment. In one of their routines, for example, the Bryants' Minstrels playfully referred to the famous observation in Act II of *Romeo and Juliet:*

> Adolphus Pompey is my name,
>   But that don't make no difference,
> For as Massa Wm. Shakespeare says,
>   A name's of no signiforance.

The minstrels loved to invoke Shakespeare as an authority: "you know what de Bird of Avon says 'bout 'De black scandal an' de foul faced reproach!" And they constantly quoted him in appropriately garbled form: "Fust to dine own self be true, an' it must follow night an' day, dou den can be false to any man." The significance of this national penchant for parodying Shakespeare is clear: Shakespeare and his drama had become by the nineteenth century an integral part of American culture. It is difficult to take familiarities with that which is not already familiar; one cannot parody that which is not well known. The minstrels' characteristic conundrums would not have been funny to an audience lacking knowledge of Shakespeare's works:

> When was Desdemona like a ship?
> When she was Moored.[4]

It is not surprising that educated Americans in the eighteenth and nineteenth centuries knew their Shakespeare. What is more interesting is how widely Shakespeare was known to the public in general. In the last half of the eighteenth century, when the reading of Shakespeare's plays was still confined to a relatively small, educated elite, substantial numbers of Americans had the chance to see his plays performed. From the first documented American performance of a Shakespearean play in 1750 until the closing of the theaters in 1778 because of the American Revolution, Shakespeare emerged as the most popular playwright in the colonies. Fourteen or fifteen of his plays were presented at least one hundred and eighty—and one scholar has estimated perhaps as many as five hundred—times. Following the Revolution, Shakespeare retained his position as the most widely performed dramatist, with five more of his plays regularly performed in an increasing number of cities and towns.[5]

Not until the nineteenth century, however, did Shakespeare come into his own—presented and recognized almost everywhere in the country. In the cities of the Northeast and Southeast, Shakespeare's plays dominated the theater. During the 1810–11 season in Philadelphia, for example, Shakespearean plays accounted for twenty-two of eighty-eight performances. The following season lasted 108 nights, of which again one-quarter—27—were devoted to Shakespeare. From 1800 to 1835, Philadelphians had the opportunity to see twenty-one of Shakespeare's thirty-seven plays. The Philadelphia theater was not exceptional; one student of the American stage concluded that in cities on the Eastern Seaboard at least one-fifth of all plays offered in a season were likely to be by Shakespeare.[6] George Makepeace Towle, an American consul in England, returned to his own country just after the Civil War and remarked with some surprise, "Shakespearian dramas are more frequently played and more popular in America than in England." Shakespeare's dominance can be attested to by what Charles Shattuck has called "the westward flow of Shakespearean actors" from England to America. In the nineteenth century, one prominent English Shakespearean actor after another—George Frederick Cooke, Edmund Kean, Junius Brutus Booth, Charles and Fanny Kemble, Ellen Tree, William Charles Macready— sought the fame and financial rewards that awaited them in their tours of the United States.[7]

It is important to understand that their journey did not end with big cities or the Eastern Seaboard. According to John Bernard, the English actor and comedian who worked in the United States from 1797 to 1819, "If an actor were unemployed, want and shame were not before him: he had merely to visit some town in the interior where no theatre existed, but 'readings' were permitted; and giving a few recitations from Shakespeare and Sterne, his pockets in a night or two were amply replenished." During his travels through the United States in the 1830s, Tocqueville found Shakespeare in "the recesses of the forests of the New World. There is hardly a pioneer's hut that does not contain a few odd volumes of Shakespeare. I remember that I read the feudal drama of *Henry V* for the first time in a log cabin."[8] Five decades later, the German visitor Karl Knortz made a similar observation:

> There is, assuredly, no other country on the face of this earth in which Shakespeare and the Bible are held in such general high esteem as in America, the very country so much decried for its lust for money. If you were to enter an isolated log cabin in the Far West and even if its inhabitant were to exhibit many of the traces of backwoods living, he will most likely have one small room nicely furnished in which to spend his few leisure

hours and in which you will certainly find the Bible and in most cases also some cheap edition of the works of the poet Shakespeare.[9]

Even if we discount the hyperbole evident in such accounts, they were far from inventions. The ability of the illiterate Rocky Mountain scout Jim Bridger to recite long passages from Shakespeare, which he had learned by hiring someone to read the plays to him, and the formative influence that the plays had upon young Abe Lincoln growing up in Salem, Illinois, became part of the nation's folklore.[10] But if books had become a more important vehicle for disseminating Shakespeare by the nineteenth century, the stage remained the primary instrument. The theater, like the church, was one of the earliest and most important cultural institutions established in frontier cities. And almost everywhere the theater blossomed Shakespeare was a paramount force. In his investigation of the theater in Louisville, Cincinnati, St. Louis, Detroit, and Lexington, Kentucky, from 1800 to 1840, Ralph Leslie Rusk concluded that Shakespeare's plays were performed more frequently than those of any other author. In Mississippi between 1814 and the outbreak of the Civil War, the towns of Natchez and Vicksburg, with only a few thousand inhabitants each, put on at least one hundred and fifty performances of Shakespeare featuring such British and American stars as Ellen Tree, Edwin Forrest, Junius Brutus Booth, J. W. Walleck, Charles Kean, J. H. Hackett, Josephine Clifton, and T. A. Cooper. Stars of this and lesser caliber made their way into the interior by boat, along the Ohio and Mississippi rivers, stopping at towns and cities on their way to New Orleans. Beginning in the early 1830s, the rivers themselves became the site of Shakespearean productions, with floating theaters in the form first of flatboats and then steamboats bringing drama to small river towns.[11]

By mid-century, Shakespeare was taken across the Great Plains and over the Rocky Mountains and soon became a staple of theaters in the Far West. During the decade following the arrival of the Forty-niners, at least twenty-two of Shakespeare's plays were performed on California stages, with *Richard III* retaining the predominance it had gained in the East and South. In 1850 the Jenny Lind Theatre, seating two thousand, opened over a saloon in San Francisco and was continuously crowded: "Miners . . . swarmed from the gambling saloons and cheap fandango houses to see *Hamlet* and *Lear*." In 1852 the British star Junius Brutus Booth and two of his sons played *Hamlet, Macbeth, Othello,* and *Richard III* from the stage of the Jenny Lind and packed the house for the two weeks of their stay. In 1856 Laura Keen brought San Franciscans not only old favorites but such relatively uncommon productions as *Coriolanus* and *A Midsummer Night's Dream*. Along with such eminent stars from abroad, American actors like McKean Buchanan and James Stark kept the hunger for Shakespeare satisfied.[12]

But Shakespeare could not be confined to the major population centers in the Far West any more than he had been in the East. If miners could not always come to San Francisco to see theater, the theater came to them. Stark, Buchanan, Edwin Booth, and their peers performed on makeshift stages in mining camps around Sacramento and crossed the border into Nevada, where they brought characterizations of Hamlet, Iago, Macbeth, Kate, Lear, and Othello to miners in Virginia City, Silver City, Dayton, and Carson City. Walter M. Leman recalled the dearth of theaters in such California towns as Tod's Valley, Chip's Flat, Cherokee Flat, Rattlesnake, Mud Springs, Red Dog, Hangtown, Drytown, and Fiddletown, which he toured in the 1850s. In the Sierra town of Downieville, Leman performed *Richard III* on the second story of a cloth and paper house in a hall without a stage: "we had to improvise one out of the two billiard tables it contained, covering them with boards for that purpose." Such conditions were by no means confined to the West Coast. In earlier years, Leman had toured the Maine towns of Bangor, Belfast, Orono, and Oldtown, not one of which had a proper theater, necessitating the use of church vestries and other improvisations. In 1816 in Lexington, Kentucky, Noah Ludlow performed *The Taming of the Shrew, Othello,* and *The Merchant of Venice* in a room on the second floor of an old brewery, next door to a saloon, before an audience seated on backless, cushionless chairs. In the summer of 1833, Sol Smith's company performed in the dining room of a hotel in Tazewell, Alabama, "on a sort of landing-place or gallery about six feet long, and two and a half feet wide." His "heavy tragedian" Mr. Lyne attempted to recite the "Seven Ages of Man" from *As You Like It* while "Persons were passing from one room to the other continually and the performer was obliged to *move* whenever any one passed."[13]

Thus Shakespeare was by no means automatically treated with reverence. Nor was he accorded universal acclaim. In Davenport and neighboring areas of Eastern Iowa, where the theater flourished in both English and German, Shakespeare was seldom performed and then usually in the form of short scenes and soliloquies rather than entire plays. As more than one theater manager learned, producing Shakespeare did not necessarily result in profits. Theatrical lore often repeated the vow attributed to Robert L. Place that he would never again produce a play by Shakespeare "no matter how many more he wrote." But these and similar incidents were exceptions to the general rule: from the large and often opulent theaters of major cities to the makeshift stages in halls, saloons, and churches of small towns and mining camps, wherever there was an audience for the theater, there Shakespeare's plays were performed prominently and frequently. Shakespeare's popularity in frontier communities in all sections of the country may not fit Frederick Jackson Turner's image of the frontier as a crucible, melting civilization down into a new amalgam, but it does fit our knowledge of human beings and their need for the comfort of familiar things under the pressure of new circumstances and surroundings. James Fenimore Cooper had this familiarity in mind when he called Shakespeare "the great author of America" and insisted that Americans had "just as good a right" as Englishmen to claim Shakespeare as their countryman.[14]

Shakespeare's popularity can be determined not only by the frequency of Shakespearean productions and the size of the audiences for them but also by the nature of the productions and the manner in which they were presented. Shakespeare was performed not merely alongside popular entertainment as an elite supplement to it; Shakespeare was performed as an integral part of it. Shakespeare *was* popular entertainment in nineteenth-century America. The theater in the first half of the nineteenth century played the role that movies played in the first half of the twentieth: it was a kaleidoscopic, democratic institution presenting a widely varying bill of fare to all classes and socioeconomic groups.

During the first two-thirds of the nineteenth century, the play may have been the thing, but it was not the only thing. It was the centerpiece, the main attraction, but an entire evening generally consisted of a long play, an afterpiece (usually a farce), and a variety of between-act specialities. In the spring of 1839, a playbill advertising the appearance of William Evans Burton in *As You Like It* at Philadelphia's American Theatre announced, "Il Diavolo Antonio And His Sons, Antonio, Lorenzo, Augustus And Alphonzo will present a most magnificent display of position in the Science of Gymnastics, portraying some of the most grand and imposing groups from the ancient masters . . . to conclude with a grand Horizontal Pyramid." It was a characteristically full evening. In addition to gymnastics and Shakespeare, "Mr. Quayle (by Desire)" sang "The Swiss Drover Boy," La Petite Celeste danced "a New Grand Pas Seul," Miss Lee danced "La Cachuca," Quayle returned to sing "The Haunted Spring," Mr. Bowman told a "Yankee Story," and "the Whole" concluded "with *Ella Rosenberg* starring Mrs. Hield."[15]

Thus Shakespeare was presented amid a full range of contemporary entertainment. During the Mexican War, a New Orleans performance of *Richard III* was accompanied by "A NEW and ORIGINAL Patriotic Drama in 3 Acts, . . . (founded in part on events which have occurred during the Mexican War,) & called: Palo Alto! Or, Our Army on the Rio Grande! . . . TRIUMPH OF AMERICAN ARMS! Surrender of Gen.

Vega to Capt. May! Grand Military Tableau!" It would be a mistake to conclude that Shakespeare was presented as the dry, staid ingredient in this exciting menu. On the contrary, Shakespearean plays were often announced as spectacles in their own right. In 1799 the citizens of Alexandria, Virginia, were promised the following in a production of *Macbeth:* "In Act 3d—A Regal Banquet in which the Ghost of Banquo appears. In Act 4th—A Solemn incantation & dance of Witches. In Act 5th—A grand Battle, with the defeat & death of Macbeth." At mid-century, a presentation of *Henry IV* in Philadelphia featured the "Army of Falstaff on the March! . . . Battlefield, Near Shrewsbury, Occupying the entire extent of the Stage, Alarms! Grand Battle! Single Combat! DEATH OF HOTSPUR ! FINALE—Grand Tableau."[16]

Shakespeare's position as part and parcel of popular culture was reinforced by the willingness of Shakespearean actors to take part in the concluding farce. Thus Mr. Parsons followed such roles as Coriolanus, Othello, Macbeth, and Lear by playing Ralph Stackpole, "A Ring-Tailed Squealer & Rip-Staver from Salt River," in *Nick of the Woods.* Even Junius Brutus Booth followed his celebrated portrayal of Richard III with the role of Jerry Sneak in *The Mayor of Garrat.*[17] In the postbellum years Edward L. Davenport referred to this very ability and willingness to mix genres when he lamented the decline of his profession: "Why, I've played an act from *Hamlet,* one from *Black-Eyed Susan,* and sung 'A Yankee Ship and a Yankee Crew' and danced a hornpipe, and wound up with a 'nigger' part, all in one night. Is there any one you know of today who can do that?"[18] It is clear that, as much as Shakespearean roles were prized by actors, they were not exalted; they did not unfit one for other roles and other tasks; they were not elevated to a position above the culture in which they appeared. Most frequently, the final word of the evening was not Shakespeare's. *Hamlet* might be followed by *Fortune's Frolic, The Merchant of Venice* by *The Lottery Ticket, Richard III* by *The Green Mountain Boy, King Lear* by *Chaos Is Come Again* on one occasion and by *Love's Laughs at Locksmiths: or, The Guardian Outwitted* on another, and, in California, *Romeo and Juliet* by *Did You Ever Send Your Wife to San Jose?.*[19]

These afterpieces and *divertissements* most often are seen as having diluted or denigrated Shakespeare. I suggest that they may be understood more meaningfully as having *integrated* him into American culture. Shakespeare was presented as part of the same milieu inhabited by magicians, dancers, singers, acrobats, minstrels, and comics. He appeared on the same playbills and was advertised in the same spirit. This does not mean that theatergoers were unable to make distinctions between Shakespearean productions and the accompanying entertainment. Of course they were. Shakespeare, after all, was what most of them came to see. But it was a Shakespeare presented as part of the culture they enjoyed, a Shakespeare rendered familiar and intimate by virtue of his context.

In 1843 the curtain of the rebuilt St. Charles Theatre featured an arresting bit of symbolism: it depicted Shakespeare in a halo of light being borne aloft on the wings of the American eagle.[20] Shakespeare was not only domesticated; he was humanized. Henry Norman Hudson, the period's most popular Shakespearean lecturer, hailed Shakespeare as "the prodigy of our race" but also stressed his decency, his humility, his "true gentleness and lowliness of heart" and concluded that "he who looks the highest will always bow the lowest."[21] In his melodrama *Shakespeare in Love,* Richard Penn Smith pictured the poet not as an awesome symbol of culture but as a poor, worried, stumbling young man in love with a woman of whose feelings he is not yet certain. In the end, of course, he triumphs and proclaims his joy in words that identify him as a well-rounded human being to whom one can relate: "I am indeed happy. A poet, a lover, the husband of the woman I adore. What is there more for me to desire?"[22] Nineteenth-century America swallowed Shakespeare, digested him and his plays, and made them part of the cultural body. If Shakespeare originally came to America as *Culture* in the libraries of the educated, he existed in pre–Civil War America as *culture.* The nature of his reception by nineteenth-century audiences confirms this conclusion.

While he was performing in Natchez, Mississippi, in 1835, the Irish actor Tyrone Power observed people on the road hurrying to the theater. Their fine horses, ornate and often antique saddles, and picturesque clothing transported him back to Elizabethan England and "the palmy days of the Globe and Bear-garden." Power's insight was sound; there *were* significant similarities between the audiences of Shakespeare's own day and those he drew in America. One of Shakespeare's contemporaries commented that the theater was "frequented by all sorts of people old and younge, rich and poore, masters and servants, papists and puritans, wise men etc., churchmen and statesmen." The nineteenth-century American audience was equally heterogeneous. In both eras the various classes saw the same plays in the same theaters—though not necessarily from the same vantage point. Until mid-century, at least, American theaters generally had a tripartite seating arrangement: the pit (orchestra), the boxes, and the gallery (balcony). Although theater prices fell substantially from 1800 to 1850, seating arrangements continued to dovetail with class and economic divisions. In the boxes sat, as one spectator put it, "the dandies, and people of the first respectability and fashion." The gallery was inhabited largely by those—apprentices, servants, poor workingmen—who could not afford better seats or by those—Negroes and often prostitutes—who were not allowed to sit elsewhere. The pit was dominated by what were rather vaguely called the "middling classes"—a "mixed multitude" that some contemporaries praised as the "honest folks" or "the sterling part of the audience."[23]

All observers agreed that the nineteenth-century theater housed under one roof a microcosm of American society. This, the actor Joseph Jefferson maintained, was what made drama a more difficult art than painting, music, or writing, which "have a direct following, generally from a class whose taste and understanding are pretty evenly balanced,—whereas a theater is divided into three and sometimes four classes." Walt Whitman warmly recalled the Bowery Theatre around the year 1840, where he could look up to the first tier of boxes and see "the faces of the leading authors, poets, editors, of those times," while he sat in the pit surrounded by the "slang, wit, occasional shirt sleeves, and a picturesque freedom of looks and manners, with a rude good-nature and restless movement" of cartmen, butchers, firemen, and mechanics. Others spoke of the mixed audience with less enthusiasm. Washington Irving wrote a series of letters to the New York *Morning Chronicle* in 1802 and 1803 describing his theater experiences. The noise in the gallery he found "is somewhat similar to that which prevailed in Noah's Ark; for we have an imitation of the whistles and yells of every kind of animal." When the "gallery gods" were roused for one reason or another, "they commenced a discharge of apples, nuts & ginger-bread, on the heads of the honest folks in the pit."[24]

Little had changed by 1832 when the English visitor Frances Trollope attended the theater in several American cities. In Cincinnati she observed coatless men with their sleeves rolled up, incessantly spitting, reeking "of onions and whiskey." She enjoyed the Shakespeare but abhorred the "perpetual" noises: "the applause is expressed by cries and thumping with the feet, instead of clapping; and when a patriotic fit seized them, and 'Yankee Doodle' was called for, every man seemed to think his reputation as a citizen depended on the noise he made." Things were no better in Philadelphia and, if anything, worse in New York theaters, where she witnessed "a lady performing the most maternal office possible . . . and a general air of contempt for the decencies of life."[25] When he published his reminiscences in 1836, Tyrone Power tried to counter such accounts by praising the attentiveness and intelligence of his American audiences, but it appears that what differed was less the audience than Power's tolerance for it. For instance, in hailing the "degree of repose and gentility of demeanour" of the audience he performed for in New Orleans in 1835, he wrote:

The least prolonged tumult of approbation even is stilled by a word to order: and when it is considered that here are assembled the wildest and

rudest specimens of the Western population, men owning no control except the laws, and not viewing these over submissively, and who admit of
no *arbiter elegantiarum* or standard of fine breeding, it confers infinite credit
on their innate good feeling, and that sense of propriety which here forms
the sole check on their naturally somewhat uproarious jollity.[26]

Evidence of this sort makes it clear that an understanding of the American theater in our own time is not adequate grounding for a comprehension of American theater in the nineteenth century. To envision
nineteenth-century theater audiences correctly, one might do well to visit
a contemporary sporting event in which the spectators not only are similarly heterogeneous but are also—in the manner of both the nineteenth
century and the Elizabethan era—more than an audience; they are participants who can enter into the action on the field, who feel a sense of
immediacy and at times even of control, who articulate their opinions
and feelings vocally and unmistakably. Washington Irving wryly observed, "The good folks of the gallery have all the trouble of ordering
the music." When the orchestra's selection displeased them, they stamped,
hissed, roared, whistled, and groaned in cadence until the musicians played
"Moll in the wad, Tally ho the grinders, and several other *airs* more suited
to their tastes." The audience's vociferousness continued during the play
itself, which was punctuated by expressions of disapproval in the form
of hisses or groans and of approval in the form of applause, whistles,
and stamping to the point that a Virginia editor felt called upon to remind his readers in 1829 that it was not "a duty to applaud at the conclusion of every sentence." A French reporter, attending a production of
Shakespeare in California in 1851, was fascinated by the audience's enthusiasm: "the more they like a play, the louder they whistle, and when
a San Francisco audience bursts into shrill whistles and savage yells, you
may be sure they are in raptures of joy." Audiences frequently demanded—and got—instant encores from performers who particularly
pleased them. "Perhaps," a New York editor wrote sarcastically in 1846,
"we'll flatter Mr. Kean by making him take poison twice."[27]

Like the Elizabethans, a substantial portion of nineteenth-century
American audiences knew their Shakespeare well. Sol Smith reported
that in 1839, when he wanted to put on an evening of acts from various
Shakespearean plays in St. Louis, he had "no difficulty in finding Hamlets, Shylocks and Richards in abundance, very glad of the opportunity
to exhibit their hidden powers." Constance Rourke has shown that as far
west as California, from miners' camps to the galleries of urban theaters,
there were many who knew large parts of the plays by heart.[28] This
knowledge easily became an instrument of control, as more than one
hapless actor found out. In the winter of 1856 Hugh F. McDermott's
depiction of Richard III did not meet the critical expectations of his

Sacramento audience. During the early scenes of Act I "a few carrots timely thrown, had made their appearance," but the full ardor of the audience was roused only when Richard's killing of Henry included a "thrust *a posteriori*, after Henry had fallen." Then, the Sacramento *Union* reported, "cabbages, carrots, pumpkins, potatoes, a wreath of vegetables, a sack of flour and one of soot, a dead goose, with other articles, simultaneously made their appearance upon the stage." The barrage woke the dead Henry, who fled followed by Richard, "his head enveloped in a halo of vegetable glory." Pleas from the manager induced the audience to allow the play to go on—but not for long. Early in Act II, McDermott's ineptness brought forth first a storm of shouts and then a renewal of the vegetable shower accompanied this time by Chinese firecrackers. As poor Richard fled for the second time, "a well directed pumpkin caused him to stagger; and with still truer aim, a potato relieved him of his cap, which was left upon the field of glory, among the cabbages."[29]

Scenes like this account for the frequent assurance on playbills that "proper officers are appointed who will rigidly enforce decorum."[30] Proper officers or not, such incidents were common enough to prompt a nineteenth-century gentleman to note in his diary, "The egg as a vehicle of dramatic criticism came into early use in this Continent."[31] Nevertheless, the same California audiences capable of driving King Richard from the stage could pay homage to a performance they recognized as superior. Irish-born Matilda Heron's portrayal of Juliet on New Year's night 1854 "so fascinated and entranced" the "walnut-cracking holiday audience," according to the San Francisco *Chronicle,* that "they sat motionless and silent for some moments after the scene was done; and then suddenly recovering themselves from the thraldom under which they had been placed, they came down in a shower of applause that shook the house."[32]

These frenetic displays of approval and disapproval were signs of engagement in what was happening on the stage—an engagement that on occasion could blur the line between audience and actors. At a performance of *Richard III* with Junius Brutus Booth at New York's Bowery Theatre in December 1832, the holiday audience was so large that some three hundred people overflowed onto the stage and entered into the spirit of things, the New York *Mirror* reported. They examined Richard's royal regalia with interest, hefted his sword, and tried on his crown; they moved up to get a close look at the ghosts of King Henry, Lady Anne, and the children when these characters appeared on stage; they mingled with the soldiers during the battle of Bosworth Field and responded to the roll of drums and blast of trumpets by racing across the stage. When Richard and Richmond began their fight, the audience "made a ring around the combatants to see fair play, and kept them at it for nearly a quarter of an hour by 'Shrewsbury's clock.' This was all done in perfect good humor, and with no intention to make a row." When Dan Rice came on to dance his famous Jim Crow, the on-stage audience made him repeat it some twenty times, "and in the afterpiece, where a supper-table [was] spread, some among the most hungry very leisurely helped themselves to the viands."[33] Frequently, members of the audience became so involved in the action on stage that they interfered in order to dispense charity to the sick and destitute, advice to the indecisive, and, as one man did during a Baltimore production of *Coriolanus* and another during a New York production of *Othello,* protection to someone involved in an unfair fight.[34]

These descriptions should make it clear how difficult it is to draw arbitrary lines between popular and folk culture. Here was professional entertainment containing numerous folkish elements, including a knowledgeable, participatory audience exerting important degrees of control. The integration of Shakespeare into the culture as a whole should bring into serious question our tendency to see culture on a vertical plane, neatly divided into a hierarchy of inclusive adjectival categories such as "high," "low," "pop," "mass," "folk," and the like. If the phenomenon of Shakespeare was not an aberration—and the diverse audiences for such art forms as Italian opera, such performers as singer Jenny Lind, and such writers as Longfellow, Dickens, and Mark Twain indicate it was not—then the study of Shakespeare's relationship to the American people helps reveal the existence of a shared public culture to which we have not paid enough attention. It has been obscured by the practice of employing such categories as "popular" aesthetically rather than literally. That is, the adjective "popular" has been utilized to describe not only those creations of expressive culture that actually had a large audience (which is the way I have tried to use it in this essay), but also, and often primarily, those that had questionable artistic merit. Thus, a banal play or a poorly written romantic novel has been categorized as popular culture, even if it had a tiny audience, while the recognized artistic attributes of a Shakespearean play have prevented it from being included in popular culture, regardless of its high degree of popularity. The use of such arbitrary and imprecise cultural categories has helped obscure the dynamic complexity of American culture in the nineteenth century.

Our difficulty also proceeds from the historical fallacy of reading the present into the past. By the middle of the twentieth century, Shakespearean drama did not occupy the place it had in the nineteenth century. As a Shakespearean scholar wrote in 1963, "the days when a Davenport and a Barry could open rival productions of *Hamlet* on the same night, as in 1875; when *Macbeth* could be seen at three different theatres in New York in 1849; when ten *Hamlets* could be produced in a single season, as in New York in 1857–58; . . . these days are unfortunately gone."[35] Although in the mid-twentieth century there was no more widely known, respected, or quoted dramatist in our culture than Shakespeare, the nature of his relationship to the American people had changed: he was no longer their familiar, no longer part of their culture, no longer at home in their theaters or on the movie and television screens that had become the twentieth-century equivalents of the stage. If Shakespeare had been an integral part of mainstream culture in the nineteenth century, in the twentieth he had become part of "polite" culture—an essential ingredient in a complex we call, significantly, "legitimate" theater. He had become the possession of the educated portions of society who disseminated his plays for the enlightenment of the average folk who were to swallow him not for their entertainment but for their education, as a respite from—not as a normal part of—their usual cultural diet. Recalling his youthful experiences with Shakespeare, the columnist Gerald Nachman wrote in 1979 that in the schools of America "Shakespeare becomes theatrical spinach: He's good for you. If you digest enough of his plays, you'll grow up big and strong intellectually like teacher." The efforts of such young producers and directors as Joseph Papp in the late 1950s and the 1960s to liberate Shakespeare from the genteel prison in which he had been confined, to restore his plays to their original vitality, and to disseminate them among what Papp called "a great dispossessed audience" is a testament to what had happened to Shakespearean drama since the mid-nineteenth century.[36]

Signs of this transformation appear throughout the twentieth century. In his 1957 treatise on how to organize community theaters, John Wray Young warned, "Most organizations will find it difficult to please with the classics. . . . Shakespeare, Ibsen, Chekhov, the Greeks, and the other masters are hard to sell in the average community situation." Shakespeare had become not only a hard-to-sell classic to average members of the community but even an alienating force. In a 1929 episode of the popular comic strip "Bringing Up Father," the neighborhood bartender, Dinty Moore, suddenly goes "high hat" when he meets and courts a wealthy woman. The symbols of his attempt to enter "society," which alienate him from his friends, are his fancy clothing, his poodle dog, his horseback riding and golf, his pretentious language, *and* his reading of Shakespeare's *Romeo and Juliet,* which so infuriates his friend Jiggs that he seizes the volume and throws it at Moore.[37] In one of his wonderful monologues on politics, published in 1905, George Washington Plunkitt, ward boss of the fifteenth assembly district in New York City and one of the powers of Tammany Hall, admonished aspiring politicians:

> If you're makin' speeches in a campaign, talk the language the people talk. Don't try to show how the situation is by quoting Shakespeare. Shake-

speare was all right in his way, but he didn't know anything about Fifteenth District politics. . . . go out and talk the language of the Fifteenth to the people. I know it's an awful temptation, the hankerin' to show off your learnin'. I've felt it myself, but I always resist it. I know the awful consequences.[38]

For Plunkitt, and obviously for his constituents, Shakespeare symbolized "learning," irrelevant, impractical, pretentious—fit only for what Plunkitt called "the name-parted-in-the-middle aristocrats." Similarly, in her account of her life as a worker, Dorothy Richardson deplored the maudlin yellowback novels that dominated the reading habits of working women at the turn of the century and pleaded for the wide dissemination of better literature:

Only, please, Mr. or Mrs. Philanthropist, don't let it be Shakespeare, or Ruskin, or Walter Pater. Philanthropists have tried before to reform degraded literary tastes with heroic treatment, and they have failed every time. That is sometimes the trouble with the college settlement folk. They forget that Shakespeare, and Ruskin, and all the rest of the really true and great literary crew, are infinite bores to every-day people.[39]

Culture is a process, not a fixed condition; it is the product of unremitting interaction between the past and the present. Thus, Shakespeare's relationship to the American people was always in flux, always changing. Still, it is possible to isolate a period during which the increasing separation of Shakespeare from "every-day people" becomes more evident. The American Theatre in San Francisco advised those attending its May 29, 1855, production of *A Midsummer Night's Dream* that "owing to the length of the play there will be NO FARCE." Similarly, in 1869 the Varieties Theatre in New Orleans announced in its playbill advertising Mrs. Scott Siddons in *As You Like It*, "In consequence of the length of this comedy, it will constitute the Evening's Entertainment." In following decades it became less and less necessary for theaters to issue such explanations. In 1873 the California Theatre in San Francisco advertised *Coriolanus* with no promise of a farce or between-act entertainment—and no apologies. This became true in city after city. There is no precise date, but everywhere in the United States during the final decades of the nineteenth century the same transformation was evidently taking place; Shakespeare was being divorced from the broader world of everyday culture. Gone were the entre-act diversions: the singers, jugglers, dancers, acrobats, orators. Gone, too, was the purple prose trumpeting the sensational events and pageantry that were part of the Shakespearean plays themselves. Those who wanted their Shakespeare had to take him alone, lured to his plays by stark playbills promising no frills or enhancements. In December 1890 Pittsburgh's Duquesne Theatre advertised productions of *The Merchant of Venice, Othello, Romeo and Juliet* and *Julius Ceasar* by announcing simply, "Engagement of Mr. Lawrence Barrett, supported by Miss Gale And a Competent Company of Players." Significantly, the frequent admonitions relating to audience behavior were now missing as well. By the early twentieth century, playbills of this type became the norm everywhere.[40] Once again, William Shakespeare had become *Culture*.

It is easier to describe this transformation than to explain it, since the transformation itself has clouded our vision of the past. So completely have twentieth-century Americans learned to accept as natural and timeless Shakespeare's status as an elite, classic dramatist, to whose plays the bulk of the populace do not or cannot relate, that we have found it difficult to comprehend nineteenth-century conceptions of Shakespeare. Too frequently, modern historians of the theater have spent less time and energy understanding Shakespeare's nineteenth-century popularity than in explaining it away. The formula is simple: how to account for the indisputable popularity of a great master in a frontier society with an "overwhelmingly uneducated" public. The consensus seems to be that Shakespeare was popular for all the wrong reasons: because of the afterpieces and *divertissements* that surrounded his plays; because the people wanted to see great actors who in turn insisted on performing Shakespeare to demonstrate their abilities; because his plays were presented in altered, simplified versions; because of his bombast, crudities, and sexual allusions rather than his poetry or sophistication; because of almost anything but his dramatic genius. "Shakespeare," we are told in a conclusion that would not be important if it were not so typical, "could communicate with the unsophisticated at the level of action and oratory while appealing to the small refined element at the level of dramatic and poetic artistry."[41]

Again and again, historians and critics have arbitrarily separated the "action and oratory" of Shakespeare's plays from the "dramatic and poetic artistry" with which they were, in reality, so intricately connected. We are asked to believe that the average member of the audience saw only violence, lewdness, and sensationalism in such plays as *Richard III, Hamlet, King Lear, Othello* and *Macbeth* and was incapable of understanding the moral and ethical dilemmas, the generational strains between parents and children, the crude ambition of Richard III or Lady Macbeth, the haunting guilt of Macbeth, the paralyzing introspection and doubts of Hamlet, the envy of Iago, the insecurities of Othello. We have been asked to believe that such human conditions and situations were beyond the powers of most of the audience and touched only a "refined element" who understood the "subtleties of Shakespeare's art."

Certainly, the relationship of an audience to the object of its focus—be it a sermon, political speech, newspaper, musical composition, or play—

is a complex one and constitutes a problem for the historian who would reconstruct it. But the problem cannot be resolved through the use of such ahistorical devices as dividing both the audience and the object into crude categories and then coming to conclusions that have more to do with the culture of the writer than that of the subject. In fact, the way to understand the popularity of Shakespeare is to enter into the spirit of the nineteenth century. Shakespeare was popular, first and foremost, because he was integrated into the culture and presented within its context. Nineteenth-century Americans were able to fit Shakespeare into their culture so easily because he *seemed* to fit—because so many of his values and tastes were, or at least appeared to be, close to their own, and were presented through figures that seemed real and came to matter to the audience. Shakespeare's characters, Henry Norman Hudson insisted, were so vivid, so alive, that they assumed the shape "of actual persons, so that we know them as well and remember them as distinctly as we do our most intimate friends." For the teenaged William Dean Howells, who memorized great chunks of Shakespeare while working as an apprentice printer in his father's newspaper office in the 1850s, the world of Shakespeare was one in which he felt as much "at home," as much like "a citizen," as he did in his small Ohio town.[42]

Both worlds enshrined the art of oratory. The same Americans who found diversion and pleasure in lengthy political debates, who sought joy and God in the sermons of church and camp meeting, who had, in short, a seemingly inexhaustible appetite for the spoken word, thrilled to Shakespeare's eloquence, memorized his soliloquies, delighted in his dialogues. Although nineteenth-century Americans stressed the importance of literacy and built an impressive system of public education, theirs remained an oral world in which the spoken word was central. In such a world, Shakespeare had no difficulty finding a place. Nor was Shakespearean oratory confined to the professional stage; it often was a part of life. Walt Whitman recalled that as a young man he rode in the Broadway omnibuses "declaiming some stormy passage from Julius Caesar or Richard" to passersby. In the 1850s Mark Twain worked as an apprentice to the pilot-master George Ealer on the steamboat *Pennsylvania:* "He would read Shakespeare to me; not just casually, but by the hour, when it was his watch, and I was steering. . . . He did not use the book, and did not need to; he knew his Shakespeare as well as Euclid ever knew his multiplication table." In Corpus Christi, Texas, in 1845, soldiers of the Fourth Infantry Regiment broke the monotony of waiting for the Mexican War to begin by staging plays, including a performance of *Othello* starring young Lieutenant Ulysses S. Grant as Desdemona. Many of Lincoln's aides and associates remembered his tendency to recite long, relevant passages from Shakespeare during the troubling days of the Civil War. Shakespeare was taught in nineteenth-century schools and colleges as declamation or rhetoric, not literature. For many youngsters Shakespeare was first encountered in schoolbooks as texts to be recited aloud and memorized. Through such means, Shakespearean phrases, aphorisms, ideas, and language helped shape American speech and became so integral a part of the nineteenth-century imagination that it is a futile exercise to separate Americans' love of Shakespeare's oratory from their appreciation for his subtle use of language.[43]

It was not merely Shakespeare's language but his style that recommended itself to nineteenth-century audiences. In a period when melodrama became one of the mainstays of the American stage, Shakespearean plays easily lent themselves to the melodramatic style. Shakespearean drama featured heroes and villains who communicated directly with the audience and left little doubt about the nature of their character or their intentions. In a series of asides during the opening scenes of the first act, Macbeth shares his "horrible imaginings" and "vaulting ambition" with the audience (I.iii–vii). Similarly, Iago confides to the audience "I hate the Moor," rehearses his schemes of "double knavery" to betray both Cassio and Othello, and confesses that his jealousy of Othello "Doth, like a poisonous mineral, gnaw my inwards; / And nothing can or shall content my soul / Till I am evened with him" (I.iii). As in melodrama, Shakespearean villains are aware not only of their own evil but also of the goodness of their adversaries. Thus Iago, even as he plots against Othello, admits that "The Moor—howbeit that I endure him not— / Is of a constant, loving, noble nature" (II.i).

Lines like these, which so easily fit the melodramatic mode, were delivered in appropriately melodramatic style. The actors who dominated the stage during the first half of the nineteenth century were vigorous, tempestuous, emotional. To describe these men, contemporaries reached for words like "hurricane," "maelstrom," "avalanche," "earthquake," "monsoon," and "whirlwind." Edmund Kean's acting, one of them noted, was "just on the edge, sometimes quite over the edge of madness." It "blinded and stunned the beholders, appalled the imagination, and chilled their blood." Walt Whitman, who saw Junius Brutus Booth perform in the late 1830s, wrote of him, "He illustrated Plato's rule that to the forming an artist of the very highest rank a dash of insanity or what the world calls insanity is indispensable."[44] The first great American-born Shakespearean actor, Edwin Forrest, carried his romantic tradition to its logical culmination. William Rounseville Alger, who saw Forrest perform, described his portrayal of Lear after Goneril rebuffs him:

> His eyes flashed and faded and reflashed. He beat his breast as if not knowing what he did. His hands clutched wildly at the air as though struggling with something invisible. Then, sinking on his knees, with upturned

look and hands straight outstretched towards his unnatural daughter, he poured out, in frenzied tones of mingled shriek and sob, his withering curse, half adjuration, half malediction.[45]

As in melodrama itself, language and style in American productions of Shakespeare were not utilized randomly; they were used to inculcate values, to express ideas and attitudes. For all of the complaints of such as Whitman that the feudal plays of Shakespeare were not altogether fitting for a democratic age, Shakespeare's attraction for nineteenth-century audiences was due in no small part to the fact that he was—or at least was taken to be—in tune with much of nineteenth-century American consciousness. From the beginning, Shakespeare's American admirers and promoters maintained that he was pre-eminently a *moral* playwright. To overcome the general prejudice against the theater in the eighteenth century, Shakespeare's plays were frequently presented as "moral dialogues" or "moral lectures." For Thomas Jefferson, "A lively and lasting sense of filial duty is more effectually impressed on the mind of a son or daughter by reading *King Lear,* than by all the dry volumes of ethics and divinity that ever were written." For Abraham Lincoln, *Macbeth* stood as "the perfect illustration of the problems of tyranny and murder." And John Quincy Adams concluded, even as he was waging his heroic fight against the power of the slave South in the House of Representatives in 1836, that the moral of *Othello* was "that the intermarriage of black and white blood is a violation of the law of nature. *That* is the lesson to be learned from the play."[46]

Regardless of specific interpretations, writers of nineteenth-century schoolbooks and readers seemed to have agreed with Henry Norman Hudson that Shakespeare's works provided "a far better school of virtuous discipline than half the moral and religious books which are now put into the hands of youth" and reprinted lines from Shakespeare not only to illustrate the art of declamation but also to disseminate moral values and patriotic principles. As late as 1870 the playbill of a New Orleans theater spelled out the meaning of *Twelfth Night:* "MORAL: In this play Shakespeare has finely penciled the portraits of Folly and Vanity in the persons of Aguecheek and Malvolio; and with a not less masterly hand, he has exhibited the weakness of the human mind when Love has usurped the place of Reason." The affinity between Shakespeare and the American people went beyond moral homilies; it extended to the basic ideological underpinnings of nineteenth-century America. When Cassius proclaimed that "The fault, dear Brutus, is not in our stars, / But in ourselves, that we are underlings" (*Julius Ceasar,* I.ii), and when Helena asserted that "Our remedies oft in ourselves do lie, / Which we ascribe to heaven: the fated sky / Gives us free scope"

(*All's Well That Ends Well,* I.i), they articulated a belief that was central to the pervasive success ethos of the nineteenth century and that confirmed the developing American worldview.[47]

Whatever Shakespeare's own designs, philosophy, and concept of humanity were, his plays had meaning to a nation that placed the individual at the center of the universe and personalized the large questions of the day. The actor Joseph Jefferson held Shakespeare responsible for the star system that prevailed for so much of the nineteenth century since "his tragedies almost without exception contain one great character on whom the interest of the play turns, and upon whom the attention of the audience is centered." Shakespeare's characters—like the Davy Crocketts and Mike Finks that dominated American folklore and the Jacksons, Websters, Clays, and Calhouns who dominated American politics—were larger than life: their passions, appetites, and dilemmas were of epic proportions. Here were forceful, meaningful people who faced, on a larger scale, the same questions as those that filled the pages of schoolbooks: the duties of children and parents, husbands and wives, governed and governors to one another. In their lives the problems of jealousy, morality, and ambition were all writ large. However flawed some of Shakespeare's central figures were, they at least acted—even the indecisive Hamlet—and bore responsibility for their own fate. If they failed, they did so because ultimately they lacked sufficient inner control. Thus Othello was undone by his jealousy and gullibility, Coriolanus by his pride, Macbeth and Richard III by their ambition. All of them could be seen as the architects of their own fortunes, masters of their own fate. All of them, Hudson taught his audiences, "contain within themselves the reason why they are there and not elsewhere, why they are so and not otherwise."[48]

How important this quality of individual will was can be seen in the fate of Sophocles' *Oedipus* in nineteenth-century America. The play was introduced twice in the century to New York audiences and failed both times, largely because of its subject matter. The New York *Tribune*'s reaction, after *Oedipus* opened in January 1882, was typical: "King Oedipus certainly carries more woe to the square inch than anybody else that ever walked upon the stage. And it is woe of the very worst kind—without solace, and without hope." Sophocles seemed guilty of determinism—an ideological stance nineteenth-century Americans rejected out of hand. "The overmastering fates that broke men and women upon the wheel of torture that destiny might be fulfilled are far away from us, the gods that lived and cast deep shadows over men's lives are turned to stone," the New York *Herald*'s reviewer wrote. "The helpful human being—who pays his way through the world finds it hard to imagine the creature kicking helpless in the traps of the gods." Similarly, critics attacked the bloodshed and immorality in *Oedipus*. The New York *Mirror* denounced "a plot like this, crammed full of murder, suicide, self-mutilation, incest, and dark deeds of a similar character."[49] Shakespearean drama, of course, was no less laced through with gore. But, while this quality in Sophocles seemed to Americans to be an end in itself, Shakespeare's thought patterns were either close enough or were made to seem close enough so that the violence had a point, and that point appeared to buttress American values and confirm American expectations.

This ideological equation, this ability of Shakespeare to connect with Americans' underlying beliefs, is crucial to an understanding of his role in nineteenth-century America. Much has been made of the adaptations of Shakespeare as instruments that made him somehow more understandable to American audiences. Certainly, the adaptations did work this way—but not primarily, as has been so widely claimed, by vulgarizing or simplifying him to the point of utter distortion but rather by heightening those qualities in Shakespeare that American audiences were particularly drawn to. The liberties taken with Shakespeare in nineteenth-century America were often similar to liberties taken with folklore: Shakespeare was frequently seen as common property to be treated as the user saw fit. Thus many small changes were made for practical and moral reasons without much fanfare or fuss: minor roles were consolidated to create richer acting parts; speeches and scenes, considered overly long or extraneous, were shortened or omitted; sexual references were rendered more palatable by shifting such words as "whores" to "wenches" or "maidenheads" to "virtue"; contemporary sensibilities were catered to by making Juliet eighteen rather than thirteen or by softening some of Hamlet's angriest diatribes against Ophelia and his mother. Some of the alterations bordered on the spectacular, such as the flying, singing witches in *Macbeth* and the elaborate funeral procession that accompanied Juliet's body to the tomb of the Capulets in *Romeo and Juliet*. On the whole, such limited changes were made with respect for—and sensitivity to—Shakespeare's purposes.[50]

It is important to realize that, while some of the alterations were imported from England and others were made in America, none were adopted indiscriminately. Of the many drastically revised editions of Shakespeare that originated in England, only three held sway in the United States during the nineteenth century: David Garrick's *Catharine and Petruchio* (1756), Nahum Tate's revision of *King Lear* (1681), and Colley Cibber's revision of *Richard III* (1700). For our purposes, the first is the least significant, since it was largely a three-act condensation of *The Taming of the Shrew*, which retained the basic thrust of Shakespeare's original and won considerable popularity as an afterpiece. If brevity was the chief virtue of Garrick's *Catharine and Petruchio*, the attractions of Cibber's

Richard and Tate's *Lear* were more complex and suggest that those alterations of Shakespeare that became most prevalent in the United States were those that best fit the values and ideology of the period and the people.

For most of the nineteenth century Colley Cibber's *Richard III* held sway everywhere.[51] Cibber's revision, by cutting one-third of the lines, eliminating half of the characters, adding scenes from other Shakespearean plays and from Cibber's own pen, succeeded in muting the ambiguities of the original and focusing all of the evil in the person of Richard. Thus, although Cibber retained Shakespeare's essential plot and much of his poetry, he refashioned the play in such a way that, while his work was done in the England of 1700, it could have been written a hundred years later in the United States, so closely did it agree with American sensibilities concerning the centrality of the individual, the dichotomy between good and evil, and the importance of personal responsibility. Richmond's speech over the body of the vanquished Richard mirrored perfectly America's moral sense and melodramatic taste:

> Farewel, Richard, and from thy dreadful end
> May future Kings from Tyranny be warn'd;
> Had thy aspiring Soul but stir'd in Vertue
> With half the Spirit it has dar'd in Evil,
> How might thy Fame have grac'd our English Annals:
> But as thou art, how fair a Page thou'st blotted.

If Cibber added lines making clear the fate of villains, he was no less explicit concerning the destiny of heroes. After defeating Richard, Richmond is informed that "the Queen and fair Elizabeth, / Her beauteous Daughter, some few miles off, are / On their way to Gratulate your Victory." His reply must have warmed America's melodramatic heart as much as it confirmed its ideological underpinnings: "Ay, there indeed my toil's rewarded."[52]

Tate's altered *King Lear*, like Cibber's *Richard III*, virtually displaced Shakespeare's own version for almost two centuries. Tate, who distorted Shakespeare far more than Cibber did, devised a happy ending for what was one of the most tragic of all of Shakespeare's plays: he created a love affair between Edgar and Cordelia and allowed Cordelia and Lear to live. Although there were certainly critics of this fundamental alteration, it proved popular with theatergoers. When in 1826 James H. Hackett chided his fellow actor Edmund Kean about his choice of Tate's ending rather than Shakespeare's, Kean replied that he had attempted to restore the original, "but when I had ascertained that a large majority of the public—whom we live to please, and must please to be popular—like Tate better than Shakespeare, I fell back upon his corruption; though in my soul I was ashamed of the prevailing taste, and of my professional condition that required me to minister unto it."[53] Still, many Americans defended the Tate version on ideological grounds. "The moral's now more complete," wrote a contemporary, "for although Goneril, Regan, and Edmond were deservedly punished for their crimes, yet Lear and Cordelia were killed without reason and without fault. But now they survive their enemies and virtue is crowned with happiness."[54] That virtue be "crowned with happiness" was essential to the beliefs of nineteenth-century Americans. Thus audiences had the pleasure of having their expectations confirmed when Edgar concludes the play by declaiming to "Divine Cordelia":

> Thy bright Example shall convince the World
> (Whatever Storms of Fortune are decreed)
> That Truth and Vertue shall at last succeed.[55]

The profound and longstanding nineteenth-century American experience with Shakespeare, then, was neither accidental nor aberrant. It was based upon the language and eloquence, the artistry and humor, the excitement and action, the moral sense and worldview that Americans found in Shakespearean drama. The more firmly based Shakespeare was in nineteenth-century culture, of course, the more difficult it is to understand why he lost so much of his audience so quickly.

A complete explanation would require a separate research project of its own, but it is appropriate here to probe tentatively into the factors underlying Shakespeare's transformation. Some of these were intricately connected to the internal history of the theater. So long as the theater was under attack on moral grounds, as it was in the eighteenth and early nineteenth centuries, Shakespeare, because of his immense reputation, could be presented more easily and could be used to help make the theater itself legitimate. Shakespearean drama also lent itself to the prevalent star system. Only the existence of a small repertory of well-known plays, in which Shakespeare's were central, made it feasible for the towering stars of England and America to travel throughout the United States acting with resident stock companies wherever they went. The relative dearth of native dramatists and the relative scarcity of competing forms of theatrical entertainment also figured in Shakespeare's popularity. As these conditions were altered, Shakespeare's popularity and centrality were affected. As important as factors peculiar to the theater were, the theater did not exist in a vacuum; it was an integral part of

American culture—of interest to the historian precisely because it so frequently and so accurately indicated the conditions surrounding it. A fuller explanation must therefore be sought in the larger culture itself.[56]

Among the salient cultural changes at the turn of the century were those in language and rhetorical style. The oratorical mode, which so dominated the nineteenth century and which helped make Shakespeare popular, hardly survived into the twentieth century. No longer did Americans tolerate speeches of several hours' duration. No longer was their attention riveted upon such political debates as that between Webster and Hayne in 1830, which consumed several days. It is true that in the closing years of the century William Jennings Bryan could still rise to national political leadership through his superb oratorical skills, but it is equally true that he lived to see himself become an anachronism, the bearer of a style redolent of an earlier culture. The surprisingly rapid decline of oratory as a force in national life has not received the study it deserves, but certainly it was affected by the influx of millions of non-English-speaking people. The more than one thousand foreign-language newspapers and magazines published in the United States by 1910 testify graphically to the existence of a substantial group for whom Shakespeare, at least in his original language, was less familiar and less accessible.[57] These immigrant folk helped constitute a ready audience for the rise of the more visual entertainments such as baseball, boxing, vaudeville, burlesque, and especially the new silent movies, which could be enjoyed by a larger and often more marginal audience less steeped in the language and the culture.

If what Reuel Denney called the "deverbalization of the forum" weakened Shakespeare among some segments of the population, the parallel growth of literacy among other groups also undermined some of the props that had sustained Shakespeare's popularity. Literacy encroached upon the pervasive oral culture that had created in nineteenth-century America an audience more comfortable with listening than with reading. Thus the generations of people accustomed to hearing and reciting things out loud—the generations for whom oral recitation of the King James version of the Bible could well have formed a bridge to the English of Shakespeare—were being depleted as America entered a new century.[58]

These language-related changes were accompanied by changes in taste and style. John Higham has argued that from the 1860s through the 1880s romantic idealism declined in the United States.[59] The melodramatic mode, to which Shakespeare lent himself so well and in which he was performed so frequently, went into a related decline. Edwin Booth, the most influential Shakespearean actor in America during the closing decades of the nineteenth century, played his roles in a less ferocious, more subtle and intellectualized fashion than his father and most of the other leading actors of the first half of the century had. When asked how his acting compared to his father's, Booth replied simply, "I think I must be somewhat quieter." The younger Booth's quietness became the paradigm.[60] The visceral, thunderous style fell into such disfavor that by 1920 the critic Francis Hackett not only berated John Barrymore for his emotional portrayal of Richard III but also took Shakespeare himself to task for the "unsophisticated" manner in which he had crafted the play—the play that nineteenth-century audiences had enjoyed above all others: "the plot, the psychology, the history, seem to me infantile. . . . Are we led to understand Richard? No, only to moralize over him. Thus platitude makes cowards of us all."[61]

These gradual and decisive changes in language, style, and taste are important but by themselves do not constitute a totally satisfying explanation for the diminished popularity of Shakespeare. As important as changes in language were, they did not prevent the development of radio as a central entertainment medium at the beginning of the 1920s or the emergence of talking movies at the end of that decade. Nor was there anything inherent in the new popular media that necessarily relegated Shakespeare to a smaller, elite audience; on the contrary, he was quite well suited to the new forms of presentation that came to dominance. His comedies had an abundance of slapstick and contrived happy endings, his tragedies and historical plays had more than their share of action. Most importantly, having written for a stage devoid of scenery, Shakespeare could and did incorporate as much spatial mobility as he desired into his plays—twenty-five scene changes in *Macbeth,* one of his shortest plays, and forty-two in *Antony and Cleopatra,* where the action gravitated from Alexandria to such locales as Rome, Messina, Athens, and Syria. This fluidity—which caused innumerable problems for the stagecraft of the nineteenth century—was particularly appropriate to the movies, which could visually reproduce whatever Shakespeare had in mind, and to radio, which, like the Elizabethan stage itself, could rely upon the imagination of its audience. That these new media did not take full advantage of so recently a popular source of entertainment as Shakespearean drama demands further explanation.[62]

Shakespeare did not, of course, disappear from American culture after the turn of the century; he was transformed from a playwright for the general public into one for a specific audience. This metamorphosis from popular culture to polite culture, from entertainment to erudition, from the property of "Everyman" to the possession of a more elite circle needs to be seen with the perspective of other transformations that took place in nineteenth-century America.

At the beginning of the century, as we have seen, the theater was a microcosm; it housed both the entire spectrum of the population and the complete range of entertainment from tragedy to farce, juggling to ballet, opera to minstrelsy. The theater drew all ranks of people to one place where they constituted what Erving Goffman has called a "focused gathering"—a set of people who relate to one another through the medium of a common activity. The term is useful in reminding us that, in the theater, people not only sat under one roof, they interacted. In this sense, the theater in the first half of the nineteenth century constituted a microcosm of still another sort: a microcosm of relations between the various socioeconomic groups in America. The descriptions of such observers as Washington Irving and Mrs. Trollope make it clear that those relations were beset by tensions and conflicts. Even so convinced a democrat as Whitman complained by 1847 that the New York theaters were becoming " 'low' places where vulgarity (not only on the stage, but in front of it) is in the ascendant, and bad-taste carries the day with hardly a pleasant point to mitigate its coarseness." Whitman excepted only the Park Theatre "because the audiences there are always intelligent, and there is a dash of superiority thrown over the Performances." Earlier in the century the Park Theater had received the patronage of the entire public; by the 1830s it had become more exclusive, while the Bowery, Chatham, and other theaters became the preserves of gallery gods and groundlings. This development was not exclusive to New York. "I have discovered that the *people* are with *us*," Tyrone Power reported from Baltimore in 1833, since the Front Theatre, at which he was performing, drew "the sturdy democracy of the good city," while its rival, the Holiday Theatre, was "considered the aristocratic house."[63]

Not only was there an increasing segregation of audiences but ultimately of actors and styles as well. On a winter evening in 1863, George William Curtis, the editor of *Harper's,* took a "rustic friend" to two New York theaters. First they went to see Edwin Forrest at Niblo's Gardens. "It was crammed with people. All the seats were full, and the aisles, and the steps. And the people sat upon the stairs that ascend to the second tier, and they hung upon the balustrade, and they peeped over shoulders and between heads." Forrest's acting, Curtis wrote, was "a boundless exaggeration of all the traditional conventions of the stage." Still he conceded that Forrest "move[d] his world nightly. . . . There were a great many young women around us crying. . . . They were not refined nor intellectual women. They were, perhaps, rather coarse. But they cried good hearty tears." After one act his friend whispered, "I have had as much as I can hold," and they went up the street to the Winter Garden, where Edwin Booth was portraying Iago. "The difference of the spectacle was striking. The house was comfortably full, not crowded. The air of the audience was that of refined attention rather than of eager interest. Plainly it was a more cultivated and intellectual audience." And just as plainly they were seeing a very different type of acting. "Pale, thin, intellectual, with long black hair and dark eyes, Shakespeare's Iago was perhaps never more articulately represented . . . ; all that we saw of Booth was admirable."[64]

In 1810 John Howard Payne complained, "The judicious few are very few indeed. They are always to be found in a Theatre, like flowers in a desert, but they are nowhere sufficiently numerous to *fill* one." By the second half of the century this was evidently no longer the case. Separate theaters, often called *legitimate* theaters, catering to the "judicious," appeared in city after city, leaving the other theaters to those whom Payne called "the idle, profligate, and vulgar."[65] The psychologist Robert Somer has shown the connections between space and status and has argued that "society compensates for blurred social distinctions by clear spatial ones." Such scholars as Burton J. Bledstein and William R. Taylor have noted the Victorian urge to structure or rationalize space.[66] As the traditional spatial distinctions among pit, gallery, and boxes within the theater were undermined by the aggressive behavior of audiences caught up in the egalitarian exuberance of the period and freed in the atmosphere of the theater from many of the demands of normative behavior, this urge gradually led to the creation of separate theaters catering to distinct audiences and shattered for good the phenomenon of theater as a social microcosm of the entire society.

This dramatic split in the American theater was part of more important bifurcations that were taking place in American culture and society. How closely the theater registered societal dissonance can be seen in the audiences' volatile reaction to anything they considered condescending behavior, out of keeping with a democratic society. The tension created by hierarchical seating arrangements helps explain the periodic rain of objects that the gallery unleashed upon those in more privileged parts of the theater. When Washington Irving was "saluted aside [his] head with a rotten pippen" and rose to shake his cane at the gallery gods, he was restrained by a man behind him who warned that this would bring down upon him the full wrath of the people; the only course of action, he was advised, was to "sit down quietly and bend your back to it."[67]

English actors, who were *ipso facto* suspected of aristocratic leanings, had to tread with particular caution. Edmund Kean failed to do so in 1821 when he cancelled his performance of *Richard III* in Boston because only twenty people were in the audience. The next day's papers denounced him for insulting and dishonoring the American people and suggested that he be taken "by the nose, and dragged . . . before the curtain to make his excuses for his conduct." Four years later, when Kean returned to Boston, he attempted to make those excuses, but it was too late. The all-male audience that packed the theater and over-flowed onto the streets allowed him neither to perform *Richard III* nor to "apologize for [his] indiscretions." A barrage of nuts, foodstuffs, and bottles of odorous drugs drove him weeping from the stage and the theater, after which the anti-Keanites in the pit and gallery turned on his supporters in the boxes and did grievous damage to the theater. Kean performed in Philadelphia, New York, and Charleston but precipitated another riot in Baltimore and finally left the country for good.[68]

In 1834 the Irishman Tyrone Power committed exactly the same er-ror—he cancelled a performance in Albany, New York, when the audi-ence numbered less than ten—and found that even his outspoken dem-ocratic sympathies could not save him from a similar fate. When he next performed two days later, he reported, "the house was filled with men, and everything foreboded a violent outbreak. . . . On my appearance the din was mighty deafening; . . . every invention for making the voice of humanity bestial was present and in full use. The boxes I observed to be occupied by well-dressed men, who generally either remained neutral, or by signs sought that I should be heard." Upon the intervention of the manager, Power was allowed to explain himself, after which "the row was resumed with added fierceness: not a word of either play or farce was heard."[69]

The full extent of class feeling and divisions existing in egalitarian America was revealed on a bloody Thursday in May 1849 at and around the Astor Place Opera House in New York City. The immediate catalyst was a longstanding feud between two leading actors, the Englishman William Charles Macready and the American Edwin Forrest, who had become symbols of antithetical values. Forrest's vigorous acting style, his militant love of his country, his outspoken belief in its citizenry, and his frequent articulation of the possibilities of self-improvement and social mobility endeared him to the American people, while Macready's cere-bral acting style, his aristocratic demeanor, and his identification with the wealthy gentry made him appear Forrest's diametric opposite. On May 7, Macready and Forrest appeared against one another in separate productions of *Macbeth*. Forrest's performance was a triumph; Mac-ready's was never heard—he was silenced by a storm of boos and cries of "Down with the codfish aristocracy," which drowned out appeals for order from those in the boxes, and by an avalanche of eggs, apples, potatoes, lemons, and, ultimately, chairs hurled from the gallery, which forced him to leave the stage in the third act.

Macready was now prepared to leave the country as well, but he was dissuaded by persons of "highest respectability," including Washington Irving and Herman Melville, who urged him not to encourage the mob by giving in to it and assured him "that the good sense and respect for order prevailing in this community will sustain you." Eighteen hundred people filled the Astor Place Opera House on the evening of May 10, with some ten thousand more on the streets outside. Assisted by the quick arrest of the most voluble opponents inside the theater, Macready completed his performance of *Macbeth,* but only under great duress. Those outside—stirred by orators' shouts of "Burn the damned den of the aristocracy!" and "You can't go in there without . . . kid gloves and a white vest, damn 'em!"—bombarded the theater with paving stones, attempted to storm the entrances, and were stopped only after detachments of militia fired point blank into the crowd. In the end at least twenty-two people were killed, and over one hundred and fifty were wounded or injured.[70]

If the eighty-six men arrested were at all typical, the crowd had been composed of workingmen—coopers, printers, butchers, carpenters, servants, sailmakers, machinists, clerks, masons, bakers, plumbers, laborers—whose feelings were probably reflected in a speech given at a rally the next day: "Fellow citizens, for what—for whom was this murder committed? . . . To please the aristocracy of the city, at the expense of the lives of unoffending citizens . . . , to revenge the aristocrats of this city against the working class." Although such observers as the New York *Tribune* saw the riot as the "absurd and incredible" result of a petty quarrel, the role of class was not ignored. The *Home Journal* viewed the riot as a protest against "aristocratizing the pit" in such new and exclusive theaters as the Astor Place Opera House and warned that in the future the republic's rich would have to "be mindful where its luxuries offend." The New York *Herald* asserted that the riot had introduced a "new aspect in the minds of many, . . . nothing short of a controversy and collision between those who have been styled the 'exclusives,' or 'upper ten,' and the great popular masses." The New York correspondent for the Philadelphia *Public Ledger* lamented a few days after the riot, "It leaves behind a feeling to which this community has hitherto been a stranger— an opposition of classes—the rich and poor . . . , a feeling that there is now in our country, in New York City, what every good patriot hitherto has considered it his duty to deny—*a high and a low class.*"[71]

The purpose of acting, Shakespeare had Hamlet say in his charge to the players, "was and is, to hold, as 'twere, the mirror up to nature; to show virtue her own feature, scorn her own image, and the very age and body of time his form and pressure" (III.ii). The functions of the nineteenth-century American stage were even broader. As a central institution, the theater not only mirrored the sweep of events in the larger society but presented an arena in which those events could unfold. The Astor Place Riot was both an indication of and a catalyst for the cultural changes that came to characterize the United States at the end of the century. Theater no longer functioned as a cultural form that embodied all classes within a shared public space, nor did Shakespeare much longer remain the common property of all Americans. The changes were not cataclysmic; they were gradual and took place in rough stages: physical or spatial bifurcation, with different socioeconomic groups becoming associated with different theaters in large urban centers, was followed inevitably by the stylistic bifurcation described by George William Curtis and ultimately culminated in a content bifurcation, which saw a growing chasm between "serious" and "popular" culture.

Increasingly in the second half of the nineteenth century, as public life became everywhere more fragmented, the concept of culture took on hierarchical connotations along the lines of Matthew Arnold's definition—"the best that has been thought and known in the world . . . , the study and pursuit of perfection." Looking back on "the disgraceful scenes of the Astor Place Riot" some thirty years later, Henry James pronounced it a manifestation of the "instinctive hostility of barbarism to culture."[72] This practice of distinguishing "culture" from lesser forms of expression became so common that by 1915 Van Wyck Brooks found it necessary to incorporate the terms "highbrow" and "lowbrow" to express the chasm between which "there is no community, no genial middle ground." "What side of American life is not touched by this antithesis?" Brooks asked. "What explanation of American life is more central or more illuminating?"[73] Walt Whitman understood the drift of events as early as 1871. "We find ourselves abruptly in close quarters with the enemy," he charged in *Democratic Vistas*, with "this word Culture, or what it has come to represent." "Refinement and delicatesse," he warned, "threaten to eat us up, like a cancer." Whitman insisted that culture should not be "restricted by conditions ineligible to the masses," should not be created "for a single class alone, or for the parlors or lecture-rooms," and placed his hopes for the creation of a classless, democratic culture in the leadership of the new "middling" groups—"men and women with occupations, well-off owners of houses and acres, and with cash in the bank."[74]

The groups to which Whitman turned were neither willing nor able to fulfill his expectations. The emergence of new middle and upper-middle classes, created by rapid industrialization in the nineteenth century, seems to have accelerated rather than inhibited the growing distinctions between elite and mass culture. When, in the waning years of the century, Thorstein Veblen constructed his concept of conspicuous consumption, he included not only the obvious material possessions but also "immaterial" goods—"the knowledge of dead languages and the occult sciences; of correct spelling; of syntax and prosody; of the various forms of domestic music . . . ; of the latest proprieties of dress, furniture, and equipage"; of the ancient "classics"—all of which constituted a conspicuous culture that helped confer legitimacy on the newly emergent groups.[75] "Culture" became something refined, ideal, removed from and elevated above the mundane events of everyday life. This helps explain the vogue during this period of manuals of etiquette, of private libraries and rare books, of European art and music displayed and performed in ornate—often neoclassical—museums and concert halls.[76]

It also helps explain the transformation of Shakespeare, who fit the new cultural equation so well. His plays had survived the test of time and were therefore immortal; his language was archaic and therefore too complex for ordinary people; his poetry was sublime and therefore elevating—especially if his plays could be seen in a theater and a style of one's own choice, devoid of constant reminders that they contained earthier elements and more universal appeals as well. The point is not that there was a conspiracy to remove Shakespeare from the American people but that a cultural development occurred which produced the same result—a result that was compounded by the fact that during these years American entertainment was shaped by many of the same forces of consolidation and centralization that molded other businesses.[77]

If the managers of the new theater chains and huge booking agencies approached their tasks with a hierarchical concept of culture, with the conviction that an unbridgeable gulf separated the tastes and predilections of the various socioeconomic groups, and with the belief that Shakespeare was "highbrow" culture, then we have isolated another decisive factor in his transformation.

The transformation of Shakespeare is important precisely because it was not unique. It was part of a larger transformation that Richard Sennett has argued characterized Western European culture after the eighteenth century, in which public culture fractured into a series of discrete private cultures that had less and less to do with one another. The audience that had been heterogenous, interactive, and participatory became homogeneous, atomized, and passive—in Sennett's phrase, "a spectator rather than a witness."[78] When George Makepeace Towle was rediscovering his native land shortly after the Civil War, opera was still part of the public domain. "*Lucretia Borgia* and *Faust, The Barber of Seville* and *Don Giovanni,* are everywhere popular," he wrote in 1870; "you may hear their airs in the drawing rooms and concert halls, as well as whistled by the street boys and ground out on the hand organs." In the twentieth century, such scenes became increasingly rare as grand opera joined Shakespeare in the elevated circles of elite culture.[79]

The journey could lead in the opposite direction as well. From 1840 to 1900, chromolithography—the process by which original paintings were reproduced lithographically in color and sold in the millions to all segments of the population—was one of the most familiar art forms in the nation. It was hailed as a vehicle for bringing art "within the reach of all classes of society" and praised as "art republicanized and naturalized in America." These very characteristics made chromolithography anathema to E. L. Godkin of *The Nation* and the genteel group for whom he spoke. To Godkin, chromolithography symbolized the packaged "pseudo-culture" that "diffused through the community a kind of smattering of all sorts of knowledge" and gave people the false confidence of being "cultured." "A society of ignoramuses who know they are ignoramuses, might lead to a tolerably happy and useful existence," he wrote, "but a society of ignoramuses each of whom thinks he is a Solon, would be an approach to Bedlam let loose. . . . The result is a kind of mental and moral chaos." Godkin's view prevailed. By the 1890s the term "chromo" had come to mean "ugly" or "offensive." Thus, while at the Philadelphia Centennial Exposition in 1876 chromolithographs were exhibited as "Fine Arts" along with sculpture, painting, and engravings, seventeen years later at Chicago's Columbian Exposition of 1893 they were classified as, and exhibited with, "Industrial" or "Commercial" arts. Indeed, the Columbian Exposition itself, with its sharp physical division between the Midway, containing common entertainments, and the Court of Honor or White City, containing monumental classic architecture, stood as a fitting symbol of the bifurcated culture that had come to characterize the United States.[80]

This is not to suggest the existence of an idyllic era when the American people experienced a cultural unity devoid of tensions. In the nineteenth-century folk paintings of Edward Hicks, the wolf and the lamb, the lion and the fatling, the leopard and the kid might occupy the same territory in harmony, but reality was more complex—as Hicks and his countrymen well knew. Still, America in the first half of the nineteenth century did experience greater cultural sharing in the sense that cultural lines were more fluid, cultural spaces less rigidly subdivided than they were to become. Certainly, what I have called a shared public culture did not disappear with the nineteenth century. Twentieth-century Americans, especially in the palaces they built to the movies and in their sporting arenas, continued to share public space and public culture. But with a difference. Cultural space became more sharply defined, more circumscribed, and less fluid than it had been. Americans might sit together to watch the same films and athletic contests, but those who also desired to experience "legitimate" theater or hear "serious" music went to segregated temples devoted to "high" or "classical" art. Cultural lines are generally porous, and there were important exceptions—Toscanini was featured on commercial radio and television, and Shakespeare's works were offered on the movie screen. But these were conscious exceptions to what normally prevailed. The cultural fare that was actively and regularly shared by all segments of the population belonged to the lower rungs of the cultural hierarchy.

As we gradually come to the realization that Fred Astaire was one of this century's fine dancers, Louis Armstrong one of its important musicians, Charlie Chaplin one of its acute social commentators, we must remember that they could be shared by all of the people only when they were devalued as "popular" art, only when they were rendered nonthreatening by being relegated to the nether regions of the cultural complex. By the twentieth century, art could not have it both ways: no longer could it simultaneously enjoy high cultural status and mass popularity. Shakespeare is a prime example. He retained his lofty position only by being limited and confined to audiences whose space was no longer shared with, and whose sensibilities no longer violated by, the bulk of the populace.

NOTES

1. Twain, *The Adventures of Huckleberry Finn* (New York, 1884), 190.

2. Laurence Hutton, *Curiosities of the American Stage* (New York, 1891), 157, 181–86; Stanley Wells, ed., *Nineteenth-Century Shakespeare Burlesques*, 5 (London, 1978): xi–xii; Charles Mathews, *Trip to America* (Baltimore, 1824), 9, 25; Charles Haywood, "Negro Minstrelsy and Shakespearean Burlesque," in Bruce Jackson, ed., *Folklore and Society: Essays in Honor of Benj. A. Botkin* (Norwood, Pa., 1976), 88; and Ray B. Browne, "Shakespeare in America: Vaudeville and Negro Minstrelsy," *American Quarterly*, 12 (1960): 381–82. For examples of parodies of *Hamlet*, see *An Old Play in a New Garb: Hamlet, Prince of Denmark*, in Wells, *Nineteenth-Century Shakespeare Burlesques;* and *Hamlet the Dainty*, in Gary D. Engle, ed., *This Grotesque Essence: Plays from the Minstrel Stage* (Baton Rouge, 1978). For the popularity of parodies of *Hamlet* in the United States, see Ralph Leslie Rusk, *The Literature of the Middle Western Frontier*, 2 vols. (New York, 1925), 2: 4n; Louis Marder, *His Exits and His Entrances: The Story of Shakespeare's Reputation* (Philadelphia, 1963), 295–96, 316–17; and Esther Cloudman Dunn, *Shakespeare in America* (New York, 1939), 108–12, 215–16.

3. For examples, see Wells, *Nineteenth-Century Shakespeare Burlesques;* and Engle, *This Grotesque Essence.* For a contemporary view of nineteenth-century parodies, see Hutton, *Curiosities of the American Stage*, 145–204. Also see Marder, *His Exits and His Entrances*, 316–17; Alice I. Perry Wood, *The Stage History of Shakespeare's* King Richard the Third (New York, 1909), 158; Browne, "Shakespeare in America," 380, 385–90; David Grimsted, *Melodrama Unveiled: American Theater and Culture, 1800–1850* (Chicago, 1968), 240; and Constance Rourke, *Troupers of the Gold Coast* (New York, 1928), 221.

4. Haywood, "Negro Minstrelsy and Shakespearean Burlesque," 80, 86–87; and Browne, "Shakespeare in America," 376–79.

5. John Quincy Adams, who was born in 1767, wrote of Shakespeare, "at ten years of age I was as familiarly acquainted with his lovers and his clowns, as with Robinson Crusoe, the Pilgrim's Progress, and the Bible. In later years I have left Robinson and the Pilgrim to the perusal of the children; but have continued to read the Bible and Shakespeare." Adams to James H. Hackett, printed in Hackett, *Notes and Comments upon Certain Plays and Actors of Shakespeare, with Criticisms and Correspondence* (New York, 1864), 229. See Alfred Van Rensselaer Westfall, *American Shakespearean Criticism, 1607–1865* (New York, 1939), 45–46, 50–55; Wood, *The Stage History of Shakespeare's* King Richard the Third, 134–35; Charles H. Shattuck, *Shakespeare on the American Stage: From the Hallams to Edwin Booth* (Washington, 1976), 3, 15–16; and Hugh Rankin, *The Theater in Colonial America* (Chapel Hill, 1960), 191–92.

6. Arthur Hobson Quinn, *A History of the American Drama* (New York, 1943), 162; Dunn, *Shakespeare in America,* 133, 171–72; and Carl Bode, *The Anatomy of American Popular Culture, 1840–1861* (Berkeley and Los Angeles, 1960), 16–17. For the reception of Shakespeare in specific Eastern and Southern cities, the following are useful: T. Allston Brown, *A History of the New York Stage from the First Performance in 1732 to 1901,* 3 vols. (New York, 1903); James H. Dorman, Jr., *Theater in the Ante-Bellum South, 1815–1861* (Chapel Hill, 1967); W. Stanley Hoole, *The Ante-Bellum Charleston Theatre* (Tuscaloosa, Ala., 1946); Reese Davis James, *Cradle of Culture, 1800–1810: The Philadelphia Stage* (Philadelphia, 1957); Martin Staples Shockley, *The Richmond Stage, 1784–1812* (Charlottesville, Va., 1977); Eola Willis, *The Charleston Stage in the XVIII Century* (Columbia, S.C., 1924); and Joseph Patrick Roppolo, "Hamlet in New Orleans," *Tulane Studies in English,* 6 (1956): 71–86. For tables showing the popularity of plays in the first half of the nineteenth century, see Grimsted, *Melodrama Unveiled,* apps. 1–2.

7. Towle, *American Society,* 2 (London, 1870): 22. The migration of English stars to America is demonstrated throughout Shattuck's *Shakespeare on the American Stage.*

8. Bernard, *Retrospections of America, 1797–1811* (New York, 1887), 263; and Tocqueville, *Democracy in America,* pt. 2 (Vintage edn., New York, 1961), 58.

9. Knortz, *Shakespeare in Amerika: Eine Literarhistorische Studie* (Berlin, 1882), 47.

10. James G. McManaway, "Shakespeare in the United States," *Publications of the Modern Language Association of America,* 79 (1964): 514; and Bernard De Voto, *Mark Twain's America* (Boston, 1932), 142–43.

11. Rusk, *The Literature of the Middle Western Frontier,* 1: 398–400, 411–14; William Bryan Gates, "Performances of Shakespeare in Ante-Bellum Mississippi," *Journal of Mississippi History,* 5 (1943): 28–37; Ashley Thorndike, "Shakespeare in America," in L. Abercrombie *et al.,* eds., *Aspects of Shakespeare* (Oxford, 1933), 116–17; Westfall, *American Shakespearean Criticism,* 59; William G. B. Carson, *The Theatre on the Frontier: The Early Years of the St. Louis Stage* (1932; reprint edn., New York, 1965); West T. Hill, Jr., *The Theatre in Early Kentucky, 1790–1820* (Lexington, Ky., 1971); Sol Smith, *Theatrical Management in the West and South for Thirty Years* (New York, 1868); and Noah Ludlow, *Dramatic Life as I Found It* (St. Louis, 1880).

12. Rourke, *Troupers of the Gold Coast* 33, 44, 101–02; George R. MacMinn,

The Theater of the Golden Era in California (Caldwell, Idaho, 1941), 23–24, 84, 87–88; and Margaret G. Watson, *Silver Theatre: Amusements of the Mining Frontier in Early Nevada, 1850–1864* (Glendale, Calif., 1964), 73.

13. Leman, *Memories of an Old Actor* (San Francisco, 1886), 212–13, 260–62, 276–77; Ludlow, *Dramatic Life as I Found It*, 89–90, 113, 116, 242–43, 256, 258, 303; and Smith, *Theatrical Management in the West and South for Thirty Years*, 90–91.

14. Place, as quoted in Dormon, *Theater in the Ante-Bellum South*, 257n; Cooper, *Notions of the Americans*, 2 (London, 1828): 100, 113. For the theater in Iowa, see Joseph S. Schick, *The Early Theater in Eastern Iowa: Cultural Beginnings and the Rise of the Theater in Davenport and Eastern Iowa, 1836–1863* (Chicago, 1939). Schick's appendixes contain a list of all plays performed in either English or German in Iowa during these years.

15. Playbill, American Theatre, Philadelphia, May 13, 1839, Folger Shakespeare Library, Washington [hereafter, FSL]. For the prevalence of this format in the eighteenth century, see Rankin, *The Theater in Colonial America*, 150, 193–94; Kenneth Silverman, *A Cultural History of the American Revolution* (New York, 1976), 62; and Garff B. Wilson, *Three Hundred Years of American Drama and Theatre* (Englewood Cliffs, N.J., 1973), 19–27.

16. Playbills, St. Charles Theatre, New Orleans, November 30, 1846, Alexandria, Virginia, July 12, 1799, and Arch Street Theatre, Philadelphia, March 2, 1857, FSL.

17. Playbills, American Theatre, Philadelphia, August 30, 31, September 1, 11, 1838, June 24, 1839, FSL.

18. Davenport, as quoted in Lloyd Morris, *Curtain Time: The Story of the American Theater* (New York, 1953), 205.

19. Playbills, Walnut Street Theater, Philadelphia, November 30, 1821, Military Hall, Newark, N.J., August 15, 1852, Montgomery Theatre, Montgomery, Alabama, March 21, 1835, and American Theatre, Philadelphia, June 25, 1839, December 14, 1837, FSL; and MacMinn, *The Theatre of the Golden Era in California*, 90. Nevertheless, it was not uncommon for *Catharine and Petruchio*, an abridged version of *The Taming of the Shrew*, to serve as an afterpiece; see playbills, American Theatre, New Orleans, April 20, 1827, American Theatre, Philadelphia, September 26, 1838, and St. Charles Theatre, New Orleans, March 25, 1864, FSL. *Catharine and Petruchio* also served as an afterpiece when plays other than Shakespeare's were presented; see playbills, American Theatre, New Orleans, April 20, 1827, and American Theatre, Philadelphia, September 26, December 8, 1838, FSL.

20. John S. Kendall, *The Golden Age of the New Orleans Theater* (Baton Rouge, 1952), 210.

21. Hudson, *Lectures on Shakespeare*, 1 (New York, 1848): 1–41.

22. Smith, *The Sentinel and Other Plays*, ed. Ralph H. Ware and H. W. Schoenberger (Bloomington, Ind., n.d.), 101–14.

23. Power, *Impressions of America*, 2 vols. (London, 1836), 2: 189–92. Shakespeare's contemporary is quoted in Alfred Harbage, *Shakespeare's Audience* (New York, 1941), 84–85. For an excellent discussion of theater audiences in the first half of the nineteenth century, see Grimsted's indispensable *Melodrama Unveiled*,

chap. 3. For a comparison with audiences in eighteenth-century England, see James T. Lynch, *Box, Pit, and Gallery: Stage and Society in Johnson's London* (New York, 1971). Claudia Johnson deals with a neglected part of the American audience in "That Guilty Third Tier: Prostitution in Nineteenth-Century Theaters," *American Quarterly*, 27 (1975): 575–84.

24. Alan S. Downer, ed., *The Autobiography of Joseph Jefferson* (Cambridge, Mass., 1964), 286; Whitman, "The Old Bowery," in Justin Kaplan, ed., *Walt Whitman: Poetry and Prose* (New York, 1982), 1189–90; and Irving, *Letters of Jonathan Oldstyle*, ed. Bruce I. Granger and Martha Hartzog (Boston, 1977), 12–25.

25. Trollope, *Domestic Manners of the Americans*, 2 vols. (London, 1832), 1: 179–84, and 2: 87–88, 194–95.

26. Power, *Impressions of America*, 2: 171–74. Also see *ibid.*, 1: 62–66, 87–89, 123–26, 210–11.

27. Irving, *Letters of Jonathan Oldstyle*, 14; the Virginia and New York editors are quoted in Grimsted, *Melodrama Unveiled*, 63–64; and the French reporter's account is reprinted in Barnard Hewitt, *Theatre U.S.A., 1665 to 1957* (New York, 1959), 164–66.

28. Smith, *Theatrical Management*, 137–38; and Rourke, *Troupers of the Gold Coast*, 149–50, 209–10.

29. Sacramento *Union*, as quoted in MacMinn, *The Theater of the Golden Era in California*, 90–91.

30. Playbill, Walnut Street Theatre, Philadelphia, November 30, 1821, FSL.

31. As quoted in Nancy Webb and Jean Francis Webb, *Will Shakespeare and His America* (New York, 1964), 84.

32. San Francisco *Chronicle*, January 1854, as quoted in MacMinn, *The Theater of the Golden Era in California*, 100.

33. New York *Mirror*, December 29, 1832, reprinted in Hewitt, *Theatre U.S.A.*, 122.

34. Grimsted, *Melodrama Unveiled*, 60; and *Harper's New Monthly Magazine*, December 1863, p. 133.

35. Marder, *His Exits and His Entrances*, 317–18.

36. Nachman, "Break a Leg, Willy," San Francisco *Chronicle*, November 30, 1982; and Papp, as quoted in Gerald M. Berkowitz, *New Broadways: Theatre across America, 1950–1980* (Totowa, N.J., 1982), 37.

37. Young, *The Community Theatre and How It Works* (New York, 1957), 126; and George McManus, *Bringing Up Father*, ed. Herb Galewitz (New York, 1973), 37.

38. Plunkitt, *Plunkitt of Tammany Hall: A Series of Very Plain Talks on Very Practical Politics*, recorded by William L. Riordon (1905; reprint edn., New York, 1963), 52, 71.

39. Richardson, *The Long Day: The Story of a New York Working Girl* (1905), reprinted in its entirety in William L. O'Neill, ed., *Women at Work* (Chicago, 1972), 300, chap. 6.

40. Playbills, American Theatre, San Francisco, May 29, 1855, Varieties Theatre, New Orleans, December 30, 1869, California Theatre, San Francisco, April 4, 1873, Mechanics Hall, Salem, Mass., February 12, 1868, San Jose Opera House,

August 22, 1870, Roberts Opera House, Hartford, Conn., November 1869, Academy of Music, Providence, R.I., November 24, 1869, Leland Opera House, Albany, N.Y., September 27, 1880, April 15, 1882, Opera House, Albany, N.Y., January 21, 22, 1874, Piper's Opera House, Virginia City, Nevada, July 29, 1878, Walnut Street Theatre, Philadelphia, November 5, 1875, Duquesne Theatre, Pittsburgh, December 23, 24, 25, 1890, Murray Hill Theatre, New York, May 4, 1903, Garden Theatre, New York City, December 24, 1900, Forty-fourth Street Theatre, New York City, February 22, 1915, Schubert Memorial Theatre, St. Louis, November 9, 1914, Olympic Theatre, St. Louis, January 6, 1902, May 6, 1907, and National Theatre, Washington, D.C., October 2, 1939, FSL.

41. Dormon, *Theatre in the Ante-Bellum South,* 256–59. Esther Dunn studied the "indifferent and vulgar stuff" accompanying Shakespeare in the theater and concluded that, "if the public could stand for this sort of entertainment, night in and night out, they could not have derived the fullest pleasure from the Shakespearean portion of the programme"; *Shakespeare in America,* 133–35, 142–45, 175. In 1926 Poet Laureate Robert Bridges spoke for many on both sides of the Atlantic when he attributed the "bad jokes and obscenities," "the mere foolish verbal trifling," and such sensationalism in Shakespeare's plays as the murder of Macduff's child or the blinding of Gloucester to Shakespeare's need to make concessions "to the most vulgar stratum of his audience, . . . those wretched beings who can never be forgiven their share in preventing the greatest poet and dramatist of the world from being the best artist"; Bridges, *The Influence of the Audience* (New York, 1926), 3, 23.

42. Hudson, *Lectures on Shakespeare,* 1: 54; and Kenneth S. Lynn, *William Dean Howells: An American Life* (New York, 1971), 67–68.

43. Whitman, *Specimen Days,* in Kaplan, *Whitman: Poetry and Prose,* 702–03; Twain, *Is Shakespeare Dead?* (New York, 1909), 4–7; William S. McFeely, *Grant: A Biography* (New York, 1982), 29; Robert N. Reeves, "Abraham Lincoln's Knowledge of Shakespeare," *Overland Monthly,* 43 (1904): 336–42; Westfall, *American Shakespearean Criticism,* 227–29; and Henry W. Simon, *The Reading of Shakespeare in American Schools and Colleges: An Historical Survey* (New York, 1932).

44. Ludlow, *Dramatic Life as I found It,* 234, 690–91, 694–95; Richard Moody, *America Takes the Stage: Romanticism in American Drama and Theatre, 1750–1900* (Bloomington, Ind., 1955), 195–96; and Whitman, "The Old Bowery," in Kaplan, *Whitman: Poetry and Prose,* 1187–88.

45. Alger, *Life of Edwin Forrest: The American Tragedian,* 2 (Philadelphia, 1877; reprint edn., New York, 1972): 786.

46. For Whitman's musings about the effects of Shakespeare's "aristocratic perfume," see his "A Thought on Shakespeare" and "A Backward Glance o'er Travel'd Roads," in Kaplan, *Whitman: Poetry and Prose,* 1150–52, 663–64. Eighteenth-century depictions of Shakespeare as a moral playwright are described in Bernard, *Retrospections of America,* 270–71; Westfall, *American Shakespearean Criticism,* 30–31; and Shattuck, *Shakespeare on the American Stage,* 16. And see Jefferson, as quoted in Lawrence A. Cremin, *American Education: The Colonial Experience, 1607–1783* (New York, 1970), 438; Lincoln, as quoted in Alan Bloom, *Shakespeare's Politics* (New York, 1964), 5; and Adams, "The Character of Des-

demona," *American Monthly Magazine,* 1 (1836): 209–17, reprinted in Hackett, *Notes and Comments,* 234–49, and "Misconceptions of Shakespeare upon the Stage," reprinted in Hackett, *Notes and Comments,* 217–28.

47. Hudson, *Lectures on Shakespeare,* 1: 79; and playbill, Varieties Theatre, New Orleans, January 3, 4, 1870, FSL. Also see Ruth Miller Elson, *Guardians of Tradition: American Schoolbooks of the Nineteenth Century* (Lincoln, Neb., 1964), 242, 283; and Simon, *The Reading of Shakespeare in American Schools and Colleges,* 19, 26, 44.

48. Downer, *The Autobiography of Joseph Jefferson,* 166–67; and Hudson, *Lectures on Shakespeare,* 1: 69.

49. For the New York reaction to Sophocles, see Doris M. Alexander, "Oedipus in Victorian New York," *American Quarterly,* 12 (1960): 417–21.

50. Grimsted, *Melodrama Unveiled,* chap. 6; George C. Branam, *Eighteenth-Century Adaptations of Shakespearean Tragedy* (Berkeley and Los Angeles, 1956), chap. 1; and Rankin, *The Theater in Colonial America,* 83–84, 191–92.

51. In 1909 Alice Wood reported that Cibber's version of *Richard III* "is still holding the stage and is still preferred by a large part of the community," and thus "the struggle for the 'Richard the Third' of Shakespeare is still 'on' "; *The Stage History of Shakespeare's* King Richard the Third, 133, 165. As late as 1930, Arthur Colby Sprague attended a performance of *Richard III* in Boston and was treated to "the Cibber text, practically in its entirety" although Cibber's name was nowhere mentioned; Sprague, *Shakespearian Players and Performances* (1953; reprint edn., New York, 1969), 151, 212 n. 3.

52. Cibber, *The Tragical History of King Richard III,* in Christopher Spencer, ed., *Five Restoration Adaptations of Shakespeare* (Urbana, Ill., 1965), 275–344. For an excellent discussion of Cibber's adaptation, see Wood, *The Stage History of Shakespeare's* King Richard the Third, chaps. 4, 6; also see Frederick W. Kilbourne, *Alterations and Adaptations of Shakespeare* (Boston, 1906), 107–12.

53. Hackett, *Notes and Comments,* 227n. For John Quincy Adams's critique of Tate, see *ibid.,* 226–28.

54. As quoted in Grimsted, *Melodrama Unveiled,* 119–20.

55. Tate, *The History of King Lear,* in Spencer, *Five Restoration Adaptations of Shakespeare,* 201–74. Also see Kilbourne, *Alterations and Adaptations of Shakespeare,* 157–72.

56. For a first-hand account of the changes the theater underwent, see Otis Skinner, *Footlights and Spotlights: Recollections of My Life on the Stage* (Indianapolis, 1924), esp. chap. 23.

57. Joshua A. Fishman, *Language Loyalty in the United States* (1966; reprint edn., New York, 1978), 59.

58. For Denney's phrase, see his essay, "The Discovery of Popular Culture," in Robert E. Spiller and Eric Larrabee, eds., *American Perspectives: The National Self-Image in the Twentieth Century* (Cambridge, Mass., 1961), 164–65. The relationships between recitation of the King James Bible and performances of Shakespeare and between the transformation of nineteenth-century religious style and the transformation of Shakespeare need further thought and research.

59. Higham, "The Reorientation of American Culture in the 1890's," in John Weiss, ed., *The Origins of Modern Consciousness* (Detroit, 1965), 25–48.

60. The questioner was the young actor Otis Skinner; see his autobiography, *Footlights and Spotlights*, 93. As he was preparing for his first portrayal of Shylock in 1893—the year of Booth's death—Skinner discovered the extent of Booth's influence: "I found myself reading speeches with the Booth cadence, using the Booth gestures, attitudes and facial expressions, in short, giving a rank imitation. The ghost of the dead actor rose between me and the part." *Ibid.*, 213. For other evidence of Booth's influence, see Hutton, *Curiosities of the American State*, 293–94; Henry Austin Clapp, *Reminiscences of a Dramatic Critic* (1902; reprint edn., Freeport, N.Y., 1972), chap. 15; and Charles H. Shattuck, *The Hamlet of Edwin Booth* (Urbana, Ill., 1969).

61. Hackett, "After the Play," *New Republic*, March 24, 1920, p. 122.

62. For the suitability of Shakespeare to modern media, see Roger Manvell, *Shakespeare and the Film* (New York, 1971), 9–10; Jan Kott, *Shakespeare, Our Contemporary*, trans. Boleslaw Taborski (Garden City, N.Y., 1964), 231–35; and John Wain, *The Living World of Shakespeare* (London, 1978), 2–7.

63. Goffman, *Encounters: Two Studies in the Sociology of Interaction* (Indianapolis, 1961); Whitman, "Miserable State of the Stage," *Brooklyn Eagle*, February 8, 1847, reprinted in Montrose J. Moses and John Mason Brown, eds., *American Theatre as Seen by Its Critics* (New York, 1934), 70–72; and Power, *Impressions of America*, 1: 141.

64. Curtis, "Editor's Easy Chair," *Harper's New Monthly Magazine*, December 1863, pp. 131–33. For the contrast between the two actors portraying Hamlet, see Hutton, *Curiosities of the American Stage*, 281.

65. Payne, as quoted in Grimsted, *Melodrama Unveiled*, 56–57.

66. Somer, *Personal Space: The Behavioral Basis of Design* (Englewood Cliffs, N.J., 1969), chap. 2; Bledstein, *The Culture of Professionalism: The Middle Class and the Development of Higher Education in America* (New York, 1976), 58–64, 80; and Taylor, "Public Space, Public Opinion, and the Origins of Mass Culture," paper presented to a joint meeting of the American Council of Learned Societies and the Hungarian Academy of Sciences, held in Budapest, August 1982.

67. Irving, *Letters of Jonathan Oldstyle*, 12.

68. Francis Courtney Wemyss, *Twenty-Six Years of the Life of an Actor and Manager* (New York, 1847), 97–99, 113–15; and Shattuck, *Shakespeare on the American Stage*, 2–43.

69. Power, *Impressions of America*, 1: 351–55.

70. My account of the Astor Place Riot is based on Richard Moody, *The Astor Place Riot* (Bloomington, Ind., 1958), 12, 172; William Toynbee, ed., *The Diaries of William Charles Macready*, 2 (London, 1912), 404–29; and Peter G. Buckley, "The Astor Place Riot and Jenny Lind," paper presented at the Ninety-Sixth Annual Meeting of the American Historical Association, held in Los Angeles, December 28–30, 1981, and " 'A Privileged Place': New York Theatre Riots, 1817–1849," paper presented at the annual meeting of the Organization of American Historians, held in St. Louis, April 8–11, 1982. I am extremely grateful to Buckley for sharing with me not only his unpublished papers but also a chapter from his draft dissertation. Moody sets the number of dead at thirty-one—twenty-two during the riot itself and nine more as a result of wounds received during the riot; in his more recent research Buckley has only been able

to account for a total of twenty-two dead—eighteen during the riot and four more as a result of wounds received.

71. New York *Tribune,* May 12, 1849; New York *Herald,* May 12, 1849; *Home Journal,* May 12, 1849, as quoted in Montrose J. Moses, *The Fabulous Forrest: The Record of an American Actor* (Boston, 1929), 262; and Philadelphia *Public Ledger,* May 16, 1849.

72. Arnold, *Culture and Anarchy* (New York, 1875), 44, 47; and James, as quoted in Moses, *The Fabulous Forrest,* 246.

73. Brooks, *America's Coming-of-Age* (New York, 1915), 6–7. Brooks popularized rather than coined the terms. According to the *Supplement* to the *Oxford English Dictionary,* "highbrow" was first used in the 1880s to describe intellectual or aesthetic superiority, while "lowbrow" came to mean someone or something neither "highly intellectual" nor "aesthetically refined" shortly after 1900. The term "middlebrow" seems to have come into use in the 1920s.

74. Whitman, *Democratic Vistas,* in Kaplan, *Whitman: Poetry and Prose,* 950–51, 961–62. For an excellent discussion of Whitman and culture after the Civil War, see Alan Trachtenberg, *The Incorporation of America: Culture and Society in the Gilded Age* (New York, 1982), 158–60.

75. Veblen, *The Theory of the Leisure Class* (1899; Penguin edn., New York, 1979), 45, 397–98.

76. My sense of late nineteenth-century American culture was enhanced by the following: Trachtenberg, *The Incorporation of America;* Lewis A. Erenberg, *Steppin' Out: New York Nightlife and the Transformation of American Culture, 1890–1930* (Westport, Conn., 1981); Daniel Walker Howe, "American Victorianism as a Culture," *American Quarterly,* 27 (1975): 507–32; John F. Kasson, *Amusing the Million: Coney Island at the Turn of the Century* (New York, 1978); John G. Sproat, *"The Best Men": Liberal Reformers in the Gilded Age* (New York, 1968); Arthur M. Schlesinger, *Learning How to Behave: A Historical Study of American Etiquette Books* (New York, 1946); John Tomisch, *A Genteel Endeavor: American Culture and Politics in the Gilded Age* (Stanford, 1971); T. J. Jackson Lears, *No Place of Grace: Antimodernism and the Transformation of American Culture, 1880–1920* (New York, 1981); Stow Persons, *The Decline of American Gentility* (New York, 1973); Robert R. Roberts, "Gilt, Gingerbread, and Realism: The Public and Its Taste," in H. Wayne Morgan, ed., *The Gilded Age: A Reappraisal* (Syracuse, N.Y., 1963), 169–95; Robert Wiebe, *The Search for Order* (New York, 1967); and George Frederickson, *The Inner Civil War: Northern Intellectuals and the Crisis of the Union* (New York, 1965).

77. See Albert F. McLean, Jr., *American Vaudeville as Ritual* (Lexington, Ky., 1965), 16–17; Foster Rhea Dulles, *A History of Recreation: America Learns to Play* (New York, 1965), 219; Russel Nye, *The Unembarrassed Muse: The Popular Arts in America* (New York, 1970), 170; and Wilson, *Three Hundred Years of American Drama and Theatre,* 301.

78. Sennett, *The Fall of Public Man* (New York, 1978), esp. 261. For the argument that by the 1880s Americans became preoccupied with the private rather than the public taste, also see Russell Lynes, *The Tastemakers: The Shaping of American Popular Taste* (1955; reprint edn., New York, 1980), 117.

79. Towle, *American Society,* 4. For a discussion of opera as popular music in

nineteenth-century America, see Charles Hamm, *Yesterdays: Popular Song in America* (New York, 1983), chap. 4.

80. This account of chromolithography is based upon Peter C. Marzio, *The Democratic Art: Pictures for a Nineteenth-Century America* (Boston, 1979). For the Columbian Exposition of 1893, see Reid Badger, *The Great American Fair: The World's Columbian Exposition and American Culture* (Chicago, 1979); David F. Burg, *Chicago's White City of 1893* (Lexington, Ky., 1976); and John C. Cawelti, "America on Display: The World's Fairs of 1876, 1893, 1933," in Frederick Cople Jaher, ed., *The Age of Industrialism in America* (New York, 1968), 317–63.

SIX

The Dream World of Mass Consumption

Rosalind Williams

THE SCHOOL OF TROCADÉRO

The arrival of the twentieth century was celebrated in Paris by a universal exposition spread over 550 acres and visited by 50 million people from around the world. The 1900 exposition was the climax of a series of similar events that began with the Crystal Palace exposition in London in 1851 and continued to be held at regular intervals during the second half of the century (in 1855, 1867, 1878, and 1889) in Paris, the undisputed if unofficial capital of European civilization. The purpose of all expositions was, in the popular phrase of the time, to teach a "lesson of things." "Things" meant, for the most part, the recent products of scientific knowledge and technical innovation that were revolutionizing daily life; the "lesson" was the social benefit of this unprecedented material and intellectual progress. The 1855 exposition featured a Palace of Industry filled with tools, machinery, and sequential exhibits of products in various stages of manufacture. The 1867 fair had an even more elaborately organized Palace of Industry (including the first displays of aluminum and of petroleum distillation), and a History of Labor exhibit showing tools from all eras. At the 1878 exposition the wonders of scientific discovery, especially electricity and photography, were stressed. In 1889, at the exposition commemorating the outbreak of the French Revolution, the "lesson of things" was taught on a grand scale. The two focal points of the 1889 fair were the Gallery of Machines, a long hall with a vault nearly 400 feet across where sightseers could gaze from a

From Rosalind Williams, *Dream Worlds* (Berkeley: University of California Press, 1982), pp. 58–106. © 1982 The Regents of the University of California.

suspended walkway at a sea of spinning wheels, clanking hammers, and whirring gears, and the Eiffel Tower, a monument at once scientific, technological, and aesthetic, the architecture of which was derived from that of iron railroad bridges; at its summit was an assortment of apparatus for meteorological, aeronautical, and communications research.

Over the decades, the dominant tone of these expositions altered. The emphasis gradually changed from instructing the visitor in the wonders of modern science and technology to entertaining him. In 1889, for all their serious didactic intent, the Eiffel Tower and Gallery of Machines were popular above all because they provided such thrilling vistas. More and more, consumer merchandise rather than productive tools was displayed. The Crystal Palace exposition had been so innocent of commercial purpose that no selling prices were posted there, but at the Paris exposition in 1855 began the tradition of placing price tags on all objects, as well as of charging admission.[1] From then on the emphasis on selling, prizes, and advertising grew until one booster of the 1900 exposition enthused:

> Expositions secure for the manufacturer, for the businessman, the most striking publicity. In one day they bring before his machine, his display, his shop windows, more people than he would see in a lifetime in his factory or store. They seek out clients in all parts of the world, bring them at a set time, so that everything is ready to receive them and seduce them. That is why the number of exhibitors increases steadily.[2]

At the 1900 exposition the sensual pleasures of consumption clearly triumphed over the abstract intellectual enjoyment of contemplating the progress of knowledge. This emphasis was evident the moment a visitor entered the grounds through the Monumental Gateway, which, according to one bemused contemporary, consisted of "two pale-blue, pierced minarets and polychrome statues surmounted by oriflammes and adorned with cabochons," terminating in "an immense flamboyant arch" above which, perched on a golden ball, "stood the flying figure of a siren in a tight skirt, the symbolic ship of the City of Paris on her head, throwing back an evening coat of imitation ermine—La Parisienne."[3] Whatever this chic madonna represented, it was certainly not science nor technology. Inside this gateway the sprawling exposition had no orderly arrangement of focal points such as previous ones had possessed. Machines were scattered throughout the grounds next to their products, an indication that tools of production now seemed hopelessly boring apart from the things they made. The vault of the Gallery of Machines had been cut up—desecrated like a "secularized temple," complained one admirer of the 1889 version[4]—and overrun by a display of food products:

[Instead of] a universal workshop . . . a festival hall has invaded the center of the structure. The extremities are abandoned to the rustic charms of agriculture and to the fattening joys of eating. No more sharp whistles, trembling, clacking transmission belts; nothing being released except champagne corks.[5]

Despite this confusion or, rather, because of it, thoughtful observers sensed that the 1900 exposition was particularly prophetic, and it was a microcosm of emerging France, a scale model of future Paris, that something rich and strange was happening there which broke decisively with the past and prefigured twentieth-century society. In 1889 and even more in 1900, the expositions attracted a host of journalists of a philosophical bent who provided not only descriptions of the various exhibits but also reflections on their significance. For the most part their sense of the exposition's prophetic value remained poorly articulated. While convinced that the fair revealed the shape of things to come, they were unsure of the contours and were vaguely apprehensive without knowing quite why. One exception was Maurice Talmeyr (1850–1933), a journalist who reported regularly on the 1900 exposition in a Catholic periodical. No less apprehensive than many of his colleagues, he was unusual in being able to explain why he found the fair so disturbing. He summarized his conclusions in his article "L'École du Trocadéro" ("The School of Trocadéro"), published in November, 1900, just as the exposition was drawing to a close, in the *Revue des deux mondes*, the most prestigious biweekly in France at that time.[6]

The Trocadéro was the section of the exposition on the Right Bank of the Seine, directly across the river from the Eiffel Tower, where all the colonial exhibits were gathered. It was in this "school," Talmeyr contended, that the true lesson of the exposition could be discerned. Exhibits of exotic places were not a new feature. As far back as 1867 expositions had included reproductions of an Egyptian temple and a Moroccan tent, and in 1889 one of the most popular attractions had been the notorious Rue du Caire ("Street of Cairo") where dark-eyed belly dancers performed seductive dances before patrons in "Oriental" cafés. In 1900, when imperial adventurism was at its height, the number of colonial exhibits expanded accordingly to become, in Talmeyr's words, a gaudy and incoherent jumble of "Hindu temples, savage huts, pagodas, souks, Algerian alleys, Chinese, Japanese, Sudanese, Senegalese, Siamese, Cambodian quarters . . . a bazaar of climates, architectural styles, smells, colors, cuisine, music." Reproductions of the most disparate places were heaped together to "settle down together, as a Lap and a Moroccan, a Malgache and a Peruvian go to bed in the same sleeping car . . . the universe in a garden!"

Even more disconcerting were the discontinuities and illogicalities found in the details of particular exhibits. Talmeyr notes, for example, that the Indian exhibit featured a carefully contrived pantomime acted out by a group of stuffed animals: an elephant with uplifted trunk trumpeted a speech to some hens between his feet, while next to him a wild boar browsed near a serpent coiled and ready to strike. In the same neighborhood a couple of stuffed jaguars were shown feeding their young, while a rose ibis, "evidently surprised," surveyed the whole tableau while standing on one foot. The wildlife of an entire subcontinent was condensed into one scene, an absurdity which was nonetheless, Talmeyr confesses, highly entertaining. "But," he asks, "the 'lesson'? The lesson they are giving us?" It is by no means the lesson the exhibit intends to teach, for we learn nothing about the realities of India. Instead, we learn

> that all trickery is childish. They don't want to show us anything serious, and we have nothing to ask that's serious. But isn't this precisely the vice of all these exoticisms of the exposition? They offer themselves as serious in not being so, and when they cannot be so.

Talmeyr finds the same vice of inherent and pervasive trickery in the rest of the Indian exhibit, which consisted of stacks of merchandise—rugs, cotton balls, plates, sacks of rice, fabrics, jams—all of which reminded him of a "sort of Louvre or Bon Marché of Tyre or Baghdad." (The Louvre and the Bon Marché were two of the largest department stores in Paris.) The spectacle of India as a land of overflowing treasure chests was as enticing and exciting a vision of the exotic as any child could imagine. But that vision hides what is "serious and adult" about India, the reality of India as a subjugated English colony:

> The notion of such an India, of an India-warehouse, so magnificent and so partially true as it may be, is true only partially, so partially as to be false, and all these overflowing rooms . . . speak to me only of an incomplete and truncated India, that of the cashiers. And the other? That of the famine? For this land of enormous and sumptuous trade is equally that of a frightening local degeneracy, of a horrifying indigenous misery. A whole phantom-race dies there and suffers in famine. India is not only a warehouse, it is a cemetery.

For the moment, Talmeyr does not dwell on this somber analysis but continues to cite amusing examples of the "nullity, buffoonery, gross alteration, or absolute falsity" that abound at the Trocadéro. At an exhibit representing Andalusian Spain at the time of the Moors he attends a sort of circus where camels replace the usual horses—"Camel exercises, camel cavalcades, trained camels that kneel, camels that bow, camels that dance"—while spectators are sold lemonade and beer by hawkers in a room lined with rugs for sale, their prices prominently marked. For two cents the public may also view licentious scenes through a stereoscope. "Perhaps, after this spectacle, there still remains something for us to learn about the Moors of Andalusia," Talmeyr comments sarcastically, so he tells how he went down a staircase to a small courtyard, "deliciously archaic," full of pretty and curious items, complete with vaults, columns, an old well, armaments, and so forth:

> We are here, it seems, in the most legendary Spain, and this time there is indeed a well-done reproduction of great fidelity and delicacy. I feel, in these old walls, in this broken well, in these small columns which are crumbling, in a coat of arms that is obliterated, five centuries of mystery and sunshine. . . . Then I look, I observe more closely, and I notice, above the door, in the patina of the stone, the tracing of Gothic letters. . . . I approach, and what is it I make out?
> Simply: *Menier Chocolate* . . .

Talmeyr concludes that behind the "ornamental delirium" of the Trocadéro, behind its seemingly mad disorder, behind its silly and serious deceptions alike, lies a strictly logical and consistent ordering principle: the submission of truth, of coherence, of taste, of all other considerations to the ends of business. He sees through the false lesson of this school of the absurd to the genuine lesson:

> An exposition must, above all, be an exposition, which is to say a certain type of didactic banking whose first goal is to attract, to hold, and to attract and to hold by the exclusive means of the bank. . . . A framework is provided for [the exhibitor of exoticism], and he will confine himself within it. Obligations of price, of economy, of placement, of health are imposed on him, and he submits to them. And the quest for success, for attraction, for show, for excitement, for everything that amuses, for all that diverts, will necessarily be his guideline. Truth, history, common sense, will be arranged afterward as best they can. So . . . why, in English India, do the panther, wild boar, partridge, elephant, monkey, ibis, and serpent present themselves all in a family and form this touching commune? Because this fable gathers them together, and what matters, above all, is to gather them together. And why is starving India incarnated in well-coiffed, well-nourished, well-clothed Indians? Because famine is not and never can be an exposition attraction. . . . And why does Andalusia—in the time of the Moors—recommend Menier Chocolate to us? Because the authentic Moors and the authentic Andalusia do not, according to all appearances, sufficiently allow for advertisements, and an exposition is not going, never has gone, and never will go without advertisements.

THE SIGNIFICANCE OF THE EXPOSITION

The exposition of 1900 provides a scale model of the consumer revolution. The cultural changes working gradually and diffusely throughout society were there made visible in a concrete and concentrated way. One change was the sheer emphasis on merchandising. Even more striking and disturbing, at least to observers like Talmeyr, was the change in how this merchandising was accomplished—by appealing to the fantasies of the consumer. The conjunction of banking and dreaming, of sales pitch and seduction, of publicity and pleasure, is far more unsettling than when each element is taken separately. As Talmeyr appreciates, the conjunction is inherently deceptive. Fantasy which openly presents itself as such keeps its integrity and may claim to point to truth beyond everyday experience, what the poet Keats called the "truth of the imagination." At the Trocadéro, on the contrary, reveries were passed off as reality, thereby losing their independent status to become the alluring handmaidens of commerce. When they assume concrete form and masquerade as objective fact, dreams lose their liberating possibilities as alternatives to daylight reality. What is involved here is not a casual level of fantasy, a kind of mild and transient wishful thinking, but a far more thoroughgoing substitution of subjective images for external reality. Talmeyr stresses the inevitable corruption that results when business exploits dreams. To him all advertising is false advertising. Blatant lies and subtle ones, lies of omission and of commission, lies in detail and in the ensemble, the exhibits claiming to represent the "real Java" or the "real China" or the real anything are not real at all. People are duped. Seeking a pleasurable escape from the workaday world, they find it in a deceptive dream world which is no dream at all but a sales pitch in disguise.

The 1900 exposition incarnates this new and decisive conjunction between imaginative desires and material ones, between dreams and commerce, between events of collective consciousness and of economic fact. It is obvious how economic goods satisfy physical needs such as those for food and shelter; less evident, but of overwhelming significance in understanding modern society, is how merchandise can fill needs of the imagination. The expression "the dream world of the consumer" refers to this non-material dimension. From earliest history we find indications that the human mind has transcended concerns of physical survival to imagine a finer, richer, more satisfying life. Through most of history, however, only a very few people ever thought of trying to approximate such dreams in daily life. Instead, art and religion provided ways to express these desires. But in the late nineteenth century, commodities that provided an approximation of these age-old longings began to be widely available. Consumer goods, rather than other facets of culture, became focal points for desire. The seemingly contrary activities of hard-headed accounting and dreamy-eyed fantasizing merged as business appealed to consumers by inviting them into a fabulous world of pleasure, comfort, and amusement. This was not at all the future that a conservative

nationalist like Talmeyr wished; it was not the vision of a workers' society
that socialists wanted; nor did it conform to traditional bourgeois virtues
of sobriety and rationality. But welcome or not, the "lesson of things"
taught by the make-believe city of the 1900 exposition was that a dream
world of the consumer was emerging in real cities outside its gates.

EXOTICISM IN DEPARTMENT STORES

One obvious confirmation of this lesson was the emergence of department stores (in French *grands magasins*, "big" or "great" stores) in Paris.
The emergence of these stores in late nineteenth-century France depended on the same growth of prosperity and transformation of merchandising techniques that lay behind the international expositions. Talmeyr was on the mark when he observed that the India exhibit at the
Trocadéro reminded him of an Oriental Louvre or Bon Marché. The
Bon Marché was the first department store, opening in Paris in 1852,
the year after the Crystal Palace exposition, and the Louvre appeared
just three years later. The objective advantages of somewhat lower prices
and larger selection which these stores offered over traditional retail outlets
were not the only reasons for their success. Even more significant factors
were their practices of marking each item with a fixed price and of
encouraging customers to inspect merchandise even if they did not
make a purchase. Until then very different customs had prevailed in
retail establishments. Prices had generally been subject to negotiation,
and the buyer, once haggling began, was more or less obligated to buy.

The department store introduced an entirely new set of social interactions to shopping. In exchange for the freedom to browse, meaning
the liberty to indulge in dreams without being obligated to buy in fact,
the buyer gave up the freedom to participate actively in establishing prices
and instead had to accept the price set by the seller.[7] Active verbal interchange between customer and retailer was replaced by the passive, mute
response of consumer to things—a striking example of how "the civilizing process" tames aggressions and feelings toward people while encouraging desires and feelings directed toward things. Department stores
were organized to inflame these material desires and feelings. Even if
the consumer was free not to buy at that time, techniques of merchandising pushed him to want to buy *sometime*. As environments of mass
consumption, department stores were, and still are, places where consumers are an audience to be entertained by commodities, where selling
is mingled with amusement, where arousal of free-floating desire is as
important as immediate purchase of particular items. Other examples
of such environments are expositions, trade fairs, amusement parks, and

(to cite more contemporary examples) shopping malls and large new airports or even subway stations. The numbed hypnosis induced by these places is a form of sociability as typical of modern mass consumption as the sociability of the salon was typical of prerevolutionary upper-class consumption.

The new social psychology created by environments of mass consumption is a major theme of *Au Bonheur des Dames*. In creating his fictional store Zola did not rely on imagination alone; he filled research notebooks with observations of contemporary department stores before writing his novel. Zola's fictional creation in turn influenced the design of actual stores. He invited his friend, architect Frantz Jourdain, to draw an imaginary plan for Au Bonheur des Dames, and not many years later Jourdain began to collaborate on an ambitious renovation and building program for La Samaritaine, a large department store in the heart of Paris. By 1907, when most of the program was completed, the store closely resembled Zola's descriptions of Au Bonheur des Dames. Ernest Cognacq, founder of La Samaritaine, was an energetic entrepreneur who probably served as a model for Octave Mouret, the imaginative and innovative owner of Au Bonheur des Dames.

In loving detail Zola describes how Mouret employed exotic décor to encourage shoppers to buy his wares. One section of the novel portrays the reaction of the public to a rug exhibit on the day of a big sale:

> [T]he vestibule [was] changed into an Oriental salon. From the doorway it was a marvel, a surprise that ravished them all. Mouret . . . had just bought in the Near East, in excellent condition, a collection of old and new carpets, those rare carpets which till then only specialty merchants had sold at very high prices, and he was going to flood the market, he gave them away at cut rates, extracting from them a splendid décor which would attract to the store the most elegant clientele. From the middle of Place Gaillon could be seen this Oriental salon made only of rugs and curtains. From the ceiling were suspended rugs from Smyrna with complicated patterns that stood out from the red background. Then, from the four sides, curtains were hung: curtains of Karamanie and Syria; zebra-striped in green, yellow, and vermilion; curtains from Diarbekir, more common, rough to the touch, like shepherds' tunics; and still more rugs, which could serve as wall hangings; strange flowerings of peonies and palms, fantasy released in a garden of dreams.[8]

Customers kept drifting into the store, attracted by this décor so similar to that of the Trocadéro, "the décor of a harem," in Zola's words. By afternoon the building was overflowing with a crush of excited, eager shoppers. At the end of the day some of them met in the Oriental salon so they could depart together; they were so enchanted by the rug display that they could talk of nothing else:

They were leaving, but it was in the midst of a babbling crisis of admira-
tion. Mme. Guibal herself was ecstatic:
"Oh! delicious! . . ."
"Isn't it just like a harem? And not expensive!"
"The Smyrnan ones, ah! the Smyrnan ones! What tones, what finesse!"
"And this one from Kurdistan, look! a Delacroix!"[9]

It was the most profitable day in the history of Au Bonheur des Dames.

The department store dominates the novel. The virtuous but pallid
Denise, Octave Mouret, the crudely drawn entrepreneur who tries unsuccessfully to seduce Denise, and the female shoppers whom Mouret
does seduce commercially, are all subordinate to the store, which seems
to overwhelm them and control their destinies. It does this through means
essentially the same as those employed at the Trocadéro exhibits. The
counters of the department store present a disconnected assortment of
"exhibits," a sort of "universe in a garden" of merchandise. The sheer
variety, the assault of dissociated stimuli, is one cause of the numbed
fascination of the customers. Furthermore, the décor of the department
store repeats the stylistic themes characteristic of the Trocadéro: syncretism, anachronism, illogicality, flamboyance, childishness. In both cases
the décor represents an attempt to express visions of distant places in
concrete terms. It is a style which may without undue flippancy be called
the chaotic-exotic. But within one exhibit not chaos but repetition is often
employed to numb the spectator even further. When rugs are placed on
the ceiling, walls, and floor of the vestibule, when the same item is repeated over and over with minor variations—just as the Andalusian exhibit at the Trocadéro had camels here, camels there, camels everywhere—the sheer accumulation becomes awesome in a way that no single
item could be. The same effect is achieved when Mouret fills an entire
hall with an ocean of umbrellas, top to bottom, along columns and bal-
ustrades and staircases; the umbrellas shed their banality and instead
become "large Venetian lanterns, illuminated for some colossal festival,"
an achievement that makes one shopper exclaim, "It's a fairyland!"[10]

Mouret's most stunning coup, however, is his creation of his own exposition, an "exposition of white," to celebrate the opening of a new
building. The description of this event forms the final chapter of Au
Bonheur des Dames, where it becomes a climactic hymn of praise to modern commerce. Mouret constructs a dreamland architecture of "white
columns . . . white pyramids . . . white castles" made from white hand-
kerchiefs, "a whole city of white bricks . . . standing out in a mirage against
an Oriental sky, heated to whiteness."[11] In this display, exotic fantasies
merge with oceanic ones, and dreams of distant places fade into dreams
of bathing in passive bliss, surrounded on all sides by comfort, a fantasy
of a return to the womb, which has become a womb of merchandise.

THE "AESTHETIC" OF EXOTICISM

To return to a question already posed: this may be impressive, but is it civilization? Is it even art? Like the displays of Versailles—the silver furniture of the palace, its frenzies of gilt, its acres of mirrors and entire rooms swirling with marble, stucco, and frescoes—department-store displays also are designed to impress the spectator. The difference is in the nature of the audience and the motivation behind the display. At Versailles the audience was the restricted one of the court. The courtiers were impressed mainly by the costliness of the décor, costliness due to the fineness of the materials and to the artistic skill used to work them. These qualities, no matter what motivated them, can be incorporated in objects which have enduring value as decorative art. In the department store, on the other hand, the audience is a large and anonymous public. The stylistic traits of repetition, variety, and exoticism used to seduce it into buying usually have little enduring aesthetic value. The motivation behind the décor is to lure people into the store in the first place and then to imbue the store's merchandise with glamor, romance, and, therefore, consumer appeal. There is no aesthetic connection between this décor and the objects it enhances, objects that generally lack any artistic merit.

To criticize the chaotic-exotic style as "bad taste," a frequent condemnation even around the turn of the century, misses the point. As a quality of aesthetic judgment, taste does not apply to transient décor whose purpose is "to attract and to hold" the spectator's attention. Why the reliance on fake mahogany, fake bronze, fake marble? Because the purpose of the materials is not to express their own character but to convey a sense of the lavish and foreign. Why the hodgepodge of visual themes? Because the purpose is not to express internal consistency but to bring together anything that expresses distance from the ordinary. Exotic décor is therefore impervious to objections of taste. It is not ladylike but highly seductive. In this aesthetic demi-monde, exotic décor exists as an intermediate form of life between art and commerce. It resembles art, it has recognizable themes and stylistic traits, its commercial purpose is wrapped in elaborate visual trappings; yet it does not participate in traditional artistic goals of creating beauty, harmony, and spiritual significance. This hybrid form is an illusion of art, a "so-called artistic element"[12] posing as the genuine article.

Zola, for one, was taken in. He praises Mouret as an aesthetic genius as well as a financial one, for in Zola's mind the two types of genius are indistinguishable. He lauds the exposition of white, the Oriental salon, and the sea of open umbrellas as artistic successes, because they attract so many customers. His judgment reflects a deep-seated confusion of commercial and aesthetic values. Talmeyr, on the other hand, clearly distinguishes the type of decoration used by modern business for its own ends from traditional forms of art. According to Talmeyr, in over fifty years universal expositions had not produced any truly artistic constructions at all, but only a "type of frightful plastered and clumsy heaviness, twisting or declamatory, of all those domes, balconies, pediments, columns."[13] True architecture involves the construction of monuments, while expositions require only *décors*, "stage sets" or "scenery." "Why . . . insist on transferring to that which is ephemeral in intention, to that which is *décor* by nature, the principles and procedures of that which is durable and permanent in essence, *monument* by raison d'être?" Exposition buildings are intended to "make . . . in their fashion a weighty and proud show," the same goal that inspires posters advertising "a new shoe polish or a new brand of champagne in a manner vaguely derived from that of Raphael." The goal is to convey an "industrial image," not an artistic one, and the search for magnitude or lavishness will never bridge the gulf in intention:

> You can imagine the [industrial] image as enormous, as ambitious as you wish, it could be stupefying, it will be no less always and necessarily inept. You can even imagine the façade, the frieze, or the columns pushed to the furthest limits of richness, they will be no less equally stupid.

Talmeyr concludes with the suggestion that décor might be able to invent an authentic style if it renounced the attempt to imitate art and instead realized its own nature. He notes that the only modern edifice of the 1900 exposition which he is tempted to praise is the Monumental Gateway surmounted by "La Parisienne." Talmeyr admits that the gateway is heavy, clumsy, bizarre, and gaudy, and that "La Parisienne" is reminiscent of a peasant girl in a cape. Nonetheless, he remarks, they possess

> a unique merit, that nothing like them has been seen anywhere, *that they resemble nothing*! They are absurd? . . . This is also true! But their quality is precisely to be absurd, in an order of ideas where it is logical to be so, and where the only true absurdity, as a result, is to wish to be reasonable.

In environments of mass consumption, the logic of art gives way to the logic of fantasy.

DISTANT VISIONS

For all its innovation in stylistic absurdity, the exotic-chaotic decorative style was traditional in its technology. Its only technical novelty involved the use of increasingly convincing imitation materials to construct "all those domes, balconies, pediments, columns." Nineteenth-century technology developed far more effective ways of creating an illusion of voyage to far-off places, techniques that were dynamic and cinematic rather than static and decorative. They proved so exhilarating and popular that, while occasionally used to publicize products, they more often became products themselves, offered as amusement attractions. At the 1900 exposition twenty-one of the thirty-three major attractions involved a dynamic illusion of voyage. This group of exhibits, like the colonial ones clustered at the Trocadéro, furnished a "lesson of things" in the form of a scale model of a dream world of the consumer.

As Maurice Talmeyr enunciated the lesson of "the school of Trocadéro," so another journalist, Michel Corday (Louis-Léonard Pollet, 1869–1937) assessed the significance of the exhibits providing "Visions Lointaines" ("Distant Visions," or "Views of Faraway Places"). This is the title Corday gave to an article on cinematic exhibits—one of a series he wrote on the exposition—published in the *Revue de Paris*.[14] Corday was well able to appreciate these exhibits from both a technical and a cultural perspective, for he had been educated as an engineer and served with distinction in the army before deciding, at the age of twenty-six, to devote himself to letters. The imprint of Corday's technical training is manifest when he begins by classifying the twenty-one "distant visions" exhibits into five categories, according to the increasing sophistication of the techniques used to convey the illusion of travel: "ensembles in relief," panoramas in which the spectator moves, those in which the panorama itself moves, those in which both move, and moving photographs. One of the more primitive exhibits, an example of the second category, was the World Tour: the tourist walked along the length of an enormous circular canvas representing "without solution of continuity, Spain, Athens, Constantinople, Suez, India, China, and Japan," as natives danced or charmed serpents or served tea before the painted picture of their homeland. The visitor was supposed to have the illusion of touring the world as he strolled by, although Corday hardly found it convincing to have "the Acropolis next-door neighbor to the Golden Horn and the Suez Canal almost bathing the Hindu forests"—the chaotic-exotic style, the universe in a garden, only on canvas! On a somewhat more ingenious level, the Trans-Siberian Panorama placed the spectator in a real railroad car that moved eighty meters from the Russian to the Chinese exhibit while a canvas was unrolled outside the window giving the impression of a journey across Siberia. Three separate machines operated at three different speeds, and their relative motion gave a faithful impression of gazing out a train window. A slight rocking motion was originally planned for the car, but the sponsoring railway company vetoed the idea because it advertised that its trains did not rock.

Corday was even more intrigued by an attraction where not canvases but photographs moved:

> This is Cinéorama, the application—it is surprising that it did not appear sooner—of cinematography to the panorama. This ingenious apparatus . . . is placed in the center of the spectacle to be reproduced. . . . [T]he projector is composed of ten cameras which work in unison and divide the horizon into ten sections, like ten slices of cake.

The Cinéorama could convey the impression of ascending from the earth in a balloon, by a series of panoramic photographs showing things below growing smaller and smaller. To make the illusion even more persuasive, spectators stood in the basket of a balloon to watch the show. Finally, Corday describes some exhibits appealing to many senses at the same time. The Maréorama reproduced a sea voyage from France to Constantinople, complete with canvas panorama, the smell of salt air, a gentle swaying motion (unlike trains, boats were expected to rock), and phonograph music "which takes on the color of the country at which the ship is calling: melancholy at departure, it . . . becomes Arabic in Africa, and ends up Turkish after having been Venetian."

Even sailing to Byzantium was not enough: the surface of the earth was too small to contain human imagination armed with such gadgetry. Corday marvels that new devices allow the masses to realize the "extraordinary voyages" of Jules Verne, to travel not only where few have ventured but also where none have. The Cinéoramatic balloon trip was only the first step in flight from earthbound reality. At another exhibit a diorama took the tourist far beneath the earth to dramatize its formation by showing vast subterranean and prehistoric landscapes strikingly lit by electricity. In the Optical Palace photographic plates were pieced together to give the impression of viewing the moon from a distance of only four kilometers. Then, according to Corday,

> the diorama makes its appearance; at first prudent, it reproduces with exactitude the lunar landscape: then, fantastically, it paints an imaginary voyage to a star; finally, leaping across centuries as easily as space, it narrates the genesis of the earth in twenty tableaux.

So convincing was this illusion that the spectator was hardly aware of crossing the line between reality and fantasy, of moving from a painstaking reproduction of the moon's surface to a wholly imaginary simulation of a journey beyond the galaxy. Real and fantastic voyages, present and future and prehistoric ones, earthbound and cosmic ones became indistinguishable when all were presented as triumphs of technical ingenuity.

Corday was considerably younger and further to the left politically than Talmeyr, and because of his democratic sentiments he saw another aspect of these exhibits besides their obvious profitability. He took seriously the educational purpose, which Talmeyr rejected as a sham. Corday lauded "the sum of ingenuity, of research and invention, spent there to amuse the masses usefully, to enrich them with new visions in all directions of the universe." Between 1889 and 1900 the masses rapidly developed "curiosity about new horizons, a confused desire to widen a little, if only in appearance, the framework of life." Because modern technology makes it possible to satisfy the curiosity of those who could never afford to travel in reality, these exhibits are part of a "great current of democratization that offers to the masses the precious joys until now reserved for a few." Even if far from perfected, technological stratagems such as these constitute "an extraordinary movement of vulgarization, an enormous scientific toy placed in the hands of the masses."

While expressing forcefully his belief in the educational and democratic benefits of the "distant visions" exhibits, Corday fails to question the reliability of what they teach. He is clearly an intelligent and thoughtful observer, but his interest in gadgetry tends to make him neglect the deeper question of veracity. In his mind the matter of truthfulness becomes transformed to a matter of mechanical ingenuity. This is how Corday invites his reader to tour the exposition with him: "Let us go to attend a veritable concourse of evocations, a sort of agreeable race where each one exerts himself to press closer to the Truth." In this context "Truth" means a mechanically faithful rendering of external sensations, the sights, smells, and sounds of travel or of a place. Corday is so intrigued by the cleverness of the means that he never stops to ask, as Talmeyr does, whether the mechanical illusion is faithful to the total social reality or only to selected external appearances. Talmeyr contends that education cannot be made into amusement without being falsified, while Corday sees no such inevitability. The façades of the Trocadéro, which Talmeyr finds so eloquently expressive of a fundamental mendacity, are dismissed by Corday as lacking in technical sophistication and therefore in crowd appeal: "Certainly, these façades speak to the eyes, teach them about distant architectural styles, but do not really constitute attractions, which is to say efforts combined for an illusion." In contrast, the "distant visions" do attract and hold the crowd precisely because the illusion they create is so convincing.

As Zola confuses aesthetic and commercial standards in evaluating department-store displays, so Corday confuses technical and commercial standards in judging the success of the "distant visions" exhibits. The extent of that confusion is evident at the end of Corday's article, when he marvels at the intoxication the exhibits can induce: "Thanks to them, one can live a long time in a few hours; travel across vast distances in a few steps; they are like liquors sparkling to the eyes, pleasing to the palate, which concentrate power and life in a small volume." This drug-induced dreaming, this magical escape from ordinary constraints—what harm can there be in this confusion of reality and fantasy so long as it provides the masses with a taste of "power and life"? Some of the dangers are suggested in the concluding paragraph, which immediately follows the one just quoted. Corday proposes that

> without injuring the interests involved, without transgressing on past contracts, the doors of these attractions might be generally opened to the people. For a few months, for two hundred days, from all points of the continent, trains are going to converge on just one point: Paris. They are like so many miniature societies in motion, which money brutally and frankly divides into three classes. Well, one has to wish that this harsh hierarchy might disappear at the doorway of the Exposition: that those who suffer from it might find in this promised land a short and charming respite from life.

Has Corday himself become unable to distinguish reality from dream? The real world of real train trips was one of first, second, and third classes, corresponding to high, middle, and low incomes. The same business world that ran these trains had invested large amounts of capital in the exposition to advertise their services by operating imaginary train rides at a profit.[15] But Corday seems to imagine that because the voyages at the exposition are illusory, the whole event might become an illusion, a "promised land" of dreams set apart from waking reality. In his muddle he hopes the exposition will not only market fantasies but also become a fantasy. Corday unwittingly testifies to the danger of the intoxication he praises when his delight in a dream world blinds him to its origins in a real social world of classes, profits, and capital.

CINEMATIC VOYAGES

The motion picture is the commercial and technological successor to the "distant visions" exhibits. Between the close of the 1900 exposition and the outbreak of World War I, films became a popular attraction in urban France. In 1907 there were two cinemas in Paris; six years later there were one hundred and sixty, and by 1914 cinema receipts in France were 16 million francs a year.[16] Large, well-financed organizations were established to prepare the décors, costumes, and special effects, to devise the script and hire actors, to shoot the film and edit it, to publicize and distribute the product.

"It is a new, and important, and very modern branch of business," wrote Louis Haugmard in 1913. "This development, extraordinary in its rapidity and extent, this swarming, this 'invasion' of cinematography is a fact which deserves to attract the attention of the casual observer who likes to meditate on things." Haugmard was such an observer. Like Corday, like many other young men in literary circles around the turn of the century, he published a considerable body of creative and critical writings without achieving lasting fame—such is the richness of French letters in that era. Haugmard's report on the movies, titled "L' 'Esthé-tique' du cinématographie" ("The 'Aesthetic' of Cinematography"), appeared in *Le Correspondant*, the Catholic journal in which Talmeyr had reported on the 1900 exposition thirteen years earlier.[17] In that interval the marketing of dreams in cinematic form had been transformed from a temporary fairground curiosity into a decisive and established fact of urban life, a phenomenon to quote Haugmard, "as immense as it is disquieting."

The jumbled chaos of the exposition had been transferred to the silver screen. Haugmard begins his article by remarking upon the way all forms of entertainment—fantastic, sentimental, comic, dramatic, scientific, historical, moralizing—are shown one after the other in the movie house, so that a Western is juxtaposed with a drawing-room comedy, a social documentary with a travelogue, a comic chase sequence with the fall of Troy. "[There is] nothing that cannot be used . . . for the confection of a film." Distinctions of significance and even of realism are obliterated when all levels of experience are reduced to the same level of technically ingenious entertainment. Haugmard further suggests that this cinematic syncretism is a result of the need to appeal to a large public with varying tastes. "In fact, the public of cinematographic spectacles is not coherent. Many 'milieux' are represented there, and all sorts of minds." Because the mass audience is incoherent rather than homogeneous, film programs are also incoherent, for they include something for everyone, just as newspapers and tourist attractions do.

In defining the cinema as a phenomenon of "the people, in the largest meaning of this term," Haugmard agrees with Corday that modern technology widens the horizons of the masses. Not only does film take people to far-off places, "reproduced in their photographic truth, luminous and trembling"; it also allows them to enter hitherto inaccessible reaches of society through "elegant and worldly dramas which introduce them to milieux where they cannot otherwise penetrate." Whether the distance is geographic or social, film allows the pleasures of mobility.

Haugmard is, however, inclined to side with Talmeyr in condemning these imaginary excursions as childish escapism. A film advertisement promises "an hour of intense emotion": who could resist this appeal, Haugmard asks? People crave concentrated doses of intense emotion (what Corday called "liquors . . . which concentrate power and life") to get away from "their sorry and monotonous existence, from which they love to escape." Haugmard notes that moviegoers much prefer fantasies to portrayals of ordinary life:

> "The masses" are like a grown-up child who demands a picture album to leaf through in order to forget his miseries . . . [T]he "cinema," which is a "circus" for adults, offers to the popular imagination and sensibility, deprived and fatigued, the "beau voyage."

People want to evade reality, not to learn about it. Certainly the technical dexterity of the medium permits convincing reproductions of visual appearances, "in their photographic truth, luminous and trembling," but "photographic truth" is not truth. Film can give "the exact reproduction of natural reality" while still being

> a factor of artifice and of falsification. . . . If it is the realm of fraud, of counterfeit, of trickery, how will a naïve public know how to make the indispensable distinctions and the necessary selection, under pain of inevitable misunderstandings and multiple errors?

Just because of its photographic realism, film offers a nearly irresistible temptation not only to inculcate political propaganda but also "to vulgarize, which is to say, to deform" the noblest novels, plays, and poems; " 'to romanticize' or falsify" history by giving a partial view; and, on current subjects, "to nourish vanities and launch imitations, for the image excites naïve souls."

Because film speaks in the language of imagery, it is at once emotionally exciting and intellectually deceptive. The rapid succession of "realistic" images captivates the imagination of the viewer without engaging his mind. As an example, Haugmard describes the way a robbery is portrayed on the screen in a series of scenes of violence, beginning with the hold-up of a delivery van,

> even down to the mark of the bullet on the wheel; then the judge is shown . . . interrogating the policemen. Imagine the influence on children's minds of the burglary scenes and the ingenious methods used to throw the pursuers off the track. The prefect of police in Berlin thought it appropriate to forbid children under fifteen to enter movie theatres.

Movies excite because they communicate through powerful, concrete, realistic images. They lie because they communicate *only* through images:

> Why does an evening at the movies, however crammed with the most diverse films, despite everything leave in the mind an impression of emptiness, of nothingness? . . . Hardly is the spectacle over and it is forgotten.
> It is because only facts are photographed. All the rest is sacrificed, all

that which is intellectual and interior life, and in the human order, only intelligence and soul really count! This exclusive capacity to reproduce only the fact entails its consequences. Action, only action, which is rapid and brutal. From this the suppression, almost absolute, of all psychology. Cinematography is a notation by image, as arithmetic and algebra are notations by figures and letters; now, it is convenient to limit as much as possible in the statement or the exposition all that which is not the sign itself. It is the triumph of simplification.

These remarks apply most directly to the silent films of that era, but even when the image is accompanied by a soundtrack its dominance is maintained. The cinema and its descendant, television, remain positivistic mediums, excluding all that is not fact, visually speaking. By excluding so much, by passing off simplification as totality, they are, to borrow Talmeyr's description of the Indian exhibit, true only partially, and so partially as to be false. Haugmard points out that movie actors become " 'types,' " which is to say that their immediately recognizable personal images come to convey a constellation of values and feelings, down to the child actor who incarnates " 'Baby.' " In the same way, the images of the exotic—the colorful rug, the belly dancer, the domed palace—are decorative "types" that incarnate exciting feelings of adventure, romance, and luxury but have little to do with Oriental reality. The language of imagery is also the language of the dream world of the consumer.

Haugmard's final condemnation of the language of imagery is that it goes in one direction only, from screen to spectator. The moviegoer has no need to make a response to be communicated to others, for in the theatre "everything takes place in the domain of silence." The screen does all the work for the viewer, who needs to put forth only the most minimal intellectual effort. "The mental tension required is feeble; fatigue, if there be fatigue at the end of the spectacle, will be purely nervous and wholly passive." Because all the details of the film are explained by a program or narrator, "mental work is already accomplished in advance to suppress the active effort of the spectators." The passive solitude of the moviegoer therefore resembles the behavior of department-store shoppers, who also submit to the reign of imagery with a strange combination of intellectual and physical passivity and emotional hyperactivity. In both cases shared social experience is replaced by uniformity of experience based on response to potent images. In the moviehouse the characteristic sociability of environments of mass consumption is taken to its limit in ordered rows of silent, hypnotized spectators.

Haugmard finds the implications of this behavior so distressing that he evaluates it not in his own words but in the words of an imaginary "man of taste, of a skepticism sometimes morose, sometimes indulgent."

In an indulgent mood, the "man of taste" muses that the movies provide tolerable and even delightful illusions, views of lovely landscapes, of strange lands, even of fairylands,

> for cinematography can realize any dream. What good are Hoffmann, Andersen, and creators of fantasy, what good are poets who invent, when cinematography is there to record scientifically, for the incredulous masses, the wildest phantasmagorias of ancestral myths?

But in the actual world (and here the "man of taste" turns morose) life will become distorted when the behavior induced by the movies becomes habitual. When movies provide the miracle of "an unlimited posthumous life, there will be no more written archives, only films, catalogued and classified, and the 'pressings' of public life, the 'preserves' of the past, often not exempt from falsification." Not only will our view of the past be altered, but action in the present will alter with an eye to how it will look on film. "Alas! in the future, notorious personalities will instinctively 'pose' for cinematographic popularity, and historical events will tend to be concocted for its sake." Already film is becoming, if not exactly the "religion of the masses," then (borrowing the title of a well-known contemporary book)[18] "the irreligion of the future":

> Through it the charmed masses will learn not to think anymore, to resist all desire to reason and to construct, which will atrophy little by little; they will know only how to open their large and empty eyes, only to look, look, look. . . . Will cinematography comprise, perhaps, the elegant solution to the social question, if the modern cry is formulated: "Bread and cinemas"? . . .
>
> And we shall progressively draw near to those menacing days when universal illusion in universal mummery will reign.

Haugmard's meditation beautifully illustrates a type of culture criticism that deserves to be rehabilitated, a type that originates in aesthetic thought but extends to far more encompassing social and moral issues. When Haugmard places "aesthetic" in quotations in his title, he registers his awareness that the term is only approximate, that no pristinely aesthetic response is possible, that, as in the case of exposition décor, appraisal of the visual phenomenon must take into account the commercial motivation behind it. Haugmard experiments with a variety of vocabularies—aesthetic, moral, sociological, psychological—in attempting to deal with a cultural phenomenon "as immense as it is disquieting," too immense, certainly, to be reduced to any one terminology. In this respect he is an experimentalist, like such other French *moralistes* of his day as Talmeyr and Corday. They are trying to devise a language appropriate for events at once significant and unbounded by traditional disciplinary categories. Like the experiences they treat, their vocabulary is hybrid and innovative: new forms of consumption demand new modes of criticism.

THE ELECTRICAL FAIRYLAND

By now it is becoming clear how momentous were the effects of nineteenth-century technological progress in altering the social universe of consumption. Besides being responsible for an increase in productivity which made possible a rise in real income; besides creating many new products and lowering the prices of traditional ones; besides all this, technology made possible the material realization of fantasies which had hitherto existed only in the realm of imagination. More than any other technological innovation of the late nineteenth century, even more than the development of cinematography, the advent of electrical power invested everyday life with fabulous qualities. The importance of an electrical power grid in transforming and diversifying production is obvious, as is its eventual effect in putting a whole new range of goods on the market. What is less appreciated, but what amounts to a cultural revolution, is the way electricity created a fairyland environment, the sense of being, not in a distant place, but in a makebelieve place where obedient genies leap to their master's command, where miracles of speed and motion are wrought by the slightest gesture, where a landscape of glowing pleasure domes and twinkling lights stretches into infinity.

Above all, the advent of large-scale city lighting by electrical power nurtured a collective sense of life in a dream world. In the 1890s nocturnal lighting in urban areas was by no means novel, since gas had been used for this purpose for decades; however, gas illumination was pale and flickering compared to the powerful incandescent and arc lights which began to brighten the night sky in that decade. The expositions provided a preview of the transformation of nighttime Paris from somber semidarkness to a celestial landscape. At the 1878 exposition an electric light at a café near but not actually on the fairgrounds caused a sensation. In 1889 a nightly show of illuminated fountains entranced crowds with a spectacle of falling rainbows, cascading jewels, and flaming liquids, while spotlights placed on the top of the Eiffel Tower swept the darkening sky as the lights of the city were being turned on. At the 1900 exposition electrical lighting was used for the first time on a massive scale, to keep the fair open well into the night. Furthermore, the special lighting effects were stunning. In one of his articles for the *Revue de Paris*, Corday describes the nightly performance:

> A simple touch of the finger on a lever, and a wire as thick as a pencil throws upon the Monumental Gateway . . . the brilliance of three thousand

incandescent lights which, under uncut gems of colored glass, become the
sparkling soul of enormous jewels.

Another touch of the finger: the banks of the Seine and the bridges are
lighted with fires whose reflection prolongs the splendor. . . . The façade
of the Palace of Electricity is embraced, a stained-glass window of light,
where all these diverse splendors are assembled in apotheosis.[19]

Like the technological marvels already mentioned, this one was at once
exploited for commercial purposes. As early as 1873 the writer Villiers
de l'Isle-Adam (1838–1889) predicted in a short story, "L'Affichage cé-
leste" (which might be loosely translated as "The Heavenly Billboard"),
that the "seeming miracles" of electrical lights could be used to generate
"an absolute Publicity" when advertising messages were projected upward to shine among the stars:

Wouldn't it be something to surprise the Great Bear himself if, suddenly,
between his sublime paws, this disturbing message were to appear: *Are
corsets necessary, yes or no?* . . . What emotion concerning dessert liqueurs
. . . if one were to perceive, in the south of Regulus, this heart of the Lion,
on the very tip of the ear of corn of the Virgin, an Angel holding a flask
in hand, while from his mouth comes a small paper on which could be
read these words: *My, it's good!*[20]

Thanks to this wonderful invention, concluded Villiers, the "sterile spaces"
of heaven could be converted "into truly and fruitfully instructive spectacles. . . . It is not a question here of feelings. Business is business. . . .
Heaven will finally make something of itself and acquire an intrinsic value."
As with so many other writers of that era, Villiers's admiration of technological wonders is tempered by the ironic consideration of the banal
commercial ends to which the marvelous means were directed. Unlike
the wonders of nature, the wonders of technology could not give rise to
unambiguous enthusiasm or unmixed awe, for they were obviously manipulated to arouse consumers' enthusiasm and awe.

The prophetic value of Villiers's story lies less in his descriptions of
the physical appearance of the nocturnal sky with its stars obscured by
neon lights, than in his forebodings of the moral consequences when
commerce seizes all visions, even heavenly ones, to hawk its wares. Villiers's prophecies were borne out by the rapid application of electrical
lighting to advertising. As he foresaw, electricity was used to spell out
trade names, slogans, and movie titles. Even without being shaped into
words, the unrelenting glare of the lights elevated ordinary merchandise
to the level of the marvelous. Department-store windows were illuminated with spotlights bounced off mirrors. At the 1900 exposition, wax
figurines modeling the latest fashions were displayed in glass cages under brilliant lights, a sight which attracted hordes of female spectators.

When electrical lighting was used to publicize another technical novelty, the automobile, the conjunction attracted mammoth crowds of both sexes. Beginning in 1898, an annual Salon de l'Automobile was held in Paris to introduce the latest models to the public. It was one of the first trade shows; the French were pioneers in advertising the automobiles as well as in developing the product itself. This innovation in merchandising—like the universal expositions the Salon de l'Automobile resembles so closely—claimed the educational function of acquainting the public with recent technological advances, a goal, however, which was strictly subordinate to that of attracting present and future customers. The opening of the 1904 Salon de l'Automobile was attended by 40,000 people (compared to 10,000 who went to the opening of the annual painting salon), and 30,000 came each day for the first week. Each afternoon during the Salon de l'Automobile, the Champs-Élysées was thronged with crowds making their way to the show, which was held in the Grand Palais, an imposing building constructed for the 1900 universal exposition. During the Salon the glass and steel domes of the Grand Palais were illuminated at dusk with 200,000 lights; the top of the building glowed in the gathering darkness like a stupendous lantern. People were enchanted: "a radiant jewel," they raved, "a colossal industrial fairyland," "a fairytale spectacle."[21]

Inside, lights transformed the automobiles themselves into glittering objects of fantasy:

> You must come at nightfall. Coming out into the world from the entrance to the Métro, you stand stupefied by so much noise, movement, and light. A rotating spotlight, with its quadruple blue ray, sweeps the sky and dazzles you; two hundred automobiles in battle formation look at you with their large fiery eyes. . . . Inside, the spectacle is of a rare and undeniable beauty. The large nave has become a prodigious temple of Fire; each of its iron arches is outlined with orange flames; its cupola is carpeted with white flames, with those fixed and as it were solid flames of incandescent lamps: fire is made matter, and they have built from it. The air is charged with a golden haze, which the moving rays of the projectors cross with their iridescent pencils. . . .[22]

Again this is an aesthetic of the exaggerated and showy, of simple but powerful imagery repeated to overwhelm the viewer (what could be more repetitious than two hundred thousand lights?). As with exotic décor, the purpose behind such a display is to win attention and to raise merchandise above the level of the everyday by associating it with exciting imagery.

Unlike images of far-off places, however, a fairyland cannot be accused of falsity because it never pretends to be a real place. Or can it? Electric lighting covers up unpleasant sights which might be revealed in the cold light of day. The illumination of the Grand Palais disguised the building itself. In the words of one visitor:

> The Grand Palais itself is almost beautiful because you hardly see it any-more: the confused scrap-iron and copperwork . . . [is] lost in the shadow; the luminous scallop decorations and chandeliers and . . . allegories, drowned in the irradiation. . . . The roof itself, that monstrous skin of a leviathan washed up there on the bank of the river, borrows a sort of beauty from the light which emanates from it.[23]

Through the obscuring glare the same visitor noted that the poles supporting the light fixtures were ridiculously ornamented with nautical motifs and garlands which were coming unstuffed. Others who viewed the décor of the Salon de l'Automobile were appalled when in the daylight they saw booths with doorways plastered to resemble those of Persian mosques, Gothic churches, or Egyptian temples, other booths constructed like bamboo huts hung with Japanese lanterns, and still others rigged with ship's masts complete with ropes, sails, and flags. The visitor quoted above, horrified by this "so-called artistic element" of the Salon, said that the exhibits showed "an incoherent heap of the most laughable imaginings" which the French should be thoroughly ashamed to display to the rest of the world, except that the displays of foreigners were equally ridiculous.[24] But all that junk miraculously disappeared when the lights came on.

Through fantasy, business provides alternatives to itself. If the world of work is unimaginative and dull, then exoticism allows an escape to a dream world. If exotic décor is heavy, unconvincing, and shabby, then another level of deception is furnished by a nightly fairyland spectacle that waves away the exotic with the magic wand of electricity. Robert de La Sizeranne, art critic for the *Revue dex deux mondes,* compared the Salons de l'Automobile to fairytale princesses fought over by "perverse and benevolent powers" so that they were "frightfully ugly all day long [and] at night [became] beauties adorned with dazzling jewels." According to La Sizeranne, this diurnal schizophrenia was being repeated all over Paris. In the day the city displayed "superfluous, ignoble, lamentable ornaments," while at nightfall "these trifling or irritating profiles are melted in a conflagration of apotheosis. . . . Everything takes on another appearance," the ugly details are lost, and diamonds, rubies, and sapphires spill over the city.[25] Instead of correcting its mistakes, the city buries them under another level of technology. In this respect the whole city is assuming the character of an environment of mass consumption. In the day as well as at night, the illusions of these environments divert attention to merchandise of all kinds and away from other things, like colonialism, class structure, and visual disasters.

How much of the history of consumption is revealed in comparing Mme. de Rambouillet's salon of witty conversation and candlelight with the twentieth-century Salon de l'Automobile, a cacophony of crowds, cars, glass, steel, noise, and light!

DREAMS OF LOVE AND WEALTH

It is neither necessary nor possible to catalog all the dreams exploited by modern business. Although their range is as boundless as that of the human imagination, the concepts already discussed should apply to them also, in a general way. One fantasy, however, is so powerful and pervasive that it deserves special mention—the desire for sexual pleasure. If dreams of distant places are materialized in exotic imagery and fairyland ones in electric-light displays, erotic dreams are incarnated in the female image. Once again the expositions provided a prophecy of the commercial exploitation of imagery. The belly dancers of the Rue du Caire at the 1889 fair and the glass-caged wax mannequins at the 1900 exposition attracted large crowds. Both female images had a compelling effect, but the dancer and mannequin were enticing in different ways to different audiences. Men gathered to see the sinuous, half-naked entertainer perform in the shadows of a cabaret, while women were held spellbound by the motionless, elegantly clothed models poised under electric lights. The charm of the dancer is closely related to the appeal of the exotic, for both invite liberation from ordinary conventions and attainment of a more romantic, exciting existence. The appeal of the wax mannequin, on the contrary, is that of a fairytale princess, who is coldly beautiful and proudly remote. The images imply a startling contrast between male and female fantasies, between what men want women to be like and what women want to be like. Can these contrary images be reconciled, in a woman at once exotic and ethereal, at once sensual and remote, at once harem slave and princess?

"La Parisienne" suggests that they can be. This penultimate female, the symbol of the 1900 exposition, was perched atop the Monumental Gateway, an icon both sexy and remote, goddess and slut, and she resembles the women who were portrayed on advertising posters all over Paris in that era when these posters became a significant art form. Indeed, the triumph of French poster art, according to Georges d'Avenel (of whom more will be said shortly), is its mating of contradictory female images in its ceaseless repetition of "the representation of a female being with teasing features, half fairy princess and half 'streetwalker.' " The preferred model of the Chéret brothers, masters of poster art, is "this Parisienne, of a desirable height, with a hieratic smile, pagan goddess intoxicated with her own apotheosis." This "illusory type" always wears the same expression whether she is shown on horseback, at the beach, smoking, writing to advertise an ink or carrying a lamp to publicize mineral oil, always "lending the charm of her petite person to all the offerings of business."[26]

If this creation is not exactly a triumph of art, it is surely a triumph of décor. This "type" (which also appeared in all the movie houses) appeals to the fantasies of both sexes at the same time. Just as cinema programs include something for everyone, business wants to deploy images that appeal to as many consumers as possible. The aim of mass publicity is to make the dream world as uniform as possible in order to entice as many people as possible. The creation of a hybrid streetwalker-princess is one way to achieve this goal.

Another is to reduce fantasies to their lowest common denominator. This is why the idea of wealth is of such importance in the symbiosis of commerce and dream. Desire for wealth is infinitely malleable. People have diverse ideas about how they would indulge themselves if they were rich, but their daydreams depend on the basic fantasy of possession of great wealth. With wealth other dreams can come true. In appealing to this fantasy, commerce can achieve a feat of reductionism and secure the broadest possible audience.

Environments of mass consumption are places where consumers can indulge temporarily in the fantasy of wealth. These environments are Versailles open to all, at least during business hours. Without having to buy, the department-store shopper can handle and try on merchandise. For the relatively low price of admission, the exposition tourist can enjoy palaces and dancing girls, gaze on luxurious goods, travel in style, and otherwise taste pleasures normally reserved for the fortunate few. In the "picture palace," the moviegoer can be transported to high society to mingle with the rich. At the Salon de l'Automobile young couples can lounge in the crushed velvet seats of luxury vehicles before taking the Métro back home to cramped and drab apartments.[27] Perhaps the consumer revolution intensified the pain of envy by bringing within the realm of possibility the acquisition of a degree of wealth that had formerly been considered out of reach. This point is stressed by Balzac, chronicler of that pain. But the consumer revolution also brought an anodyne in the form of environments of mass consumption, where envy is transformed into pleasure by producing a temporary but highly intense satisfaction of the dream of wealth.

The satisfaction of this dream on a less intense but more lasting basis was another long-term accomplishment of the consumer revolution. The outpouring of new commodities in the late nineteenth century created a world where a consumer could possess images of wealth without actually having a large income. This magic was wrought, in the first place, through

the alchemy of scientific and technological advances that permitted hitherto expensive articles to be made much more cheaply or to be imitated
convincingly and inexpensively.

The other major advance making possible a widespread illusion of
wealth was the vast expansion of credit. . . . [C]ourtiers had custom-
arily bought their luxuries with borrowed money; at the other end of
the social scale, the poor had long purchased food on credit. During the
consumer revolution the habit of borrowing permeated the ranks of the
bourgeoisie, and credit buying began to be used for a wide range of
consumer goods. Credit became a branch of big business. French retailers of food, drink, and pharmaceuticals had long offered credit (and
had traditionally been expensive in consequence), but they did so on a
personal, unsystematic, unwritten basis. During the consumer revolution borrowing was transformed into a large-scale, impersonal, rationalized system of installment purchase which made possible the acquisition of goods without ready cash—indeed a fantasy come true.

Installment plans were "developed into a national institution" in France
by Georges Dufayel (1855–1916), beginning in the 1870s. His clients
generally paid 20 percent of the standard purchase price for household
goods at over 400 stores accepting Dufayel's tokens, and repaid the rest
in small weekly installments. Dufayel received 18 percent commission on
his sales. By the turn of the century the Dufayel firm had served over
three million customers and had branches in every large French town.
In Paris alone 3,000 clerks were employed to handle the orders and
another 800 went out each day to collect repayments.[28]

These figures, however, do not fully convey the significance of credit
purchase in allowing an ordinary wage-earner to enjoy a convincing illusion of wealth. The power of that illusion is expressed more vividly in
the magnificent store, costing $10,000,000, that Dufayel built in the Rue
de Clignancourt just after the turn of the century. "On entering Dufayel's store by the principal door," remarked one admiring observer, "it
seems as though you are entering a palace rather than a shop." The
entrance porch was richly ornamented with carvings and statues representing themes like "Credit" and "Publicity" and surmounted by a dome
180 feet high. Inside the building were 200 statues, 180 paintings, pillars, decorative panels, bronze allegorical figures holding candelabras,
painted ceramics and glass, and grand staircases, as well as a theatre
seating 3000 that was decorated with silk curtains, white-and-gold fo-
liage wreaths, and immense mirrors. But Dufayel's establishment was
more than a reproduction of a palace of the *ancien régime:* it also incorporated the most up-to-date attractions of consumer society. If there was
a traditional cut-glass chandelier inside the dome, on the outside, at the
very top, was a revolving light of ten million candlepower (almost as

powerful as the searchlight on top of the Eiffel Tower) visible for twelve
miles—"which makes an excellent advertisement at night." If the theatre
was "an object of astonishment and admiration to all visitors," who attended monthly musical performances there, the far plainer Cinematograph Hall in the basement was far more popular. There 1,500 people
paid admission to attend each of four hour-long performances every
day. "The cinematograph attracts many people to the store, and is an
ingenious and profitable method of advertising." Dufayel's genius was
to transform the traditional décor of an aristocratic palace into a modern, democratic environment of mass consumption.[29] The décor of the
building faithfully symbolized its merchandise: to sell credit was to sell
the illusion of princely wealth to the masses.

Dufayel's firm was so successful that rival credit companies were established, and department stores, beginning with the Samaritaine in 1913,
began to organize their own credit companies.[30] The proliferation of
credit, together with the proliferation of inexpensive imitation goods,
permitted (in a phrase then popular) "the democratization of luxury."
As the word *democratization* suggests, the dream of wealth, more than any
other dream yet mentioned, has a social dimension, and it is therefore
worthy of special attention.

GEORGES D'AVENEL ON THE DEMOCRATIZATION OF LUXURY

Georges d'Avenel (1855–1939) was the most perceptive French analyst
of the democratization of luxury. Around the turn of the century, he
published a lively series of articles for the *Revue des deux mondes,* collectively titled "Le Mécanisme de la vie moderne" ("The Mechanism of
Modern Life"), which appeared from 1894 to 1905 and which, simultaneously published in book form, went through numerous editions.[31] The
title of the series is intriguing. The word *mechanism,* traditionally associated with means of production, was applied by d'Avenel to means of
consumption. In each of his articles he discusses one aspect of modern
consumption: institutions like department stores and supermarkets; the
manufacture (but this is not emphasized) and retailing (this *is* emphasized) of items like paper, silk, porcelain, clothing, and alcoholic beverages; systems of credit, advertising, and insurance; methods of transportation such as steamships, buses, and the Métro; entertainments such as
the racetrack and theater; and domestic consumption in the form of
lighting, heating, and home decoration. All these things and more are
subsumed under d'Avenel's exceptionally broad understanding of what
mass consumption encompasses. The principal value of his commentary
lies in his multiplicity of perspectives. He defines the phenomenon as an

area for general social inquiry. In the words of one admirer, d'Avenel wields "statistics like an engineer, caprices like a caricaturist, motives like a sociologist, and recollections like an historian."[32]

The historical perspective, the ingrained habit of viewing contemporary events in the light of history, enables d'Avenel to assess his own times with exceptional lucidity. He wrote some well-received traditional historical studies of the aristocracy and Church in seventeenth-century France. In the course of this research, however, he became convinced that the doings of eminent political and ecclesiastical figures bore little relevance to the lives of ordinary people. "The public life of a people is a very small thing in comparison to its private life."[33] No doubt this conclusion reflected d'Avenel's disdain for contemporary public life. The Third Republic of his day was sullied by the adventures of Boulanger and the sordid Panama scandal, and d'Avenel's contempt for its political shabbiness was by no means unique or unjustified. A wealthy aristocrat with the title of viscount, he was not predisposed to favor Third Republic politics, although he was sincerely liberal in religion and social outlook.

Instead of retreating to the anti-Semitic and legitimist fanaticism of many of his social peers in the Faubourg Saint-Germain, d'Avenel used his criticism of contemporary society to enrich his historical work. Turning off the well-trodden path of public history, he ventured into a realm of private history few had explored—the history of slow changes in material life, in food, clothing, furnishings, lodgings, and lighting, to name only a few examples. The bedrock of his research was a statistical compilation of private incomes and expenditures over seven centuries. Gathering these data involved staggering labor: d'Avenel claimed he examined as many as 75,000 prices as part of his research. He was convinced, however, that household budgets were the key to penetrating lost worlds of private history. From these budgets he concluded that material life had changed radically, that it had been "transformed from top to bottom"[34] over the centuries, and that this transformation had progressed independent of political or legal events, even so-called revolutionary ones. But statistics were only the means to his ultimate goal, which was "to penetrate into the intimacy of humble homes of yesteryear, to scrutinize the relations formerly established between rich and poor, finally, to discover, buried beneath the heap of dead statistics, a thousand secret emotions of our fathers."[35] The dry figures of prices and incomes provided the key to the mental life of the past: "the history of figures becomes the history of men."[36] Spending patterns had never been based on a logical and sober assessment of material well-being; instead, spending was motivated primarily by mental pleasures ranging from the thrill of success in doubling one's income to the "vaporous reveries of inebriation." D'Avenel concluded that "for the poor as for the rich, this question of income and expenses is above all a *matter of imagination*."[37]

If his dissatisfaction with contemporary society enriched d'Avenel's historical outlook, his research into the consumption patterns of the past made him an astute observer of the consumer society evolving around him and, above all, of the imaginative pleasures it afforded. In "The Mechanism of Modern Life" he demonstrates over and over how ordinary citizens of his own day could enjoy the illusion of wealth; the backdrop, stated or implied, is the preceding seven centuries, when striking differences in appearance and possessions erected a "brutal barrier" between peasants and courtiers. The consumer revolution had toppled that barrier. In his article on porcelain, for example, d'Avenel describes how the rich used to eat off porcelain and the poor off clay or wood; now Frenchmen from millionaire to peasant eat out of the same dish, as it were. The industrial changes that made possible large-scale production of tableware also revolutionized interior decoration, so that the working classes could afford factorymade rugs and wallpapers that offered some appearance of wealth in the place of the reality. The illusion of riches could be enjoyed in dress, especially in "the democratization of the 'silk dress,' that ancient symbol of opulence, thus procuring the illusion of similarity in clothing—a great comfort for the feminine half of the human race."[38] Although mass-produced silks selling for a franc and a half a meter in department stores were less beautiful than fine Lyonnais ones costing six hundred francs a meter, "they make more people happy." Technological advances had also transformed the feather industry: cheap and persuasive facsimiles of the rarest varieties, or even of totally imaginary ones, could be purchased by any shopgirl. Rabbit pelts could be turned into exotic furs like "Mongolian chinchilla." Artificial flowers with brilliant colors, flexible rubber stems, and papyrus corollas were available to all. The pleasures of novelty could also be enjoyed by everyone. The privilege of following changes in clothing fashions had spread to both men and women, people whose grandparents had probably purchased only a few new outfits in their lives.[39]

D'Avenel wholeheartedly welcomes the mass of cheap imitations flooding the marketplace. Instead of living with constant frustration, the humble could now enjoy the pleasures of being rich:

> Each time [industries] extended their reach, the life of a great number of individuals gains a new satisfaction; they allow the pale and illusory but sweet reflection of opulence to penetrate even to the humble. These vulgarizations are the work of our century: they honor it greatly.[40]

To those who protested the banality of the pleasure derived from these vulgarizations, d'Avenel responds:

The character of the new luxury is to be banal. Let us not complain too much, if you please: before, there was nothing banal but misery. Let us not fall into this childish but nevertheless common contradiction which consists of welcoming the development of industry while deploring the results of industrialism.[41]

And to those who complained that the democratization of luxury meant the proliferation of "bad taste," d'Avenel suggests that the cause of decline in workmanship is not only technological—the replacement of handwork by machinery—but also social and psychological—the desire to have consumer goods resembling those of the rich. The shopgirl prefers a shoddy, mass-produced silk to a sturdy, handsome cotton because silk, originally valued for its intrinsic beauty, is now valued by the masses for conveying an aura of moneyed glamor. The illusion, and not the fabric, is the source of the consumer's pleasure. D'Avenel defends this subjective satisfaction. When a manufacturer admits to him that the lovely tints of mass-produced silks do not last long, d'Avenel remarks:

> I am not pleading here the cause of the "shoddy"; it doesn't need a lawyer, and if it needed a poet the dyers could say: "Qu'importe le flacon pourvu qu'on ait l'ivresse? . . ." ["What does it matter what's in the bottle as long as it gets you drunk?"][42]

D'Avenel's defense of the joys of cheap imitations stands in refreshing contrast to the frequent condescending dismissals of them by those who can afford better. On the other hand, he is condescending in another way. His very defense of these goods implies the acceptance of a social system where significant inequalities in income endure despite the growing equality in merchandise. Indeed, d'Avenel not only accepts this system but praises the democratization of luxury for strengthening it. In modern society, technology makes possible an "equalization of enjoyments" without a corresponding "equalization of incomes."[43] From his statistical research d'Avenel knew that incomes had in fact become less equal during the nineteenth century: he himself estimated that bourgeois had multiplied their real income by three or four times, the very rich by six to eight times, and the masses by only two times. But he contends that the rich man's increase in fortune has little real meaning, that his additional income buys only "artificial" luxuries, in the form of rarities, rather than genuine comforts. "Leveling consists of this: that the common people have acquired more real well-being, more useful luxury than the wealthy."[44] Mechanical invention diminished meaningful class differences by overturning the traditional relationship between the utility of an object and its monetary value. "There is more difference between a peasant lighted by a resin candle and the lord lighted by wax tapers than between a worker lighted by oil and a bourgeois lighted by electricity."[45] The bicycle is another example: it is much more useful to the poor than the automobile is to the bourgeois, and the Paris Métro would soon give all urban workers the dream come true of a vehicle always at their service. According to d'Avenel, socialist "egalophiles" are not only futile, since improvement in living standards proceeds regardless of political events, but are also unnecessary. "What does inequality in money matter, when it no longer gives rise to inequality in actual enjoyments?"[46]

CRITICAL REMARKS

Does it matter? D'Avenel correctly stresses the radical differences between modern levels of consumption and those of preceding centuries. His historical research gives him a clear-eyed recognition of what industrialization means to the vast majority, in practical terms. Many other social critics who contrast past and present regard only differences in production methods. They portray a former utopia of small shops, craftsmanship, and good will, and a present hell of grinding factories, industrial strife, and degrading labor. D'Avenel looks instead at the level of consumption each productive system is capable of supporting. The contrast he draws is between the physical and psychological miseries of ill-fed, ill-clothed, and ill-lodged masses and the far more comfortable and uniform conditions of contemporary life. But his emphasis on higher consumer standards leads him to underestimate the costs of the physically taxing and psychologically unrewarding labor that is often involved in producing modern goods. D'Avenel could argue that working conditions are no worse than before and that they are more than compensated for by the new pleasures of consumption. These responses deserve consideration by anyone proposing an impossible marriage of past production and present consumption. Still, gains in consumption should not be used as an excuse for the persistence of bad working conditions. Improvement of those conditions does not necessarily entail a return to primitive consumer levels. D'Avenel himself cannot be accused of having used this excuse directly, and to fault him for slighting production is to blame him for not covering a topic he never intended to discuss at length. The point is that his arguments could readily be turned into evasions of or excuses for the failings of modern production methods, or even into a defense of consumerism as an opiate to lull workers into forgetfulness of their dissatisfactions.

D'Avenel was aware that many wage-earners remained unhappy despite the leveling of enjoyments. In his article on alcoholic beverages in "The Mechanism of Modern Life," he notes that an enormous number of workers did not use their high wages to gather a nest-egg or to enjoy a more comfortable life, but only to fill their goblets and empty their heads with drink like some "fetishist Negro" of the Sudan. Why would the most cultivated, proud workers in the world behave in this manner, drinking not in jolly festivity but rapidly, silently, grimly?

> You would have to understand their interior life, probably better than they understand it. . . . Only in drink are promises never eluded. . . . The more his reason takes flight and his head strays, the alcoholic, in stupefying himself, loses himself and, however crude be his dream, he dreams![47]

"Qu'importe le flacon pourvu qu'on ait l'ivresse. . . ." In describing the inebriated worker, d'Avenel comes disconcertingly close to describing the dream world of the consumer, whose pleasures he has defended so vigorously. Is there any great difference between solitary drinking and solitary moviegoing, between "stupefying" oneself with a bottle or with a department store, exposition, or Salon de l'Automobile? Does not Corday describe the "distant visions" exhibits as draughts of highly distilled liquor which give the masses a taste of power and life? Perhaps d'Avenel is right in claiming that the worker himself does not know why he craves dreams, but clearly something is desired which is not found in the leveling of enjoyments. Why this flight, by whatever method, from reality to illusion—from sobriety to drunkenness, from reason to stupor, from waking to dream?

One possibility frequently mentioned in twentieth-century analyses of mass culture is that the pleasures of consumption fail to compensate for the dreary work the drinker has to do all day long. Another possibility, raised by d'Avenel's own writings, is that the illusion of equality is not so convincing as he suggests. His social theory assumes that a shoddy silk dress or a "Mongolian chinchilla" gives the same sense of wealth as a handmade silk dress from Lyon or a mink coat. D'Avenel understands the objective differences in quality, but he assumes that the masses won't notice or won't care. Still, if the rich seek the unique and genuine, the work of art rather than the mass-produced, why shouldn't ordinary people want them too? If the rich take pride in having an educated "good taste" that appreciates the difference between a cheap imitation and an expensive original, why shouldn't that education be available to all? Even without a high degree of education, people are aware of the desirability of unique or rare items. In the "Mechanism" series d'Avenel often reminds his readers that wealth consists of the ability to possess, not beautiful or comfortable things, but rare ones. However, he adds, an object cannot be rare and also be possessed by the masses. No matter how desirable the item, no matter what its former associations with wealth, as soon as it becomes cheap enough to find a mass market it loses its rarity and therefore its desirability. D'Avenel notes that department stores tend to accelerate the dissipation of the illusion of wealth. These stores offer objects for mass consumption whose great attraction has been the difficulty of obtaining them because of their costliness (for example, Mouret offered Oriental rugs at cut rates). The pleasure of the illusion of wealth disappears into the distance as the mass market keeps encroaching, transforming the rare into the commonplace. When everyone can afford an imitation or cheap Oriental rug, then people want a handmade tapestry. The genuine continues to signify wealth, and common people continue to suffer from the vision of unattainable merchandise. There can be no authentic democratization of luxury because by definition luxury is a form of consumption limited to a few. Modern society has instead introduced the proliferation of superfluity.

D'Avenel fails to distinguish luxury from superfluity, and so his theory of the leveling of enjoyments attempts to base social harmony on deception rather than reality. Dreams may be solitary, but reality is inescapably collective. D'Avenel's conviction that change in private life is far more consequential than change in public life leads him to ignore the public consequences that follow from even the most seemingly private acts of consumption. In part the consequences are psychological. When a shopgirl buys a silk dress to fulfill a personal fantasy, she steps out onto the street and discovers that thousands of other women have had the same dream and bought the same type of dress. For all of them the illusion of wealth is shattered. On a more objective level, too, the pleasures of possession may be destroyed when many dream the same dream. As d'Avenel himself concedes, some goods cannot be democratized without losing their inherent charm:

> [It] would doubtless be more pleasant for each Parisian to own the Bois de Boulogne all by himself, or with a small number of friends, rather than share its enjoyment on holidays with 500,000 other proprietors. But it is precisely the glory of Progress to have created this congestion in making accessible to all an outing which used to be very remote.[48]

A "glory," perhaps, but the judgment would be more convincing if d'Avenel himself had to spend his holidays in this congested park. In an imaginary exposition voyage, many people can pretend to visit an unspoiled, uncrowded place; the actual Bois de Boulogne loses its charm because it is invaded by masses of other pleasure-seekers.

The basic weakness of d'Avenel's social theory lies deeper than this, however: it is his assumption that as consumers people seek enjoyment above all. As d'Avenel himself admits:

> If the mass of citizens does not appear to appreciate the . . . new enjoyments with which the nineteenth century has endowed it, it is because the "money question" is not a question of enjoyment, but one of equality; a matter of self-respect and not at all one of pleasure. "To have money,"

isn't it basically "to have more money than others," and how can it be arranged so that each Frenchman has more money than the others?[49]

With this admission collapses the theory of social harmony through the leveling of enjoyments. Differences in income are objective and measurable; intangible, subjective similarities in enjoyment may be claimed but cannot be demonstrated. People are more aware of tangible class differences than of illusory similarities, more aware of their disadvantages compared with wealthier contemporaries than of their advantages over their ancestors. An obvious conclusion is that people should have real equality in income and seek whatever illusions they crave on their own. But d'Avenel immediately jumps to the conclusion that people will not rest satisfied with equality but will demand superiority of income. The moment he approaches the issue of equalizing incomes rather than consumer pleasures, equalizing realities rather than dreams, he evades the issue in the despairing observation that people will never be happy anyway. It would be more accurate to say that people will remain dissatisfied with equality in consumer goods when so many other differences remain. D'Avenel looks too much at the objects people own and not enough at the flesh-and-blood owners—at the differences in their mortality, education, health, manners, taste, social contacts, leisure, and social and political power. These human distinctions remain despite a democratization of goods.

CONCLUDING REMARKS

D'Avenel is the historian of the material side of "the civilizing process" whereby consumer enjoyments originally limited to a small courtly circle gradually spread among a mass public. His contribution in defining and describing this process endures despite the inadequacies of his social theory. Its inadequacy did not keep it from being shared by moderate liberals who also approved of this democratization and even wanted it extended, while at the same time opposing more radical policies of equalization. Other social critics openly lamented the end of elitism in consumption . . . , and still others argued that democratization had not gone nearly far enough, that the mass of consumers needed to acquire far more political and economic powers. . . . Nevertheless, all these turn-of-the-century thinkers—moderate, elitist, and democratic alike—agreed that the historical evolution traced by d'Avenel raises fundamental and portentous issues for the future.

Surely it is instructive that in confronting those issues so decent a man as d'Avenel enthusiastically endorsed the idea of equalizing enjoyments rather than money, for, at the bottom, he was approving a vast delusion whereby human inequalities are masked by material appearances. The appeal of the theory only demonstrates how seductive are all the illusions of the dream world of consumption. By imperceptible degrees the charming and seemingly innocent fantasies of Mongolian chinchilla and Moorish courtyards lead to far more serious social deceits.

It is just because the transition is so gradual and easy, Talmeyr warns, that the deception of mass consumption must be resisted from the outset. That is the final lesson he extracts from the school of Trocadéro: truthfulness demands constant effort, and, in particular, effort to use the imagination more rather than less. If people only stare at the Indian bazaar and buy its rugs and fabrics unquestioningly, the realities of colonialism will remain forever buried beneath a mountain of merchandise. Talmeyr's imagination is too active to stop at the barrier of décor. He sees beyond what is displayed to what is not displayed, envisioning the emaciated Indians who are omitted and, furthermore, seeing why they are omitted. Talmeyr contends that laziness is responsible for the successful exploitation of dreams by commerce. The Trocadéro is a commercial success because everyone wants to see distant places but no one wants to go to the trouble of traveling:

> We don't go to the mountain but the mountain comes to us! Only, is it the real Japan, the real New World, and the genuine Honolulu which come? Isn't it a suspect Japan, a contraband New World, a Honolulu from a menu? . . .
>
>   Bah! We don't look too closely, and our whole concern has become to avoid any effort above all.[50]

This widespread passivity, both physical and mental, is responsible for other distressing social trends. People love to believe that there is a short cut, an easy way out, and they want to be deceived because it is a way to avoid confronting real problems:

> Neither the voyage difficult to make, nor the language difficult to speak, nor the marriage difficult to endure, we want no more of that, and the same psychology is at the basis of the law on divorce, the decrees which suppress participles, and that which authorizes the opening of a Malaysian section at the exposition. The first tells us, "To be married, you don't need to be." The second: "To write French, you don't need to know it." And the third: "To go to Malaysia, you don't need to go there." Easy methods! But are we really sure of swimming in the ocean by putting a box of salt in our bathtub, and of returning from China, India, or the Sudan by returning from the Trocadéro?[51]

Are we so sure social justice can be achieved by the mass distribution of inexpensive Oriental rugs and silk dresses? An easy method! But truth is not found by dreaming. Time-consuming, unceasing effort is needed to replace confusion with lucidity, simplification with complexity, and deception with reality.

NOTES

1. Many of these details are from Richard D. Mandell, *Paris 1900: The Great World's Fair* (n.p.: University of Toronto Press, 1967), chapter 1. For an excellent short summary of the French universal expositions, see Raymond Isay, *Panorama des expositions universelles* (3rd ed., Paris: Gallimard, 1937).

2. Henri Chardon, "L'Exposition de 1900," *Revue de Paris* 1 (February 1, 1896): 644. Chardon was participating in a debate as to whether another exposition should be held in 1900. Because of the commercialism of the 1889 event, there was strong opposition to the proposal. On the debate see Mandell, *Paris 1900,* pp. 25–51.

3. This description is from Paul Morand, *1900 A.D.*, trans. Mrs. Romilly Fedden (New York: William Farquhar Payson, 1931), p. 66. See also pp. 65–66 and the photograph facing p. 67.

4. Eugène-Melchior de Vogüé, "La Défunte Exposition," *Revue des deux mondes,* 4th per., 162 (November 15, 1900): 384–85.

5. Michel Corday [Louis-Léonard Pollet], "La Force à l'Exposition," *Revue de Paris* 1 (January 15, 1900): 439.

6. Maurice Talmeyr, "L'École du Trocadéro," *Revue des deux mondes.* All quotations from Talmeyr are from this article unless otherwise noted. He also wrote a series "Notes sur l'Exposition" that appeared in *Le Correspondant* between April 10, 1899, and April 25, 1900. Altogether the series included thirteen articles.

7. Richard D. Sennett, *The Fall of Public Man* (New York: Alfred A. Knopf, 1976), pp. 141–49.

8. Emile Zola, *Au Bonheur des Dames* (Lausanne: Éditions Rencontre, n.d.), pp. 122–23.

9. Ibid., p. 153.

10. Ibid., p. 288.

11. Ibid., pp. 472–73.

12. Roger de Félice, "Le Salon de l'Automobile," *Les Arts de la vie* 3 (January, 1905): 12.

13. These quotations from Talmeyr about exposition décor are from his "Notes sur l'Exposition," *Le Correspondant* 199 (April 25, 1900): 401.

14. Michel Corday, "À l'Exposition.—Visions lointaines," *Revue de Paris* 2 (March 15, 1900): 422–38. Quotations from Corday are from this article unless otherwise noted. Corday's reports on the exposition are summarized in his book *Comment on a fait l'Exposition* (Paris: E. Flammarion, 1900).

15. For information on the capital investments and profits of expositions, see Charles Gide, "La Liquidation de l'Exposition universelle," *Revue d'économie politique* 15 (June, 1901): 674–77; Louis Joubert, "Fin de rêve. L'Exposition universelle de 1900," *Le Correspondant* 201 (November 24, 1900): 771–84; and Paul Leroy-Beaulieu, "Les Grands Inconvénients des foires universelles et la nécessité d'y renoncer," *L'Économiste français* 2 (December 7, 1895):729–31.

16. Theodore Zeldin, *France 1848–1945*, Vol. II: *Intellect, Taste and Anxiety* (Oxford: Clarendon Press, 1977), in *Oxford History of Modern Europe*, ed. Lord Bullock and Sir William Deakin, p. 389.

17. Louis Haugmard, "L'Esthétique de cinématographie," *Le Correspondant* 251 (May 25, 1913), pp. 762–71.

18. By Jean-Marie Guyau (1854–1888).

19. Michel Corday, "À l'Exposition.—La Force à l'Exposition," *Revue de Paris* 1 (January 15, 1900): 438–39. See his note at the bottom of p. 438 regarding the number of kilowatts involved in this display.

20. In Villiers de l'Isle-Adam, *Oeuvres*, ed. Jacques-Henry Bornecque (n.p.: Le Club Français du Livre, 1957), p. 57. The short story was first published in *La Renaissance littéraire et artistique* (November 30, 1873) and was republished in 1883 as part of Villiers's *Contes cruels*.

21. Robert de La Sizeranne, "La Beauté des machines, à propos du Salon de l'Automobile," *Revue des deux mondes*, 5th per., 42 (December 1, 1907): 657; Camille Mauclair, "La Décoration lumineuse," *Revue bleue* 8 (November 23, 1907): 656; and Émile Berr, "Une Exposition parisienne.—Le 'Salon' des chauffeurs," *Revue bleue* 11 (December 24, 1904): 829.

22. De Félice, "Le Salon de l'Automobile," pp. 11–12.

23. Ibid.

24. Ibid.

25. La Sizeranne, "La Beauté," p. 657–58.

26. Georges d'Avenel, "Le Mécanisme de la vie moderne: la publicité," *Revue des deux mondes*, 5th per., 1 (February 1, 1901): 657, 659.

27. This scene is amusingly, and pathetically, described by Berr, "Exposition parisienne," p. 829.

28. Zeldin, *France*, vol. 2, pp. 627–29.

29. Pierre Calmettes, "The 'Big Store' of Paris," *Architectural Record* 12 (September, 1902): 431–44.

30. Zeldin, *France*, vol. 2, p. 628.

31. The *Revue des deux mondes* series ran from July 15, 1894, to August 1, 1905, and included twenty-eight installments. The book *Le Mécanisme de la vie moderne* was published in five editions, plus several reprintings, from 1896 to 1905. D'Avenel was president of the Supervisory Board and editor of the Political Chronicle of the *Revue des deux mondes*.

32. In a review of d'Avenel's *Le Mécanisme de la vie moderne* by Paul Dudon, S.J., in *Études publiées par les pères de la Compagnie de Jésus* 83 (June, 1900): 703.

33. D'Avenel, *Les Français de mon temps*, intro. Charles Sardea (Paris: Plon-Nourrit, 1904), p. 1.

34. Georges d'Avenel, *Le Nivellement des jouissances* (Paris: Ernest Flammarion, 1913), pp. 303–4.

35. Quoted by Ernest Seillière in "Georges d'Avenel, historien et moraliste," *Revue des deux mondes*, 8th per., 53 (September 15, 1939): 445.

36. Ibid., p. 446.

37. D'Avenel, *Nivellement*, p. 4. D'Avenel's research into the history of consumption resulted in the monumental four-volume *Histoire économique de la propriété, des salaires, des denrées, et de tous les prix en générale, depuis l'an 1200 jusqu'en*

l'an 1800 (1894–1898), later condensed for a more general audience in *La Fortune privée à travers sept siècles* (1895), *Paysans et ouvriers depuis sept cent ans* (1889), and *Les Riches depuis sept cent ans* (1909).

38. D'Avenel, "Mécanisme: la soie," *Revue des deux mondes,* 4th per., 138 (December 15, 1896): 790–91.

39. Ibid., p. 820.

40. D'Avenel, "Mécanisme: la maison parisienne.—L'Intérieur," *Revue des deux mondes,* 4th per., 140 (April 15, 1897): 800–801.

41. Ibid., p. 800.

42. D'Avenel, "Mécanisme: la soie," p. 805. The quotation is from a poem by Alfred de Musset titled "La Coupe et les lèvres": "Aimer est le grand point, qu'importe la maîtresse? / Qu'importe le flacon pourvu qu'on ait l'ivresse?"

43. Quoted by Seillière, "Georges d'Avenel," p. 448.

44. D'Avenel, *Nivellement,* p. 313.

45. Ibid., p. 315.

46. Ibid., p. 310.

47. D'Avenel, "Mécanisme: L'alcool et les liqueurs," *Revue des deux mondes,* 4th per., 151 (January 1, 1899): 129–30.

48. D'Avenel, *Nivellement,* p. 151. In his recent book *Social Limits to Growth,* A Twentieth Century Fund Study (Cambridge, Mass., and London: Harvard University Press, 1976), Fred Hirsch uses the terms "material economy" and "positional economy" to distinguish goods that can be multiplied indefinitely without losing any of their desirability from those that cannot.

49. D'Avenel, *Les Français,* pp. 256–57.

50. Talmeyr, "L'École," pp. 212–13.

51. Ibid., p. 213. The laws to which Talmeyr refers had recently been promulgated by the French national assembly.

PART TWO

Popular Culture in Anthropological Studies

SEVEN

Deep Play

Notes on the Balinese Cockfight

Clifford Geertz

THE RAID

Early in April of 1958, my wife and I arrived, malarial and diffident, in a Balinese village we intended, as anthropologists, to study. A small place, about five hundred people, and relatively remote, it was its own world. We were intruders, professional ones, and the villagers dealt with us as Balinese seem always to deal with people not part of their life who yet press themselves upon them: as though we were not there. For them, and to a degree for ourselves, we were nonpersons, specters, invisible men.

We moved into an extended family compound (that had been arranged before through the provincial government) belonging to one of the four major factions in village life. But except for our landlord and the village chief, whose cousin and brother-in-law he was, everyone ignored us in a way only a Balinese can do. As we wandered around, uncertain, wistful, eager to please, people seemed to look right through us with a gaze focused several yards behind us on some more actual stone or tree. Almost nobody greeted us; but nobody scowled or said anything unpleasant to us either, which would have been almost as satisfactory. If we ventured to approach someone (something one is powerfully inhibited from doing in such an atmosphere), he moved, negligently but definitely, away. If, seated or leaning against a wall, we had him trapped, he said nothing at all, or mumbled what for the Balinese is the ultimate nonword—"yes." The indifference, of course, was studied; the villagers were watching every move we made, and they had an enormous amount

Reprinted by permission of *Daedalus,* Journal of the American Academy of Arts and Sciences, "Myth, Symbol, and Culture," 101, no. 1 (Winter 1972), Boston, MA.

of quite accurate information about who we were and what we were going to be doing. But they acted as if we simply did not exist, which, in fact, as this behavior was designed to inform us, we did not, or anyway not yet.

This is, as I say, general in Bali. Everywhere else I have been in Indonesia, and more latterly in Morocco, when I have gone into a new village, people have poured out from all sides to take a very close look at me, and, often an all-too-probing feel as well. In Balinese villages, at least those away from the tourist circuit, nothing happens at all. People go on pounding, chatting, making offerings, staring into space, carrying baskets about while one drifts around feeling vaguely disembodied. And the same thing is true on the individual level. When you first meet a Balinese, he seems virtually not to relate to you at all; he is, in the term Gregory Bateson and Margaret Mead made famous, "away."[1] Then—in a day, a week, a month (with some people the magic moment never comes)—he decides, for reasons I have never quite been able to fathom, that you *are* real, and then he becomes a warm, gay, sensitive, sympathetic, though, being Balinese, always precisely controlled, person. You have crossed, somehow, some moral or metaphysical shadow line. Though you are not exactly taken as a Balinese (one has to be born to that), you are at least regarded as a human being rather than a cloud or a gust of wind. The whole complexion of your relationship dramatically changes to, in the majority of cases, a gentle, almost affectionate one—a low-keyed, rather playful, rather mannered, rather bemused geniality.

My wife and I were still very much in the gust-of-wind stage, a most frustrating, and even, as you soon begin to doubt whether you are really real after all, unnerving one, when, ten days or so after our arrival, a large cockfight was held in the public square to raise money for a new school.

Now, a few special occasions aside, cockfights are illegal in Bali under the Republic (as, for not altogether unrelated reasons, they were under the Dutch), largely as a result of the pretensions to puritanism radical nationalism tends to bring with it. The elite, which is not itself so very puritan, worries about the poor, ignorant peasant gambling all his money away, about what foreigners will think, about the waste of time better devoted to building up the country. It sees cockfighting as "primitive," "backward," "unprogressive," and generally unbecoming an ambitious nation. And, as with those other embarrassments—opium smoking, begging, or uncovered breasts—it seeks, rather unsystematically, to put a stop to it.

Of course, like drinking during Prohibition or, today, smoking marijuana, cockfights, being a part of "The Balinese Way of Life," nonetheless go on happening, and with extraordinary frequency. And, as with

Prohibition or marijuana, from time to time the police (who, in 1958 at least, were almost all not Balinese but Javanese) feel called upon to make a raid, confiscate the cocks and spurs, fine a few people, and even now and then expose some of them in the tropical sun for a day as object lessons which never, somehow, get learned, even though occasionally, quite occasionally, the object dies.

As a result, the fights are usually held in a secluded corner of a village in semisecrecy, a fact which tends to slow the action a little—not very much, but the Balinese do not care to have it slowed at all. In this case, however, perhaps because they were raising money for a school that the government was unable to give them, perhaps because raids had been few recently, perhaps, as I gathered from subsequent discussion, there was a notion that the necessary bribes had been paid, they thought they could take a chance on the central square and draw a larger and more enthusiastic crowd without attracting the attention of the law.

They were wrong. In the midst of the third match, with hundreds of people, including, still transparent, myself and my wife, fused into a single body around the ring, a superorganism in the literal sense, a truck full of policemen armed with machine guns roared up. Amid great screeching cries of "pulisi! pulisi!" from the crowd, the policemen jumped out, and, springing into the center of the ring, began to swing their guns around like gangsters in a motion picture, though not going so far as actually to fire them. The superorganism came instantly apart as its components scattered in all directions. People raced down the road, disappeared headfirst over walls, scrambled under platforms, folded themselves behind wicker screens, scuttled up coconut trees. Cocks armed with steel spurs sharp enough to cut off a finger or run a hole through a foot were running wildly around. Everything was dust and panic.

On the established anthropological principle, "When in Rome," my wife and I decided, only slightly less instantaneously than everyone else, that the thing to do was run too. We ran down the main village street, northward, away from where we were living, for we were on that side of the ring. About halfway down another fugitive ducked suddenly into a compound—his own, it turned out—and we, seeing nothing ahead of us but rice fields, open country, and a very high volcano, followed him. As the three of us came tumbling into the courtyard, his wife, who had apparently been through this sort of thing before, whipped out a table, a tablecloth, three chairs, and three cups of tea, and we all, without any explicit communication whatsoever, sat down, commenced to sip tea, and sought to compose ourselves.

A few moments later, one of the policemen marched importantly into the yard, looking for the village chief. (The chief had not only been at the fight, he had arranged it. When the truck drove up he ran to the river, stripped off his sarong, and plunged in so he could say, when at length they found him sitting there pouring water over his head, that he had been away bathing when the whole affair had occurred and was ignorant of it. They did not believe him and fined him three hundred rupiah, which the village raised collectively.) Seeing me and my wife, "White Men," there in the yard, the policeman performed a classic double take. When he found his voice again he asked, approximately, what in the devil did we think we were doing there. Our host of five minutes leaped instantly to our defense, producing an impassioned description of who and what we were, so detailed and so accurate that it was my turn, having barely communicated with a living human being save my landlord and the village chief for more than a week, to be astonished. We had a perfect right to be there, he said, looking the Javanese upstart in the eye. We were American professors; the government had cleared us; we were there to study culture; we were going to write a book to tell Americans about Bali. And we had all been there drinking tea and talking about cultural matters all afternoon and did not know anything about any cockfight. Moreover, we had not seen the village chief all day; he must have gone to town. The policeman retreated in rather total disarray. And, after a decent interval, bewildered but relieved to have survived and stayed out of jail, so did we.

The next morning the village was a completely different world for us. Not only were we no longer invisible, we were suddenly the center of all attention, the object of a great outpouring of warmth, interest, and most especially, amusement. Everyone in the village knew we had fled like everyone else. They asked us about it again and again (I must have told the story, small detail by small detail, fifty times by the end of the day), gently, affectionately, but quite insistently teasing us: "Why didn't you just stand there and tell the police who you were?" "Why didn't you just say you were only watching and not betting?" "Were you really afraid of those little guns?" As always, kinesthetically minded and, even when fleeing for their lives (or, as happened eight years later, surrendering them), the world's most poised people, they gleefully mimicked, also over and over again, our graceless style of running and what they claimed were our panic-stricken facial expressions. But above all, everyone was extremely pleased and even more surprised that we had not simply "pulled out our papers" (they knew about those too) and asserted our Distinguished Visitor status, but had instead demonstrated our solidarity with what were now our covillagers. (What we had actually demonstrated was our cowardice, but there is fellowship in that too.) Even the Brahmana priest, an old, grave, halfway-to-heaven type who because of its associations with the underworld would never be involved, even distantly, in a cockfight, and was difficult to approach even to other Balinese, had us called into his courtyard to ask us about what had happened, chuckling happily at the sheer extraordinariness of it all.

In Bali, to be teased is to be accepted. It was the turning point so far as our relationship to the community was concerned, and we were quite literally "in." The whole village opened up to us, probably more than it ever would have otherwise (I might actually never have gotten to that priest, and our accidental host became one of my best informants), and certainly very much faster. Getting caught, or almost caught, in a vice raid is perhaps not a very generalizable recipe for achieving that mysterious necessity of anthropological field work, rapport, but for me it worked very well. It led to a sudden and unusually complete acceptance into a society extremely difficult for outsiders to penetrate. It gave me the kind of immediate, inside-view grasp of an aspect of "peasant mentality" that anthropologists not fortunate enough to flee headlong with their subjects from armed authorities normally do not get. And, perhaps most important of all, for the other things might have come in other ways, it put me very quickly on to a combination emotional explosion, status war, and philosophical drama of central significance to the society whose inner nature I desired to understand. By the time I left I had spent about as much time looking into cockfights as into witchcraft, irrigation, caste, or marriage.

OF COCKS AND MEN

Bali, mainly because it is Bali, is a well-studied place. Its mythology, art, ritual, social organization, patterns of child rearing, forms of law, even styles of trance, have all been microscopically examined for traces of that elusive substance Jane Belo called "The Balinese Temper."[2] But, aside from a few passing remarks, the cockfight has barely been noticed, although as a popular obsession of consuming power it is at least as important a revelation of what being a Balinese "is really like" as these more celebrated phenomena.[3] As much of America surfaces in a ball park, on a golf links, at a race track, or around a poker table, much of Bali surfaces in a cock ring. For it is only apparently cocks that are fighting there. Actually, it is men.

To anyone who has been in Bali any length of time, the deep psychological identification of Balinese men with their cocks is unmistakable. The double entendre here is deliberate. It works in exactly the same way in Balinese as it does in English, even to producing the same tired jokes, strained puns, and uninventive obscenities. Bateson and Mead have even suggested that, in line with the Balinese conception of the body as a set of separately animated parts, cocks are viewed as detachable, self-operating penises, ambulant genitals with a life of their own.[4] And while I do not have the kind of unconscious material either to confirm or disconfirm this intriguing notion, the fact that they are masculine symbols par excellence is about as indubitable, and to the Balinese about as evident, as the fact that water runs downhill.

The language of everyday moralism is shot through, on the male side of it, with roosterish imagery. *Sabung*, the word for cock (and one which appears in inscriptions as early as A.D. 922), is used metaphorically to mean "hero," "warrior," "champion," "man of parts," "political candidate," "bachelor," "dandy," "lady-killer," or "tough guy." A pompous man whose behavior presumes above his station is compared to a tailless cock who struts about as though he had a large, spectacular one. A desperate man who makes a last, irrational effort to extricate himself from an impossible situation is likened to a dying cock who makes one final lunge at his tormentor to drag him along to a common destruction. A stingy man, who promises much, gives little, and begrudges that, is compared to a cock which, held by the tail, leaps at another without in fact engaging him. A marriageable young man still shy with the opposite sex or someone in a new job anxious to make a good impression is called "a fighting cock caged for the first time."[5] Court trials, wars, political contests, inheritance disputes, and street arguments are all compared to cockfights.[6] Even the very island itself is perceived from its shape as a small, proud cock, poised, neck extended, back taut, tail raised, in eternal challenge to large, feckless, shapeless Java.[7]

But the intimacy of men with their cocks is more than metaphorical. Balinese men, or anyway a large majority of Balinese men, spend an enormous amount of time with their favorites, grooming them, feeding them, discussing them, trying them out against one another, or just gazing at them with a mixture of rapt admiration and dreamy self-absorption. Whenever you see a group of Balinese men squatting idly in the council shed or along the road in their hips down, shoulders forward, knees up fashion, half or more of them will have a rooster in his hands, holding it between his thighs, bouncing it gently up and down to strengthen its legs, ruffling its feathers with abstract sensuality, pushing it out against a neighbor's rooster to rouse its spirit, withdrawing it toward his loins to calm it again. Now and then, to get a feel for another bird, a man will fiddle this way with someone else's cock for a while, but usually by moving around to squat in place behind it, rather than just having it passed across to him as though it were merely an animal.

In the houseyard, the high-walled enclosures where the people live, fighting cocks are kept in wicker cages, moved frequently about so as to maintain the optimum balance of sun and shade. They are fed a special diet, which varies somewhat according to individual theories but which is mostly maize, sifted for impurities with far more care than it is when mere humans are going to eat it, and offered to the animal kernel by kernel. Red pepper is stuffed down their beaks and up their anuses to give them spirit. They are bathed in the same ceremonial preparation of tepid water, medicinal herbs, flowers, and onions in which infants are bathed, and for a prize cock just about as often. Their combs are cropped, their plumage dressed, their spurs trimmed, and their legs massaged, and they are inspected for flaws with the squinted concentration of a diamond merchant. A man who has a passion for cocks, an enthusiast in the literal sense of the term, can spend most of his life with them, and even those, the overwhelming majority, whose passion though intense has not entirely run away with them, can and do spend what seems not only to an outsider, but also to themselves, an inordinate amount of time with them. "I am cock crazy," my landlord, a quite ordinary *afficionado* by Balinese standards, used to moan as he went to move another cage, give another bath, or conduct another feeding. "We're all cock crazy."

The madness has some less visible dimensions, however, because although it is true that cocks are symbolic expressions or magnifications of their owner's self, the narcissistic male ego writ out in Aesopian terms, they are also expressions—and rather more immediate ones—of what the Balinese regard as the direct inversion, aesthetically, morally, and metaphysically, of human status: animality.

The Balinese revulsion against any behavior regarded as animal-like can hardly be overstressed. Babies are not allowed to crawl for that reason. Incest, though hardly approved, is a much less horrifying crime than bestiality. (The appropriate punishment for the second is death by drowning, for the first being forced to live like an animal.)[8] Most demons are represented—in sculpture, dance, ritual, myth—in some real or fantastic animal form. The main puberty rite consists in filing the child's teeth so they will not look like animal fangs. Not only defecation but eating is regarded as a disgusting, almost obscene activity, to be conducted hurriedly and privately, because of its association with animality. Even falling down or any form of clumsiness is considered to be bad for these reasons. Aside from cocks and a few domestic animals—oxen, ducks—of no emotional significance, the Balinese are aversive to animals and treat their large number of dogs not merely callously but with a phobic cruelty. In identifying with his cock, the Balinese man is identifying not just with his ideal self, or even his penis, but also, and at the same time, with what he most fears, hates, and ambivalence being what it is, is fascinated by—"The Powers of Darkness."

The connection of cocks and cockfighting with such Powers, with the animalistic demons that threaten constantly to invade the small, cleared-off space in which the Balinese have so carefully built their lives and devour its inhabitants, is quite explicit. A cockfight, any cockfight, is in the first instance a blood sacrifice offered, with the appropriate chants and oblations, to the demons in order to pacify their ravenous, cannibal hunger. No temple festival should be conducted until one is made. (If it is omitted, someone will inevitably fall into a trance and command with the voice of an angered spirit that the oversight be immediately corrected.) Collective responses to natural evils—illness, crop failure, volcanic eruptions—almost always involve them. And that famous holiday in Bali, "The Day of Silence" *(Njepi)*, when everyone sits silent and immobile all day long in order to avoid contact with a sudden influx of demons chased momentarily out of hell, is preceded the previous day by large-scale cockfights (in this case legal) in almost every village on the island.

In the cockfight, man and beast, good and evil, ego and id, the creative power of aroused masculinity and the destructive power of loosened animality fuse in a bloody drama of hatred, cruelty, violence, and death. It is little wonder that when, as is the invariable rule, the owner of the winning cock takes the carcass of the loser—often torn limb from limb by its enraged owner—home to eat, he does so with a mixture of social embarrassment, moral satisfaction, aesthetic disgust, and cannibal joy. Or that a man who has lost an important fight is sometimes driven to wreck his family shrines and curse the gods, an act of metaphysical (and social) suicide. Or that in seeking earthly analogues for heaven and hell the Balinese compare the former to the mood of a man whose cock has just won, the latter to that of a man whose cock has just lost.

THE FIGHT

Cockfights *(tetadjen; sabungan)* are held in a ring about fifty feet square. Usually they begin toward late afternoon and run three or four hours until sunset. About nine or ten separate matches *(sehet)* comprise a program. Each match is precisely like the others in general pattern: there is no main match, no connection between individual matches, no variation in their format, and each is arranged on a completely ad hoc basis. After a fight has ended and the emotional debris is cleaned away—the bets have been paid, the curses cursed, the carcasses possessed—seven, eight, perhaps even a dozen men slip negligently into the ring with a cock and seek to find there a logical opponent for it. This process, which rarely takes less than ten minutes, and often a good deal longer, is conducted in a very subdued, oblique, even dissembling manner. Those not immediately involved give it at best but disguised, sidelong attention; those who, embarrassedly, are, attempt to pretend somehow that the whole thing is not really happening.

A match made, the other hopefuls retire with the same deliberate indifference, and the selected cocks have their spurs *(tadji)* affixed—razor-sharp, pointed steel swords, four or five inches long. This is a delicate job which only a small proportion of men, a half-dozen or so in most villages, know how to do properly. The man who attaches the spurs also provides them, and if the rooster he assists wins, its owner awards him the spur-leg of the victim. The spurs are affixed by winding a long length of string around the foot of the spur and the leg of the cock. For reasons I shall come to presently, it is done somewhat differently from case to case, and is an obsessively deliberate affair. The lore about spurs is extensive—they are sharpened only at eclipses and the dark of the moon, should be kept out of the sight of women, and so forth. And they are handled, both in use and out, with the same curious combination of fussiness and sensuality the Balinese direct toward ritual objects generally.

The spurs affixed, the two cocks are placed by their handlers (who may or may not be their owners) facing one another in the center of the ring.[9] A coconut pierced with a small hole is placed in a pail of water, in which it takes about twenty-one seconds to sink, a period known as a *tjeng* and marked at beginning and end by the beating of a slit gong. During these twenty-one seconds the handlers *(pengangkeb)* are not permitted to touch their roosters. If, as sometimes happens, the animals have not fought during this time, they are picked up, fluffed, pulled, prodded, and otherwise insulted, and put back in the center of the ring and the process begins again. Sometimes they refuse to fight at all, or one keeps running away, in which case they are imprisoned together under a wicker cage, which usually gets them engaged.

Most of the time, in any case, the cocks fly almost immediately at one another in a wing-beating, head-thrusting, leg-kicking explosion of animal fury so pure, so absolute, and in its own way so beautiful, as to be almost abstract, a Platonic concept of hate. Within moments one or the other drives home a solid blow with his spur. The handler whose cock has delivered the blow immediately picks it up so that it will not get a return blow, for if he does not the match is likely to end in a mutually mortal tie as the two birds wildly hack each other to pieces. This is particularly true if, as often happens, the spur sticks in its victim's body, for then the aggressor is at the mercy of his wounded foe.

With the birds again in the hands of their handlers, the coconut is now sunk three times after which the cock which has landed the blow must be set down to show that he is firm, a fact he demonstrates by wandering idly around the ring for a coconut sink. The coconut is then sunk twice more and the fight must recommence.

During this interval, slightly over two minutes, the handler of the wounded cock has been working frantically over it, like a trainer patching a mauled boxer between rounds, to get it in shape for a last, desperate try for victory. He blows in its mouth, putting the whole chicken head in his own mouth and sucking and blowing, fluffs it, stuffs its wounds with various sorts of medicines, and generally tries anything he can think of to arouse the last ounce of spirit which may be hidden somewhere within it. By the time he is forced to put it back down he is usually drenched in chicken blood, but, as in prize fighting, a good handler is worth his weight in gold. Some of them can virtually make the dead walk, at least long enough for the second and final round.

In the climactic battle (if there is one; sometimes the wounded cock simply expires in the handler's hands or immediately as it is placed down again), the cock who landed the first blow usually proceeds to finish off his weakened opponent. But this is far from an inevitable outcome, for if a cock can walk, he can fight, and if he can fight, he can kill, and what counts is which cock expires first. If the wounded one can get a stab in and stagger on until the other drops, he is the official winner, even if he himself topples over an instant later.

Surrounding all this melodrama—which the crowd packed tight around the ring follows in near silence, moving their bodies in kinesthetic sympathy with the movement of the animals, cheering their champions on with wordless hand motions, shiftings of the shoulders, turnings of the head, falling back en masse as the cock with the murderous spurs careens toward one side of the ring (it is said that spectators sometimes lose eyes and fingers from being too attentive), surging forward again as they glance off toward another—is a vast body of extraordinarily elaborate and precisely detailed rules.

These rules, together with the developed lore of cocks and cockfighting which accompanies them, are written down in palm-leaf manuscripts *(lontar; rontal)* passed on from generation to generation as part of the general legal and cultural tradition of the villages. At a fight, the umpire *(saja komong; djuru kembar)*—the man who manages the coconut—is in charge of their application and his authority is absolute. I have never seen an umpire's judgment questioned on any subject, even by the more despondent losers, nor have I ever heard, even in private, a charge of unfairness directed against one, or, for that matter, complaints about umpires in general. Only exceptionally well trusted, solid, and, given the complexity of the code, knowledgeable citizens perform this job, and in fact men will bring their cocks only to fights presided over by such men. It is also the umpire to whom accusations of cheating, which, though rare in the extreme, occasionally arise, are referred; and it is he who in the not infrequent cases where the cocks expire virtually together decides which (if either, for, though the Balinese do not care for such an outcome, there can be ties) went first. Likened to a judge, a king, a priest, and a policeman, he is all of these, and under his assured direction the animal passion of the fight proceeds within the civic certainty of the law. In the dozens of cockfights I saw in Bali, I never once saw an altercation about rules. Indeed, I never saw an open altercation, other than those between cocks, at all.

This crosswise doubleness of an event which, taken as a fact of nature, is rage untrammeled and, taken as a fact of culture, is form perfected, defines the cockfight as a sociological entity. A cockfight is what, searching for a name for something not vertebrate enough to be called a group and not structureless enough to be called a crowd, Erving Goffman has called a "focused gathering"—a set of persons engrossed in a common flow of activity and relating to one another in terms of that flow.[10] Such gatherings meet and disperse; the participants in them fluctuate; the activity that focuses them is discrete—a particulate process that reoccurs rather than a continuous one that endures. They take their form from the situation that evokes them, the floor on which they are placed, as Goffman puts it; but it is a form, and an articulate one, nonetheless. For the situation, the floor is itself created, in jury deliberations, surgical operations, block meetings, sit-ins, cockfights, by the cultural preoccupations—here, as we shall see, the celebration of status rivalry—which not only specify the focus but, assembling actors and arranging scenery, bring it actually into being.

In classical times (that is to say, prior to the Dutch invasion of 1908), when there were no bureaucrats around to improve popular morality, the staging of a cockfight was an explicitly societal matter. Bringing a cock to an important fight was, for an adult male, a compulsory duty of citizenship; taxation of fights, which were usually held on market day, was a major source of public revenue; patronage of the art was a stated responsibility of princes; and the cock ring, or *wantilan,* stood in the center of the village near those other monuments of Balinese civility—the council house, the origin temple, the marketplace, the signal tower, and the banyan tree. Today, a few special occasions aside, the newer rectitude makes so open a statement of the connection between the excitements of collective life and those of blood sport impossible, but, less directly expressed, the connection itself remains intimate and intact. To expose it, however, it is necessary to turn to the aspect of cockfighting around which all the others pivot, and through which they exercise their force, an aspect I have thus far studiously ignored. I mean, of course, the gambling.

ODDS AND EVEN MONEY

The Balinese never do anything in a simple way that they can contrive to do in a complicated one, and to this generalization cockfight wagering is no exception.

In the first place, there are two sorts of bets, or *toh*.[11] There is the single axial bet in the center between the principals *(toh ketengah)*, and there is the cloud of peripheral ones around the ring between members of the audience *(toh kesasi)*. The first is typically large; the second typically small. The first is collective, involving coalitions of bettors clustering around the owner; the second is individual, man to man. The first is a matter of deliberate, very quiet, almost furtive arrangement by the coalition members and the umpire huddled like conspirators in the center of the ring; the second is a matter of impulsive shouting, public offers, and public acceptances by the excited throng around its edges. And most curiously, and as we shall see most revealingly, *where the first is always, without exception, even money, the second, equally without exception, is never such.* What is a fair coin in the center is a biased one on the side.

The center bet is the official one, hedged in again with a webwork of rules, and is made between the two cock owners, with the umpire as overseer and public witness.[12] This bet, which, as I say, is always relatively and sometimes very large, is never raised simply by the owner in whose name it is made, but by him together with four or five, sometimes seven or eight, allies—kin, village mates, neighbors, close friends. He may, if he is not especially well-to-do, not even be the major contributor; though, if only to show that he is not involved in any chicanery, he must be a significant one.

Of the fifty-seven matches for which I have exact and reliable data on the center bet, the range is from fifteen ringgits to five hundred, with a mean at eighty-five and with the distribution being rather noticeably trimodal: small fights (15 ringgits either side of 35) accounting for about 45 percent of the total number; medium ones (20 ringgits either side of 70) for about 25 percent; and large (75 ringgits either side of 175) for about 20 percent, with a few very small and very large ones out at the extremes. In a society where the normal daily wage of a manual laborer—a brickmaker, an ordinary farmworker, a market porter—was about three ringgits a day, and considering the fact that fights were held on the average about every two-and-a-half days in the immediate area I studied, this is clearly serious gambling, even if the bets are pooled rather than individual efforts.

The side bets are, however, something else altogether. Rather than the solemn, legalistic pactmaking of the center, wagering takes place rather in the fashion in which the stock exchange used to work when it was out on the curb. There is a fixed and known odds paradigm which runs in a continuous series from ten-to-nine at the short end to two-to-one at the long: 10–9, 9–8, 8–7, 7–6, 6–5, 5–4, 4–3, 3–2, 2–1. The man who wishes to back the *underdog cock* (leaving aside how favorites, *kebut*, and underdogs, *ngai*, are established for the moment) shouts the short-side number indicating the odds he wants *to be given*. That is, if he shouts *gasal*, "five," he wants the underdog at five-to-four (or, for him, four-to-five); if he shouts "four," he wants it at four-to-three (again, he putting up the "three"); if "nine," at nine-to-eight, and so on. A man backing the favorite, and thus considering giving odds if he can get them short enough, indicates the fact by crying out the color-type of that cock—"brown," "speckled," or whatever.[13]

As odds-takers (backers of the underdog) and odds-givers (backers of the favorite) sweep the crowd with their shouts, they begin to focus in on one another as potential betting pairs, often from far across the ring. The taker tries to shout the giver into longer odds, the giver to shout the taker into shorter ones.[14] The taker, who is the wooer in this situation, will signal how large a bet he wishes to make at the odds he is shouting by holding a number of fingers up in front of his face and vigorously waving them. If the giver, the wooed, replies in kind, the bet is made; if he does not, they unlock gazes and the search goes on.

The side betting, which takes place after the center bet has been made and its size announced, consists then in a rising crescendo of shouts as backers of the underdog offer their propositions to anyone who will accept them, while those who are backing the favorite but do not like the price being offered, shout equally frenetically the color of the cock to show they too are desperate to bet but want shorter odds.

Almost always odds-calling, which tends to be very consensual in that at any one time almost all callers are calling the same thing, starts off toward the long end of the range—five-to-four or four-to-three—and then moves, also consensually, toward the short end with greater or lesser speed and to a greater or lesser degree. Men crying "five" and finding themselves answered only with cries of "brown" start crying "six," either drawing the other callers fairly quickly with them or retiring from the scene as their too-generous offers are snapped up. If the change is made and partners are still scarce, the procedure is repeated in a move to "seven," and so on, only rarely, and in the very largest fights, reaching the ultimate "nine" or "ten" levels. Occasionally, if the cocks are clearly mismatched, there may be no upward movement at all, or even a movement down the scale to four-to-three, three-to-two, very, very rarely two-to-one, a shift which is accompanied by a declining number of bets as a shift upward is accompanied by an increasing number. But the general pattern is for the betting to move a shorter or longer distance up the scale toward the, for sidebets, nonexistent pole of even money, with the overwhelming majority of bets falling in the four-to-three to eight-to-seven range.[15]

As the moment for the release of the cocks by the handlers approaches, the screaming, at least in a match where the center bet is large, reaches almost frenzied proportions as the remaining unfulfilled bettors try desperately to find a last-minute partner at a price they can live with. (Where the center bet is small, the opposite tends to occur: betting dies off, trailing into silence, as odds lengthen and people lose interest.) In a large-bet, well-made match—the kind of match the Balinese regard as "real cockfighting"—the mob scene quality, the sense that sheer chaos is about to break loose, with all those waving, shouting, pushing, clambering men is quite strong, an effect which is only heightened by the intense stillness that falls with instant suddenness, rather as if someone had turned off the current, when the slit gong sounds, the cocks are put down, and the battle begins.

When it ends, anywhere from fifteen seconds to five minutes later, *all bets are immediately paid.* There are absolutely no IOUs, at least to a betting opponent. One may, of course, borrow from a friend before offering or accepting a wager, but to offer or accept it you must have the money already in hand and, if you lose, you must pay it on the spot, before the next match begins. This is an iron rule, and as I have never heard of a disputed umpire's decision (though doubtless there must sometimes be some), I have also never heard of a welshed bet, perhaps because in a worked-up cockfight crowd the consequences might be, as they are reported to be sometimes for cheaters, drastic and immediate.

It is, in any case, this formal asymmetry between balanced center bets and unbalanced side ones that poses the critical analytical problem for a theory which sees cockfight wagering as the link connecting the fight to the wider world of Balinese culture. It also suggests the way to go about solving it and demonstrating the link.

The first point that needs to be made in this connection is that the higher the center bet, the more likely the match will in actual fact be an even one. Simple considerations of rationality suggest that. If you are betting fifteen ringgits on a cock, you might be willing to go along with even money even if you feel your animal somewhat the less promising. But if you are betting five hundred you are very, very likely to be loathe to do so. Thus, in large-bet fights, which of course involve the better animals, tremendous care is taken to see that the cocks are about as evenly matched as to size, general condition, pugnacity, and so on as is humanly possible. The different ways of adjusting the spurs of the animals are often employed to secure this. If one cock seems stronger, an agreement will be made to position his spur at a slightly less advantageous angle—a kind of handicapping, at which spur affixers are, so it is said, extremely skilled. More care will be taken, too, to employ skillful handlers and to match them exactly as to abilities.

In short, in a large-bet fight the pressure to make the match a genuinely fifty-fifty proposition is enormous, and is consciously felt as such.

For medium fights the pressure is somewhat less, and for small ones less yet, though there is always an effort to make things at least approximately equal, for even at fifteen ringgits (five days' work) no one wants to make an even money bet in a clearly unfavorable situation. And, again, what statistics I have tend to bear this out. In my fifty-seven matches, the favorite won thirty-three times overall, the underdog twenty-four, a 1.4:1 ratio. But if one splits the figures at sixty ringgits center bets, the ratios turn out to be 1.1:1 (twelve favorites, eleven underdogs) for those above this line, and 1.6:1 (twenty-one and thirteen) for those below it. Or, if you take the extremes, for very large fights, those with center bets over a hundred ringgits the ratio is 1:1 (seven and seven): for very small fights, those under forty ringgits, it is 1.9:1 (nineteen and ten).[16]

Now, from this proposition—that the higher the center bet the more exactly a fifty-fifty proposition the cockfight is—two things more or less immediately follow: (1) the higher the center bet is, the greater the pull on the side betting toward the short-odds end of the wagering spectrum, and vice versa; (2) the higher the center bet is, the greater the volume of side betting, and vice versa.

The logic is similar in both cases. The closer the fight is in fact to even money, the less attractive the long end of the odds will appear and, therefore, the shorter it must be if there are to be takers. That this is the case is apparent from mere inspection, from the Balinese's own analysis of the matter, and from what more systematic observations I was able to collect. Given the difficulty of making precise and complete recordings of side betting, this argument is hard to cast in numerical form, but in all my cases the odds-giver, odds-taker consensual point, a quite pronounced mini-max saddle where the bulk (at a guess, two-thirds to three-quarters in most cases) of the bets are actually made, was three or four points further along the scale toward the shorter end for the large-center-bet fights than for the small ones, with medium ones generally in between. In detail, the fit is not, of course, exact, but the general pattern is quite consistent: the power of the center bet to pull the side bets toward its own even-money pattern is directly proportional to its size, because its size is directly proportional to the degree to which the cocks are in fact evenly matched. As for the volume question, total wagering is greater in large-center-bet fights because such fights are considered more "interesting," not only in the sense that they are less predictable, but, more crucially, that more is at stake in them—in terms of money, in terms of the quality of the cocks, and consequently, as we shall see, in terms of social prestige.[17]

The paradox of fair coin in the middle, biased coin on the outside is thus a merely apparent one. The two betting systems, though formally incongruent, are not really contradictory to one another, but are part of a single larger system in which the center bet is, so to speak, the "center of gravity," drawing, the larger it is the more so, the outside bets toward the short-odds end of the scale. The center bet thus "makes the game," or perhaps better, defines it, signals what, following a notion of Jeremy Bentham's, I am going to call its "depth."

The Balinese attempt to create an interesting, if you will, "deep," match by making the center bet as large as possible so that the cocks matched will be as equal and as fine as possible, and the outcome, thus, as unpredictable as possible. They do not always succeed. Nearly half the matches are relatively trivial, relatively uninteresting—in my borrowed terminology, "shallow"—affairs. But that fact no more argues against my interpretation than the fact that most painters, poets, and playwrights are mediocre argues against the view that artistic effort is directed toward profundity and, with a certain frequency, approximates it. The image of artistic technique is indeed exact: the center bet is a means, a device, for creating "interesting," "deep" matches, *not* the reason, or at least not the main reason, *why* they are interesting, the source of their fascination, the substance of their depth. The question of why such matches are interesting—indeed, for the Balinese, exquisitely absorbing—takes us out of the realm of formal concerns into more broadly sociological and social-psychological ones, and to a less purely economic idea of what "depth" in gaming amounts to.[18]

PLAYING WITH FIRE

Bentham's concept of "deep play" is found in his *The Theory of Legislation*.[19] By it he means play in which the stakes are so high that it is, from his utilitarian standpoint, irrational for men to engage in it at all. If a man whose fortune is a thousand pounds (or ringgits) wages five hundred of it on an even bet, the marginal utility of the pound he stands to win is clearly less than the marginal disutility of the one he stands to lose. In genuine deep play, this is the case for both parties. They are both in over their heads. Having come together in search of pleasure they have entered into a relationship which will bring the participants, considered collectively, net pain rather than net pleasure. Bentham's conclusion was, therefore, that deep play was immoral from first principles and, a typical step for him, should be prevented legally.

But more interesting than the ethical problem, at least for our concerns here, is that despite the logical force of Bentham's analysis men do engage in such play, both passionately and often, and even in the face of law's revenge. For Bentham and those who think as he does (nowadays mainly lawyers, economists, and a few psychiatrists), the explanation is, as I have said, that such men are irrational—addicts, fetishists,

children, fools, savages, who need only to be protected against themselves. But for the Balinese, though naturally they do not formulate it in
so many words, the explanation lies in the fact that in such play, money
is less a measure of utility, had or expected, than it is a symbol of moral
import, perceived or imposed.

It is, in fact, in shallow games, ones in which smaller amounts of money
are involved, that increments and decrements of cash are more nearly
synonyms for utility and disutility, in the ordinary, unexpanded sense—
for pleasure and pain, happiness and unhappiness. In deep ones, where
the amounts of money are great, much more is at stake than material
gain: namely, esteem, honor, dignity, respect—in a word, though in Bali
a profoundly freighted word, status.[20] It is at stake symbolically, for (a
few cases of ruined addict gamblers aside) no one's status is actually altered by the outcome of a cockfight; it is only, and that momentarily,
affirmed or insulted. But for the Balinese, for whom nothing is more
pleasurable than an affront obliquely delivered or more painful than
one obliquely received—particularly when mutual acquaintances, unde-
ceived by surfaces, are watching—such appraisive drama is deep indeed.

This, I must stress immediately, is *not* to say that the money does not
matter, or that the Balinese is no more concerned about losing five
hundred ringgits than fifteen. Such a conclusion would be absurd. It is
because money *does*, in this hardly unmaterialistic society, matter and
matter very much that the more of it one risks, the more of a lot of other
things, such as one's pride, one's poise, one's dispassion, one's masculinity, one also risks, again only momentarily but again very publicly as well.
In deep cockfights an owner and his collaborators, and, as we shall see,
to a lesser but still quite real extent also their backers on the outside, put
their money where their status is.

It is in large part *because* the marginal disutility of loss is so great at
the higher levels of betting that to engage in such betting is to lay one's
public self, allusively and metaphorically, through the medium of one's
cock, on the line. And though to a Benthamite this might seem merely
to increase the irrationality of the enterprise that much further, to the
Balinese what it mainly increases is the meaningfulness of it all. And as
(to follow Weber rather than Bentham) the imposition of meaning on
life is the major end and primary condition of human existence, that
access of significance more than compensates for the economic costs involved.[21] Actually, given the even-money quality of the larger matches,
important changes in material fortune among those who regularly participate in them seem virtually nonexistent, because matters more or less
even out over the long run. It is, actually, in the smaller, shallow fights,
where one finds the handful of more pure, addict-type gamblers involved—those who *are* in it mainly for the money—that "real" changes

in social position, largely downward, are affected. Men of this sort, plungers, are highly dispraised by "true cockfighters" as fools who do not understand what the sport is all about, vulgarians who simply miss the point of it all. They are, these addicts, regarded as fair game for the genuine enthusiasts, those who do understand, to take a little money away from—something that is easy enough to do by luring them, through the force of their greed, into irrational bets on mismatched cocks. Most of them do indeed manage to ruin themselves in a remarkably short time, but there always seems to be one or two of them around, pawning their land and selling their clothes in order to bet, at any particular time.[22]

This graduated correlation of "status gambling" with deeper fights and, inversely, "money gambling" with shallower ones is in fact quite general. Bettors themselves form a sociomoral hierarchy in these terms. As noted earlier, at most cockfights there are, around the very edges of the cockfight area, a large number of mindless, sheer-chance-type gambling games (roulette, dice throw, coin-spin, pea-under-the-shell) operated by concessionaires. Only women, children, adolescents, and various other sorts of people who do not (or not yet) fight cocks—the extremely poor, the socially despised, the personally idiosyncratic—play at these games, at, of course, penny ante levels. Cockfighting men would be ashamed to go anywhere near them. Slightly above these people in standing are those who though they do not themselves fight cocks, bet on the smaller matches around the edges. Next, there are those who fight cocks in small, or occasionally medium matches, but have not the status to join in the large ones, though they may bet from time to time on the side in those. And finally, there are those, the really substantial members of the community, the solid citizenry around whom local life revolves, who fight in the larger fights and bet on them around the side. The focusing element in these focused gatherings, these men generally dominate and define the sport as they dominate and define the society. When a Balinese male talks, in that almost venerative way, about "the true cockfighter," the *bebatoh* ("bettor") or *djuru kurung* ("cage keeper"), it is this sort of person, not those who bring the mentality of the pea-and-shell game into the quite different, inappropriate context of the cockfight, the driven gambler (*potét*, a word which has the secondary meaning of thief or reprobate), and the wistful hanger-on, that they mean. For such a man, what is really going on in a match is something rather closer to an *affaire d'honneur* (though, with the Balinese talent for practical fantasy, the blood that is spilled is only figuratively human) than to the stupid, mechanical crank of a slot machine.

What makes Balinese cockfighting deep is thus not money in itself, but what, the more of it that is involved the more so, money causes to happen: the migration of the Balinese status hierarchy into the body of

the cockfight. Psychologically an Aesopian representation of the ideal/
demonic, rather narcissistic, male self, sociologically it is an equally
Aesopian representation of the complex fields of tension set up by the
controlled, muted, ceremonial, but for all that deeply felt, interaction of
those selves in the context of everyday life. The cocks may be surrogates
for their owners' personalities, animal mirrors of psychic form, but the
cockfight is—or more exactly, deliberately is made to be—a simulation
of the social matrix, the involved system of cross-cutting, overlapping,
highly corporate groups—villages, kingroups, irrigation societies, temple congregations, "castes"—in which its devotees live.[23] And as prestige,
the necessity to affirm it, defend it, celebrate it, justify it, and just plain
bask in it (but not, given the strongly ascriptive character of Balinese
stratification, to seek it), is perhaps the central driving force in the society, so also—ambulant penises, blood sacrifices, and monetary exchanges aside—is it of the cockfight. This apparent amusement and
seeming sport is, to take another phrase from Erving Goffman, "a status
bloodbath."[24]

The easiest way to make this clear, and at least to some degree to
demonstrate it, is to invoke the village whose cockfighting activities I
observed the closest—the one in which the raid occurred and from which
my statistical data are taken.

Like all Balinese villages, this one—Tihingan, in the Klungkung region of southeast Bali—is intricately organized, a labyrinth of alliances
and oppositions. But, unlike many, two sorts of corporate groups, which
are also status groups, particularly stand out, and we may concentrate
on them, in a part-for-whole way, without undue distortion.

First, the village is dominated by four large, patrilineal, partly endogamous descent groups which are constantly vying with one another
and form the major factions in the village. Sometimes they group two
and two, or rather the two larger ones versus the two smaller ones plus
all the unaffiliated people; sometimes they operate independently. There
are also subfactions within them, subfactions within the subfactions, and
so on to rather fine levels of distinction. And second, there is the village
itself, almost entirely endogamous, which is opposed to all the other villages round about in its cockfight circuit (which, as explained, is the market region), but which also forms alliances with certain of these neighbors against certain others in various supravillage political and social
contexts. The exact situation is thus, as everywhere in Bali, quite distinctive; but the general pattern of a tiered hierarchy of status rivalries between highly corporate but various based groupings (and, thus, between
the members of them) is entirely general.

Consider, then, as support of the general thesis that the cockfight,
and especially the deep cockfight, is fundamentally a dramatization of

status concerns, the following facts, which to avoid extended ethnographic description I shall simply pronounce to be facts—though the
concrete evidence, examples, statements, and numbers that could be
brought to bear in support of them, is both extensive and unmistakable:

1. A man virtually never bets against a cock owned by a member of
   his own kingroup. Usually he will feel obliged to bet for it, the
   more so the closer the kin tie and the deeper the fight. If he is
   certain in his mind that it will not win, he may just not bet at all,
   particularly if it is only a second cousin's bird or if the fight is a
   shallow one. But as a rule he will feel he must support it and, in
   deep games, nearly always does. Thus the great majority of the
   people calling "five" or "speckled" so demonstratively are expressing their allegiance to their kinsman, not their evaluation of
   his bird, their understanding of probability theory, or even their
   hopes of unearned income.

2. This principle is extended logically. If your kingroup is not involved you will support an allied kingroup against an unallied
   one in the same way, and so on through the very involved networks of alliances which, as I say, make up this, as any other,
   Balinese village.

3. So, too, for the village as a whole. If an outsider cock is fighting
   any cock from your village, you will tend to support the local one.
   If, what is a rarer circumstance but occurs every now and then, a
   cock from outside your cockfight circuit is fighting one inside it,
   you will also tend to support the "home bird."

4. Cocks which come from any distance are almost always favorites,
   for the theory is the man would not have dared to bring it if it
   was not a good cock, the more so the further he has come. His
   followers are, of course, obliged to support him, and when the
   more grand-scale legal cockfights are held (on holidays, and so
   on) the people of the village take what they regard to be the best
   cocks in the village, regardless of ownership, and go off to support them, although they will almost certainly have to give odds
   on them and to make large bets to show that they are not a cheap-
   skate village. Actually, such "away games," though infrequent, tend
   to mend the ruptures between village members that the constantly occurring "home games," where village factions are opposed rather than united, exacerbate.

5. Almost all matches are sociologically relevant. You seldom get
   two outsider cocks fighting, or two cocks with no particular group
   backing, or with group backing which is mutually unrelated in
   any clear way. When you do get them, the game is very shallow,

betting very slow, and the whole thing very dull, with no one save the immediate principals and an addict gambler or two at all interested.

6. By the same token, you rarely get two cocks from the same group, even more rarely from the same subfaction, and virtually never from the same sub-subfaction (which would be in most cases one extended family) fighting. Similarly, in outside village fights two members of the village will rarely fight against one another, even though, as bitter rivals, they would do so with enthusiasm on their home grounds.

7. On the individual level, people involved in an institutionalized hostility relationship, called *puik*, in which they do not speak or otherwise have anything to do with each other (the causes of this formal breaking of relations are many: wife-capture, inheritance arguments, political differences) will bet very heavily, sometimes almost maniacally, against one another in what is a frank and direct attack on the very masculinity, the ultimate ground of his status, of the opponent.

8. The center bet coalition is, in all but the shallowest games, *always* made up by structural allies—no "outside money" is involved. What is "outside" depends upon the context, of course, but given it, no outside money is mixed in with the main bet; if the principals cannot raise it, it is not made. The center bet, again especially in deeper games, is thus the most direct and open expression of social opposition, which is one of the reasons why both it and matchmaking are surrounded by such an air of unease, furtiveness, embarrassment, and so on.

9. The rule about borrowing money—that you may borrow *for* a bet but not *in* one—stems (and the Balinese are quite conscious of this) from similar considerations: you are never at the *economic* mercy of your enemy that way. Gambling debts, which can get quite large on a rather short-term basis, are always to friends, never to enemies, structurally speaking.

10. When two cocks are structurally irrelevant or neutral so far as *you* are concerned (though, as mentioned, they almost never are to each other) you do not even ask a relative or a friend whom he is betting on, because if you know how he is betting and he knows you know, and you go the other way, it will lead to strain. This rule is explicit and rigid; fairly elaborate, even rather artificial precautions are taken to avoid breaking it. At the very least you must pretend not to notice what he is doing, and he what you are doing.

11. There is a special word for betting against the grain, which is also

the word for "pardon me" *(mpura)*. It is considered a bad thing to
do, though if the center bet is small it is sometimes all right as
long as you do not do it too often. But the larger the bet and the
more frequently you do it, the more the "pardon me" tack will
lead to social disruption.

12. In fact, the institutionalized hostility relation, *puik,* is often formally initiated (though its causes always lie elsewhere) by such a
"pardon me" bet in a deep fight, putting the symbolic fat in the
fire. Similarly, the end of such a relationship and resumption of
normal social intercourse is often signalized (but, again, not actually brought about) by one or the other of the enemies supporting the other's bird.

13. In sticky, cross-loyalty situations, of which in this extraordinarily
complex social system there are of course many, where a man is
caught between two more or less equally balanced loyalties, he
tends to wander off for a cup of coffee or something to avoid
having to bet, a form of behavior reminiscent of that of American
voters in similar situations.[25]

14. The people involved in the center bet are, especially in deep fights,
virtually always leading members of their group—kinship, village, or whatever. Further, those who bet on the side (including
these people) are, as I have already remarked, the more established members of the village—the solid citizens. Cockfighting is
for those who are involved in the everyday politics of prestige as
well, not for youth, women, subordinates, and so forth.

15. So far as money is concerned, the explicitly expressed attitude
toward it is that it is a secondary matter. It is not, as I have said,
of no importance; Balinese are no happier to lose several weeks'
income than anyone else. But they mainly look on the monetary
aspects of the cockfight as self-balancing, a matter of just moving
money around, circulating it among a fairly well-defined group
of serious cockfighters. The really important wins and losses are
seen mostly in other terms, and the general attitude toward wagering is not any hope of cleaning up, of making a killing (addict
gamblers again excepted), but that of the horseplayer's prayer:
"Oh, God, please let me break even." In prestige terms, however,
you do not want to break even, but, in a momentary, punctuate
sort of way, win utterly. The talk (which goes on all the time) is
about fights against such-and-such a cock of So-and-So which your
cock demolished, not on how much you won, a fact people, even
for large bets, rarely remember for any length of time, though
they will remember the day they did in Pan Loh's finest cock for
years.

16. You must bet on cocks of your own group aside from mere loy-

alty considerations, for if you do not people generally will say, "What! Is he too proud for the likes of us? Does he have to go to Java or Den Pasar [the capital town] to bet, he is such an important man?" Thus there is a general pressure to bet not only to show that you are important locally, but that you are not so important that you look down on everyone else as unfit even to be rivals. Similarly, home team people must bet against outside cocks or the outsiders will accuse them—a serious charge—of just collecting entry fees and not really being interested in cockfighting, as well as again being arrogant and insulting.

17. Finally, the Balinese peasants themselves are quite aware of all this and can and, at least to an ethnographer, do state most of it in approximately the same terms as I have. Fighting cocks, almost every Balinese I have ever discussed the subject with has said, is like playing with fire only not getting burned. You activate village and kingroup rivalries and hostilities, but in "play" form, coming dangerously and entrancingly close to the expression of open and direct interpersonal and intergroup aggression (something which, again, almost never happens in the normal course of ordinary life), but not quite, because, after all, it is "only a cockfight."

More observations of this sort could be advanced, but perhaps the general point is, if not made, at least well-delineated, and the whole argument thus far can be usefully summarized in a formal paradigm:

THE MORE A MATCH IS . . .
1. Between near status equals (and/or personal enemies)
2. Between high status individuals

THE DEEPER THE MATCH.

THE DEEPER THE MATCH . . .
1. The closer the identification of cock and man (or, more properly, the deeper the match the more the man will advance his best, most closely-identified-with cock).
2. The finer the cocks involved and the more exactly they will be matched.
3. The greater the emotion that will be involved and the more the general absorption in the match.
4. The higher the individual bets center and outside, the shorter the outside bet odds will tend to be, and the more betting there will be overall.
5. The less an "economic" and the more a "status" view of gaming will be involved, and the "solider" the citizens who will be gaming.[26]

Inverse arguments hold for the shallower the fight, culminating, in a reversed-signs sense, in the coin-spinning and dice-throwing amusements. For deep fights there are no absolute upper limits, though there are of course practical ones, and there are a great many legendlike tales of great Duel-in-the-Sun combats between lords and princes in classical times (for cockfighting has always been as much an elite concern as a popular one), far deeper than anything anyone, even aristocrats, could produce today anywhere in Bali.

Indeed, one of the great culture heroes of Bali is a prince, called after his passion for the sport, "The Cockfighter," who happened to be away at a very deep cockfight with a neighboring prince when the whole of his family—father, brothers, wives, sisters—were assassinated by commoner usurpers. Thus spared, he returned to dispatch the upstart, regain the throne, reconstitute the Balinese high tradition, and build its most powerful, glorious, and prosperous state. Along with everything else that the Balinese see in fighting cocks—themselves, their social order, abstract hatred, masculinity, demonic power—they also see the archetype of status virtue, the arrogant, resolute, honor-mad player with real fire, the ksatria prince.[27]

FEATHERS, BLOOD, CROWDS, AND MONEY

"Poetry makes nothing happen," Auden says in his elegy of Yeats, "it survives in the valley of its saying . . . a way of happening, a mouth." The cockfight, too, in this colloquial sense, makes nothing happen. Men go on allegorically humiliating one another and being allegorically humiliated by one another, day after day, glorying quietly in the experience if they have triumphed, crushed only slightly more openly by it if they have not. *But no one's status really changes.* You cannot ascend the status ladder by winning cockfights; you cannot, as an individual, really ascend it at all. Nor can you descend it that way.[28] All you can do is enjoy and savor, or suffer and withstand, the concocted sensation of drastic and momentary movement along an aesthetic semblance of that ladder, a kind of behind-the-mirror status jump which has the look of mobility without its actuality.

Like any art form—for that, finally, is what we are dealing with—the cockfight renders ordinary, everyday experience comprehensible by presenting it in terms of acts and objects which have had their practical consequences removed and been reduced (or, if you prefer, raised) to the level of sheer appearances, where their meaning can be more powerfully articulated and more exactly perceived. The cockfight is "really real" only to the cocks—it does not kill anyone, castrate anyone, reduce anyone to animal status, alter the hierarchical relations among people, or refashion the hierarchy; it does not even redistribute income in any significant way. What it does is what, for other peoples with other temperaments and other conventions, *Lear* and *Crime and Punishment* do; it catches up these themes—death, masculinity, rage, pride, loss, beneficence, chance—and, ordering them into an encompassing structure, presents them in such a way as to throw into relief a particular view of their essential nature. It puts a construction on them, makes them, to those historically positioned to appreciate the construction, meaningful—visible, tangible, graspable—"real," in an ideational sense. An image, fiction, a model, a metaphor, the cockfight is a means of expression; its function is neither to assuage social passions nor to heighten them (though, in its playing-with-fire way it does a bit of both), but, in a medium of feathers, blood, crowds, and money, to display them.

The question of how it is that we perceive qualities in things—paintings, books, melodies, plays—that we do not feel we can assert literally to be there has come, in recent years, into the very center of aesthetic theory.[29] Neither the sentiments of the artist, which remain his, nor those of the audience, which remain theirs, can account for the agitation of one painting or the serenity of another. We attribute grandeur, wit, despair, exuberance, to strings of sounds; lightness, energy, violence, fluidity to blocks of stone. Novels are said to have strength, buildings eloquence, plays momentum, ballets repose. In this realm of eccentric predicates, to say that the cockfight, in its perfected cases at least, is "disquietful" does not seem at all unnatural, merely, as I have just denied it practical consequence, somewhat puzzling.

The disquietfulness arises, "somehow," out of a conjunction of three attributes of the fight: its immediate dramatic shape; its metaphoric content; and its social context. A cultural figure against a social ground, the fight is at once a convulsive surge of animal hatred, a mock war of symbolical selves, and a formal simulation of status tensions, and its aesthetic power derives from its capacity to force together these diverse realities. The reason it is disquietful is not that it has material effects (it has some, but they are minor); the reason that it is disquietful is that, joining pride to selfhood, selfhood to cocks, and cocks to destruction, it brings to imaginative realization a dimension of Balinese experience normally well-obscured from view. The transfer of a sense of gravity into what is in itself a rather blank and unvarious spectacle, a commotion of beating wings and throbbing legs, is effected by interpreting it as expressive of something unsettling in the way its authors and audience live, or, even more ominously, what they are.

As a dramatic shape, the fight displays a characteristic that does not seem so remarkable until one realizes that it does not have to be there: a radically atomistical structure.[30] Each match is a world unto itself, a particulate burst of form. There is the matchmaking, there is the betting, there is the fight, there is the result—utter triumph and utter defeat—and there is the hurried, embarrassed passing of money. The loser is not consoled. People drift away from him, look around him, leave him to assimilate his momentary descent into nonbeing, reset his face, and return, scarless and intact, to the fray. Nor are winners congratulated, or events rehashed; once a match is ended the crowd's attention turns totally to the next, with no looking back. A shadow of the experience no doubt remains with the principals, perhaps even with some of the witnesses of a deep fight, as it remains with us when we leave the theater after seeing a powerful play well-performed; but it quite soon fades to become at most a schematic memory—a diffuse glow or an abstract shudder—and usually not even that. Any expressive form lives only in its own present—the one it itself creates. But, here, that present is severed into a string of flashes, some more bright than others, but all of them disconnected, aesthetic quanta. Whatever the cockfight says, it says in spurts.

But . . . the Balinese live in spurts. Their life, as they arrange it and perceive it, is less a flow, a directional movement out of the past, through the present, toward the future than an on-off pulsation of meaning and vacuity, an arhythmic alternation of short periods when "something" (that is, something significant) is happening, and equally short ones where "nothing" (that is, nothing much) is—between what they themselves call "full" and "empty" times, or, in another idiom, "junctures" and "holes." In focusing activity down to a burning-glass dot, the cockfight is merely being Balinese in the same way in which everything from the monadic encounters of everyday life, through the clanging pointillism of *gamelan* music, to the visiting-day-of-the-gods temple celebrations are. It is not an imitation of the punctuateness of Balinese social life, nor a depiction of it, nor even an expression of it; it is an example of it, carefully prepared.[31]

If one dimension of the cockfight's structure, its lack of temporal directionality, makes it seem a typical segment of the general social life, however, the other, its flat-out, head-to-head (or spur-to-spur) aggressiveness, makes it seem a contradiction, a reversal, even a subversion of it. In the normal course of things, the Balinese are shy to the point of obsessiveness of open conflict. Oblique, cautious, subdued, controlled, masters of indirection and dissimulation—what they call *alus*, "polished," "smooth"—they rarely face what they can turn away from, rarely resist what they can evade. But here they portray themselves as wild and murderous, with manic explosions of instinctual cruelty. A powerful rendering of life as the Balinese most deeply do not want it (to adapt a phrase Frye has used of Gloucester's blinding) is set in the context of a sample of it as they do in fact have it.[32] And, because the context suggests that the rendering, if less than a straightforward description, is nonetheless more than an idle fancy; it is here that the disquietfulness—the disquietfulness of the *fight,* not (or, anyway, not necessarily) its patrons, who seem in fact rather thoroughly to enjoy it—emerges. The slaughter in the cock ring is not a depiction of how things literally are among men, but, what is almost worse, of how, from a particular angle, they imaginatively are.[33]

The angle, of course, is stratificatory. What, as we have already seen, the cockfight talks most forcibly about is status relationships, and what it says about them is that they are matters of life and death. That prestige is a profoundly serious business is apparent everywhere one looks in Bali—in the village, the family, the economy, the state. A peculiar fusion of Polynesian title ranks and Hindu castes, the hierarchy of pride is the moral backbone of the society. But only in the cockfight are the sentiments upon which that hierarchy rests revealed in their natural colors. Enveloped elsewhere in a haze of etiquette, a thick cloud of euphemism and ceremony, gesture and allusion, they are here expressed in only the thinnest disguise of an animal mask, a mask which in fact demonstrates them far more effectively than it conceals them. Jealousy is as much a part of Bali as poise, envy as grace, brutality as charm; but without the cockfight the Balinese would have a much less certain understanding of them, which is, presumably, why they value it so highly.

Any expressive form works (when it works) by disarranging semantic contexts in such a way that properties conventionally ascribed to certain things are unconventionally ascribed to others, which are then seen actually to possess them. To call the wind a cripple, as Stevens does, to fix tone and manipulate timbre, as Schoenberg does, or, closer to our case, to picture an art critic as a dissolute bear, as Hogarth does, is to cross conceptual wires; the established conjunctions between objects and their qualities are altered, and phenomena—fall weather, melodic shape, or cultural journalism—are clothed in signifiers which normally point to other referents.[34] Similarly, to connect—and connect, and connect—the collision of roosters with the divisiveness of status is to invite a transfer of perceptions from the former to the latter, a transfer which is at once a description and a judgment. (Logically, the transfer could, of course, as well go the other way; but, like most of the rest of us, the Balinese are a great deal more interested in understanding men than they are in understanding cocks.)

What sets the cockfight apart from the ordinary course of life, lifts it from the realm of everyday practical affairs, and surrounds it with an aura of enlarged importance is not, as functionalist sociology would have it, that it reinforces status discriminations (such reinforcement is hardly

necessary in a society where every act proclaims them), but that it provides a metasocial commentary upon the whole matter of assorting human beings into fixed hierarchical ranks and then organizing the major
part of collective existence around that assortment. Its function, if you
want to call it that, is interpretive: it is a Balinese reading of Balinese
experience, a story they tell themselves about themselves.

SAYING SOMETHING OF SOMETHING

To put the matter this way is to engage in a bit of metaphorical refocus-
ing of one's own, for it shifts the analysis of cultural forms from an endeavor in general parallel to dissecting an organism, diagnosing a symp-
tom, deciphering a code, or ordering a system—the dominant analogies
in contemporary anthropology—to one in general parallel with penetrating a literary text. If one takes the cockfight, or any other collectively
sustained symbolic structure, as a means of "saying something of something" (to invoke a famous Aristotelian tag), then one is faced with a
problem not in social mechanics but social semantics.[35] For the anthropologist, whose concern is with formulating sociological principles, not
with promoting or appreciating cockfights, the question is, what does
one learn about such principles from examining culture as an assemblage of texts?

Such an extension of the notion of a text beyond written material,
and even beyond verbal, is, though metaphorical, not, of course, all that
novel. The *interpretatio naturae* tradition of the middle ages, which, culminating in Spinoza, attempted to read nature as Scripture, the Nietsz-
chean effort to treat value systems as glosses on the will to power (or the
Marxian one to treat them as glosses on property relations), and the
Freudian replacement of the enigmatic text of the manifest dream with
the plain one of the latent, all offer precedents, if not equally recom-
mendable ones.[36] But the idea remains theoretically undeveloped; and
the more profound corollary, so far as anthropology is concerned, that
cultural forms can be treated as texts, as imaginative works built out of
social materials, has yet to be systematically exploited.[37]

In the case at hand, to treat the cockfight as a text is to bring out a
feature of it (in my opinion, the central feature of it) that treating it as a
rite or a pastime, the two most obvious alternatives, would tend to obscure: its use of emotion for cognitive ends. What the cockfight says it
says in a vocabulary of sentiment—the thrill of risk, the despair of loss,
the pleasure of triumph. Yet what it says is not merely that risk is exciting, loss depressing, or triumph gratifying, banal tautologies of affect,
but that it is of these emotions, thus exampled, that society is built and
individuals are put together. Attending cockfights and participating in

them is, for the Balinese, a kind of sentimental education. What he learns there is what his culture's ethos and his private sensibility (or, anyway, certain aspects of them) look like when spelled out externally in a collective text; that the two are near enough alike to be articulated in the symbolics of a single such text; and—the disquieting part—that the text in which this revelation is accomplished consists of a chicken hacking another mindlessly to bits.

Every people, the proverb has it, loves its own form of violence. The cockfight is the Balinese reflection on theirs: on its look, its uses, its force, its fascination. Drawing on almost every level of Balinese experience, it brings together themes—animal savagery, male narcissism, opponent gambling, status rivalry, mass excitement, blood sacrifice—whose main connection is their involvement with rage and the fear of rage, and, binding them into a set of rules which at once contains them and allows them play, builds a symbolic structure in which, over and over again, the reality of their inner affiliation can be intelligibly felt. If, to quote Northrop Frye again, we go to see *Macbeth* to learn what a man feels like after he has gained a kingdom and lost his soul, Balinese go to cockfights to find out what a man, usually composed, aloof, almost obsessively self-absorbed, a kind of moral autocosm, feels like when, attacked, tormented, challenged, insulted, and driven in result to the extremes of fury, he has totally triumphed or been brought totally low. The whole passage, as it takes us back to Aristotle (though to the *Poetics* rather than the *Hermeneutics*), is worth quotation:

> But the poet [as opposed to the historian], Aristotle says, never makes any real statements at all, certainly no particular or specific ones. The poet's job is not to tell you what happened, but what happens: not what did take place, but the kind of thing that always does take place. He gives you the typical, recurring, or what Aristotle calls universal event. You wouldn't go to *Macbeth* to learn about the history of Scotland—you go to it to learn what a man feels like after he's gained a kingdom and lost his soul. When you meet such a character as Micawber in Dickens, you don't feel that there must have been a man Dickens knew who was exactly like this: you feel that there's a bit of Micawber in almost everybody you know, including yourself. Our impressions of human life are picked up one by one, and remain for most of us loose and disorganized. But we constantly find things in literature that suddenly coordinate and bring into focus a great many such impressions, and this is part of what Aristotle means by the typical or universal human event.[38]

It is this kind of bringing of assorted experiences of everyday life to focus that the cockfight, set aside from that life as "only a game" and reconnected to it as "more than a game," accomplishes, and so creates what, better than typical or universal, could be called a paradigmatic human event—that is, one that tells us less what happens than the kind of thing that would happen if, as is not the case, life were art and could be as freely shaped by styles of feeling as *Macbeth* and *David Copperfield* are.

Enacted and re-enacted, so far without end, the cockfight enables the Balinese, as, read and reread, *Macbeth* enables us, to see a dimension of his own subjectivity. As he watches fight after fight, with the active watching of an owner and a bettor (for cockfighting has no more interest as a pure spectator sport than does croquet or dog racing), he grows familiar with it and what it has to say to him, much as the attentive listener to string quartets or the absorbed viewer of still life grows slowly more familiar with them in a way which opens his subjectivity to himself.[39]

Yet, because—in another of those paradoxes, along with painted feelings and unconsequenced acts, which haunt aesthetics—that subjectivity does not properly exist until it is thus organized, art forms generate and regenerate the very subjectivity they pretend only to display. Quartets, still lifes, and cockfights are not merely reflections of a pre-existing sensibility analogically represented; they are positive agents in the creation and maintenance of such a sensibility. If we see ourselves as a pack of Micawbers, it is from reading too much Dickens (if we see ourselves as unillusioned realists, it is from reading too little); and similarly for Balinese, cocks, and cockfights. It is in such a way, coloring experience with the light they cast it in, rather than through whatever material effects they may have, that the arts play their role, as arts, in social life.[40]

In the cockfight, then, the Balinese forms and discovers his temperament and his society's temper at the same time. Or, more exactly, he forms and discovers a particular facet of them. Not only are there a great many other cultural texts providing commentaries on status hierarchy and self-regard in Bali, but there are a great many other critical sectors of Balinese life besides the stratificatory and the agonistic that receive such commentary. The ceremony consecrating a Brahmana priest, a matter of breath control, postural immobility, and vacant concentration upon the depths of being, displays a radically different, but to the Balinese equally real, property of social hierarchy—its reach toward the numinous transcendent. Set not in the matrix of the kinetic emotionality of animals, but in that of the static passionlessness of divine mentality, it expresses tranquillity not disquiet. The mass festivals at the village temples, which mobilize the whole local population in elaborate hostings of visiting gods—songs, dances, compliments, gifts—assert the spiritual unity of village mates against their status inequality and project a mood of amity and trust.[41] The cockfight is not the master key to Balinese life, any more than bullfighting is to Spanish. What it says about that life is not unqualified nor even unchallenged by what other equally eloquent cultural statements say about it. But there is nothing more surprising in this than in the fact that Racine and Molière were contemporaries, or that the same people who arrange chrysanthemums cast swords.[42]

The culture of a people is an ensemble of texts, themselves ensembles, which the anthropologist strains to read over the shoulders of those to whom they properly belong. There are enormous difficulties in such an enterprise, methodological pitfalls to make a Freudian quake, and some moral perplexities as well. Nor is it the only way that symbolic forms can be sociologically handled. Functionalism lives, and so does psychologism. But to regard such forms as "saying something of something," and saying it to somebody, is at least to open up the possibility of an analysis which attends to their substance rather than to reductive formulas professing to account for them.

As in more familiar exercises in close reading, one can start anywhere in a culture's repertoire of forms and end up anywhere else. One can stay, as I have here, within a single, more or less bounded form, and circle steadily within it. One can move between forms in search of broader unities or informing contrasts. One can even compare forms from different cultures to define their character in reciprocal relief. But whatever the level at which one operates, and however intricately, the guiding principle is the same: societies, like lives, contain their own interpretations. One has only to learn how to gain access to them.

NOTES

1. G. Bateson and M. Mead, *Balinese Character: A Photographic Analysis* (New York, 1942), p. 68.

2. J. Belo, "The Balinese Temper," in *Traditional Balinese Culture*, ed. J. Belo (New York, 1970) (originally published in 1935), pp. 85–110.

3. The best discussion of cockfighting is again Bateson and Mead's *Balinese Character*, pp. 24–25, 140; but it, too, is general and abbreviated.

4. Ibid., pp. 25–26. The cockfight is unusual within Balinese culture in being a single-sex public activity from which the other sex is totally and expressly excluded. Sexual differentiation is culturally extremely played down in Bali and most activities, formal and informal, involve the participation of men and women on equal ground, commonly as linked couples. From religion, to politics, to economics, to kinship, to dress, Bali is a rather "unisex" society, a fact both its customs and its symbolism clearly express. Even in contexts where women do not in fact play much of a role—music, painting, certain agricultural activities—their absence, which is only relative in any case, is more a mere matter of fact than socially enforced. To this general pattern, the cockfight, entirely of, by, and for men (women—at least *Balinese* women—do not even watch), is the most striking exception.

5. C. Hooykaas, *The Lay of the Jaya Prana* (London, 1958), p. 39. The lay has

a stanza (no. 17) with the reluctant bridgegroom use. Jaya Prana, the subject of a Balinese Uriah myth, responds to the lord who has offered him the loveliest of six hundred servant girls: "Godly King, my Lord and Master / I beg you, give me leave to go / such things are not yet in my mind; / like a fighting cock encaged / indeed I am on my mettle / I am alone / as yet the flame has not been fanned."

6. For these, see V. E. Korn, *Het Adatrecht van Bali*, 2d ed. (The Hague, 1932), index under *toh*.

7. There is indeed a legend to the effect that the separation of Java and Bali is due to the action of a powerful Javanese religious figure who wished to protect himself against a Balinese culture hero (the ancestor of two Ksatria castes) who was a passionate cockfighting gambler. See C. Hooykaas, *Agama Tirtha* (Amsterdam, 1964), p. 184.

8. An incestuous couple is forced to wear pig yokes over their necks and crawl to a pig trough and eat with their mouths there. On this, see J. Belo, "Customs Pertaining to Twins in Bali," in *Traditional Balinese Culture*, ed. J. Belo, p. 49; on the abhorrence of animality generally, Bateson and Mead, *Balinese Character*, p. 22.

9. Except for unimportant, small-bet fights (on the question of fight "importance," see below) spur affixing is usually done by someone other than the owner. Whether the owner handles his own cock or not more or less depends on how skilled he is at it, a consideration whose importance is again relative to the importance of the fight. When spur affixers and cock handlers are someone other than the owner, they are almost always a quite close relative—a brother or cousin—or a very intimate friend of his. They are thus almost extensions of his personality, as the fact that all three will refer to the cock as "mine," say "I" fought So-and-So, and so on, demonstrates. Also, owner-handler-affixer triads tend to be fairly fixed, though individuals may participate in several and often exchange roles within a given one.

10. E. Goffman, *Encounters: Two Studies in the Sociology of Interaction* (Indianapolis, 1961), pp. 9–10.

11. This word, which literally means an indelible stain or mark, as in a birthmark or a vein in a stone, is used as well for a deposit in a court case, for a pawn, for security offered in a loan, for a stand-in for someone else in a legal or ceremonial context, for an earnest advanced in a business deal, for a sign placed in a field to indicate its ownership is in dispute, and for the status of an unfaithful wife from whose lover her husband must gain satisfaction or surrender her to him. See Korn, *Het Adatrecht van Bali;* Th. Pigeaud, *Javaans-Nederlands Handwoordenboek* (Groningen, 1938); H. H. Juynboll, *Oudjavaansche-Nederlandsche Woordenlijst* (Leiden, 1923).

12. The center bet must be advanced in cash by both parties prior to the actual fight. The umpire holds the stakes until the decision is rendered and then awards them to the winner, avoiding, among other things, the intense embarrassment both winner and loser would feel if the latter had to pay off personally following his defeat. About 10 percent of the winner's receipts are subtracted for the umpire's share and that of the fight sponsors.

13. Actually, the typing of cocks, which is extremely elaborate (I have col-

lected more than twenty classes, certainly not a complete list), is not based on color alone, but on a series of independent, interacting, dimensions, which include—besides color—size, bone thickness, plumage, and temperament. (But *not* pedigree. The Balinese do not breed cocks to any significant extent, nor, so far as I have been able to discover, have they ever done so. The *asil*, or jungle cock, which is the basic fighting strain everywhere the sport is found, is native to southern Asia, and one can buy a good example in the chicken section of almost any Balinese market for anywhere from four or five ringgits up to fifty or more.) The color element is merely the one normally used as the type name, except when the two cocks of different types—as on principle they must be—have the same color, in which case a secondary indication from one of the other dimensions ("large speckled" v. "small speckled," etc.) is added. The types are coordinated with various cosmological ideas which help shape the making of matches, so that, for example, you fight a small, headstrong, speckled brown-on-white cock with flat-lying feathers and thin legs from the east side of the ring on a certain day of the complex Balinese calendar, and a large, cautious, all-black cock with tufted feathers and stubby legs from the north side on another day, and so on. All this is again recorded in palm-leaf manuscripts and endlessly discussed by the Balinese (who do not all have identical systems), and a full-scale componential-cum-symbolic analysis of cock classifications would be extremely valuable both as an adjunct to the description of the cockfight and in itself. But my data on the subject, though extensive and varied, do not seem to be complete and systematic enough to attempt such an analysis here. For Balinese cosmological ideas more generally see Belo, ed., *Traditional Balinese Culture*, and J. L. Swellengrebel, ed., *Bali: Studies in Life, Thought, and Ritual* (The Hague, 1960).

14. For purposes of ethnographic completeness, it should be noted that it is possible for the man backing the favorite—the odds-giver—to make a bet in which he wins if his cock wins or there is a tie, a slight shortening of the odds (I do not have enough cases to be exact, but ties seem to occur about once every fifteen or twenty matches). He indicates his wish to do this by shouting *sapih* ("tie") rather than the cock-type, but such bets are in fact infrequent.

15. The precise dynamics of the movement of the betting is one of the most intriguing, most complicated, and, given the hectic conditions under which it occurs, most difficult to study, aspects of the fight. Motion picture recording plus multiple observers would probably be necessary to deal with it effectively. Even impressionistically—the only approach open to a lone ethnographer caught in the middle of all this—it is clear that certain men lead both in determining the favorite (that is, making the opening cock-type calls which always initiate the process) and in directing the movement of the odds, these "opinion leaders" being the more accomplished cockfighters-cum-solid-citizens to be discussed below. If these men begin to change their calls, others follow; if they begin to make bets, so do others and—though there are always a large number of frustrated bettors crying for shorter or longer odds to the end—the movement more or less ceases. But a detailed understanding of the whole process awaits what, alas, it is not very likely ever to get: a decision theorist armed with precise observations of individual behavior.

16. Assuming only binomial variability, the departure from a fifty-fifty expectation in the sixty-ringgits-and-below case is 1.38 standard deviations, or (in a one direction test) an eight in one hundred possibility by chance alone; for the below-forty-ringgits case it is 1.65 standard deviations, or about five in one hundred. The fact that these departures though real are not extreme merely indicates, again, that even in the smaller fights the tendency to match cocks at least reasonably evenly persists. It is a matter of relative relaxation of the pressures toward equalization, not their elimination. The tendency for high-bet contests to be coin-flip propositions is, of course, even more striking, and suggests the Balinese know quite well what they are about.

17. The reduction in wagering in smaller fights (which, of course, feeds on itself; one of the reasons people find small fights uninteresting is that there is less wagering in them, and contrariwise for large ones) takes place in three mutually reinforcing ways. First, there is a simple withdrawal of interest as people wander off to have a cup of coffee or chat with a friend. Second, the Balinese do not mathematically reduce odds, but bet directly in terms of stated odds as such. Thus, for a nine-to-eight bet, one man wagers nine ringgits, the other eight; for five-to-four, one wagers five, the other four. For any given currency unit, like the ringgit, therefore, 6.3 times as much money is involved in a ten-to-nine bet as in a two-to-one bet, for example, and, as noted, in small fights betting settles toward the longer end. Finally, the bets which are made tend to be one- rather than two-, three-, or in some of the very largest fights, four- or five-finger ones. (The fingers indicate the *multiples* of the stated bet odds at issue, not absolute figures. Two fingers in a six-to-five situation means a man wants to wager ten ringgits on the underdog against twelve, three in an eight-to-seven situation, twenty-one against twenty-four, and so on.)

18. Besides wagering there are other economic aspects of the cockfight, especially its very close connection with the local market system which, though secondary both to its motivation and to its function, are not without importance. Cockfights are open events to which anyone who wishes may come, sometimes from quite distant areas, but well over 90 percent, probably over 95, are very local affairs, and the locality concerned is defined not by the village, nor even by the administrative district, but by the rural market system. Bali has a three-day market week with the familiar "solar-system"-type rotation. Though the markets themselves have never been very highly developed, small morning affairs in a village square, it is the microregion such rotation rather generally marks out— ten or twenty square miles, seven or eight neighboring villages (which in contemporary Bali is usually going to mean anywhere from five to ten or eleven thousand people) from which the core of any cockfight audience, indeed virtually all of it, will come. Most of the fights are in fact organized and sponsored by small combines of petty rural merchants under the general premise, very strongly held by them and indeed by all Balinese, that cockfights are good for trade because "they get money out of the house, they make it circulate." Stalls selling various sorts of things as well as assorted sheer-chance gambling games (see below) are set up around the edge of the area so that this even takes on the quality of a small fair. This connection of cockfighting with markets and market sellers is

very old, as, among other things, their conjunction in inscriptions [R. Goris, *Prasasti Bali,* 2 vols. (Bandung, 1954)] indicates. Trade has followed the cock for centuries in rural Bali, and the sport has been one of the main agencies of the island's monetization.

19. The phrase is found in the Hildreth translation, International Library of Psychology (1931), note to p. 106; see L. L. Fuller, *The Morality of Law* (New Haven, 1964), p. 6 ff.

20. Of course, even in Bentham, utility is not normally confined as a concept to monetary losses and gains, and my argument here might be more carefully put in terms of a denial that for the Balinese, as for any people, utility (pleasure, happiness . . .) is merely identifiable with wealth. But such terminological problems are in any case secondary to the essential point: the cockfight is not roulette.

21. M. Weber, *The Sociology of Religion* (Boston, 1963). There is nothing specifically Balinese, of course, about deepening significance with money, as Whyte's description of corner boys in a working-class district of Boston demonstrates: "Gambling plays an important role in the lives of Cornerville people. Whatever game the corner boys play, they nearly always bet on the outcome. When there is nothing at stake, the game is not considered a real contest. This does not mean that the financial element is all-important. I have frequently heard men say that the honor of winning was much more important than the money at stake. The corner boys consider playing for money the real test of skill and, unless a man performs well when money is at stake, he is not considered a good competitor." W. F. Whyte, *Street Corner Society,* 2d ed. (Chicago, 1955), p. 140.

22. The extremes to which this madness is conceived on occasion to go—and the fact that it is considered madness—is demonstrated by the Balinese folk tale *I Tuhung Kuning.* A gambler becomes so deranged by his passion that, leaving on a trip, he orders his pregnant wife to take care of the prospective newborn if it is a boy but to feed it as meat to his fighting cocks if it is a girl. The mother gives birth to a girl, but rather than giving the child to the cocks she gives them a large rat and conceals the girl with her own mother. When the husband returns, the cocks, crowing a jingle, inform him of the deception and, furious, he sets out to kill the child. A goddess descends from heaven and takes the girl up to the skies with her. The cocks die from the food given them, the owner's sanity is restored, the goddess brings the girl back to the father, who reunites him with his wife. The story is given as "Geel Komkommertje" in J. Hooykaas-van Leeuwen Boomkamp, *Sprookjes en Verhalen van Bali* (The Hague, 1956), pp. 19–25.

23. For a fuller description of Balinese rural social structure, see C. Geertz, "Form and Variation in Balinese Village Structure," *American Anthropologist* 61 (1959): pp. 94–108; "Tihingan, A Balinese Village," in R. M. Koentjaraningrat, *Villages in Indonesia* (Ithaca, 1967), pp. 210–243; and, though it is a bit off the norm as Balinese villages go, V. E. Korn, *De Dorpsrepubliek tnganan Pagringsingan* (Santpoort, Netherlands, 1933).

24. Goffman, *Encounters,* p. 78.

25. B. R. Berelson, P. F. Lazersfeld, and W. N. McPhee, *Voting: A Study of Opinion Formation in a Presidential Campaign* (Chicago, 1954).

26. As this is a formal paradigm, it is intended to display the logical, not the

causal, structure of cockfighting. Just which of these considerations leads to which, in what order, and by what mechanisms, is another matter—one I have attempted to shed some light on in the general discussion.

27. In another of Hooykaas-van Leeuwen Boomkamp's folk tales ("De Gast," *Sprookjes en Verhalen van Bali,* pp. 172–180), a low caste *Sudra,* a generous, pious, and carefree man who is also an accomplished cockfighter, loses, despite his accomplishment, fight after fight until he is not only out of money but down to his last cock. He does not despair, however—"I bet," he says, "upon the Unseen World."

His wife, a good and hard-working woman, knowing how much he enjoys cockfighting, gives him her last "rainy day" money to go and bet. But, filled with misgivings due to his run of ill luck, he leaves his own cock at home and bets merely on the side. He soon loses all but a coin or two and repairs to a food stand for a snack, where he meets a decrepit, odorous, and generally unappetizing old beggar leaning on a staff. The old man asks for food, and the hero spends his last coins to buy him some. The old man then asks to pass the night with the hero, which the hero gladly invites him to do. As there is no food in the house, however, the hero tells his wife to kill the last cock for dinner. When the old man discovers this fact, he tells the hero he has three cocks in his own mountain hut and says the hero may have one of them for fighting. He also asks for the hero's son to accompany him as a servant, and, after the son agrees, this is done.

The old man turns out to be Siva and, thus, to live in a great palace in the sky, though the hero does not know this. In time, the hero decides to visit his son and collect the promised cock. Lifted up into Siva's presence, he is given the choice of three cocks. The first crows: "I have beaten fifteen opponents." The second crows, "I have beaten twenty-five opponents." The third crows, "I have beaten the king." "That one, the third, is my choice," says the hero, and returns with it to earth.

When he arrives at the cockfight, he is asked for an entry fee and replies, "I have no money; I will pay after my cock has won." As he is known never to win, he is let in because the king, who is there fighting, dislikes him and hopes to enslave him when he loses and cannot pay off. In order to insure that this happens, the king matches his finest cock against the hero's. When the cocks are placed down, the hero's flees, and the crowd, led by the arrogant king, hoots in laughter. The hero's cock then flies at the king himself, killing him with a spur stab in the throat. The hero flees. His house is encircled by the king's men. The cock changes into a Garuda, the great mythic bird of Indic legend, and carries the hero and his wife to safety in the heavens.

When the people see this, they make the hero king and his wife queen and they return as such to earth. Later their son, released by Siva, also returns and the hero-king announces his intention to enter a hermitage. ("I will fight no more cockfights. I have bet on the Unseen and won.") He enters the hermitage and his son becomes king.

28. Addict gamblers are really less declassed (for their status is, as everyone else's, inherited) than merely impoverished and personally disgraced. The most prominent addict gambler in my cockfight circuit was actually a very high caste *satria* who sold off most of his considerable lands to support his habit. Though

everyone privately regarded him as a fool and worse (some, more charitable, regarded him as sick), he was publicly treated with the elaborate deference and politeness due his rank. . . .

29. For four, somewhat variant, treatments, see S. Langer, *Feeling and Form* (New York, 1953); R. Wollheim, *Art and Its Objects* (New York, 1968); N. Goodman, *Languages of Art* (Indianapolis, 1968); M. Merleau-Ponty, "The Eye and the Mind," in his *The Primacy of Perception* (Evanston, Ill., 1964), pp. 159–190.

30. British cockfights (the sport was banned there in 1840) indeed seem to have lacked it, and to have generated, therefore, a quite different family of shapes. Most British fights were "mains," in which a preagreed number of cocks were aligned into two teams and fought serially. Score was kept and wagering took place both on the individual matches and on the main as a whole. There were also "battle Royales," both in England and on the Continent, in which a large number of cocks were let loose at once with the one left standing at the end the victor. And in Wales, the so-called Welsh main followed an elimination pattern, along the lines of a present-day tennis tournament, winners proceeding to the next round. As a genre, the cock fight has perhaps less compositional flexibility than, say, Latin comedy, but it is not entirely without any. On cockfighting more generally, see A. Ruport, *The Art of Cockfighting* (New York, 1949); G. R. Scott, *History of Cockfighting* (London, 1957); and L. Fitz-Barnard, *Fighting Sports* (London, 1921).

31. For the necessity of distinguishing among "description," "representation," "exemplification," and "expression" (and the irrelevance of "imitation" to all of them) as modes of symbolic reference, see Goodman, *Languages of Art*, pp. 61–110, 45–91, 225–241.

32. N. Frye, *The Educated Imagination* (Bloomington, Ind., 1964), p. 99.

33. There are two other Balinese values and disvalues which, connected with punctuate temporality on the one hand and unbridled aggressiveness on the other, reinforce the sense that the cockfight is at once continuous with ordinary social life and a direct negation of it: what the Balinese call *ramé*, and what they call *paling*. *Ramé* means crowded, noisy, and active, and is a highly sought-after social state: crowded markets, mass festivals, busy streets are all *ramé*, as, of course, is, in the extreme, a cockfight. *Ramé* is what happens in the "full" times (its opposite, *sepi*, "quiet," is what happens in the "empty" ones). *Paling* is social vertigo, the dizzy, disoriented, lost, turned-around feeling one gets when one's place in the coordinates of social space is not clear, and it is a tremendously disfavored, immensely anxiety-producing state. Balinese regard the exact maintenance of spatial orientation ("not to know where north is" is to be crazy), balance, decorum, status relationships, and so forth, as fundamental to ordered life *(krama)* and *paling*, the sort of whirling confusion of position the scrambling cocks exemplify as its profoundest enemy and contradiction. On *ramé*, see Bateson and Mead, *Balinese Character*, pp. 3, 64; on *paling*, ibid., p. 11, and Belo, ed., *Traditional Balinese Culture*, p. 90 ff.

34. The Stevens reference is to his "The Motive for Metaphor" ("You like it under the trees in autumn, / Because everything is half dead. / The wind moves like a cripple among the leaves / And repeats words without meaning") [Copyright 1947 by Wallace Stevens, reprinted from *The Collected Poems of Wallace Ste-*

vens by permission of Alfred A. Knopf, Inc., and Faber and Faber Ltd.]; the Schoenberg reference is to the third of his *Five Orchestral Pieces* (Opus 16), and is borrowed from H. H. Drager, "The Concept of 'Tonal Body,' " in *Reflections on Art*, ed. S. Langer (New York, 1961), p. 174. On Hogarth, and on this whole problem—there called "multiple matrix matching"—see E. H. Gombrich, "The Use of Art for the Study of Symbols," in *Psychology and the Visual Arts*, ed. J. Hogg (Baltimore, 1969), pp. 149–170. The more usual term for this sort of semantic alchemy is "metaphorical transfer," and good technical discussions of it can be found in M. Black, *Models and Metaphors* (Ithaca, N.Y., 1962), p. 25 ff; Goodman, *Languages of Art*, p. 44 ff; and W. Percy, "Metaphor as Mistake," *Sewanee Review* 66 (1958): 78–99.

35. The tag is from the second book of the *Organon, On Interpretation*. For a discussion of it, and for the whole argument for freeing "the notion of text . . . from the notion of scripture or writing" and constructing, thus, a general hermeneutics, see P. Ricoeur, *Freud and Philosophy* (New Haven, 1970), p. 20 ff.

36. Ibid.

37. Lévi-Strauss' "structuralism" might seem an exception. But it is only an apparent one, for, rather than taking myths, totem rites, marriage rules, or whatever as texts to interpret, Lévi-Strauss takes them as ciphers to solve, which is very much not the same thing. He does not seek to understand symbolic forms in terms of how they function in concrete situations to organize perceptions (meanings, emotions, concepts, attitudes); he seeks to understand them entirely in terms of their internal structure, *independent de tout sujet, de tout objet, et de toute contexte. . . .*

38. Frye, *The Educated Imagination*, pp. 63–64.

39. The use of the, to Europeans, "natural" visual idiom for perception— "see," "watches," and so forth—is more than usually misleading here, for the fact that, as mentioned earlier, Balinese follow the progress of the fight as much (perhaps, as fighting cocks are actually rather hard to see except as blurs of motion, more) with their bodies as with their eyes, moving their limbs, heads, and trunks in gestural mimicry of the cocks' maneuvers, means that much of the individual's experience of the fight is kinesthetic rather than visual. If ever there was an example of Kenneth Burke's definition of a symbolic act as "the dancing of an attitude" [*The Philosophy of Literary Form*, rev. ed. (New York, 1957), p. 9] the cockfight is it. On the enormous role of kinesthetic perception in Balinese life, Bateson and Mead, *Balinese Character*, pp. 84–88; on the active nature of aesthetic perception in general, Goodman, *Languages of Art*, pp. 241–244.

40. All this coupling of the occidental great with the oriental lowly will doubtless disturb certain sorts of aestheticians as the earlier efforts of anthropologists to speak of Christianity and totemism in the same breath disturbed certain sorts of theologians. But as ontological questions are (or should be) bracketed in the sociology of religion, judgmental ones are (or should be) bracketed in the sociology of art. In any case, the attempt to deprovincialize the concept of art is but part of the general anthropological conspiracy to deprovincialize all important social concepts—marriage, religion, law, rationality—and though this is a threat to aesthetic theories which regard certain works of art as beyond the reach of sociological analysis, it is no threat to the conviction, for which Robert Graves

claims to have been reprimanded at his Cambridge tripos, that some poems are better than others.

41. For the consecration ceremony, see V. E. Korn, "The Consecration of the Priest," in Swellengrebel, ed., *Bali: Studies*, pp. 131–154; for (somewhat exaggerated) village communion, R. Goris, "The Religious Character of the Balinese Village," ibid., pp. 79–100.

42. That what the cockfight has to say about Bali is not altogether without perception and the disquiet it expresses about the general pattern of Balinese life is not wholly without reason is attested by the fact that in two weeks of December 1965, during the upheavals following the unsuccessful coup in Djakarta, between forty and eighty thousand Balinese (in a population of about two million) were killed, largely by one another—the worst outburst in the country. [J. Hughes, *Indonesian Upheaval* (New York, 1967), pp. 173–183. Hughes' figures are, of course, rather casual estimates, but they are not the most extreme.] This is not to say, of course, that the killings were caused by the cockfight, could have been predicted on the basis of it, or were some sort of enlarged version of it with real people in the place of the cocks—all of which is nonsense. It is merely to say that if one looks at Bali not just through the medium of its dances, its shadowplays, its sculpture, and its girls, but—as the Balinese themselves do—also through the medium of its cockfight, the fact that the massacre occurred seems, if no less appalling, less like a contradiction to the laws of nature. As more than one real Gloucester has discovered, sometimes people actually get life precisely as they most deeply do not want it.

EIGHT

La Pensée Bourgeoise

Western Society as Culture

Marshall Sahlins

The field of political economy, constructed exclusively on the two values of exchange and use, falls to pieces and must be entirely reanalyzed in the form of a GENERALIZED POLITICAL ECONOMY, which will imply the production of symbolic exchange value [valeur d'echange/signe] *as the same thing and in the same movement as the production of material goods and of economic exchange value. The analysis of the production of symbols and culture is not thus posed as external, ulterior, or "superstructural" in relation to material production; it is posed as a* revolution of political economy itself, *generalized by the theoretical and practical intervention of symbolic exchange value.*

BAUDRILLARD
1972

Historical materialism is truly a self-awareness of bourgeois society—yet an awareness, it would seem, within the terms of that society. In treating production as a natural-pragmatic process of need satisfaction, it risks an alliance with bourgeois economics in the work of raising the alienation of persons and things to a higher cognitive power. The two would join in concealing the meaningful system in the praxis by the practical explanation of the system. If that concealment is allowed, or smuggled in as premise, everything would happen in a Marxist anthropology as it does in the orthodox economics, as if the analyst were duped by the same commodity fetishism that fascinates the participants in the process. Conceiving the creation and movement of goods solely from their pecuniary quantities (exchange-value), one ignores the cultural code of concrete properties governing "utility" and so remains unable to account for what is in fact produced. The explanation is satisfied to recreate the self-deception of the society to which it is addressed, where the logical system of objects and social relations proceeds along an unconscious plane,

Reprinted by permission of the author and the University of Chicago Press from Marshall Sahlins, *Culture and Practical Reason* (Chicago: University of Chicago Press), pp. 166–178, © 1976 by the University of Chicago.

manifested only through market decisions based on price, leaving the impression that production is merely the precipitate of an enlightened rationality. The structure of the economy appears as the objectivized consequence of practical behavior, rather than a social organization of things, by the institutional means of the market, but according to a cultural design of persons and goods.

Utilitarianism, however, is the way the Western economy, indeed the entire society, is experienced: the way it is lived by the participating subject, thought by the economist. From all vantages, the process seems one of material maximization: the famous allocation of scarce means among alternative ends to obtain the greatest possible satisfaction—or, as Veblen put it, getting something for nothing at the cost of whom it may concern. On the productive side, material advantage takes the form of added pecuniary value. For the consumer, it is more vaguely understood as the return in "utility" to monetary disbursements; but even here the appeal of the product consists in its purported functional superiority to all available alternatives (cf. Baudrillard 1968). The latest model automobile—or refrigerator, style of clothing, or brand of toothpaste—is by some novel feature or other more convenient, better adapted to "modern living," more comfortable, more healthful, sexier, longer-lasting, or better-tasting than any competing product.[1] In the native conception, the economy is an arena of pragmatic action. And society is the formal outcome. The main relations of class and politics, as well as the conceptions men entertain of nature and of themselves, are generated by this rational pursuit of material happiness. As it were, cultural order is sedimented out of the interplay of men and groups severally acting on the objective logic of their material situations:

> Till jarring interests of themselves create
> The according music of a well-mixed state. . . .
> Thus God and Nature linked the general frame,
> And bade Self-love and Social be the same.
> [Alexander Pope, *Essay on Man*]

Such is the mode of appearance of our bourgeois society, and its common average social science wisdom. On the other hand, it is also common anthropological knowledge that the "rational" and "objective" scheme of any given human group is never the only one possible. Even in very similar material conditions, cultural orders and finalities may be quite dissimilar. For the material conditions, if always indispensable, are potentially "objective" and "necessary" in many different ways—according to the cultural selection by which they become effective "forces." Of course in one sense nature is forever supreme. No society can live on miracles, thinking to exist by playing her false. None can fail to provide for the biological continuity of the population in determining it culturally—can neglect to provide shelter in producing houses, or nourishment in distinguishing the edible from the inedible. Yet men do not merely "survive." They survive in a definite way. They reproduce themselves as certain kinds of men and women, social classes and groups, not as biological organisms or aggregates of organisms ("populations"). True that in so producing a cultural existence, society must remain within the limits of physical-natural necessity. But this has been considered axiomatic at least since Boas, and not even the most biological of cultural ecologies can claim any more: "limits of viability" are the mode of the practical intervention of nature in culture (cf. Rappaport 1967). Within these limits, any group has the possibility of great range of "rational" economic intentions, not even to mention the options of production strategy that can be conceived from the diversity of existing techniques, the example of neighboring societies, or the negation of either.

Practical reason is an indeterminate explanation of cultural form; to do any better, it would have to assume what it purports to explain—the cultural form. But allow me a justifiable "nervousness." Insofar as this applies to historical materialism, it is Marx who here criticizes Marx, if through the medium of a later anthropology. The point of these objections had already been anticipated in Marx's understanding of production as devoted not simply to the reproduction of the producers, but also to the social relations under which it is carried out. The principle is, moreover, interior to Marx's work in an even more general form. I repeat a seminal passage of *The German Ideology:* "This mode of production must not be considered simply as being the reproduction of physical existence of individuals. Rather it is a definite form of activity of these individuals, a definite form of expressing their life, a definite *mode of life* on their part" (Marx and Engels 1965, p. 32). Thus it was Marx who taught that men never produce absolutely, that is, as biological beings in a universe of physical necessity. Men produce objects for given *social* subjects, in the course of reproducing subjects by *social* objects.

Not even capitalism, despite its ostensible organization by and for pragmatic advantage, can escape this cultural constitution of an apparently objective praxis. For as Marx also taught, all production, even where it is governed by the commodity-form, by exchange-value, remains the production of use-values. Without consumption, the object does not complete itself as a product: a house left unoccupied is no house. Yet use-value cannot be specifically understood on the natural level of "needs" and "wants"—precisely because men do not merely produce "housing" or "shelter": they produce dwellings of definite sorts, as a peasant's hut, or a nobleman's castle. This determination of use-values, of a particular type of house as a particular type of home, represents a continuous process of social life in which men reciprocally define objects in terms of themselves and themselves in terms of objects.

Production, therefore, is something more and other than a practical logic of material effectiveness. It is a cultural intention. The material process of physical existence is organized as a meaningful process of social being—which is for men, since they are always culturally defined in determinate ways, the only mode of their existence. If it was Saussure who foresaw the development of a general semiology devoted to "the role played by signs in social life," it was Marx who provided the *mise-en-scène*. Situating society in history, and production in society, Marx framed the problematic of an anthropological science yet unborn. For the question he proposed to it contains its own answer, inasmuch as the question is the definition of symbol itself: How can we account for an existence of persons and things that cannot be recognized in the physical nature of either?

We have seen that Marx nevertheless reserved the symbolic quality to the object in its commodity-form (fetishism). Assuming that use-values transparently serve human needs, that is, by virtue of their evident properties, he gave away the meaningful relations between men and objects essential to the comprehension of production in any historical form. He left the question without an answer: "About the *system of needs* and the *system of labours*—at what point is this to be dealt with?"

In order to frame an answer, to give a cultural account of production, it is critical to note that the social meaning of an object that makes it useful to a certain category of persons is no more apparent from its physical properties than is the value it may be assigned in exchange. Use-value is not less symbolic or less arbitrary than commodity-value. For "utility" is not a quality of the object but a significance of the objective qualities. The reason Americans deem dogs inedible and cattle "food" is no more perceptible to the senses than is the price of meat. Likewise, what stamps trousers as masculine and skirts as feminine has no necessary connection with their physical properties or the relations arising therefrom. It is by their correlations in a symbolic system that pants are produced for men and skirts for women, rather than by the nature of the object per se or its capacity to satisfy a material need—just as it is by the cultural values of men and women that the former normally undertake this production and the latter do not. No object, no thing, has being or movement in human society except by the significance men can give it.[2]

Production is a functional moment of a cultural structure. This understood, the rationality of the market and of bourgeois society is put in another light. The famous logic of maximization is only the manifest appearance of another Reason, for the most part unnoticed and of an

entirely different kind. We too have our forebears. It is not as if we had
no culture: no symbolic code of objects—in relation to which the mechanism of supply-demand-price, ostensibly in command, is in reality the
servant.

Consider, for example, just what Americans do produce in satisfying
basic "needs" for food. . . .[3]

FOOD PREFERENCE AND TABU IN AMERICAN DOMESTIC ANIMALS

The aim of these remarks on American uses of common domestic animals will be modest: merely to suggest the presence of a cultural reason
in our food habits, some of the meaningful connections in the categorical distinctions of edibility among horses, dogs, pigs, and cattle. Yet the
point is not only of consuming interest; the productive relation of American society to its own and the world environment is organized by specific
valuations of edibility and inedibility, themselves qualitative and in no
way justifiable by biological, ecological, or economic advantage. The
functional consequences extend from agricultural "adaptation" to international trade and world political relations. The exploitation of the
American environment, the mode of relation to the landscape, depends
on the model of a meal that includes a central meat element with the
peripheral support of carbohydrates and vegetables—while the centrality of the meat, which is also a notion of its "strength," evokes the masculine pole of a sexual code of food which must go back to the Indo-
European identification of cattle or increasable wealth with virility.[4] The
indispensability of meat as "strength," and of steak as the epitome of
virile meats, remains a basic condition of American diet (note the training table of athletic teams, in football especially). Hence also a corresponding structure of agricultural production of feed grains, and in turn
a specific articulation to world markets—all of which would change over-
night if we ate dogs. By comparison with this meaningful calculus of
food preferences, supply, demand, and price offer the interest of institutional means of a system that does not include production costs in its
own principles of hierarchy. The "opportunity costs" of our economic
rationality are a secondary formation, an expression of relationships already given by another kind of thought, figured a posteriori within the
constraints of a logic of meaningful order. The tabu on horses and dogs
thus renders unthinkable the consumption of a set of animals whose
production is practically feasible and which are nutritionally not to be
despised. Surely it must be practicable to raise *some* horses and dogs for
food in combination with pigs and cattle. There is even an enormous
industry for raising horses as food for dogs. But then, America is the
land of the sacred dog.

A traditional Plains Indian or a Hawaiian (not to mention a Hindu) might be staggered to see how we permit dogs to flourish under the strictest interdictions on their consumption. They roam the streets of major American cities at will, taking their masters about on leashes and depositing their excrements at pleasure on curbs and sidewalks. A whole system of sanitation procedures had to be employed to get rid of the mess—which in the native thought, and despite the respect owed the dogs themselves, is considered "pollution." (Nevertheless, a pedestrian excursion on the streets of New York makes the hazards of a midwestern cow pasture seem like an idyllic walk in the country.) Within the houses and apartments, dogs climb upon chairs designed for humans, sleep in people's beds, and sit at table after their own fashion awaiting their share of the family meal. All this in the calm assurance that they themselves will never be sacrificed to necessity or deity, nor eaten even in the case of accidental death. As for horses, Americans have some reason to suspect they are edible. It is rumored that Frenchmen eat them. But the mention of it is usually enough to evoke the totemic sentiment that the French are to Americans as "frogs" are to people.

In a crisis, the contradictions of the system reveal themselves. During the meteoric inflation of food prices in the spring of 1973, American capitalism did not fall apart—quite the contrary; but the cleavages in the food system did surface. Responsible government officials suggested that the people might be well-advised to buy the cheaper cuts of meat such as kidneys, heart, or entrails—after all, they are just as nutritious as hamburger. To Americans, this particular suggestion made Marie Antoinette seem like a model of compassion. The reason for the disgust seems to go to the same logic as greeted certain unsavory attempts to substitute horsemeat for beef during the same period. The following item is reprinted in its entirety from the *Honolulu Advertiser* of 15 April 1973:

PROTEST BY HORSE LOVERS

WESTBROOK, Conn. (UPI)—About 25 persons on horseback and on foot paraded outside Carlson's Mart yesterday to protest the store's selling horsemeat as a cheap substitute for beef.

"I think the slaughter of horses for human consumption in this country is disgraceful," said protest organizer Richard Gallagher. "We are not at a stage yet in the United States where we are forced to kill horses for meat."

"Horses are to be loved and ridden," Gallagher said. "In other words, horses are shown affection, where cattle that are raised for beef . . . they've never had someone pet them or brush them, or anything like that. To buy someone's horse up and slaughter it, that, I just don't see it."

The market began selling horsemeat—as "equine round," "horsemeat porterhouse" and "horseburger"—on Tuesday, and owner Kenneth Carlson said about 20,000 pounds were sold in the first week.

Most butchers who sell horsemeat have purchased "real old, useless

horses" which would otherwise be sold "for dogfood and stuff like that,"
Gallagher said. But "now they're picking up the young horses. We can't
buy these horses now, because the killers are outbidding us."

The principal reason postulated in the American meat system is the
relation of the species to human society. "Horses are shown affection,
where cattle that are raised for beef . . . they've never had someone pet
them or brush them, or anything like that."[5] Let us take up in more
detail the domesticated series cattle-pigs-horses-dogs. All of these are in
some measure integrated in American society, but clearly in different
statuses, which correspond to degrees of edibility. The series is divisible,
first, into the two classes of edible (cattle-pigs) and inedible (horses-dogs),
but then again, within each class, into higher and less preferable categories of food (beef vs. pork) and more and less rigorous categories of
tabu (dogs vs. horses). The entire set appears to be differentiated by
participation as subject or object in the company of men. Moreover, the
same logic attends the differentiations of the edible animal into "meat"
and the internal "organs" or "innards." To adopt the conventional in-
cantations of structuralism, "everything happens as if" the food system
is inflected throughout by a principle of metonymy, such that taken as a
whole it composes a sustained metaphor on cannibalism.

Dogs and horses participate in American society in the capacity of
subjects. They have proper personal names, and indeed we are in the
habit of conversing with them as we do not talk to pigs and cattle.[6] Dogs
and horses are thus deemed inedible, for, as the Red Queen said, "It
isn't etiquette to cut anybody you've been introduced to." But as domestic cohabitants, dogs are closer to men than are horses, and their consumption is more unthinkable: they are "one of the family." Traditionally horses stand in a more menial, working relationship to people; if
dogs are as kinsmen, horses are as servants and nonkin. Hence the consumption of horses is at least conceivable, if not general, whereas the
notion of eating dogs understandably evokes some of the revulsion of
the incest tabu.[7] On the other hand, the edible animals such as pigs and
cattle generally have the status of objects to human subjects, living their
own lives apart, neither the direct complement nor the working instrument of human activities. Usually, then, they are anonymous, or if they
do have names, as some milk cows do, these are mainly terms of reference in the conversations of men. Yet as barnyard animals and scaven-
gers of human food, pigs are contiguous with human society, more so
than cattle (cf. Leach 1964, pp. 50–51). Correspondingly, cut for cut,
pork is a less prestigious meat than beef. Beef is the viand of higher
social standing and greater social occasion. A roast of pork does not have
the solemnity of prime rib of beef, nor does any part of the pig match
the standing of steak.

Edibility is inversely related to humanity. The same holds in the preferences and common designations applied to edible portions of the animal. Americans frame a categorical distinction between the "inner" and "outer" parts which represents to them the same principle of relation to humanity, metaphorically extended. The organic nature of the flesh (muscle and fat) is at once disguised and its preferability indicated by the general term "meat," and again by particular conventions such as "roast," "steak," "chops," or "chuck"; whereas the internal organs are frankly known as such (or as "innards"), and more specifically as "heart," "tongue," "kidney," and so on—except as they are euphemistically transformed by the process of preparation into such products as "sweetbreads."[8] The internal and external parts, in other words, are respectively assimilated to and distinguished from parts of the human body—on the same model as we conceive our "innermost selves" as our "true selves"—and the two categories are accordingly ranked as more or less fit for human consumption. The distinction between "inner" and "outer" thus duplicates within the animal the differentiation drawn between edible and tabu species, the whole making up a single logic on two planes with the consistent implication of a prohibition on cannibalism.

It is this symbolic logic which organizes demand. The social value of steak or roast, as compared with tripe or tongue, is what underlies the difference in economic value. From the nutritional point of view, such a notion of "better" and "inferior" cuts would be difficult to defend. Moreover, steak remains the most expensive meat even though its absolute supply is much greater than that of tongue; there is much more steak to the cow than there is tongue. But more, the symbolic scheme of edibility joins with that organizing the relations of production to precipitate, through income distribution and demand, an entire totemic order, uniting in a parallel series of differences the status of persons and what they eat. The poorer people buy the cheaper cuts, cheaper because they are socially inferior meats. But poverty is in the first place ethnically and racially encoded. Blacks and whites enter differentially into the American labor market, their participation ordered by an invidious distinction of relative "civilization." Black is in American society as the savage among us, objective nature in culture itself. Yet then, by virtue of the ensuing distribution of income, the "inferiority" of blacks is realized also as a culinary defilement. "Soul food" may be made a virtue. But only as the negation of a general logic in which cultural degradation is confirmed by dietary preferences akin to cannibalism, even as this metaphorical attribute of the food is confirmed by the status of those who prefer it.

I would not invoke "the so-called totemism" merely in casual analogy to the *pensée sauvage*. True that Lévi-Strauss writes as if totemism had retreated in our society to a few marginal resorts or occasional practices

(1963; 1966). And fair enough—in the sense that the "totemic operator," articulating differences in the cultural series to differences in natural species, is no longer a main architecture of the cultural system. But one must wonder whether it has not been replaced by species and varieties of manufactured objects, which like totemic categories have the power of making even the demarcation of their individual owners a procedure of social classification. (My colleague Milton Singer suggests that what Freud said of national differentiation might well be generalized to capitalism, that it is narcissism in respect of minor differences.) And yet more fundamental, do not the totemic and product-operators share a common basis in the cultural code of natural features, the significance assigned to contrasts in shape, line, color and other object properties presented by nature? The "development" that is effected by the *pensée bourgeoise* may consist mainly in the capacity to duplicate and combine such variations at will, and within society itself. But in that event, capitalist production stands as an exponential expansion of the same kind of thought, with exchange and consumption as means of its communication.

For, as Baudrillard writes in this connection, consumption itself is an exchange (of meanings), a discourse—to which practical virtues, "utilities," are attached only post facto:

> As it is true of the communication of speech, so it is likewise true of goods and products: consumption is exchange. A consumer is never isolated, any more than a speaker. It is in this sense that we must have a total revolution in the analysis of consumption. In the same way as there is no language simply because of an individual need to speak, but first of all language— not as an absolute, autonomous system but as a contemporary structure of the exchange of meaning, to which is articulated the individual interaction of speech—in the same sense neither is there consumption because of an objective need to consume, a final intention of the subject toward the object. There is a social production, in a system of exchange, of differentiated materials, of a code of meanings and constituted values. The functionality of goods comes afterward, adjusting itself to, rationalizing and at the same time repressing these fundamental structural mechanisms. [Baudrillard 1972, pp. 76–77][9]

The modern totemism is not contradicted by a market rationality. On the contrary, it is promoted precisely to the extent that exchange-value and consumption depend on decisions of "utility." For such decisions turn upon the social significance of concrete contrasts among products. It is by their meaningful differences from other goods that objects are rendered exchangeable: they thus become use-values to certain persons, who are correspondingly differentiated from other subjects. At the same time, as a modular construction of concrete elements combined by human invention, manufactured goods uniquely lend themselves to this type of discourse. Fashioning the product, man does not merely alienate his labor, congealed thus in objective form, but by the physical modifications he effects he sediments a thought. The object stands as a human concept outside itself, as man speaking to man through the medium of things. And the systematic variation in objective features is capable of serving, even better than the differences between natural species, as the medium of a vast and dynamic scheme of thought: because in manufactured objects many differences can be varied at once, and by a godlike manipulation—and the greater the technical control, the more precise and diversified this manipulation—and because each difference thus developed by human intervention with a view toward "utility" must have a significance and not just those features, existing within nature for their own reasons, which lend themselves to cultural notice. The bourgeois totemism, in other words, is potentially more elaborate than any "wild" (*sauvage*) variety, not that it has been liberated from a natural-material basis, but precisely because nature has been domesticated. "Animals produce only themselves," as Marx taught, "while men reproduce the whole of nature."[10]

Yet if it is not mere existence which men produce but a "definite *mode of life* on their part," it follows that this reproduction of the whole of nature constitutes an objectification of the whole of culture. By the systematic arrangement of meaningful differences assigned the concrete, the cultural order is realized also as an order of goods. The goods stand as an object code for the signification and valuation of persons and occasions, functions and situations. Operating on a specific logic of correspondence between material and social contrasts, production is thus the reproduction of the culture in a system of objects.

NOTES

1. Of course we know at some level that these claims are fraudulent, but this knowledge is only further evidence of the same principle, namely, the ordering power of gain. Having penetrated the secrets of advertising, taken away all substance and sense, what else is left but the gainful motive underneath all social form? Now, by the very abstractness and nakedness in which we discover it, its power is confirmed—even more so by the illusion that we have been able to determine it behind the mask of false claims.

2. In one respect, that of being less bound to a specific situation, use-value is more arbitrary than exchange-value, although in stricter association with concrete properties of the object. Marx was surely correct in understanding the commodity-value as a differential meaning established in the discourse of things, i.e., standing as the concept (*le signifié*) of a given object only by relations developed in the commercial discourse and not by reference to concrete properties.

In the latter respect, commodity-value is the more abstract. In order to enter into these determining relations, however, the object must be a use-value, i.e., have a conventional meaning assigned to its objective properties, such as to give it "utility" to certain persons. Since this meaning is a differential *valuation* of the properties, it cannot be grasped by the senses; but it is always connected to the sensible—hence use-value is the more concrete value. On the other hand, the utility-meaning can be invoked outside any specific action, being taken as the meaning of the object as such. But exchange-value is determinable only from the economic interaction of commodities, and differently in each such situation. It is bound to and stipulated within the discourse of commodities; outside the context of exchange, the object resumes the status of a use-value. Viewed thus, use-value is the more arbitrary; exchange-value is a pragmatic "shifter."

3. The discussion which follows is but a marginal gloss on the larger analysis of notions of edibility and relations to domestic animals launched by Douglas (1966, 1971); Leach (1964), and Lévi-Strauss (1966). See also Barthes (1961), R. Valeri (1971), and, on certain correspondences between social and zoological categories, Bulmer (1967) and Tambiah (1969). The intent here is not so much to contribute to the semiotic analysis as to stress the economic implications.

4. Cf. Benveniste (1969, vol. I) on Indo-European *pasu vīra;* for example: "it is as an element of mobile wealth that one must take the avestic *vīra* or *pasu vīra.* One designates by that term the ensemble of movable private property, men as well as animals" (p. 49). Or see the extensive discussion of the Latin *pecu, pecunia,* and *peculium* (pp. 55 ff.).

5. "Supposing an individual accustomed to eating dogs should inquire among us for the reason why we do not eat dogs, we could only reply that it is not customary; and he would be justified in saying that dogs are tabooed among us, just as much as we are justified in speaking of taboos among primitive people. If we were hard pressed for reasons, we should probably base our aversion to eating dogs or horses on the seeming impropriety of eating animals that live with us as our friends" (Boas 1965 [1938], p. 207).

6. French and American naming practices appear to differ here. Lévi-Strauss's observations on the names the French give animals (1966, pp. 204 ff.) apply only fractionally to American custom. A brief ethnographic inquiry is enough to show that the latter is quite complex in this regard. The general rule, however, is that named/unnamed : inedible/edible. The names of both dogs and horses (excluding racehorses) are sometimes "like stage names, forming a series parallel to the names people bear in ordinary life, or, in other words, metaphorical names" (ibid., p. 205)—e.g., Duke, King, Scout, Trigger. More often, however, the names used in English are descriptive terms, likewise metaphorical, but taken from the chain of discourse, Smokey, Paint, Blue, Snoopy, Spot, etc. The French reserve such names for cattle. Our cattle are generally unnamed, except for milk cows, which often have two-syllable human names (Bessie, Ruby, Patty, Rena—these were collected from informants). Work horses—as distinguished from riding horses—also had human names. Differences between related societies in these regards, as Lévi-Strauss (1973) points out, represent different cultural *découpages* or superpositions of the animal on the human series.

7. Leach develops this point in his important paper on English animal cate-

gories as fitting into a systematic set of correspondences between relations to people and relations to animals according to degrees of distance from self (1964, pp. 42–47 and appendix). Leach claims the scheme has wide validity, although not universality; of course, it would require some permutation for peoples who (for example) eat domestic dogs. The Hawaiians treat dogs destined for eating with great compassion, "and not infrequently, condescend to treat them with Poi [pounded taro] from their mouths" (Dampier 1971, p. 50). Dogs destined for eating, however, are never allowed to touch meat (Corney 1896 [1821], p. 117). It is not clear whether they are eaten by the family who raised them, or like Melanesian pigs, similarly coddled in the household, reserved for prestations to others.

8. The meat taxonomy is of course much more complex than these common appellations. Steak, for instance, has a whole vocabulary of its own, in which some organic reference occurs, although usually not the terms applied to the human body (sirloin, T-bone, etc.). Calves' liver is an exception to this entire discussion, the reasons for which I do not know.

9. Moreover, there is to this notion of communication a fundamental base, set down by Rousseau in his running debate with Hobbes: "But when it should prove true that this unlimited and indomitable covetousness shall have developed in all men to the point supposed by our sophist, still it would not produce that universal war of each against all of which Hobbes ventures to trace the odious *tableau*. This unchecked desire to appropriate all things is incompatible with that of destroying all fellow beings; and having killed everyone the victor would have only the misfortune of being alone in the world, and could enjoy nothing even as he had everything. Wealth in itself: What good does it do if it cannot be communicated; and what would it serve a man to possess the entire universe, if he were its only inhabitant?" (Rousseau 1964, 3:601).

10. "Les objets ne constituent ni une flore ni une faune. Pourtant ils donnent bien l'impression d'une végétation proliférante et d'une jungle, où le nouvel homme sauvage des temps modernes a du mal à retrouver les réflexes de la civilisation. Cette faune et cette flore, que l'homme a produit et qui reviennent l'encercler et l'investir . . . il faut tenter de les décrire . . . en n'oubliant jamais, dans leur faste et leur profusion, qu'elles sont le *produit d'une activité humaine,* et qu'elles sont dominées, non par des lois écologiques naturelles, mais par la loi de la valeur d'échange" (Baudrillard 1970, pp. 19–20).

BIBLIOGRAPHY

Barthes, Roland. 1961. Pour une psycho-sociologie de l'alimentation contemporaine. *Annales,* pp. 977–86.

Baudrillard, Jean. 1968. *Le système des objets.* Paris: Denoël-Gonthier.

1970. *La société de consommation.* Paris: S.G.P.P.

1972. *Pour une critique de l'économie politique du signe.* Paris: Gallimard.

Benveniste, Emile. 1969. *Le vocabulaire des institutions indo-européennes.* Vol. 1. *Economie, parenté, société.* Paris: Editions de Minuit.

Boas, Franz. 1965 (1938). *The Mind of Primitive Man.* New York: Free Press.

Bulmer, R. 1967. Why is the cassowary not a bird? A problem of zoological taxonomy among the Karam of the New Guinea highlands. *Man*, n.s., 2:5–25.

Corney, Peter. 1896 (1821). *Voyages in the Northern Pacific.* Honolulu: Thos. G. Thrum.

Dampier, Robert. 1971. *To the Sandwich Islands on H.M.S. Blonde.* Honolulu: University of Hawaii Press.

Douglas, Mary. 1966. *Purity and danger.* London: Routledge and Kegan Paul.

———. 1971. Deciphering a meal. In *Myth, symbol and culture,* ed. Clifford Geertz. New York: Norton.

Leach, Edward. 1964. Anthropological aspects of language: animal categories and verbal abuse. In *New directions in the study of language,* ed. Eric H. Lenneberg, pp. 23–63. Cambridge: MIT Press.

Lévi-Strauss, Claude. 1963. *Totemism.* Boston: Beacon Press.

———. 1966. *The Savage mind.* Chicago: University of Chicago Press.

———. 1973. Religion, langue et histoire: A propos d'un texte inédit de Ferdinand de Saussure. In *Méthodologie de l'histoire et des sciences humaines* (Mélanges en l'honneur de Fernand Braudel), pp. 325–33. Paris: Privat.

Marx, Karl, and Friedrich Engels. 1965. *The German Ideology.* London: Lawrence and Wishart.

Rappaport, Roy A. 1967. *Pigs for the ancestors.* New Haven: Yale University Press.

Rousseau, Jean Jacques. 1964. *Oeuvres complètes.* Vol. 3. *Du contrat social; écrits politiques.* Paris: Bibliothèque de la Pléiade.

Tambiah, S. J. 1969. Animals are good to think and good to prohibit. *Ethnology* 8: 423–59.

Valeri, Valerio. 1971. Study of traditional food supply in the southwest of France. *Ethnologia Scandinavica,* pp. 86–95.

NINE

Jokes

Mary Douglas

Anthropologists tend to approach ritual joking from scratch, with merely an introspective glance at the cases in which they themselves feel impelled to joke. Consequently they have treated joking rituals as if they arise spontaneously from social situations and as if the anthropologist's sole task is to classify the relations involved. The jokes have not been considered as jokes in themselves, nor has our own cultural tradition been applied to interpreting the joke situation. Certain new trends invite us now to make a more open approach. Anthropology has moved from the simple analysis of social structures current in the 1940s to the structural analysis of thought systems. One of the central problems now is the relation between categories of thought and categories of social experience. Joking as one mode of expression has yet to be interpreted in its total relation to other modes of expression.

Such an approach suggests that the alternatives of joking and of not joking would be susceptible to the kind of structural analysis which Leach (1961: 23) has applied to controlled and uncontrolled modes of mystical power. His original model for this was the linguistic patterning of voiced and unvoiced consonants; his sole concern to show that the contrasts were used in regular patterns. It was not relevant to his argument to ask whether the patterning of contrasted elements in the system of communication was arbitrary or not. But it is possible that the patterning of articulate and less articulate sounds corresponds to a similar patterning in the experiences which they are used to express. This question raises the general problem of the relation between symbolic systems and ex-

From Mary Douglas, *Implicit Meanings* (London: Routledge & Kegan Paul, 1975), pp. 90–114. Reproduced by permission of the publisher and the author.

perience. It is true that in language the process of symbolic differentiation may start with arbitrarily selected elements at the simple phonemic level and combine them into consistent patterns. But at more complex levels each sign carries into the patterning an ever richer load of association. To return to Leach's case of modes of mystical power, I have elsewhere argued (Douglas, 1966: 101–3) that the discrimination of articulate and inarticulate forms of mystical power is not arbitrary. The use of spell and rite is attributed to people occupying articulate areas of the social structure, the use of unconscious psychic powers to others in inarticulate areas. There is a play upon articulateness and its absence, both in the kinds of mystic power being wielded and in the areas of the social structure to which they are allocated. The same appropriateness of symbolic forms to the situations they express can be illustrated with ritual joking. I am confident that where the joke rite is highly elaborated, joking is not used merely diacritically to contrast with seriousness, but that the full human experience of the joke is exploited. If we could be clear about the nature of joking, we could approach the interpretation of the joke rite at a more profound level than hitherto.

Fortunately, a new, more general trend enables this generation to make a fresh approach to joke rites. At the turn of the century when European thought turned an analytic eye upon humour, anthropologists were either antiquarians or specialists, or both. It would not have been in the tradition to look to recent thinkers for illumination. When Radcliffe-Brown wrote on joking relations in the 1940s (Radcliffe-Brown, 1940, 1949) it was still natural that he should not have taken account of Bergson or Freud. Still less would he have turned to the surrealist movement, whose passionate frivolity would estrange one who wished above all to establish the scientific status of his subject. He therefore wrote on the subject of joking in a very desiccated perspective. But there is a great difference in the form in which Freud's ideas are now available to the ordinary public. For us, thanks largely to the surrealists, it is not possible to read new fiction, to go to the theatre, to read the catalogue of any exhibition of painting or sculpture without taking note of an attitude which derives from the thinkers of the beginning of this century. Awareness of the contrast between form and formlessness, and awareness of the subjective character of the categories in which experience is structured have become the cultural premises of our age. They are no longer erudite preoccupations of the learned, but get expressed at an entirely popular level. Continual experimentation with form has given us now an intuitive sympathy for symbolic behaviour which is, after all, a play upon form. What is implicit in some other cultures has become an implicit part of our own. At the same time we can also bring to bear a tradition of explicit analysis.

Thus we can have insights at the two levels necessary for understanding joking.

African joking institutions combine the following elements: first, a crude scatology; second, a range of specific relationships; and third, certain ritual occasions (namely funerals and purifications) expressed scatologically. The subject is therefore closely related to ritual pollution in general. I myself am drawn to it because I hope that it will prove possible to distinguish jokes from pollutions by analysing some aspects of humour. This is a task which I shirked in my essay on ritual pollution (1966).

As a key question in this exercise I take Griaule's controversy with Radcliffe-Brown about the whole status of so-called 'joking relationships'. According to Griaule (1948), the Dogon joking partners do not exchange witticisms but rather gross insults. Although Dogon find these exchanges very hilarious, Griaule found it arbitrary to fasten on the laughter-provoking aspect of a complex institution. Now what is the difference between an insult and a joke? When does a joke get beyond a joke? Is the perception of a joke culturally determined so that the anthropologist must take it on trust when a joke has been made? Is no general culture-free analysis of joking possible? When people throw excrement at one another whenever they meet, either verbally or actually, can this be interpreted as a case of wit, or merely written down as a case of throwing excrement? This is the central problem of all interpretation.

First, let me bracket aside the whole subject of laughter. It would be wrong to suppose that the acid test of a joke is whether it provokes laughter or not. It is not necessary to go into the physiology and psychology of laughter, since it is generally recognised that one can appreciate a joke without actually laughing, and one can laugh for other reasons than from having perceived a joke. As the two experiences are not completely congruent, I shall only touch on laughter incidentally. Here I am following Bergson, whose essay on laughter was first published in 1899 in the *Revue de Paris,* and Freud (1916), whose analysis of wit, first published in 1905, says very little about laughter.

Both Bergson and Freud assume that it is possible to identify a structure of ideas characteristic of humour. If this were a valid assumption, all that would be necessary here would be to identify this joke form in the African joke rite. But in practice, it is a very elusive form to nail down. We face the dilemma either of finding that all utterances are capable of being jokes, or that many of those which pass for jokes in Africa do not conform to the laid-down requirements. My argument will be that the joke form rarely lies in the utterance alone, but that it can be identified in the total social situation.

Bergson and Freud are in fact very close: the difference between them lies in the different place of joke analysis in their respective philosophies. Bergson's reflections on laughter are a distillation of his general philosophy on the nature of man. He takes humour as a field in which to demonstrate the superiority of intuition to logic, of life to mechanism. It is part of his general protest against the threatened mechanisation of humanity. According to Bergson the essence of man is spontaneity and freedom: laughter asserts this by erupting whenever a man behaves in a rigid way, like an automaton no longer under intelligent control. 'Humour consists in perceiving something mechanical encrusted on something living' (1950: 29). It is funny when persons behave as if they were inanimate things. So a person caught in a repetitive routine, such as stammering or dancing after the music has stopped, is funny. Frozen posture, too rigid dignity, irrelevant mannerism, the noble pose interrupted by urgent physical needs, all are funny for the same reason. Humour chastises insincerity, pomposity, stupidity.

This analysis is adequate for a vast number of funny situations and jokes. There is no denying that it covers the style of much African joking, the grotesque tricks of Lodagaba funeral partners (Goody, 1962) and the obscene insults of Dogon and Bozo joking partners (Griaule, 1948). But I find it inadequate for two reasons. First, it imports a moral judgment into the analysis. For Bergson the joke is always a chastisement: something 'bad', mechanical, rigid, encrusted is attacked by something 'good', spontaneous, instinctive. I am not convinced either that there is any moral judgment, nor that if there is one, it always works in this direction. Second, Bergson includes too much. It is not always humorous to recognise 'something encrusted on something living': it is more usually sinister, as the whole trend of Bergson's philosophy asserts. Bergson's approach to humour does not allow for punning nor for the more complex forms of wit in which two forms of life are confronted without judgment being passed on either.

If we leave Bergson and turn to Freud, the essence of wit is neatly to span gulfs between different ideas. The pleasure of a joke lies in a kind of economy. At all times we are expending energy in monitoring our subconscious so as to ensure that our conscious perceptions come through a filtering control. The joke, because it breaks down the control, gives the monitoring system a holiday. Or, as Freud puts it, since monitoring costs effort, there is a saving in psychic expenditure. For a moment the unconscious is allowed to bubble up without restraint, hence the sense of enjoyment and freedom.

The late Anton Ehrenzweig (1953) extended the Freudian analysis of wit to aesthetic pleasure. In appreciating a work of art there is a perception of form, and underlying the articulate or dominant form there are other submerged forms half-perceived. These are inarticulate areas, subpatternings or reversals of the main theme. Ehrenzweig argues that the perception of inarticulate forms is itself a direct source of pleasure. The inarticulate forms are experienced as an image of the subconscious. As they are perceived there is a release of energy, for they allow the subconscious itself to be expressed. Aesthetic pleasure would then have this in common with the joy of a joke; something is saved in psychic effort, something which might have been repressed has been allowed to appear, a new improbable form of life has been glimpsed. For Bergson it is lifeless encrustation which is attacked in the joke, for Freud the joke lies in the release from control. If I may sum up the differences of emphasis between Bergson and Freud I would suggest that for Bergson the man who slips on a banana peel would be funny because he has lost his bodily control and so becomes a helpless automaton: for Freud this man would be funny because his stiff body has for two seconds moved with the swiftness of a gazelle, as if a new form of life had been hidden there. In short, they have a common approach which Freud uses more abstractly and flexibly. For both the essence of the joke is that something formal is attacked by something informal, something organised and controlled, by something vital, energetic, an upsurge of life for Bergson, of libido for Freud. The common denominator underlying both approaches is the joke seen as an attack on control.

Here we can see why scatology is potentially funny. Take any pun or funny story: it offers alternative patterns, one apparent, one hidden: the latter, by being brought to the surface impugns the validity of the first. Bergson said: 'Est comique tout incident qui appelle notre attention sur le physique d'une personne alors que le moral est en cause' (1950: 391). Reference to the physical pattern of events takes the dignity out of the moral pattern, yes. But this is not all. The symbols are not necessarily loaded the same way. Freud's approach is more complex because it allows that the relation of physical and moral could equally well be the other way round. What is crucial is that one accepted pattern is confronted by something else.

All jokes have this subversive effect on the dominant structure of ideas. Those which bring forward the physiological exigencies to which moral beings are subject, are using one universal, never-failing technique of subversion. But it would be a great mistake to think that humour can be reduced to scatology. Beidelman (1966) seems to do this, I think unintentionally, when he reduces Kaguru joking relations to cosmological ideas about dirt and sex. Structural analysis does not work by reducing all symbols to one or two of their number; rather, it requires an abstract statement of the patterned relations of all the symbols to one another. The same applies to moral bias. It may be incidentally worked into the structure of many jokes, but it is not the essence of joking. Compare the

Comedy of Errors with *Le Jeu de l'amour et du hazard.* In the latter, Beaumarchais makes the girl of noble birth pretend to be her own hand-
maiden so as to spy on her suitor; he adopts the same trick to observe
her unrecognised. The joke lies in the ridiculous display of valet and
handmaid disguised as lord and lady. In Bergson's terms the essence of
the joke is that 'something living', natural nobility, triumphs over 'something encrusted', false imitation of breeding. Shakespeare, on the other
hand, does not moralise when he successfully entangles the separate worlds
of twin brothers and their twin servants and disengages them at the end.
His is no less a comedy for all that the social messages are weaker.

By this stage we seem to have a formula for identifying jokes. A joke
is a play upon form. It brings into relation disparate elements in such a
way that one accepted pattern is challenged by the appearance of another which in some way was hidden in the first. I confess that I find
Freud's definition of the joke highly satisfactory. The joke is an image
of the relaxation of conscious control in favour of the subconscious. For
the rest of this article I shall be assuming that any recognisable joke falls
into this joke pattern which needs two elements, the juxtaposition of a
control against that which is controlled, this juxtaposition being such
that the latter triumphs. Needless to say, a successful subversion of one
form by another completes or ends the joke, for it changes the balance
of power. It is implicit in the Freudian model that the unconscious does
not take over the control system. The wise sayings of lunatics, talking
animals, children and drunkards are funny because they are not in control; otherwise they would not be an image of the subconscious. The joke
merely affords opportunity for realising that an accepted pattern has no
necessity. Its excitement lies in the suggestion that any particular ordering of experience may be arbitrary and subjective. It is frivolous in that
it produces no real alternative, only an exhilarating sense of freedom
from form in general.

SOCIAL CONTROL OF PERCEPTION

While hailing this joke pattern as authentic, it is a very different matter
to use it for identifying jokes. First we should distinguish standardised
jokes, which are set in a conventional context, from spontaneous jokes.
Freud's claim to have found the same joke pattern in all joking situations
hides an important shift in levels of analysis. The standard joke, starting
for instance with 'Have you heard this one?' or 'There were three men,
an Irishman, etc.', contains the whole joke pattern within its verbal form.
So does the pun. The joke pattern can easily be identified within the
verbal form of standard jokes and puns. But the spontaneous joke or-
ganises the total situation in its joke pattern. Thus we get into difficulties

in trying to recognise the essence of a spontaneous joke if we only have
the utterance or the gesture and not the full pattern of relationships. If
the Kaguru think it witty to throw excrement at certain cousins or the
Lodagaba to dance grotesquely at funerals or the Dogon to refer to the
parents' sexual organs when they meet a friend, then to recognise the
joke that sends all present into huge enjoyment we need not retreat into
cultural relativism and give up a claim to interpret. The problem has
merely shifted to the relation between joking and the social structure.

The social dimension enters at all levels into the perception of a joke.
Even its typical patterning depends on a social valuation of the elements.
A twentieth-century audience finds the Beaumarchais comedy weak because it one-sidedly presents the aristocrats' manners as live and their
servants' manners as lifeless imitations. But to an eighteenth-century audience of French aristocrats any dramatist presenting both lords and
commoners as equally lively in their own right would have had, not a
comedy, but a theme of social reform to tempt only a Bernard Shaw in
his most tendentious vein. In every period there is a pile of submerged
jokes, unperceived because they are irrelevant or wrongly balanced for
the perspective of the day. Here let me try to save the definition of the
joke pattern from the charge that it does not include modern forms of
humour, such as the shaggy dog story or the sick joke. The shaggy dog
is only told in a society which has been satiated with joke stories. The
joke of the tale that goes on in a declining spiral to a nadir of pointless-
ness lies in the dashed expectations of the listeners: the humour is not
in the verbal utterances but in the total situation in which it is a practical
joke. The sick joke expresses a parallel sophistication in joke forms. It
plays with a reversal of the values of social life; the hearer is left uncertain which is the man and which the machine, who is the good and who
the bad, or where is the legitimate pattern of control. There is no need
to labour the point that such a joke form relates to a particular kind of
social experience and could not be perceived by those who have not been
exposed to a thoroughgoing relativising of moral values.

So much for the social control of perception. As to the permitting of
a joke, there are jokes which can be perceived clearly enough by all present but which are rejected at once. Here again the social dimension is
at work. Social requirements may judge a joke to be in bad taste, risky,
too near the bone, improper, or irrelevant. Such controls are exerted
either on behalf of hierarchy as such, or on behalf of values which are
judged too precious and too precarious to be exposed to challenge.
Whatever the joke, however remote its subject, the telling of it is potentially subversive. Since its form consists of a victorious tilting of uncon-
trol against control, it is an image of the levelling of hierarchy, the triumph
of intimacy over formality, of unofficial values over official ones. Our

question is now much clearer. We must ask what are the social conditions for a joke to be both perceived and permitted. We could start to answer it by examining the literature of various joking situations. My hypothesis is that a joke is seen and allowed when it offers a symbolic pattern of a social pattern occurring at the same time. As I see it, all jokes are expressive of the social situations in which they occur. The one social condition necessary for a joke to be enjoyed is that the social group in which it is received should develop the formal characteristics of a 'told' joke: that is, a dominant pattern of relations is challenged by another. If there is no joke in the social structure, no other joking can appear.

Take as an example Fredrik Barth's (1966) analysis of the social situation on board a Norwegian fishing boat. Here the skipper is in full charge of the crew until the boats are lowered into the water. Then the net boss takes over. Before that point the net boss is not subject to the skipper as are other crew members. He is there on the boat, nominally under the skipper, but potentially a source of authority which will supplant the skipper for a brief period. There is in this social pattern the perfect joke form. All the time that the skipper and the other members of the crew are busily expressing superordination and subordination within the frame of common commitment to the enterprise, the net boss expresses his detachment and individuality by witty sallies. As soon as he takes over responsibility, however, his joking stops short. The essential point is that the joking by the net boss expresses a pattern of authority which arises out of the technicalities of fishing: it does nothing to create the situation, it merely expresses it.

Take as a second example the rather unexpected story about laughter in the beginning of The *Iliad*. At first sight the social situation seems to be all wrong, if my account of a proper joke form is accepted. Thersites, a common soldier, insults the Greek leaders; Odysseus strikes him brutally with a metal studded rod; Thersites is crushed and the troops have a hearty laugh at his expense. On this showing there seems to be no joke to provoke the laughter, for the Greek leaders represent the dominant elements in the social structure. Odysseus's act merely asserts their authority. But this would be to take the story out of context. The Greek leaders' plan to mount a new attack on Troy is about to be thwarted by their men. The argument between Odysseus and Thersites takes place when the former has been trying singlehanded to check a wild dash for the ships by hordes of men who have been nine years away from home. In the context of threatened mob rule, the leaders are not the dominant element in the pattern, but the weak, endangered element. One could say that everyone laughs with relief that their scramble for home is not allowed to overwhelm the delicate balance of power between a handful of leaders and a mass of followers. Thersites, the rude and ugly cripple, usually takes Odysseus and Achilles for his butts; this time the pattern is reversed. The men laugh to find themselves on the side of the leaders, in reverse of their behaviour a short time before.

As a final example, I would like to turn to the parables in the New Testament to suggest that when the social structure is not depicted, it is unlikely that we can perceive 'told' jokes even when the joke form is clearly present in the verbal utterance. Many of the parables have an obvious joke pattern: the kingdom of heaven likened to a mustard seed (Luke 13: 19; Mark 4: 31–2), the prayers of the complacent Pharisee placed second after the humble prayer of the publican (Luke 18: 10–14), the guest who takes the lowest place and is brought up to the top, to cite a few. Many incidents in the Gospel narrative itself also have a joke form, the wedding at Cana to take only one. But whereas the Gospel incidents present little difficulty in the light of the messages that 'the things that are impossible with men are possible with God' (Luke 18: 27), some of the parables do. Why was the poor fellow with no wedding garment bound and cast into the place of darkness with weeping and gnashing of teeth (Matthew 22: 11–14)? Why was the unjust steward commended for making friends with Mammon (Luke 16: 1–9)? How does this accord with the message of love and truth? I suggest that the difficulties arise because we are lacking signals from the social situation. Suppose that the Galilee audience, as soon as it heard 'Let me tell you a parable' settled into the same expectant joking mood that we do on hearing 'Do you know the riddle about . . . ?' Then we could interpret the parables frankly as jokes, told at a rattling pace, with dramatic pauses for effect, each reaching higher and higher climaxes of absurdity and ridicule. The punishment of the man with no wedding garment then appears as a necessary correction to the obviously funny story of the rich man whose social equals, having refused his invitation to a feast, found their places were filled by beggars from the street (Matthew 22: 2–10). Could the kingdom of heaven be filled with any kind of riff-raff then? No—that would be to miss the point of the story. True, the socially uppermost are not necessarily the best qualified for the kingdom of heaven. But to correct the wrong impression about riff-raff, a new joke has to be introduced against the gate-crasher. There will be more to say later about the joke form as a vehicle of religious thought.

I hope that I have established that a joke cannot be perceived unless it corresponds to the form of the social experience: but I would go a step further and even suggest that the experience of a joke form in the social structure calls imperatively for an explicit joke to express it. Hence the disproportionate joy which a feeble joke often releases. In the case of a bishop being stuck in the lift, a group of people are related together in a newly relevant pattern which overthrows the normal one: when one of them makes the smallest jest, something pertinent has been said about the social structure. Hence the enthusiasm with which a joke at the right time is always hailed. Whatever happens next will be seen to be funny: whether the lowliest in the no longer relevant hierarchy discovers the right switch and becomes saviour of the mighty, or whether the bishop himself turns out to be the best mechanic, the atmosphere will become heady with joy, unless the bishop has made the mistake of imposing the external hierarchy.

To the pleasure of the joke itself, whatever that may be, is added enjoyment of a hidden wit, the congruence of the joke structure with the social structure. With laughter there is a third level of appositeness: for disturbed bodily control mirrors both the joke structure and the social structure. Here there is the germ of an answer to the puzzle of why tickling should provoke laughter, discussed by Koestler (1964).

Tickling, says Koestler, using the same Bergson-Freud analysis of wit, is funny because it is interpreted as a mock attack. The baby laughs more when it is tickled by its own mother than by a stranger; with strangers one can never be sure (Koestler, 1964: 80–2). But to the uncertainty about whether a stranger is really making a serious or a mock attack add the fact that there is no social relation with strangers. Hence the wit is not in play in the social dimension to anything like the same extent. From the content of the joke, to the analogy of the joke structure with the social structure, on to the analogy of these two with the physical experience, the transfer of formal patterns goes on even to a fourth level, that revealed by Freud. A joke unleashes the energy of the subconscious against the control of the conscious. This, I argue, is the essential joke experience, a fourfold perception of the congruence of a formal pattern.

JOKES AS RITES

In classing the joke as a symbol of social, physical and mental experience, we are already treating it as a rite. How then should we treat the joke which is set aside for specified ritual occasions?

Once again, as with standardised and spontaneous jokes, it is necessary to distinguish spontaneous rites from routinised or standard rites. The joke, in its social context as we have discussed it so far, is a spontaneous symbol. It expresses something that is happening, but that is all. The social niche in which it belongs is quite distinct from that of ritual which is enacted to express what ought to happen. Similarly, the spontaneous rite is morally neutral, while the standard rite is not. Indeed, there is a paradox in talking about joke rites at all, for the peculiar expressive character of the joke is in contrast with ritual as such. Here I need to return to the general idea of joke structure derived from Freud, and to contrast the way a joke relates disparate ideas with the way a standard ritual does the same.

A standard rite is a symbolic act which draws its meaning from a cluster of standard symbols. When I use the word 'rite' in what follows, I combine the action and the cluster of symbols associated with it. A joke has it in common with a rite that both connect widely differing concepts. But the kind of connection of pattern A with pattern B in a joke is such that B disparages or supplants A, while the connection made in a rite is such that A and B support each other in a unified system. The rite imposes order and harmony, while the joke disorganises. From the physical to the personal, to the social, to the cosmic, great rituals create unity in experience. They assert hierarchy and order. In doing so, they affirm the value of the symbolic patterning of the universe. Each level of patterning is validated and enriched by association with the rest. But jokes have the opposite effect. They connect widely differing fields, but the connection destroys hierarchy and order. They do not affirm the dominant values, but denigrate and devalue. Essentially a joke is an anti-rite.

I have analysed elsewhere (Douglas, 1966: 114–28) rituals which use bodily symbolism to express ideas about the body politic. The caste system in India is a case in point. The symbolism underlying the ideas about pollution and purification has something in common with wit; it transfers patterns of value on a declining slope of prestige from one context to another with elegant economy. The lowest social ranks in the caste system are those required to perform social functions equivalent to the excretory functions of the body. There is the basis for a joke in the congruence of bodily and social symbolism, but the joke is absent since two patterns are related without either being challenged. The hierarchy is not undermined by the comparison, but rather reinforced.

Totemic systems make play with formal analogues. The same patterns are transposed from context to context with exquisite economy and grace. But they are not funny. One of the essential requirements of a joke is absent, the element of challenge. I give an example from Madame Calame-Griaule's recent book (1966) on Dogon language. She has analysed something that might be called a kind of linguistic totemism. The Dogon use a limited number of classes of speech as a basis for classifying wide ranges of other experience. With speech of the market place, for instance, are classified commerce and weaving. There is an obvious analogy from two kinds of constructive interaction. Here we have economy in connecting up disparate activities, but no humour. Take the class of speech that Dogon call 'trivial speech', the speech of women. This includes certain forms of insect, animal and human life. The controlling idea for the class associated with 'trivial speech' is dissipation. The work in this class is the sower's broadcasting of seed; the red monkey who comes to eat the crops after the farmer has planted is the appropriate animal in the class; the despised Fulani herder who pastures his cattle on the stubble after harvesting it is the human associated with it. The insect is the grasshopper, alleged to defecate as fast as it eats, an obvious type of fruitless effort. The references to despised forms of activity and to uncontrolled bowel movements has a derogatory implication for the idle chatter of women. The range of behaviour on which the pattern of 'trivial speech' is imposed degenerates from human Dogon to human Fulani, from human to animal pest, then to insect pest and finally to the excretory functions of the body. As the classification moves down from one context to the next, it slights and devalues. There is the possibility of a joke here. If it were challenging the known pretensions of women to utter important speech, it would have the making of a joke. But, given the low place of women in Dogon esteem, it is more likely to be the deadly earnest affirmation of male superiority, in which case this classification supports the established social order. The message of a standard rite is that the ordained patterns of social life are inescapable. The message of a joke is that they are escapable. A joke is by nature an anti-rite.

When joking is used in a ritual, it should be approached none the less as a rite. Like any other rite the joke rite is first and foremost a set of symbols. Its symbolism draws on the full experience of joking, just as communion rites draw on the full experience of eating, right down to the digestive process, and sexual rites and sacrifice draw on the experience of sex and death. So we should expect the joke rite to exploit all the elements of the joke in its essential nature. This will give the full explanation of ritual joking. Jokes, being themselves a play upon forms, can well serve to express something about social forms. Recall that the joke connects and disorganises. It attacks sense and hierarchy. The joke rite then must express a comparable situation. If it devalues social structure, perhaps it celebrates something else instead. It could be saying something about the value of individuals as against the value of the social relations in which they are organised. Or it could be saying something about different levels of social structure; the irrelevance of one obvious level and the relevance of a submerged and unappreciated one.

John Barnes (1954: 43) used the term 'network' to indicate an undifferentiated field of friendship and acquaintance. In his Morgan Lectures, Victor Turner has suggested that the word 'community' could be applied to this part of social life. In 'community' the personal relations of men and women appear in a special light. They form part of the ongoing process which is only partly organised in the wider social 'structure'. Whereas 'structure' is differentiated and channels authority through the system, in the context of 'community', roles are ambiguous, lacking hierarchy, disorganised. 'Community' in this sense has positive values associated with it; good fellowship, spontaneity, warm contact. Turner sees some dionysian ritual as expressing the value of 'community' as against 'structure'. This analysis gives a better name to, and clarifies, what I have elsewhere crudely called the experience of the non-structure in contrast to the structure (Douglas, 1966: 102). Laughter and jokes, since they attack classification and hierarchy, are obviously apt symbols for expressing community in this sense of unhierarchised, undifferentiated social relations.

Peter Rigby (1968) has developed this approach in his survey of all types of relationship in which joking is required in Gogo culture. He starts with interclan joking, then goes on to affinal joking, grandparent / grandchild joking, and finally joking between mother's brother and sister's sons and between cross-cousins. Each kind of joking has its own rules and quality of joke required. He concludes from his survey that he needs the concept of 'community' as distinct from 'structure' in order to interpret this pattern of behaviour: 'In Gogo society it is relationships with and through women which establish the "community"; that is affinal, matrilateral and uterine kin' (Rigby, 1968: 152).

Interclan links and links with aliens and enemies are included in a general class along with links through women. Starting from an ego-centred universe of kin, the Gogo have developed a cosmic model: joking categories are contrasted with control categories; joking categories are links or mediators between different organised domains. Gogo use the idea of joking categories to express the fading out of social control at all points and in all directions. It is a boundary image, but the boundaries are fuzzy and face two ways; one is structured, the other is unstructured. Boundaries connect as well as separate. Women are the boundaries of the patrilineal lineage. Affines stand out of reach of clan and lineage control but they are links. Clans are bounded as clans, but are linked by exogamy. 'Grandfathers are links or mediators with the unstructured world of the spirits of the dead who are not distinguished on the basis of lineal descent' (Rigby, 1968: 152).

Here we have an analysis which brings out cosmological implications hidden in the nature of joking. A joke confronts one relevant structure by another less clearly relevant, one well-differentiated view by a less coherent one, a system of control by another independent one to which it does not apply. By using jokes at social boundary points the Gogo are being witty at several levels: they comment on the nature of society, and on the nature of life and death. Their joke rites play upon one central abstraction, the contrast of articulation, and they develop the application of this symbol with the energy of inveterate punners. At the division of meat at a funeral, the heirs are told by the elders to speak clearly: if they mumble the sister's son will take everything (Rigby, 1968: 149). Here is an explicit reference to articulateness in speech as the symbol of structured relationships and inarticulateness as the symbol of the personal, undifferentiated network.

The interpretation of the Gogo joke rites as an abstract statement of two kinds of social interaction is highly satisfactory. The interpretation of Kaguru joke rites as an expression of an association made between sex, filth and liminality I find dubious. According to Beidelman, the Kaguru use joking to express 'liminal' relations, that is ambiguous ones. The range of relationships in which Kaguru require joking is much the same as the range of Gogo joking relations. It would seem plausible that the ego-oriented view of social life (as either differentiated by a pattern of control or undifferentiated), is enough to warrant joking between these categories, and that dirt is an apt enough expression of undifferentiated, unorganised, uncontrolled relations.

It still remains to distinguish jokes in general from obscenity as such. They are obviously very close. A joke confronts one accepted pattern with another. So does an obscene image. The first amuses, the second shocks. Both consist of the intrusion of one meaning on another, but whereas the joke discloses a meaning hidden under the appearance of the first, the obscenity is a gratuitous intrusion. We are unable to identify joke patterns without considering the total social situation. Similarly for obscenity, abominations depend upon social context to be perceived as such. Language which is normal in male company is regarded as obscene in mixed society; the language of intimacy is offensive where social distance reigns and, similarly, the language of the dissecting room where intimacy belongs. Inevitably, the best way of stating the difference between joking and obscenity is by reference to the social context. The joke works only when it mirrors social forms; it exists by virtue of its congruence with the social structure. But the obscenity is identified by its opposition to the social structure, hence its offence.

In the modern industrial world the categories of social life do not embrace the physical universe in a single moral order. If there is a social offence, there are moral implications such as cruelty, impiety, corruption of the innocent, and so on. But the social offence is not thought to release floods, famines or epidemics. Obscenity for us is a mild offence, since it can now be accounted for entirely in terms of offence against social categories. This leaves us unqualified to comprehend the much greater offence of obscenity in a primitive culture. For there the categories of social life co-ordinate the whole of experience: a direct attack on social forms is as disturbing as an attack on any of the symbolic categories in which the social forms are expressed—and vice versa. The idea of obscenity then has a much greater range and power, and the response it triggers is stronger. It is better to use a quite different word, such as abomination or ritual pollution, for the primitive cultures' equivalent to obscenity and to look for a much more whole-hearted and systematic wiping out of the offence than we can muster for dealing with obscenity.

Abomination is an act or event which contradicts the basic categories of experience and in doing so threatens both the order of reason and the order of society. A joke does nothing of the sort. It represents a temporary suspension of the social structure, or rather it makes a little disturbance in which the particular structuring of society becomes less relevant than another. But the strength of its attack is entirely restricted by the consensus on which it depends for recognition.

THE JOKER

Now we should turn to the role of the joker. He appears to be a privileged person who can say certain things in a certain way which confers immunity. He is by no means anything like a taboo breaker whose polluting act is a real offence to society. He *is* worth contrasting with persons undergoing rituals of transition, mourners and initiands. Symbolically, they are in marginal states, passing from one clearly defined status to another. They are held to be dangerous to themselves and to others until they have gone through the whole ritual of redefinition. In the symbolisation of the social structure, they have let go their moorings and are temporarily displaced. But the joker is not exposed to danger. He has a firm hold on his own position in the structure and the disruptive comments which he makes upon it are in a sense the comments of the social group upon itself. He merely expresses consensus. Safe within the permitted range of attack, he lightens for everyone the oppressiveness of social reality, demonstrates its arbitrariness by making light of formality in general, and expresses the creative possibilities of the situation.

From this we can see the appropriateness of the joker as ritual purifier. Among the Kaguru, certain common sexual offences such as sexual intercourse between affines are thought to bring illness, sterility or death on the kin of the two offenders. There are other graver sexual offences, but these relatively minor ones can be ritually cleansed by the joking partners of the transgressors (Beidelman, 1966: 361–2). A similar responsibility falling on joking partners among the Dogon led Griaule to describe their partnership as cathartic (1948). Rites of purification are a very widespread responsibility of joking partners in central and east Africa, as Stefaniszyn (1950) has pointed out. I myself commented (Tew, 1951) that the joking aspects of the relationships could not be understood without an analysis of the relation between joking and purification.

Now I suggest that the relevance of joking to purification emerges as another elaborate ritual pun. These rites make a double play on the joke experience: laughter itself is cathartic at the level of emotions; the joke consists in challenging a dominant structure and belittling it; the joker who provokes the laughter is chosen to challenge the relevance of the dominant structure and to perform with immunity the act which wipes out the venial offence.

The joker's own immunity can be derived philosophically from his apparent access to other reality than that mediated by the relevant structure. Such access is implied in the contrast of forms in which he deals. His jokes expose the inadequacy of realist structurings of experience and so release the pent-up power of the imagination.

Perhaps the joker should be classed as a kind of minor mystic. Though only a mundane and border-line type, he is one of those people who pass beyond the bounds of reason and society and give glimpses of a truth which escapes through the mesh of structured concepts. Naturally he is only a humble, poor brother of the true mystic, for his insights are given by accident. They do not combine to form a whole new vision of life, but remain disorganised as a result of the technique which produces them. He is distinctly gimmicky. One would expect him to be the object of a hilarious mythology, as among the Winnebago, but hardly the focus of a religious cult. And yet there he is, enshrined—Proteus in ancient Greece; the elephant god who gives luck and surprises in Hinduism; and the unpredictable, disruptive, creative force called Legba in Yoruba religion (Wescott, 1962). Needless to say, he is always a subordinate deity in a complex pantheon. The joker as god promises a wealth of new, unforeseeable kinds of interpretation. He exploits the symbol of creativity which is contained in a joke, for a joke implies that anything is possible.

It is much easier now to see the role of the joker at a funeral. By restraining excessive grief he asserts the demands of the living. I would expect joking at funerals to be more possible and more required the more the community is confident that it will turn the mourner's desolation into a temporary phase. Then the question is: who must joke and what should be his precise degree of relationship with the bereaved and the dead? The central African joking partner is a friend cultivated by gifts and hospitality, and is by definition not a close kinsman: his role at a funeral is to cheer the bereaved and to relieve them of the polluting duties of burial. There are here the elements of another ritual pun; for it is the kin who are ritually endangered by contact with the dead, the kin who are involved in the social structure of inheritance and succession, and it is the personal friend, the joking partner, who is uninvolved in the social structure and is the person who is immune from pollution of death.

There are many ways in which it can be appropriate to joke at a funeral. When a man dies his friends fall to reviewing his life. They try to see in it some artistic pattern, some fulfilment which can comfort him and them. At this moment obvious inconsistencies and disharmonies are distressing. If he is a great man, a national figure, of course his achievements are cited, but it seems important to be able to say that in his private life he also had fulfilled his family roles. If he is an ordinary citizen then the assessment of his success goes on entirely at the level of family and community. He is judged as a man, not as an item of social structure.

The role of the joker at the funeral could call attention to his individual personality. Indeed, in the Jewish *shib'ah*, a week of mourning after burial, the friends who come in to comfort the bereaved and praise the departed, invariably find themselves joking at his expense. Thus they affirm that he was an individual, not only a father or brother in a series of descending generations, but a man. So much for the social symbolism.

On the subject of funeral joking it is tempting to consider some metaphysical implications. A joke symbolises levelling, dissolution and recreation. As a symbol of social relations it is destructive (somewhat like fire?) and regenerative (somewhat like water?). The joke, working on its own materials, mimics a kind of death. Its form in itself suggests the theme of rebirth. It is no coincidence that practical jokes are common in initiation rites, along with more concrete expressions of dying and being reborn. When Jan Vansina underwent the Bushong boys' initiation (1955) he was continually involved in practical joking, either at the expense of non-initiates or at the expense of the group of novices to which he belonged. One after another the much dreaded ordeals were revealed to be only tricks.

METAPHYSICAL JOKES

If the joke form can symbolise so much, it could be capable of saying something about death itself in the context of religion.

We have traced the pun from its social to its psychological form, from these to its physical expression in laughter, and from the spontaneous symbol of social relationships to the standardised joke rite, expressing the value of less articulate sectors of social relationships compared with formalised structures. At funerals it expresses the value of the man himself, or the value of disinterested friendship or the value of the level of community in which most of a man's life is effective. It seems, after all this, not too bold to suggest that by the path of ritual joking these African cultures too have reached a philosophy of the absurd. By revealing the arbitrary, provisional nature of the very categories of thought, by lifting their pressure for a moment and suggesting other ways of structuring reality, the joke rite in the middle of the sacred moments of religion hints at unfathomable mysteries. This is the message which Turner attributes to the practical joke at the centre of the cult of Chihamba performed by the Ndembu tribe in Zambia.

First the initiates pay homage to the great white spirit, Kavula, as the source of all power; then as they approach his tabernacle, they are told to strike his effigy under a white cloth with their rattles, and then that they have killed him. Soon after they are told that they are innocent, and that he is not dead, and the paraphernalia under the white cloth is revealed to be no more than some everyday implements. Everyone then laughs joyfully. Following an elaborate exegesis, Turner (1962: 87) says:

> we have in Chihamba the local expression of a universal-human problem, that of expressing what cannot be *thought of*, in view of thought's subjugation to essences. It is a problem which has engaged the passionate attention of ritual man in all places and ages. It is a problem, furthermore, which has confronted artists, musicians and poets whenever these have gone beyond the consideration of aesthetic form and social manners.

It is unfortunate that Turner presented his novel interpretation of a primitive cult in neo-scholastic terms. The only serious consideration which his study has received attacks this presentation. Horton (1964) argues that the whole complex of ontological problems with which Turner has saddled Ndembu theologians, the distinction between the act-of-being itself (an act) and the concept of being (an essence) only makes sense in the terms of Thomist-Aristotelian philosophy. He deftly applies the logical positivist criticism to this approach. Further, Horton rejects the idea that 'a dominant concern to "say the unsayable" about the ultimate ground of all particular forms of existence' can be found in all African religions (1964: 96–7), still less, as Turner says, universally in all religions whatever.

These criticisms by-pass the main challenge of Turner's thesis. Merely to dare to interpret a ritual mock-killing of a god in one particular African religion as an attempt to express unfathomable mysteries about the inadequacy of the categories of thought for expressing the nature of existence is bold enough. Leave out Turner's claim that this is a universal human pre-occupation; it may be or it may not be. Forget his presentation in scholastic terms; it could as well have been presented through Kant or Kierkegaarde or modern phenomenologists as through Aquinas. It is still a daring claim that he makes for the profound meaning of an African joke rite. For all the subtlety and complexity with which he spins out the symbolism, my own first response was one of doubt. It was the first serious suggestion by a contemporary anthropologist that rituals which have no formal philosophical exegesis in their native culture could be concerned with problems about the relation of thought to experience which are, undeniably, a universal pre-occupation of philosophy. After reflecting on the use of the joke rite in Africa, I am now much more convinced that Turner may be right. African cultures have clearly reached an apotheosis of wit by playing upon the joke at various levels of meaning. It is not a great leap from attributing to the joke rite a subtle image of society to attributing also to it an image of the conditions of human knowledge.

But this is not the point at which I would wish to end this article. There is another implication which should be underlined: the social control of experience. It is here argued that the patterning of social forms limits and conditions the apprehension of symbolic forms. This may be extended from the perception of the joke form to the perception of other patterns, hierarchy, part-whole relations, unity, schism, incorporation, exclusion. The control exerted by experience in the social dimension over the perception of conceptual patterns is already taken into account in learning theory and in religious sociology. This study of the joke rite suggests that the achievement of consonance between different realms of experience is a source of profound satisfaction. It suggests that the drive to reduce dissonance may work at a more abstract level than has been recognised hitherto. The exercise of tracing the analogies drawn in joke rites gives additional meaning to Kandinsky's famous saying that the impact of an acute triangle on a circle produces an effect no less powerful than the finger of God touching the finger of Adam in Michelangelo's famous fresco.

BIBLIOGRAPHY

Barnes, J. A. (1954), 'Class and committees in a Norwegian island parish', *Hum. Relat.*, 7, 39–58.

Barth, Fredrik (1966), *Models of Social Organisation* (Occasional Papers Royal Anthropological Institute, 23), London, Royal Anthropological Institute.

Beidelman, T. O. (1966), '*Utani:* some Kagura notions of death, sexuality and affinity', *SWest. J. Anthrop.*, 22–4, 354–80.

Bergson, Henri (1950), *Le Rire: essai sur la signification du comique*, first published Paris, Presses Universitaires de France.

Calame-Griaule, G. (1966), *Ethnologie et langage: la parole chez les Dogon*, Paris, Gallimard.

Douglas, M. (1966), *Purity and Danger: an Analysis of Concepts of Pollution and Taboo*, London, Routledge & Kegan Paul.

Ehrenzweig, Anton (1953), *The Psychoanalysis of Artistic Vision and Hearing: a Theory of Unconscious Perception*, London, Routledge & Kegan Paul.

Freud, Sigmund (1916), *Wit and its Relation to the Unconscious* (trans. A. A. Brill), London, Fisher & Unwin.

Goody, J. R. (1962), *Death, Property and the Ancestors*, London, Tavistock Publications.

Griaule, Marcel (1948), 'L'Alliance cathartique', *Africa, 16,* 242–58.

Horton, R. (1964), 'Ritual Man in Africa', *Africa, 34,* 85–104.

Koestler, A. (1964), *The Act of Creation*, London, Hutchinson.

Leach, E. R. (1961), *Re-thinking Anthropology* (London School of Economics Monographs in Social Anthropology, 22), London, Athlone Press.

Radcliffe-Brown, A. R. (1940), 'On joking relationships', *Africa, 13,* 195–210.

Radcliffe-Brown, A. R. (1949), 'A further note on joking relationships', *Africa, 19,* 133–40.

Rigby, P. (1968), 'Joking relationships, kin categories and clanship among the Gogo', *Africa, 38,* 133–55.

Stefaniszyn, B. (1950), 'Funeral friendship in central Africa', *Africa, 20,* 290–306.

Tew, Mary (1951), 'A further note on funeral friendship', *Africa, 21,* 122–4.

Turner, V. W. (1962), *Chihamba, the White Spirit (Rhodes-Livingstone Papers, 33)*, Manchester University Press.

Vansina, J. (1955), 'Initiation rituals of the Bushong', *Africa, 25,* 138–52.

Wescott, J. (1962), 'The sculpture and myths of Eshu-Elegba the Yoruba trickster: definition and interpretation in Yoruba iconography', *Africa, 32,* 336–65.

PART III

Popular Culture in Sociological Studies

TEN

Processing Fads and Fashions

An Organization-Set
Analysis of Cultural Industry Systems[1]

Paul M. Hirsch

Some years ago I had the opportunity to study rather extensively and at
first hand the women's fashion industry. I was forcibly impressed by the
fact that the setting or determination of fashion takes place actually through
an intense process of selection. At a seasonal opening of a major Parisian
fashion house there may be presented a hundred or more designs of wom-
en's evening wear before an audience of from one to two hundred buyers.
The managerial corps of the fashion house is able to indicate a group of
about thirty designs of the entire lot, inside of which will fall the small
number, usually about six to eight designs, that are chosen by the buyers,
but the managerial staff is typically unable to predict this small number on
which the choices converge. Now, these choices are made by the buyers—
a highly competitive and secretive lot—independently of each other and
without knowledge of each other's selections. Why should their choices
converge on a few designs as they do? When the buyers were asked why
they chose one dress in preference to another—between which my inex-
perienced eye could see no appreciable difference—the typical, honest, yet
largely uninformative answer was that the dress was "stunning." [Blumer
1969, pp. 278–79]

The preselection of goods for potential consumption is a feature common to all industries. In order for new products or ideas to reach consumers, they must first be processed favorably through a system of organizations whose units filter out a large proportion of candidates before
they arrive at the consumption stage (Barnett 1953). Much theory and
research on complex organizations is concerned with isolated aspects of
this process by which innovations flow through organization systems—
such as the relation of research and development units to the industrial

This article first appeared in the *American Journal of Sociology* 77 (1972): 639–59. Reprinted
by permission of the author and the University of Chicago.

firm (Burns and Stalker 1961; Wilensky 1968); or problems encountered by public agencies attempting to implement new policy decisions (Selznick 1949; Bailey and Mosher 1968; Moynihan 1969).

Most studies of the "careers" of innovations, however, treat only the invention and the ultimate adoption stages as problematic. The "throughput" sector, comprised of organizations which filter the overflow of information and materials intended for consumers, is generally ignored.[2] Literature on the diffusion of innovations, for example, is concerned solely with the reception accorded a new product by consumers *subsequent* to its release into the marketplace by sponsoring organizations (Rogers 1962). From an organizational perspective, two questions pertaining to any innovation are logically prior to its experience in the marketplace: (1) by what criteria was it selected for sponsorship over available alternatives? and (2) might certain characteristics of its organizational sponsor, such as prestige or the size of an advertising budget, substantially aid in explaining the ultimate success or failure of the new product or idea?

In modern, industrial societies, the production and distribution of both fine art and popular culture entail relationships among a complex network of organizations which both facilitate and regulate the innovation process. Each object must be "discovered," sponsored, and brought to public attention by entrepreneurial organizations or nonprofit agencies before the originating artist or writer can be linked successfully to the intended audience. Decisions taken in organizations whose actions can block or facilitate communication, therefore, may wield great influence over the access of artist and audience to one another. The content of a nation's popular culture is especially subject to economic constraints due to the larger scale of capital investment required in this area to link creators and consumers effectively.[3]

This paper will outline the structure and operation of entrepreneurial organizations engaged in the production and mass distribution of three types of "cultural" items: books, recordings, and motion pictures. Entrepreneurial organizations in cultural industries confront a set of problems especially interesting to students of interorganizational relations, mainly: goal dissensus, boundary-spanning role occupants with nonorganizational norms, legal and value constraints against vertical integration, and, hence, dependence on autonomous agencies (especially mass-media gatekeepers) for linking the organization to its customers. In response to environmental uncertainties, mainly a high-risk element and changing patterns of distribution, they have evolved a rich assortment of adaptive "coping" strategies and, thus, offer a promising arena in which to develop and apply tentative propositions derived from studies of other types of organizations and advanced in the field of organization studies. Our focal organizations (Evan 1963) are the commercial publishing house, the movie studio, and the record company. My description of their operation is based on information and impressions gathered from (1) an extensive sampling of trade papers directed at members of these industries, primarily: *Publishers' Weekly, Billboard,* and *Variety;* (2) 53 open-ended interviews with individuals at all levels of the publishing, recording, and broadcasting industries;[4] and (3) a thorough review of available secondary sources.

DEFINITIONS AND CONCEPTUAL FRAMEWORK

Cultural products may be defined tentatively as "nonmaterial" goods directed at a public of consumers, for whom they generally serve an esthetic or expressive, rather than a clearly utilitarian function. Insofar as one of its goals is to create and satisfy consumer demand for new fads and fashions, every consumer industry is engaged to some extent in the production of cultural goods, and any consumer good can thus be placed along the implied continuum between cultural and utilitarian products. The two poles, however, should be intuitively distinct. Movies, plays, books, art prints, phonograph records, and pro football games are predominantly cultural products; each is nonmaterial in the sense that it embodies a live, one-of-a-kind performance and/or contains a unique set of ideas. Foods and detergents, on the other hand, serve more obvious utilitarian needs. The term "cultural organization" refers here only to *profit-seeking firms producing cultural products for national distribution.* Noncommercial or strictly local organizations, such as university presses and athletic teams, respectively, are thus excluded from consideration. A fundamental difference between entrepreneurial organizations and nonprofit agencies is summarized by Toffler (1965, pp. 181–82):

> In the non-profit sector the end-product is most frequently a live performance—a concert, a recital, a play. If for purposes of economic analysis we consider a live performance to be a commodity, we are immediately struck by the fact that, unlike most commodities offered for sale in our society, this commodity is not standardized. It is not machine made. It is a handicrafted item. . . . Contrast the output of the non-profit performing arts with that of the record manufacturer. He, too, sells what appears to be a performance. But it is not. It is a replica of a performance, a mass-produced embodiment of a performance. . . . The book publisher, in effect, does the same. The original manuscript of the poem or novel represents the author's work of art, the individual, the prototype. The book in which it is subsequently embodied is a [manufactured] replica of the original. Its form of production is fully in keeping with the level of technology in the surrounding society.

Our frame of reference is the cultural industry system, comprised of all organizations engaged in the process of filtering new products and ideas as they flow from "creative" personnel in the technical subsystem to the managerial, institutional, and societal levels of organization (Parsons 1960). Each industry system is seen as a single, concrete, and stable network of identifiable and interacting components. The concept of organization levels, proposed initially to analyze transactions within the boundaries of a single, large-scale organization, is easily applied to the analysis of interorganizational systems. Artist and mass audience are linked by an ordered sequence of events: before it can elicit any audience response, an art object first must succeed in *(a)* competition against others for selection and promotion by an entrepreneurial organization, and then in *(b)* receiving mass-media coverage in such forms as book reviews, radio-station air play, and film criticism. It must be ordered by retail outlets for display or exhibition to consumers and, ideally, its author or performer will appear on television talk shows[5] and be written up as an interesting news story. Drawing on a functionalist model of organizational control and facilitation of innovations proposed by Boskoff (1964), we view the mass media in their gatekeeping role as a primary "institutional regulator of innovation."

A number of concepts and assumptions implicit in this paper are taken from the developing field of interorganizational relations and elaborated on more fully by Thompson (1967).[6] Studies in this emerging tradition typically view all phenomena from the standpoint of the organization under analysis. It seldom inquires into the functions performed by the organization for the social system but asks rather, as a temporary partisan, how the goals of the organization may be constrained by society. The organization is assumed to act under norms of rationality, and the subject of analysis becomes its forms of adaptation to constraints imposed by its technology and "task environment." The term "organization-set" has been proposed by Evan (1963) as analogous to the role-set concept developed by Merton (1957) for analyzing role relationships:

> Instead of taking a particular status as the unit of analysis, as Merton does in his role-set analysis, I take ... an organization, or a class of organizations, and trace its interactions with the network of organizations in its environment, i.e., with elements of its organization-set. As a partial social system, a focal organization depends on input organizations for various types of resources: personnel, matériel, capital, legality, and legitimacy. . . . The focal organization in turn produces a product or a service for a market, an audience, a client system, etc. [Evan 1963, pp. 177–79]

After examining transactions between the focal organization and elements of its task environment,[7] we will describe three adaptive strategies developed by cultural organizations to minimize uncertainty. Finally, variations within each industry will be reviewed.

INPUT AND OUTPUT ORGANIZATION-SETS

The publishing house, movie studio, and record company each invests entrepreneurial capital in the creations and services of affiliated organizations and individuals at its input (product selection) and output (marketing) boundaries. Each effects volume sales by linking individual creators and producer organizations with receptive consumers and mass-media gatekeepers. New material is sought constantly because of the rapid turnover of books, films, and recordings.

Cultural organizations constitute the managerial subsystems of the industry systems in which they must operate. From a universe of innovations proposed by "artists" in the "creative" (technical) subsystem, they select ("discover") a sample of cultural products for organizational sponsorship and promotion. A distinctive feature of cultural industry systems at the present time is the organizational segregation of functional units and subsystems. In the production sector, the technical and managerial levels of organization are linked by boundary-spanning talent scouts—for example, acquisitions editors, record "producers," and film directors—located on the input boundary of the focal organization.

To this point, cultural industries resemble the construction industry and other organization systems characterized by what Stinchcombe (1959) calls "craft administration of production." The location of professionals in the technical subsystem, and administrators in the managerial one, indicates that production may be organized along craft rather than bureaucratic lines (Stinchcombe 1959). In the cultural industry system, lower-level personnel (artists and talent scouts) are accorded professional status and seldom are associated with any one focal organization for long time periods. Although company executives may tamper with the final product of their collaborations, contracted artists and talent scouts are *delegated* the responsibility of producing marketable creations, with little or no interference from the front office beyond the setting of budgetary limits (Peterson and Berger 1971). Due to widespread uncertainty over the precise ingredients of a best-seller formula, administrators are forced to trust the professional judgment of their employees. Close supervision in the production sector is impeded by ignorance of relations between cause and effect.[8] A highly placed spokesman for the recording industry (Brief 1964, pp. 4–5) has stated the problem as follows:

> We have made records that appeared to have all the necessary ingredients—artist, song, arrangements, promotion, etc.—to guarantee they wind up as best sellers. . . . Yet they fell flat on their faces. On the other hand we have produced records for which only a modest success was anticipated that became runaway best sellers. . . . There are a large number of companies in our industry employing a large number of talented performers and creative producers who combine their talents, their ingenuity and their

creativity to produce a record that each is sure will captivate the American public. The fact that only a small proportion of the output achieves hit status is not only true of our industry. . . . There are no formulas for producing a hit record . . . just as there are no pat answers for producing hit plays, or sell-out movies or best-selling books.

Stinchcombe's (1959, 1968) association of craft administration with a minimization of fixed overhead costs is supported in the case of cultural organizations. Here, we find, for example, artists (i.e., authors, singers, actors) contracted on a *royalty* basis and offered no tenure beyond the expiration of the contract. Remuneration (less advance payment on royalties) is contingent on the number of books, records, or theater tickets sold *after* the artist's product is released into the marketplace.[9] In addition, movie-production companies minimize overhead by hiring on a per-picture basis and renting sets and costumes as needed (Stinchcombe 1968), and publishers and record companies frequently subcontract out standardized printing and record-pressing jobs.

The organization of cultural industries' technical subsystems along craft lines is a function of *(a)* demand uncertainty and *(b)* a "cheap" technology. Demand uncertainty is caused by: shifts in consumer taste preferences and patronage (Gans 1964; Meyersohn and Katz 1957); legal and normative constraints on vertical integration (Conant 1960; Brockway 1967); and widespread variability in the criteria employed by mass-media gatekeepers in selecting cultural items to be awarded coverage (Hirsch 1969). A cheap technology enables numerous cultural organizations to compete in producing a surplus of books, records, and low-budget films on relatively small capital investments. The cost of producing and manufacturing a new long-play record or hard-cover book for the general public is usually less than $25,000 (Brief 1964; Frase 1968). Once sales pass the break-even point (about 7,000 copies for books and 12,000 for records, *very roughly*), the new product begins to show a profit.[10] On reaching sales of 20,000 a new book is eligible for best-seller status; "hit records" frequently sell over several hundred thousand copies each. Mass media exposure and volume sales of a single item generally cover earlier losses and yield additional returns. Sponsoring organizations tend to judge the success of each new book or record on the basis of its performance in the marketplace during the first six weeks of its release. Movies require a far more substantial investment but follow a similar pattern.[11]

These sources of variance best account for the craft administration of production at the input boundary of the cultural organization. It is interesting to note that in an earlier, more stable environment, that is, less heterogeneous markets and fewer constraints on vertical integration, the production of both films and popular records was administered more bureaucratically: lower-level personnel were delegated less responsibility, overhead costs were less often minimized, and the status of artists resembled more closely the salaried employee's than the free-lance professional's (Coser 1965; Brown 1968; Powdermaker 1950; Rosten 1941; Hughes 1959; Montagu 1964; Peterson and Berger 1971).

At their output boundaries, cultural organizations confront high levels of uncertainty concerning the commercial prospects of goods shipped out to national networks of promoters and distributors. Stratification within each industry is based partly on each firm's ability to control the distribution of marginally differentiated products. Competitive advantage lies with firms best able to link available input to reliable and established distribution channels. In the book industry, distribution "for the the great majority of titles is limited, ineffective, and costly. In part this weakness in distribution is a direct consequence of the strength of the industry in issuing materials. . . . If it were harder to get a book published, it would be easier to get it distributed" (Lacy 1963, pp. 53–54).[12]

The mass distribution of cultural items requires more *bureaucratic* organizational arrangements than the administration of production, for example, a higher proportion of salaried clerks to process information, greater continuity of personnel and ease of supervision, less delegation of responsibility, and higher fixed overhead (Stinchcombe 1959). Whereas the building contractor produces custom goods to meet the specifications of a clearly defined client-set, cultural organizations release a wide variety of items which must be publicized and made attractive to thousands of consumers in order to succeed. Larger organizations generally maintain their own sales forces, which may contract with smaller firms to distribute their output as well as the parent company's.

The more highly bureaucratized distribution sector of cultural industries is characterized by more economic concentration than the craft-administered production sector, where lower costs pose fewer barriers to entry. Although heavy expenditures required for product promotion and marketing may be reduced by contracting with independent sales organizations on a commission basis, this practice is engaged in primarily by smaller, weaker, and poorly capitalized firms. As one publishing company executive explains:

> If a company does not have a big sales force, it's far more difficult for them to have a best seller. But unless a firm does $7,500,000 worth of trade book business a year, they can't afford to maintain an adequate sales force. Many publishing houses, consequently, do not have any sales force at all. They rely on middlemen—jobbers—to get their books into bookstores. But jobbers, of course, don't attend sales conferences. They handle so many books for so many publishers that they can't be expected to "push" certain books from a certain house. [Mann 1967, p. 14]

Contracting with autonomous sales organizations places the entrepreneurial firm in a position of dependence on outsiders, with the attendant risk of having cultural products regarded highly by the sponsoring organization assigned a low priority by its distributor. In the absence of media coverage and/or advertising by the sponsoring organization, retail outlets generally fail to stock new books or records.

A functional equivalent of direct advertising for cultural organizations is provided by the selective coverage afforded new styles and titles in books, recordings, and movies by the mass media. Cultural products provide "copy" and "programming" for newspapers, magazines, radio stations, and television programs; in exchange, they receive "free" publicity. The presence or absence of coverage, rather than its favorable or unfavorable interpretation, is the important variable here. Public awareness of the existence and availability of a new cultural product often is contingent on feature stories in newspapers and national magazines, review columns, and broadcast talk shows, and, for recordings, radio-station air play. While the total number of products to be awarded media coverage may be predicted in the aggregate, the estimation of *which ones* will be selected from the potential universe is problematic.

The organizational segregation of the producers of cultural items from their disseminators places definite restrictions on the forms of power which cultural organizations may exercise over mass-media gatekeepers to effect the selection of particular items for coverage. Widely shared social norms mandate the independence of book-review editors, radio-station personnel, film critics, and other arbiters of coverage from the special needs and commercial interests of cultural organizations.[13] Thus, autonomous gatekeepers present the producer organization with the "control" problem of favorably influencing the probability that a given new release will be selected for exposure to consumers.

For publishing houses and record firms, especially, it would be uneconomical to engage in direct, large-scale advertising campaigns to bring more than a few releases to public attention.[14]

> The fact that each one of the thousands of titles every year must be separately advertised imposes almost insuperable obstacles in the way of effective national advertising. It is as though General Motors for each tenth Chevrolet had to change the name, design, and characteristics of the car and launch a new national advertising campaign to sell the next ten cars. . . . The advertising problem . . . is thus wholly different from that of the advertiser of a single brand that remains on sale indefinitely. [Lacy 1963, pp. 54–55]
> The publisher's advertising problem is greatly aggravated by what we have all agreed is true—too many books are published, most of them doomed in advance to a short and inglorious life. . . . Many a novel is dead the day

it is published, many others survive a month or two or three. The sales of such books are always small, and what little advertising they get may be rendered doubly useless by the fact that the bookseller tends to return to the publisher his stock of slow-moving books before they have had time to be exposed to very many potential customers. . . . Well then, what does make a book sell? Charles Darwin gave the right answer to Samuel Butler when he was asked this question: "Getting talked about is what makes a book sell." [Knopf 1964, p. 17]

Record companies are dependent on radio . . . to introduce new artists as well as to introduce new records of all artists and to get them exposed to the public. . . . [We] cannot expose their performances because it's just on grooves and the public will not know what they sound like. (Q.) "Would it be fair to say that radio accounts for 75, or 90 percent of the promotion of new releases?" (A.) I think your figures are probably accurate, yes. [Davis 1967, p. 5]

For book publishers, record companies, and, to a lesser extent, movie studios, then, the crucial target audience for promotional campaigns consists of autonomous gatekeepers, or "surrogate consumers" such as disk jockeys, film critics, and book reviewers, employed by mass-media organizations to serve as fashion experts and opinion leaders for their respective constituencies.

The mass media constitute the institutional subsystem of the cultural industry system. *The diffusion of particular fads and fashions is either blocked or facilitated at this strategic checkpoint.* Cultural innovations are seen as originating in the technical subsystem. A sample selected for sponsorship by cultural organizations in the managerial subsystem is introduced into the marketplace. This output is filtered by mass-media gatekeepers serving as "institutional regulators of innovation" (Boskoff 1964). Organizations in the managerial subsystem are highly responsive to feedback from institutional regulators: styles afforded coverage are imitated and reproduced on a large scale until the fad has "run its course" (Boskoff 1964; Meyersohn and Katz 1957).[15]

We see the consumer's role in this process as essentially one of rank ordering cultural styles and items "preselected" for consideration by role occupants in the managerial and institutional subsystems. Feedback from consumers, in the form of sales figures and box-office receipts, cues producers and disseminators of cultural innovations as to which experiments may be imitated profitably and which should probably be dropped.[16] This process is analogous to the preselection of electoral candidates by political parties, followed by voter feedback at the ballot box. The orderly sequence of events and the possibility of only two outcomes at each checkpoint resemble a Markov process.

This model assumes a surplus of available "raw material" at the outset (e.g., writers, singers, politicians) and pinpoints a number of strategic checkpoints at which the oversupply is filtered out. It is "value added" in the sense that no product can enter the societal subsystem (e.g., retail outlets) until it has been processed favorably through each of the preceding levels of organization, respectively.[17]

ORGANIZATIONAL RESPONSE TO TASK-ENVIRONMENT UNCERTAINTIES

Our analysis suggests that organizations at the managerial level of cultural industry systems are confronted by (1) constraints on output distribution imposed by mass-media gatekeepers, and (2) contingencies in recruiting creative "raw materials" for organizational sponsorship. To minimize dependence on these elements of their task environments, publishing houses, record companies, and movie studios have developed three proactive strategies: (1) the allocation of numerous personnel to boundary-spanning roles; (2) overproduction and differential promotion of new items; and (3) cooptation of mass-media gatekeepers.

Proliferation of Contact Men

Entrepreneurial organizations in cultural industries require competent intelligence agents and representatives to actively monitor developments at their input and output boundaries. Inability to locate and successfully market new cultural items leads to organizational failure: new manuscripts must be located, new singers recorded, and new movies produced. Boundary-spanning units have therefore been established, and a large proportion of personnel allocated to serve as "contact men" (Wilensky 1956), with titles such as talent scout, promoter, press coordinator, and vice-president in charge of public relations. The centrality of information on boundary developments to managers and executives in cultural organizations is suggested in these industries' trade papers: coverage of artist relations and selections by mass-media gatekeepers far exceeds that of matters managed more easily in a standardized manner, such as inflation in warehousing, shipping, and physical production costs.

Contact men linking the cultural organization to the artist community contract for creative raw material on behalf of the organization and supervise its production. Much of their work is performed in the field. In publishing, for example:

> "You have to get out to lunch to find out what's going on out there—and what's going on out there is where an editor's books come from," says James Silberman, editor-in-chief of Random House. "Over the years, I've watched people in the book business stop having lunch, and they stop getting books."

There are, in general, three kinds of publishing lunches. The first, and most common, takes place between editor and agent: its purpose is to generate book ideas for the agent's clients; also, it provides an opportunity for the agent to grow to like the editor enough to send him completed manuscripts. The second kind is set up by publicists with whomever they want to push their books: television people, critics, book-review editors. . . .

The third kind takes place between authors and editors, and it falls into three phases: the precontract phase, where the editor woos the author with good food and book ideas; the postcontract phase, where the author is given assistance on his manuscript and the impetus to go on; and the postpublication phase, where the editor explains to the author why the publishing house took so few advertisements for his book. [Ephron 1969, p. 8]

Professional agents on the input boundary must be allowed a great deal of discretion in their activities on behalf of the cultural organization. Successful editors, record "producers," and film directors and producers thus pose control problems for the focal organization. In fields characterized by uncertainty over cause/effect relations, their talent has been "validated" by the successful marketplace performance of "their discoveries"—providing high visibility and opportunities for mobility outside a single firm. Their value to the cultural organization as recruiters and intelligence agents is indicated by high salaries, commissions, and prestige within the industry system.

Cultural organizations deploy additional contact men at their output boundaries, linking the organization to (1) retail outlets and (2) surrogate consumers in mass-media organizations. The tasks of promoting and distributing new cultural items are analytically distinct, although boundary units combining both functions may be established. Transactions between retailers and boundary personnel at the wholesale level are easily programmed and supervised. In terms of Thompson's (1962) typology of output transactions, the retailer's "degree of nonmember discretion" is limited to a small number of fixed options concerning such matters as discount schedules and return privileges.[18] In contrast, where organizations are dependent on "surrogate consumers" for coverage of new products, the latter enjoy a high degree of discretion: tactics employed by contact men at this boundary entail more "personal influence"; close supervision by the organization is more difficult and may be politically inexpedient. Further development of Thompson's typology would facilitate tracing the flow of innovations through organization systems by extending the analysis of transactions "at the end of the line"— that is, between salesmen and consumers or bureaucrats and clients—to encompass boundary transactions at all levels of organization through which new products are processed.

A high ratio of promotional personnel to surrogate consumers ap-

pears to be a structural feature of any industry system in which: *(a)* goods
are marginally differentiated; *(b)* producers' access to consumer markets
is regulated by independent gatekeepers; and *(c)* large-scale, *direct* advertising campaigns are uneconomical or prohibited by law. Cultural
products are advertised *indirectly* to independent gatekeepers within the
industry system in order to reduce demand uncertainty over which
products will be selected for exposure to consumers. Where independent gatekeepers neither filter information nor mediate between producer and consumer, the importance of contact men at the organization's output boundary is correspondingly diminished. In industry systems
where products are advertised more directly to consumers, the contact
man is superseded by full-page advertisements and sponsored commercials, purchased outright by the producer organization and directed at
the lay consumer.

Overproduction and Differential Promotion of Cultural Items

Differential promotion of new items, in conjunction with overproduction, is a second proactive strategy employed by cultural organizations
to overcome dependence on mass-media gatekeepers. Overproduction
is a rational organizational response in an environment of low capital
investments and demand uncertainty. "Fortunately, from a cultural point
of view if not from the publisher's, the market is full of uncertainties.
. . . A wise publisher will hedge his bets" (Bailey 1970, pp. 144, 170).

Under these conditions it apparently is more efficient to produce many
"failures" for each success than to sponsor fewer items and pretest each
on a massive scale to increase media coverage and consumer sales. The
number of books, records, and low-budget films released annually far
exceeds coverage capacity and consumer demand for these products.[19]
The publisher's "books cannibalize one another. And even if he hasn't
deliberately lowered his editorial standards (and he almost certainly has)
he is still publishing more books than he can possibly do justice to" (Knopf
1964, p. 18). While over 15,000 new titles are issued annually, the probability of any one appearing in a given bookstore is only 10% (Lacy 1963).
Similarly, fewer than 20% of over 6,000 (45 rpm) "singles" appear in
retail record outlets (Shemel and Krasilovsky 1964). Movie theaters exhibit a larger proportion of approximately 400 feature films released
annually, fewer than half of which, however, are believed to recoup the
initial investment. The production of a surplus is facilitated further by
contracts negotiated with artists on a royalty basis and other cost-mini-
mizing features of the craft administration of production.

Cultural organizations ideally maximize profits by mobilizing promotional resources in support of volume sales for a small number of items.
These resources are not divided equally among each firm's new releases.

Only a small proportion of all new books and records "sponsored" by cultural organizations is selected by company policy makers for large-scale promotion within the industry system. In the record industry:

> The strategy of massive promotion is employed by policymakers in an attempt to influence the coverage of their product by media over which they exert little control. They must rely on independently owned trade papers to bring new records to the attention of radio programmers and disk jockeys, and upon radio airplay and journalists to reach the consumer market. For this reason, selected artists are sent to visit key radio stations, and parties are arranged in cities throughout the country to bring together the artist and this advanced audience. It seems likely that if . . . policymakers could better predict exposure for particular releases, then fewer would be recorded. . . . Records are released (1) with no advance publicity, (2) with minimal fanfare, or (3) only after a large-scale advance promotional campaign. The extent of a record's promotion informs the policymakers' immediate audience of regional promoters and Top 40 programmers of their expectations for, and evaluation of, their product. In this way the company rank orders its own material. The differential promotion of records serves to sensitize Top 40 programmers to the names of certain songs and artists. Heavily promoted records are publicized long before their release through full-page advertisements in the trade press, special mailings, and personal appearances by the recording's artists. The program director is made familiar with the record long before he receives it. It is "expected" to be a hit. In this way, though radio stations receive records gratis, anticipation and "demand" for selected releases are created. . . . The best indicator of a record's potential for becoming a hit at this stage is the amount of promotion it is allocated. [Hirsch 1969, pp. 34, 36]

Similarly, in the publishing industry:

> Publishers' advertising has several subsidiary functions to perform besides that of selling books, or even making readers. Among them are:
>
> 1. Influencing the "trade"—that is impressing book jobbers and retail booksellers with the fact that the publisher is actively backing a certain title and that it would be good business for them to stock and push it.
> 2. Influencing authors and their agents. Many an author has left one publisher for another because he felt that the first publisher was not giving his book enough advertising support.
> 3. Influencing reviewers. The implication here is not that any reputable reviewer can be "bought" by the use of his paper's advertising columns, but reviewers are apt to watch publishers' announcements (particularly those that appear in the trade papers) for information which will aid them in selecting books for review, and in deciding which ones to feature or to review at length.
> 4. Influencing the sale of book club, reprint, and other subsidiary rights. Publishers sometimes advertise solely to keep a book on the best-seller

list while a projected movie sale is in prospect. Occasionally this works the other way round: movie producers have been known to contribute generously to the ad budget of the initial hardcover edition so as to reap the benefit of the best-seller publicity for their film when it finally appears. [Spier 1967, pp. 155–56]

Most cultural items are allocated minimal amounts for promotion and are "expected" to fail (recall the description of postpublication author-editor luncheons cited earlier). Such long shots constitute a pool of "understudies," from which substitutes may be drawn in the event that either mass-media gatekeepers or consumers reject more heavily plugged items.[20] We see the strategy of differential promotion as an attempt by cultural organizations to "buffer" their technical core from demand uncertainties by smoothing out output transactions (Thompson 1967).

Cooptation of "Institutional Regulators"

Mass-media gatekeepers report a wide variety of mechanisms developed by cultural organizations to influence and manipulate their coverage decisions. These range from "indications" by the sponsoring organization of high expectations for particular new "discoveries" (e.g., full-page advertisements in the trade press, parties arranged to introduce the artist to recognized opinion leaders) to personal requests and continuous barrages of indirect advertising, encouraging and cajoling the gatekeeper to "cover," endorse, and otherwise contribute toward the fulfillment of the organization's prophecy of great success for its new product.

The goals of cultural and mass-media organizations come into conflict over two issues. First, public opinion, professional ethics, and, to a lesser extent, job security, all require that institutional gatekeepers maintain independent standards of judgment and quality rather than endorse only those items which cultural organizations elect to promote. Second, the primary goal of commercial mass-media organizations is to maximize revenue by "delivering" audiences for sponsored messages rather than to serve as promotional vehicles for particular cultural items. Hit records, for example, are featured by commercial radio stations primarily to sell advertising:

Q. Do you play this music because it is the most popular?
A. Exactly for that reason. . . . We use the entertainment part of our programming, which is music, essentially, to attract the largest possible audience, so that what else we have to say . . . in terms of advertising message . . . [is] exposed to the largest number of people possible—and the way to get the largest number to tune in is to play the kind of music they like . . . so that you have a mass audience at the other end.
Q. If, let's say that by some freak of nature, a year from now the most popular music was chamber music, would you be playing that?

A. Absolutely . . . , and the year after that, if it's Chinese madrigals, we'll be playing them. [Strauss 1966, p. 3][21]

Goal conflict and value dissensus are reflected in frequent disputes among cultural organizations, mass-media gatekeepers, and public representatives concerning the legitimacy (or legality) of promoters' attempts to acquire power over the decision autonomy of surrogate consumers.

Cultural organizations strive to control gatekeepers' decision autonomy to the extent that coverage for new items is *(a)* crucial for building consumer demand, and *(b)* problematic. Promotional campaigns aimed at coopting institutional gatekeepers are most likely to require proportionately large budgets and illegitimate tactics when consumers' awareness of the product hinges almost exclusively on coverage by these personnel. As noted earlier, cultural organizations are less likely to deploy boundary agents or sanction high-pressure tactics for items whose sale is less contingent on gatekeepers' actions.

VARIABILITY WITHIN CULTURAL INDUSTRIES

Up to this point, we have tended to minimize variability among cultural organizations, cultural products, and the markets at which they are directed. Our generalizations apply mainly to the most *speculative* and entrepreneurial segments of the publishing, recording, and motion picture industries, that is, adult trade books, popular records, and low-budget movies.[22] Within each of these categories, organizations subscribe, in varying degrees, to normative as well as to the more economic goals we have assumed thus far. Certain publishing houses, record companies, and movie producers command high prestige within each industry system for financing cultural products of high quality but of doubtful commercial value. To the extent they do *not* conform to economic norms of rationality, these organizations should be considered separately from the more dominant pattern of operations described above.[23]

Whether our generalizations might also characterize less-uncertain industry segments, such as educational textbook and children's-book publishing divisions, or classical record production is also subject to question. In each of these instances, cost factors and/or degree of demand uncertainty may be quite different, which, in turn, would affect the structure and operation of the producer organizations. Textbook publishers, for example, face a more predictable market than do publishers (or divisions) specializing in trade books: more capital investment is required, and larger sales forces must be utilized for school-to-school canvassing (Brammer 1967). In the case of children's books, some differences might be expected in that libraries rather than retail stores account for 80% of sales (Lacy 1968).

Within the adult-trade-book category, coverage in book-review columns is more crucial to the success of literary novels than to detective stories or science-fiction books (Blum 1959). Review coverage is also problematic: "Even *The New York Times,* which reviews many more books than any other journal addressed to the general public, covers only about 20 percent of the annual output. Many books of major importance in specialized fields go entirely unnoticed in such general media, and it is by no means unknown for even National Book Award winners to go unreviewed in the major national journals" (Lacy 1963, p. 55). We would therefore expect publishers' agents to push novels selected for national promotion more heavily than either detective stories or science-fiction works. Serious novels should be promoted more differentially than others.

Similarly, coverage in the form of radio-station air play is far more crucial in building consumer demand for recordings of popular music than for classical selections. Control over the selection of new "pop" releases by radio-station programmers and disk jockeys is highly problematic. Record companies are dependent on radio air play as the *only* effective vehicle of exposure for new pop records. In this setting—where access to consumers hinges almost exclusively on coverage decisions by autonomous gatekeepers—institutionalized side payments ("payola") emerged as a central tactic in the overall strategy of cooptation employed by producer organizations to assure desired coverage.

Radio air play for classical records is less crucial for building consumer demand; the probability of obtaining coverage for classical releases is also easier to estimate. Whereas producers and consumers of pop records are often unsure about a song's likely sales appeal or musical worth, criteria of both musical merit and consumer demand are comparatively clear in the classical field. Record companies, therefore, allocate proportionately fewer promotional resources to assure coverage of classical releases by mass-media gatekeepers, and record-company agents promoting classical releases employ more legitimate tactics to influence coverage decisions than promoters of pop records employ to coopt the decision autonomy of institutional regulators.

Thompson (1967, p. 36) has proposed that "when support capacity is concentrated but demand dispersed, the weaker organization will attempt to handle its dependence through coopting." In our analysis, cultural organizations represent a class of weaker organizations, dependent on support capacity concentrated in mass-media organizations; demand is dispersed among retail outlets and consumers. While all cultural organizations attempt to coopt autonomous consumer surrogates, the intensity of the tactics employed tends to vary with degree of dependence. Thus, cultural organizations most dependent on mass-media gatekeepers (i.e., companies producing pop records) resorted to the most costly and illegitimate tactics; the institution of payola may be seen as an indication of their weaker power position.

CONCLUSION

This paper has outlined the structure of entrepreneurial organizations engaged in the production and distribution of cultural items and has examined three adaptive strategies employed to minimize dependence on elements of their task environments: the deployment of contact men to organizational boundaries, overproduction and differential promotion of new items, and the cooptation of mass-media gatekeepers. It is suggested that in order for new products or ideas to reach a public of consumers, they first must be processed favorably through a system of organizations whose units filter out large numbers of candidates before they arrive at the consumption stage. The concept of an industry system is proposed as a useful frame of reference in which to (1) trace the flow of new products and ideas as they are filtered at each level or organization, and (2) examine relations among organizations.

NOTES

1. This paper was developed in connection with a study of the popular music industry and its audience conducted at the Survey Research Center, University of Michigan, under the supervision of Dr. Stephen B. Withey and supported by grant numbers 1-RO1-MH17064-01 and 1-FO1-MH48847-01 from the National Institute of Mental Health. I wish to thank Edward O. Laumann, Albert J. Reiss, Jr., Randall Collins, Theodore L. Reed, David R. Segal, and an anonymous reviewer for critical comments on an earlier version of this paper, presented at the sixty-fifth annual meeting of the American Sociological Association, August 1970.

2. A notable exception is Alfred Chandler's classic study of corporate innovation (1962). In the areas of fine art and popular culture, this problem has been noted by Albrecht (1968), Barnett (1959), Baumol and Bowen (1968), and Gans (1966).

3. As Lane (1970*a*, p. 240) puts it, a central sociological question is the extent to which sponsoring organizations "manage and control values and knowledge rather than simply purvey." An organizational approach to the study of American mass culture suggests that changes in content can be caused by shrinking markets only partially due to shifts in consumer taste preferences. Industry observers see increased public access since 1955 to "art" films (Houston 1963; Gubeck 1969) and popular-song lyrics with protest themes (Carey 1969) as reflecting the near-total loss of a once-dependable audience, whose unchanged predispositions now receive confirmation from television fare. The advent of

television forced movie exhibitors and radio-station managers to relinquish the majority audience and alter program content to attract minority subcultures *previously neglected for economic reasons*. The production of "rock 'n' roll" records and films by independent producers was stimulated by unprecedented opportunity for radio air play and exhibition (Hirsch 1971). While the altered content represents the best market share now available to many producers and distributors, it is directed at the teenage and intellectual markets, respectively, and not to former patrons.

4. Large firms and record-industry personnel are disproportionately represented.

5. An excellent, first-person account of this experience is provided by Cowan (1970).

6. For a more far-ranging consideration of the genesis and life cycle of fads and fashions from the standpoint of classic sociological theories, see Meyersohn and Katz (1957), Blumer (1968), and Denzin (1970).

7. A focal organization's task environment consists of other organizations located on its input and output boundaries.

8. "Production" here refers to the performances or manuscripts created by artists and talent scouts for later replication in the form of books, film-negative prints, and phonograph records. The physical manufacture of these goods is sufficiently amenable to control as to be nearly irrelevant to our discussion.

9. Royalty payments in the motion-picture industry are an alternative to costly, long-term contracts with established movie stars and permit producers to partially defer expenditures until the picture is in exhibition. Contracts specifying royalties (in addition to negotiated fees) are limited to well-known actors with proven "track records." Author-publisher contracts are more uniform, specifying royalties of at least 10% to all authors. Record companies seldom provide royalties higher than 3%–5% of sales. Since popular records are frequently purchased in greater quantities than best-selling books, however, musicians' royalties may equal or exceed those of authors.

10. The cost of producing and manufacturing (45 rpm) record "singles" averages only $2,500 (Brief 1964).

11. Low-budget feature films range in cost from $100,000 to $2 million each. The break-even point for movies is believed to be $4 in box-office receipts for each dollar invested in the film. A recent film, *Easy Rider*, produced on a low budget of $360,000, is reported to have earned $50 million in box-office receipts and netted its producers approximately $10 million. "Rather than make one expensive film, with all the correct box-office insurance in the way of story and star-casting, and see the whole thing go down the drain," many producers have tried putting "the same kind of money into three or four cheap films by young directors, gambling that at least one of them would prove [to be a smash]" (Houston 1963, p. 101). Houston's description of French filmmaking has since come to characterize its American counterpart.

12. Prior to implementation of a (1948) judgment by the U.S. Supreme Court, independent and foreign film-production companies without powerful distribution arms were blocked most effectively from access to consumers through movie exhibition. The *Paramount Decrees* divested movie-theater-chain ownership from nine major film producers and distributors (Conant 1960).

13. Public reaction to the "payola" scandals in the late 1950s demonstrated a widespread belief that the disseminators of mass culture should be independent of its producers. Disk jockeys, book reviewers, and film critics are expected to remain free from the influence or manipulations of record companies, book publishers, and movie studios, respectively. This feeling is shared generally by members of each industry system as well as embodied in our legal system.

14. New movies, faced with fewer competitors and representing far greater investment per capita, are advertised more heavily directly.

15. Boskoff (1964, p. 224) sees the sources of innovations within any social system as the "technical and/or managerial levels of organization, or external sources. . . . By its very nature, the institutional level is uncongenial to innovative roles for itself." Changes occur at an increasing rate when "the institutional level is ineffective in controlling the cumulation of variations. . . . This may be called change by institutional default." Changes in pop-culture content consistently follow this pattern.

16. Two interesting formal models of aspects of this process are presented by McPhee (1963).

17. For a more detailed discussion of the *role-set* engaged in the processing of fads and fashions, with particular application to "hit" records, see Hirsch (1969).

18. Sponsoring organizations without access to established channels of distribution, however, experience great difficulty in obtaining orders for their products from retail outlets and consumers. Thompson's (1962) typology of interaction between organization members and nonmembers consists of two dimensions: Degree of nonmember discretion, and specificity of organizational control over members in output roles. Output roles are defined as those which arrange for the distribution of an organization's ultimate product (or service) to other agents in society.

19. This is not to say that "uneconomical" selections may not appeal to a fair number of consumers. Each industry defines consumer demand according to its own costs and convenience. Thus, a network television program with only 14 million viewers fails for inadequate consumer demand.

20. Two recent successful long shots are the best-selling reissue of turn-of-the-century Sears Roebuck catalogs and the film *Endless Summer*. For a discussion of criteria employed to choose pop records for differential promotion, see Hirsch 1969.

21. Similarly, the recent demise of the *Saturday Evening Post* was precipitated by an inability to attract sufficient advertising revenue: too many of its 6 million subscribers lived in rural areas and fell into low-income categories (Friedrich 1970).

22. Adult trade books account for less than 10% of all sales in the book-publishing industry, excluding book-club sales (Bowker 1969). Recordings of popular music (subsuming folk and country and western categories) provide the majority of sales in the record industry (Brief 1964). Figures on the contribution of low-budget films to movie industry sales were not obtained. Low-budget films are more speculative than high-budget "blockbusters" on a *per picture* basis only, where their probability of box-office success as well as their costs appear to be lower.

23. Lane (1970b) presents a valuable portrait of one such publishing house;

Miller (1949) provides an excellent study of cross-pressures within the book industry.

REFERENCES

Albrecht, Milton C. 1968. "Art as an Institution." *American Sociological Review* 33 (June): 383–96.

Bailey, Herbert S. 1970. *The Art and Science of Book Publishing.* New York: Harper & Row.

Bailey, Stephen K., and Edith K. Mosher. 1968. *ESEA: The Office of Education Administers a Law.* Syracuse, N.Y.: Syracuse University Press.

Barnett, H. G. 1953. *Innovation: The Basis of Cultural Change.* New York: McGraw-Hill.

Barnett, James H. 1959. "The Sociology of Art." In *Sociology Today,* edited by Robert K. Merton, Leonard Broom, and Leonard S. Cottrell, Jr. New York: Basic.

Baumol, William J., and William G. Bowen. 1968. *Performing Arts: The Economic Dilemma.* Cambridge, Mass.: M.I.T. Press.

Blum, Eleanor. 1959. "Paperback Book Publishing: A Survey of Content." *Journalism Quarterly* 36 (Fall): 447–54.

Blumer, Herbert. 1968. "Fashion." In *International Encyclopedia of the Social Sciences.* 2d ed. New York: Macmillan.

———. 1969. "Fashion: From Class Differentiation to Collective Selection." *Sociological Quarterly* 10 (Summer): 275–91.

Boskoff, Alvin. 1964. "Functional Analysis as a Source of a Theoretical Repertory and Research Tasks in the Study of Social Change." In *Explorations in Social Change,* edited by George K. Zollschan and Walter Hirsch. Boston: Houghton Mifflin.

Bowker, R. R., Co. 1969. *The Bowker Annual of Library and Book Trade Information.* New York: R. R. Bowker Co.

Brammer, Mauck. 1967. "Textbook Publishing." In *What Happens in Book Publishing,* edited by Chandler B. Grannis. 2d ed. New York: Columbia University Press.

Brief, Henry. 1964. *Radio and Records: A Presentation by the Record Industry Association of America at the 1964 Regional Meetings of the National Association of Broadcasters.* New York: Record Industry Association of America.

Brockway, George P. 1967. "Business Management and Accounting." In *What Happens in Book Publishing,* edited by Chandler B. Grannis. 2d ed. New York: Columbia University Press.

Brown, Roger L. 1968. "The Creative Process in the Popular Arts." *International Social Science Journal* 20 (4): 613–24.

Burns, Tom, and G. M. Stalker. 1961. *The Management of Innovation.* London: Tavistock.

Carey, James T. 1969. "Changing Courtship Patterns in the Popular Song." *American Journal of Sociology* 74 (May): 720–31.

Chandler, Alfred D., Jr. 1962. *Strategy and Structure: Chapters in the History of the American Industrial Enterprise.* Cambridge, Mass.: M.I.T. Press.

Conant, Michael. 1960. *Antitrust in the Motion Picture Industry*. Berkeley: University of California Press.

Coser, Lewis A. 1965. *Men of Ideas*. New York: Free Press.

Cowan, Paul. 1970. "Electronic Vaudeville Tour: Miking of an Un-American." *Village Voice*, April 16, 1970, p. 5.

Davis, Clive. 1967. "The Truth About Radio: A WNEW Inquiry." Transcript of interview with general manager CBS Records. Mimeographed. New York: WNEW.

Denzin, Norman K. 1970. "Problems in Analyzing Elements of Mass Culture: Notes on the Popular Song and Other Artistic Productions." *American Journal of Sociology* 75 (May): 1035–38.

Ephron, Nora. 1969. "Where Bookmen Meet to Eat." *New York Times Book Review*, June 22, 1969, pp. 8–12.

Evan, William M. 1963. "Toward a Theory of Inter-Organizational Relations." *Management Science* 11:B217–30. Reprinted in *Approaches to Organizational Design*, edited by James D. Thompson. Pittsburgh: University of Pittsburgh Press, 1966.

Frase, Robert W. 1968. "The Economics of Publishing." In *Trends in American Publishing*, edited by Kathryn L. Henderson. Champaign: Graduate School of Library Science, University of Illinois.

Friedrich, Otto. 1970. *Decline and Fall*. New York: Harper & Row.

Gans, Herbert J. 1964. "The Rise of the Problem Film." *Social Problems* 11 (Spring): 327–36.

———. 1966. "Popular Culture in America: Social Problem in a Mass Society or Social Asset in a Pluralist Society?" In *Social Problems: A Modern Approach*, edited by Howard S. Becker. New York: Wiley.

Guback, Thomas H. 1969. *The International Film Industry: Western Europe and America Since 1945*. Bloomington: Indiana University Press.

Hirsch, Paul M. 1969. *The Structure of the Popular Music Industry*. Ann Arbor: Survey Research Center, University of Michigan.

———. 1971. "Sociological Approaches to the Pop Music Phenomenon." *American Behavioral Scientist* 14 (January): 371–88.

Houston, Penelope. 1963. *The Contemporary Cinema: 1945–1963*. Baltimore: Penguin.

Hughes, Richard, ed. 1959. *Film: The Audience and the Filmmaker*. Vol. 1. New York: Grove.

Knopf, Alfred A. 1964. "Publishing Then and Now, 1912–1964." Twenty-first of the R. R. Bowker Memorial Lectures. New York: New York Public Library.

Lacy, Dan. 1963. "The Economics of Publishing, or Adam Smith and Literature." In "The American Reading Public," edited by Stephen R. Graubard. *Daedalus* (Winter), pp. 42–62.

———. 1968. "Major Trends in American Book Publishing." In *Trends in American Book Publishing*, edited by Kathryn L. Henderson. Champaign: Graduate School of Library Science, University of Illinois.

Lane, Michael. 1970a. "Books and Their Publishers." In *Media Sociology*, edited by Jeremy Tunstall. Urbana: University of Illinois Press.

———. 1970b. "Publishing Managers, Publishing House Organization and Role Conflict." *Sociology* 4: 367–83.

McPhee, William. 1963. "Survival Theory in Culture," and "Natural Exposure and the Theory of Popularity." In *Formal Theories of Mass Behavior*. Glencoe, Ill.: Free Press.

Mann, Peggy. 1967. "A Dual Portrait and Market Report: Harper and Row." *Writer's Yearbook* 37: 10–17.

Merton, Robert K. 1957. *Social Theory and Social Structure*. Rev. ed. Glencoe, Ill.: Free Press.

Meyersohn, Rolf, and Elihu Katz. 1957. "Notes on a Natural History of Fads." *American Journal of Sociology* 62 (May): 594–601.

Miller, William. 1949. *The Book Industry: A Report of the Public Library Inquiry of the Social Science Research Council*. New York: Columbia University Press.

Montagu, Ivor. 1964. *Film World*. Baltimore: Penguin.

Moynihan, Daniel P. 1969. *Maximum Feasible Misunderstanding*. New York: Free Press.

Parsons, Talcott. 1960. *Structure and Process in Modern Societies*. Glencoe, Ill.: Free Press.

Peterson, Richard, and David Berger. 1971. "Entrepreneurship in Organizations: Evidence from the Popular Music Industry." *Administrative Science Quarterly* 16 (March): 97–107.

Powdermaker, Hortense. 1950. *Hollywood: The Dream Factory*. New York: Grosset & Dunlap.

Rogers, Everett. 1962. *Diffusion of Innovations*. Glencoe, Ill.: Free Press.

Rosten, Leo. 1941. *Hollywood*. New York: Harcourt Brace.

Selznick, Phillip. 1949. *TVA and the Grass Roots*. Berkeley: University of California Press.

Shemel, Sidney, and M. William Krasilovsky. 1964. *This Business of Music*. New York: Billboard.

Spier, Franklin. 1967. "Book Advertising." In *What Happens in Book Publishing*, edited by Chandler B. Grannis. 2d ed. New York: Columbia University Press.

Stinchcombe, Arthur L. 1959. "Bureaucratic and Craft Administration of Production: A Comparative Study." *Administrative Science Quarterly* 4 (September): 168–87.

———. 1968. *Constructing Social Theories*. New York: Harcourt, Brace & World.

Strauss, R. Peter. 1966. "The Truth About Radio: A WNEW Inquiry." Transcript of interview. Mimeographed. New York: WNEW.

Thompson, James D. 1962. "Organizations and Output Transactions." *American Journal of Sociology* 68 (November): 309–24.

———. 1967. *Organizations in Action*. New York: McGraw-Hill.

Toffler, Alvin. 1965. *The Culture Consumers*. Baltimore: Penguin.

Wilensky, Harold. 1956. *Intellectuals in Labor Unions*. Glencoe, Ill.: Free Press.

———. 1968. "Organizational Intelligence." In *International Encyclopedia of the Social Sciences*. 2d ed. New York: Macmillan.

ELEVEN

Movies of the Week

Todd Gitlin

The television-industrial complex manufactures not series alone, but the one-shot movies that vary the networks' weekly routines. Each year, the three networks together underwrite more original movies than all the studios combined. In 1982–83, ABC, CBS, and NBC scheduled some ninety movies that they had ordered, financed, and shaped explicitly for television; and that number was down from earlier peaks. In sheer volume, the network departments of TV movies and miniseries (which the industry calls "long form") have therefore become the mass-production studios of this time. Their pictures no doubt make less of an impression on society than series, for they don't stay long enough to inspire sustained identification. Rather than producing personality cults, they exploit them. These B movies come and go, leaving who knows what traces in the consciousness of our time. They are the pills and modules the networks drop into their schedules for relief from the series habit. But whatever their precise consequence, they add up to a considerable portion of the prime-time schedule. Although they did not become staples of the schedule until the mid-sixties, they took up twelve and a half hours a week in 1980–81, or almost 20 percent of the prime time. The corporate deputies who develop and license these regular stopgaps are the functional equivalents of David O. Selznick, Louis B. Mayer, Irving Thalberg, Samuel Goldwyn, and Jack Warner, although their names don't circulate through American households the way their products do.

If the economics of production determined content all by itself, TV movies should be more diverse in style and ideology than either feature films or series, for they are far cheaper and therefore less risky as business propositions. In the early eighties a two-hour TV movie cost about $2 million, compared to an average of $9.4 million for a feature film and $14.3 million for a season's worth of an hour-long series. There is enough money in TV movies to pay for months of writing and about three weeks of shooting, making possible in sheer technical terms more complex scripts, more sophisticated direction and editing, more accomplished acting. Between the lure of money and the chance for less standardized material, TV movies attract not only the major suppliers but forty or fifty low-overhead independent producers, most of them in Los Angeles and a few in New York. Indeed, the long form lends itself to the indie prods, who should be—and sometimes are—more adventuresome than the major suppliers. Because TV movies don't syndicate well (although they often go into theatrical distribution abroad), they theoretically wouldn't have to look like the money machines that series promise to be. And their very evanescence means that characters don't have to survive intact for next week's resuscitation. They can be killed off, or descend to bad ends, making tragedy possible at least in the technical sense. Months and years can elapse. Upheavals and revelations can interrupt and transform a character's life. Since movies are usually singular, any producers so inclined ought to be able to carve out some freedom from formula. Since they are transitory, they have less chance to offend that offendable public the networks are always so concerned to protect. And so, one might think, the definitions of permissible subject matter and form should be free to open up.

At times, of course, the networks do take chances, largely for prestige's sake. The format of the "docudrama"—or as some in the industry prefer to call it, the "motion picture based on fact"—has taken on subjects foreclosed to series. In recent years CBS has aired *Fear on Trial,* about TV's own blacklist, and *Playing for Time,* about Auschwitz; ABC has put on *Roots, Attica,* and *Friendly Fire,* which explored anti–Vietnam War sentiments; NBC, *Holocaust, Kent State, Bitter Harvest*—about chemical pollution—and, in a much different spirit, a version of G. Gordon Liddy's *Will.* Yet what stands out about most docudramas is how unexceptional they really are. Mostly they are special events made routine—precisely by the same network system of market calculations that dominates series. TV movies, like series, are deficit-financed. Overhead and huge interest payments pile up long before there is any prospect of income. In effect, the networks are banks, and for their cash they exert control. Since, as ever, the networks seek the sure accumulation of maximum audiences, TV movies become just another set of predictable interruptions in the series stream.

Because movies are rarely aired twice, though, they pose a special marketing problem that radically shapes the networks' decision-making process. As posed by Stu Samuels, the energetic, outspoken young vice-president for TV movies at ABC, the question is, "How are you going to get people into the tent?" Each episode of a series advertises the entire season; the early episodes of a miniseries can build interest in the later; a regular feature film can do well on word of mouth, reviews, and multiple viewings; but the one-shot TV movie cannot advertise itself. Therefore, network executives in charge of movies think first and foremost about promotability.

Since the networks are their own best advertising medium—with *TV Guide* and the local newspaper listings second, newspaper ads and critics' columns third—network executives focus not so much on how the movie will look as a movie but on how its "summary" will play. A TV movie, it's believed, has to have a story line that can be summarized in a line or two in *TV Guide*. As examples of clear concepts, the agent Bill Haber offers "Mine collapses, family separated," or "Train hijacked over Alps."

"If you can't define [a TV movie] in a television log line, how can you get the audience to it?" says Deanne Barkley, former vice-president for movies at NBC and ABC, summing up industry wisdom on the subject. "You've only got one shot to get them, you know. It doesn't matter how good it is or how bad it is. *Jaws* is a perfect television movie. If you can describe it in one sentence so they know what they're coming to, and it stars Angie Dickinson, or someone that they've heard of, they'll come to it."

Since marketing is of the essence, it seems only reasonable that one of the most successful executives in the field of TV movies should have begun his career in advertising.[1] Uncustomarily for television, Brandon Stoddard is a white Anglo-Saxon Protestant who came from a Connecticut lawyer's family, went to private schools and Yale. He worked at the Grey and BBD&O ad agencies for nine years before making his way through every major department in ABC's programming hierarchy. Starting at daytime in 1970, Stoddard headed both daytime and children's programs, next TV movies, then dramatic series development and movies, and finally, beginning in 1979, all ABC TV movies, plays, miniseries, and its newly developing theatrical films as well. "The most important thing for a television movie," he says, "is the capacity for a movie to be understood by an audience after watching a ten-second film clip. The problem—or advantage—of the television movie is that an audience decides whether they're going to watch it or not watch it, a huge audience of fifteen million people, in roughly four days, which is miraculous, and they do it primarily off the on-air promotion. So if you have a movie that takes a long time to explain, or it is a movie that is somewhat diffuse, you're going to have a very very difficult time telling the audience about it."

The second most important factor in the selling of TV movies is the star, who by himself or herself may be the magnet drawing that audience in. That is why the network's favored stars have such leverage. A commitment from Ron Howard or Sally Struthers can get a project made that otherwise might fail to reduce neatly to the ten-second clip or the *TV Guide* blurb. As CBS vice-president in charge of movies for television Steve Mills said, "There are only so many different story lines. Let's just say a picture where a man in a midlife crisis has an affair with a younger woman is not a new story idea. We have done it many times, and everybody else has, too. That's okay; it depends on how you do it, how you cast it. We did it last year with Ed Asner having an affair with Meredith Baxter Birney while married to Anne Jackson, and we could predict that it would do five share points higher than if we did it with a non–television star; and it did. If I had to predict what that would do, a midlife-crisis man having an affair with a younger woman, I'd say a thirty-two, thirty-three share. But Alan Alda or Ed Asner[2] in it and I would say a thirty-seven, thirty-eight share, getting up into the forty range."

Finally there are the prestigious exceptions, projects that some network executives may have especially cared about and all make a point of singling out. "You sometimes say," as Brandon Stoddard puts it, "All right, I really love this movie. It's not very easy to sell it in a promo or in an ad, but we're going to make it because we really care about this idea, and we are going to spend a year selling it, publicity, promotion, screenings, teacher's guides, and all the rest of that kind of stuff. *Friendly Fire*'s a pretty good example of that. Now that was also helped by Carol Burnett in her first dramatic debut on television. But *Friendly Fire* was an example where we just decided we really want to make that movie. We felt it's a really important movie, and we spent a great deal of time and effort selling it beyond the normal four days and the *TV Guide* ads."

In fact, the 1980 ABC version of C. D. B. Bryan's popular book *Friendly Fire* was launched by Stoddard's friendship with Bryan, going back to college days at Yale, and ABC produced it itself through its own movie department, ABC Circle Films. But the typical development process is more elusive. "We put into work a hundred and fifty to two hundred scripts a year," says Steve Mills of CBS. "We probably have five thousand ideas pitched to us in various forms, in oral presentations, an idea at lunch, or over cocktails, a few pages prepared by a writer or a producer, sometimes a step outline, sometimes a completed script." Eventually those 5,000 ideas and 150 to 200 scripts will generate fifty or sixty movies.

(ABC takes as many pitches, develops about half as many scripts, and makes twenty to thirty movies a year.)

Mills, like Stoddard, says that, important as the star is in attracting the requisite numbers, "Very seldom do we have a star or a director and then start off and have to find something for them to do. We go the other way. We go for material first." Even commitments to current or former series stars—and CBS has forty or fifty of them—rarely determine what the movie will be about. "When we do make that kind of a commitment, as in the case of Liz Montgomery," Mills says, "we know that from our batch of one hundred fifty or two hundred scripts we will find at least one property that a woman in her thirties or early forties can play very well." But which projects to develop in the first place, which scripts to commission? As with series, there is no neat logic for generating salable stories. The networks want "good stories," yes, but what are they? "Usually it's something that I respond to on a gut level," says Janey Rosenthal, who works under Steve Mills and, in her early twenties, is probably the youngest high-ranking woman in network entertainment. "Is it intriguing, is it interesting, is it entertaining, is the character sympathetic, or do I want to watch him because I'm curious about him and want to know more and want to go deeper?"

Even when they talk up light entertainment and escape, the executives in charge of movies operate under the sign of a distinct form, which might be called television realism. Always they want "high concept," clear stories that tell viewers instantly whom to care about and root for. Movies have to be "believable" and sensational at the same time. The characters have to fit the familiarity of the home screen. The network idea is that people will venture out to movie theaters to be voyeurs of other worlds, but if they stay home they want stay-at-home figures. It's felt spy stories don't work on television, for example, because spies are not the folks next door. Industry lore also has it that the audience is fickle and expects instant clarity. The finger is always poised near the dial, so all salient elements have to be established with breathtaking haste. In network logic, it follows that characters have to be stripped down to unequivocal moral emblems; their troubles spotlit; their traits, like trademarks, leaping out of the screen.

The rare historical dramas are no exceptions to this rule. Abraham Lincoln strides into Ford's Theatre; FDR or JFK or Richard Nixon sits behind his desk in the Oval Office: These are the moments to be immortalized as History. The rest of historical time is an unpopulated void between the great moments. Private life is best consigned to the present. History-as-pageant is normally reserved for the realm of special miniseries and movies: There are the adventures of the imperial explorer as

outsider and hero *(Shōgun, Marco Polo);* the docudramas of pivotal moments in the lives of presidents *(Truman and MacArthur, Eleanor and
Franklin, The Missiles of October);* the Watergate shows *(Blind Ambition,
Washington: Behind Closed Doors, Will);* and tales of tyrants *(The Bunker*
and *Inside the Third Reich).* The "docudrama" was aptly named, for it
exists not to comprehend but to document, to authenticate the validity
of surface detail, to establish that this really happened.

Docudrama is melodrama whose stereotypes, however, sometimes
disclose the point of view of historical victims. Whatever its limits as historical chronicle, the 1977 *Roots* was not only an unanticipated record-
breaking ratings blockbuster, but a national purgation that kept blacks
and whites alike tuned in in acts of moral witness, of expiation as well as
curiosity and compassion. *Holocaust* in 1978 had sufficient impact to seize
the moral high ground not only in the United States but in West Germany, where it helped mobilize public feeling for an extension of the
statue of limitations on atrocity crimes.

Roots got on the air partly on the strength of Alex Haley's bestselling
book and partly because of a favorable run of network circumstances.
Aside from making money by appealing to the largest audiences, *Roots*
producer Stan Margulies says, the networks have consciences. He also
recalls, as "a joke that had some truth in it," telling ABC while it was
wavering, "What have you got to lose? You're number three. If *Roots*
fails, you'll still be number three. But what if the show takes off? Since
there's nothing else like it on the air, that's a possibility. Maybe the novelty of it will drive everyone crazy."

ABC had already committed to its first, precedent-setting limited-run
miniseries, *Rich Man, Poor Man,* which was to run once a week for twelve
weeks. Stan Margulies gives credit to Fred Silverman for what he calls
the "very daring and yet safe maneuver of scheduling *Roots* during a
single week." "We first started talking about it as five two-hour shows,"
he says. "Half in jest I said, 'Why don't we have a *Roots* week?' And
someone at the network said, 'Because if the first show doesn't do well,
we've lost the whole week.' I thought, Well, that made sense. So it was
considered that it would run probably five consecutive Sunday nights,
or whatever. When we got down to where they really had to schedule
the show, that's where I thought Freddie Silverman showed a touch of
genius. [ABC was] breaking new ground by doing the show. Why not
break new ground by finding a new way to show the show? And so, what
Silverman did that was incredible was he scheduled the show so that we
were a one-hour show on certain nights. It meant a lot of reediting. On
those nights, he therefore protected the known hit shows, so that if *Roots*
went straight down the toilet he still wouldn't lose the week, because he
had not affected *Laverne and Shirley* and *Happy Days*. By putting us on at

ten o'clock, he kept his eight to ten schedule intact; he knew he would win those nights, and, if *Roots* did nothing, what the hell?"

The networks came to regard the successes of *Roots* and, later, *Holocaust* largely as flukes. Executives concluded nothing more than that anything might work once. If the miniseries form made for success, or if socially charged material made the difference, why had later "relevant" miniseries like *Loose Change* (campus radicals in the sixties) and *King* rated badly? Stan Margulies, who produced *Roots,* noted that *Roots* was upbeat while *King* ended in assassination. Indeed, ABC's promotion department had billed *Roots* as "The Triumph of an American Family." But public curiosity is not so simple: The hardly upbeat *Holocaust* rated splendidly.

Executives might conclude that miniseries and movies do well when they create identification with families, so that audiences can enact in ritual what they feel in reality: anxiety about family stability in a churning world, sweetened by a message that family feeling persists amid the most atrocious conditions. Or they might conclude that *Roots* and *Holocaust* were national rites of exorcism and expiation, with a touch of the soap opera version of the theater of cruelty. (The Hollywood joke was that in the South, *Roots* was shown with the episodes in reverse order.) But instead of theorizing in this vein, most network executives and advertising agencies and many producers did what managers and gamblers always do: They simply went right back to what they saw as the low-risk gamble. They decided that the successes were not precedents but unrepeatable exceptions in violation of the odds. Perhaps they worked because they were pioneering; perhaps they belonged to singular historical moments like the liberal upwelling of the early Carter administration. Such arguments may be plausible. What is certain is that network belief has made them self-fulfilling, for no one will ever know how other serious historical dramas might rate as long as the networks refuse to invest in them.

If the networks like a dollop of controversy now and then, they usually want it manageable: social significance with a lifted face. This normally means little personal stories that executives think a mass audience will take as revelations of the contemporary. To spot emblematic stories when they see them, the executives have to stay current—by their lights. "I look at television commercials to look for a trend," says Deanne Barkley. "Or places where money is spent, not free stuff like television. What's on the cover of magazines? What are advertisers using to sell soap? What are they saying about what's going on in the country?" To her, AT&T's "Reach out and touch someone" campaign is a sign of growing desire for family connection, a desire she faults current executives for failing to tap. Other executives find inspiration in commercial television's own "reality" forms. Brandon Stoddard says that the idea for *Pray TV*, a 1982 movie about a television evangelist, was launched when he watched a piece on the subject on ABC's news magazine show, *20/20*.

Stu Samuels looks at it this way: "It's not just a question of giving the people what it wants. That's a gross oversimplification. Sometimes you don't know. It's not a science. Anyone who tells you it is is a fool." Then what do you do? "You look at what worked before," he says. "You look at what's just happening, so you come in on the crest. And you look at fundamentals: acting, directors, and so on." When I asked Samuels how he knew "what's just happening," he fell back on Deanne Barkley's reasoning, but with a more explicit rationale: "In a free society, in a free capitalist society, the public pays for what it's interested in. They buy what they're interested in."

Like all half-truths, this one is notable for what it omits. Gatekeepers like Barkley, Stoddard, and Samuels select; so do commercial makers, magazine editors, and *20/20* producers. From the great pool of demonstrable and potential public interest they choose and recirculate those images that match their sales sense and their own values. From among these the public chooses, but they can't choose what they don't know exists.

I asked Stu Samuels to give me an example of the normal development process at work, and he described the origins of a TV movie then in development this way: "About forty-eight hours after the hostages came home from Iran, the story started to break that Vietnam vets were disgruntled. About three months before that, there was a little tiny segment on *Real People* about a reunion of World War II veterans. These were guys who had been in some German POW camps, and I think there were also people who'd been in the Japanese theater. It started off very nicely, and then, halfway through, started listing some of the aftershocks—some of the injuries, some difficulties they had getting benefits. I saw it in my home. I got very angry and very moved. I came in the next morning, I called in somebody in this department, and I said, 'I want to do a story about two generations of vets, World War II and Vietnam, about how they're not getting what they're entitled to.' The piece that we're doing is called *A Little Piece of America*—that's a phrase used in the *Real People* piece. Now I'm betting that if we do a show about two generations of vets, I think we're going to strike a nerve with that picture."

I asked Samuels if he had thought about the plight of veterans before he saw the *Real People* piece. He shifted from his own feeling to his politically couched assessment of what the traffic would bear. "I'd heard stories," he said. "But something said to me that this country is swinging to the right. And I thought that with this swing to the right we could possibly strike a resonance here with viewers. But I'm not talking about something political, I'm talking about something emotional. . . . Reagan is touching the patriotic impulse, saying, 'Don't be ashamed about patriotism.' I want to do a film that will ask you to take a look at your government, at agencies like the VA, and say, 'You don't like it? Change it! Make government responsive to the people!' " This traditional fusion of feeling for nation with hostility to government bureaucracy was precisely the right-wing mixture Reagan had brewed for his own mass medium, the American electorate.

Network executives are not, themselves, right-wing. Samuels's best guess, and mine, is that in 1980 they supported John Anderson in disproportionate numbers. (So did many top producers, including Norman Lear and Grant Tinker.) These people admire getting the job done; they thought Jimmy Carter was inefficient, and between Anderson and Reagan, as Samuels says, "Anderson probably represented pragmatism, and network people are pragmatic."

Efficiency and pragmatism are core values for all managers. At the center of their lives efficiency and pragmatism funnel into the great and enduring American drama of personal success. Network executives are skilled in negotiating the heights of the corporate bureaucracy. Their own hard-won skill testifies to the possibility of personal triumph. Their own lives are "upbeat." If this sounds like a television movie, there is good reason for it. Men and women of this character gravitate toward the upbeat formula, partially because they believe it's what the mass audience desires, but also because their own experience enshrines it.

If an idea rings bells for subordinate and chief alike in a network TV-movie division, then they go after producers and writers to write scripts. Ninety percent of the time, though, producers and agents pitch their ideas first. Either way, the network has the upper hand. It knows what it doesn't want even if it doesn't know what it wants. Producers have to tailor their pitches to the standard conventions, and eventually the script has to match the network's version of the dramatic verities—characters should be simple and simply motivated, heroes familiar, stories full of conflict, endings resolved, uplift apparent, and each act should end on a note of suspense sufficient to carry the viewer through the commercial break. Wherever the idea originates, the development and approval process is the same. Aspiring producers and writers learn that it makes sense to arrive for the pitch meeting with appropriate article or book in hand, certifying that the project comes already equipped with mass popularity and significance.

When a project snakes its way into a producer's hands from more obscure sources, it is harder to sell, though not impossible. When the project is out of the ordinary and the sell is harder, then the television-industrial complex must come into play, and personal connections count all the more heavily. The disposition of a single executive or a star might make all the difference. The production company has to have a solid track record. The paradox is that when all these usual elements are in place, the product stands a chance of being unusual. A case in point is *Bitter Harvest,* a 1981 movie made for NBC, based on the actual poisoning of most of Michigan's cattle by a mispackaged chemical, and loosely derived from the 1978 book of the same name written by a Michigan farmer, Frederic Halbert, and his wife, Sandra.

Bitter Harvest starred Ron Howard, onetime child star in *The Music Man* and the long-running *Andy Griffith Show* and later a teenage star in *Happy Days.* Howard played a farmer whose cattle sicken, whose child develops rashes, and who gradually, against the lassitude and callousness of the state's health bureaucracy, traces the illness to a toxic fire retardant, polybrominated biphenyl, PBB, that had been mistakenly mixed into cattle feed. More children and adults sicken; the state still refuses to quarantine the poisoned cattle or ban their milk. Finally, to alert the populace, the farmer kills his own cattle. The show drew a good Nielsen rating of 18.0 and a handsome 29 percent share of the viewing audience, although promotion had been botched[3] and major affiliates in Philadelphia and Dallas didn't carry the movie at all. It drew four Emmy nominations. The writer won a Writers Guild award, among others, for his script. Yet the picture came within inches of not getting made.

Bitter Harvest began with an earnest, unflashy young man named Richard Friedenberg, who had directed, among other films, a feature called *Grizzly Adams* he thought so contemptible its enormous box-office success filled him with disgust. He had also directed on television for a while until he lost interest, whereupon he decided to see if he could write. In his diffident way, Friedenberg admired Italian neorealism, especially DeSica's *The Bicycle Thief* and *Umberto D,* from which he extracted the idea that TV movies could tell small personal stories that revealed the larger society. Like most young Hollywood writers trying to get noticed, he wrote "spec scripts," scripts on speculation, and sold nothing. "I have a totally uncommercial mind," he says, and so he was unemployed for months on end. Whenever he came up with an idea, his agent told him, "Forget it," and Friedenberg started looking for a new agent.

Friedenberg was a loner, a conscientious objector to the Hollywood glad-handing circuit; and he had the odd habit, from a Hollywood point of view, of reading a magazine called *Country Journal,* where one day in early 1979 he noticed an article about a Michigan farmer, Ric Halbert, who had campaigned to get the state to do something about his poisoned cattle. To Friedenberg this sounded like a television story, a large issue on a small scale, but his old agent was as usual less than enthusiastic. Friedenberg liked the Michigan idea well enough to try it out, among other ideas, on a sympathetic agent named Norman Stevens.

Any television deal brings a producer, a writer, and often a star into conjunction with an executive, often through the mediation of an agent, and all at the right time. Accidents happen, yet even accidents have a history; happy accidents happen to people who get into the right places often enough at the right times. Friedenberg's new agent happened to intersect with a bright young producer, Tony Ganz, who had been to Harvard, worked in documentaries on PBS's *Great American Dream Machine*, and then gone to work for a successful producer named Charles Fries at the Metromedia conglomerate. When Fries went off and set up his own company, Ganz went with him as a producer. Charles Fries Productions became one of the pillars of the TV-movie business, and over the years sold some forty movies to the networks.

In the spring of 1979, just as the Love Canal chemical dump was becoming national news, Three Mile Island was stopping the national heart, and *The China Syndrome* was growing into a national media event, Charles Fries happened to go to a meeting that Fred Silverman also attended. Within Fries's earshot, Silverman turned to Norman Lear and said that the Love Canal story was interesting and that someone should do a movie-of-the-week about it. The next day Fries sent a note to Ganz and Malcolm Stuart, his partner in the Fries Productions development department, repeating this conversation and saying, "Is this of any interest to you? See if you can follow this up."

Ganz knew barely anything about Love Canal, by his own account, so he did some research that convinced him Love Canal "wasn't the right story, but a story about chemical pollution seemed like an exciting idea."[4] He began talking to Hollywood agents, writers, and New York agents who handled new nonfiction manuscripts. After several months of looking, he had failed to find anything that lent itself to the dramatic boundaries of a small-screen movie. "One day—this is where the accident happened—" he recalls, "I went into Malcolm's office, and he was on the phone, so the man who was sitting in his office had no one to talk to until I walked in, and his name was Norman Stevens, and he was Friedenberg's agent—I guess he had just signed him. None of this would have happened if Malcolm hadn't been on the phone, because I would have asked him what I was going to ask him and left. Stevens said, 'What are you looking for?'—typical agent kind of question—and usually the answer to that question is 'Jesus Christ, anything I can, anything that's interesting that I can sell.' But in this case I had a better answer." Ganz told Stevens he was looking for something like Love Canal.

The next day, Friedenberg was in Stevens's office reeling off a list of possible story ideas. Halfway through the Michigan cattle story, Stevens stopped him. "Hold the thought," he said. Stevens picked up the phone, dialed Tony Ganz, and set up an appointment.

Ganz didn't treat his first conversation with Stevens all that seriously until Friedenberg came in and told him Ric Halbert's story. Then he paid attention, for he heard Friedenberg tick off what he thought were the hallmarks of a workable story: character, visible consequences, visible accomplishment, and the symbolic accoutrements of a morality tale. "I thought it was one of the best stories I had ever heard, period," Ganz says. "It had at its center a character, which was crucial and something that was missing in most of the other stories that I had heard. They tended to be group efforts at stopping chemical dumping, and that sort of thing. And there was a victory involved, but it wasn't too pat—I mean, it was a sort of hollow victory, or Pyrrhic, in the end. Nine million people were contaminated. There was just this guy, who at least sounded the alarm, and made certain connections that everyone else refused to believe in. And it had strong central characters. And it was in the middle of the country, which is a landscape that appealed to me."

Ganz has his own recombinant repertoire of movie precedents. "It was the same landscape as *Friendly Fire*. I didn't think *Friendly Fire* was a masterpiece . . . but I loved the way it looked, and I loved that it wasn't New York or Los Angeles or on either coast. I went to school in Vermont, so I knew cows a little, and I liked cows. They're big, stupid, and dumb. They're sort of like us, in fact. They do what they're told. They don't fight back. In the end, they go into the pit, and they get slaughtered, which is what we're doing to ourselves. The cows also made visible the effects of the poison. In most of those other stories no one really gets sick. It's an *it*, in the water table, or where there's radiation leaking from a *China Syndrome* plant, and you can't really dramatize it. The cows got sick, and you had to take them out back and shoot them, just like in *Hud*. It was a terrific story. It just all worked."

The idea went first to CBS, where executives passed, saying that the *Lou Grant* series had already done an episode on the PBB poisoning; they didn't want movies to duplicate series.[5] *Bitter Harvest* then went to ABC, where an executive said she liked the story but, after all, the switch of the fire retardant for the cattle growth additive was an accident, so where was the drama, where were the good guys and the bad guys? Reasoning of this sort has the effect of prohibiting TV movies from depicting the social structures that make accidents routine, even, paradoxically, predictable. A company that permitted the two chemicals to be packed in similar sacks, one pile next to the other, could not be held accountable by a dramatic form that refused to recognize the normality of evil.

NBC, the third buyer in town, was widely believed to be so overloaded with commitments and so short of capital that there seemed no sense pitching to them. The idea of *Bitter Harvest* therefore languished for several months. Then it received the blessing of the Hollywood gods, who move through revolving doors.

One of Ganz's producer colleagues at Fries Productions was an experienced TV hand named Irv Wilson, a magnetic, gregarious man who had shuttled through every cranny of the TV business, from ad agency to Universal Studios to talent agency to the NBC programming department. In fact, Irv Wilson had helped pioneer the development of TV movies at NBC. He was not always averse to TV fluff. He owned up to having devised *The Harlem Globetrotters on Gilligan's Island* during his second tenure at NBC, and while he was there NBC aired *Enola Gay,* a romance about the bomber mission that dropped the atomic bomb on Hiroshima. But Wilson was possessed of an uncommonly active social conscience. Born into a Depression-era working-class family in the Bronx, he had been instructed by the social-problem movies that Warner Brothers produced in the thirties and forties. He had worked for Henry Wallace in the presidential campaign of 1948. Although Wilson was no longer committed to any particular political position, he did think television entertainment had a responsibility to be more than entertaining, at least some of the time.

While still with Fries, Wilson bought his *Los Angeles Times* one morning and read the first in a series of articles called "The Poisoning of America." "It was incredible," he recalls, "and Tony came in one morning, and we were talking about it, and he said he had met a writer who had a story that he had heard, Richard Friedenberg, that was a true story, and he thought it was fantastic. I see, 'Gee, you ought to do something about that.' "

Then Fred Silverman tapped his old friend Irv Wilson to run NBC's West Coast specials department, which was to include whatever Wilson could pass off as "a special movie." As soon as Wilson told Ganz about his impending move, Ganz enlisted him for an unusual sort of pitch meeting at NBC with an executive named Dennis Considine. "Dennis," as Ganz put it later, "was in the curious position of being pitched to by the man who was about to be his boss, and he knew it. So at the end of [Friedenberg's] telling the story, he looked at Irv and said, 'Well, what do you think?' And Irv said, 'I think it's great and we should buy it.' I had never been in a meeting like that; it was really fun."

Wilson was sold by the time he got to NBC, but NBC was piled high with movie commitments that extended back years. Ganz kept calling Wilson and Wilson kept saying, "Someday I'll get it through for you," but right now NBC was only making movies to fulfill existing commit-

ments. There was no money for new deals. Six more months passed.
Dick Friedenberg gave up for the second time, and busied himself with
other futile projects. But Wilson was biding his time. Then *Time* magazine came out with a cover story called "The Poisoning of America." As
Wilson remembers it, "On the cover of *Time* was a guy being swallowed
up by this crap in the ground. And I showed it to Brandon Tartikoff,
and he says, 'All right, write the script.' " Wilson was sure that the *Time*
cover had made the difference.

Ganz and Friedenberg were jubilant, but almost immediately they had
to worry about possible network censorship. As soon as NBC headquar-
ters in New York learned of the project, they "red-flagged" it as a possible legal risk. Ganz didn't know how seriously to take New York's concern, but he decided to test the waters. He called up an NBC attorney
named Barbara Hering, whose job was to inspect movies based on fact
for potentially litigable issues. He found Hering to be, as he put it, "at
once supportive and pleasant and, on the other hand, guarded and realistic that it was not going to be an easy project." Ganz made an astute
decision. He decided to level with Hering. "If you're too careful in the
beginning and you write a sort of compromise script keeping one eye
open for legal problems, you won't even get to test the legal problems.
So I said to her, 'Look, it seems to me, unless you disagree, that we
should just proceed now as best we can, being somewhat careful but
writing the story as it happened.' And she said, 'Yes, do it that way, and
then let me see it.' " Ganz was still apprehensive about how to handle the
company, the governor, and the Michigan bureaucracy, but decided to
save his worries for later. "It is impossible to get reliable, consistent answers from anybody about what you can and cannot do. So if you react
too soon you could be reacting to the wrong thing."

Instead of handing in the usual first or second version, Friedenberg
and Ganz were inordinately careful and handed in a fourth or fifth draft.
NBC program executives waxed enthusiastic, asking them only routine
questions about dramatic structure: What was the proper balance between the time before and after the farmer ascertains the source of the
illness? Couldn't there be more scenes between the farmer and his wife?
"They asked a lot of questions," Ganz recalls, "and I think without exception they were questions that we had asked ourselves and tried eleven
different ways."

Irv Wilson knew, meanwhile, that success would depend on the hero's
appeal, and had for a long time been thinking about Ron Howard, a
sure-fire TV draw. Wilson later thought his major achievement at NBC
was to have nudged Ron Howard's career toward serious drama. The
first movie Wilson had pushed through at NBC was *Act of Love*, a movie
about euthanasia committed by one brother on another. He had per-

suaded the producers that Ron Howard had just the kind of likable image to sweep the audience into sympathy. And—all-important to getting
a movie about euthanasia made—NBC had commitments to Howard.

Now Wilson saw Howard as box office again: "The first time I met
him I loved him, because he reminded me of today's Jimmy Stewart.
Every Frank Capra picture you want to make, you could recast Ron
Howard, and it's smashing, because he is the all-American boy who is so
pure and so fucking honest, and good, and decent." *Act of Love* should
have been depressing, by TV standards, yet it garnered high numbers,
a 21.7 rating and 35 share. So in the case of *Bitter Harvest*, Wilson's argument for Ron Howard met no resistance. "Jimmy Stewart could have
played that part, right?" Wilson said. *"Bitter Harvest* was a Frank Capra
movie," one idealistic, responsible man against the system. Karen Dan-
aher, a forceful and socially conscious former junior-high-school teacher
and TV newswoman whom Wilson had brought into the NBC movie
department, had the same feeling. "When I read the script," she says, "I
knew we had to get a TV star that people could trust." When Ganz saw
a cassette of Howard's dramatic performance in *Act of Love*, he was convinced. Wilson fired the script off to Howard, and he was sold on it
immediately.

So the *Time* cover made possible the writing of the script; the script
garnered Ron Howard; Howard sold the show. For the smaller part of
Howard's farmer neighbor, NBC brought up Art Carney, another piece
of offbeat casting. Carney was expensive, but the network was willing to
spend the money for what, in effect, was insurance. Howard's agreement, and Carney's, neutralized the opposition of the affable and cautious Perry Lafferty, NBC's West Coast senior vice-president for programs, who reported directly to Brandon Tartikoff. "I had a lot of
reservations about it," Lafferty says, "because I didn't know whether the
audience would be interested in such a disagreeable subject. It's got Ron
Howard and Art Carney and you can make a good promo on it and take
a good ad. But for me, I thought it was very tough, and material that
I've heard about before." Novelty that was *too* novel was out of bounds;
novelty not novel enough was stale. "You've had the chemical wastes and
all that stuff over and over and over. I didn't think it was going to be
that big a ratings-gatherer." Lafferty had often been a conservative voice
in high NBC circles; he had resisted *Hill Street Blues* as well. This time he
was overruled.

From then on, *Bitter Harvest* went through the network screening process without much tampering. Ganz remained apprehensive, but Hering
was satisfied. "They really did a first-class job on the hard facts," she says,
"whether there had been real negligence bordering on reckless negligence in the factory, which led to the mix-up; whether the Agriculture

Department had really been bound down by red tape, or whatever the cause, but failing to do what was necessary to take strong steps to stop a problem that was clearly very serious. All of those things were very, very heavily substantiated. You get into charges like that, and you have to worry a little bit, because you're making serious claims against important institutions and organizations. If justified by the facts, the program performs a public service, but if the facts are not as portrayed, the possible undermining of the public's faith in their institutions would be not only unfair to the institutions but a real disservice to our audience. It's not the same when the story is about a guy who is truly anonymous, in that he might be any one of hundreds of people, and whose story, however interesting, is simply personal."

A few changes were dictated for legal reasons. For one thing, Fries Productions' insurance company demanded that the name of the state of Michigan be taken out. Ganz wanted to keep Michigan, for verisimilitude's sake, but NBC backed the insurance company and Ganz went along. Michigan became "the state." Later on, Ganz regretted the sacrifice of realism. But it could equally well be argued that the very generality of "the state" made the story more universal and more powerful. This poisoning did happen somewhere, but it could have happened—it could still happen—anywhere. The names of the Michigan Chemical Co. and Michigan Farm Bureau Services, Inc., the companies responsible for the chemical switch, were also changed, but this was Friedenberg's doing. Even the earliest outlines Friedenberg worked up for Ganz used the pseudonym United Chemical. Ganz felt no particular moral outrage toward these particular companies. After all, they had paid millions of dollars in claims. So he did not care about this change, any more than he cared about the change in the farmer-hero's name from Ric Halbert to Ned DeVries. Such changes are standard in the movie-based-on-fact format. They afford legal protection and may even contribute to the movie's aura of familiarity. If the audience knows that a character is no more than "based on" a living person, the character comes closer to Everyman. The farmer Ned escapes from the singularity of Ric Halbert and is pulled closer to Ron Howard playing Ned, and therefore to Ron Howard, the trustable, Jimmy Stewart–style actor.

Hering intervened on only one script issue. Late in the movie comes a scene in which Ned tries to alert another farmer, a tense and conscience-stricken man who has unknowingly—or so he says—sold his poisoned milk on the market. The farmer pulls at his son's hair to show Ned—it is a wig. There are bald patches all over the child's scalp. Barbara Hering questioned the accuracy of this vignette. "If the bald patches and wig were true, they could be shown; but not otherwise." Ganz was also asked not to linger on this shot, "because," he was told, "we are not out to scare people needlessly." No matter. Brief as it is, the moment in the film when the farmer pulls away his child's hair remains shocking. Real people were really hurt. That was what happened when Michigan was poisoned.

As the script went through refinement after refinement, though, one potentially troublesome line kept nagging at Ganz. When Ned finds out the nature of the toxic chemical in his cattle feed, he races home, triumphant, to tell his wife about PBB. "What on earth is that?" she asks. In early versions of the script, Ned answers, "It's a fire retardant. It's used for TV sets so they don't burn up. . . ." Ganz knew that RCA, which owned NBC, also manufactured television sets. "I knew NBC would say something." He consulted with friendly West Coast programming executives. Although Barbara Hering had never flagged this line—it was a problem of corporate public relations, after all, not the law—one executive feared that someone above Hering in the New York chain of command might raise a fuss. Knowing that the red flag of controversy was already flying over the project, and not caring exactly what PBB was used for, Ganz decided on discretion—self-censorship, some might call it. "I was concerned," he said afterward, "that something like that could blow the whole goddamned project." At a late stage of the script he changed the line to: "It's a fire retardant. They put it in plastics or something."

Another political point flattened during the shooting was a borderline case that couldn't be laid at the door of the network—or, for that matter, the audience. Dr. Freeman, Ned's medical angel, testifies before a state committee in favor of a cattle quarantine. In the middle of a long speech about the effects of PBB—about its permanent presence in the bodies of those who eat the meat or drink the milk from the poisoned cattle, about effects that might even skip a generation—the script had Freeman say, "And don't think it's an isolated case. There are thirty-five thousand other chemicals out there that are unsafe, and they're being spilled and dumped and buried all over the *planet*." During the shooting in the dairy country of Northern California, at the last minute, Tony Ganz and the director, Roger Young, decided Freeman's speech was too long—almost a minute and a half. These lines seemed to them the most expendable. "We didn't want to get didactic," Ganz said. "It seemed too much a documentary statement. We felt that, given the reality of that little courtroom in that little town, nobody was thinking about anything but the nightmare of one particular chemical." Friedenberg agreed. To him the issue mattered so little, in fact, that when I asked him about it just after the shooting, he couldn't remember whether the line had stayed in or not. But Richard Dysart, the actor who played Freeman, was disturbed about the cut. He thought this was the one moment when *Bitter Harvest*

generalized from PBB to make a larger point about the chemical industry. Freeman was speaking directly to the audience. After the cut, was
the story of PBB narrowed into a single dreadful exception, "an isolated
case"?

Ganz and Friedenberg thought not. They believed they made the larger
point by hewing close to the story of PBB. They adhered to the prevailing aesthetic of small scale, in which the general point is inherent in the
particular, and indeed their claim cannot be dismissed out of hand. True,
any cut, in a literal sense, changes the meaning of the whole. To make
this simple point is my bias; it is the bias of all close readers of texts,
especially those who aim to ferret out the traces of political censorship
or the virtues of political expression. But I confess I am not altogether
convinced by the literal-mindedness of such criticism, especially as it bears
on a medium that rushes lines past us at an irreversibly fast pace. Lines
that break radically with the expected level of discourse might be more
memorable, therefore more effective, especially when they come from
the authoritative Freeman; or conceivably a general message buried amid
the specific, in the context of the small-scale story, goes by so fast as to
be lost with or without such individual lines. The tools for assessing the
effects of lines are too crude to tell us anything.

Whatever the effect of this or that line, it is clear that Ganz, Friedenberg, and all other "docudramatists," simply by accepting the conventions of their form, are committing a kind of self-censorship. Television
docudrama abhors what it considers polemic, didacticism, speechifying.
Convention clamps a tight frame around the story. It doesn't want the
larger public world leaking in. The soapbox is forbidden furniture. This
convention of the small, restricted, realistic story has ideological consequences. It has the effect of keeping the show compact, narrow, simplified. Indeed, coherence is defined as narrowness, and not just in the
thinking of the writers but audiences, too. It is the dramatic aesthetic
that prevails in this culture. Such conventions are shared, not imposed.
When they are shared long enough and deeply enough, they harden
into the collective second nature of a cultural style. True, against restric-
tion there arises a counterconvention based on audience identification
with the normal. If Ron Howard is Everyman and if his fictional state is
Everystate, and if Ron Howard's cows and child and neighbors are at
risk, then in imagination everyone is at risk. But there is still a difference
between saying that PBB is in the body cells of virtually everyone in
Everystate, and warning that there are thousands of other dangerous
chemicals—that PBB is, in a way, Everychemical.

Bitter Harvest further restricts the meaning of the problem of chemicals. What, after all, is the source of Ned's troubles? It is expressed most
pointedly in NBC's promo, where the voice-over says breathlessly, "And

now: Ron Howard in *Bitter Harvest,* the true story of one man's triumphant battle against the bureaucracy. His cattle were dying and no one would help." This accurately defines the movie's main line of tension: Ned's care played off against the heedlessness of the agricultural bureaucrats. The state is no true guardian of bucolic peace; from the opening shot—acoustic guitar and flute sounding a sweet, wistful melody over a shot of Ned and his wife feeding their calves from giant baby bottles— we understand that Ned is that guardian. Later, when the cattle start drying up, Ned gets the bureaucrats to conduct tests, which come out negative. The bureaucrats outrage Ned by suggesting that he is guilty of bad management. These unkind and uncaring men claim knowledge, and impugn both his skill and his care. But Ned has been to college and can't be so easily intimidated. He fights to reclaim his title to both knowledge and care.

The question the movie poses is, Who really knows and who really cares? When Ned presses the agricultural inspectors to undertake further tests, they protest that they aren't a research laboratory. In other words, they really aren't in the business of knowing. He has to shame them with direct evidence. He trusts his intuitions about his cattle and his methods; while bureaucrats play by the book, the farmer and lover of animals is the real investigator. Persistence leads Ned to direct action. Behind a wall in his barn he finds a pile of rats that have died from eating his feed; and when the bureaucrats continue to put him off, he dumps the rats onto their conference table. Ned's devoted search for the truth pays off when he shames a state technician into performing one more test. This gives him the data to find help in the person of Dr. Freeman, the good scientist freed from bureaucratic fetters, the crusty spirit of truth-seeking incarnate. In the end, though, even antibureaucratic truth-seeking proves insufficient and Ned has to take direct action again. The cost is terrible, all those cows shot down; but even at this traumatic moment Ned demonstrates he is closer to the cows than any remote bureaucrat.

The written text ("crawl") and simultaneous voice-over that follow give Ned credit for a victory but indicate that bureaucrats will still be bureaucrats: "After Ned DeVries killed his herd, public pressure forced the state to start testing livestock for contamination. Over five hundred farms were closed. Thirty thousand cattle were driven into mass graves and slaughtered. It was not until two years later, in 1976, that testing was finally begun on state residents. Ninety percent of the people tested showed levels of PBB. Another year passed before a law was enacted to eliminate all contaminated meat and milk from the marketplace. It is now estimated that eight million men, women, and children carry the toxic chemical PBB inside their bodies."[6]

Ned expects the state to help; he is a citizen and he feels entitled to public health. When the bureaucracy derails his rights, he crusades. But never in *Bitter Harvest* does he couple his fury against the state with any comparable attack on the company. There is one scene in which he joins a state team investigating the factory where the PBBs were substituted for a cattle feed additive. Ned shows disgust, but he never takes up the cudgels against the company. He claims no entitlement against the private economy. The corporate decisions that produced PBB and similar chemicals, the mentality that relies on them, the slack shop-floor conditions that permitted such substitutions are never mentioned; by the convention of the hero-centered narrative, the corporate bureaucracy remains invisible.

Ned, and the movie, accept the political-economic division of labor: The company should manufacture, the government should regulate. This keeps the movie on the normal side of American ideology—yet without making it conservative, as Americans measure the term. The corporation is more forgotten than forgiven, while the most visible blame is the government's for not regulating well. Although Ned is a lone hero, his rugged individualism departs from the kind celebrated in the speeches of Ronald Reagan. In fact, *Bitter Harvest* cleverly turns the Reagan view of the world on its head. In Reaganism, "bureaucracy" and "regulation" are inseparable evils. In the movie, bureaucracy, not regulation, is to blame. Ned shows that the public urgently needs regulation, while bureaucracy obstructs it. Citizens then have to act to force the government to live up to its legitimate calling. If this sounds familiar, it is not only the Frank Capra formula of the thirties, but also the crusading image that brought both Jimmy Carter and Ronald Reagan to power. All hail to the outsider who takes up the call to clean the Augean stables! The hero's foray into politics brings about the public good. In that sense, *Bitter Harvest* was deep in the grain of American political mythology.

If the forte of everyday American screenwriting is the short, flat line, *Bitter Harvest* put it to good use. The movie was moving, understated, sharply directed, and well photographed (including a lovely sequence of the live birth of a calf)—in short, one of the best of its breed. Shot in a breathtakingly intense and under-average eighteen days, on a budget of $1.8 million—at the low end of the TV movie range—it didn't look as if it had been prefabricated on the back lot. On the weakest network, even without two major affiliates, Philadelphia and Dallas—Fort Worth, the show won its time-slot handily.[7] As a rural show, it had the advantage of a lead-in from a rural series, the popular *Little House on the Prairie* (from which, significantly, it lost no audience). It beat out *M*A*S*H* and *Lou Grant* on CBS, and another serious movie on ABC.

Under such conditions, an above-average share might have suggested that Americans were concerned about major social issues and interested in straightforward dramatic representations of likable Americans grappling with them. Yet *Bitter Harvest* made barely a ripple on network consciousness. The day after it aired, I overheard one ABC executive say to another, "They claim this *Bitter Harvest* was high [i.e., clear and simple] concept. What high concept? All it was was a bunch of sick cows." Robert Greenwald, an independent producer who was pushing hard to make a CBS movie about Love Canal, grumbled that the networks would attribute *Bitter Harvest*'s success to Ron Howard, period. The networks were more comfortable drawing negative conclusions from the ratings failure of a run of social-issue movies than taking the chance of offending their nervous affiliates, or advertisers, or any other powerful institutions, or blocs of viewers. Only an executive with conviction would have bothered to use the success of *Bitter Harvest* to fight such a drift toward the bland; and politically committed executives, even politically interested ones, were rare.

NOTES

1. Nor is it surprising that one of his successors, Stu Samuels, came to television from eight years at *TV Guide*.

2. This was before Asner's press conference on behalf of Medical Aid for El Salvador, and the cancellation of *Lou Grant*.

3. NBC promotion and scheduling were in chaos that year. The network decided on *Bitter Harvest*'s May 18 screening date only two weeks in advance. By that time, Ron Howard had gone on three talk shows giving a previously announced date of May 11. The switch also cost *Bitter Harvest* any chance at a cover of *TV Guide* or the newspaper logs.

4. Another producer, Robert Greenwald, independently sold CBS on a movie about the Love Canal housewife, Lois Gibbs, who led the neighborhood in a movement to get government help. Greenwald, who had a considerable track record with TV movies like *Lady Truckers, Portrait of an Escort,* and *Portrait of a Centerfold,* was shifting his territory to liberal morality tales. On the strength of his record, and the interest of a big television star (who later lost interest), Greenwald persuaded CBS's Steve Mills to buy what he called "the story of a woman who'd do anything to protect her children." He pitched for fifteen minutes, in fact, before he let fall the words "Love Canal." Mills could see the tale as an uplift piece about personal triumph over adversity; it also borrowed from the woman-in-jeopardy genre. To Mills—as to Greenwald and Gibbs herself—it was a little Frank Capra movie, *Mrs. Smith Goes to Washington.* There followed months of haggling about casting, with Greenwald arguing for an actress with "an everywoman quality," "not a movie star." In the end, CBS settled on Marsha Mason, who was no one's first choice, and finally committed to the movie. Like *Bitter*

Harvest, it was framed as hero-versus-heedless-government, not hero-versus-corporation. *Lois Gibbs and the Love Canal* aired February 17, 1982, and for whatever reasons rated a miserable 12.5, with a meager 20 share.

5. Interestingly, that *Lou Grant* episode had been scheduled to air the night before the 1978 Michigan gubernatorial primary in which then Governor Milliken was being challenged in part on the ground that he had not acted swiftly enough to stop the spread of the PBB infestation. The *Lou Grant* producers had decided to delay the show a week in order not to affect the primary results.

6. Until the last minute Ganz wasn't sure exactly what to put in the crawl, or whether to accentuate it with a voice-over. He thought of resurrecting the point he had earlier excised from Dr. Freeman's speech, about the proliferation of dangerous chemicals in the environment, then decided against it. After he satisfied Barbara Hering about the validity of the facts he finally selected, his version was the one that ran.

In April of 1982, the results of fuller tests on Michigan residents were released, showing that an estimated 97 percent of them carried PBB in their bodies five years after the contamination.

7. To beef up May sweeps ratings, the Philadelphia NBC affiliate, in the nation's fourth-largest market, ran the movie *The Night They Raided Minsky's,* ironically the last feature product of television's Mr. Social Consciousness, Norman Lear. The Dallas–Fort Worth affiliate, in the eleventh-largest market, ran a baseball game. When Tony Ganz heard about the Philadelphia decision, a few weeks before air date, he called up the affiliate to try to change its mind. NBC's affiliate relations and promotions departments were so chaotic that the Philadelphia man hadn't been told that Ron Howard was the star. "*Act of Love* got a thirty-five share," Ganz said to him. "If I told you about a movie in which a guy goes into a hospital room and blows his brother's brains out with a shotgun, you wouldn't think it would get big numbers, would you?" He failed to convince the Philadelphian.

TWELVE

Sport and Social Class

Pierre Bourdieu

I think that, without doing too much violence to reality, it is possible to consider the whole range of sporting activities and entertainments offered to social agents—rugby, football, swimming, athletics, tennis, golf, etc.—as a *supply* intended to meet a *social demand*. If such a model is adopted, two sets of questions arise. First, is there an area of production, endowed with its own logic and its own history, in which 'sports products' are generated, i.e. the universe of the sporting activities and entertainments socially realized and acceptable at a given moment in time? Secondly, what are the social conditions of possibility of the appropriation of the various 'sports products' that are thus produced—playing golf or reading *L'Équipe,* cross-country skiing or watching the World Cup on TV? In other words, how is the demand for 'sports products' produced, how do people acquire the 'taste' for sport, and for one sport rather than another, whether as an activity or as a spectacle? The question certainly has to be confronted, unless one chooses to suppose that there exists a natural need, equally widespread at all times, in all places and in all social milieux, not only for the expenditure of muscular energy, but more precisely, for this or that form of exertion. (To take the example most favourable to the 'natural need' thesis, we know that swimming, which most educators would probably point to as the most necessary sporting activity, both on account of its 'life-saving' functions and its physical effects, has at times been ignored or refused—e.g. in medieval Europe—and still has to be imposed by means of national 'campaigns'.) More precisely, according to what principles do agents choose

A slightly longer version of this article first appeared in *Social Science Information* 17, no. 6 (1978): 819–40. Reprinted by permission of the author and Sage Publications.

between the different sports activities or entertainments which, at a given moment in time, are offered to them as being possible?

THE PRODUCTION OF SUPPLY

It seems to me that it is first necessary to consider the historical and social conditions of possibility of a social phenomenon which we too easily take for granted: 'modern sport'. In other words, what social conditions made possible the constitution of the system of institutions and agents directly or indirectly linked to the existence of sporting activities and entertainments? The system includes public or private 'sports associations', whose function is to represent and defend the interests of the practitioners of a given sport and to draw up and impose the standards governing that activity,[1] the producers and vendors of goods (equipment, instruments, special clothing, etc.) and services required in order to pursue the sport (teachers, instructors, trainers, sports doctors, sports journalists, etc.) and the producers and vendors of sporting entertainments and associated goods (tee shirts, photos of stars, the *tiercé*,[2] etc.). How was this body of specialists, living directly or indirectly off sport, progressively constituted (a body to which sports sociologists and historians also belong—which probably does not help the question to emerge)? And, more exactly, when did this system of agents and institutions begin to function as a *field of competition*, the site of confrontations between agents with specific interests linked to their positions within the field? If it is the case, as my questions tend to suggest, that the system of the institutions and agents whose interests are bound up with sport tends to function as a field, it follows that one cannot directly understand what sporting phenomena are at a given moment in a given social environment by relating them directly to the economic and social conditions of the corresponding societies: the history of sport is a relatively autonomous history which, even when marked by the major events of economic and social history, has its own tempo, its own evolutionary laws, its own crises, in short, its specific chronology.

One of the tasks of the social history of sport might be to lay the real foundations of the legitimacy of a social science of sport as a *distinct scientific object* (which is not at all self-evident), by establishing from what moment, or rather, from what set of social conditions, it is really possible to speak of sport (as opposed to the simple playing of games—a meaning that is still present in the English word 'sport' but not in the use made of the word in countries outside the Anglo-Saxon world where it was introduced *at the same time* as the radically new social practices which it designated). How was this terrain constituted, with its specific logic, as the site of quite specific social practices, which have defined themselves in the course of a specific history and can only be understood in terms of that history (e.g. the history of sports laws or the history of *records,* an interesting word that recalls the contribution which historians, with their task of *recording* and celebrating noteworthy exploits, make to the constitution of a field and its esoteric culture)?

The Genesis of a Relatively Autonomous Field of Production and Circulation of Sports Products

It seems to be indisputable that the shift from games to sports in the strict sense (which, as Defrance points out, must be distinguished from gymnastics[3]) took place in the educational establishments reserved for the 'élites' of bourgeois society, the English public schools, where the sons of aristocratic or upper-bourgeois families took over a number of *popular*—i.e. *vulgar*—games, simultaneously changing their meaning and function in exactly the same way as the field of learned music transformed the folk dances—bourrées, sarabands, gavottes, etc.—which it introduced into high-art forms such as the suite.

To characterize this transformation briefly, i.e. as regards its *principle,*[4] we can say that the bodily exercises of the 'élite' are disconnected from the ordinary social occasions with which folk games remained associated (agrarian feasts, for example) and divested of the social (and, *a fortiori,* religious) functions still attached to a number of traditional games (such as the ritual games played in a number of precapitalist societies at certain turning-points in the farming year). The school, the site of *skhole,* leisure, is the place where practices endowed with social functions and integrated into the collective calendar are converted into *bodily exercises,* activities which are an end in themselves, a sort of physical art for art's sake, governed by specific rules, increasingly irreducible to any functional necessity, and inserted into a specific calendar. The school is the site, *par excellence,* of what are called gratuitous exercises, where one acquires a distant, neutralizing disposition towards language and the social world, the very same one which is implied in the bourgeois relation to art, language and the body: gymnastics makes a use of the body which, like the scholastic use of language, is an end in itself. (This no doubt explains why sporting activity, whose frequency rises very markedly with educational level, declines more slowly with age, as do cultural practices, when educational level is higher. It is known that among the working classes, the abandonment of sport, an activity whose play-like character seems to make it particularly appropriate to adolescence, often coincides with marriage and entry into the serious responsibilities of adulthood.) What is acquired in and through experience of school, a sort of retreat from the world and from real practice, of which the great boarding schools of the 'élite' represent the fully developed form, is the propensity towards activity for no purpose, a fundamental aspect of the ethos of bourgeois 'élites', who always pride themselves on disinterestedness and define themselves by an elective distance—manifested in art and sport—from material interests. 'Fair play' is the way of playing the game characteristic of those who do not get so carried away by the game as to forget that it *is* a game, those who maintain the 'rôle distance', as Goffman puts it, that is implied in all the rôles designated for the future leaders.

The autonomization of the field of sport is also accompanied by a process of *rationalization* intended, as Weber expresses it, to ensure predictability and calculability, beyond local differences and particularisms: the constitution of a corpus of specific rules and of specialized governing bodies recruited, initially at least, from the 'old boys' of the public schools, come hand in hand. The need for a body of fixed, universally applicable rules makes itself felt as soon as sporting 'exchanges' are established between different educational institutions, then between regions, etc. The relative autonomy of the field of sport is most clearly affirmed in the powers of self-administration and rule-making, based on a historical tradition or guaranteed by the State, which sports associations are acknowledged to exercise: these bodies are invested with the right to lay down the standards governing participation in the events which they organize, and they are entitled to exercise a disciplinary power (banning, fines, etc.) in order to ensure observance of the specific rules which they decree. In addition, they award specific titles, such as championship titles and also, as in England, the status of trainer.

The constitution of a field of sports practices is linked to the development of a philosophy of sport which is necessarily a *political* philosophy of sport. The theory of amateurism is in fact one dimension of an aristocratic philosophy of sport as a disinterested practice, a finality without an end, analogous to artistic practice, but even more suitable than art (there is always something residually feminine about art: consider the piano and watercolours of genteel young ladies in the same period) for affirming the manly virtues of future leaders: sport is conceived as a training in courage and manliness, 'forming the character' and inculcating the 'will to win' which is the mark of the true leader, but a will to win within the rules. This is 'fair play', conceived as an aristocratic disposition utterly opposed to the plebeian pursuit of victory at all costs. What is at stake, it seems to me, in this debate (which goes far beyond sport), is a definition of bourgeois education which contrasts with the petty-bourgeois and academic definition: it is 'energy', 'courage', 'willpower', the virtues of leaders (military or industrial), and perhaps above all personal initiative, (private) 'enterprise', as opposed to knowledge, erudition, 'scholastic' submissiveness, symbolized in the great lycée-barracks and its disciplines, etc. In short, it would be a mistake to forget that the modern definition of sport is an integral part of a 'moral ideal', i.e. an ethos which is that of the dominant fractions of the dominant class and is brought to fruition in the major private schools intended primarily for the sons of the heads of private industry, such as the École des Roches, the paradigmatic realization of this ideal. To value *education* over *instruction, character* or *willpower* over *intelligence, sport* over *culture,* is to affirm, within the educational universe itself, the existence of a hierarchy irreducible to the strictly scholastic hierarchy which favours the second term in those oppositions. It means, as it were, disqualifying or discrediting the values recognized by other fractions of the dominant class or by other classes (especially the intellectual fractions of the petty-bourgeoisie and the 'sons of schoolteachers', who are serious challengers to the sons of the bourgeoisie on the terrain of purely scholastic competence); it means putting forward other criteria of 'achievement' and other principles for legitimating achievement as alternatives to 'academic achievement'. (In a recent survey of French industrialists,[5] I was able to demonstrate that the opposition between the two conceptions of education corresponds to two routes into managerial positions in large firms, one from the École des Roches or the major Jesuit schools via the Law Faculty or, more recently, the Institut des Sciences Politiques, the Inspection des Finances or the École des Hautes Études Commerciales, the other from a provincial lycée via the École Polytechnique.) Glorification of sport as the training-ground of character, etc., always implies a certain anti-intellectualism. When one remembers that the dominant fractions of the dominant class always tend to conceive their relation to the dominated fraction—'intellectuals', 'artists', 'professors'—in terms of the opposition between the male and the female, the virile and the effeminate, which is given different contents depending on the period (e.g. nowadays short hair/long hair; 'economico-political' culture/'artistico-literary' culture etc.), one understands one of the most important implications of the exaltation of sport and especially of 'manly' sports like rugby, and it can be seen that sport, like any other practice, is an object of struggles between the fractions of the dominant class and also between the social classes.

At this point I shall take the opportunity to emphasize, in passing, that the *social definition of sport* is an object of struggles, that the field of sporting practices is the site of struggles in which what is at stake, *inter alia,* is the monopolistic capacity to impose the legitimate definition of sporting practice and of the legitimate function of sporting activity— amateurism vs. professionalism, participant sport vs. spectator sport, distinctive (élite) sport vs. popular (mass) sport; that this field is itself part of the larger field of struggles over the definition of the *legitimate body* and the *legitimate use of the body,* struggles which, in addition to the agents engaged in the struggle over the definition of sporting uses of the body, also involve moralists and especially the clergy, doctors (especially health specialists), educators in the broadest sense (marriage guidance counsellors, etc.), pacemakers in matters of fashion and taste (couturiers, etc.). One would have to explore whether the struggles for the monopolistic power to impose the legitimate definition of a particular *class* of body uses, sporting uses, present any *invariant* features. I am thinking, for example, of the opposition, from the point of view of the definition of legitimate exercise, between the professionals in physical education (gymnasiarchs, gymnastics teachers, etc.) and doctors, i.e. between two forms of specific *authority* ('pedagogic' vs. 'scientific'), linked to two sorts of *specific capital;* or the recurrent opposition between two antagonistic philosophies of the use of the body, a more ascetic one (*askesis* = training) which, in the paradoxical expression *culture physique* ('physical culture') emphasizes culture, *antiphysis,* the counter-natural, straightening, rectitude, effort, and another, more hedonistic one which privileges nature, *physis,* reducing culture to the body, physical culture to a sort of 'laisser-faire', or return to 'laisser-faire'—as *expression corporelle* ('physical expression'—'anti-gymnastics') does nowadays, teaching its devotees to unlearn the superfluous disciplines and restraints imposed, among other things, by ordinary gymnastics.

Since the relative autonomy of the field of bodily practices entails, by definition, a relative dependence, the development within the field of practices oriented towards one or the other pole, asceticism or hedonism, depends to a large extent on the state of the power relations within the field of struggles for monopolistic definition of the legitimate body and, more broadly, in the field of struggles between fractions of the dominant class and between the social classes over morality. Thus the progress made by everything that is referred to as 'physical expression' can only be understood in relation to the progress, seen for example in parent-child relations and more generally in all that pertains to pedagogy, of a new variant of bourgeois morality, preached by certain rising fractions of the bourgeoisie (and petty bourgeoisie) and favouring liberalism in child-rearing and also in hierarchical relations and sexuality, in place of ascetic severity (denounced as 'repressive').

The Popularization Phase

It was necessary to sketch in this first phase, which seems to me a determinant one, because in states of the field that are nonetheless quite different, sport still bears the marks of its origins. Not only does the aristocratic ideology of sport as disinterested, gratuitous activity, which lives on in the ritual themes of celebratory discourse, help to mask the true nature of an increasing proportion of sporting practices, but the practice of sports such as tennis, riding, sailing or golf doubtless owes part of its 'interest', just as much nowadays as at the beginning, to its distinguishing function and, more precisely, to the *gains in distinction* which it brings (it is no accident that the majority of the most select, i.e. selective, clubs are organized around sporting activities which serve as a focus or pretext for elective gatherings). We may even consider that the distinctive gains are increased when the distinction between noble—distinguished and distinctive—practices, such as the 'smart' sports, and the 'vulgar' practices which popularization has made of a number of sports originally reserved for the 'élite', such as football (and to a lesser extent rugby, which will perhaps retain for some time to come a dual status and a dual social recruitment), is combined with the yet sharper opposition between participation in sport and the mere consumption of sporting entertainments. We know that the probability of practising a sport beyond adolescence (and *a fortiori* beyond early manhood or in old age) declines markedly as one moves down the social hierarchy (as does the probability of belonging to a sports club), whereas the probability of watching one of the reputedly most popular sporting spectacles, such as football or rugby, on television (stadium attendance as a spectator obeys more complex laws) declines markedly as one rises in the social hierarchy.

Thus, without forgetting the importance of taking part in sport—particularly team sports like football—for working-class and lower middle-class adolescents, it cannot be ignored that the so-called popular sports, cycling, football or rugby, *also* function as spectacles (which may owe part of their interest to imaginary participation based on past experience of real practice). They are 'popular' but in the sense this adjective takes on whenever it is applied to the material or cultural products of mass production, cars, furniture or songs. In brief, sport, born of truly popular games, i.e. games produced by the people, returns to the people, like 'folk music', in the form of spectacles produced for the people. We may consider that sport as a spectacle would appear more clearly as a mass commodity, and the organization of sporting entertainments as one branch among others of show business (there is a difference of degree rather than kind between the spectacle of professional boxing, or Holiday on Ice shows, and a number of sporting events that are perceived as legitimate, such as the various European football championships or ski competitions), if the value collectively bestowed on practising sports (especially now that sports contests have become a measure of relative national strength and hence a political objective) did not help to mask the divorce between practice and consumption and consequently the functions of simple passive consumption.

It might be wondered, in passing, whether some recent developments in sporting practices are not in part an effect of the evolution which I have too rapidly sketched. One only has to think, for example, of all that is implied in the fact that a sport like rugby (in France—but the same is true of American football in the USA) has become, through television, a mass spectacle, transmitted far beyond the circle of present or past 'practitioners', i.e. to a public very imperfectly equipped with the specific competence needed to decipher it adequately. The 'connoisseur' has schemes of perception and appreciation which enable him to see what the layman cannot see, to perceive a necessity where the outsider sees only violence and confusion, and so to find in the promptness of a movement, in the unforeseeable inevitability of a successful combination or the near-miraculous orchestration of a team strategy, a pleasure no less intense and learned than the pleasure a music-lover derives from a particularly successful rendering of a favourite work. The more superficial the perception, the less it finds its pleasure in the spectacle contemplated in itself and for itself, and the more it is drawn to the search for the 'sensational', the cult of obvious feats and visible virtuosity and, above all, the more exclusively it is concerned with that other dimension of the sporting spectacle, suspense and anxiety as to the result, thereby encouraging players and especially organizers to aim for victory at all costs. In other words, everything seems to suggest that, in sport as in music, extension of the public beyond the circle of amateurs helps to reinforce the reign of the pure professionals.

More than by the encouragement it gives to chauvinism and sexism, it is undoubtedly through the division it makes between professionals, the virtuosi of an esoteric technique, and laymen, reduced to the role of mere consumers, a division that tends to become a deep structure of the collective consciousness, that sport produces its most decisive political effects. Sport is not the only area in which ordinary people are reduced to fans, the extreme caricatural form of the militant, condemned to an imaginary participation which is only an illusory compensation for the dispossession they suffer to the advantage of the experts.

In fact, before taking further the analysis of the effects, we must try to analyse more closely the determinants of the shift whereby sport as an élite practice reserved for amateurs became sport as a spectacle produced by professionals for consumption by the masses. It is not sufficient to invoke the relatively autonomous logic of the field of production of sporting goods and services or, more precisely, the development, within this field, of a sporting entertainments industry which, subject to the laws of profitability, aims to maximize its efficiency while minimizing its risks. (This leads, in particular, to the need for specialized executive personnel and scientific management techniques that can rationally organize the training and upkeep of the physical capital of the professional players: one thinks, for example, of American football, in which the squad of trainers, doctors and public-relations men is more numerous than the team of players, and which almost always serves as a publicity medium for the sports equipment and accessories industry.)

In reality, the development of sporting activity itself, even among working-class youngsters, doubtless results partly from the fact that sport was predisposed to fulfil, on a much larger scale, the very same functions which underlay its *invention* in the late nineteenth century English public schools. Even before they saw sport as a means of 'improving character' in accordance with the Victorian belief, the public schools, 'total institutions' in Goffman's sense, which have to carry out their supervisory task twenty-four hours a day, seven days a week, saw sport as 'a means of filling in time', an economical way of occupying the adolescents who were their full-time responsibility. When the pupils are on the sports field, they are easy to supervise, they are engaged in healthy activity and they are venting their violence on each other rather than destroying the buildings or shouting down their teachers; that is why, Ian Weiberg concludes, "organized sport will last as long as the public schools".[6] So it would not be possible to understand the popularization of sport and the growth of sports associations, which, originally organized on a *voluntary* basis, progressively received recognition and aid from the public authorities,[7] if we did not realize that this *extremely economical* means of mobilizing, occupying and controlling adolescents was predisposed to become an instrument and an objective in struggles between all the institutions totally or partly organized with a view to the mobilization and symbolic conquest of the masses and therefore competing for the symbolic conquest of youth. These include political parties, unions, and churches, of course, but also paternalistic bosses, who, with the aim of ensuring *complete and continuous containment* of the working population, provided their employees not only with hospitals and schools but also with stadiums and other sports facilities (a number of sports clubs were founded with the help and under the control of private employers, as is still attested today by the number of stadiums named after employers). We are familiar with the competition which has never ceased to be fought out in the various political arenas over questions of sport from the level of the village (with the rivalry between secular or religious clubs, or more recently, the debates over the priority to be given to sports facilities, which is one of the issues at stake in political struggles on a municipal scale) to the level of the nation as a whole (with, for example, the opposition between the Fédération du Sport de France, controlled by the Catholic Church, and the Fédération Sportive et Gymnique du Travail controlled by the left-wing parties.) And indeed, in an increasingly disguised way as State recognition and subsidies increase, and with them the apparent neutrality of sports organizations and their officials, sport is an object of political struggle. This competition is one of the most important factors in the development of a social, i.e. socially constituted, need for sporting practices and for all the accompanying equipment, instruments, personnel and services. Thus the imposition of sporting needs is most evident in rural areas where the appearance of facilities and teams, as with youth clubs and senior citizens' clubs nowadays, is almost always the result of the work of the village petty-bourgeoisie or bourgeoisie, which finds here an opportunity to impose its political services of organization and leadership[8] and to accumulate or maintain a political capital of renown and honourability which is always potentially reconvertible into political power.

It goes without saying that the popularization of sport, down from the élite schools (where its place is now contested by the 'intellectual' pursuits imposed by the demands of intensified social competition) to the mass sporting associations, is necessarily accompanied by a change in the functions which the sportsmen and their organizers assign to this practice, and also by a transformation of the very logic of sporting practices which corresponds to the transformation of the expectations and demands of the public in correlation with the increasing autonomy of the spectacle vis-à-vis past or present practice. The exaltation of 'manliness' and the cult of 'team spirit'[9] that are associated with playing rugby—not to mention the aristocratic ideal of 'fair play'—have a very different meaning and function for bourgeois or aristocratic adolescents in English public schools and for the sons of peasants or shopkeepers in southwest France. This is simply because, for example, a sporting career, which is practically excluded from the field of acceptable trajectories for a child of the bourgeoisie—setting aside tennis or golf—represents one of the few paths of upward mobility open to the children of the dominated classes; the sports market is to the boys' physical capital what the system of beauty prizes and the occupations to which they lead—hostess, etc.—is to the girls' physical capital; and the working-class cult of sportsmen of working-class origin is doubtless explained in part by the fact that these 'success stories' symbolize the only recognized route to wealth and fame. Everything suggests that the 'interests' and values which practitioners from the working and lower-middle classes bring into the conduct of sports are in harmony with the corresponding requirements of *professionalization* (which can, of course, coexist with the appearances of amateurism) and of the rationalization of preparation for and performance of the sporting exercise that are imposed by the pursuit of maximum specific efficiency (measured in 'wins', 'titles', or 'records') combined with the minimization of risks (which we have seen is itself linked to the development of a private or State sports entertainments industry).

THE LOGIC OF DEMAND: SPORTING PRACTICES AND ENTERTAINMENTS IN THE UNITY OF LIFE-STYLES

We have here a case of a supply, i.e. the particular definition of sporting practice and entertainment that is put forward at a given moment in time, meeting a demand, i.e. the expectations, interests and values that agents bring into the field, with the actual practices and entertainments evolving as a result of the permanent confrontation and adjustment between the two. Of course, at every moment each new entrant must take account of a determinate state of the division of sporting activities and entertainments and their distribution among the social classes, a state which he cannot alter and which is the result of the whole previous history of the struggles and competition among the agents and institutions engaged in the 'sporting field'. For example, the appearance of a new sport or a new way of practising an already established sport (e.g. the 'invention' of the crawl by Trudgen in 1893) causes a restructuring of the space of sporting practices and a more or less complete redefinition of the meaning attached to the various practices. But while it is true that, here as elsewhere, the field of production helps to produce the need for its own products, nonetheless the logic whereby agents incline towards this or that sporting practice cannot be understood unless their dispositions towards sport, which are themselves one dimension of a *particular relation to the body*, are reinserted into the unity of the system of dispositions, the habitus, which is the basis from which life-styles are generated. One would be likely to make serious mistakes if one attempted to study sporting practices (more so, perhaps, than with any other practices, since their basis and object is the body, the synthesizing agent *par excellence,* which integrates everything that it incorporates), without re-placing them in the universe of practices that are bound up with them because their common origin is the system of tastes and preferences that is a class habitus (for example, it would be easy to demonstrate the homologies between the relation to the body and the relation to language that are characteristic of a class or class fraction).[10] Insofar as the 'body-for-others' is the visible manifestation of the person, of the 'idea it wants to give of itself', its 'character', i.e. its values and capacities, the sports practices which have the aim of shaping the body are realizations, among others, of an aesthetic and an ethic in the practical state. A postural norm such as uprightness ('stand up straight') has, like a direct gaze or a close haircut, the function of symbolizing a whole set of moral 'virtues'—rectitude, straightforwardness, dignity (face to face confrontation as a demand for respect)—and also physical ones—vigour, strength, health.

An explanatory model capable of accounting for the distribution of sporting practices among the classes and class fractions must clearly take account of the positive or negative determining factors, the most important of which are *spare time* (a transformed form of economic capital), *economic capital* (more or less indispensable depending on the sport), and *cultural capital* (again, more or less necessary depending on the sport). But such a model would fail to grasp what is most essential if it did not take account of the variations in the meaning and function given to the various practices by the various classes and class fractions. In other words, faced with the distribution of the various sporting practices by social class, one must give as much thought to the variations in the meaning and function of the different sports among the social classes as to the variations in the intensity of the statistical relationship between the different practices and the different social classes. To answer this question, one might be tempted to turn to the *specialists*, who, like nutritionists for food and drink, claim to possess a purely technical definition of what bodily exercise ought to be by reference to a purely technical definition of what the body ought to be. In reality, the sociology and social history of sport, which establish the variations, according to the period, society or social class, of the functions assigned to bodily exercise, also enable us to characterize the illusion that there exists *a* technical definition, i.e. one that is socially neutral and objectively based (on nature), of sporting exercise, as the occupational ideology of the professionals who produce and sell sporting goods and services. As is clearly seen in the case of a diet, which will vary depending on whether the objective—which the dietician's technique cannot of itself determine—is to get fatter or thinner, to approach a weight defined in terms of an ideal which varies with time, place and milieu, the 'choice' of the 'aims' of sporting exercise is determined by a system of principles which orient the whole set of practices, i.e. sexual practices and eating habits, aesthetic preferences and style of dress, and so on.

It would not be difficult to show that the different social classes do not agree as to the effects expected from bodily exercise, whether on the outside of the body (bodily hexis), such as the visible strength of prominent muscles which some prefer or the elegance, ease and beauty favoured by others, or inside the body, health, mental equilibrium, etc. In other words, the class variations in these practices derive not only from the variations in the factors which make it possible or impossible to meet their *economic or cultural costs* but also from the *variations in the perception and appreciation of the immediate or deferred profits* accruing from the different sporting practices. (It can be seen, incidentally, that specialists are able to make use of the specific authority conferred by their status to put forward a perception and appreciation defined as the only legitimate ones, in opposition to the perceptions and appreciations structured by the dispositions of a class habitus. I am thinking of the national campaigns to impose a sport like swimming, which seems to be unanimously approved by the specialists in the name of its strictly 'technical' functions, on those who "can't see the use of it".) As regards the profits actually perceived, Jacques Defrance convincingly shows that gymnastics may be asked to produce either a strong body, bearing the outward signs of strength—this is the working-class demand, which is satisfied by body-building—or a healthy body—this is the bourgeois demand, which is satisfied by a gymnastics or other sports whose function is essentially hygienic.[11]

But this is not all: class habitus defines the meaning conferred on sporting activity, the profits expected from it; and not the least of these profits is the social value accruing from the pursuit of certain sports by virtue of the distinctive rarity they derive from their class distribution. In short, to the 'intrinsic' profits (real or imaginary, it makes little difference—real in the sense of being really anticipated, in the mode of belief) which are expected from sport for the body itself, one must add the social profits, those accruing from any distinctive practice, which are very unequally perceived and appreciated by the different classes (for whom they are, of course, very unequally accessible). It can be seen, for example, that in addition to its strictly health-giving functions, golf, like caviar, *foie gras* or whisky, has a *distributional significance* (the meaning which practices derive from their distribution among agents distributed in social classes), or that weight-lifting, which is supposed to develop the muscles, was for many years, especially in France, the favourite working-class sport; nor is it an accident that the Olympic authorities took so long to grant official recognition to weight-lifting, which, in the eyes of the aristocratic founders of modern sport, symbolized mere strength, brutality and intellectual poverty, in short the working classes.

We can now try to account for the distribution of these practices among the classes and class fractions. The probability of practising the different sports depends, to a different degree for each sport, primarily on economic capital and secondarily on cultural capital and spare time; it also depends on the affinity between the ethical and aesthetic dispositions characteristic of each class or class fraction and the objective potentialities of ethical or aesthetic accomplishment which are or seem to be contained in each sport. The relationship between the different sports and age is more complex, since it is only defined—through the intensity of the physical effort required and the disposition towards that effort which is an aspect of class ethos—within the relationship between a sport and a class. The most important property of the 'popular sports' is the fact that they are tacitly associated with youth, which is spontaneously and implicitly credited with a sort of *provisional licence* expressed, among other ways, in the squandering of an excess of physical (and sexual) energy, and are abandoned very early (usually at the moment of entry into adult life, marked by marriage). By contrast, the 'bourgeois' sports, mainly practised for their functions of physical maintenance and for the social profit they bring, have in common the fact that their age-limit lies far beyond youth and perhaps comes correspondingly later the more prestigious and exclusive they are (e.g. golf). This means that the probability of practising those sports which, because they demand only 'physical' qualities and bodily competences for which the conditions of early apprenticeship seem to be fairly equally distributed, are doubtless equally accessible within the limits of the spare time and, secondarily, the physical energy available, would undoubtedly increase as one goes up the social hierarchy, if the concern for distinction and the absence of ethico-aesthetic affinity or 'taste' for them did not turn away members of the dominant class, in accordance with a logic also observed in other fields (photography, for example).[12] Thus, most of the team sports—basketball, handball, rugby, football—which are most common among office workers, technicians and shopkeepers, and also no doubt the most typically working-class individual sports, such as boxing or wrestling, combine all the reasons to repel the upper classes. These include the social composition of their public which reinforces the vulgarity implied by their popularization, the values and virtues demanded (strength, endurance, the propensity to violence, the spirit of 'sacrifice', docility and submission to collective discipline, the absolute antithesis of the 'rôle distance' implied in bourgeois rôles, etc.), the exaltation of competition and the contest, etc. To understand how the most distinctive sports, such as golf, riding, skiing or tennis, or even some less recherché ones, like gymnastics or mountaineering, are distributed among the social classes and especially among the fractions of the dominant class, it is even more difficult to appeal solely to variations in economic and cultural capital or in spare time. This is firstly because it would be to forget that, no less than the economic obstacles, it is the hidden entry requirements, such as family tradition and early training, and also the obligatory clothing, bearing and techniques of sociability which keep these sports closed to the working classes and to individuals rising from the lower-middle and even upper-middle classes; and secondly because economic constraints define the field of possibilities and impossibilities without determining within it an agent's positive orientation towards this or that particular form of practice. In reality, even apart from any search for distinction, it is the relation to one's own body, a fundamental aspect of the habitus, which distinguishes the working classes from the privileged classes, just as, within the latter, it distinguishes fractions that are separated by the whole universe of a life-style. On one side, there is the *instrumental* relation to the body which the working classes express in all the practices centred on the body, whether in dieting or beauty care, relation to illness or medication, and which is also manifested in the choice of sports requiring a considerable investment of effort, sometimes of pain and suffering (e.g. boxing) and sometimes a *gambling with the body itself* (as in motor-cycling, parachute-jumping, all forms of acrobatics, and, to some extent, all sports involving fighting, among which we may include rugby). On the other side, there is the tendency of the privileged classes to treat the body as an *end in itself*, with variants according to whether the emphasis is placed on the intrinsic functioning of the body as an organism, which leads to the macrobiotic cult of health, or on the appearance of the body as a perceptible configuration, the 'physique', i.e. the body-for-others. Everything seems to suggest that the concern to cultivate the body appears, in its most elementary form, i.e. as the cult of health, often implying an ascetic exaltation of sobriety and dietetic rigour, among the lower middle classes, i.e. among junior executives, clerical workers in the medical services and especially primary-school teachers, who indulge particularly intensively in gymnastics, the ascetic sport *par excellence* since it amounts to a sort of training *(askesis)* for training's sake.

Gymnastics or strictly health-oriented sports like walking or jogging, which, unlike ball games, do not offer any competitive satisfaction, are highly rational and rationalized activities. This is firstly because they presuppose a resolute faith in reason and in the deferred and often intangible benefits which reason promises (such as protection against ageing, an abstract and negative advantage which only exists by reference to a thoroughly theoretical referent); secondly, because they generally only have meaning by reference to a thoroughly theoretical, abstract knowledge of the effects of an exercise which is itself often reduced, as in gymnastics, to a series of abstract movements, decomposed and reorganized by reference to a specific and technically-defined end (e.g. 'the abdominals') and is opposed to the total movements of everyday situations, oriented towards practical goals, just as marching, broken down into elementary movements in the sergeant-major's handbook, is opposed to ordinary walking. Thus it is understandable that these activities can only be rooted in the ascetic dispositions of upwardly mobile individuals who are prepared to find their satisfaction in effort itself and to accept—such is the whole meaning of their existence—the deferred satisfactions which will reward their present sacrifice.

In sports like mountaineering (or, to a lesser extent, walking), which are most common among secondary or university teachers, the purely health-oriented function of maintaining the body is combined with all the symbolic gratifications associated with practising a highly distinctive activity. This gives to the highest degree the sense of mastery of one's own body as well as the free and exclusive appropriation of scenery inaccessible to the vulgar. In fact, the health-giving functions are always more or less strongly associated with what might be called aesthetic functions (especially, other things being equal, in women, who are more imperatively required to submit to the norms defining what the body ought to be, not only in its perceptible configuration but also in its motion, its gait, etc.). It is doubtless among the professions and the well-established business bourgeoisie that the health-giving and aesthetic functions are combined with social functions; there, sports take their place, along with parlour games and social exchanges (receptions, dinners, etc.), among the 'gratuitous' and 'disinterested' activities which enable the accumulation of social capital. This is seen in the fact that, in the extreme form it assumes in golf, shooting, and polo in smart clubs, sporting activity is a mere pretext for select encounters or, to put it another way, a technique of sociability, like bridge or dancing. Indeed, quite apart from its socializing functions, dancing is, of all the social uses of the body, the one which, treating the body as a sign, a sign of one's own ease, i.e. one's own mastery, represents the most accomplished realization of the bourgeois uses of the body: if this way of comporting the body is most successfully affirmed in dancing, this is perhaps because it is recognizable above all by its *tempo*, i.e. by the measured, self-assured slowness which also characterizes the bourgeois use of language, in contrast to working-class abruptness and petty-bourgeois eagerness.

This article is a translation of a paper given at the International Congress of the History of Sports and Physical Education Association, held in March 1978 at the Institut National des Sports et de l'Education Physique, Paris. The original title was "Pratiques sportives et pratiques sociales".

The translation is by Richard Nice.

NOTES

1. Cf. J. Meynaud, *Sport et politique*, Paris, Payot, 1966.
2. One of the options available in the French state-run system of betting on horses. (Translator's note.)
3. J. Defrance, "Esquisse d'une histoire sociale de la gymnastique (1760–1870)", *Actes de la Recherche en Sciences Sociales* 6, 1976, pp. 22–46.
4. For a more detailed analysis, see C. Pociello, "Pratiques sportives et pratiques sociales", *Informations Sociales* 5, 1977, pp. 33–45.
5. P. Bourdieu, M. de Saint Martin, "Le patronat", *Actes de la Recherche en Sciences Sociales* 20/21, 1978, pp. 3–82.
6. I. Weinberg, *The English public schools*, New York, Atherton Press, 1967, pp. 69–70.

7. Cf. Meynaud, op. cit., pp. 58 sq.

8. Cf. P. Bourdieu, "Célibat et condition paysanne," *Etudes Rurales* 5–6, 1962, pp. 32–136.

9. Cf. Weinberg, op. cit., pp. 111–112.

10. Cf. P. Bourdieu, "The economics of linguistic exchanges", *Social Science Information* 16 (6), 1977, pp. 645–668.

11. Defrance, op. cit.

12. Cf. P. Bourdieu et al., *Un art moyen, essai sur les usages sociaux de la photographie*, Paris, Editions de Minuit, 1965.

THIRTEEN

Cultural Entrepreneurship in Nineteenth-Century Boston

The Creation of an Organizational Base for High Culture in America

Paul DiMaggio

Sociological and political discussions of culture have been predicated on a strong dichotomy between high culture—what goes on in museums, opera houses, symphony halls and theatres—and popular culture, of both the folk and commercial varieties. Such culture critics as Dwight Mc-Donald (1957) and Theodor Adorno (1941) have based on this dichotomy thorough-going critiques of popular culture and the mass media. Defenders of popular culture (Lowenthal, 1961; Gans, 1974) have questioned the normative aspect of the critique of popular culture, but have, for the most part, accepted the basic categories. The distinction between high and popular culture has been implicit, as well, in the discussion of public policy towards culture in both the United States and Great Britain (DiMaggio and Useem, 1978).

Yet high and popular culture can be defined neither by qualities inherent to the work of art, nor, as some have argued, by simple reference to the class character of their publics. The distinction between high and popular culture, in its American version, emerged in the period between 1850 and 1900 out of the efforts of urban elites to build organizational forms that, first, isolated high culture and, second, differentiated it from popular culture. Americans did not merely adopt available European models. Instead they groped their way to a workable distinction. Not until two distinct organizational forms—the private or semi-private, non-profit cultural institution and the commercial popular-culture industry—took shape did the high/popular-culture dichotomy emerge in its modern form. Once these organizational models developed, the first in the bosom of elite urban status communities, the second in the relative

This article first appeared in *Media, Culture and Society*, 4 (1982): 33–50. Reprinted with permission of Sage Publications.

impersonality of emerging regional and national markets, they shaped the rôle that cultural institutions would play, the careers of artists, the nature of the works created and performed, and the purposes and publics that cultural organizations would serve.

In this paper I will address only one side of this process of classification, the institutionalization of high culture and the creation of distinctly high-cultural organizations. While high culture could be defined only in opposition to popular culture, it is the process by which urban elites forged an institutional system embodying their ideas about the high arts that will engage us here. In order to grasp the extent to which the creation of modern high-cultural institutions was a task that involved elites as an organic group, we will focus on that process in one American city. Boston in the nineteenth century was the most active center of American culture; and its elite—the Boston Brahmins—constituted the most well defined status group of any of the urban upper classes of this period. For this reason the processes with which I am concerned appear here in particularly clear relief.[1]

When we look at Boston before 1850 we see a culture defined by the pulpit, the lectern and a collection of artistic efforts, amateurish by modern standards, in which effort rarely was made to distinguish between art and entertainment, or between culture and commerce. The arts in Boston were not self-conscious; they drew few boundaries. While intellectuals and ministers distinguished culture that elevated the spirit from that which debased it, there was relatively little agreement on what works or genres constituted which (see Hatch, 1962; Harris, 1966). Harvard's Pierian Sodality mixed popular songs with student compositions and works by European fine-arts composers. The Philharmonic Society played classical concerts, but also backed visiting popular vocalists. Throughout this period, most of Boston music was in the hands of commercial entrepreneurs. Gottlieb Graupner, the city's leading impresario in the 1830s, sold sheet music and instruments, published songs and promoted concerts at which religious, classical and popular tunes mingled freely. (One typical performance included a bit of Italian opera, a devotional song by Mrs Graupner, a piece by Verdi, 'Bluebell of Scotland' and 'The Origin of Common Nails', recited by Mr Bernard, a comedian.) The two exceptions, the Handel and Haydn Society and the Harvard Musical Association, founded in the 1840s and 1850s respectively, were associations of amateurs and professionals that appealed only to a relatively narrow segment of the elite.

The visual arts were also organized on a largely commercial basis in this era. In the 1840s, the American Art Union sold paintings by national lottery (Lynnes, 1953). These lotteries were succeeded, in Boston, New York and Philadelphia, by private galleries. Museums were mod-

elled on Barnum's (Barnum, 1879; Harris, 1973): fine art was inter-
spersed among such curiosities as bearded women and mutant animals,
and popular entertainments were offered for the price of admission to
a clientele that included working people as well as the upper middle
class. Founded as a commercial venture in 1841, Moses Kemball's Boston Museum exhibited works by such painters as Sully and Peale alongside Chinese curiosities, stuffed animals, mermaids and dwarves. For the
entrance fee visitors could also attend the Boston Museum Theatre, which
presented works by Dickens and Shakespeare as well as performances
by gymnasts and contortionists, and brought to Boston the leading players of the American and British stage (McGlinchee, 1940). The promis-
cuous combination of genres that later would be considered incompatible was not uncommon. As late as the 1880s, American circuses employed
Shakespearian clowns who recited the bard's lines in full clown make-up
(Fellows and Freeman, 1936).

By 1910, high and popular culture were encountered far less frequently in the same settings. The distinction towards which Boston's clerics
and critics had groped 50 years before had emerged in institutional form.
The Boston Symphony Orchestra was a permanent aggregation, wrest-
ing the favor of Boston's upper class decisively from the commercial and
co-operative ensembles with which it first competed. The Museum of
Fine Arts, founded in 1873, was at the center of the city's artistic life, its
exhibitions complemented by those of Harvard and the eccentric Mrs
Gardner. Music and art critics might disagree on the merits of individual
conductors or painters; but they were united in an aesthetic ideology
that distinguished sharply between the nobility of art and the vulgarity
of mere entertainment. The distinction between true art, distributed by
not-for-profit corporations managed by artistic professionals and governed closely by prosperous and influential trustees, and popular entertainment, sponsored by entrepreneurs and distributed via the market to
whomever would buy it, had taken a form that has persisted to the present. So, too, had the social distinctions that would differentiate the publics for high and popular culture.

The sacralization of art, the definition of high culture and its opposite, popular culture and the institutionalization of this classification, was
the work of men and women whom I refer to as *cultural capitalists*. I use
the term in two senses to describe the capitalists (and the professionals
whose wealth came from the participation of their families in the industrial ventures—textiles, railroads and mining—of the day) who founded
the museums and the symphony orchestras that embodied and elaborated the high-cultural ideal. They were capitalists in the sense that their
wealth came from the management of industrial enterprises from which
they extracted a profit, and cultural capitalists in that they invested some

of these profits in the foundation and maintenance of distinctly cultural enterprises. They also—and this is the second sense in which I use the term—were collectors of what Bourdieu has called 'cultural capital', knowledge and familiarity with styles and genres that are socially valued and that confer prestige upon those who have mastered them (Bourdieu and Passeron, 1977, 1979). It was the vision of the founders of the institutions that have become, in effect, the treasuries of cultural capital upon which their descendants have drawn that defined the nature of cultural capital in American society.[2]

To create an institutional high culture, Boston's upper class had to accomplish three concurrent, but analytically distinct, projects: entrepreneurship, classification and framing. By entrepreneurship, I mean the creation of an organizational form that members of the elite could control and govern. By classification, I refer to the erection of strong and clearly defined boundaries between art and entertainment, the definition of a high art that elites and segments of the middle class could appropriate as their own cultural property; and the acknowledgment of that classification's legitimacy by other classes and the state. Finally, I use the term framing to refer to the development of a new etiquette of appropriation, a new relationship between the audience and the work of art.[3]

THE PREDECESSORS: ORGANIZATIONAL MODELS BEFORE THE GILDED AGE

By the close of the Civil War, Boston was in many ways the hub of America's cultural life. But, as Martin Green (1966) has illustrated, the unity of the city's economic and cultural elite, the relative vibrancy of Harvard and the vitality of the communal cultural associations of the elite—the Handel and Haydn Society, the Athenaeum, the Dante Circle, the singing clubs—made Boston unique among America's cities. Godkin called Boston 'the one place in America where wealth and the knowledge of how to use it are apt to coincide' (ibid.: 41).

Yet at the close of the Civil War, Boston lacked the organizational arrangements that could sustain a public 'high culture' distinct and insulated from more popular forms. As we have seen, the boundaries between high art and mass art were poorly drawn; artists and performers had not yet segmented elite and popular markets. It is not that the wealthy were uninterested in art. Henry Lee Higginson, later head of the Lee, Higginson brokerage house and founder of the Boston Symphony Orchestra, could reminisce of his not atypical student days in Cambridge in the mid-1850s:

we had been to the Italian opera, getting there seats for twenty-five cents in the upper gallery enjoying it highly. I had an inborn taste for music, which was nourished by a few concerts in Boston and by the opera (Perry, 1921: 29).

His wife recollected

There were private theatricals, sometimes in German, there was a German class, and there were readings which finished with a delightful social gathering in the evening. He [Higginson] belonged to a private singing club in Boston, and often went to James Savage's room in Holworthy, where there was much informal singing and music (ibid.: 81).

Many young Brahmins, like Higginson, spent time in Europe, studying art or music (e.g. Adams, 1928). And many more learned and played music in or around Boston (Whipple, n.d.), or attended public lectures on the arts.

Nor was there a lack of theories about the nature of good art. Although aesthetic philosophies blossomed after the high-culture institutions were established, even the mid-1850s nurtured aesthetic philosophers like Brook Farmer John S. Dwight, editor of *Dwight's Journal of Music*. Some Bostonians were aware of the latest developments in European music and acquainted with classical standards in the visual arts.

High culture (and by this I mean a strongly classified, consensually defined body of art distinct from 'popular' fare) failed to develop in Boston prior to the 1870s because the organizational models through which art was distributed were not equipped to define and sustain such a body and a view of art. Each of the three major models for organizing the distribution of aesthetic experience before 1870—the for-profit firm, the co-operative enterprise and the communal association—was flawed in some important way.

The problems of the privately owned, for-profit firm are most obvious. As Weber (1968, vol. 2, sec. 9: 937) has argued, the market declassifies culture: presenters of cultural events mix genres and cross boundaries to reach out to larger audiences. The Boston Museum, founded in the 1840s, mixed fine art and sideshow oddities, Shakespeare and theatrical ephemerata. For-profit galleries exhibited art as spectacle: when James Jackson Jarves showed his fine collection of Italian primitives at Derby's Institute of Fine Arts in New York, 'the decor of this . . . dazzlingly ornate commercial emporium . . . caused much more favorable comment than Jarves' queer old pictures' (Burt, 1977: 57).

If anything, commerce was even less favorable to the insulation of high art in the performance media. Fine-art theatre in Boston never seems to have got off the ground. And the numerous commercial orchestras that either resided in or toured Boston during this period mixed fine-arts and light music indiscriminately. A memoir of the period recalls a concert of the Germania Society (one of the better orchestras of this type):

> One of the numbers was the "Railway Gallop,"—composer forgotten— during the playing of which a little mock steam-engine kept scooting about the floor of the hall, with black cotton wool smoke coming out of the funnel.

The same writer describes the memorable

> evening when a fantasia on themes from Wallace's "Maritana" was played as a duet for mouth harmonica and the Great Organ; a combination, as the program informed us, "never before attempted in the history of music!" (William F. Apthorp, quoted in Howe, 1914).

As with the visual arts, the commercial treatment of serious music tended to the extravagant rather than to the sacred. In 1869, an entrepreneur organized a Peace Jubilee to celebrate the end of the Civil War. A structure large enough to accommodate 30,000 people was built (at what would later be the first site of the Museum of Fine Arts) and 'star' instrumentalists and vocalists were contracted to perform along with an orchestra of 1000 and a chorus of 10,000. As a finale, the orchestra (which included 330 strings, 75 drums and 83 tubas) played the anvil chorus with accompaniment from a squadron of firemen beating anvils, and the firing of live cannon (Fisher, 1918: 45–46).

An alternative form of organization, embraced by some musical societies, was the workers' co-operative, in which each member had a vote, shared in the profits of the enterprise and elected a conductor from among their number.[4] The co-operative was vulnerable to market incentives. Perhaps more important, however, it was (also like its privately owned counterpart) unable to secure the complete allegiance of its members, who supported themselves by playing many different kinds of music in a wide range of settings. The early New York Philharmonic, for example, performed as a group only monthly. Members anticipated the concert

> as a pleasant relief from more remunerative occupational duties, and the rehearsal periods were cluttered up with routine business matters, from which members could absent themselves with relative impunity (Mueller, 1951: 41).

The lines dividing non-profit, co-operative, for-profit and public enterprise were not as strong in the nineteenth century as they would become in the twentieth. Civic-minded guarantors might hold stock in commercial ventures with no hope of gaining a profit (e.g. Symphony

Hall at the end of the century). The goals of the charitable corporation were usually defined into its charter, but otherwise it legally resembled its for-profit counterpart. Even less clearly defined was what I call the voluntary association: closed associations of individuals (sometimes incorporated, sometimes not) to further the aims of the participating members, rather than of the community as a whole. For associations like the Handel and Haydn Society, which might give public concerts, or the Athenaeum, which took an active rôle in public affairs, privateness was relative. But, ultimately, each was a voluntary and exclusive instrument of its members.

Why were these communal associations ill-suited to serve as the organizational bases for high culture in Boston? Why could the Athenaeum, a private library, or the Boston Art Club, which sponsored contemporary art shows (Boston Art Club, 1878), not have developed continuous programs of public exhibitions? Could not the Handel and Haydn Society, the Harvard Musical Association (formed by Harvard graduates who wished to pursue after graduation musical interests developed in the College's Pierian Sodality) or one of the numerous singing circles have developed into a permanent orchestra? They faced no commercial temptations to study, exhibit or perform any but the highest art. (Indeed, the Harvard Musical Association's performances were so austere as to give rise to the proverb 'dull as a symphony concert' (Howe, 1914: 8).

None of them, however, could, by the late nineteenth century, claim to speak for the community as a whole, even if they chose to. Each represented only a fraction (although, in the case of Athenaeum, a very large and potent fraction) of the elite; and, in the case of the musical associations and the Art Club, members of the middle class and artistic professionals were active as well. The culture of an elite status group must be monopolized, it must be legitimate and it must be sacralized. Boston's cultural capitalists would have to find a form able to achieve all these aims: a single organizational base for each art form; institutions that could claim to serve the community, even as they defined the community to include only the elite and the upper-middle classes; and enough social distance between artist and audience, between performer and public, to permit the mystification necessary to define a body of artistic work as sacred.

This they did in the period between 1870 and 1900. By the end of the century, in art and music (but not in theatre [see Twentieth Century Club, 1919; Poggi, 1968]), the differences between high- and popular-culture artists and performers were becoming distinct, as were the physical settings in which high and popular art were presented.

The form that the distribution of high culture would take was the non-profit corporation, governed by a self-perpetuating board of trustees who, eventually, would delegate most artistic decisions to professional artists or art historians (Zolberg, 1974, 1981). The charitable corporation was not designed to define a high culture that elites could monopolize; nor are non-profit organizations by their nature exclusive. But the non-profit corporation had five virtues that enabled it to play a key rôle in this instance. First, the corporation was a familiar and successful tool by which nineteenth-century elites organized their affairs (see Fredrickson, 1965; Story, 1980; Hall, forthcoming). In the economic realm it enabled them to raise capital for such profitable ventures as the Calumet and Hecla Mines, the western railroads and the telephone company. In the non-profit arena, it had been a useful instrument for elite communal governance at Harvard, the Massachusetts General Hospital and a host of charitable institutions (Story, 1980). Second, by entrusting governance decisions to trustees who were committed either to providing financial support or to soliciting it from their peers, the non-profit form effectively (if not completely) insulated museums and orchestras from the pressures of the market. Third, by vesting control in a well integrated social and financial elite, the charitable corporation enabled its governors to rule without interference from the state or from other social classes. Fourth, those organizations whose trustees were able to enlist the support of the greater part of the elite could provide the stability needed for a necessarily lengthy process of defining art and developing ancillary institutions to insulate high-cultural from popular-cultural work, performance and careers. Finally, and less obviously, the goals of the charitable corporation, unlike those of the profit-seeking firm, are diffuse and ambiguous enough to accommodate a range of conflicting purposes and changing ends. The broad charters of Boston's major cultural organizations permitted their missions to be redefined with time, and enabled their governors to claim (and to believe) that they pursued communitarian goals even as they institutionalized a view and vision of art that made elite culture less and less accessible to the vast majority of Boston's citizens.

THE CONTEXT OF CULTURAL CAPITALISM

In almost every literate society, dominant status groups or classes eventually have developed their own styles of art and the institutional means of supporting them. It was predictable that this would happen in the United States, despite the absence of an hereditary aristocracy. It is more difficult, however, to explain the timing of this process. Dwight and others wished (but failed) to start a permanent professional symphony orchestra from at least the 1840s. The Athenaeum's proprietors tried to raise a public subscription to purchase the Jarves collection in the late 1850s, but they failed. What had changed?

Consider, first, the simple increase in scale and wealth between 1800 and 1870. At the time of the revolution, Boston's population was under 10,000. By 1800 it had risen to 25,000; by 1846 it was 120,000. By 1870, over a quarter of a million people lived in Boston (Lane, 1975). The increase in the size of the local cultural market facilitated a boom in theatre building in the 1830s (Nye, 1960: 264), a rise in the number and stability of book and music stores (Fisher, 1918: 30) and the growth of markets for theatre, music, opera, dancing and equestrian shows (Nye, 1960: 143). The growth of population was accompanied by an increase in wealth. Boston's first fortunes were mercantile, the fruits of the China trade, large by local, but small by national standards. In 1840, Boston had but a handful of millionaires. By 1890, after post–Civil War booms in railroads, mining, banking and communications, there were 400 (Jaher, 1968, 1972; Story, 1980). Even the physical scale of the city changed during this period: beginning in 1856, developers began filling in the waters of the Back Bay, creating a huge tract of publicly owned land, partially devoted to civic and cultural buildings. As wealthy outlanders from Lawrence, Lynn and Lexington migrated to Beacon Hill and Cambridge, streetcars reduced the cost and the difficulty of travel to Boston from its suburbs (Warner, 1970). In short, Boston was larger, wealthier and more compact in 1870 than it had been 50 years before.

With growth came challenges to the stability of the community and to the cultural authority (Starr, forthcoming) of elites. Irish immigrants flowed into Boston from the 1840s to work in the city's industrial enterprises (Handlin, 1972; Thernstrom, 1972); industrial employment rôles doubled between 1845 and 1855 (Handlin, 1972). With industry and immigration came disease, pauperism, alcoholism, rising infant mortality and vice. The Catholic Irish were, by provenance and religion, outside the consensus that the Brahmins had established. By 1900, 30% of Boston's residents were foreign-born and 70% were of foreign parentage (Green, 1966: 102). By the close of the Civil War, Boston's immigrants were organizing to challenge the native elite in the political arena (Solomon, 1956).

If immigration and industrialization wrought traumatic changes in the city's social fabric, the political assault on Brahmin institutions by native populists proved even more frightening. The Know-Nothings who captured state government in the 1850s attacked the social exclusivity of Harvard College frontally, amending its charter and threatening state control over its governance, hiring and admissions policies (Story, 1980). Scalded by these attacks, Boston's leadership retreated from the public sector to found a system of non-profit organizations that permitted them to maintain some control over the community even as they lost their command of its political institutions.[5]

Story (1980) argues persuasively that this political challenge, and the wave of institution-building that followed it, transformed the Brahmins from an elite into a social class.[6] As a social class, the Brahmins built institutions (schools, almshouses and charitable societies) aimed at securing control over the city's social life (Huggins, 1971; Vogel, 1981). As a status group, they constructed organizations (clubs, prep schools and cultural institutions) to seal themselves off from their increasingly unruly environment. Thus Vernon Parrington's only partially accurate observation that 'The Brahmins conceived the great business of life to be the erection of barriers against the intrusion of the unpleasant' (quoted in Shiverick, 1970: 129). The creation of a network of private institutions that could define and monopolize high art was an essential part of this process of building cultural boundaries.

The Brahmin class, however, was neither large enough to constitute a public for large-scale arts organizations, nor was it content to keep its cultural achievements solely to itself. Alongside of, and complicating, the Brahmins' drive towards exclusivity was a conflicting desire, as they saw it, to educate the community. The growth of the middle class during this period—a class that was economically and socially closer to the working class and thus in greater need of differentiating itself from it culturally—provided a natural clientele for Boston's inchoate high culture. While we have all too little information about the nature of the visitors to Boston's Museum or of the audiences for the Symphony, it seems certain from contemporary accounts (and sheer arithmetic) that many of them were middle class. The same impulse that created the markets for etiquette and instruction books in the mid-nineteenth century helped populate the galleries and concert halls of the century's last quarter (Nye, 1960; Douglas, 1978).

CULTURAL ENTREPRENEURSHIP: THE MUSEUM OF FINE ARTS AND THE BOSTON SYMPHONY ORCHESTRA

The first step in the creation of a high culture was the centralization of artistic activities within institutions controlled by Boston's cultural capitalists. This was accomplished with the foundings of the Museum of Fine Arts and the Boston Symphony Orchestra. These institutions were to provide a framework, in the visual arts and music, respectively, for the definition of high art, for its segregation from popular forms and for the elaboration of an etiquette of appropriation.

Bostonians had sought to found a museum for some time before 1870. In 1858, the state legislature, dominated by factions unfriendly to Boston's elite, refused to provide Back Bay land for a similar venture (Harris, 1962: 548). The immediate impetus for the Museum, however, was a bequest by Colonel Timothy Bigelow Lawrence of an armor collection too large for the Athenaeum's small gallery to accommodate. Three years earlier the Athenaeum's Fine Arts Committee had suggested that the galleries be expanded, but nothing had been done. With the Lawrence bequest, and his widow's offer to contribute a wing to a new gallery, the trustees voted that

> the present is a proper time for making an appeal to the public and especially to the friends of the Fine Arts, to raise the sum required to make available Mrs. Lawrence's proposed donation, and, if possible, to provide even larger means to carry out so noble a design in the confident hope that it may be attended with success . . . (Whitehill, 1970: 6–8).

A new museum promised to solve problems for several of Boston's elite institutions: Harvard had a collection of prints for which it sought a fire-safe depository, and MIT and the American Social Science Association possessed collections of architectural casts too large for them to store conveniently. After a series of meetings between the Athenaeum trustees and other public and private decision makers, it was decided to raise money for a museum on a tract of land in the Back Bay. (The land, owned by the Boston Water Power Company, was made available through the intervention of Mathias Denman Ross, a local developer who was keenly aware of the effects of public and cultural buildings on the value of nearby real estate.) In 1870 the state legislature chartered the enterprise and, with the help of the Athenaeum, which sponsored exhibitions throughout this period, fund-raising began.[7]

The initial aspirations of the Museum founders were somewhat modest. The key figure in the founding was Charles Callahan Perkins, great-nephew of a China-trade magnate, kinsman of the chairman of the Athenaeum's Fine Arts Committee and himself President of the Boston Art Club. Perkins wrote two books on Italian sculpture in the 1860s, championed arts education in Boston's public schools and served as head of the American Social Science Association's arts-education panel in 1869. (He had studied painting and sculpture in Europe for almost 10 years, before concluding that he lacked the creativity to be a good artist.) Perkins, in a report to the ASSA had asserted 'the feasibility of establishing a regular Museum of Art at moderate expense', with primarily educational aims. Since Boston's collections had few originals, he recommended that the new collection consist of reproductions, primarily plaster casts of sculpture and architecture.

The breadth of response to the first appeal for funds for the museum is striking. Although the economy was not robust, $261,425 was collected for the building. Of this amount, the largest gift was $25,000, only two were larger than $5000 and all but $100,000 came from over 1000 gifts of less than $2000 from such sources as local newspapers, public-school teachers and workers at a piano factory. (By contrast, when the Museum sought to raise $400,000 for new galleries and an endowment 15 years later, $218,000 of the·initial $240,000 in contributions came from a mere 58 donors (Whitehill, 1970: 42).)

One reason for the breadth of early support was that the Museum, although in private hands, was to be a professedly communitarian and educational venture. The Board of Trustees contained a large segment of the Brahmin class: All but one of the first 23 trustees were proprietors of the Athenaeum; 11 were members of the Saturday Club, while many others were members of the Somerset and St Botolph's clubs; most were graduates of Harvard and many were active in its affairs. The public nature of the Board was further emphasized by the inclusion on it of permanent and *ex-officio* appointments: from Harvard, MIT and Athenaeum; the Mayor, the Chairman of the Boston Public Library's board, the trustee of the Lowell Institute, the Secretary of the State Board of Education and the Superintendent of Boston's schools. The trustees dedicated the institution to education; one hoped that the breadth of the board's membership would ensure that the Museum's managers would be 'prevented from squandering their funds upon the private fancies of would-be connoisseurs'. Indeed, the articles of incorporation required that the Museum be open free of charge at least four times a month. The public responded by flooding the Museum on free weekend days in the early years (Harris, 1962: 48–52).

The centralization of the visual arts around a museum required only the provision of a building and an institution controlled by a board of civic-minded members of the elite. The Museum functioned on a relatively small budget in its early years, under the direction of Charles Greely Loring, a Harvard graduate and Civil War general, who had studied Egyptology when his physician sent him to the banks of the Nile. The Museum's founders, facing the need to raise substantial funds, organized both private and public support carefully, mobilizing a consensus in favor of their project from the onset.

By contrast, the Boston Symphony Orchestra was, for its first years at least, a one-man operation, forced to wrest hegemony over Boston's musical life from several contenders, each with its own coterie of elite support. That Henry Lee Higginson, a partner in the brokerage firm of Lee, Higginson, was able to do so was a consequence of the soundness of his organizational vision, the firmness of his commitment, and, equally important, his centrality to Boston's economic and social elite.

In a sense, Higginson began as a relative outsider. Although his father, founder of the family firm, made a fortune in shipping, Henry was the first of his line to matriculate at Harvard; and soon he dropped out (claiming poor vision), visiting Europe and returning to private tutelage in Cambridge. Upon completing his education, he studied music in Europe for several years, ultimately against the wishes of his father, as their tense and sometimes acrimonious correspondence suggests (Perry, 1921: 121–135). After an accident lamed his arm, he returned to the United States for good, fought in the Civil War, married a daughter of the Harvard scientist Louis Agassiz and, following a disastrous venture in southern farming and a lucrative investment in the Calumet and Hecla copper mines, finally joined his father's State Street firm.[8]

Higginson was a knowledgeable student of music, and a follower of the aesthetic doctrines of John S. Dwight. As early as 1840, Dwight had called for the founding of a permanent orchestra in Boston. 'This promises something', he wrote of an amateur performance.

> We could not but feel that the materials that evening collected might, if they could be kept together through the year, and induced to practice, form an orchestra worthy to execute the grand works of Haydn and Mozart. . . . To secure these ends might not a plan of this kind be realized? Let a few of our most accomplished and refined musicians institute a series of cheap instrumental concerts. . . . Let them engage to perform quartettes, etc., occasionally a symphony, by the best masters and no others. Let them repeat the best and most characteristic pieces enough to make them a study to the audiences (Howe, 1914: 4–5).

As we have seen, a number of ensembles attempted to realize Dwight's ambitions. But it was Higginson's organizational skills (and his money) that gave Boston the nation's first permanent, philanthropically supported and governed, full-season symphony orchestra. In achieving the dream of a large permanent orchestra devoted to fine-arts music, Higginson faced and overcame two challenges: first, establishing control over fine-arts music in Boston as a whole; and, second, enforcing internal discipline over the orchestra's members. Against him were arrayed the supporters of Boston's existing ensembles, principally the Philharmonia and the Harvard Musical Association, and the city's musicians, jealous of their personal and professional autonomy.

Higginson published his plans for the orchestra in a column, headed 'In the Interest of Good Music', that appeared in several of Boston's newspapers:

> Notwithstanding the development of musical taste in Boston, we have never yet possessed a full and permanent orchestra, offering the best music at low prices, such as may be found in all the large European cities. . . . The

essential condition of such orchestras is their stability, whereas ours are necessarily shifting and uncertain, because we are dependent upon musicians whose work and time are largely pledged elsewhere. To obviate this difficulty the following plan is offered. It is an effort made simply in the interest of good music, and though individual in as much as it is independent of societies or clubs, it is in no way antagonistic to any previously existing musical organization (Howe, 1914: 41).

In this last sentence, Higginson treads on delicate ground. He goes on to praise, specifically, the Handel and Haydn Society and the Harvard Musical Association, the two musical societies with the closest Brahmin connections, while indicating implicitly that there will be no further need for the services of the latter. To launch this new enterprise, Higginson proposes to spend, annually, $20,000 of his own money until the orchestra becomes self-supporting.

Despite a measure of public incredulity, and some resentment at Higginson's choice of European conductor, George Henschel, over local candidates, the BSO opened in December 1881 to the enthusiastic response of the musical public. (The demand for tickets was great; lines formed outside the box office the evening before they went on sale.) The social complexion of the first night's audience is indicated by a report in a Boston newspaper that 'the spirit of the music so affected the audience that when the English national air was recognized in Weber's Festival Overture, the people arose en masse and remained standing until the close'. By employing local musicians and permitting them to play with the Philharmonic Society and the Harvard Musical Association (both of which, like the BSO, offered about 20 concerts that season), Higginson earned the gratitude of the city's music lovers.

The trouble began in February 1882, when the players received Higginson's terms for the following season. To continue to work for the Symphony, they would be required to make themselves available for rehearsals and performances from October through April, four days a week, and to play for no other conductor or musical association. (The Handel and Haydn Society, which had strong ties to the Athenaeum, was exempted from this prohibition.) The implications of the contract, which the players resisted unsuccessfully, were clear: Boston's other orchestras, lacking the salaries that Higginson's subsidies permitted, would be unable to compete for the services of Boston's musicians. (To make matters worse, a number of the city's journeymen musicians received no offers from Higginson at all.)

The response of the press, particularly of the Brahmin *Transcript*, suggests that loyalists of the other ensembles responded to Higginson's actions with outrage. The *Transcript* editorialized of Higginson

He thus "makes a corner" in orchestral players, and monopolizes these for his own concerts and those of the Handel and Haydn Society. . . . Mr. Higginson's gift becomes an imposition, it is something that we must receive, or else we look musical starvation in the face. It is as if a man should make a poor friend a present of several baskets of champagne and, at the same time, cut off his whole water supply.

A more populist newspaper complained that the 'monopoly of music' was 'an idea that could scarcely have emanated from any association except that of deluded wealth with arrant charlatanism'. Even *Music,* a New York publication originally friendly to Higginson's efforts, called his contract

a direct stab at the older organizations and rival conductors of Boston. It means that one or two organizations may make efforts to place their concerts on the off days which Mr. Henschel has been pleased to allow them, but some must be left in the cold, orchestraless and forlorn. . . . The manner in which the proposal was made was also one that forebodes tyranny. Some of the oldest members of the Orchestra, men whose services to music in Boston have entitled them to deference and respect, were omitted altogether, and will be left out of the new organization. It was intimated strongly that in case the offer was rejected by the men, their places would be filled from the ranks of European orchestras (Howe, 1914: 67–69).

Higginson and his orchestra weathered the storm. Attendance stayed up and, within a year, his was the only orchestral association in Boston, co-existing peacefully with the smaller Handel and Haydn Society. In order to achieve the kind of ensemble he desired, however, Higginson had to ensure that his musicians would commit their time and their attention to the BSO alone, and accept his (and his agent's, the conductor's) authority as inviolate. Since, in the past, all musicians, whatever their affiliations, were freelancers upon whom no single obligation weighed supreme, accomplishing these aspirations required a fundamental change in the relationship between musicians and their employers.

In part, effecting this internal monopolization of attention was simply a matter of gaining an external monopoly of classical-music performance. With the surrender of the Philharmonic Society and the Harvard Musical Association, two major competitors for the working time of Boston's musicians disappeared. Nonetheless, while his musicians were now more dependent upon the BSO for their livelihoods, and thus more amenable to his demands, his control over the work force was still challenged by the availability of light-music or dance engagements, teaching commitments and the tradition of lax discipline to which the players were accustomed.

Throughout his life, Higginson fought to maintain control over the

Orchestra's employees, and the issue of discipline was foremost in his mind from the beginning. In an early plan for the Orchestra, he suggested engaging a conductor and eight to ten exceptionally good younger musicians from outside Boston at a fixed salary, 'who would be ready at my call to play anywhere, and then to draw around them the best of our Boston musicians, thus refreshing and renewing the present orchestra, and getting more nearly possession of it . . .' (Howe, 1914: 28). At that time, exclusive employment contracts were so rare that the more timid Henschel, after agreeing to serve as conductor, tried to convince Higginson to abandon his insistence on total commitment. 'I assure you', he wrote as the first orchestra was being assembled,

> that is the best thing we can do, and if you have any confidence in my judgment, pray drop all conditions in the contract except those relating to our own welfare. I mean now the conditions of discipline, etc. (Perry, 1921: 299).

Despite his frequent assertions that he yielded in all cases to his conductors' advice on orchestral matters, Higginson, as we have seen, insisted on exclusive contracts in the orchestra's second year, threatening to break any strike with the importation of European players. Although he won that battle, he nonetheless replaced the locals gradually, over the course of the next decade, with new men with few Boston ties, mostly European, of greater technical accomplishment, upon whose loyalty he could count (Howe, 1914: 121–123).

In this, Higginson was not merely following a European model. 'My contracts', he wrote an associate in 1888, 'are very strong, indeed much stronger than European contracts usually are . . .' (Perry, 1921: 398). Characteristic of the orchestra contract was section 12:

> If said musician fails to play to the satisfaction of said Higginson, said Higginson may dismiss said musician from the Orchestra, paying his salary to the time of dismissal, and shall not be liable to pay him any compensation or damages for such dismissal (Perry, 1921: 398).

Higginson was undeniably an autocrat. In later years he rejected the suggestions of friends to place the Orchestra under a board of trustees; and he used the threat of discontinuing his annual subventions as a bludgeon to forestall the unionization of the players. Yet Higginson accomplished what all orchestras would have to achieve if orchestral work was to be separated permanently from the playing of popular music and Dwight's dream of a permanent orchestra devoted to high-art music achieved: the creation of a permanent musical work force, under exclusive contract, willing to accept without question the authority of the conductor.

THE BRAHMINS AS AN ORGANIZATION-FORMING CLASS

The Museum of Fine Arts and the Boston Symphony Orchestra were both organizations embedded in a social class, formal organizations whose official structure was draped around the ongoing life of the group that governed, patronized, and staffed them.[9] They were not separate products of different segments of an elite; or of artists and critics who mobilized wealthy men to bankroll their causes. Rather they were the creations of a densely connected self-conscious social group intensely unified by multiple ties among its members based in kinship, commerce, club life and participation in a wide range of philanthropic associations. Indeed, if, as Stinchcombe (1965) has argued, there are 'organization-forming organizations'—organizations that spawn off other organizations in profusion—there are also organization-forming status groups, and the Brahmins were one of these. This they could be not just because of their cultural or religious convictions (to which Green (1966), Baltzell (1979) and Hall (forthcoming) have called attention), but because they were integrated by their families' marriages, their Harvard educations, their joint business ventures, their memberships in a web of social clubs and their trusteeships of charitable and cultural organizations. This integration is exemplified in the associations of Higginson, and in the ties between the Museum and the Orchestra during the last 20 years of the nineteenth century.

It is likely that Higginson's keen instinct for brokerage—and the obligations he accrued as principal in one of Boston's two major houses—served him well in his efforts to establish the Orchestra. At first glance, Higginson's achievement in creating America's first elite-governed permanent symphony orchestra in Boston appears to be the work of a rugged individualist. On closer inspection, we see that it was precisely Higginson's centrality to the Brahmin social structure that enabled him to succeed. Only a lone, centrally located entrepreneur could have done what Higginson did, because to do so ruffled so many feathers: a committee would have compromised with the supporters of other musical associations and with the patrons of the more established local musicians. Nonetheless, if Higginson's youthful marginality permitted the attempt, it was his eventual centrality that enabled him to succeed. His career illustrates the importance of kinship, commerce, clubs and philanthropy in Boston elite life. Ties in each of these areas reinforced those in the others; each facilitated the success of the Orchestra, and each brought him into close connection with the cultural capitalists active in the MFA and led, eventually, to his selection as a Museum trustee.

Higginson was born a cousin to some of the leading families in Boston: the Cabots, the Lowells, the Perkinses, the Morses, the Jacksons, the

Channings and the Paines, among others (Perry, 1921: 14). (The first four of these families produced trustees of the Museum of Fine Arts during Higginson's lifetime. His kinsman Frances W. Higginson was also a Museum trustee.) In Cambridge, he was close to Charles Lowell and, after his first European adventure, he studied with Samuel Eliot, a cousin of Harvard President Charles W. Eliot, and later a trustee of the Museum. During this period, he spent a great deal of time in the salon-like household of Louis Agassiz, befriending the scientist's son and marrying his daughter. So close did Henry remain to his Harvard classmates that, despite his withdrawal after freshman year, they permitted him to take part in their class's Commencement exercises.

When Henry went into business, he brought his family and college ties with him. A contemporary said of the Lee, Higginson firm, it 'owed in some measure to family alliances its well-advised connections with the best financial enterprises of the day' (Perry, 1921: 272). Indeed, Higginson's first successful speculation was his investment in the Calumet and Hecla mines, at the behest of his in-laws Agassiz and Shaw (the latter an early donor of paintings to the Museum). The family firm was instrumental in the development of the western railroads, through the efforts of cousin Charles Jackson Paine. In this enterprise, Higginson associated with John M. Forbes and with Charles H. Perkins (kinsman of the MFA founder). Higginson was so intimate with the latter that he invested Perkins' money without consultation. Lee, Higginson made a fortune in the telephone company, and Higginson, in later years, was a director of General Electric. In some of these ventures, the firm co-operated with other Boston financiers. Higginson was on close terms with his competitors Kidder of Kidder, Peabody (the Museum's first treasurer) and Endicott, President of the New England Trust and Suffolk Savings (and the Museum's second treasurer). Gardiner Martin Lane was a partner in Lee, Higginson when he resigned his position to assume the Museum's presidency in 1907.

Higginson was also an active clubman, a member of the Tavern Club (and its President for twenty years), the Wednesday Evening Club, the Wintersnight, Friday Night and Officers Clubs, New York's Knickerbocker Club and, from 1893, the Saturday Club. Among his Tavern Club colleagues were Harvard's Charles Eliot Norton (spiritual godfather of the Museum's aesthetes), William Dean Howells and Henry Lee. At the Friday Club he consorted with Howells, William James and Henry Adams. At the Saturday Club, his clubmates included the MFA's Thomas Gold Appleton and Martin Brimmer.

In the 1890s, Higginson's career in Boston philanthropy blossomed. (By now he was on the MFA's Board. Earlier, when the Museum's first President, Martin Brimmer, asked Charles Eliot Norton if Higginson should be invited, Norton wrote back that 'Higginson would be excellent, but he never attends meetings' (Harris, 1962: 551).) He lavished most of his attention (beyond that devoted to the Orchestra) on Harvard, which elected him a Fellow in 1893. He gave Harvard Soldiers Field and a new student union, was Treasurer of Radcliffe College, played a key rôle in the founding of the Graduate School of Business, patronized the medical school and gave anonymous gifts to deserving faculties.[10] Higginson's position as Fellow of Harvard placed him at the summit of Boston's institutional life and undoubtedly reinforced his contacts with the Museum's trustees and friends. His personal art collection, which included Turners, Corots and Rodins, encouraged such interactions as well. (In 1893, he donated a valuable Dutch master to the MFA.)

Thus was the Orchestra's founder embedded in the Brahmin community. When Lee, Higginson furnished an emergency loan of $17,000 to the Museum of Fine Arts in 1889, with little prospect of repayment, was this because he was on the Board; was it a consequence of Higginson's kinship ties with the Cabots, Perkinses or Lowells; his business alliances with Kidder or Endicott; his club friendship with Norton; Harvard ties to the Eliots? The range of possibilities renders the question trivial and illustrates how closely knit was Higginson's world.

In 1893, when Higginson demanded that Boston build him a new and suitable Symphony Hall, lest he abandon the Orchestra to bankruptcy and dissolution, the initial appeal for funds was signed by a broad cross section of the city's elite: his friends and kinsmen Agassiz, Lodge, Lowell, Lee and John Lowell Gardner; Harvard's Eliot, Norton, Longfellow, Shattuck and Parkman; Peabody of Kidder Peabody, to name a few. Present on the list were at least four of Higginson's fellow MFA trustees: the President (Martin Brimmer), the Treasurer (by now, John L. Gardner), Eliot and Norton.[11] The group raised over $400,000, a substantial stake in that financially troubled year.

CONCLUSIONS

The Museum of Fine Arts and the Boston Symphony Orchestra were creations of the Brahmins, and the Brahmins alone. As such, their origins are easier to understand than were British or Continental efforts in which aristocrats and bourgeoisie played complex and interrelated rôles (Wolff, 1982). The Brahmins were a status group, and as such they strove towards exclusivity, towards the definition of a prestigious culture that they could monopolize as their own. Yet they were also a social class, and they were concerned, as is any dominant social class, with establishing hegemony over those they dominated. Some Marxist students of culture have misinterpreted the cultural institutions as efforts to dictate taste or to inculcate the masses with the ideas of elites. Certainly, the cultural capitalists, consummate organizers and intelligent men and woman, were wise enough to understand the impossibility of socializing the masses in institutions from which they effectively were barred. Their concern with education, however, was not simply window-dressing or an effort at public relations. Higginson, for example, devoted much of his fortune to American universities and secondary schools. He once wrote a kinsman, from whom he sought a donation of $100,000 for Harvard, 'Educate, and save ourselves and our families and our money from the mobs!' (Perry, 1921: 329). Moreover, a secret or thoroughly esoteric culture could not have served to legitimate the status of American elites; it would be necessary to share it, at least partially. The tension between monopolization and hegemony, between exclusivity and legitimation, was a constant counterpoint to the efforts at classification of American urban elites.

This explains, in part, the initial emphasis on education at the Museum of Fine Arts. Yet, from the first, the Museum managers sought to educate through distinguishing true from vulgar art—at first, cautiously, later with more confidence. In the years that followed they would place increased emphasis on the original art that became available to them, until they abandoned reproductions altogether and with them their emphasis on education. In a less dramatic way, the Orchestra, which began with an artistic mandate, would further classify the contents of its programs and frame the aesthetic experience in the years to come.

In structure, however, the Museum and the Orchestra were similar innovations. Each was private, controlled by members of the Brahmin class, and established on the corporate model, dependent on private philanthropy and relatively long-range financial planning; each was sparely staffed and relied for much of its management on elite volunteers; and each counted among its founders wealthy men with considerable scholarly or artistic credentials who were centrally located in Boston's elite social structure. The Museum was established under broad auspices for the education of the community as a whole; the Orchestra was created by one man in the service of art and of those in the community with the sophistication or motivation to appreciate it. Within 40 years, the logic of cultural capitalism would moderate sharply, if not eliminate, these historically grounded differences. The Symphony would come to resemble the Museum in charter and governance, and the Museum would abandon its broad social mission in favor of aestheticism and an elite clientele.

The creation of the MFA, the BSO and similar organizations throughout the United States created a base through which the ideal of high culture could be given institutional flesh. The alliance between class and culture that emerged was defined by, and thus inseparable from, its

organizational mediation. As a consequence, the classification 'high cul-
ture/popular culture' is comprehensible only in its dual sense as characterizing both a ritual classification and the organizational systems that
give that classification meaning.

NOTES

1. The process, in other American cities, was to a large extent influenced by
the Boston model. A final, more mundane, consideration recommends Boston
as the focus for this study. The work in this paper is still in an exploratory stage,
at which I am plundering history rather than writing it; the prolixity of nineteenth-century Boston's men and women of letters and the dedication and quality of her local historians makes Boston an ideal site for such an enterprise.

2. In a third sense, 'cultural capital' might refer to the entrepreneurs of popular culture—the Barnums, the Keiths, the Shuberts and others—who turned
culture into profits. While we will not consider this group at any length, we must
remember that it was in opposition to their activities that the former defined
their own.

3. My debt to Bernstein (1975*a, b*) and to Mary Douglas (1966) is evident
here. My use of the terms 'classification' and 'framing' is similar to Bernstein's.

4. See Couch (1976*a, b*) and Mueller (1951: 37ff.) for more detailed descriptions of this form.

5. Shiverick (1970) notes the contrast between the founding of the public
library in the 1850s and that of the private art museum 20 years later, both
enterprises in which Athenaeum members were central.

6. I use the term 'class' to refer to a self-conscious elite united by bonds of
economic interest, kinship and culture (see Thompson, 1966: 8; Story, 1980: xi).

7. This section relies heavily upon Walter Muir Whitehill's classic two-volume
history of the Museum (1970) and, to a lesser extent, on Neil Harris' fine paper
(1962) for its facts, albeit not for their interpretation.

8. In Henry Adams' words, 'Higginson, after a desperate struggle, was forced
into State Street' (Adams, 1928: 210). In later years, Higginson told a relative
that 'he never walked into 44 State Street without wanting to sit down on the
doorstep and cry' (Perry, 1921: 135).

9. In James Thompson's terms, they were organizations whose resource dependencies all coincided. For their financial support, for their governance and
for their clients, they looked to a class whose members were 'functionally inter-
dependent and interact[ed] regularly with respect to religious, economic, recreational, and governmental matters' (Thompson, 1967: 27).

10. Higginson, whose vision extended beyond Boston, also gave generously
to Princeton, Williams, the University of Virginia and Middlesex, and sent the
Orchestra to play, at his expense, at Williams, Princeton and Yale.

11. Higginson's relationship with Gardner and his mildly scandalous wife
Isabella Stewart Gardner, is revealing. When Isabella, a New Yorker, entered
Boston society in the 1880s, she was accorded a frosty reception. According to
Morris Carter, her biographer and the first Director of her collection, she won

social acceptance by employing the BSO to entertain at one of her parties (Carter, 1925), an action that would have required Higginson's approval. After her palace opened (more or less) to the public in 1909, Higginson presented her with a book compiled by her admirers (Green, 1966: 112).

ACKNOWLEDGMENTS

For advice and encouragement I am indebted to Randall Collins, David Karen, Michael Schudson, Ann Swidler and to the members of Professor Mary Douglas's 'Mass Media and Mythology' seminar at the New York University Institute for the Humanities, of Theda Skocpol's graduate research seminar at Harvard University and of Paul Hirsch's production-of-culture session at the 1980 Sociology and the Arts conference in Chicago. Research and institutional support from the Andrew W. Mellon Foundation and from Yale University's Program on Non-Profit Organizations is gratefully acknowledged.

REFERENCES

Adams, H. (1928). *The Education of Henry Adams: An Autobiography*, New York, Book League of America

Adorno, T. W. (1941). On popular music, *Studies in Philosophy and Social Science*, vol. 9, no. 1

Baltzell, E. D. (1979). *Puritan Boston and Quaker Philadelphia*, New York, Free Press

Barnum, P. T. (1879). *Struggles and Triumphs; or Forty Years Recollections*, Buffalo, New York, The Courier Company

Bernstein, B. (1975a). On the classification and framing of educational knowledge, in *Class, Codes and Control*, vol. 3, London, Routledge and Kegan Paul

Bernstein, B. (1975b). Ritual in education, in *Class, Codes and Control*, vol. 3, London, Routledge and Kegan Paul

Boston Art Club (1878). *Constitution and By-Laws of the Boston Art Club, With a Sketch of its History*, Boston, E. H. Trulan

Bourdieu, P. and Passeron, J.-C. (1977). *Reproduction in Education, Society and Culture*, Beverly Hills, Sage

Bourdieu, P. and Passeron, J.-C. (1979). *The Inheritors: French Students and their Relation to Culture*, Chicago, University of Chicago Press

Burt, N. (1977). *Palaces for the People*, Boston, Little, Brown and Co.

Carter, M. (1925). *Isabella Stewart Gardner and Fenway Court*, Boston, Houghton Mifflin

Couch, S. R. (1976a). Class, politics and symphony orchestras. *Society*, vol. 14, no. 1

Couch, S. R. (1976b). The symphony orchestra in London and New York: some political considerations, presented at the Third Annual Conference on Social Theory and the Arts, Albany, New York

DiMaggio, P. and Useem, M. (1978). Cultural property and public policy: Emerging tensions in government support for the arts, *Social Research,* vol. 45, Summer

Douglas, A. (1978). *The Feminization of American Culture,* New York, Avon

Douglas, M. (1966). *Purity and Danger: An Analysis of Pollution and Taboo,* London, Routledge and Kegan Paul

Fellows, D. W. and Freeman, A. A. (1936). *This Way to the Big Show: The Life of Dexter Fellows,* New York, Viking Press

Fisher, W. A. (1918). *Notes on Music in Old Boston,* Boston, Oliver Ditson

Fredrickson, G. M. (1965). *The Inner Civil War: Northern Intellectuals and the Crisis of the Union,* New York, Harper and Row

Gans, H. J. (1974). *Popular Culture and High Culture,* New York, Basic Books

Green, M. (1966). *The Problem of Boston,* New York, Norton

Hall, P. D. (forthcoming). *Institutions and the Making of American Culture,* Westport, Connecticut, Greenwood

Handlin, O. (1972). *Boston's Immigrants, 1790–1880,* New York, Atheneum

Harris, N. (1962). The Gilded Age revisited: Boston and the museum movement, *American Quarterly,* vol. 14, Winter

Harris, N. (1966). *The Artist in American Society: The Formative Years, 1790–1860,* New York, George Braziller

Harris, N. (1973). *Humbug: The Art of P. T. Barnum,* Boston, Little, Brown and Co.

Hatch, C. (1962). Music for America: A cultural controversy of the 1850s, *American Quarterly,* vol. 14, Winter

Howe, M. A. D. (1914). *The Boston Symphony Orchestra: An Historical Sketch,* Boston, Houghton Mifflin

Huggins, N. J. (1971). *Protestants against Poverty: Boston's Charities, 1870–1900,* Westport, Connecticut, Greenwood

Jaher, F. C. (1968). The Boston Brahmins in the age of industrial capitalism, in Jaher, F. C. (ed.), *The Age of Industrialism in America,* New York, Oxford University Press

Jaher, F. C. (1972). Nineteenth-century elites in Boston and New York, *Journal of Social History,* vol. 6, Spring

Lane, R. (1975). *Policing the City: Boston, 1822–85,* New York, Atheneum

Lowenthal, L. (1961). *Literature, Popular Culture, and Society,* Englewood Cliffs, Prentice-Hall

Lynes, R. (1953). *The Tastemakers,* New York, Grosset and Dunlap

McDonald, D. (1957). A theory of mass culture, in Rosenberg, B. and White, D. M. (eds). *Mass Culture: The Popular Arts in America,* Glencoe, Illinois, Free Press

McGlinchee, C. (1940). *The First Decade of the Boston Museum,* Boston, Bruce Humphries

Mueller, J. H. (1951). *The American Symphony Orchestra: A Social History of Musical Taste,* Bloomington, Indiana University Press

Nye, R. B. (1960). *The Cultural Life of the New Nation, 1776–1830,* New York, Harper and Row

Perry, B. (1921). *Life and Letters of Henry Lee Higginson,* Boston, Atlantic Monthly Press

Poggi, J. (1968). *Theater in America: The Impact of Economic Forces, 1870–1967,* Ithaca, Cornell University Press

Ryan, K. (1915). *Old Boston Museum Days,* Boston, Little, Brown and Co.

Shiverick, N. C. (1970). The social reorganization of Boston, in Williams, A. W., *A Social History of the Greater Boston Clubs,* New York, Barre

Solomon, B. M. (1956). *Ancestors and Immigrants,* New York, John Wiley

Starr, P. (1983). *The Social Transformation of American Medicine,* New York, Basic Books

Stinchcombe, A. L. (1965). Social structure and organizations, in March, J. G. (ed.), *Handbook of Organizations,* Chicago, Rand McNally

Story, R. (1980). *The Forging of an Aristocracy: Harvard and the Boston Upper Class, 1800–1870,* Middletown, Connecticut, Wesleyan University Press

Thernstrom, S. (1972). *Poverty and Progress: Social Mobility in a Nineteenth-Century City,* New York, Atheneum

Thompson, E. P. (1966). *The Making of the English Working Class,* New York, Random House

Thompson, J. D. (1967). *Organizations in Action,* New York, McGraw-Hill

Twentieth Century Club (1910). *The Amusement Situation in Boston,* Boston

Vogel, M. (1981). *The Invention of the Modern Hospital,* Chicago, University of Chicago Press

Warner, S. B. (1970). *Streetcar Suburbs: The Process of Growth in Boston, 1870–1900,* New York, Atheneum

Weber, M. (1968). *Economy and Society,* 3 volumes, New York, Bedminster Press

Whipple, G. M. (n.d.). *A Sketch of Musical Societies of Salem,* Salem, Massachusetts, Essex Institute

Whitehill, W. M. (1970). *Museum of Fine Arts, Boston: A Centennial History,* Cambridge, Harvard University Press

Wolff, J. (1982). The problem of ideology in the sociology of art: a case study of Manchester in the nineteenth century, *Media, Culture and Society,* vol. 4. no. 1

Zolberg, V. L. (1974). The art institute of Chicago: the sociology of a cultural institution, Ph.D. Dissertation, Department of Sociology, University of Chicago

Zolberg, V. L (1981). Conflicting visions of American art museums, *Theory and Society,* vol. 10, January

FOURTEEN

The Public Sphere

Jürgen Habermas

CONCEPT

By "public sphere" we mean first of all a domain of our social life in which such a thing as public opinion can be formed. Access to the public sphere is open in principle to all citizens. A portion of the public sphere is constituted in every conversation in which private persons come together to form a public. They are then acting neither as business or professional people conducting their private affairs, nor as legal consociates subject to the legal regulations of a state bureaucracy and obligated to obedience. Citizens act as a public when they deal with matters of general interest without being subject to coercion; thus with the guarantee that they may assemble and unite freely, and express and publicize their opinions freely. When the public is large, this kind of communication requires certain means of dissemination and influence; today, newspapers and periodicals, radio and television are the media of the public sphere. We speak of a political public sphere (as distinguished from a literary one, for instance) when the public discussions concern objects connected with the practice of the state. The coercive power of the state is the counterpart, as it were, of the political public sphere, but it is not a part of it. State power is, to be sure, considered "public" power, but it owes the attribute of publicness to its task of caring for the public, that is, providing for the common good of all legal consociates. Only when the exercise of public authority has actually been subordinated to the

From *Jürgen Habermas on Society and Politics: A Reader* (Boston: Beacon Press, 1989), edited by Steven Seidman, translated by Shierry Weber Nicholsen. Originally published as "Öffentlichkeit" in Jürgen Habermas, *Kultur und Kritik*, © 1973 by Suhrkamp Verlag, Frankfurt.

requirement of democratic publicness does the political public sphere acquire an institutionalized influence on the government, by way of the legislative body. The term "public opinion" refers to the functions of criticism and control of organized state authority that the public exercises informally, as well as formally during periodic elections. Regulations concerning the publicness (or publicity *[Publizität]* in its original meaning) of state-related activities, as, for instance, the public accessibility required of legal proceedings, are also connected with this function of public opinion. To the public sphere as a sphere mediating between state and society, a sphere in which the public as the vehicle of public opinion is formed, there corresponds the principle of publicness—the publicness that once had to win out against the secret politics of monarchs and that since then has permitted democratic control of state activity.

It is no accident that these concepts of the public sphere and public opinion were not formed until the eighteenth century. They derive their specific meaning from a concrete historical situation. It was then that one learned to distinguish between opinion and public opinion, or *opinion publique*. Whereas mere opinions (things taken for granted as part of a culture, normative convictions, collective prejudices and judgments) seem to persist unchanged in their quasi-natural structure as a kind of sediment of history, public opinion, in terms of its very idea, can be formed only if a public that engages in rational discussion exists. Public discussions that are institutionally protected and that take, with critical intent, the exercise of political authority as their theme have not existed since time immemorial—they developed only in a specific phase of bourgeois society, and only by virtue of a specific constellation of interests could they be incorporated into the order of the bourgeois constitutional state.

HISTORY

It is not possible to demonstrate the existence of a public sphere in its own right, separate from the private sphere, in the European society of the High Middle Ages. At the same time, however, it is not a coincidence that the attributes of authority at that time were called "public." For a public representation of authority existed at that time. At all levels of the pyramid established by feudal law, the status of the feudal lord is neutral with respect to the categories "public" and "private"; but the person possessing that status represents it publicly; he displays himself, represents himself as the embodiment of a "higher" power, in whatever degree. This concept of representation has survived into recent constitutional history. Even today the power of political authority on its highest level, however much it has become detached from its former basis, requires representation through the head of state. But such elements derive from a pre-bourgeois social structure. Representation in the sense of the bourgeois public sphere, as in "representing" the nation or specific clients, has nothing to do with *representative publicness,* which inheres in the concrete existence of a lord. As long as the prince and the estates of his realm "are" the land, rather than merely "representing" it, they are capable of this kind of representation; they represent their authority "before" the people rather than for the people.

The feudal powers (the church, the prince, and the nobility) to which this representative publicness adheres disintegrated in the course of a long process of polarization; by the end of the eighteenth century they had decomposed into private elements on the one side and public on the other. The position of the church changed in connection with the Reformation; the tie to divine authority that the church represented, that is, religion, became a private matter. Historically, what is called the freedom of religion safeguarded the first domain of private autonomy; the church itself continued its existence as one corporate body under public law among others. The corresponding polarization of princely power acquired visible form in the separation of the public budget from the private household property of the feudal lord. In the bureaucracy and the military (and in part also in the administration of justice), institutions of public power became autonomous vis-à-vis the privatized sphere of the princely court. In terms of the estates, finally, elements from the ruling groups developed into organs of public power, into parliament (and in part also into judicial organs); elements from the occupational status groups, insofar as they had become established in urban corporations and in certain differentiations within the estates of the land, developed into the sphere of bourgeois society, which would confront the state as a genuine domain of private autonomy.

Representative publicness gave way to the new sphere of "public power" that came into being with the national and territorial states. Ongoing state activity (permanent administration, a standing army) had its counterpart in the permanence of relationships that had developed in the meantime with the stock market and the press, through traffic in goods and news. Public power became consolidated as something tangible confronting those who were subject to it and who at first found themselves only negatively defined by it. These are the "private persons" who are excluded from public power because they hold no office. "Public" no longer refers to the representative court of a person vested with authority; instead, it now refers to the competence-regulated activity of an apparatus furnished with a monopoly on the legitimate use of force. As those to whom this public power is addressed, private persons subsumed under the state form the public.

As a private domain, society, which has come to confront the state, as it were, is on the one hand clearly differentiated from public power; on the other hand, society becomes a matter of public interest insofar as with the rise of a market economy the reproduction of life extends beyond the confines of private domestic power. The *bourgeois public sphere* can be understood as the sphere of private persons assembled to form a public. They soon began to make use of the public sphere of informational newspapers, which was officially regulated, against the public power itself, using those papers, along with the morally and critically oriented weeklies, to engage in debate about the general rules governing relations in their own essentially privatized but publicly relevant sphere of commodity exchange and labor.

THE LIBERAL MODEL OF THE PUBLIC SPHERE

The medium in which this debate takes place—public discussion—is unique and without historical prototype. Previously the estates had negotiated contracts with their princes in which claims to power were defined on a case-by-case basis. As we know, this development followed a different course in England, where princely power was relativized through parliament, than on the Continent, where the estates were mediatized by the monarch. The "third estate" then broke with this mode of equalizing power, for it could no longer establish itself as a ruling estate. Given a commercial economy, a division of authority accomplished through differentiation of the rights of those possessing feudal authority (liberties belonging to the estates) was no longer possible—the power under private law of disposition of capitalist property is nonpolitical. The bourgeois are private persons; as such, they do not "rule." Thus their claims to power in opposition to public power are directed not against a concentration of authority that should be "divided" but rather against the principle of established authority. The principle of control, namely publicness, that the bourgeois public opposes to the principle of established authority aims at a transformation of authority as such, not merely the exchange of one basis of legitimation for another.

In the first modern constitutions the sections listing basic rights provide an image of the liberal model of the public sphere: they guarantee society as a sphere of private autonomy; opposite it stands a public power limited to a few functions; between the two spheres, as it were, stands the domain of private persons who have come together to form a public and who, as citizens of the state, mediate the state with the needs of bourgeois society, in order, as the idea goes, to thus convert political authority to "rational" authority in the medium of this public sphere. Under the presuppositions of a society based on the free exchange of commodities, it seemed that the general interest, which served as the criterion by which this kind of rationality was to be evaluated, would be assured if the dealings of private persons in the marketplace were emancipated from social forces and their dealings in the public sphere were emancipated from political coercion.

The political daily press came to have an important role during this same period. In the second half of the eighteenth century, serious competition to the older form of news writing as the compiling of items of information arose in the form of literary journalism. Karl Bücher describes the main outlines of this development: "From mere institutions for the publication of news, newspapers became the vehicles and guides of public opinion as well, weapons of party politics. The consequence of this for the internal organization of the newspaper enterprise was the insertion of a new function between the gathering of news and its publication: the editorial function. For the newspaper publisher, however, the significance of this development was that from a seller of new information he became a dealer in public opinion." Publishers provided the commercial basis for the newspaper without, however, commercializing it as such. The press remained an institution of the public itself, operating to provide and intensify public discussion, no longer a mere organ for the conveyance of information, but not yet a medium of consumer culture.

This type of press can be observed especially in revolutionary periods, when papers associated with the tiniest political coalitions and groups spring up, as in Paris in 1789. In the Paris of 1848 every halfway prominent politician still formed his own club, and every other one founded his own *journal:* over 450 clubs and more than 200 papers came into being there between February and May alone. Until the permanent legalization of a public sphere that functioned politically, the appearance of a political newspaper was equivalent to engagement in the struggle for a zone of freedom for public opinion, for publicness as a principle. Not until the establishment of the bourgeois constitutional state was a press engaged in the public use of reason relieved of the pressure of ideological viewpoints. Since then it has been able to abandon its polemical stance and take advantage of the earning potential of commercial activity. The ground was cleared for this development from a press of viewpoints to a commercial press at about the same time in England, France, and the United States, during the 1830s. In the course of this transformation from the journalism of writers who were private persons to the consumer services of the mass media, the sphere of publicness was changed by an influx of private interests that achieved privileged representation within it.

THE PUBLIC SPHERE IN MASS WELFARE-STATE DEMOCRACIES

The liberal model of the public sphere remains instructive in regard to the normative claim embodied in institutionalized requirements of publicness; but it is not applicable to actual relationships within a mass democracy that is industrially advanced and constituted as a social-welfare state. In part, the liberal model had always contained ideological aspects; in part, the social presuppositions to which those aspects were linked have undergone fundamental changes. Even the forms in which the public sphere was manifested, forms which made its idea seem to a certain extent obvious, began to change with the Chartist movement in England and the February Revolution in France. With the spread of the press and propaganda, the public expanded beyond the confines of the bourgeoisie. Along with its social exclusivity the public lost the cohesion given it by institutions of convivial social intercourse and by a relatively high standard of education. Accordingly, conflicts which in the past were pushed off into the private sphere now enter the public sphere. Group needs, which cannot expect satisfaction from a self-regulating market, tend toward state regulation. The public sphere, which must now mediate these demands, becomes a field for competition among interests in the cruder form of forcible confrontation. Laws that have obviously originated under the "pressure of the streets" can scarcely continue to be understood in terms of a consensus achieved by private persons in public discussion; they correspond, in more or less undisguised form, to compromises between conflicting private interests. Today it is social organizations that act in relation to the state in the political public sphere, whether through the mediation of political parties or directly, in interplay with public administration. With the interlocking of the public and private domains, not only do political agencies take over certain functions in the sphere of commodity exchange and social labor; societal powers also take over political functions. This leads to a kind of "refeudalization" of the public sphere. Large-scale organizations strive for political compromises with the state and with one another, behind closed doors if possible; but at the same time they have to secure at least plebiscitarian approval from the mass of the population through the deployment of a staged form of publicity.

The political public sphere in the welfare state is characterized by a singular weakening of its critical functions. Whereas at one time publicness was intended to subject persons or things to the public use of reason and to make political decisions susceptible to revision before the tribunal of public opinion, today it has often enough already been enlisted in the aid of the secret policies of interest groups; in the form of "publicity" it now acquires public prestige for persons or things and renders them capable of acclamation in a climate of nonpublic opinion. The term "public relations" itself indicates how a public sphere that formerly emerged from the structure of society must now be produced circumstantially on a case-by-case basis. The central relationship of the public, political parties, and parliament is also affected by this change in function.

This existing trend toward the weakening of the public sphere, as a principle, is opposed, however, by a welfare-state transformation of the functioning of basic rights: the requirement of publicness is extended by state organs to all organizations acting in relation to the state. To the extent to which this becomes a reality, a no longer intact public of private persons acting as individuals would be replaced by a public of organized private persons. Under current circumstances, only the latter could participate effectively in a process of public communication using the channels of intra-party and intra-organizational public spheres, on the basis of a publicness enforced for the dealings of organizations with the state. It is in this process of public communication that the formation of political compromises would have to achieve legitimation. The idea of the public sphere itself, which signified a rationalization of authority in the medium of public discussions among private persons, and which has been preserved in mass welfare-state democracy, threatens to disintegrate with the structural transformation of the public sphere. Today it could be realized only on a different basis, as a rationalization of the exercise of social and political power under the mutual control of rival organizations committed to publicness in their internal structure as well as in their dealings with the state and with one another.

PART FOUR

Popular Culture in Cultural Criticism

FIFTEEN

Base and Superstructure in Marxist Cultural Theory

Raymond Williams

Any modern approach to a Marxist theory of culture must begin by considering the proposition of a determining base and a determined superstructure. From a strictly theoretical point of view this is not, in fact, where we might choose to begin. It would be in many ways preferable if we could begin from a proposition which originally was equally central, equally authentic: namely the proposition that social being determines consciousness. It is not that the two propositions necessarily deny each other or are in contradiction. But the proposition of base and superstructure, with its figurative element, with its suggestion of a fixed and definite spatial relationship, constitutes, at least in certain hands, a very specialized and at times unacceptable version of the other proposition. Yet in the transition from Marx to Marxism, and in the development of mainstream Marxism itself, the proposition of the determining base and the determined superstructure has been commonly held to be the key to Marxist cultural analysis.

It is important, as we try to analyse this proposition, to be aware that the term of relationship which is involved, that is to say 'determines', is of great linguistic and theoretical complexity. The language of determination and even more of determinism was inherited from idealist and especially theological accounts of the world and man. It is significant that it is in one of his familiar inversions, his contradictions of received propositions, that Marx uses the word which becomes, in English translation, 'determines' (the usual but not invariable German word is *bestimmen*). He is opposing an ideology that had been insistent on the power of certain forces outside man, or, in its secular version, on an abstract determining

Reprinted from *Problems in Materialism and Culture,* by Raymond Williams, Verso Editions and NLB, pp. 31–49, © 1980 by Raymond Williams. Reproduced by permission of Verso.

consciousness. Marx's own proposition explicitly denies this, and puts the origin of determination in men's own activities. Nevertheless, the particular history and continuity of the term serves to remind us that there are, within ordinary use—and this is true of most of the major European languages—quite different possible meanings and implications of the word 'determine'. There is, on the one hand, from its theological inheritance, the notion of an external cause which totally predicts or prefigures, indeed totally controls a subsequent activity. But there is also, from the experience of social practice, a notion of determination as setting limits, exerting pressures.[1]

Now there is clearly a difference between a process of setting limits and exerting pressures, whether by some external force or by the internal laws of a particular development, and that other process in which a subsequent content is essentially prefigured, predicted and controlled by a preexisting external force. Yet it is fair to say, looking at many applications of Marxist cultural analysis, that it is the second sense, the notion of prefiguration, prediction or control, which has often explicitly or implicitly been used.

SUPERSTRUCTURE: QUALIFICATIONS AND AMENDMENTS

The term of relationship is then the first thing that we have to examine in this proposition, but we have to do this by going on to look at the related terms themselves. 'Superstructure' (Überbau) has had most attention. In common usage, after Marx, it acquired a main sense of a unitary 'area' within which all cultural and ideological activities could be placed. But already in Marx himself, in the later correspondence of Engels, and at many points in the subsequent Marxist tradition, qualifications were made about the determined character of certain superstructural activities. The first kind of qualification had to do with delays in time, with complications, and with certain indirect or relatively distant relationships. The simplest notion of a superstructure, which is still by no means entirely abandoned, had been the reflection, the imitation or the reproduction of the reality of the base in the superstructure in a more or less direct way. Positivist notions of reflection and reproduction of course directly supported this. But since in many real cultural activities this relationship cannot be found, or cannot be found without effort or even violence to the material or practice being studied, the notion was introduced of delays in time, the famous lags; of various technical complications; and of indirectness, in which certain kinds of activity in the cultural sphere—philosophy, for example—were situated at a greater distance from the primary economic activities. That was the first stage of qualification of the notion of superstructure: in effect, an operational qualification. The second stage was related but more fundamental, in that the process of the relationship itself was more substantially looked at. This was the kind of reconsideration which gave rise to the modern notion of 'mediation', in which something more than simple reflection or reproduction—indeed something radically different from either reflection or reproduction—actively occurs. In the later twentieth century there is the notion of 'homologous structures', where there may be no direct or easily apparent similarity, and certainly nothing like reflection or reproduction, between the superstructural process and the reality of the base, but in which there is an essential homology or correspondence of structures, which can be discovered by analysis. This is not the same notion as 'mediation', but it is the same kind of amendment in that the relationship between the base and the superstructure is not supposed to be direct, nor simply operationally subject to lags and complications and indirectnesses, but that of its nature it is not direct reproduction.

These qualifications and amendments are important. But it seems to me that what has not been looked at with equal care is the received notion of the 'base' (Basis, Grundlage). And indeed I would argue that the base is the more important concept to look at if we are to understand the realities of cultural process. In many uses of the proposition of base and superstructure, as a matter of verbal habit, 'the base' has come to be considered virtually as an object, or in less crude cases, it has been considered in essentially uniform and usually static ways. 'The base' is the real social existence of man. 'The base' is the real relations of production corresponding to a stage of development of the material productive forces. 'The base' is a mode of production at a particular stage of its development. We make and repeat propositions of this kind, but the usage is then very different from Marx's emphasis on productive activities, in particular structural relations, constituting the foundation of all other activities. For while a particular stage of the development of production can be discovered and made precise by analysis, it is never in practice either uniform or static. It is indeed one of the central propositions of Marx's sense of history that there are deep contradictions in the relationships of production and in the consequent social relationships. There is therefore the continual possibility of the dynamic variation of these forces. Moreover, when these forces are considered, as Marx always considers them, as the specific activities and relationships of real men, they mean something very much more active, more complicated and more contradictory than the developed metaphorical notion of 'the base' could possibly allow us to realize.

THE BASE AND THE PRODUCTIVE FORCES

So we have to say that when we talk of 'the base', we are talking of a process and not a state. And we cannot ascribe to that process certain fixed properties for subsequent translation to the variable processes of the superstructure. Most people who have wanted to make the ordinary proposition more reasonable have concentrated on refining the notion of superstructure. But I would say that each term of the proposition has to be revalued in a particular direction. We have to revalue 'determination' towards the setting of limits and the exertion of pressure, and away from a predicted, prefigured and controlled content. We have to revalue 'superstructure' towards a related range of cultural practices, and away from a reflected, reproduced or specifically dependent content. And, crucially, we have to revalue 'the base' away from the notion of a fixed economic or technological abstraction, and towards the specific activities of men in real social and economic relationships, containing fundamental contradictions and variations and therefore always in a state of dynamic process.

It is worth observing one further implication behind the customary definitions. 'The base' has come to include, especially in certain twentieth-century developments, a strong and limiting sense of basic industry. The emphasis on heavy industry, even, has played a certain cultural role. And this raises a more general problem, for we find ourselves forced to look again at the ordinary notion of 'productive forces'. Clearly what we are examining in the base is primary productive forces. Yet some very crucial distinctions have to be made here. It is true that in his analysis of capitalist production Marx considered 'productive work' in a very particular and specialized sense corresponding to that mode of production. There is a difficult passage in the *Grundrisse* in which he argues that while the man who makes a piano is a productive worker, there is a real question whether the man who distributes the piano is also a productive worker; but he probably is, since he contributes to the realization of surplus value. Yet when it comes to the man who plays the piano, whether to himself or to others, there is no question: he is not a productive worker at all. So piano-maker is base, but pianist superstructure. As a way of considering cultural activity, and incidentally the economics of modern cultural activity, this is very clearly a dead-end. But for any theoretical clarification it is crucial to recognize that Marx was there engaged in an analysis of a particular kind of production, that is capitalist commodity production. Within his analysis of this mode, he had to give to the notion of 'productive labour' and 'productive forces' a specialized sense of primary work on materials in a form which produced commodities. But this has narrowed remarkably, and in a cultural context very damagingly, from his more central notion of *productive forces*, in which, to give just brief reminders, the most important thing a worker ever produces is himself, himself in the fact of that kind of labour, or the broader historical emphasis of men producing themselves, themselves and their history. Now when we talk of the base, and of primary productive forces, it matters very much whether we are referring, as in one degenerate form of this proposition became habitual, to primary production within the terms of capitalist economic relationships, or to the primary production of society itself, and of men themselves, the material production and reproduction of real life. If we have the broad sense of productive forces, we look at the whole question of the base differently, and we are then less tempted to dismiss as superstructural, and in that sense as merely secondary, certain vital productive social forces, which are in the broad sense, from the beginning, basic.

USES OF TOTALITY

Yet, because of the difficulties of the ordinary proposition of base and superstructure, there was an alternative and very important development, an emphasis primarily associated with Lukács, on a social 'totality'. The totality of social practices was opposed to this layered notion of base and a consequent superstructure. This concept of a totality of practices is compatible with the notion of social being determining consciousness, but it does not necessarily interpret this process in terms of a base and a superstructure. Now the language of totality has become common, and it is indeed in many ways more acceptable than the notion of base and superstructure. But with one very important reservation. It is very easy for the notion of totality to empty of its essential content the original Marxist proposition. For if we come to say that society is composed of a large number of social practices which form a concrete social whole, and if we give to each practice a certain specific recognition, adding only that they interact, relate and combine in very complicated ways, we are at one level much more obviously talking about reality, but we are at another level withdrawing from the claim that there is any process of determination. And this I, for one, would be very unwilling to do. Indeed, the key question to ask about any notion of totality in cultural theory is this: whether the notion of totality includes the notion of intention.

If totality is simply concrete, if it is simply the recognition of a large variety of miscellaneous and contemporaneous practices, then it is essentially empty of any content that could be called Marxist. Intention, the notion of intention, restores the key question, or rather the key emphasis. For while it is true that any society is a complex whole of such practices, it is also true that any society has a specific organization, a specific structure, and that the principles of this organization and structure can be seen as directly related to certain social intentions, intentions by which we define the society, intentions which in all our experience have been the rule of a particular class. One of the unexpected consequences of the crudeness of the base/superstructure model has been the too easy acceptance of models which appear less crude—models of totality or of a complex whole—but which exclude the facts of social intention, the class character of a particular society and so on. And this reminds us of how much we lose if we abandon the superstructural emphasis altogether. Thus I have great difficulty in seeing processes of art and thought as superstructural in the sense of the formula as it is commonly used. But in many areas of social and political thought—certain kinds of ratifying theory, certain kinds of law, certain kinds of institution, which after all in Marx's original formulations were very much part of the superstructure—in all that kind of social apparatus, and in a decisive area of political and ideological activity and construction, if we fail to see a superstructural element we fail to recognize reality at all. These laws, constitutions, theories, ideologies, which are so often claimed as natural, or as having universal validity or significance, simply have to be seen as expressing and ratifying the domination of a particular class. Indeed the difficulty of revising the formula of base and superstructure has had much to do with the perception of many militants—who have to fight such institutions and notions as well as fighting economic battles—that if these institutions and their ideologies are not perceived as having that kind of dependent and ratifying relationship, if their claims to universal validity or legitimacy are not denied and fought, then the class character of the society can no longer be seen. And this has been the effect of some versions of totality as the description of cultural process. Indeed I think we can properly use the notion of totality only when we combine it with that other crucial Marxist concept of 'hegemony'.

THE COMPLEXITY OF HEGEMONY

It is Gramsci's great contribution to have emphasized hegemony, and also to have understood it at a depth which is, I think, rare. For hegemony supposes the existence of something which is truly total, which is not merely secondary or superstructural, like the weak sense of ideology, but which is lived at such a depth, which saturates the society to such an extent, and which, as Gramsci put it, even constitutes the substance and limit of common sense for most people under its sway, that it corresponds to the reality of social experience very much more clearly than any notions derived from the formula of base and superstructure. For if ideology were merely some abstract, imposed set of notions, if our social and political and cultural ideas and assumptions and habits were merely the result of specific manipulation, of a kind of overt training which might be simply ended or withdrawn, then the society would be very much easier to move and to change than in practice it has ever been or is. This notion of hegemony as deeply saturating the consciousness of a society seems to me to be fundamental. And hegemony has the advantage over general notions of totality, that it at the same time emphasizes the facts of domination.

Yet there are times when I hear discussions of hegemony and feel that it too, as a concept, is being dragged back to the relatively simple, uniform and static notion which 'superstructure' in ordinary use had become. Indeed I think that we have to give a very complex account of hegemony if we are talking about any real social formation. Above all we have to give an account which allows for its elements of real and constant change. We have to emphasize that hegemony is not singular; indeed that its own internal structures are highly complex, and have continually to be renewed, recreated and defended; and by the same token, that they can be continually challenged and in certain respects modified. That is why instead of speaking simply of 'the hegemony', 'a hegemony', I would propose a model which allows for this kind of variation and contradiction, its sets of alternatives and its processes of change.

For one thing that is evident in some of the best Marxist cultural analysis is that it is very much more at home in what one might call *epochal* questions than in what one has to call *historical* questions. That is to say, it is usually very much better at distinguishing the large features of different epochs of society, as commonly between feudal and bourgeois, than at distinguishing between different phases of bourgeois society, and different moments within these phases: that true historical process which demands a much greater precision and delicacy of analysis than the always striking epochal analysis which is concerned with main lineaments and features.

The theoretical model which I have been trying to work with is this. I would say first that in any society, in any particular period, there is a central system of practices, meanings and values, which we can properly call dominant and effective. This implies no presumption about its value. All I am saying is that it is central. Indeed I would call it a corporate system, but this might be confusing, since Gramsci uses 'corporate' to mean the subordinate as opposed to the general and dominant elements of hegemony. In any case what I have in mind is the central, effective and dominant system of meanings and values, which are not merely abstract but which are organized and lived. That is why hegemony is not to be understood at the level of mere opinion or mere manipulation. It is a whole body of practices and expectations; our assignments of energy, our ordinary understanding of the nature of man and of his world. It is a set of meanings and values which as they are experienced as practices appear as reciprocally confirming. It thus constitutes a sense of reality for most people in the society, a sense of absolute because experienced reality beyond which it is very difficult for most members of the society to move, in most areas of their lives. But this is not, except in the operation of a moment of abstract analysis, in any sense a static system. On the contrary we can only understand an effective and dominant culture if we understand the real social process on which it depends: I mean the process of incorporation. The modes of incorporation are of great social significance. The educational institutions are usually the main agencies of the transmission of an effective dominant culture, and this is now a major economic as well as a cultural activity; indeed it is both in the same moment. Moreover, at a philosophical level, at the true level of theory and at the level of the history of various practices, there is a process which I call the *selective tradition*: that which, within the terms of an effective dominant culture, is always passed off as '*the* tradition', '*the* significant past'. But always the selectivity is the point; the way in which from a whole possible area of past and present, certain meanings and practices are chosen for emphasis, certain other meanings and practices are neglected and excluded. Even more crucially, some of these meanings and practices are reinterpreted, diluted, or put into forms which support or at least do not contradict other elements within the effective dominant culture. The processes of education; the processes of a much wider social training within institutions like the family; the practical definitions and organization of work; the selective tradition at an intellectual and theoretical level: all these forces are involved in a continual making and remaking of an effective dominant culture, and on them, as experienced, as built into our living, its reality depends. If what we learn there were merely an imposed ideology, or if it were only the isolable meanings and practices of the ruling class, or of a section of the ruling class, which gets imposed on others, occupying merely the top of our minds, it would be—and one would be glad—a very much easier thing to overthrow.

It is not only the depths to which this process reaches, selecting and organizing and interpreting our experience. It is also that it is continually active and adjusting; it isn't just the past, the dry husks of ideology which we can more easily discard. And this can only be so, in a complex society, if it is something more substantial and more flexible than any abstract imposed ideology. Thus we have to recognize the alternative meanings and values, the alternative opinions and attitudes, even some alternative senses of the world, which can be accommodated and tolerated within a particular effective and dominant culture. This has been much underemphasized in our notions of a superstructure, and even in some notions of hegemony. And the under-emphasis opens the way for retreat to an indifferent complexity. In the practice of politics, for example, there are certain truly incorporated modes of what are nevertheless, within those terms, real oppositions, that are felt and fought out. Their existence within the incorporation is recognizable by the fact that, whatever the degree of internal conflict or internal variation, they do not in practice go beyond the limits of the central effective and dominant definitions. This is true, for example, of the practice of parliamentary politics, though its internal oppositions are real. It is true about a whole range of practices and arguments, in any real society, which can by no means be reduced to an ideological cover, but which can nevertheless be properly analysed as in my sense corporate, if we find that, whatever the degree of internal controversy and variation, they do not in the end exceed the limits of the central corporate definitions.

But if we are to say this, we have to think again about the sources of that which is not corporate; of those practices, experiences, meanings, values which are not part of the effective dominant culture. We can express this in two ways. There is clearly something that we can call alternative to the effective dominant culture, and there is something else that we can call oppositional, in a true sense. The degree of existence of these alternative and oppositional forms is itself a matter of constant historical variation in real circumstances. In certain societies it is possible to find areas of social life in which quite real alternatives are at least left alone. (If they are made available, of course, they are part of the corporate organization.) The existence of the possibility of opposition, and of its articulation, its degree of openness, and so on, again depends on very precise social and political forces. The facts of alternative and oppositional forms of social life and culture, in relation to the effective and dominant culture, have then to be recognized as subject to historical variation, and as having sources which are very significant as a fact about the dominant culture itself.

RESIDUAL AND EMERGENT CULTURES

I have next to introduce a further distinction, between *residual* and *emergent* forms, both of alternative and of oppositional culture. By 'residual' I mean that some experiences, meanings and values, which cannot be verified or cannot be expressed in terms of the dominant culture, are nevertheless lived and practised on the basis of the residue—cultural as well as social—of some previous social formation. There is a real case of this in certain religious values, by contrast with the very evident incorporation of most religious meanings and values into the dominant system. The same is true, in a culture like Britain, of certain notions derived from a rural past, which have a very significant popularity. A residual culture is usually at some distance from the effective dominant culture, but one has to recognize that, in real cultural activities, it may get incorporated into it. This is because some part of it, some version of it—and especially if the residue is from some major area of the past—will in many cases have had to be incorporated if the effective dominant culture is to make sense in those areas. It is also because at certain points a dominant culture cannot allow too much of this kind of practice and experience outside itself, at least without risk. Thus the pressures are real, but certain genuinely residual meanings and practices in some important cases survive.

By 'emergent' I mean, first, that new meanings and values, new practices, new significances and experiences, are continually being created. But there is then a much earlier attempt to incorporate them, just because they are part—and yet not a defined part—of effective contemporary practice. Indeed it is significant in our own period how very early this attempt is, how alert the dominant culture now is to anything that can be seen as emergent. We have then to see, first, as it were a temporal relation between a dominant culture and on the one hand a residual and on the other hand an emergent culture. But we can only understand this if we can make distinctions, that usually require very precise analysis, between residual-incorporated and residual not incorporated, and between emergent-incorporated and emergent not incorporated. It is an important fact about any particular society, how far it reaches into the whole range of human practices and experiences in an attempt at incorporation. It may be true of some earlier phases of bourgeois society, for example, that there were some areas of experience which it was willing to dispense with, which it was prepared to assign as the sphere of private or artistic life, and as being no particular business of society or the state. This went along with certain kinds of political tolerance, even if the reality of that tolerance was malign neglect. But I am sure it is true of the society that has come into existence since the last war, that progressively, because of developments in the social character of labour, in the social character of communications, and in the social character of decision, it extends much further than ever before in capitalist society into certain hitherto resigned areas of experience and practice and meaning. Thus the effective decision, as to whether a practice is alternative or oppositional, is often now made within a very much narrower scope. There is a simple theoretical distinction between alternative and oppositional, that is to say between someone who simply finds a different way to live and wishes to be left alone with it, and someone who finds a different way to live and wants to change the society in its light. This is usually the difference between individual and small-group solutions to social crisis and those solutions which properly belong to political and ultimately revolutionary practice. But it is often a very narrow line, in reality, between alternative and oppositional. A meaning or a practice may be tolerated as a deviation, and yet still be seen only as another particular way to live. But as the necessary area of effective dominance extends, the same meanings and practices can be seen by the dominant culture, not merely as disregarding or despising it, but as challenging it.

Now it is crucial to any Marxist theory of culture that it can give an adequate explanation of the sources of these practices and meanings. We can understand, from an ordinary historical approach, at least some of the sources of residual meanings and practices. These are the results of earlier social formations, in which certain real meanings and values were generated. In the subsequent default of a particular phase of a dominant culture, there is then a reaching back to those meanings and values which were created in real societies in the past, and which still seem to have some significance because they represent areas of human experience, aspiration and achievement, which the dominant culture under-values or opposes, or even cannot recognise. But our hardest task, theoretically, is to find a non-metaphysical and non-subjectivist explanation of emergent cultural practice. Moreover, part of our answer to this question bears on the process of persistence of residual practices.

CLASS AND HUMAN PRACTICE

We have indeed one source to hand from the central body of Marxist theory. We have the formation of a new class, the coming to consciousness of a new class. This remains, without doubt, quite centrally important. Of course, in itself, this process of formation complicates any simple model of base and superstructure. It also complicates some of the ordinary versions of hegemony, although it was Gramsci's whole purpose to see and to create by organization that hegemony of a proletarian kind which would be capable of challenging the bourgeois hegemony. We have then one central source of new practice, in the emergence of a new class. But we have also to recognize certain other kinds of source, and in cultural practice some of these are very important. I would say that we can recognize them on the basis of this proposition: that no mode of production, and therefore no dominant society or order of society, and therefore no dominant culture, in reality exhausts the full range of human practice, human energy, human intention (this range is not the inventory of some original 'human nature' but, on the contrary, is that extraordinary range of variations, both practised and imagined, of which human beings are and have shown themselves to be capable). Indeed it seems to me that this emphasis is not merely a negative proposition, allowing us to account for certain things which happen outside the dominant mode. On the contrary, it is a fact about the modes of domination that they select from and consequently exclude the full range of actual and possible human practice. The difficulties of human practice outside or against the dominant mode are, of course, real. It depends very much whether it is in an area in which the dominant class and the dominant culture have an interest and a stake. If the interest and the stake are explicit, many new practices will be reached for, and if possible incorporated, or else extirpated with extraordinary vigour. But in certain areas, there will be in certain periods practices and meanings which are not reached for. There will be areas of practice and meaning which, almost by definition from its own limited character, or in its profound deformation, the dominant culture is unable in any real terms to recognize. This gives us a bearing on the observable difference between, for example, the practices of a capitalist state and a state like the contemporary Soviet Union in relation to writers. Since from the whole Marxist tradition literature was seen as an important activity, indeed a crucial activity, the Soviet state is very much sharper in investigating areas where different versions of practice, different meanings and values, are being attempted and expressed. In capitalist practice, if the thing is not making a profit, or if it is not being widely circulated, then it can for some time be overlooked, at least while it remains alternative. When it becomes oppositional in an explicit way, it does, of course, get approached or attacked.

I am saying then that in relation to the full range of human practice at any one time, the dominant mode is a conscious selection and organization. At least in its fully formed state it is conscious. But there are always sources of actual human practice which it neglects or excludes. And these can be different in quality from the developing and articulate interests of a rising class. They can include, for example, alternative perceptions of others, in immediate personal relationships, or new perceptions of material and media, in art and science, and within certain limits these new perceptions can be practised. The relations between the two kinds of source—the emerging class and either the dominatively excluded or the more generally new practices—are by no means necessarily contradictory. At times they can be very close, and on the relations between them much in political practice depends. But culturally and as a matter of theory the areas can be seen as distinct.

Now if we go back to the cultural question in its most usual form—what are the relations between art and society, or literature and society?—in the light of the preceding discussion, we have to say first that there are no relations between literature and society in that abstracted way. The literature is there from the beginning as a practice in the society. Indeed until it and all other practices are present, the society cannot be seen as fully formed. A society is not fully available for analysis until each of its practices is included. But if we make that emphasis we must make a corresponding emphasis: that we cannot separate literature and art from other kinds of social practice, in such a way as to make them subject to quite special and distinct laws. They may have quite specific features as practices, but they cannot be separated from the general social process. Indeed one way of emphasizing this is to say, to insist, that literature is not restricted to operating in any one of the sectors I have been seeking to describe in this model. It would be easy to say, it is a familiar rhetoric, that literature operates in the emergent cultural sector, that it represents the new feelings, the new meanings, the new values. We might persuade ourselves of this theoretically, by abstract argument, but when we read much literature, over the whole range, without the sleight-of-hand of calling Literature only that which we have already selected as embodying certain meanings and values at a certain scale of intensity, we are bound to recognize that the act of writing, the practices of discourse in writing and speech, the making of novels and poems and plays and theories, all this activity takes place in all areas of the culture.

Literature appears by no means only in the emergent sector, which is always, in fact, quite rare. A great deal of writing is of a residual kind, and this has been deeply true of much English literature in the last half-century. Some of its fundamental meanings and values have belonged to the cultural achievements of long-past stages of society. So widespread is this fact, and the habits of mind it supports, that in many minds 'literature' and 'the past' acquire a certain identity, and it is then said that there is now no literature: all that glory is over. Yet most writing, in any period, including our own, is a form of contribution to the effective dominant culture. Indeed many of the specific qualities of literature—its capacity to embody and enact and perform certain meanings and values, or to create in single particular ways what would be otherwise merely general truths—enable it to fulfil this effective function with great power. To literature, of course, we must add the visual arts and music, and in our own society the powerful arts of film and of broadcasting. But the general theoretical point should be clear. If we are looking for the relations between literature and society, we cannot either separate out this one practice from a formed body of other practices, nor when we have identified a particular practice can we give it a uniform, static and ahistorical relation to some abstract social formation. The arts of writing and the arts of creation and performance, over their whole range, are parts of the cultural process in all the different ways, the different sectors, that I have been seeking to describe. They contribute to the effective dominant culture and are a central articulation of it. They embody residual meanings and values, not all of which are incorporated, though many are. They express also and significantly some emergent practices and meanings, yet some of these may eventually be incorporated, as they reach people and begin to move them. Thus it was very evident in the sixties, in some of the emergent arts of performance, that the dominant culture reached out to transform, or seek to transform, them. In this process, of course, the dominant culture itself changes, not in its central formation, but in many of its articulated features. But then in a modern society it must always change in this way, if it is to remain dominant, if it is still to be felt as in real ways central in all our many activities and interests.

CRITICAL THEORY AS CONSUMPTION

What then are the implications of this general analysis for the analysis of particular works of art? This is the question towards which most discussion of cultural theory seems to be directed: the discovery of a method, perhaps even a methodology, through which particular works of art can be understood and described. I would not myself agree that this is the central use of cultural theory, but let us for a moment consider it. What seems to me very striking is that nearly all forms of contemporary critical theory are theories of *consumption*. That is to say, they are concerned with understanding an object in such a way that it can profitably or correctly be consumed. The earliest stage of consumption theory was the theory of 'taste', where the link between the practice and the theory was direct in the metaphor. From taste there came the more elevated notion of 'sensibility', in which it was the consumption by sensibility of elevated or insightful works that was held to be the essential practice of reading, and critical activity was then a function of this sensibility. There were then more developed theories, in the 1920s with I. A. Richards, and later in New Criticism, in which the effects of consumption were studied directly. The language of the work of art as object then became more overt. 'What effect does this work ("the poem" as it was ordinarily described) have on me?' Or, 'what impact does it have on me?', as it was later to be put in a much wider area of communication studies. Naturally enough, the notion of the work of art as *object*, as *text*, as an isolated artefact, became central in all these later consumption theories. It was not only that the practices of *production* were then overlooked, though this fused with the notion that most important literature anyway was from the past. The real social conditions of production were in any case neglected because they were believed to be at best secondary. The true relationship was seen always as between the taste, the sensibility or the training of the reader and this isolated work, this object 'as in itself it really is', as most people came to put it. But the notion of the work of art as object had a further large theoretical effect. If you ask questions about the work of art seen as object, they may include questions about the components of its production. Now, as it happened, there was a use of the formula of base and superstructure which was precisely in line with this. The components of a work of art were the real activities of the base, and you could study the object to discover these components. Sometimes you even studied the components and then projected the object. But in any case the relationship that was looked for was one between an object and its components. But this was not only true of Marxist suppositions of a base and a superstructure. It was true also of various kinds of psychological theory, whether in the form of archetypes, or the images of the collective unconscious, or the myths and symbols which were seen as the *components* of particular works of art. Or again there was biography, or psychobiography and its like, where the components were in the man's life and the work of art was an object in which components of this kind were discovered. Even in some of the more rigorous forms of New Criticism and of structuralist criticism, this essential procedure of regarding the work as an object which has to be reduced to its components, even if later it may be reconstituted, came to persist.

OBJECTS AND PRACTICES

Now I think the true crisis in cultural theory, in our own time, is between this view of the work of art as object and the alternative view of art as a practice. Of course it is at once argued that the work of art *is* an object: that various works have survived from the past, particular sculptures, particular paintings, particular buildings, and these are objects. This is of course true, but the same way of thinking is applied to works which have no such singular existence. There is no *Hamlet,* no *Brothers Karamazov,* no *Wuthering Heights,* in the sense that there is a particular great painting. There is no *Fifth Symphony,* there is no work in the whole area of music and dance and performance, which is an object in any way comparable to those works in the visual arts which have survived. And yet the habit of treating all such works as objects has persisted because this is a basic theoretical and practical presupposition. But in literature (especially in drama), in music and in a very wide area of the performing arts, what we permanently have are not objects but *notations.* These notations have then to be interpreted in an active way, according to the particular conventions. But indeed this is true over an even wider field. The relationship between the making of a work of art and its reception is always active, and subject to conventions, which in themselves are forms of (changing) social organization and relationship, and this is radically different from the production and consumption of an object. It is indeed an activity and a practice, and in its accessible forms, although it may in some arts have the character of a singular object, it is still only accessible through active perception and interpretation. This makes the case of notation, in arts like drama and literature and music, only a special case of a much wider truth. What this can show us here about the practice of analysis is that we have to break from the common procedure of isolating the object and then discovering its components. On the contrary we have to discover the nature of a practice and then its conditions.

Often these two procedures may in part resemble each other, but in many other cases they are of radically different kinds, and I would conclude with an observation on the way this distinction bears on the Marxist tradition of the relation between primary economic and social practices, and cultural practices. If we suppose that what is produced in cultural practice is a series of objects, we shall, as in most current forms of sociological-critical procedure, set about discovering their components. Within a Marxist emphasis these components will be from what we have been in the habit of calling the base. We then isolate certain features which we can so to say recognize *in component form,* or we ask what processes of transformation or mediation these components have gone through before they arrived in this accessible state.

But I am saying that we should look not for the components of a product but for the conditions of a practice. When we find ourselves looking at a particular work, or group of works, often realizing, as we do so, their essential community as well as their irreducible individuality, we should find ourselves attending first to the reality of their practice and the conditions of the practice as it was then executed. And from this I think we ask essentially different questions. Take for example the way in which an object—'a text'—is related to a genre, in orthodox criticism. We identify it by certain leading features, we then assign it to a larger category, the genre, and then we may find the components of the genre in a particular social history (although in some variants of criticism not even that is done, and the genre is supposed to be some permanent category of the mind).

It is not that way of proceeding that is now required. The recognition of the relation of a collective mode and an individual project—and these are the only categories that we can initially presume—is a recognition of related practices. That is to say, the irreducibly individual projects that particular works are, may come in experience and in analysis to show resemblances which allow us to group them into collective modes. These are by no means always genres. They may exist as resemblances within and across genres. They may be the practice of a group in a period, rather than the practice of a phase in a genre. But as we discover the nature of a particular practice, and the nature of the relation between an individual project and a collective mode, we find that we are analysing, as two forms of the same process, both its active composition and its conditions of composition, and in either direction this is a complex of extending active relationships. This means, of course, that we have no built-in procedure of the kind which is indicated by the fixed character of an object. We have the principles of the relations of practices, within a discoverably intentional organization, and we have the available hypotheses of dominant, residual and emergent. But what we are actively seeking is the true practice which has been alienated to an object, and the true conditions of practice—whether as literary conventions or as social relationships—which have been alienated to components or to mere background.

As a general proposition this is only an emphasis, but it seems to me to suggest at once the point of break and the point of departure, in practical and theoretical work, within an active and self-renewing Marxist cultural tradition.

NOTE

1. For a further discussion of the range of meanings in "determine" see Raymond Williams, *Keywords,* London 1976, pp. 87–91.

SIXTEEN

The Suit and the Photograph

John Berger

What did August Sander tell his sitters before he took their pictures? And how did he say it so that they all believed him in the same way?

They each look at the camera with the same expression in their eyes. Insofar as there are differences, these are the results of the sitter's experience and character—the priest has lived a different life from the paper-hanger; but to all of them Sander's camera represents the same thing.

Did he simply say that their photographs were going to be a recorded part of history? And did he refer to history in such a way that their vanity and shyness dropped away, so that they looked into the lens telling themselves, using a strange historical tense: *I looked like this.* We cannot know. We simply have to recognise the uniqueness of his work, which he planned with the overall title of "Man of the 20th Century."

His full aim was to find, around Cologne in the area in which he was born in 1876, archetypes to represent every possible type, social class, sub-class, job, vocation, privilege. He hoped to take, in all, 600 portraits. His project was cut short by Hitler's Third Reich.

His son Erich, a socialist and anti-nazi, was sent to a concentration camp where he died. The father hid his archives in the countryside. What remains today is an extraordinary social and human document. No other photographer, taking portraits of his own countrymen, has ever been so translucently documentary.

Walter Benjamin wrote in 1931 about Sander's work: "It was not as a scholar, advised by race theorists or social researchers, that the author [Sander] undertook his enormous task, but, in the publisher's words, 'as

From *About Looking,* by John Berger. Copyright © 1980 by John Berger. Reprinted by permission of Pantheon Books, a Division of Random House, Inc.

the result of immediate observation.' It is indeed unprejudiced observation, bold and at the same time delicate, very much in the spirit of Goethe's remark: 'There is a delicate form of the empirical which identifies itself so intimately with its object that it thereby becomes theory.' Accordingly it is quite proper that an observer like Döblin should light upon precisely the scientific aspects of this opus and point out: 'Just as there is a comparative anatomy which enables one to understand the nature and history of organs, so here the photographer has produced a comparative photography, thereby gaining a scientific standpoint which places him beyond the photographer of detail.' It would be lamentable if economic circumstances prevented the further publication of this extraordinary corpus . . . Sander's work is more than a picture book, it is an atlas of instruction."

In the inquiring spirit of Benjamin's remarks I want to examine Sander's well-known photograph of three young peasants on the road in the evening, going to a dance. There is as much descriptive information in this image as in pages by a descriptive master like Zola. Yet I only want to consider one thing: their suits.

The date is 1914. The three young men belong, at the very most, to the second generation who ever wore such suits in the European countryside. Twenty or 30 years earlier, such clothes did not exist at a price which peasants could afford. Among the young today, formal dark suits have become rare in the villages of at least western Europe. But for most of this century most peasants—and most workers—wore dark three-piece suits on ceremonial occasions, Sundays and fêtes.

When I go to a funeral in the village where I live, the men of my age and older are still wearing them. Of course there have been modifications of fashion: the width of trousers and lapels, the length of jackets change. Yet the physical character of the suit and its message does not change.

Let us first consider its physical character. Or, more precisely, its physical character when worn by village peasants. And to make generalisation more convincing, let us look at a second photograph of a village band.

Sander took this group portrait in 1913, yet it could well have been the band at the dance for which the three with their walking sticks are setting out along the road. Now make an experiment. Block out the faces of the band with a piece of paper, and consider only their clothed bodies.

By no stretch of the imagination can you believe that these bodies belong to the middle or ruling class. They might belong to workers, rather than peasants; but otherwise there is no doubt. Nor is the clue their hands—as it would be if you could touch them. Then why is their class so apparent?

Is it a question of fashion and the quality of the cloth of their suits? In real life such details would be telling. In a small black and white photograph they are not very evident. Yet the static photograph shows, perhaps more vividly than in life, the fundamental reason why the suits, far from disguising the social class of those who wore them, underlined and emphasised it.

Their suits deform them. Wearing them, they look as though they were physically mis-shapen. A past style in clothes often looks absurd until it is re-incorporated into fashion. Indeed the economic logic of fashion depends on making the old-fashioned look absurd. But here we are not faced primarily with that kind of absurdity; here the clothes look less absurd, less "abnormal" than the men's bodies which are in them.

The musicians give the impression of being uncoordinated, bandy-legged, barrel-chested, low-arsed, twisted or scalene. The violinist on the right is made to look almost like a dwarf. None of their abnormalities is extreme. They do not provoke pity. They are just sufficient to undermine physical dignity. We look at bodies which appear coarse, clumsy, brute-like. And incorrigibly so.

Now make the experiment the other way round. Cover the bodies of the band and look only at their faces. They are country faces. Nobody could suppose that they are a group of barristers or managing directors. They are five men from a village who like to make music and do so with a certain self-respect. As we look at the faces we can imagine what the bodies would look like. And what we imagine is quite different from what we have just seen. In imagination we see them as their parents might remember them when absent. We accord them the normal dignity they have.

To make the point clearer, let us now consider an image where tailored clothes, instead of deforming, *preserve* the physical identity and therefore the natural authority of those wearing them. I have deliberately chosen a Sander photograph which looks old-fashioned and could easily lend itself to parody: the photograph of four Protestant missionaries in 1931.

Despite the portentousness, it is not even necessary to make the experiment of blocking out the faces. It is clear that here the suits actually confirm and enhance the physical presence of those wearing them. The clothes convey the same message as the faces and as the history of the bodies they hide. Suits, experience, social formation and function coincide.

Look back now at the three on the road to the dance. Their hands look too big, their bodies too thin, their legs too short. (They use their walking sticks as though they were driving cattle.) We can make the same experiment with the faces and the effect is exactly the same as with the band. They can wear only their hats as if they suited them.

Where does this lead us? Simply to the conclusion that peasants can't buy good suits and don't know how to wear them? No, what is at issue here is a graphic, if small, example (perhaps one of the most graphic which exists) of what Gramsci called class hegemony. Let us look at the contradictions involved more closely.

Most peasants, if not suffering from malnutrition, are physically strong and well-developed. Well-developed because of the very varied hard physical work they do. It would be too simple to make a list of physical characteristics—broad hands through working with them from a very early age, broad shoulders relative to the body through the habit of carrying, and so on. In fact many variations and exceptions also exist. One can, however, speak of a characteristic physical rhythm which most peasants, both women and men, acquire.

This rhythm is directly related to the energy demanded by the amount of work which has to be done in a day, and is reflected in typical physical movements and stance. It is an extended sweeping rhythm. Not necessarily slow. The traditional acts of scything or sawing may exemplify it. The way peasants ride horses makes it distinctive, as also the way they walk, as if testing the earth with each stride. In addition peasants possess a special physical dignity: this is determined by a kind of functionalism, a way of being *fully at home in effort.*

The suit, as we know it today, developed in Europe as a professional ruling class costume in the last third of the 19th century. Almost anonymous as a uniform, it was the first ruling class costume to idealise purely *sedentary* power. The power of the administrator and conference table. Essentially the suit was made for the gestures of talking and calculating abstractly. (As distinct, compared to previous upper class costumes, from the gestures of riding, hunting, dancing, duelling.)

It was the English *gentleman*, with all the apparent restraint which that new stereotype implied, who launched the suit. It was a costume which inhibited vigorous action, and which action ruffled, uncreased and spoilt. "Horses sweat, men perspire and women glow." By the turn of the century, and increasingly after the first world war, the suit was mass-produced for mass urban and rural markets.

The physical contradiction is obvious. Bodies which are fully at home in effort, bodies which are used to extended sweeping movement: clothes idealising the sedentary, the discrete, the effortless. I would be the last to argue for a return to traditional peasant costumes. Any such return is bound to be escapist, for these costumes were a form of capital handed down through generations, and in the world today, in which every corner is dominated by the market, such a principle is anachronistic.

We can note, however, how traditional peasant working or ceremonial clothes respected the specific character of the bodies they were clothing. They were in general loose, and only tight in places where they were gathered to allow for freer movement. They were the antithesis of tailored clothes, clothes cut to follow the idealised shape of a more or less stationary body and then to hang from it!

Yet nobody forced peasants to buy suits, and the three on their way to the dance are clearly proud of them. They wear them with a kind of panache. This is exactly why the suit might become a classic and easily taught example of class hegemony.

Villagers—and, in a different way, city workers—were persuaded to choose suits. By publicity. By pictures. By the new mass media. By salesmen. By example. By the sight of new kinds of travellers. And also by political developments of accommodation and state central organisation. For example: in 1900, on the occasion of the great Universal Exhibition, all the mayors of France were, for the first time ever, invited to a banquet in Paris. Most of them were the peasant mayors of village communes. Nearly 30,000 came! And, naturally, for the occasion the vast majority wore suits.

The working classes—but peasants were simpler and more naïve about it than workers—came to accept *as their own* certain standards of the class that ruled over them—in this case standards of chic and sartorial worthiness. At the same time their very acceptance of these standards, their very conforming to these norms which had nothing to do with either their own inheritance or their daily experience, condemned them, within the system of those standards, to being always, and recognisably to the classes above them, second-rate, clumsy, uncouth, defensive. That indeed is to succumb to a cultural hegemony.

Perhaps one can nevertheless propose that when the three arrived and had drunk a beer or two, and had eyed the girls (whose clothes had not yet changed so drastically), they hung up their jackets, took off their ties, and danced, maybe wearing their hats, until the morning and the next day's work.

SEVENTEEN

Written Clothing

Roland Barthes

"A leather belt, with a rose stuck in it, worn above the waist, on a soft shetland dress."

THE THREE GARMENTS

Image-Clothing and Written Clothing

I open a fashion magazine; I see that two different garments are being dealt with here. The first is the one presented to me as photographed or drawn—it is image-clothing. The second is the same garment, but described, transformed into language; this dress, photographed on the right, becomes on the left: *a leather belt, with a rose stuck in it, worn above the waist, on a soft shetland dress;* this is a written garment. In principle these two garments refer to the same reality (this dress worn on this day by this woman), and yet they do not have the same structure,[1] because they are not made of the same substances and because, consequently, these substances do not have the same relations with each other: in one the substances are forms, lines, surfaces, colors, and the relation is spatial; in the other, the substance is words, and the relation is, if not logical, at least syntactic; the first structure is plastic, the second verbal. Is this to say that each of these structures is indistinguishable from the general system from which it derives—image-clothing from photography, written clothing from language? Not at all: the Fashion photograph is not just any photograph, it bears little relation to the news photograph or to the snapshot, for example; it has its own units and rules; within photographic communication, it forms a specific language which no doubt has its own lexicon and syntax, its own banned or approved "turns of phrase."[2]

Similarly, the structure of written clothing cannot be identified with the structure of a sentence; for if clothing coincided with discourse, changing a term in the discourse would suffice to alter, at the same time, the identity of the described clothing; but this is not the case; a magazine can state: "Wear shantung in summer" as easily as "Shantung goes with summer," without fundamentally affecting the information transmitted to its readership. Written clothing is carried by language, but also resists it, and is created by this interplay. So we are dealing with two original structures, albeit derived from more general systems, in the one case language, in the other the image.

Real Clothing

At the least we might suppose that these two garments recover a single identity at the level of the real garment they are supposed to represent, that the described dress and the photographed dress are united in the actual dress they both refer to. Equivalent, no doubt, but not identical; for just as between image-clothing and written clothing there is a difference in substances and relations, and thus a difference of structure, in the same way, from these two garments to the real one there is a transition to other substances and other relations; thus, the real garment forms a third structure, different from the first two, even if it serves them as model, or more exactly, even if the model which guides the information transmitted by the first two garments belongs to this third structure. We have seen that the units of image-clothing are located at the level of forms, those of written clothing at the level of words; as for the units of real clothing, they cannot exist at the level of language, for, as we know, language is not a tracing of reality;[3] nor can we locate them, although here the temptation is great, at the level of forms, for "seeing" a real garment, even under privileged conditions of presentation, cannot exhaust its reality, still less its structure; we never see more than part of a garment, a personal and circumstantial usage, a particular way of wearing it; in order to analyze the real garment in systematic terms, i.e., in terms sufficiently formal to account for all analogous garments, we should no doubt have to work our way back to the actions which governed its manufacture. In other words, given the plastic structure of image-clothing and the verbal structure of written clothing, the structure of real clothing can only be technological. The units of this structure can only be the various traces of the actions of manufacture, their materialized and accomplished goals: a seam is what has been sewn, the cut of a coat is what has been cut;[4] there is then a structure which is constituted at the level of substance and its transformations, not of its representations or significations; and here ethnology might provide relatively simple structural models.[5]

SHIFTERS

Translation of Structures

There are, then, for any particular object (a dress, a tailored suit, a belt) three different structures, one technological, another iconic, the third verbal. These three structures do not have the same circulation pattern. The technological structure appears as a mother tongue of which the real garments derived from it are only instances of "speech." The two other structures (iconic and verbal) are also languages, but if we believe Fashion magazines, which always claim to discuss a primary real garment, these are derived languages, "translated" from the mother tongue; they intervene as circulation relays between this mother tongue and its instances of "speech" (the real garments). In our society, the circulation of Fashion thus relies in large part on an activity of *transformation:* there is a transition (at least according to the order invoked by Fashion magazines) from the technological structure to the iconic and verbal structures. Yet this transition, as in all structures, can only be discontinuous: the real garment can only be *transformed* into "representation" by means of certain operators which we might call *shifters,* since they serve to transpose one structure into another, to pass, if you will, from one code to another code.[6]

The Three Shifters

Since we are dealing with three structures, we must have three kinds of shifters at our disposal: from the real to the image, from the real to language, and from the image to language. For the first translation, from the technological garment to the iconic garment, the principal shifter is the sewing pattern, whose (schematic) design analytically reproduces the stages of the garment's manufacture; to which should be added the processes, graphic or photographic, intended to reveal the technical substratum of a look or an "effect": accentuation of a movement, enlargement of a detail, angle of vision. For the second translation, from the technological garment to the written garment, the basic shifter is what might be called the sewing program or formula: it is generally a text quite apart from the literature of Fashion; its goal is to outline not what is but what is *going to be* done; the sewing program, moreover, is not given in the same kind of writing as the Fashion commentary; it contains almost no nouns or adjectives, but mostly verbs and measurements.[7] As a shifter, it constitutes a transitional language, situated midway between the making of the garment and its being, between its origin and its form, its technology and its signification. We might be tempted to include within this basic shifter all Fashion terms of clearly technological origin (*a seam, a cut*), and to consider them as so many translators from the real to the spoken; but this would ignore the fact that the value of a word is not found in its origin but in its place in the language system; once these terms pass into a descriptive structure, they are simultaneously detached from their origin (what has been, at some point, sewn, cut) and their goal (to contribute to an assemblage, to stand out in an ensemble); in them the creative act is not perceptible, they no longer belong to the technological structure and we cannot consider them as *shifters*.[8] There remains a third translation, one which allows the transition from the iconic structure to the spoken structure, from the representation of the garment to its description. Since Fashion magazines take advantage of the ability to deliver *simultaneously* messages derived from these two structures—here a dress photographed, there the same dress described—they can take a notable shortcut by using elliptical *shifters:* these are no longer pattern drawings or the texts of the sewing pattern, but simply the anaphorics of language, given either at the maximum degree (*"this" tailored suit, "the" shetland dress*) or at degree zero (*"a rose stuck into a belt"*).[9] Thus, by the very fact that the three structures have well-defined translation-operators at their disposal, they remain perfectly distinct.

THE TERMINOLOGICAL RULE

Choice of the Oral Structure

To study the garment of Fashion would first be to study each of these three structures separately and exhaustively, for a structure cannot be defined apart from the substantial identity of the units which constitute it: we must study either acts, or images, or words, but not all these substances at once, even if the structures which they form combine to constitute a generic object which, for convenience' sake, we call the garment of Fashion. Each of these structures calls for an original analysis, and we must choose. The study of the garment "represented" (by image and text), i.e., the garment dealt with by the Fashion magazine, affords an immediate methodological advantage over the analysis of real clothing.[10] Clothing "in print" provides the analyst what human languages deny the linguist: a pure synchrony; the synchrony of Fashion changes abruptly each year, but during the year it is absolutely stable; by studying the clothing in magazines, it is possible to study a state of Fashion without having to cut it artificially, as a linguist must cut the tangled continuum of messages. The choice remains between image-clothing and written (or, more precisely, described) clothing. Here again, from the methodological point of view, it is the structural "purity" of the object which influences the choice.[11] "Real" clothing is burdened with practical considerations (protection, modesty, adornment); these finalities disappear from "represented" clothing, which no longer serves to protect, to cover, or to adorn, but at most to signify protection, modesty, or adornment; but image-clothing retains one set of values which risks complicating its analysis considerably, i.e., its plastic quality; only written clothing has no practical or aesthetic function: it is entirely constituted with a view to a signification: if the magazine describes a certain article of clothing verbally, it does so solely to convey a message whose content is: *Fashion;* we might say, then, that the being of the written garment resides completely in its meaning, it is there that we stand the greatest chance of discovering the semantic pertinence in all its purity; written clothing is unencumbered by any parasitic function and entails no vague temporality: for these reasons, we have chosen to explore the verbal structure. This does not mean that we will simply be analyzing the language of Fashion; it is true that the nomenclature under study is a specialized part of the main territory of (the French) language; this part, however, will not be studied from the point of view of language, but only from the point of view of the structure of the clothing it alludes to; it is not a part of a subcode of (the French) language which is the object of the analysis, but rather of the "supercode" which words impose on the real garment, for words, as we shall see, take over an object, the garment, which itself is already a system of signification.

Semiology and Sociology

Although the choice of oral structure corresponds to reasons immanent in its object, it finds some reinforcement from sociology; first of all because the propagation of Fashion by magazines (i.e., in particular by the text) has become so vast; half of all French-women read magazines at least partially devoted to Fashion on a regular basis; the description of the garment of Fashion (and no longer its production) is therefore a social fact, so that even if the garment of Fashion remained purely imaginary (without affecting real clothing), it would constitute an incontestable element of mass culture, like pulp fiction, comics, and movies; second, the structural analysis of written clothing can also effectively pave the way for the inventory of real clothing that sociology will require for its eventual study of the circuits and circulation-rhythms of real Fashion. Nonetheless, the objectives of sociology and semiology are, in the present case, entirely different: the sociology of Fashion (even if it remains to be constituted) [12] starts from a *model* of imagined origin (the garment conceived of by the *fashion group*) and follows (or should follow) its actualization through a series of real garments (this is the problem of the circulation of models); it therefore seeks to systematize certain actions and to relate them to social conditions, standards of living, and roles. Semiology does not follow the same path at all; it describes a garment which from beginning to end remains imaginary, or, if one prefers, purely intellective; it leads us to recognize not practices but images. The sociology of Fashion is entirely directed toward real clothing; the semiology of Fashion is directed toward a set of collective representations. The choice of oral structure therefore leads not to sociology but rather to that *sociologics* postulated by Durkheim and Mauss; [13] the function of the description of Fashion is not only to propose a model which is a copy of reality but also and especially to circulate Fashion broadly as a *meaning*.

The Corpus

Once the oral stucture has been decided upon, what corpus should be chosen for study? [14] Thus far, we have referred only to Fashion magazines; this is because, on the one hand, descriptions from literature proper, although important in a number of great authors (Balzac, Michelet, Proust), are too fragmentary, too variable historically to be of use; and on the other, descriptions from department-store catalogues can be easily assimilated into the descriptions of Fashion; Fashion magazines thus constitute the best corpus. All Fashion magazines? By no means. Two limiting factors can intervene here, justified by the goal intended, which is not to describe a concrete Fashion but to reconstitute a formal system. The first selection concerns time; seeking to constitute a structure, it would be most useful to limit one's work to a state of Fashion, i.e., a synchrony. Now, as has been stated, the synchrony of Fashion is established by Fashion itself: the Fashion of a year. [15] We have chosen to work here on magazines from the year 1958–59 (from June to June), but this date obviously has no methodological importance; one could choose any other year, for we are not attempting to describe some Fashion in particular but Fashion in general. As soon as it is gathered, extracted from its year, the raw material (the utterance) must take its place in a purely formal system of functions; [16] hence, no indication will be given here as to any contingent Fashion, and a fortiori no history of Fashion: we have not sought to deal with any particular substance of Fashion, but only with the structure of its written signs. [17] Similarly (and this will be the second limit imposed on the corpus), it would be of interest to study all the magazines of a single year only if one were concerned with the substantial differences among them (ideological, aesthetic, or social); from a sociological viewpoint, this would be an important problem, since each magazine refers both to a socially defined public and to a specific body of representations, but this differential sociology of magazines, readerships, and ideologies is not the declared object of this inquiry, which aims only at finding the (written) "language" of Fashion. Thus, we have exhaustively studied only two magazines (*Elle* and *Le Jardin des Modes*), with a few forays into other publications (notably, *Vogue* and *L'Echo de la*

Mode)[18] as well as the weekly Fashion page to be found in some of the daily papers. The semiological project requires the constitution of a corpus reasonably saturated with all the possible *differences* in clothing signs. On the other hand, it matters far less that these differences are more or less often repeated, for it is difference that makes meaning, not repetition. Structurally, a rare feature of Fashion is as important as a common one, a gardenia as important as a long skirt; the objective here is to *distinguish* units, not to count them.[19] Last, we have further eliminated, within this reduced corpus, any notations which might imply a finality other than signification: advertisements, even when they claim to account for Fashion, and technical instructions for the manufacture of clothing. We have considered neither hairstyles nor makeup, since these elements contain their own particular variants which would have encumbered the inventory of clothing proper.[20]

The Terminological Rule

We will thus be dealing here with written clothing exclusively. The preliminary rule that determines the constitution of the corpus to be analyzed is *to retain no other raw material for study than the language provided by the Fashion magazines.* No doubt, this considerably limits the material for analysis; on the one hand it rules out any recourse to related documents (such as dictionary definitions), and on the other it deprives us of the rich resources of photography; in short, it treats the Fashion magazine only marginally, where it seems to duplicate the image. But this impoverishment of the raw material, aside from being methodologically inevitable, has perhaps its own rewards: to reduce the garment to its oral version is thereby to encounter a new problem which can be formulated thus: *What happens when an object, whether real or imaginary, is converted into language?* or rather, *when an object encounters language?* If the garment of Fashion appears to be a paltry thing in the face of so broad a question, we would do well to keep in mind that the same relation is established between literature and the world: isn't literature the institution which seems to convert the real into language and place its being in that conversion, just like our written garment? Moreover, isn't written Fashion a literature?

DESCRIPTION

Literary Description and Fashion Description

Fashion and literature in fact utilize a common technique whose end is seemingly to transform an object into language: it is *description*. This technique, however, is used quite differently in each case. In literature, description is brought to bear upon a hidden object (whether real or imaginary): it must make that object exist. In Fashion the described object is actualized, given separately in its plastic form (if not real form, since it is nothing other than a photograph). The functions of Fashion description are thus reduced, but also, thereby, original: since it need not render the object itself, the information which language communicates, unless it is pleonastic, is by definition the very information which photography or drawing cannot transmit. The importance of the written garment confirms the fact that specific language-functions exist which the image, whatever its development in contemporary society may be, could not possibly assume. For the written garment in particular, what then are the specific functions of language in relation to the image?

Immobilization of Levels of Perception

The primary function of speech is to immobilize perception at a certain level of intelligibility (or, as the theoreticians of information would say, of prehensibility). We know in fact that an image inevitably involves several levels of perception, and that the reader of images has at his disposal a certain amount of freedom in his choice of the level (even if he is not aware of this freedom): this choice is of course not without limits: there are *optimum* levels: precisely those where the intelligibility of the message is highest; but from the grain of the paper to this tip of the collar, then from this collar to the whole dress, every glance cast at an image inevitably implies a decision; i.e., the meaning of an image is never certain.[21] Language eliminates this freedom, but also this uncertainty; it conveys a choice and imposes it, it requires the perception of this dress to stop here (i.e., neither before nor beyond), it arrests the level of reading at its fabric, at its belt, at the accessory which adorns it. Thus, every written word has a function of authority insofar as *it* chooses—by proxy, so to speak—instead of the eye. The image freezes an endless number of possibilities; words determine a single certainty.[22]

Function of Knowledge

The second function of speech is a function of knowledge. Language makes it possible to deliver information which photography delivers poorly or not at all: the color of a fabric (if the photograph is black and white), the nature of a detail inaccessible to view *(decorative button, pearl stitch)*, the existence of an element hidden because of the two-dimensional character of the image (the back of a garment); in a general way, what language adds to the image is *knowledge*.[23] And since Fashion is a phenomenon of initiation, speech naturally fulfills a didactic function: the Fashion text represents as it were the authoritative voice of someone who knows all there is behind the jumbled or incomplete appearance of the visible forms; thus, it constitutes a technique of opening the invisible, where

one could almost rediscover, in secular form, the sacred halo of divina-
tory texts; especially since the knowledge of Fashion is not without its
price: those who exclude themselves from it suffer a sanction: the stigma
of being *unfashionable*. Such a function of knowledge is obviously possible only because language, which sustains it, constitutes in itself a system of abstraction; not that the language of Fashion intellectualizes the
garment; on the contrary, in many cases it helps to grasp it much more
concretely than the photograph, restoring to such notation all the
com80ctness of a gesture *(with a rose stuck in it)*; but because it permits
dealing with discrete concepts *(whiteness, suppleness, velvetiness)*, and not
with physically complete objects; by its abstract character, language permits isolating certain functions (in the mathematical sense of the term),
it endows the garment with a system of functional oppositions (for example, fantasy/classic), which the real or photographed garment is not
able to manifest in as clear a manner.[24]

Function of Emphasis

It also happens—and frequently—that speech seems to duplicate elements of a garment which are clearly visible in the photograph: *the large
collar, the absence of buttons, the flared line of the skirt*, etc. This is because
speech also has an emphatic function; the photograph presents a garment no part of which is privileged and which is consumed as an immediate whole; but from this ensemble the commentary can single out certain elements in order to stress their value: this is the explicit *note (Note:
the neckline cut on the bias, etc.)*.[25] This emphasis obviously rests upon an
intrinsic quality of language: its discontinuity; the described garment is
a fragmentary garment; in relation to the photograph, it is the result of
a series of choices, of amputations; in *the soft shetland dress with a belt worn
high and with a rose stuck in it*, we are told certain parts (the material, the
belt, the detail) and spared others (the sleeves, the collar, the shape, the
color), as if the woman wearing this garment went about dressed only in
a rose and softness. This is because, in fact, the limits of written clothing
are no longer material limits, but limits of value: if the magazine tells us
that this belt is made of leather, it is because its leather has an absolute
value (and not its shape, for example); if it tells us of a rose on a dress,
it is because the rose is worth as much as the dress; a neckline, a pleat, if
put into words, become clothing with full status, with the same "standing" as a whole coat. Applied to clothing, the order of language decides
between the essential and the accessory; but it is a Spartan order: it rel-
egates the accessory to the nothingness of the unnamed.[26] This emphasis
of language involves two functions. On the one hand, it permits reviving
the general information conveyed by the photograph when the latter,
like all informative entities, tends to wear out: the more photographed

dresses I see, the more banal becomes the information I receive; verbalized notation helps to reinvigorate the information; furthermore, when it is explicit *(note . . .)* it generally does not deal with eccentric details whose very novelty guarantees its informative power, but with elements so commonly offered in the variations of Fashion (collars, trim, pockets)[27] that it is necessary to recharge the message they contain; here Fashion behaves like language itself, for which the novelty of a turn of phrase or of a word always constitutes an emphasis destined to repair the wear in its system.[28] On the other hand, the emphasis language places on certain vestimentary features by naming them remains perfectly functional; description does not aim at isolating certain elements in order to praise their aesthetic value, but simply to render intelligible in an analytical way precisely those reasons which make an organized whole out of a collection of details: description here is an instrument of structuration; in particular, it permits orienting the perception of the image: in itself, a photographed dress does not begin or end anywhere; none of its limits is privileged; it can be looked at indefinitely or in the blink of an eye; the look we give it has no duration because it has no regular itinerary;[29] whereas, when described, this same dress (we saw only it) begins at its belt, continues on to a rose and ends in shetland; the dress itself is barely mentioned. Thus, by introducing an organized duration into the representation of the Fashion garment, description institutes, so to speak, a protocol of unveiling: the garment is unveiled according to a certain order, and this order inevitably implies certain goals.

Finality of Description

Which goals? It must be understood that from a practical point of view, the description of a Fashion garment serves no purpose; we could not make a garment by relying solely on its Fashion description. The goal of a sewing pattern is transitive: it involves making something; the goal of a written garment seems purely reflexive: the garment seems to *speak itself*, to refer to itself, enclosed in a sort of tautology. The functions of description, whether they are fixation, exploration, or emphasis, aim only at manifesting a certain state of being for the garment of Fashion, and this being can only coincide with Fashion itself; image-clothing can most certainly be *fashionable* (it is so by its very definition), but it cannot be *Fashion* directly; its materiality, its very totality, its evidence, so to speak, make the Fashion it represents an attribute and not a being; *this* dress, which is represented to me (and not described), may well be something other than fashionable; it may be warm, strange, attractive, modest, protective, etc., *before* being fashionable; on the contrary, this same dress, described, can only be Fashion itself; no function, no accident succeeds in barring the evidence of its existence, since functions and accidents

themselves, if they are noted, proceed from a declared intention of Fashion.[30] In short, the proper aim of description is to direct the immediate
and diffuse knowledge of image-clothing through a mediate and specific
knowledge of Fashion. Here we find once again the considerable difference, of an anthropological order, which opposes looking to reading: we
look at image-clothing, we read a described garment, and it is probable
that two different audiences correspond to these two activities; the image makes the purchase unnecessary, it replaces it; we can intoxicate
ourselves on images, identify ourselves oneirically with the model, and,
in reality, follow Fashion merely by purchasing a few boutique accessories; speech, on the contrary, rids the garment of all corporal actuality;
being no more than a system of impersonal objects whose mere assemblage creates Fashion, the described garment encourages the purchase.
The image provokes a fascination, speech an appropriation; the image
is complete, it is a saturated system; speech is fragmentary, it is an open
system: when combined, the latter serves to *disappoint* the former.

Language and Speech, Clothing and Dress

We will gain a still better understanding of the relation between image-
clothing and written clothing, between the represented object and the
described object, by referring to a conceptual opposition which has become classic since Saussure:[31] that of language and speech. Language is
an institution, an abstract body of constraints; speech is the momentary
part of this institution which the individual extracts and actualizes for
purposes of communication; language issues from the mass of spoken
words, and yet all speech is itself drawn from language; in history this is
a dialectic between the structure and the event, and in communication
theory between the code and the message.[32] Now, in relation to image-
clothing, written clothing has a structural purity which is more or less
that of language in relation to speech: description is, in a necessary and
sufficient manner, based on the manifestation of institutional constraints
which make *this* garment, represented here, fashionable; it is in no way
concerned with the manner in which the garment is worn by a particular
individual, even if that person is "institutional," as, for example, a cover
girl. Here is an important difference, and, when necessary, we might
agree to call the structural, institutional form of what is worn *clothing*
(that which corresponds to language), and this same form when actualized, individualized, worn, *dress* (that which corresponds to speech). Undoubtedly, described clothing is not entirely general, it remains *chosen;*
it is, if you will, an example of grammar, it is not grammar itself; but at
least, in order to speak an informative language, it produces no *static,*
i.e., nothing that disturbs the pure meaning it transmits: it is entirely
meaning: description is speech without static. However, this opposition is

valuable only at the level of the vestimentary system; for at the level of the linguistic system, it is evident that description itself is sustained by particular instances of speech (the one in *this* magazine, on *this* page); description is, if you will, an abstract garment entrusted to a concrete speech; written clothing is at once institution ("language") on the level of clothing, and action ("speech") on the level of language. This paradoxical status is important: it will govern the entire structural analysis of written clothing.

NOTES

1. It would be preferable to have only objects to define and not words; but since so much is expected today from the word *structure,* we will assign it here the meaning it has in linguistics: "an autonomous entity of internal dependencies" (L. Hjelmslev, *Essays in Linguistics,* 1959).

2. We touch here on the paradox of photographic communication: being in principle purely analogical, the photograph can be defined as *a message without a code;* yet there is actually no photograph without signification. So we must postulate a photographic code which obviously operates only on a second level which we shall later call the level of connotation. (Cf. "Le message photographique," *Communications,* no. 1, 1961, pp. 127–38, and "La rhétorique de l'image," *Communications,* no. 4, 1964, pp. 40–51.) In the case of Fashion illustration, the question is simpler, since the *style* of a drawing refers to an openly cultural code.

3. Cf. A. Martinet, *Elements of General Linguistics,* 1.6.

4. Provided, of course, these terms are given in a technological context as, for example, in a program of manufacture; otherwise, these terms of technological origin have a different value (cf., below, "Choice of the Oral Structure").

5. For example, A. Leroi-Gourhan differentiates clothing that hangs straight with parallel edges, clothing which is cut and open, cut and closed, cut and double-breasted, etc. (*Milieu et techniques,* Paris, Albin-Michel, 1945, p. 208).

6. Jakobson reserves the term *shifter* for the elements intermediary between the code and the message (*Essais de linguistique générale,* Paris, Editions de Minuit, 1963, chap. 9). We have broadened the sense of the term here.

7. For example: *"Place all the pieces on the lining you are cutting and baste. Baste a vertical fold three cm. wide on each side, one cm. from the ends of the shoulders."* This is a transitive language.

8. We might regard the catalogue garment as a shifter, since it is intended to effect an actual purchase by means of the relay of language. In fact, however, the catalogue garment obeys the norms of Fashion description altogether: it seeks not so much to account for the garment as to persuade us that it is in Fashion.

9. Anaphora, according to L. Tesnières (*Eléments de syntaxe structurale,* Paris, Klincksieck, 1959, p. 85), is "a supplementary semantic connection without a corresponding structural one." There is no structural link between the demonstrative "this" and the photographed skirt, but rather, so to speak, a pure and simple collision of two structures.

10. Troubetskoy postulated the possibility of the semantic analysis of real clothing in his *Principles of Phonology*, 1949.

11. These are reasons contingent upon operational method.

12. As early as Herbert Spencer, Fashion became a privileged sociological object; first of all, it constitutes "a collective phenomenon which shows us with particular immediacy . . . what is social about our own behavior" (J. Stoetzel, *La psychologie sociale*, Paris, Flammarion, 1963, p. 245); it then presents a dialectic of conformity and change which can only be explained sociologically; finally, its transmission seems to depend on those relay systems studied by P. Lazarsfeld and E. Katz (*Personal Influence: The Part Played by People in the Flow of Mass-Communications*, Glencoe, Illinois, The Free Press, 1955). Nonetheless, the actual circulation of models has not yet been the object of a complete sociological study.

13. "Essai sur quelques formes primitives de classification," *Année Sociologique*, vol. 6, 1901–2, pp. 1–72.

14. Corpus: "intangible synchronic collection of statements on which one works" (Martinet, *Elements*).

15. There are seasonal Fashions within the year, but here the seasons constitute less a diachronic series than a table of different signifieds within the lexicon of a year. The synchronic unit is indeed the "line," which is annual.

16. On occasion, we have even drawn on other synchronies for a control or an interesting example.

17. This does not rule out, of course, a general reflection on the diachrony of Fashion.

18. This choice is not altogether arbitrary, however. *Elle* and *L'Echo de la Mode* seem to have a more "popular" appeal than *Vogue* and *Le Jardin des Modes*.

19. Disparity of frequencies is of sociologic but not of systematic importance; it informs us about the "tastes" (the obsessions) of a magazine (and thus of a readership), not about the general structure of the object; the frequency of signifying units is relevant only for the comparison of magazines with one another.

20. The statements of Fashion will be quoted without sources, like examples from grammar.

21. As we know from Ombredanne's experiment with the perception of the film image (cf. E. Morin, *Le cinéma ou l'homme imaginaire*, Editions de Minuit, 1956, p. 115).

22. That is why all news photographs are captioned.

23. From the photograph to the drawing, from the drawing to the diagram, from the diagram to language, there is a progressive investment of knowledge (cf. J.-P. Sartre, *L'imaginaire*, Paris, Gallimard, 1947).

24. In relation to photography, language has a role somewhat analogous to that of phonology in relation to phonetics, since it permits isolating the phenomenon "as an abstraction drawn from sound, or as groups of functional characteristics of a sound" (N. S. Troubetskoy, quoted by E. Buyssens, "La nature du signe linguistique," *Acta Linguistica*, II: 2, 1941, 82–86).

25. In fact, all Fashion commentary is an implicit *note*.

26. By antiphrasis, what is called the *accessory*, in Fashion, is very often the essential, the spoken system having precisely the task of making the *almost nothing* signify. *Accessory* is a term derived from the real, economic structure.

27. These are the vestimentary genera which best lend themselves to the significant variation.

28. Cf. Martinet, *Elements*, 6.17.

29. A dubious experiment conducted in the United States by a clothing firm (cited by A. Rothstein, *Photo-journalism*, New York, Photographic Book Publishing Co., 1956, pp. 85, 99) nonetheless tried to discover the itinerary of the look that "reads" the representation of a human silhouette: the privileged zone of reading, what the look most often returns to, is apparently the neck—in vestimentary terms, the collar: it is true that the firm in question sold shirts.

30. The functionalization of the Fashion garment (a dance skirt) is a phenomenon of connotation; hence, it is entirely a part of the Fashion system.

31. F. de Saussure, *Cours de linguistique générale*, Paris, Payot, 4th ed., 1949, chap. III.

32. Martinet, *Elements*, 1.18—The identity of the code and of the language, of the message and of speech, has been discussed by P. Guiraud, "La mécanique de l'analyse quantitative en linguistique," in *Etudes de linguistique appliquée*, no. 2, Didier, 1963, p. 37.

EIGHTEEN

What Is an Author?

Michel Foucault

In proposing this slightly odd question, I am conscious of the need for an explanation. To this day, the "author" remains an open question both with respect to its general function within discourse and in my own writings; that is, this question permits me to return to certain aspects of my own work which now appear ill-advised and misleading. In this regard, I wish to propose a necessary criticism and reevaluation.

For instance, my objective in *The Order of Things* had been to analyse verbal clusters as discursive layers which fall outside the familiar categories of a book, a work, or an author. But while I considered "natural history," the "analysis of wealth," and "political economy" in general terms, I neglected a similar analysis of the author and his works; it is perhaps due to this omission that I employed the names of authors throughout this book in a naive and often crude fashion. I spoke of Buffon, Cuvier, Ricardo, and others as well, but failed to realize that I had allowed their names to function ambiguously. This has proved an embarrassment to me in that my oversight has served to raise two pertinent objections.

It was argued that I had not properly described Buffon or his work and that my handling of Marx was pitifully inadequate in terms of the totality of his thought.[1] Although these objections were obviously justified, they ignored the task I had set myself: I had no intention of describing Buffon or Marx or of reproducing their statements or implicit meanings, but, simply stated, I wanted to locate the rules that formed a certain number of concepts and theoretical relationships in their works.[2] In addition, it was argued that I had created monstrous families by bringing together names as disparate as Buffon and Linnaeus or in placing Cuvier next to Darwin in defiance of the most readily observable family resemblances and natural ties.[3] This objection also seems inappropriate since I had never tried to establish a genealogical table of exceptional individuals, nor was I concerned in forming an intellectual daguerreotype of the scholar or naturalist of the seventeenth and eighteenth century. In fact, I had no intention of forming any family, whether holy or perverse. On the contrary, I wanted to determine—a much more modest task—the functional conditions of specific discursive practices.

Then why did I use the names of authors in *The Order of Things*? Why not avoid their use altogether, or, short of that, why not define the manner in which they were used? These questions appear fully justified and I have tried to gauge their implications and consequences in a book that will appear shortly.[4] These questions have determined my effort to situate comprehensive discursive units, such as "natural history" or "political economy," and to establish the methods and instruments for delimiting, analyzing, and describing these unities. Nevertheless, as a privileged moment of individualization in the history of ideas, knowledge, and literature, or in the history of philosophy and science, the question of the author demands a more direct response. Even now, when we study the history of a concept, a literary genre, or a branch of philosophy, these concerns assume a relatively weak and secondary position in relation to the solid and fundamental role of an author and his works.

For the purposes of this paper, I will set aside a sociohistorical analysis of the author as an individual and the numerous questions that deserve attention in this context: how the author was individualized in a culture such as ours; the status we have given the author, for instance, when we began our research into authenticity and attribution; the systems of valorization in which he was included; or the moment when the stories of heroes gave way to an author's biography; the conditions that fostered the formulation of the fundamental critical category of "the man and his work." For the time being, I wish to restrict myself to the singular relationship that holds between an author and a text, the manner in which a text apparently points to this figure who is outside and precedes it.

Beckett supplies a direction: "What matter who's speaking, someone said, what matter who's speaking."[5] In an indifference such as this we must recognize one of the fundamental ethical principles of contemporary writing. It is not simply "ethical" because it characterizes our way of speaking and writing, but because it stands as an immanent rule, endlessly adopted and yet never fully applied. As a principle, it dominates writing as an ongoing practice and slights our customary attention to the finished product.[6] For the sake of illustration, we need only consider two of its major themes. First, the writing of our day has freed itself from the necessity of "expression"; it only refers to itself, yet it is not restricted to the confines of interiority. On the contrary, we recognize it in its exterior deployment.[7] This reversal transforms writing into an interplay of signs, regulated less by the content it signifies than by the very nature of the signifier. Moreover, it implies an action that is always testing the limits of its regularity, transgressing and reversing an order that it accepts and manipulates. Writing unfolds like a game that inevitably moves beyond its own rules and finally leaves them behind. Thus, the essential basis of this writing is not the exalted emotions related to the act of composition or the insertion of a subject into language. Rather, it is primarily concerned with creating an opening where the writing subject endlessly disappears.[8]

The second theme is even more familiar: it is the kinship between writing and death. This relationship inverts the age-old conception of Greek narrative or epic, which was designed to guarantee the immortality of a hero. The hero accepted an early death because his life, consecrated and magnified by death, passed into immortality; and the narrative redeemed his acceptance of death. In a different sense, Arabic stories, and *The Arabian Nights* in particular, had as their motivation, their theme and pretext, this strategy for defeating death. Storytellers continued their narratives late into the night to forestall death and to delay the inevitable moment when everyone must fall silent. Scheherazade's story is a desperate inversion of murder; it is the effort, throughout all those nights, to exclude death from the circle of existence.[9] This conception of a spoken or written narrative as a protection against death has been transformed by our culture. Writing is now linked to sacrifice and to the sacrifice of life itself; it is a voluntary obliteration of the self that does not require representation in books because it takes place in the everyday existence of the writer. Where a work had the duty of creating immortality, it now attains the right to kill, to become the murderer of its author. Flaubert, Proust, and Kafka are obvious examples of this reversal.[10] In addition, we find the link between writing and death manifested in the total effacement of the individual characteristics of the writer; the quibbling and confrontations that a writer generates between himself and his text cancel out the signs of his particular individuality. If we wish to know the writer in our day, it will be through the singularity of his absence and in his link to death, which has transformed him into a victim of his own writing. While all of this is familiar in philosophy, as in literary criticism, I am not certain that the consequences derived from the disappearance or death of the author have been fully explored or that the importance of this event has been appreciated. To be specific, it seems to me that the themes destined to replace the privileged position accorded the author have merely served to arrest the possibility of genuine change. Of these, I will examine two that seem particularly important.

To begin with, the thesis concerning a work. It has been understood that the task of criticism is not to reestablish the ties between an author and his work or to reconstitute an author's thought and experience through his works and, further, that criticism should concern itself with the structures of a work, its architectonic forms, which are studied for their intrinsic and internal relationships.[11] Yet, what of a context that questions the concept of a work? What, in short, is the strange unit designated by the term, work? What is necessary to its composition, if a work is not something written by a person called an "author"? Difficulties arise on all sides if we raise the question in this way. If an individual is not an author, what are we to make of those things he has written or said, left among his papers or communicated to others? Is this not properly a work? What, for instance, were Sade's papers before he was consecrated as an author? Little more, perhaps, than rolls of paper on which he endlessly unravelled his fantasies while in prison.

Assuming that we are dealing with an author, is everything he wrote and said, everything he left behind, to be included in his work? This problem is both theoretical and practical. If we wish to publish the complete works of Nietzsche, for example, where do we draw the line? Certainly, everything must be published, but can we agree on what "everything" means? We will, of course, include everything that Nietzsche himself published, along with the drafts of his works, his plans for aphorisms, his marginal notations and corrections. But what if, in a notebook filled with aphorisms, we find a reference, a reminder of an appointment, an address, or a laundry bill, should this be included in his works? Why not? These practical considerations are endless once we consider how a work can be extracted from the millions of traces left by an individual after his death. Plainly, we lack a theory to encompass the questions generated by a work and the empirical activity of those who naively undertake the publication of the complete works of an author often suffers from the absence of this framework. Yet more questions arise. Can we say that *The Arabian Nights,* and *Stromates* of Clement of Alexandria, or the *Lives* of Diogenes Laertes constitute works? Such questions only begin to suggest the range of our difficulties, and, if some have found it convenient to bypass the individuality of the writer or his status as an author to concentrate on a work, they have failed to appreciate the equally problematic nature of the word "work" and the unity it designates.

Another thesis has detained us from taking full measure of the author's disappearance. It avoids confronting the specific event that makes it possible and, in subtle ways, continues to preserve the existence of the author. This is the notion of *écriture*.[12] Strictly speaking, it should allow us not only to circumvent references to an author, but to situate his recent absence. The conception of *écriture*, as currently employed, is concerned with neither the act of writing nor the indications, as symptoms or signs within a text, of an author's meaning; rather, it stands for a remarkably profound attempt to elaborate the conditions of any text, both the conditions of its spatial dispersion and its temporal deployment.

It appears, however, that this concept, as currently employed, has merely transposed the empirical characteristics of an author to a transcendental anonymity. The extremely visible signs of the author's empirical activity are effaced to allow the play, in parallel or opposition, of religious and critical modes of characterization. In granting a primordial status to writing, do we not, in effect, simply reinscribe in transcendental terms the theological affirmation of its sacred origin or a critical belief in its creative nature? To say that writing, in terms of the particular history it made possible, is subjected to forgetfulness and repression, is this not to reintroduce in transcendental terms the religious principle of hidden meanings (which require interpretation) and the critical assumption of implicit significations, silent purposes, and obscure contents (which give rise to commentary)? Finally, is not the conception of writing as absence a transposition into transcendental terms of the religious belief in a fixed and continuous tradition or the aesthetic principle that proclaims the survival of the work as a kind of enigmatic supplement of the author beyond his own death?[13]

This conception of *écriture* sustains the privileges of the author through the safeguard of the a priori; the play of representations that formed a particular image of the author is extended within a gray neutrality. The disappearance of the author—since Mallarmé, an event of our time—is held in check by the transcendental. Is it not necessary to draw a line between those who believe that we can continue to situate our present discontinuities within the historical and transcendental tradition of the nineteenth century and those who are making a great effort to liberate themselves, once and for all, from this conceptual framework?[14]

It is obviously insufficient to repeat empty slogans: the author has disappeared; God and man died a common death.[15] Rather, we should reexamine the empty space left by the author's disappearance; we should attentively observe, along its gaps and fault lines, its new demarcations, and the reapportionment of this void; we should await the fluid functions released by this disappearance. In this context we can briefly consider the problems that arise in the use of an author's name. What is the name of an author? How does it function? Far from offering a solution,

I will attempt to indicate some of the difficulties related to these questions.

The name of an author poses all the problems related to the category of the proper name. (Here, I am referring to the work of John Searle,[16] among others.) Obviously not a pure and simple reference, the proper name (and the author's name as well) has other than indicative functions. It is more than a gesture, a finger pointed at someone; it is, to a certain extent, the equivalent of a description. When we say "Aristotle," we are using a word that means one or a series of definite descriptions of the type: "the author of the *Analytics*," or "the founder of ontology," and so forth.[17] Furthermore, a proper name has other functions than that of signification: when we discover that Rimbaud has not written *La Chasse spirituelle*, we cannot maintain that the meaning of the proper name or this author's name has been altered. The proper name and the name of an author oscillate between the poles of description and designation, and, granting that they are linked to what they name, they are not totally determined either by their descriptive or designative functions.[18] Yet—and it is here that the specific difficulties attending an author's name appear—the link between a proper name and the individual being named and the link between an author's name and that which it names are not isomorphous and do not function in the same way; and these differences require clarification.

To learn, for example, that Pierre Dupont does not have blue eyes, does not live in Paris, and is not a doctor does not invalidate the fact that the name, Pierre Dupont, continues to refer to the same person; there has been no modification of the designation that links the name to the person. With the name of an author, however, the problems are far more complex. The disclosure that Shakespeare was not born in the house that tourists now visit would not modify the functioning of the author's name, but, if it were proved that he had not written the sonnets that we attribute to him, this would constitute a significant change and affect the manner in which the author's name functions. Moreover, if we establish that Shakespeare wrote Bacon's *Organon* and that the same author was responsible for both the works of Shakespeare and those of Bacon, we would have introduced a third type of alteration which completely modifies the functioning of the author's name. Consequently, the name of an author is not precisely a proper name among others.

Many other factors sustain this paradoxical singularity of the name of an author. It is altogether different to maintain that Pierre Dupont does not exist and that Homer or Hermes Trismegistes have never existed. While the first negation merely implies that there is no one by the name of Pierre Dupont, the second indicates that several individuals have been referred to by one name or that the real author possessed none of the traits traditionally associated with Homer or Hermes. Neither is it the same thing to say that Jacques Durand, not Pierre Dupont, is the real name of X and that Stendhal's name was Henri Beyle. We could also examine the function and meaning of such statements as "Bourbaki is this or that person," and "Victor Eremita, Climacus, Anticlimacus, Frater Taciturnus, Constantin Constantius, all of these are Kierkegaard."

These differences indicate that an author's name is not simply an element of speech (as a subject, a complement, or an element that could be replaced by a pronoun or other parts of speech). Its presence is functional in that it serves as a means of classification. A name can group together a number of texts and thus differentiate them from others. A name also establishes different forms of relationships among texts. Neither Hermes not Hippocrates existed in the sense that we can say Balzac existed, but the fact that a number of texts were attached to a single name implies that relationships of homogeneity, filiation, reciprocal explanation, authentification, or of common utilization were established among them. Finally, the author's name characterizes a particular manner of existence of discourse. Discourse that possesses an author's name is not to be immediately consumed and forgotten; neither is it accorded the momentary attention given to ordinary, fleeting words. Rather, its status and its manner of reception are regulated by the culture in which it circulates.

We can conclude that, unlike a proper name, which moves from the interior of a discourse to the real person outside who produced it, the name of the author remains at the contours of texts—separating one from the other, defining their form, and characterizing their mode of existence. It points to the existence of certain groups of discourse and refers to the status of this discourse within a society and culture. The author's name is not a function of a man's civil status, nor is it fictional; it is situated in the breach, among the discontinuities, which gives rise to new groups of discourse and their singular mode of existence.[19] Consequently, we can say that in our culture, the name of an author is a variable that accompanies only certain texts to the exclusion of others: a private letter may have a signatory, but it does not have an author; a contract can have an underwriter, but not an author; and, similarly, an anonymous poster attached to a wall may have a writer, but he cannot be an author. In this sense, the function of an author is to characterize the existence, circulation, and operation of certain discourses within a society.

In dealing with the "author" as a function of discourse, we must consider the characteristics of a discourse that support this use and determine its difference from other discourses. If we limit our remarks to only those books or texts with authors, we can isolate four different features.

First, they are objects of appropriation; the form of property they have become is of a particular type whose legal codification was accomplished some years ago. It is important to notice, as well, that its status as property is historically secondary to the penal code controlling its appropriation. Speeches and books were assigned real authors, other than mythical or important religious figures, only when the author became subject to punishment and to the extent that his discourse was considered transgressive. In our culture—undoubtedly in others as well—discourse was not originally a thing, a product, or a possession, but an action situated in a bipolar field of sacred and profane, lawful and unlawful, religious and blasphemous. It was a gesture charged with risks long before it became a possession caught in a circuit of property values.[20] But it was at the moment when a system of ownership and strict copyright rules were established (toward the end of the eighteenth and beginning of the nineteenth century) that the transgressive properties always intrinsic to the act of writing became the forceful imperative of literature.[21] It is as if the author, at the moment he was accepted into the social order of property which governs our culture, was compensating for his new status by reviving the older bipolar field of discourse in a systematic practice of transgression and by restoring the danger of writing which, on another side, had been conferred the benefits of property.

Secondly, the "author-function"[22] is not universal or constant in all discourse. Even within our civilization, the same types of texts have not always required authors; there was a time when those texts which we now call "literary" (stories, folk tales, epics, and tragedies) were accepted, circulated, and valorized without any question about the identity of their author. Their anonymity was ignored because their real or supposed age was a sufficient guarantee of their authenticity. Texts, however, that we now call "scientific" (dealing with cosmology and the heavens, medicine or illness, the natural sciences or geography) were only considered truthful during the Middle Ages if the name of the author was indicated. Statements on the order of "Hippocrates said . . ." or "Pliny tells us that . . ." were not merely formulas for an argument based on authority; they marked a proven discourse. In the seventeenth and eighteenth centuries, a totally new conception was developed when scientific texts were accepted on their own merits and positioned within an anonymous and coherent conceptual system of established truths and methods of verification. Authentification no longer required reference to the individual who had produced them; the role of the author disappeared as an index of truthfulness and, where it remained as an inventor's name, it was merely to denote a specific theorem or proposition, a strange effect, a property, a body, a group of elements, or pathological syndrome.

At the same time, however, "literary" discourse was acceptable only if it carried an author's name; every text of poetry or fiction was obliged to state its author and the date, place, and circumstance of its writing. The meaning and value attributed to the text depended on this information. If by accident or design a text was presented anonymously, every effort was made to locate its author. Literary anonymity was of interest only as a puzzle to be solved as, in our day, literary works are totally dominated by the sovereignty of the author. (Undoubtedly, these remarks are far too categorical. Criticism has been concerned for some time now with aspects of a text not fully dependent on the notion of an individual creator; studies of genre or the analysis of recurring textual motifs and their variations from a norm other than the author. Furthermore, where in mathematics the author has become little more than a handy reference for a particular theorem or group of propositions, the reference to an author in biology and medicine, or to the date of his research has a substantially different bearing. This latter reference, more than simply indicating the source of information, attests to the "reliability" of the evidence, since it entails an appreciation of the techniques and experimental materials available at a given time and in a particular laboratory.)

The third point concerning this "author-function" is that it is not formed spontaneously through the simple attribution of a discourse to an individual. It results from a complex operation whose purpose is to construct the rational entity we call an author. Undoubtedly, this construction is assigned a "realistic" dimension as we speak of an individual's "profundity" or "creative" power, his intentions or the original inspiration manifested in writing. Nevertheless, these aspects of an individual, which we designate as an author (or which comprise an individual as an author), are projections, in terms always more or less psychological, of our way of handling texts: in the comparisons we make, the traits we extract as pertinent, the continuities we assign, or the exclusions we practice. In addition, all these operations vary according to the period and the form of discourse concerned. A "philosopher" and a "poet" are not constructed in the same manner; and the author of an eighteenth-century novel was formed differently from the modern novelist. There are, nevertheless, transhistorical constants in the rules that govern the construction of an author.

In literary criticism, for example, the traditional methods for defining an author—or, rather, for determining the configuration of the author from existing texts—derive in large part from those used in the Christian tradition to authenticate (or to reject) the particular texts in its possession. Modern criticism, in its desire to "recover" the author from a work, employs devices strongly reminiscent of Christian exegesis when it wished to prove the value of a text by ascertaining the holiness of its author. In *De Viris Illustribus,* Saint Jerome maintains that homonymy is not proof of the common authorship of several works, since many individuals could have the same name or someone could have perversely appropriated another's name. The name, as an individual mark, is not sufficient as it relates to a textual tradition. How, then, can several texts be attributed to an individual author? What norms, related to the function of the author, will disclose the involvement of several authors? According to Saint Jerome, there are four criteria: the texts that must be eliminated from the list of works attributed to a single author are those inferior to the others (thus, the author is defined as a standard level of quality); those whose ideas conflict with the doctrine expressed in the others (here the author is defined as a certain field of conceptual or theoretical coherence); those written in a different style and containing words and phrases not ordinarily found in the other works (the author is seen as a stylistic uniformity); and those referring to events or historical figures subsequent to the death of the author (the author is thus a definite historical figure in which a series of events converge). Although modern criticism does not appear to have these same suspicions concerning authentication, its strategies for defining the author present striking similarities. The author explains the presence of certain events within a text, as well as their transformations, distortions, and their various modifications (and this through an author's biography or by reference to his particular point of view, in the analysis of his social preferences and his position within a class or by delineating his fundamental objectives). The author also constitutes a principle of unity in writing where any unevenness of production is ascribed to changes caused by evolution, maturation, or outside influence. In addition, the author serves to neutralize the contradictions that are found in a series of texts. Governing this function is the belief that there must be—at a particular level of an author's thought, of his conscious or unconscious desire—a point where contradictions are resolved, where the incompatible elements can be shown to relate to one another or to cohere around a fundamental and originating contradiction. Finally, the author is a particular source of expression who, in more or less finished forms, is manifested equally well, and with similar validity, in a text, in letters, fragments, drafts, and so forth. Thus, even while Saint Jerome's four principles of authenticity might seem largely inadequate to modern critics, they, nevertheless, define the critical modalities now used to display the function of the author.[23]

However, it would be false to consider the function of the author as a pure and simple reconstruction after the fact of a text given as passive material, since a text always bears a number of signs that refer to the author. Well known to grammarians, these textual signs are personal pronouns, adverbs of time and place, and the conjugation of verbs.[24] But it is important to note that these elements have a different bearing on texts with an author and on those without one. In the latter, these "shifters" refer to a real speaker and to an actual deictic situation, with certain exceptions such as the case of indirect speech in the first person. When discourse is linked to an author, however, the role of "shifters" is more complex and variable. It is well known that in a novel narrated in the first person, neither the first person pronoun, the present indicative tense, nor, for that matter, its signs of localization refer directly to the writer, either to the time when he wrote, or to the specific act of writing; rather, they stand for a "second self"[25] whose similarity to the author is never fixed and undergoes considerable alteration within the course of a single book. It would be as false to seek the author in relation to the actual writer as to the fictional narrator; the "author-function" arises out of their scission—in the division and distance of the two. One might object that this phenomenon only applies to novels or poetry, to a context of "quasi-discourse," but, in fact, all discourse that supports this "author-function" is characterized by this plurality of egos. In a mathematical treatise, the ego who indicates the circumstances of composition in the preface is not identical, either in terms of his position or his function, to the "I" who concludes a demonstration within the body of the text. The former implies a unique individual who, at a given time and place, succeeded in completing a project, whereas the latter indicates an instance and plan of demonstration that anyone could perform provided the same set of axioms, preliminary operations, and an identical set of symbols were used. It is also possible to locate a third ego: one who speaks of the goals of his investigation, the obstacles encountered, its results, and the problems yet to be solved and this "I" would function in a field of existing or future mathematical discourses. We are not dealing with a system of dependencies where a first and essential use of the "I" is reduplicated, as a kind of fiction, by the other two. On the contrary, the "author-function" in such discourses operates so as to effect the simultaneous dispersion of the three egos.[26]

Further elaboration would, of course, disclose other characteristics of the "author-function," but I have limited myself to the four that seemed the most obvious and important. They can be summarized in the following manner: the "author-function" is tied to the legal and institutional systems that circumscribe, determine, and articulate the realm of discourses; it does not operate in a uniform manner in all discourses, at all times, and in any given culture; it is not defined by the spontaneous attribution of a text to its creator, but through a series of precise and complex procedures; it does not refer, purely and simply, to an actual individual insofar as it simultaneously gives rise to a variety of egos and to a series of subjective positions that individuals of any class may come to occupy.

I am aware that until now I have kept my subject within unjustifiable limits; I should also have spoken of the "author-function" in painting, music, technical fields, and so forth. Admitting that my analysis is restricted to the domain of discourse, it seems that I have given the term "author" an excessively narrow meaning. I have discussed the author only in the limited sense of a person to whom the production of a text, a book, or a work can be legitimately attributed. However, it is obvious that even within the realm of discourse a person can be the author of much more than a book—of a theory, for instance, of a tradition or a discipline within which new books and authors can proliferate. For convenience, we could say that such authors occupy a "transdiscursive" position.

Homer, Aristotle, and the Church Fathers played this role, as did the first mathematicians and the originators of the Hippocratic tradition. This type of author is surely as old as our civilization. But I believe that the nineteenth century in Europe produced a singular type of author who should not be confused with "great" literary authors, or the authors of canonical religious texts, and the founders of sciences. Somewhat arbitrarily, we might call them "initiators of discursive practices."

The distinctive contribution of these authors is that they produced not only their own work, but the possibility and the rules of formation of other texts. In this sense, their role differs entirely from that of a novelist, for example, who is basically never more than the author of his own text. Freud is not simply the author of *The Interpretation of Dreams* or of *Wit and its Relation to the Unconscious* and Marx is not simply the author of the *Communist Manifesto* or *Capital:* they both established the endless possibility of discourse. Obviously, an easy objection can be made. The author of a novel may be responsible for more than his own text; if he acquires some "importance" in the literary world, his influence can have significant ramifications. To take a very simple example, one could say that Ann Radcliffe did not simply write *The Mysteries of Udolpho* and a few other novels, but also made possible the appearance of Gothic Romances at the beginning of the nineteenth century. To this extent, her function as an author exceeds the limits of her work. However, this objection can be answered by the fact that the possibilities disclosed by the initiators of discursive practices (using the examples of Marx and

Freud, whom I believe to be the first and the most important) are significantly different from those suggested by novelists. The novels of Ann Radcliffe put into circulation a certain number of resemblances and analogies patterned on her work—various characteristic signs, figures, relationships, and structures that could be integrated into other books. In short, to say that Ann Radcliffe created the Gothic Romance means that there are certain elements common to her works and to the nineteenth-century Gothic romance: the heroine ruined by her own innocence, the secret fortress that functions as a countercity, the outlaw-hero who swears revenge on the world that has cursed him, etc. On the other hand, Marx and Freud, as "initiators of discursive practices," not only made possible a certain number of analogies that could be adopted by future texts, but, as importantly, they also made possible a certain number of differences. They cleared a space for the introduction of elements other than their own, which, nevertheless, remain within the field of discourse they initiated. In saying that Freud founded psychoanalysis, we do not simply mean that the concept of libido or the techniques of dream analysis reappear in the writings of Karl Abraham or Melanie Klein, but that he made possible a certain number of differences with respect to his books, concepts, and hypotheses, which all arise out of psychoanalytic discourse.

Is this not the case, however, with the founder of any new science or of any author who successfully transforms an existing science? After all, Galileo is indirectly responsible for the texts of those who mechanically applied the laws he formulated, in addition to having paved the way for the production of statements far different from his own. If Cuvier is the founder of biology and Saussure of linguistics, it is not because they were imitated or that an organic concept or a theory of the sign was uncritically integrated into new texts, but because Cuvier, to a certain extent, made possible a theory of evolution diametrically opposed to his own system and because Saussure made possible a generative grammar radically different from his own structural analysis. Superficially, then, the initiation of discursive practices appears similar to the founding of any scientific endeavor, but I believe there is a fundamental difference.

In a scientific program, the founding act is on an equal footing with its future transformations: it is merely one among the many modifications that it makes possible. This interdependence can take several forms. In the future development of a science, the founding act may appear as little more than a single instance of a more general phenomenon that has been discovered. It might be questioned, in retrospect, for being too intuitive or empirical and submitted to the rigors of new theoretical operations in order to situate it in a formal domain. Finally, it might be thought a hasty generalization whose validity should be restricted. In other words, the founding act of a science can always be rechanneled through the machinery of transformations it has instituted.[27]

On the other hand, the initiation of a discursive practice is heterogeneous to its ulterior transformations. To extend psychoanalytic practice, as initiated by Freud, is not to presume a formal generality that was not claimed at the outset; it is to explore a number of possible applications. To limit it is to isolate in the original texts a small set of propositions or statements that are recognized as having an inaugurative value and that mark other Freudian concepts or theories as derivative. Finally, there are no "false" statements in the work of these initiators; those statements considered inessential or "prehistoric," in that they are associated with another discourse, are simply neglected in favor of the more pertinent aspects of the work. The initiation of a discursive practice, unlike the founding of a science, overshadows and is necessarily detached from its later developments and transformations. As a consequence, we define the theoretical validity of a statement with respect to the work of the initiator, whereas in the case of Galileo or Newton, it is based on the structural and intrinsic norms established in cosmology or physics. Stated schematically, the work of these initiators is not situated in relation to a science or in the space it defines; rather, it is science or discursive practice that relate to their works as the primary points of reference.

In keeping with this distinction, we can understand why it is inevitable that practitioners of such discourses must "return to the origin." Here, as well, it is necessary to distinguish a "return" from scientific "rediscoveries" or "reactivations." "Rediscoveries" are the effects of analogy or isomorphism with current forms of knowledge that allow the perception of forgotten or obscured figures. For instance, Chomsky in his book on Cartesian grammar[28] "rediscovered" a form of knowledge that had been in use from Cordemoy to Humboldt. It could only be understood from the perspective of generative grammar because this later manifestation held the key to its construction: in effect, a retrospective codification of an historical position. "Reactivation" refers to something quite different: the insertion of discourse into totally new domains of generalization, practice, and transformations. The history of mathematics abounds in examples of this phenomenon as the work of Michel Serres on mathematical anamnesis shows.[29]

The phrase, "return to," designates a movement with its proper specificity, which characterizes the initiation of discursive practices. If we return, it is because of a basic and constructive omission, an omission that is not the result of accident or incomprehension.[30] In effect, the act of initiation is such, in its essence, that it is inevitably subjected to its own distortions; that which displays this act and derives from it is, at the same time, the root of its divergences and travesties. This nonaccidental omis-

sion must be regulated by precise operations that can be situated, analysed, and reduced in a return to the act of initiation. The barrier imposed by omission was not added from the outside; it arises from the
discursive practice in question, which gives it its law. Both the cause of
the barrier and the means for its removal, this omission—also responsible for the obstacles that prevent returning to the act of initiation—can
only be resolved by a return. In addition, it is always a return to a text in
itself, specifically, to a primary and unadorned text with particular attention to those things registered in the interstices of the text, its gaps and
absences. We return to those empty spaces that have been masked by
omission or concealed in a false and misleading plenitude. In these rediscoveries of an essential lack, we find the oscillation of two characteristic responses: "This point was made—you can't help seeing it if you
know how to read"; or, inversely, "No, that point is not made in any of
the printed words in the text, but it is expressed through the words, in
their relationships and in the distance that separates them." It follows
naturally that this return, which is a part of the discursive mechanism,
constantly introduces modifications and that the return to a text is not a
historical supplement that would come to fix itself upon the primary
discursivity and redouble it in the form of an ornament which, after all,
is not essential. Rather, it is an effective and necessary means of transforming discursive practice. A study of Galileo's works could alter our
knowledge of the history, but not the science, of mechanics; whereas, a
reexamination of the books of Freud or Marx can transform our understanding of psychoanalysis or Marxism.

A last feature of these returns is that they tend to reinforce the enigmatic link between an author and his works. A text has an inaugurative
value precisely because it is the work of a particular author, and our
returns are conditioned by this knowledge. The rediscovery of an unknown text by Newton or Cantor will not modify classical cosmology or
group theory; at most, it will change our appreciation of their historical
genesis. Bringing to light, however, *An Outline of Psychoanalysis,* to the
extent that we recognize it as a book by Freud, can transform not only
our historical knowledge, but the field of psychoanalytic theory—if only
through a shift of accent or of the center of gravity. These returns, an
important component of discursive practices, form a relationship between "fundamental" and mediate authors, which is not identical to that
which links an ordinary text to its immediate author.

These remarks concerning the initiation of discursive practices have
been extremely schematic, especially with regard to the opposition I have
tried to trace between this initiation and the founding of sciences. The
distinction between the two is not readily discernible; moreover, there is
no proof that the two procedures are mutually exclusive. My only pur-

pose in setting up this opposition, however, was to show that the "author-function," sufficiently complex at the level of a book or a series of texts that bear a definite signature, has other determining factors when analysed in terms of larger entities—groups of works or entire disciplines.

Unfortunately, there is a decided absence of positive propositions in this essay, as it applies to analytic procedures or directions for future research, but I ought at least to give the reasons why I attach such importance to a continuation of this work. Developing a similar analysis could provide the basis for a typology of discourse. A typology of this sort cannot be adequately understood in relation to the grammatical features, formal structures, and objects of discourse, because there undoubtedly exist specific discursive properties or relationships that are irreducible to the rules of grammar and logic and to the laws that govern objects. These properties require investigation if we hope to distinguish the larger categories of discourse. The different forms of relationships (or nonrelationships) that an author can assume are evidently one of these discursive properties.

This form of investigation might also permit the introduction of an historical analysis of discourse. Perhaps the time has come to study not only the expressive value and formal transformations of discourse, but its mode of existence: the modifications and variations, within any culture, of modes of circulation, valorization, attribution, and appropriation. Partially at the expense of themes and concepts that an author places in his work, the "author-function" could also reveal the manner in which discourse is articulated on the basis of social relationships.

Is it not possible to reexamine, as a legitimate extension of this kind of analysis, the privileges of the subject? Clearly, in undertaking an internal and architectonic analysis of a work (whether it be a literary text, a philosophical system, or a scientific work) and in delimiting psychological and biographical references, suspicions arise concerning the absolute nature and creative role of the subject. But the subject should not be entirely abandoned. It should be reconsidered, not to restore the theme of an originating subject, but to seize its functions, its intervention in discourse, and its system of dependencies. We should suspend the typical questions: how does a free subject penetrate the density of things and endow them with meaning; how does it accomplish its design by animating the rules of discourse from within? Rather, we should ask: under what conditions and through what forms can an entity like the subject appear in the order of discourse; what position does it occupy; what functions does it exhibit; and what rules does it follow in each type of discourse? In short, the subject (and its substitutes) must be stripped of its creative role and analysed as a complex and variable function of discourse.

The author—or what I have called the "author-function"—is undoubtedly only one of the possible specifications of the subject and, considering past historical transformations, it appears that the form, the complexity, and even the existence of this function are far from immutable. We can easily imagine a culture where discourse would circulate without any need for an author. Discourses, whatever their status, form, or value, and regardless of our manner of handling them, would unfold in a pervasive anonymity. No longer the tiresome repetitions:

"Who is the real author?"
"Have we proof of his authenticity and originality?"
"What has he revealed of his most profound self in his language?"

New questions will be heard:

"What are the modes of existence of this discourse?"
"Where does it come from; how is it circulated; who controls it?"
"What placements are determined for possible subjects?"
"Who can fulfill these diverse functions of the subject?"

Behind all these questions we would hear little more than the murmur of indifference:
"What matter who's speaking?"

NOTES

[All footnotes supplied by Donald F. Bouchard, editor.]

1. See "Entretiens sur Michel Foucault" (directed by J. Proust), *La Pensée*, No. 137 (1968), pp. 6–7 and 11; and also Sylvie le Bon, "Un Positivisme désesperée," *Esprit*, No. 5 (1967), pp. 1317–1319.

2. Foucault's purpose, concerned with determining the "codes" of discourse, is explicitly stated in the Preface to Michael Foucault, *The Order of Things* (New York: Pantheon, 1973), p. xx. These objections—see "Entretiens sur Michel Foucault"—are obviously those of specialists who fault Foucault for his apparent failure to appreciate the facts and complexities of their theoretical field.

3. For an appreciation of Foucault's technique, see Jonathan Culler, "The Linguistic Basis of Structuralism," *Structuralism: An Introduction*, ed. David Robey (Oxford: Clarendon Press, 1973), pp. 27–28.

4. *The Archaeology of Knowledge*, trans. A. M. Sheridan Smith (London: Tavistock, 1972) was published in France in 1969; for discussion of the author, see esp. pp. 92–96, 122.

5. Samuel Beckett, *Texts for Nothing*, trans. Beckett (London: Calder & Boyars, 1974), p. 16.

6. Cf. Edward Said, "The Ethics of Language," *Diacritics*, 4 (1974), 32.

7. On "expression" and writing as self-referential, see Jean-Marie Benoist, "The End of Structuralism," *Twentieth Century Studies*, 3 (1970), 39; and Roland Barthes, *Critique et vérité* (Paris: Collection Tel Quel, 1966). As the following sentence implies, the "exterior deployment" of writing relates to Ferdinand de Saussure's emphasis of the acoustic quality of the signifier, an external phenomena of speech which, nevertheless, responds to its own internal and differential articulation.

8. On "transgression," see "A Preface to Transgression," p. 42; and "Language to Infinity," p. 56 in *Language, Counter-Memory, Practice: Selected Essays by Michel Foucault*, ed. Donald F. Bouchard (Ithaca: Cornell University Press, 1977). Cf. Blanchot, *L'Espace littéraire* (Paris, 1955), p. 58; and David P. Funt, "Newer Criticism and Revolution," *Hudson Review*, 22 (1969), 87–96.

9. See "Language to Infinity," p. 58.

10. The recent stories of John Barth, collected in *Lost in the Funhouse* and *Chimera*, supply interesting examples of Foucault's thesis. The latter work includes, in fact, a novelistic reworking of *Arabian Nights*.

11. Plainly a prescription for criticism as diverse as G. Wilson Knight's *The Wheel of Fire* (London, 1930) and Roland Barthes' *On Racine*, trans. Richard Howard (New York: Hill & Wang, 1964).

12. We have kept the French, *écriture*, with its double reference to the act of writing and to the primordial (and metaphysical) nature of writing as an entity in itself, since it is the term that best identifies the program of Jacques Derrida. Like the theme of a self-referential writing, it too builds on a theory of the sign and denotes writing as the interplay of presence and absence in that "signs represent the present in its absence" ("Differance," in *Speech and Phenomena*, trans. David B. Allison [Evanston, Ill.: Northwestern Univ. Press, 1973], p. 138). See J. Derrida, *De la grammatologie* (Paris: Editions de Minuit, 1967).

13. On "supplement," see *Speech and Phenomena*, pp. 88–104.

14. This statement is perhaps the polemical ground of Foucault's dissociation from phenomenology (and its evolution through Sartre into a Marxist discipline) on one side and structuralism on the other. It also marks his concern that his work be judged on its own merits and not on its reputed relationship to other movements. This insistence informs his appreciation of Nietzsche in "Nietzsche, Genealogy, History" as well as his sense of his own position in the Conclusion of *The Archaeology of Knowledge*.

15. Nietzsche, *The Gay Science*, III, 108.

16. John Searle, *Speech Acts: An Essay in the Philosophy of Language* (Cambridge: Cambridge University Press, 1969), pp. 162–174.

17. Ibid., p. 169.

18. Ibid., p. 172.

19. This is a particularly important point and brings together a great many of Foucault's insights concerning the relationship of an author (subject) to discourse. It reflects his understanding of the traditional and often unexamined unities of discourse whose actual discontinuities are resolved in either of two ways: by reference to an originating subject or to a language, conceived as plenitude, which supports the activities of commentary or interpretation. But since

Foucault rejects the belief in the presumed fullness of language that underlies discourse, the author is subjected to the same fragmentation which characterizes discourse and he is delineated as a discontinuous series; for example, see *L'Ordre du discours* (Paris: Gallimard, 1971), pp. 54–55 and 61–62.

20. In a seminar entitled "L'Epreuve et L'enquête," which Foucault conducted at the University of Montreal in the spring of 1974, he centered the debate around the following question: is the general conviction that truth derives from and is sustained by knowledge not simply a recent phenomenon, a limited case of the ancient and widespread belief that truth is a function of events? In an older time and in other cultures, the search for truth was hazardous in the extreme and truth resided in a danger zone, but if this was so and if truth could only be approached after a long preparation or through the details of a ritualized procedure, it was because it represented power. Discourse, for these cultures, was an active appropriation of power and to the extent that it was successful, it contained the power of truth itself, charged with all its risks and benefits.

21. Cf. *The Order of Things*, p. 300; "A Preface to Transgression," pp. 30–33.

22. Foucault's phrasing of the "author-function" has been retained. This concept should not be confused (as it was by Goldmann in the discussion that followed Foucault's presentation) with the celebrated theme of the "death of man" in *The Order of Things* (pp. 342 and 386). On the contrary, Foucault's purpose is to revitalize the debate surrounding the subject by situating the subject, as a fluid function, within the space cleared by archaeology.

23. See Evaristo Arns, *La Technique du livre d'après Saint Jerome* (Paris, 1953).

24. On personal pronouns ("shifters"), see R. Jakobson, *Selected Writings* (Paris: Mouton, 1971), II, 130–132; and *Essais de linguistique générale* (Paris, 1966), p. 252. For its general implications, see Eugenio Donato, "Of Structuralism and Literature," *MLN*, 82 (1967), 556–558. On adverbs of time and place, see Emile Benveniste, *Problèmes de la linguistique générale* (Paris, 1966), pp. 237–250.

25. Cf. Wayne C. Booth, *The Rhetoric of Fiction* (Chicago: Univ. of Chicago Press, 1961), pp. 67–77.

26. This conclusion relates to Foucault's concern in developing a "philosophy of events" as described in *L'Ordre du discours*, pp. 60–61: "I trust that we can agree that I do not refer to a succession of moments in time, nor to a diverse plurality of thinking subjects; I refer to a caesura which fragments the moment and disperses the subject into a plurality of possible positions and functions."

27. Cf. the discussion of disciplines in *L'Ordre du discours*, pp. 31–38.

28. Noam Chomsky, *Cartesian Linguistics* (New York: Harper & Row, 1966).

29. *La Communication: Hermes I* (Paris: Editions de Minuit, 1968), pp. 78–112.

30. For a discussion of the recent reorientation of the sign, see Foucault's "Nietzsche, Freud, Marx," in *Nietzsche* (Cahiers de Royaumont, Philosophie VI, 1967). On the role of repetition, Foucault writes in *L'Ordre du discours:* "The new is not found in what is said, but in the event of its return" (p. 28).

NINETEEN

Interpretive Communities and Variable Literacies

The Functions of Romance Reading

Janice Radway

One of the most engaging volumes yet published on the subject of reading is the marvelous collection of photographs by André Kertész titled simply, *On Reading*.[1] Presented without commentary, this series of images of readers absorbed in apparently diverse materials, in both expected and unexpected contexts, is eloquent in its insistence that books and reading serve myriad purposes and functions for a wide variety of individuals. For that reason alone, this simple photographic essay provides an implicit but nonetheless profound commentary on some entrenched and familiar assumptions about literacy.

By grouping together readers as different as the well-dressed man perched on a library ladder in a book-lined study and the ragged young boy sprawled across a pile of discarded newspapers in the street, Kertész is able to suggest that whatever the differences and merits of the materials they peruse, all are engaged in some form of the engrossing behavior through which print is transformed into a world.[2] The very inclusiveness of the series equalizes readers and reading processes that would, in other contexts, be ranked hierarchically on an imaginary literary scale. On that scale, the grade of "truly literate" would be reserved for those educated individuals who were not only capable of reading texts that the culture deems "literature," but who also regularly choose to read such texts for utilitarian purposes, however broadly conceived. As Raymond Williams has observed, literature and literacy within this sort of system would be inextricably linked with the bourgeois ideology of taste and its concomitant construction of the "literary tradition."[3]

Reprinted by permission of *Daedalus*, Journal of the American Academy of Arts and Sciences, "Anticipations," 113, no. 3 (Summer 1974).

Kertész's book is useful, therefore, precisely because its resolutely
democratic presentation of reading refuses to make the usual distinctions through which the truly literate are distinguished from the merely
functionally literate or illiterate, and "literature" is segregated from all
that is subliterature, paraliterature, or simple entertainment. Although
his photographs are all in some sense "about" reading, what they demonstrate is the astonishing variety of circumstances within which reading
occurs. Because they function at least partially as signifiers of "context"
and difference, the photographs direct our attention to the question of
whether such contexts are mere "settings" within which a single unitary
process is carried on, or whether they are more significant situations that
actively affect the character of that process and thus differentially transform the valence of the act. Kertész's photographs seem to suggest that
we must give up our search for the essence and effects of literacy as a
single process and look instead at the varied kinds of literate behaviors
that people really engage in. The photographs, I would argue, pose the
question of *how* each of these unique readers is literate in a particular
time and place.

In effect, I am suggesting that Kertész's book echoes John Szwed's
call for ethnographic studies of different kinds of literate behavior.[4] Like
Kertész, Szwed foregrounds context and argues that in place of the usual
theoretical accounts of the unavoidable psychological consequences of
acquiring print literacy, we must have more specific studies of what people do with printed texts. I would repeat Szwed's call and suggest, addi-
tionally, that such ethnographies can be made more effective investiga-
tive tools for the study of literacy if they are grounded upon some recent
theoretical arguments in reader-response criticism. Although reader
criticism has been developed to explain the interpretation of literary texts,
it has implications for the way we think about how people operate upon
and use all sorts of printed matter.[5]

The reader and the reading process have come to occupy a central
place in literary criticism in recent years, but investigators of these phenomena share no unified theoretical position. Indeed, reception theory
or reader-response criticism includes approaches as diverse as the *rezep-
tionästhetik* of the Constance school, the structuralism of Roland Barthes,
the semiotics of Umberto Eco and Jonathan Culler, the "interactionist"
work of Louise Rosenblatt and Stanley Fish, and the subjectivist arguments of David Bleich and Norman Holland. Most of these reader theories were developed in response to the textual formalism associated
with New Criticism and its caveat against the "affective fallacy." As participants in a widespread conceptual shift in the intellectual community
from positivist positions to contextual or interpretive schemas, the various reader theorists sought to challenge the New Critical insistence on

the absolute autonomy of the text. Troubled by the complete exclusion of the reader from accounts of the interpretive process, these theorists sought ways to reassert the essential dependency of meaning upon the interaction between the reader and the text.[6]

Yet, despite their preoccupation with the activities of readers, the theorists show a lingering tendency to grant primacy and ultimate power to the text itself. Although willing to acknowledge the reader's contribution to the process of producing a reading of a text, theorists like Roman Ingarden and Wolfgang Iser eventually claim priority for the text because they believe it inevitably directs, governs, controls, indeed, determines the reader's response to it.[7] To name their theories "reception theories" and their method "reader-response criticism" is entirely accurate, since they continue to posit a confrontation between two distinct and quite different entities, the reader and the text. The reader receives the text and responds to it in such a manner that the meaning—what its author desired to communicate and embodied within its textual structures—is, in Iser's words, "concretized" by the reader. Theories like Iser's are variations of the simple transmission-reception model of communication, whereby a sender's message is transmitted to a receiver via the medium of the printed text.

In continuing to accord primacy to texts, the theories remain compatible with the determinism inherent in many traditional conceptions of literacy and, accordingly, in the understanding of reading they imply. Previous theories of literacy have assumed that the character of print itself determines what can be done with it, and thus what it means to be literate. These more recent reading theories also argue implicitly that reading is a singular, skilled process, which many readers only partially master and some texts do not fully require. Thus their adherents can continue to accept the division of texts into the complex, or "great," and the simple, or subliterary, as well as the distinction between readers who are fully literate and those who are not. Despite their apparent interest in readers and reading activities, such theories continue to support the notion that all readers are alike and all reading really one, simply because they assume that the technology of print and the character of individual texts together determine the activities they initiate.

There are other reading theories, however, that call for a rethinking of the concept of literacy, precisely because they maintain it is the reader who controls the reading process, not the text. Although these theories are often lumped together with other reader-oriented criticisms as "reception theory" or "response criticism," they should not be so labeled. In fact, such versions of reader theory conceive of reading as "production" or "construction," as opposed to reception or even simple consumption. The individuals who have elaborated these theories do not belong to a single school, nor do they adhere to the same theoretical approach. Yet all hold that reading is a productive activity in which a reader actively *makes* sense of the verbal inscriptions on the page. The most important theorists in this branch of reader theory are Umberto Eco, Stanley Fish, Louise Rosenblatt, and Jonathan Culler.[8] The four vary in the degree to which they employ the jargon now associated with semiotic theory, but each has nonetheless elaborated a model of the text-reader interaction that can be called semiotic.

All, that is, conceive of textual meaning as the product of a complex transaction between an inert textual structure, composed of verbal signifiers, and an actively productive reader, who constructs those signifiers as meaningful signs on the basis of previously learned interpretive procedures and cultural codes. Although the reader often attempts to construe the text by referring to the codes and strategies she believes the author intended her to use, nothing in the text constrains her to do so, nor, if she does, is she necessarily successful. As Eco has observed, "The multiplicity of codes, contexts, and circumstances shows us that the same message can be decoded from different points of view and by reference to diverse systems of conventions."[9] Interpretation and textual meaning, then, are as dependent on who the reader is, on how she understands the process of reading, and on the cultural context within which she operates, as they are on the text's verbal structure itself.

Print is not determinant in such a view, nor is reading a simple mechanical matter of processing what is on the page. Rather, print functions as a kind of material with which and upon which readers operate in order to produce meaning. Reading, then, is a complicated semiotic and fundamentally social process that varies both in place and in time. That is to say, different readers read differently because they belong to what are known as various interpretive communities, each of which acts upon print differently and for different purposes.

The concept of the interpretive community, of course, has been discussed most recently by Stanley Fish.[10] Fish defines the notion rather narrowly, however, because he is interested only in different forms of academic literary criticism. For him, an interpretive community is a loosely connected group of literary scholars who share basic assumptions about the nature of literature, about the goals of literary criticism, and about the nature of the interpretive process. Different interpretive communities, therefore, at least as Fish discusses them, are composed of readers who may disagree about how to construct a literary interpretation, but who are nonetheless equally and similarly literate because all can produce coherent readings of difficult texts.

In spite of Fish's own lack of interest in other than professional readers, his concept of the interpretive community can be fruitfully rethought to apply more generally to readers outside the literary academy to help us understand why some readers prefer Westerns to the classics, detective stories to poetry, or the *Enquirer* to Shakespeare. Interpretive communities may not simply differ over what to do with metaphors and tropes; they may disagree even more fundamentally over the nature and purpose of reading itself. Different interpretive communities may actually be differently literate. We need to know, therefore, what exactly divides the vast community of individuals who buy and read books—in short, how book or print-related behaviors vary according to place and over time.

To call for such a project, however, is to confront obvious methodological problems almost at once. Because we do not know what an interpretive community actually is, we cannot identify one in order to study the ways in which its members are literate. Are such communities formally constituted groups to which individual members *know* they belong? Or are they much larger collections of people who, by virtue of a common social position and demographic character, unconsciously share certain assumptions about reading as well as preferences for reading material? Assuming that the latter is true, it is not at all obvious how we could ferret out the existence of such a group without first sharpening our understanding of how more formalized interpretive communities operate. If we can detect exactly what it is the readers in a formally recognized group share, and how this common fund of knowledge affects what they "do" with printed texts, we may be able to ask certain questions of apparently unconnected individuals that will also reveal the particular ways in which they behave with printed texts and, therefore, how they are literate.

A logical way to start such a project would be to make use of the publishing industry's own understanding of the book-buying public. The industry recognizes that certain readers are particularly interested in a specific "category" of books, and it therefore identifies mass-produced texts as belonging to one or another, usually by cover iconography. This has proved to be a reliable technique because there is indeed a portion of the book-buying community that reads only one kind of text. Time after time, such "category" readers, as they are known in the trade, will choose books from only this category. Many students of mass-produced literature, furthermore, assume that such readers choose their category because essential features of their social life create needs and demands that are somehow addressed and fulfilled by these books.[11] If this is true, an investigation of their preferences for, and interaction with, books of a particular category may in fact amount to an investigation of the place and function of literacy in their lives.

In this paper, I shall detail my attempt at just such a study, but must point out first that the group I investigated was even more formalized than the loose conglomerate who read a particular category—in this case, the romance.[12] It was necessary to begin with a small group of romance readers, one clustered about a bookstore clerk in "Smithton," because not enough information about this audience is available from publishers to construct a representative sample of romance readers as a whole. Thus my findings about the nature of romance reading are based on a self-selected group of women united by their reliance on a single individual who advises them about "good" and "bad" romances. Since all of the women in the group have been consulting Dorothy Evans, the bookstore clerk, for several years, I was not surprised to learn that as readers they are united by common purposes, preferences, and interpretive procedures. I also found that these aspects of their reading behavior seem to be a function of certain common social factors of their lives, a point I shall return to.

I must add, however, that my interpretive community of romance readers may not extend beyond the area served by this particular bookstore. These women, in fact, may not be part of a larger, genre-based interpretive community. We will know that only when we can test my findings against those of a much larger study, one that attempts to survey the behavior of *all* women who think of themselves as romance readers. While all may read romances, they may do so differently or for different purposes. They may indeed be category readers, but they may not constitute an interpretive community in the sense that they all select, use, and operate on printed texts in certain socially specific ways.

In turning now to the Smithton women and to their characteristic reading behavior, it seems important to describe first exactly how information was elicited about what they "did" with texts. Because I was interested in the women's own self-perceptions and understanding of romances and romance reading, I relied on ethnographic interviewing techniques to map the "world" of the romance reader. I interviewed sixteen women in two groups about all aspects of their leisure activity, and then talked more extensively with five, including Evans. Because I was well aware of the romance reader's wariness about the general public's scorn for her activity, I hoped the group situation would reassure each enough to answer my questions honestly. I was also aware, however, that the group situation might lead to a greater uniformity in response than actually existed, because of the influence of a single reader. I therefore also administered an anonymous questionnaire to the sixteen women as well as to twenty-six others. Since I found little discrepancy between my informants' oral and written responses and between the responses of the sixteen and others of Evans's customers, I concluded that the material elicited in the oral interviews was a reasonably accurate account of what the women thought they were up to.

My first task was to determine exactly how the members of the group made the necessary discriminations in order to select the texts they wanted. Because they are category readers, what was at issue was their definition of the category or genre and how they identified individual texts as examples of it. I sought such a definition through a variety of related questions to see whether their conscious understanding of the genre coincided with the definition they actually relied on in selecting reading matter.

What I found was that a definition of the genre was implicit in the way they used cover blurbs and illustrations, in their reliance on previous readings of certain authors, and in their use of Evans's recommendations to select their texts. Indeed, all of these activities seemed to be governed by their sense that "romance" had something to do with the manner and tone of presentation of a love relationship. Once I had determined the rudimentary content of the genre, I asked them to provide a "definition" of it to see whether their genre theory actually coincided with how they used individual instances of the category. What they told me was interesting, both because it tended to confirm their implicitly reported requirements and proved to be at once formalist and functional.

Their definition—"a man and a woman meeting, the problems they encounter, whether the relationship will gel or not"—not only identified the fundamental characters and events in the story, but also specified the evolution of the action and, implicitly, the nature of the response (tension or anxiety) it ought to evoke in the reader. By beginning with the definition, I was led to mark off two areas for further study. First, I pursued the issue of the plot structure itself by attempting to determine exactly how the women processed textual inscriptions to arrive at that particular abstract structure. I was trying, essentially, to describe their manner of textual production, to discover what they did with the text to produce their characteristic interpretation. At the same time, I attempted to explore the nature of their reaction to the plot structure, and thus got involved with questions of how the text made them feel and how it functioned in their daily lives. Here, I was investigating the readers' use of the activity of reading, asking what they accomplished *by* or *in* the process of reading these books. Before I pursue this aspect of their reading behavior, I would like to return briefly to the interpretive process itself and explore some of the problems encountered in trying to determine how people in real life arrive at a given reading of a particular book, and some of the possibilities as well.

It is somewhat difficult to shed light on the interpretive process simply because so much of it occurs automatically and unconsciously. While most readers can easily summarize a book or recount its plot, we have no sure way of knowing exactly what interpretive operations come into play in the redaction of a 200- or 300-page text. After hearing a plot summary, the investigator might read the text, noting both what the reader has designated as significant in her account and what she has ignored. These observations can then be used to infer the selection criteria that prompted the reader to identify the relevant textual features from which she constructed her final reading.[13] Those selection criteria themselves then point to what the romantic story is "about," at least for the individual summarizing the plot.

In the case of the romance readers, every plot summary ignored the fact that the hero and heroine were contrasted with foil figures with whom they were sometimes entangled. Their refusal to acknowledge these contrasts as essential to the plot suggested that the women's interest in the romance came not from any interest in sexual competition, same sex friendships, or contrasts, but from a deep-seated need to see an ideal relationship worked out between a man and a woman. Their responses to questions about the qualities of good and bad romances seemed to validate this inference. An ideal romance focused on "one woman-one man," while a poor example of the genre often involved the hero and heroine with too many other secondary characters. Their sense that the romance should be "about" a single relationship governed their selective perception of the significant features and events in each tale. This fundamental desire was ultimately responsible for the particular story they constructed.

With the women's essential evaluative criteria thus established, I then questioned them about their understanding or interpretation of the story they had constructed from each text's myriad details and events. Although this led to further observations about how the women treated language, particularly declarative statements, it went beyond simple textual operations and their conscious understanding of the story to the covert consequences of those operations and the tacit significance of that understanding. It was surprising to discover that the women saw these tales of "a man and a woman meeting" as stories about a woman's triumph, surprising, because so many feminist literary critics of the genre have argued that romances are about helpless, passive, weak women who relinquish their sense of self in the arms of the more important man.[14] I was tempted to attribute the interpretive difference to varying standards of judgment about female behavior, but certain of the women's statements about the authors' attitudes toward their heroines caused me to think twice about formulating such a conclusion.

Several of the women had observed repeatedly that their favorite writers always wrote about intelligent and independent heroines, so I decided to check this against the texts. If one focused only on verbal assertion, this was indeed the case. The authors always declared at the outset that their heroines were unusual, special, bright, and self-reliant, but later portrayed them as victims of circumstance. Apparently, the Smithton readers do not see this as contradictory because they do not use subsequent narrative action to revise a character portrait established by description at the beginning. Feminist literary critics, of course, applying what Jonathan Culler has described as a rule of unity, *do* try to produce a unified characterization that takes all of these details into account.[15] In their literary universe, character behavior is meant to comment on and alter preliminary portraiture[16]—hence, their final and quite different account of the romantic heroine as only a superficially independent woman, who is, in reality, deeply dependent and incapable of action herself. The argument for the accuracy of their interpretation is that as feminist critics, they are formally trained and thus fully literate. Romance readers, on the other hand, are neither well-educated nor fully conscious of what they do, and therefore simply don't know what the story *really* means. And because these women are somehow incompletely literate, they don't know how to interpret characters correctly. Nonetheless, the romantic text manages to exert its conservative power over them and thus functions to reinforce the patriarchal status quo.

I would like to suggest, however, that there is another equally plausible explanation of this difference in interpretations. The romance reader's failure to unify action and description may, in fact, be a function of a particular "philosophy" of language that effectively precludes such an operation. Their portrait of the heroine, in such a view, is not a result of their ignorance or lack of self-awareness, but a product of a particular attitude toward language. The women believe that words have meanings that are fixed and definite. Because those meanings are essentially contained *in* words, the women also believe that people choose words to say what they mean. Words are always already meaningful and can be selected for what they accurately say about a character or event. The Smithton readers assume that romance authors choose their words very carefully because they intend those words to describe correctly the characters in question. As a result, they do not judge verbal assertion by comparing it with the character's actions. If the writer says that her heroine is intelligent and independent, nothing she does or does not do later can alter her basic character. Consequently, the women believe that they are reading a story about an extraordinary woman who is overcome by unforeseen circumstances, but who nevertheless manages to teach the hero how to care for her and to appreciate her as she wishes to be appreciated. Because he always learns the lesson she has to teach and proposes a permanent commitment, the women can interpret this as the triumph of her values. Their interpretation follows logically from their textual operations, which are themselves dictated by a prior understanding of words and language. It seems to me that what we have here is not a form of partial literacy, but a different form of literacy altogether, founded on its own conception of the word and what can be done with it.

Another consequence of this attitude toward language surfaced again in a discussion about the women's reasons for reading romantic fiction. Although they agreed overwhelmingly that they read principally for enjoyment and to escape their daily problems, the Smithton women also maintained that they read romances to learn—not, as one might expect, about how to conduct a relationship but, rather, because they acquired factual information about geography, culture, and history from these books. This is so because they operate under two assumptions.

To begin with, they firmly believe that all romance authors research the historical and physical backgrounds of their stories. In fact, this is true. One has only to read the prefaces to romantic fiction to detect how important it is to the author to portray accurately both the physical setting of the story and the period in which it takes place. Indeed, romance writers constantly thank librarians and archivists for their assistance, and for those authors who travel to the foreign locales that form the backgrounds to their stories, there is gratitude to their guides as well.[17] Second, romance readers assume that when an author makes a factual statement about the background, she does so because it is "true." They therefore mark that statement as "information" and commit it to memory as "knowledge." Their *attitude* toward language, then, rather than the text alone, is responsible for one of their most important claims about the worth and function of romance reading. Although the books are works of fiction, the women use them as primers about the world. The romance for them is a kind of encyclopedia, and reading, a process of education.[18]

Romance readers are perhaps not alone in treating novels as compendia about the world. A good deal of popular fiction places important emphasis on setting and background. The readers of Irving Wallace and Arthur Hailey, for instance, believe they authentically experience the worlds of Hollywood, big city hotels, Hawaiian history, and Israeli culture because of the extensive research these authors conduct for their books. Louis L'Amour, perhaps the most popular writer of Westerns, is also well known as a careful student of the history of the American West. If his readers, as well as those of Wallace and Hailey, treat their texts as seriously as do the Smithton romance readers, it may well be that a large portion of the American public has learned its history and geography from the popular book. They must be considered literate despite the fact that they are uninterested in that large body of material sanctioned by the culture as "literature."

But for romance readers, we need to go beyond this level of analysis. Although romances clearly both provide an education and reassure their readers about the triumphant superiority of women and their values, it is likely that when the texts provide the opportunity for the women to realize these benefits through particular kinds of interpretive operations, those operations carry other tacit consequences and effects that the women are not aware of. This is the most difficult interpretive move in any reader study, since it is not at all clear either what constitutes evidence for an effect or how one validates an intuition that a reader benefits in ways other than those she can attest to explicitly. However, because reading and comprehension are surely not entirely conscious activities, it seems advisable to attempt to infer possible meanings to the reader and the effects of interpretive operations that she carries out but which she may not fully apprehend.

As an example, let me cite something I inferred from my observations about how the Smithton women treated the language of romantic texts. In exploring their methods for formulating character portraits and for processing "factual" material, I noticed that one of the reasons they operate on the texts as they do is a function of the fact that the authors had selected a vocabulary and syntax readily familiar to a middle-class housewife and mother with a year or two of college education. I inferred that this simple and resolutely familiar language use actually permits the women to rely heavily on their memory of previously learned cultural codes. When they encounter such a linguistic structure, they simply supply the most common referents for the words and phrases in question and thus actually construct a fictional duplicate of the world they are familiar with. Although the process of construction appears to the women as automatic and natural comprehension—as learning, in fact—it is actually a form of production that has the ultimate effect of naturalizing and therefore ratifying the world in which the women ordinarily live. Reading is a highly reassuring process, because it prompts them to use their most familiar methods for apprehending the world, and rewards them by enabling them to "find" only what they would have expected. Romance reading, it appears, allows a woman to believe she is learning and changing herself at the very same time it is reassuring her that she already knows how to make sense of an existence which always is as she expects, even in fiction.

Assessing the ultimate impact of these contradictory effects of the romance reader's interpretive activity is as difficult a task as trying to validate the fact that the covert consequences one detects or infers are actually experienced by the reader. One might argue that in learning more and more about her world, the romance reader comes to value herself and her abilities more, and thus feels powerful enough to seek change. Yet it is equally possible that the conservative nature of the interpretive process actually reassures her that nothing need be changed at all, precisely because the world *is* readable and hence fully meaningful. Corroboration of either effect can be sought in the reader's daily activities, but even then it would be virtually impossible to state positively that the interpretive activities performed in reading romantic novels resulted in changed behavior.

This is the point at which the analyst of reading becomes aware of the limits of the ethnographic method, an awareness that is quite like the anthropologist's recognition of how difficult it is to pierce the veil of cultural behavior to fathom its meaning and its fundamental roots in ideology. Even though reading can be investigated empirically, and the readers' own interpretations of texts taken into account, analytic interpretation cannot be done away with entirely. As Clifford Geertz reminded ethnographic anthropologists, "What we call our data are really our own constructions of other people's constructions of what they and their compatriots are up to. Cultural analysis," he concludes, "is . . . guessing at meanings, assessing the guesses, and drawing explanatory conclusions from the better guesses."[19] My account of what romance readers do to a text in the process of constructing an interpretation is just such a guess; but I think it is a better guess than it would have been if I had merely inferred the existence of such behavior on the basis of my own reading of the texts, a reading that none of the Smithton readers would have recognized as an interpretation of the books she knows so well.

Not only, however, do the Smithton women have an elaborate theory about the meaning and the significance of the romance as a literary form, but they can articulate to themselves a coherent explanation of the meaning of the act of reading itself as well. It is true, of course, that all acts of reading involve particular texts, and thus the overall significance of each complex act is intimately bound up with the meaning of the text and its implication in the reader's social and ideological life. Still, because the act of picking up a book is a form of social behavior that permits the reader to suspend momentarily all connections with the outside world, I think it is essential to make a distinction between book reading itself and the text constructed as a consequence of it.[20] Beyond knowing what the romantic story means to the Smithton reader, one wants to know also how she uses the activity of burying herself in the pages of a book. To ask this question is, in effect, to ask what she understands herself to be doing in reading, as well as to ask what she believes she conveys to others by reading.

The importance of these questions was made clear to me by the women themselves. Early in my initial interview with Evans, for example, I asked her what romantic novels "do" better than other novels available today. In posing the question, I expected her to concern herself with plots and ideas, that is, with the meaning and value of the romantic story. But she misconstrued my use of "do" and thought I had asked about the effects the reading of such novels has upon the reader. She talked at great length about the benefits these books provide the traditional wife and mother. The typical woman, she said, has many, many caretaking duties that are part of those intertwined roles, but her labors are inadequately appreciated by her family. Because individual family members do not sufficiently recognize her efforts nor compensate her for them by "taking care" of her, Evans believes such a woman must find a legitimate way of releasing her from her duties temporarily and of replenishing the energy that is constantly being drained in performing them. Romance reading, she explained, is the perfect solution. I think it would be worthwhile to quote Evans herself here, precisely because her remarks indicate so tellingly how conscious she is of reading as an activity that is an integral part of the readers' daily existence.

> As a mother, I have run 'em to the orthodontist. I have run 'em to the swimming pool. I have run 'em to baton twirling lessons. I have run up to school because they forgot their lunch. You know, I mean, really! And you do it. And it isn't that you begrudge it. That isn't it. Then my husband would walk in the door and he'd say, "Well, what did you do today?" You know, it was like, "Well, tell me how you spent the last eight hours, because I've been out working." And I finally got to the point where I would say, "Well, I read four books, and I did all the wash and got the meal on the table and the beds are all made, and the house is tidy." And I would get defensive like, "So what do you call all this? Why should I have to tell you because I certainly don't ask you what you did for eight hours, step by step."—But their husbands *do* do that. We've compared notes. They hit the house and it's like "Well all right, I've been out earning a living. Now what have you been doin' with your time?" And you begin to be feeling, "Now really, why is he questioning me?"

Evans maintains, in effect, that romance reading is a "declaration of independence" for her and her customers. She believes that in picking up a book, each is effectively erecting a barrier between herself and the arena of her regular family ministrations. Because husband and children are told, "This is my time, my space, now leave me alone," they are expected to respect the signal of the book and to avoid interrupting her.

Book reading allows the woman to free herself from her duties and responsibilities and provides a "space" or "time" within which she can attend to her own interests and needs.

It is here that the demographic character of this particular group of readers is relevant. For the most part, the Smithton women are married, middle-class mothers of children other than infants. More than 60 percent were between twenty-five and forty-four at the time of the study, and 70 percent had children younger than eighteen. Although 42 percent work outside the home, they nevertheless felt that family care was primarily their responsibility. In discussion after discussion, they referred to the unrelenting family demands made upon them and to the "tensions" these produced. Then, with a combination of defensiveness and belligerence, the women asserted repeatedly that the very difficulty of their double work burden earned them the right to do something pleasurable for themselves alone.

In assessing the correlation between the social character of the lives of these women and their understanding of the value of romance reading, it seems clear that what the women are doing is allowing themselves to abandon temporarily the self-abnegation that had been engrained in them all their lives as the proper attitude for a wife and mother. Within the context of their lives, romance reading appeared to be both an assertion of a deeply felt psychological need and a means for satisfying that need. Although the women themselves accept their need for respite and replenishment and for self-involvement as part of a role they willingly adopt, that they feel their romance reading is not simply pleasurable but necessary testifies to the enduring force of that need. Several of the women equated their reading to a form of addiction, and most were quite comfortable with a view of themselves as dependent on romances. Something specific and integral to their situation as wives and mothers apparently is the ultimate source of the romance's significance to them and, consequently, of their preference for the category.

It was at this point that I moved beyond the women's own construction of their behavior to look for a structural explanation of the social facts of their existence that led not only to the behavior itself but to their construction of it as well. Here, I was helped by recent work on the nature of patriarchy and middle-class marriage.[21] Within the context of such work, it seemed clear that the Smithton readers' need for respite and replenishment was a function of the fact that within traditional patriarchal marriage, no one is charged with the affective and emotional reconstitution of women.[22] Indeed, as one of Evans's customers put it, "You always have to be a Mary Poppins. You can't be sad, you can't be mad, you have to keep everything bottled up inside." Even if a woman is depleted by her efforts to care for others, she is nonetheless expected to restore and sustain herself within such a family structure, precisely because other family members do not conceive of their role as being one of nurturance. The women turn to romance reading because the activity itself temporarily permits them to identify with a heroine who receives all the attention and care of an extraordinary man. In effect, when they buy a romance, they are purchasing personal space and vicarious attention.

Before exploring exactly how the stories supply the longed-for reassurance and nurturance, we might take note of the fact that the Smithton readers feel a bit guilty about the time and money spent on indulging themselves in this way. Given their willing acceptance of the traditional female role with its implicit self-denial and self-abnegation, this is quite understandable. Although the women defiantly assert that they, too, have a right to some time for themselves (they often point to the amount of time their husbands spend watching televised sports), they worry about their families' disapproval of their book expenses and their self-preoccupation. Indeed, many of the women asked somewhat rhetorically whether I agreed that they had a right to do something for themselves alone, even though as a wife and mother they were supposed to be concerned with the interests of others. Their defensiveness and uncertainty suggests that their chronic reading causes them to experience a certain amount of role conflict. They feel a need to replenish the self and to attend to emotional needs created by the role they have willingly accepted, yet are not sure that this should be done at the expense of family responsibilities or through an activity that is so obviously pleasurable.

It is here that the other "use" of romance reading becomes important, because it acts to justify the time and money spent on books and reading. The Smithton women read primarily "to escape"—literally, to deny their presence in the family context. But they also read to learn. They enjoy the travelog and documentary aspects of the romance immensely, and even categorize books on the basis of their historical and geographic settings. More important, however, they actively use the factual materials they learn through reading to demonstrate to their skeptical families that they have indeed acquired something valuable in exchange for their expenditure of time and money. This strategy cannily defines the *act* of romance reading as goal-directed work, and therefore assigns to it a higher value in the male world, which is preoccupied with labor, self-improvement, and achievement.

Although the women are well aware of the fact that they use this aspect of romance reading to convince their husbands of the activity's validity, they are unaware of the benefits they derive by construing the activity in this way. Again, I am making an interpretive leap here, but it seems to be justified, given all the women have said about the confining aspects of domestic work and our culture's propensity to disparage women. By storing factual material as "information," and by displaying it to others as their own "knowledge," the women convince themselves that they have not languished as "mere housewives" but have continued to better themselves and to demonstrate their fundamental abilities. Thus, at the same time that romance reading gives them much needed personal time and space, it also enables them to believe that they are capable individuals and that they are changing for the better. Both "uses" of romance reading, therefore, act to deny the immediate present and to propel the women elsewhere. The act of romance reading first walls off pressing demands and then demonstrates to the participants that they are making themselves better or "other" than they were.

I think it can be seen from this example why it is so helpful to distinguish between the book read by an individual and the act of reading itself carried on within a specific social context. Although it is true that the two are not actually distinct components of the individual's behavior—simply because the act of reading must involve a text, which cannot help but contribute to the meaning of the larger activity—by separating them analytically, one can then isolate the social and material situation surrounding the actual event of reading. Books are always read within a set of specific circumstances, and their final meaning and impact may well be a function of the way those circumstances constitute the reader as a social being. In thus developing an account of how the act of book reading fits within the complex set of relations and behaviors that characterize the reader's social world, we can understand better why she might select such specific reading material in the first place. An important correlation may exist, in fact, between the needs that prompt the decision to read and the character of the books that are chosen for that activity. By taking account of that possibility, one is better prepared, finally, to return to the issue of textual interpretation in an effort to understand how the reader's particular construction of a text provides certain forms of intellectual and emotional gratification. Having sketched out how a reader actually uses her literacy, one is then prepared to investigate why she does so on these particular texts.

I can best demonstrate how intricate the connections can be between the social context surrounding a reader's activity and the texts that an individual chooses to read by referring one last time to Dorothy Evans and the Smithton women. Although I cannot detail all the ways in which the texts they selected addressed the specific needs and concerns that originated with their social role and their situation in the family context, I can at least show that by reading romances, their reading activity was made even more meaningful and beneficial to them. I discovered the special significance of the romance to them when I asked whether all romances were the same. Of course they weren't, the women replied, and then showed me that they could clearly distinguish the good romances from the bad. I then began to probe more deeply into their evaluative procedures and to examine more carefully the differences between the books they actually read and those they rejected.

Their favorite books were indeed characterized by the "one woman/ one man" plot they claimed to prefer, stories in which the romantic hero focused all of his attention on a heroine with whom they identified. Although the initial interaction between the pair was characterized by the usual misunderstandings and emotional distance, the hero's treatment of the heroine was decidedly less cruel and violent than it was in what they considered to be poorer versions of the genre. In fact, his mistreatment of the heroine was always mitigated by temporary softenings of his demeanor, and his ultimate attitude toward her was transformed much earlier in the tale. Ideal heroes, it seemed, were also a good deal more androgynous than their less satisfying counterparts in that they combined masculine strength and power with a more feminine sensitivity and tenderness.

In indulging themselves in a few hundred pages of the hero's response to the heroine, the Smithton women allowed themselves to exist vicariously as the center of a spectacular man's attention. Not only did their reading activity permit them to give up their actively nurturant or servicing role in the family, but it also, because of the nature of the text, enabled them to become the passive recipient of another's total and tender care. What they achieved through romance reading was twofold: a temporary release from the demands of the social role that defined them, and psychological gratification for the needs they experienced because they had adopted that role. It might be said that romance reading functioned for the women as a kind of tacit, minimal protest against the patriarchal constitution of women: it enabled them to mark off a space where they could temporarily deny the selflessness usually demanded of them, to acknowledge the validity of the desires and needs created by the demeanor they otherwise accepted as part of that constitution, and to meet those needs by acquiring vicariously the nurturance and care that was lacking in their daily lives.

Before characterizing romance reading as incipiently subversive or oppositional behavior, however, we would do well to look carefully at the second way in which the reading of romances specifically addressed the Smithton readers' social situation as women. This aspect of romance reading was revealed to me through my exploration of their assertion that the stories were those of a woman's triumph. In looking at their favorite books very carefully, in fact, I could see a way in which their assertion was true. The typical ideal romance establishes at the outset that there is a clear opposition between the male and female worlds, the former dominated by competition, the desire for wealth, and the quest for social position, the latter characterized by the value placed on love and intimate human interactions. The romantic heroine, of course, as an inhabitant of the female world, understands the value of love, while the hero does not. Preoccupied with the goals of the typical male quest, he has no time in the beginning for sensitivity and tender gestures. In the course of the story, however, he learns the value of such things because he almost loses the heroine. In a sense, he is converted by the heroine into an occupant and proponent of the female world of love and emotional commitment—hence, the Smithton readers' understanding of these stories as tales of a woman's victory.

Romance reading, then, also demonstrates to these women that the domestic world they occupy is eminently valuable. They are told, in fact, that it is the way to true happiness, just as they are shown that it has the evangelical power to convert doubters to its purpose. The romance thus assures its readers that the world they have chosen already, or will likely choose in the future, is the world they ought to occupy. We might logically conclude, therefore, that one consequence of romance reading might be a reinforcement of the patriarchal constitution of women. Despite the fact that it enables women to resist some of that constitution's most difficult demands, romance reading might ultimately conserve patriarchy, because it reassures women that the sphere they occupy is right and fulfilling, and that all of their needs can be met within it. If so, this aspect of romance reading would contradict its existence as incipient opposition, and might override any positive force it could exert upon women to develop more effective ways of coping with their needs for nurturance and attentive care.

Unfortunately, assessment of the relative power of these two aspects of this highly complex form of behavior is nearly impossible without long-range, extensive observation of the women's actual behavior in the family. And should such a study be undertaken, it would still be extremely difficult to isolate and identify the causes of specific behavioral changes. Greater assertiveness on the part of the women might have nothing to do with the positive effects of romance reading, but might be the result of changes in the culture at large. In addition, continued acceptance of the traditional female role might in fact be the result of persistent economic dependence rather than the conservative impact of romance reading. Here again, we run up against the limitations of the ethnographic method. Although we can ask our informants what they believe they are accomplishing in reading—just as we can ask them to explain how they affect others *by* reading—we must get beyond their conscious comprehension and self-understanding if we are to make some sort of judgment about the cumulative impact of that activity both on them and on others. To ask about such an effect is, in fact, to pose a question about the relationship between the imaginary realm and the realm of material behavior in the world of actual social relations. The answer to this question can only be found through careful observation of just those behavioral changes over time. However, even when ethnographic observation leads to conclusions about significant alterations in women's behavior, attribution of those changes to specific causes will remain an inherently interpretive procedure, because the link between imagination and action will always be an inferred one.

Because I could not observe the behavior of the Smithton women over a long period of time, my account of their reading activity ends with an explanation of the multiple meanings that the activity has within the context of their daily lives. That explanation locates the ultimate source of the group's existence as an interpretive community in their roles as wives and mothers. Their preference for the romance genre, in my view, is a function of their particular social situation. The nature of their literacy, therefore—which is to say, the way they choose, understand, and use their books—is deeply affected by the circumstances of their lives. These, in fact, are both the very source of their desire to read and the set of conditions that determine and give meaning to the particular way in which they do.

The ultimate test of such an argument, of course, would be a series of related studies of romance readers that would begin by defining differently the interpretive communities to be investigated. One such study would have to begin with a group of unrelated romance readers who were demographically similar to the Smithton women. If these readers also read romances to escape and to learn, and chose only those books that supplied vicarious nurturance, then I think we might reasonably conclude that at least one form of romance reading is a function of the social and psychological consequences of patriarchal marriage. If a more extensive study of a demographically varied group of romance readers demonstrated that young, unmarried women, say, read different romances for different reasons, this would not necessarily upset that initial correlation. It is entirely possible, I think, that the interpretive community of romance readers, defined only by its members' preference for the romance category, may be subdivided into more specialized groups, whose reading behaviors vary with the particular circumstances of their daily lives. Although the interest of romance readers in the genre may be a function of the fact that all are women in a patriarchal society, and thus all fantasize about achieving self-definition through attachment to a spectacular man, the character of the man, the nature of the attachment, and the process of self-realization that are longed for may be determined by the particular situation of these women in patriarchal culture. All components of literate behavior, in short, including the desire to read, the decision to read a certain kind of material, the interpretation of that material, and the uses to which both the interpretation and the act of constructing it are put, may well be a consequence of the diverse material and social features that characterize the lives of real individuals. There may be, in fact, as many different forms of literate behavior as there are interpretive communities who buy and use books.

NOTES

Writing of this paper was supported by a commission from the Annenberg Scholars Program, Annenberg School of Communications, University of Southern California, and delivered at the Scholars Conference, "Creating Meaning: Literacies of Our Time," February 1984. Copyright, Annenberg School of Communications. I would like to thank Horace Newcomb for his very helpful comments and suggestions on an earlier version of this paper.

1. André Kertész, *On Reading* (New York: Penguin Books, 1982).

2. Ibid., pp. 37, 10.

3. Raymond Williams, *Marxism and Literature* (Oxford: Oxford University Press, 1977), pp. 45–54.

4. John Szwed, "The Ethnography of Literacy," in *Writing: The Nature, Development, and Teaching of Written Communication*, vol. 1. *Variation in Writing: Functional and Linguistic Cultural Differences*, edited by Marcia Farr Whiteman (Hillsdale, N.J.: Lawrence Erlbaum Associates, 1981). I am grateful to Judy Levin for bringing this article to my attention in one of our many helpful conversations about literacy and romance reading.

5. For a good introduction to reader-response criticism, see Jane P. Tompkins, *Reader-Response Criticism: From Formalism to Post-Structuralism* (Baltimore: Johns Hopkins University Press, 1980), and Susan B. Suleiman and Inge Crosman, *The Reader in the Text: Essays on Audience and Interpretation* (Princeton: Princeton University Press, 1980).

6. For historical and critical discussion of reader theory, see Jonathan Culler, *The Pursuit of Signs: Semiotics, Literature, Deconstruction* (Ithaca, N.Y.: Cornell University Press, 1981), pp. 47–131, and *On Deconstruction: Theory and Criticism after Structuralism* (Ithaca, N.Y.: Cornell University Press, 1982), pp. 31–83. See also Terry Eagleton, *Literary Theory: An Introduction* (Minneapolis: University of Minnesota Press, 1983), pp. 54–90.

7. See Roman Ingarden, *The Literary Work of Art: An Investigation on the Borderlines of Ontology, Logic, and Theory of Literature*, translated by George Grabowicz (Evanston, Ill.: Northwestern University Press, 1973), and Wolfgang Iser, *The Act of Reading: A Theory of Aesthetic Response* (Baltimore: Johns Hopkins University Press, 1978).

8. See, especially, Umberto Eco, *The Role of the Reader: Explorations in the Semiotics of Texts* (Bloomington: Indiana University Press, 1979) and *A Theory of Semi-*

otics (Bloomington: Indiana University Press, 1976); Jonathan Culler, *Structuralist Poetics: Structuralism, Linguistics, and the Study of Literature* (Ithaca, N.Y.: Cornell University Press, 1975); Stanley Fish, *Is There a Text in This Class?: The Authority of Interpretive Communities* (Cambridge: Harvard University Press, 1980); Louise Rosenblatt, *The Reader, the Text, the Poem: The Transactional Theory of the Literary Work* (Carbondale: Southern Illinois University Press, 1978).

9. Eco, *A Theory of Semiotics*, p. 139.

10. See especially part 2 of *Is There a Text in This Class?*, pp. 303–71.

11. See, for example, John Cawelti, *Adventure, Mystery, and Romance: Formula Stories as Art and Popular Culture* (Chicago: University of Chicago Press, 1976).

12. The present discussion of romance reading is based on my full-length study, *Reading the Romance: Women, Patriarchy, and Popular Literature* (Chapel Hill: University of North Carolina Press, 1984). For another summary of my findings, see "Women Read the Romance: The Interaction of Text and Context," *Feminist Studies* 9 (Spring 1983): 53–78. The names Dorothy Evans and the Smithton women are pseudonyms designed to protect the privacy of my informants.

13. As Stanley Fish has argued, "Linguistic and textual facts, rather than being the objects of interpretation, are its products" (*Is There a Text in This Class?* p. 9). Accordingly, the literary features used by the Smithton readers as the internal skeleton of their readings are actually isolated and deemed significant by them precisely because they come to the texts with a prior conception of what the stories should and usually do mean.

14. See Ann Douglas, "Soft Porn Culture," *The New Republic*, August 30, 1980, pp. 25–29; Tania Modleski, "The Disappearing Act: A Study of Harlequin Romances," *Signs* 5 (Spring 1980): 435–48; Ann Barr Snitow, "Mass Market Romance: Pornography for Women is Different," *Radical History Review* 20 (Spring/Summer 1979): 141–61.

15. Culler, *Structuralist Poetics*, pp. 230–38. See also his *Ferdinand de Saussure* (New York: Penguin Books, 1976), pp. 117–18.

16. For a demonstration of how such a reading strategy works, see William Veeder's discussion of *Portrait of a Lady*, in *Henry James—The Lessons of the Master: Popular Fiction and Personal Style in the Nineteenth Century* (Chicago: University of Chicago Press, 1975), pp. 106–83.

17. In her acknowledgments to *The Proud Breed* (New York: Fawcett Crest Books, 1978), p. 7, for instance, Celeste De Blasis thanks the San Bernardino County library system as well as the Bancroft Library at Berkeley. She continues, "The Roman Catholic pastors of St. Joan of Arc, Victorville, St. David's, Apple Valley, Christ the Good Shepherd, Adelanto, and San Juan Capistrano Mission, and a noted historian of the Archdiocese of Los Angeles were generous with their knowledge of early California's church ritual."

18. In an essay on Ian Fleming's thrillers ("Narrative Structures in Fleming," in *The Role of the Reader*, pp. 144–72), Umberto Eco has argued that Fleming also indulges in minute description of familiar objects that appear in the background to the melodramatic action. Eco calls this strategy "the technique of the aimless glance" and maintains that it functions to seduce the reader into identifying with a character who thus appears to be "real" even though his activities are otherwise preposterous. Because Fleming rarely describes the unusual, Eco

concludes, those descriptions do not occur as "encyclopedic information." Although the description in romances appears somewhat similar to that found in Fleming, it differs precisely because it focuses on the historically and spatially distant and thus can function encyclopedically.

19. Clifford Geertz, "Thick Description: Toward an Interpretive Theory of Culture," in *The Interpretation of Cultures* (New York: Basic Books, 1973), pp. 9, 20.

20. See Robert Escarpit's discussion of reading in *The Sociology of Literature*, translated by Ernest Pick (Painesville, Ohio: Lake Erie College Press, 1965), p. 88.

21. See, for example, Kate Millett, *Sexual Politics* (Garden City, N.Y.: Doubleday, 1970), pp. 23–58; Heidi Hartmann, "The Unhappy Marriage of Marxism and Feminism: Towards a More Progressive Union," *Capital and Class* 8 (Summer 1979), pp. 1–33 and "The Family as Locus of Gender, Class, and Political Struggle: The Example of Housework," *Signs* 6 (Spring, 1981), pp. 366–94; Annette Kuhn, "Structures of Patriarchy and Capitalism in the Family," in *Feminism and Materialism: Women and Modes of Production*, edited by Annette Kuhn and AnnMarie Wolpe (London: Routledge & Kegan Paul, 1978), pp. 42–67; and Roisin McDonough and Rachel Harrison, "Patriarchy and Relations of Production," in *Feminism and Materialism*, pp. 11–41.

22. See Nancy Chodorow, *The Reproduction of Mothering: Psychoanalysis and the Sociology of Gender* (Berkeley: University of California Press, 1978).

CONTRIBUTORS

Roland Barthes (1915–1980) was professor at the Collège de France, Paris, and the author, among other works, of *Writing Degree Zero, Elements of Semiology, Mythologies, S/Z, The Pleasure of the Text, The Fashion System,* and *The Eiffel Tower.*

John Berger lives in a small peasant community in France, where he writes fiction and essays. He has produced films with Alain Tanner, including *La Salamandre* and *Jonah Who Will Be 25 in the Year 2000.* His books include *Ways of Seeing, Art and Revolution, The Success and Failure of Picasso,* and *About Looking.*

Pierre Bourdieu is professor of sociology at the Collège de France, Paris, and director of studies at the Ecole des hautes études. His books include *The Inheritors: French Students and Their Relation to Culture* (with Jean-Claude Passeron), *Reproduction in Education, Society, and Culture* (also with Jean-Claude Passeron), *Outline of a Theory of Practice, Distinction: A Social Critique of the Judgement of Taste,* and *Homo Academicus.*

Robert Darnton is Shelby Cullom Davis Professor of European History at Princeton University. His books include *The Literary Underground of the Old Regime, The Great Cat Massacre and Other Episodes in French Cultural History,* and *The Kiss of Lamourette: Reflections on Cultural History.*

Natalie Zemon Davis is Henry Charles Lea Professor of History at Princeton University. She is the author of *Society and Culture in Early Modern France, The Return of Martin Guerre,* and *Fiction in the Archives: Pardon Tales and Their Tellers in Sixteenth-Century France.*

Paul DiMaggio is associate professor of sociology at Yale University. He is the editor of *Nonprofit Enterprises in the Arts,* coeditor (with Sharon Zukin) of *Structures of Capital: The Social Organization of the Economy*, and coeditor (with Walter Powell) of *The New Institutionalism in Organizational Studies*.

Mary Douglas is visiting professor in religion, sociology, and anthropology at Princeton University. She is the author of *Purity and Danger, Natural Symbols: Explorations in Cosmology, Implicit Meanings: Essays in Anthropology, Cultural Bias, The World of Goods* (with Baron Isherwood), and other works.

Michel Foucault (1926–1984) was professor of the history of systems of ideas at the Collège de France. His books include *The Archaeology of Knowledge, Madness and Civilization, The Order of Things, Discipline and Punish*, and *A History of Sexuality*.

Clifford Geertz is Harold F. Linder Professor of Social Science at the Institute for Advanced Study, Princeton, New Jersey. Among his books are *The Religion of Java, The Interpretation of Cultures: Selected Essays, Local Knowledge: Further Essays in Interpretive Anthropology*, and *Works and Lives: The Anthropologist as Author*.

Todd Gitlin is professor of sociology at the University of California, Berkeley. His works include *The Whole World is Watching, Inside Prime Time*, and *The Sixties: Years of Hope, Days of Rage*.

Jürgen Habermas is professor of philosophy at the University of Frankfurt. His many books include *Toward A Rational Society, Legitimation Crisis, The Theory of Communicative Action, The Philosophical Discourse of Modernity, The Social Transformation of the Public Sphere*, and *The New Conservatism*.

Paul Hirsch is James Allen Distinguished Professor of Strategy and Organizational Behavior at the Kellogg Graduate School of Management and professor of sociology at Northwestern University. He is the author of *The Structure of the Popular Music Industry* and *Pack Your Own Parachute: How to Survive Mergers, Takeovers, and Other Corporate Disasters*.

Lawrence Levine is professor of history at the University of California, Berkeley. He is the author of *Defender of the Faith: William Jennings Bryan, The Last Decade, 1915–1925, Black Culture and Black Consciousness*, and *Highbrow/Lowbrow: The Emergence of Cultural Hierarchy in America*.

Chandra Mukerji is professor of communication and sociology at the University of California, San Diego. Her previous books are *From Graven Images: Patterns of Modern Materialism* and *A Fragile Power: Scientists and the State*.

Janice Radway is professor of literature at Duke University and the author of *Reading the Romance: Women, Patriarchy, and Popular Literature*.

She is currently working on a project tentatively entitled The Book-of-the-Month Club and the General Reader: Mapping the Middle Ground in the Twentieth Century.

Roy Rosenzweig is professor of history at George Mason University and the author of *Eight Hours for What We Will: Workers and Leisure in an Industrial City.* He is also editor (with Susan Porter Benson and Steven Brier) of *Presenting the Past: Essays on History and the Public,* and editor (with Warren Leon) of *History Museums in the United States: A Critical Assessment.*

Marshall Sahlins is professor of anthropology at the University of Chicago. His books include *Stone Age Economics, The Uses and Abuses of Biology: An Anthropological Critique of Sociobiology, Culture and Practical Reason,* and *Islands of History.*

Michael Schudson is professor of communication and sociology at the University of California, San Diego. His previous books are *Discovering the News: A Social History of American Newspapers* and *Advertising: The Uneasy Persuasion.* He edited, with Robert Manoff, *Reading the News.*

Raymond Williams (1921–1988) was a fellow of Jesus College, Cambridge University. His many books of cultural and political analysis include *Culture and Society, 1780–1950, The Long Revolution, The Country and the City, Marxism and Literature, Problems in Materialism and Culture, Television: Technology and Culture Form,* and *Keywords.* He also wrote several novels.

Rosalind Williams is associate professor in the Writing Program at the Massachusetts Institute of Technology. She is the author of *Dream Worlds: Mass Consumption in Late Nineteenth-Century France* and *Notes on the Underground: An Essay on Technology, Society, and the Imagination.*

INDEX

Compositor:	Maple-Vail Composition Services
Text:	10/12 Baskerville
Display:	Baskerville
Printer and Binder:	The Maple-Vail Book Manufacturing Group